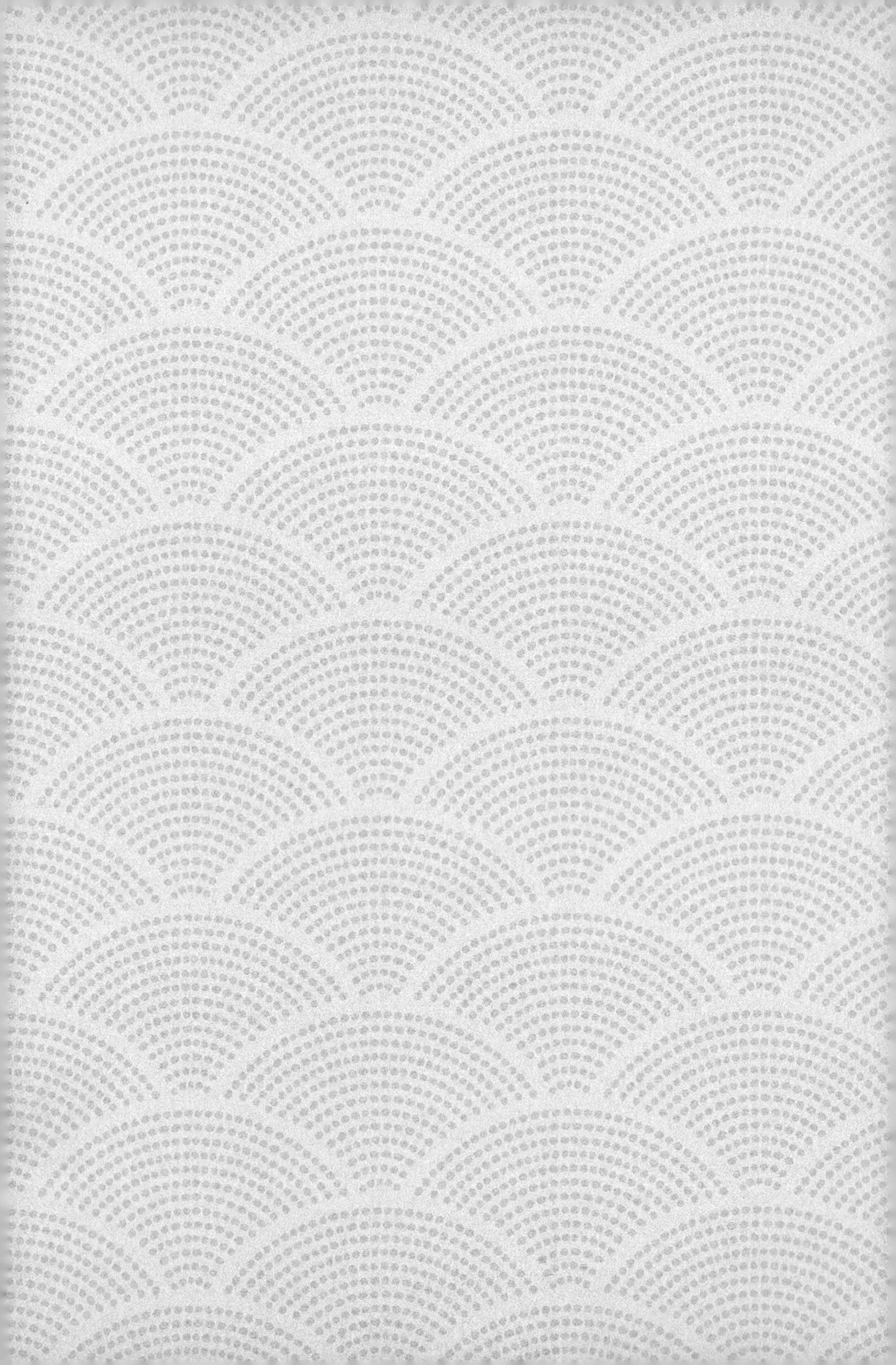

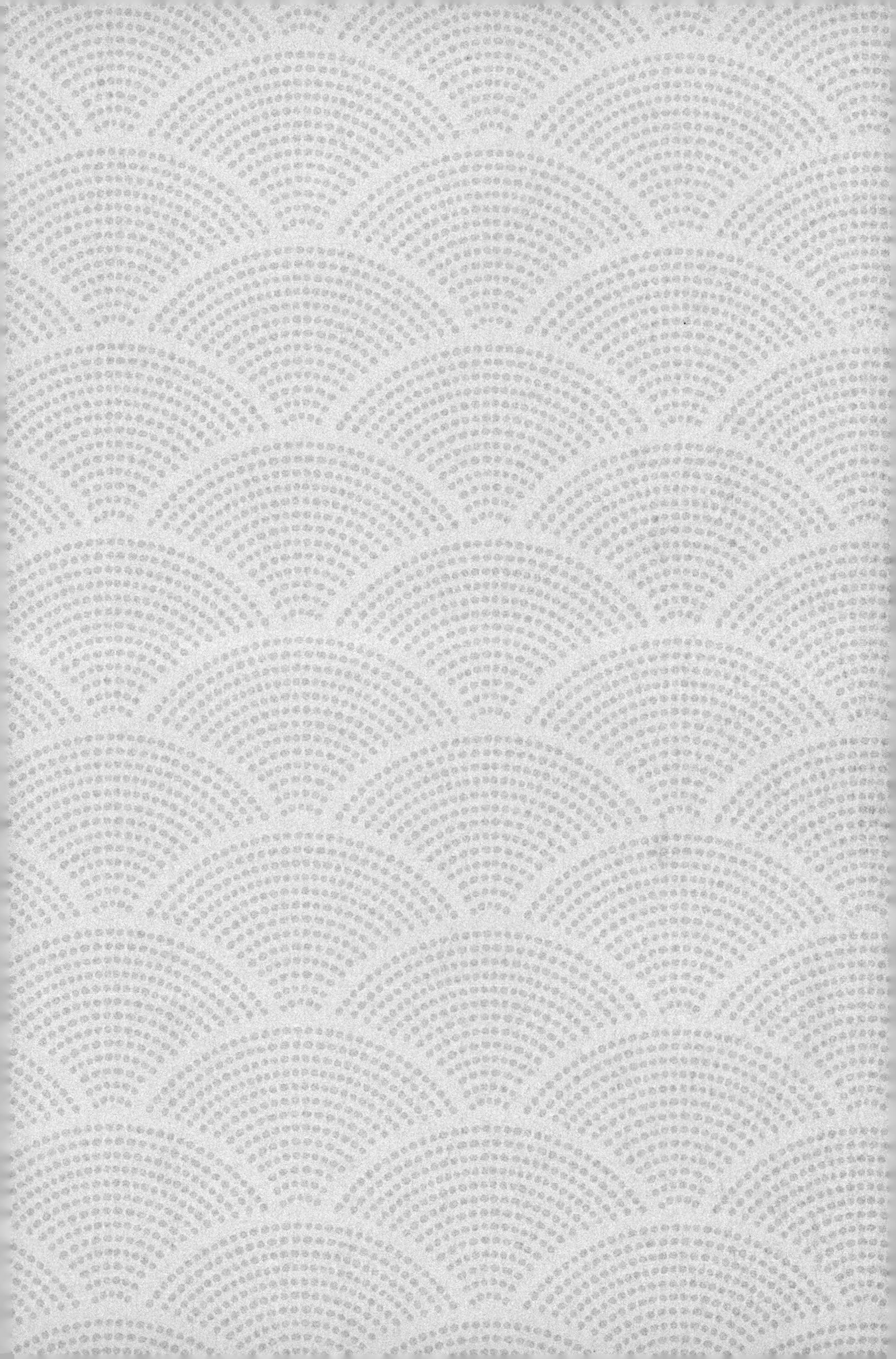

KEN NIIMURA

NEVER OPEN IT

THE TABOO TRILOGY

Yen
Press

New York

NEVER OPEN IT
THE TABOO TRILOGY

KEN NIIMURA

Translation: Stephen Blanford
Rewrite: Josh Tierney and Antonio Núñez Sánchez
Lettering: Abigail Blackman

Yen Press
150 West 30th Street, 19th Floor
New York, NY 10001

Visit us at yenpress.com • facebook.com/yenpress • twitter.com/yenpress
yenpress.tumblr.com • instagram.com/yenpress

First Yen Press Edition: October 2021

Yen Press is an imprint of Yen Press, LLC.
The Yen Press name and logo are trademarks of Yen Press, LLC.

The publisher is not responsible for websites (or their content) that are not owned by the publisher.

Library of Congress Control Number: 2021943671

ISBNs: 978-1-9753-2583-1 (paperback)
978-1-9753-2584-8 (ebook)

10 9 8 7 6 5 4 3 2 1

WOR

Printed in the United States of America

KEN NIIMURA

NEVER OPEN IT

THE TABOO TRILOGY

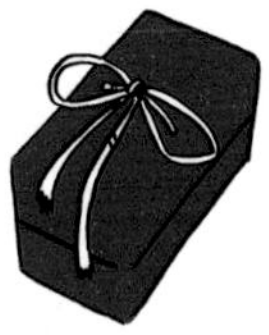

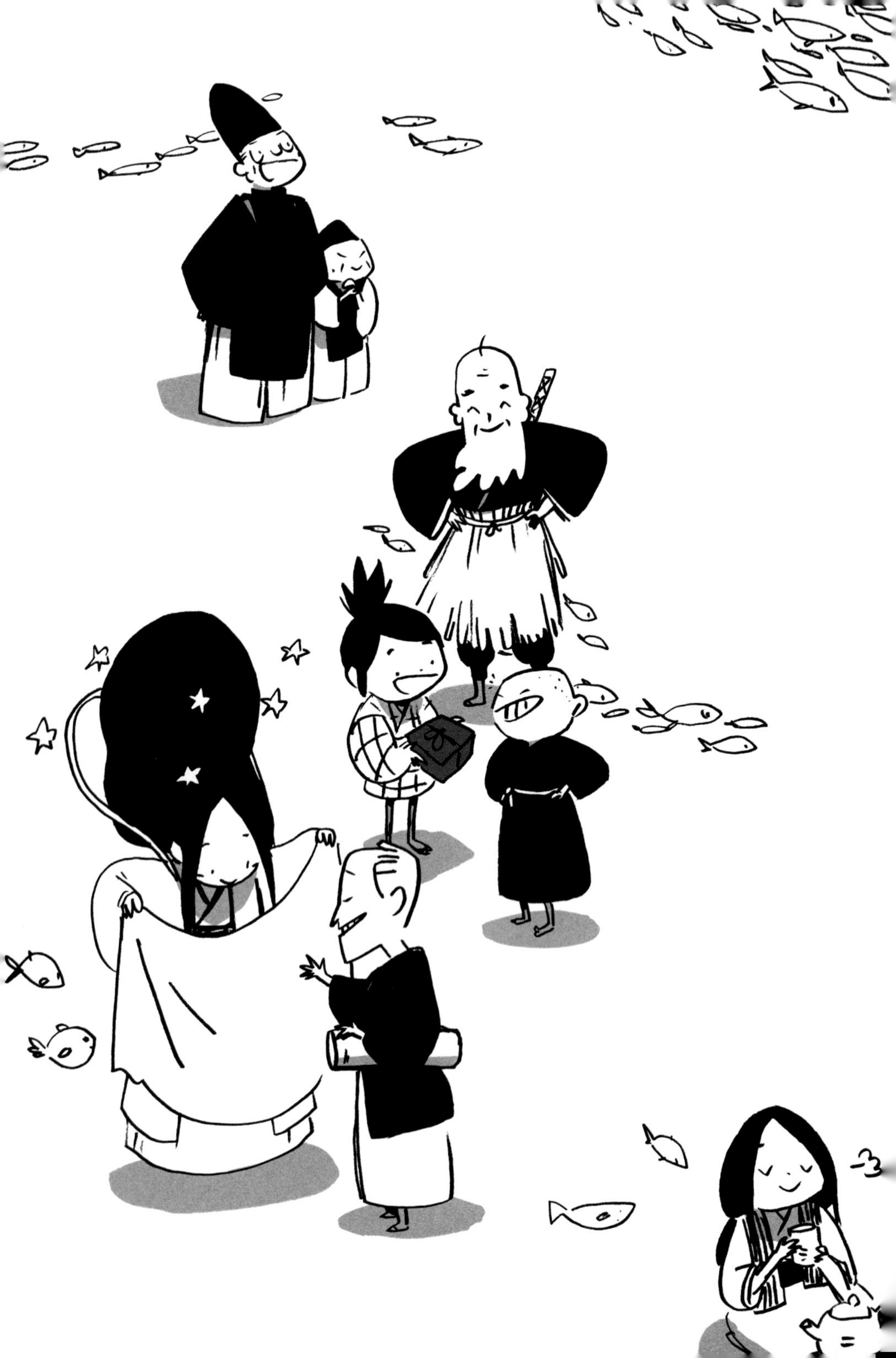

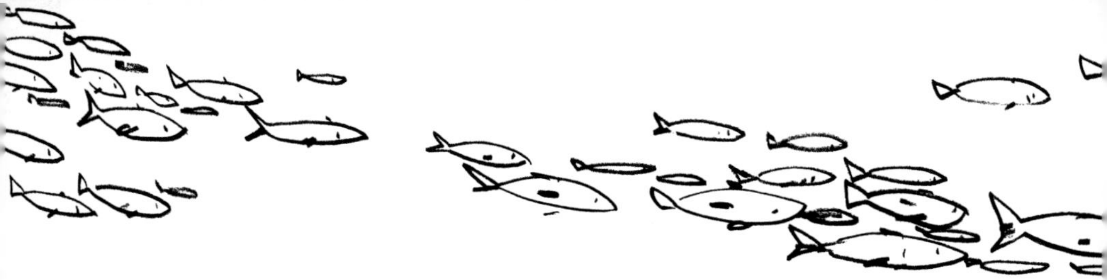

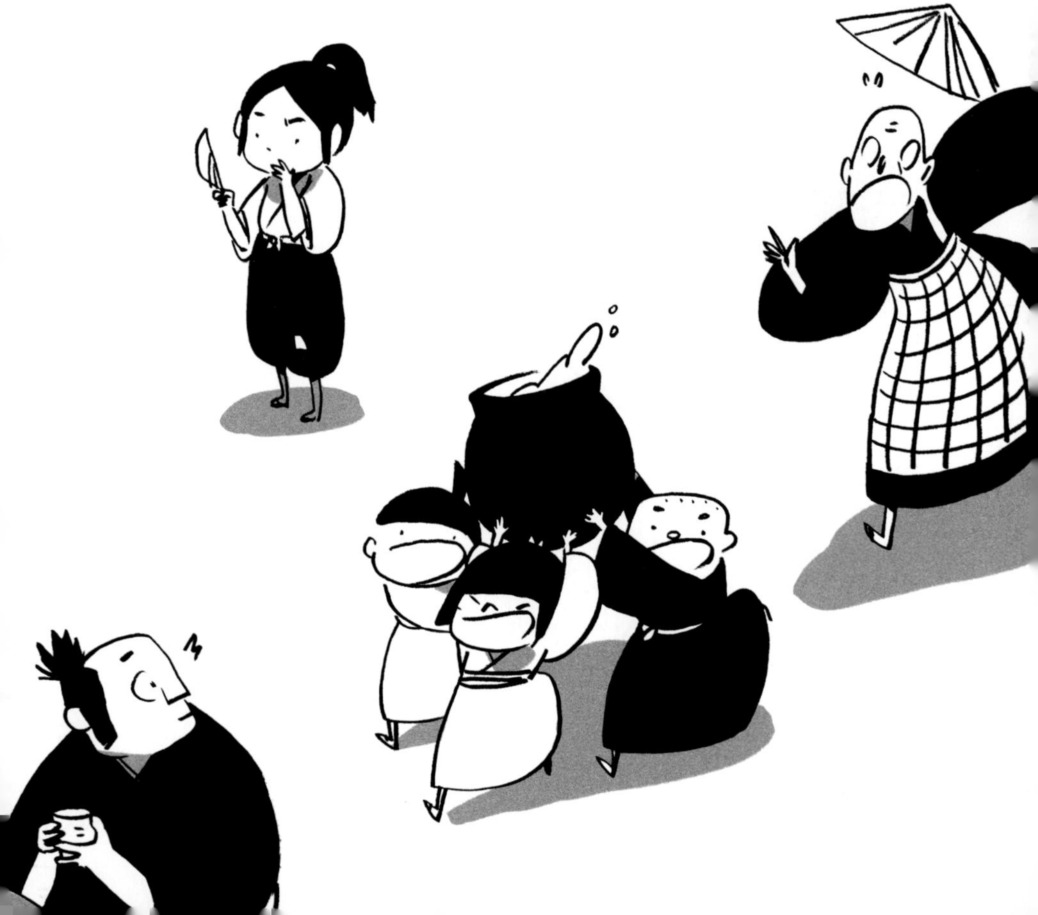

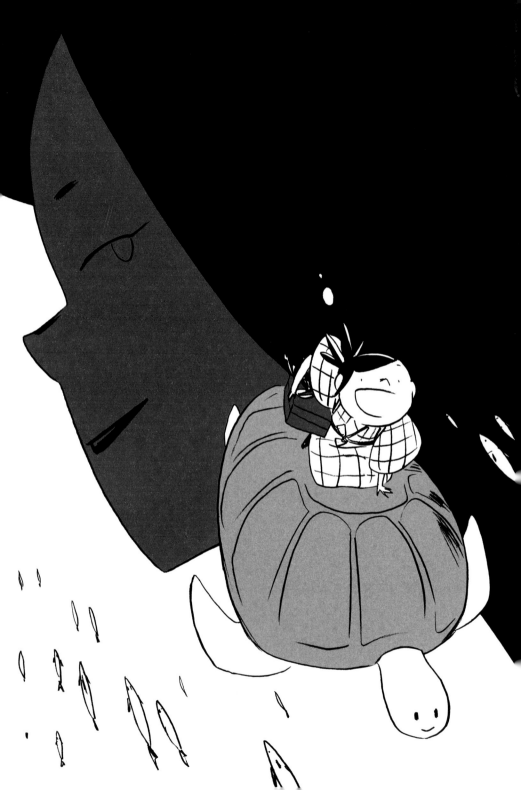

NEVER OPEN IT

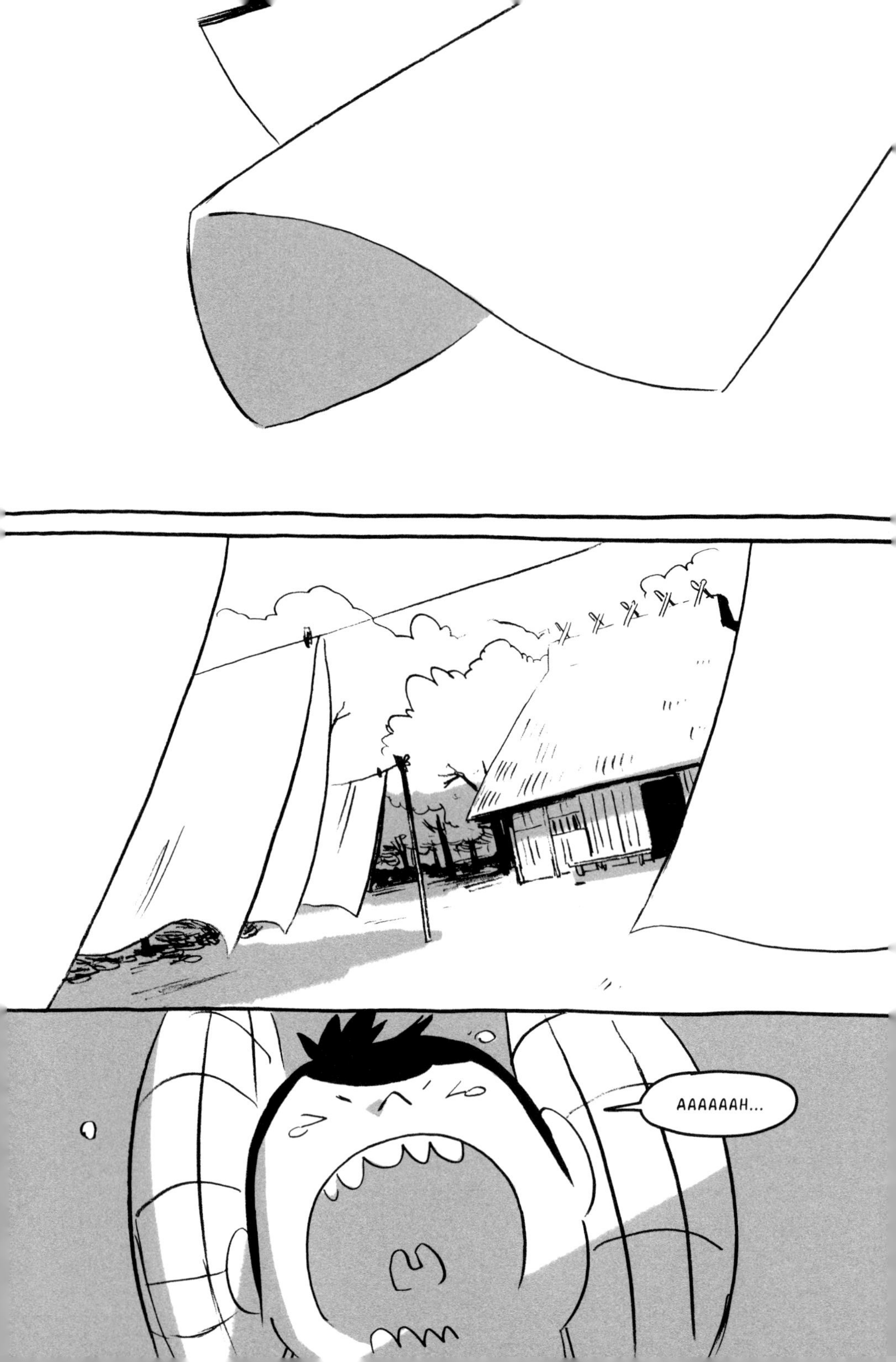
AAAAAAH...

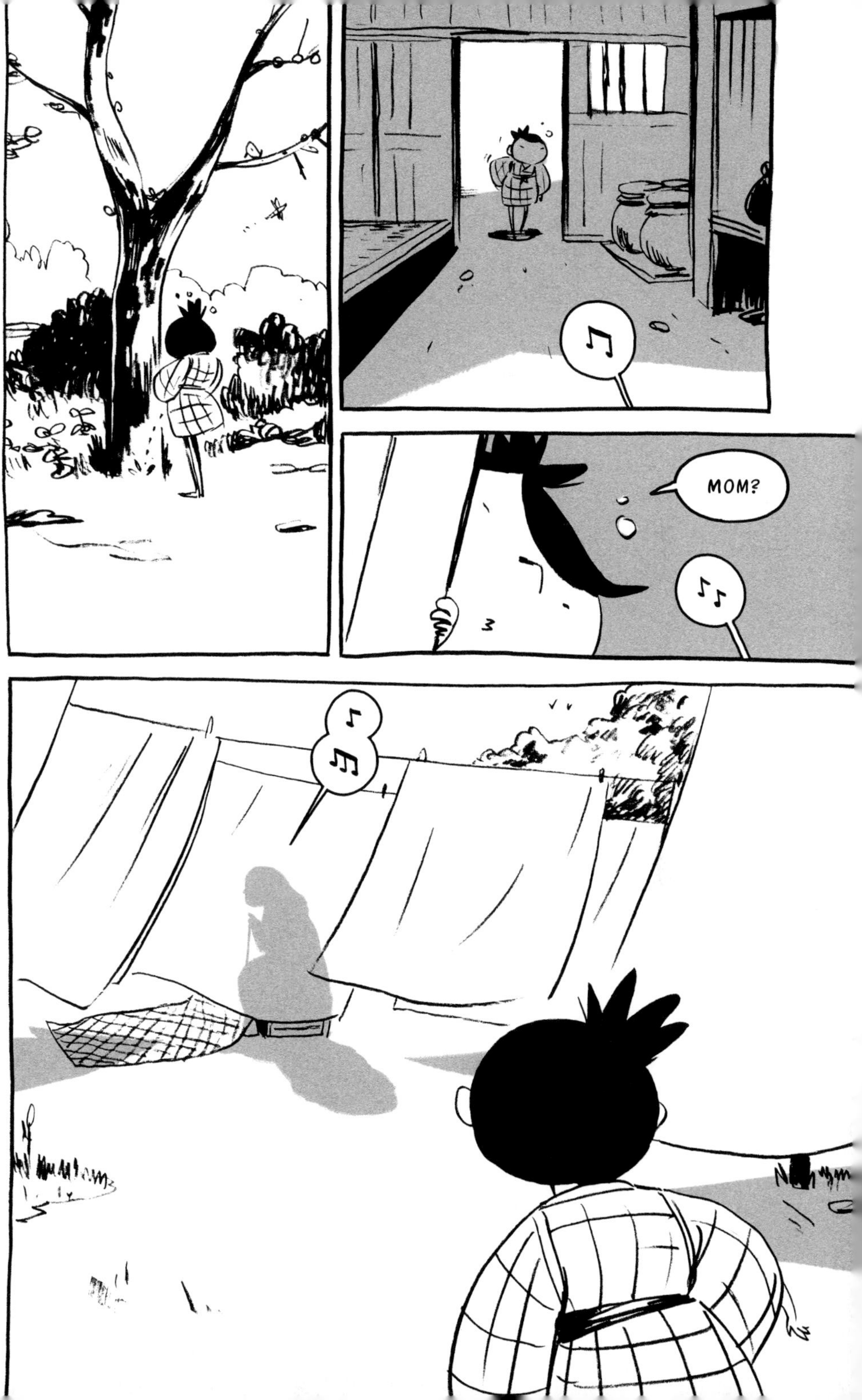
MOM?

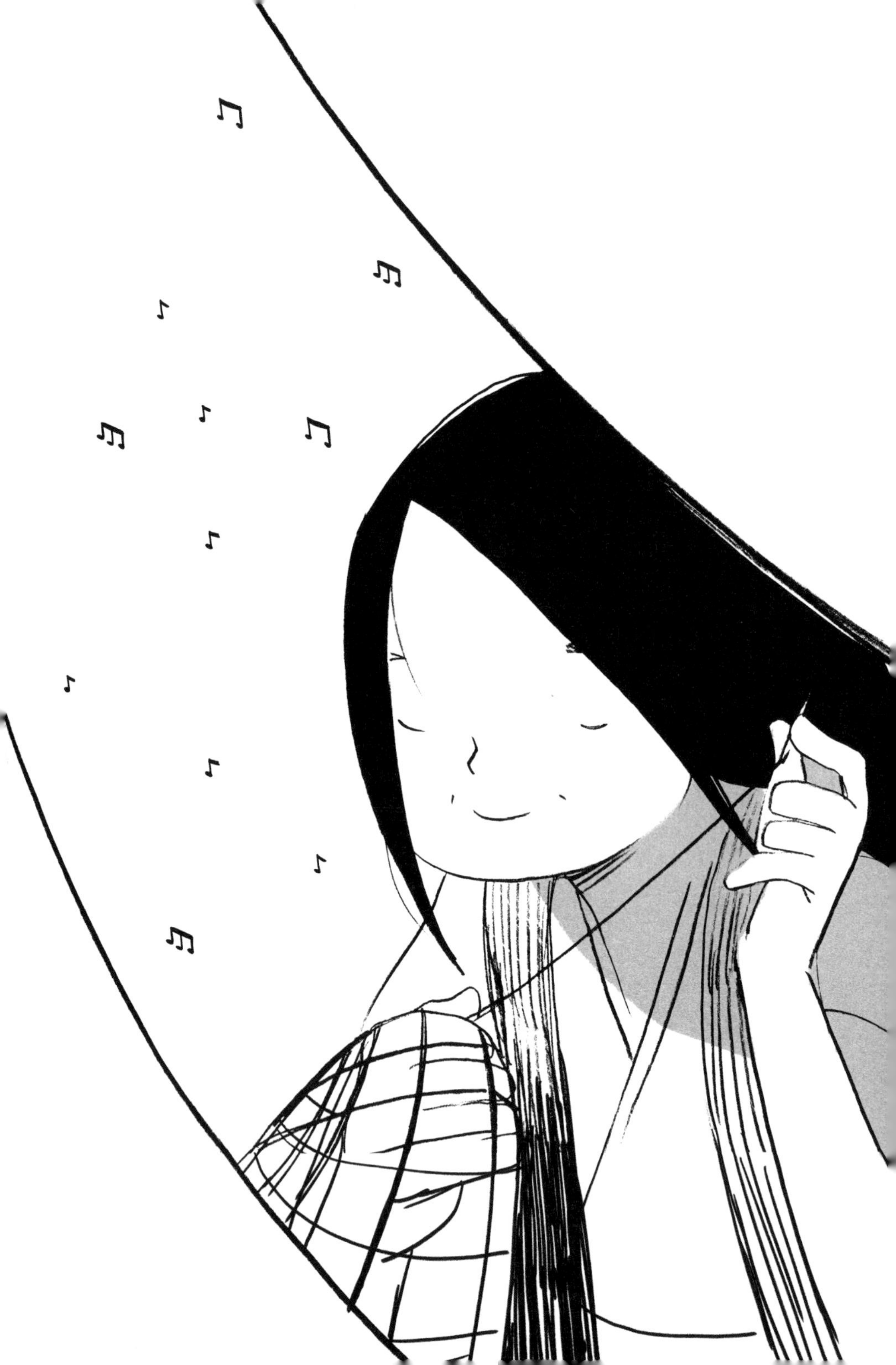

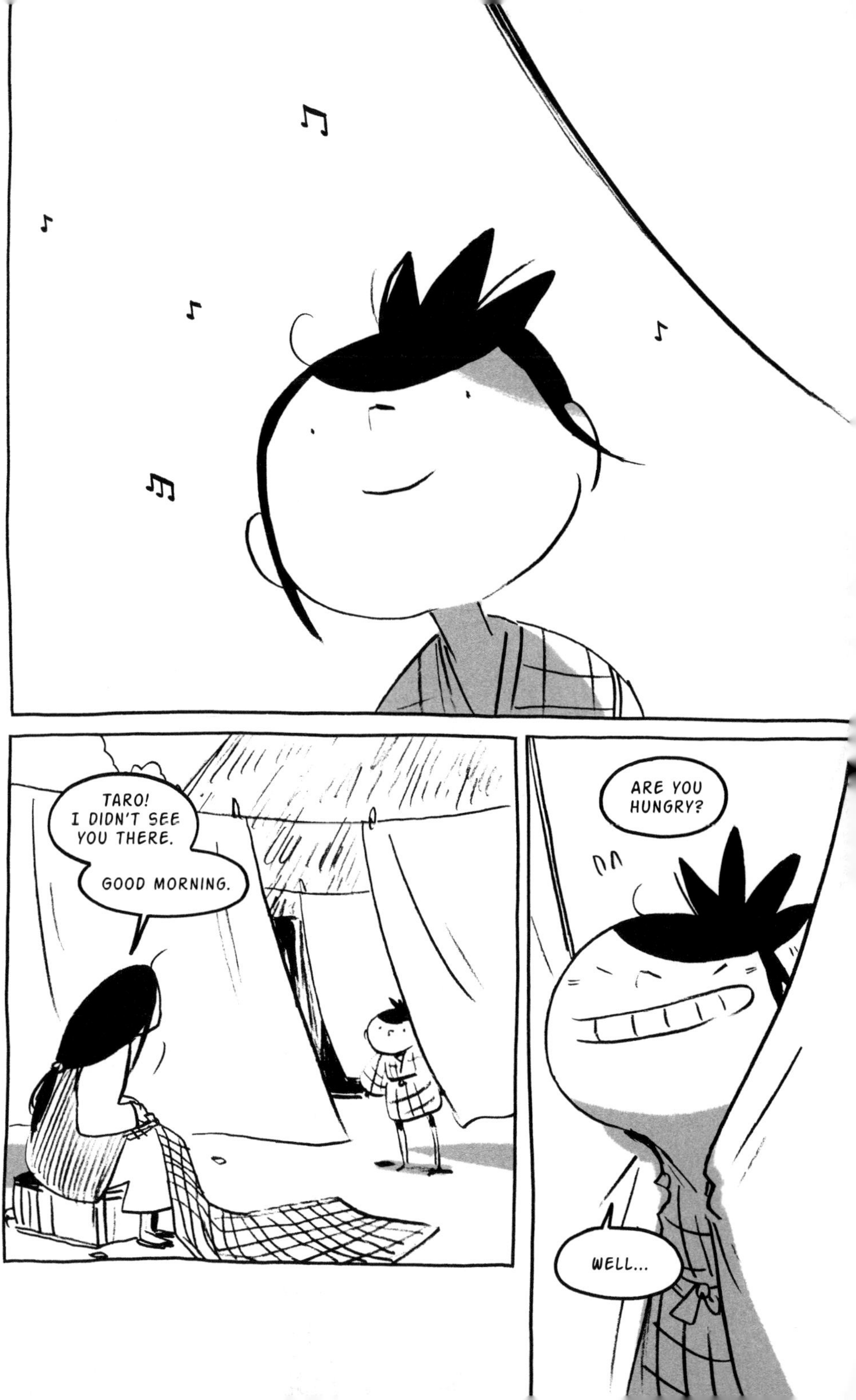
TARO!
I DIDN'T SEE YOU THERE.
GOOD MORNING.
ARE YOU HUNGRY?
WELL...

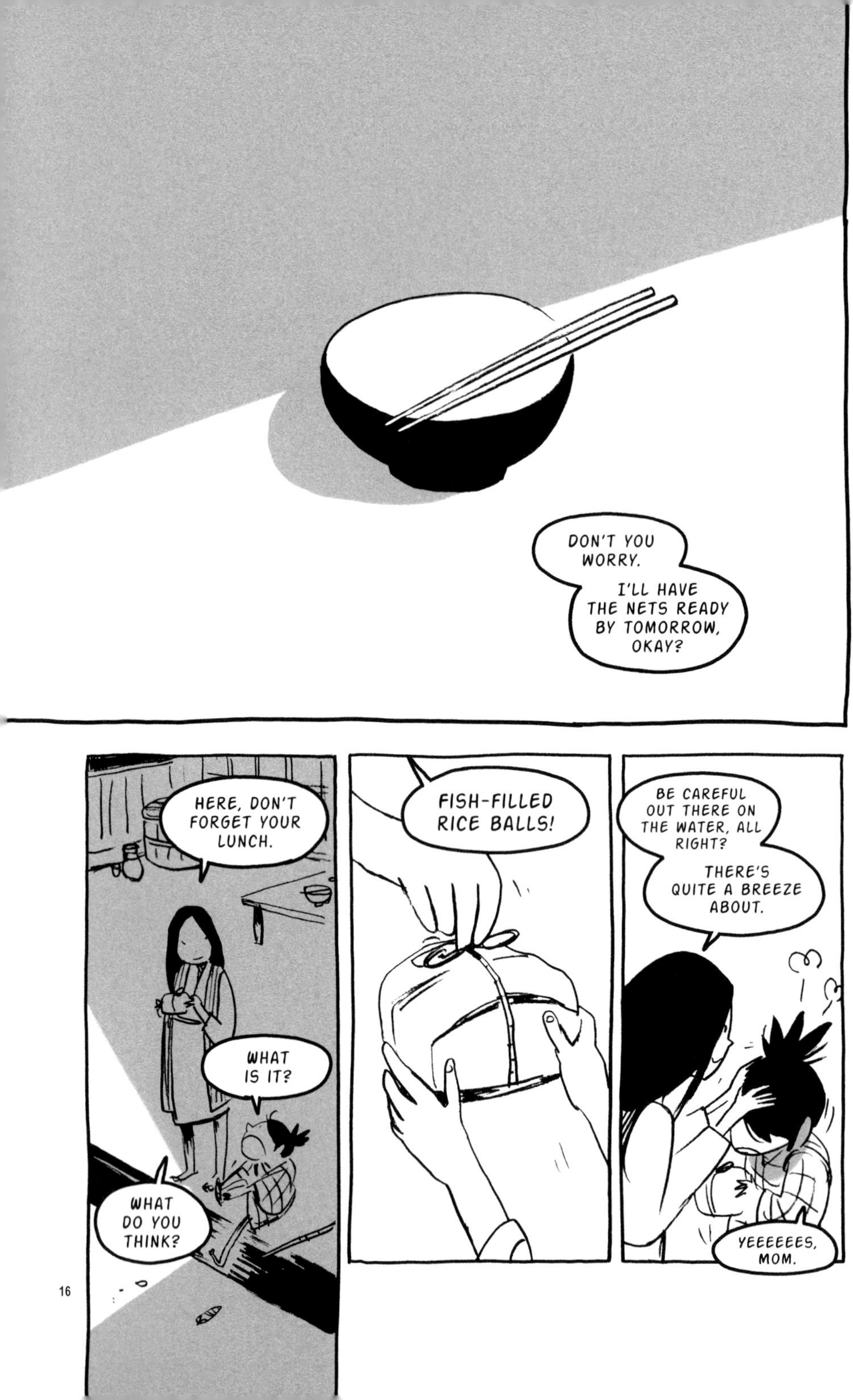
DON'T YOU WORRY.
I'LL HAVE THE NETS READY BY TOMORROW, OKAY?
HERE, DON'T FORGET YOUR LUNCH.
WHAT IS IT?
WHAT DO YOU THINK?
FISH-FILLED RICE BALLS!
BE CAREFUL OUT THERE ON THE WATER, ALL RIGHT?
THERE'S QUITE A BREEZE ABOUT.
YEEEEEES, MOM.

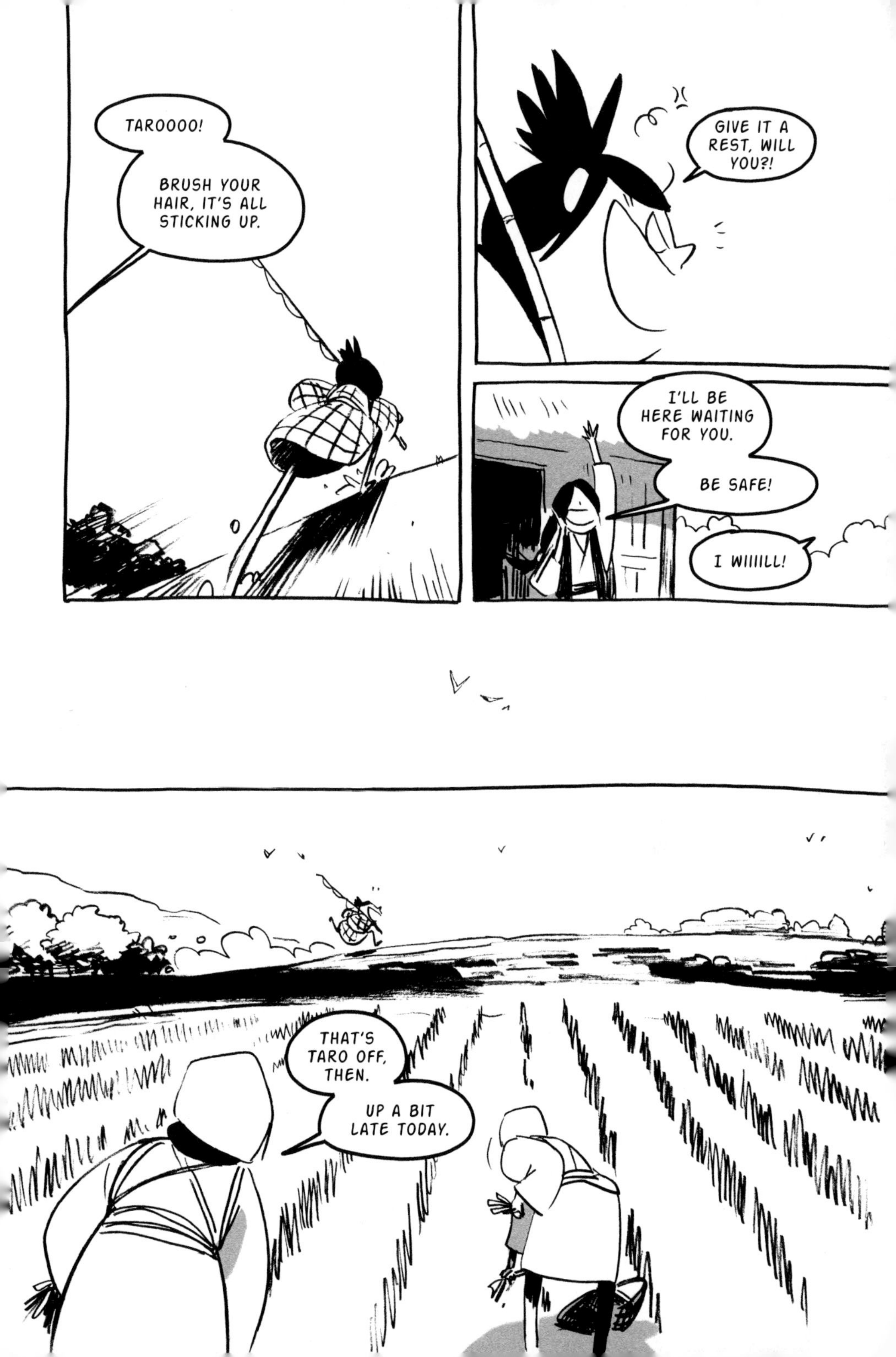
TAROOOO!
BRUSH YOUR HAIR, IT'S ALL STICKING UP.
GIVE IT A REST, WILL YOU?!
I'LL BE HERE WAITING FOR YOU.
BE SAFE!
I WIIIILL!
THAT'S TARO OFF, THEN.
UP A BIT LATE TODAY.

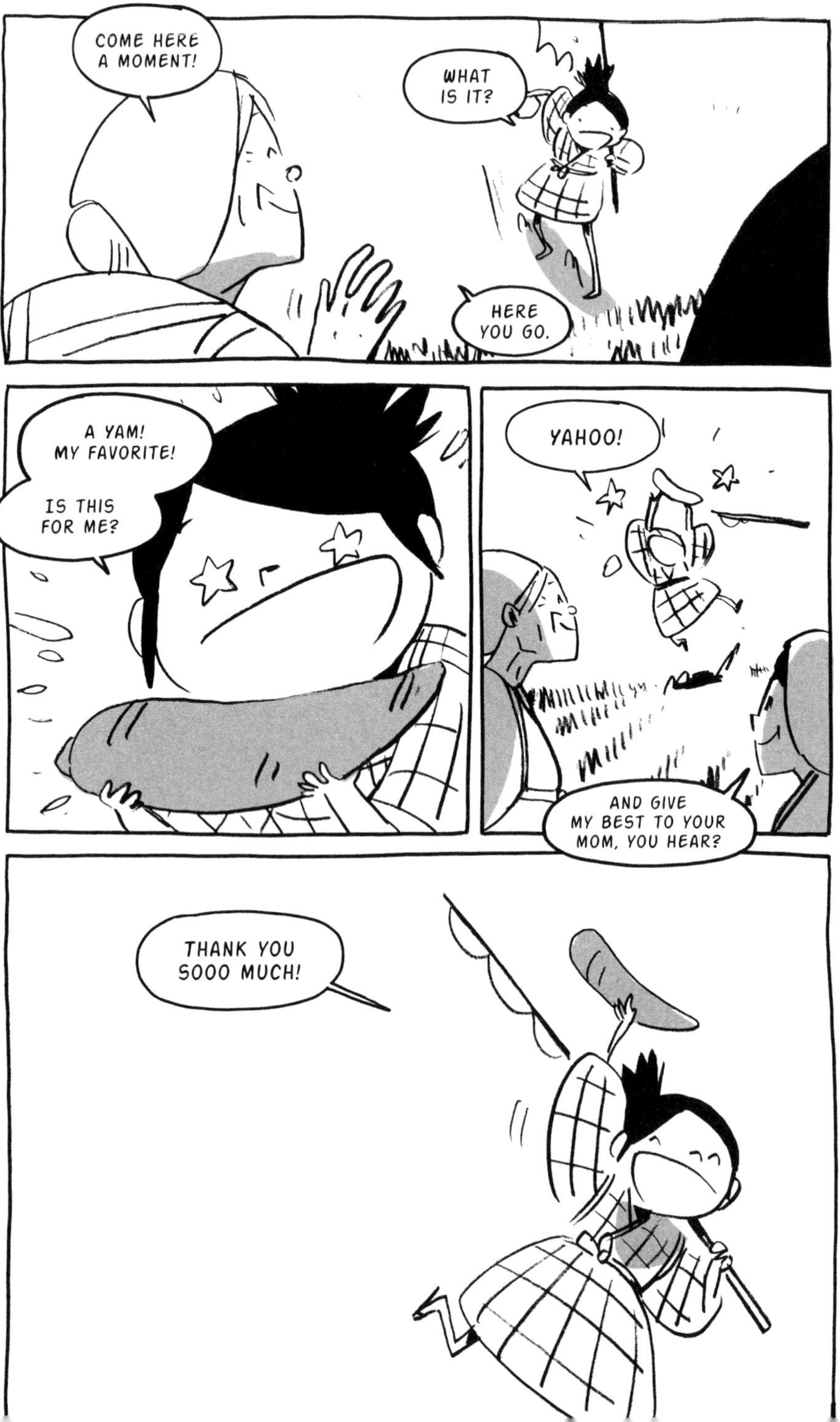
COME HERE A MOMENT!
WHAT IS IT?
HERE YOU GO.
A YAM! MY FAVORITE!
IS THIS FOR ME?
YAHOO!
AND GIVE MY BEST TO YOUR MOM, YOU HEAR?
THANK YOU SOOO MUCH!

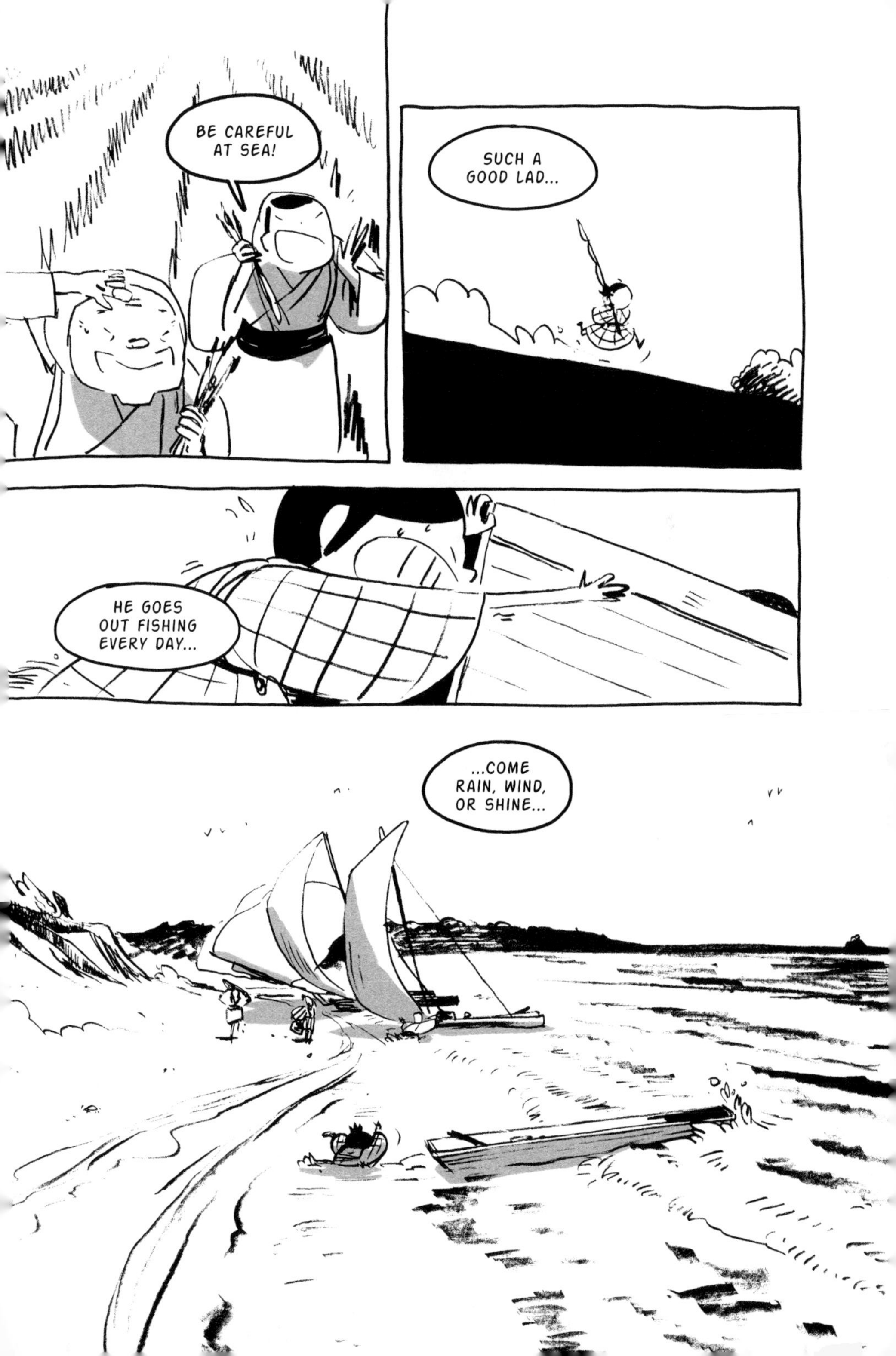
BE CAREFUL AT SEA!
SUCH A GOOD LAD...
HE GOES OUT FISHING EVERY DAY...
...COME RAIN, WIND, OR SHINE...

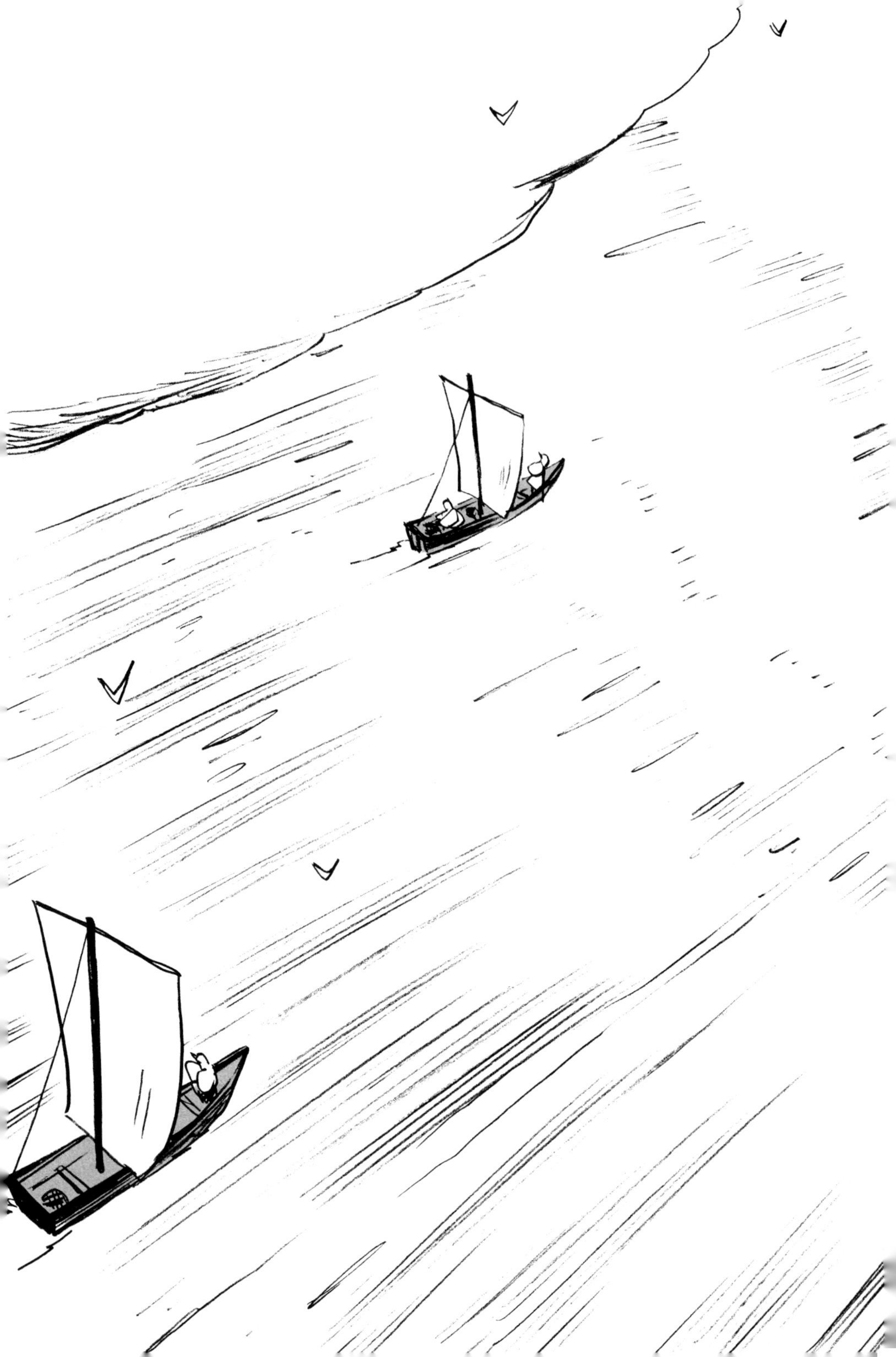

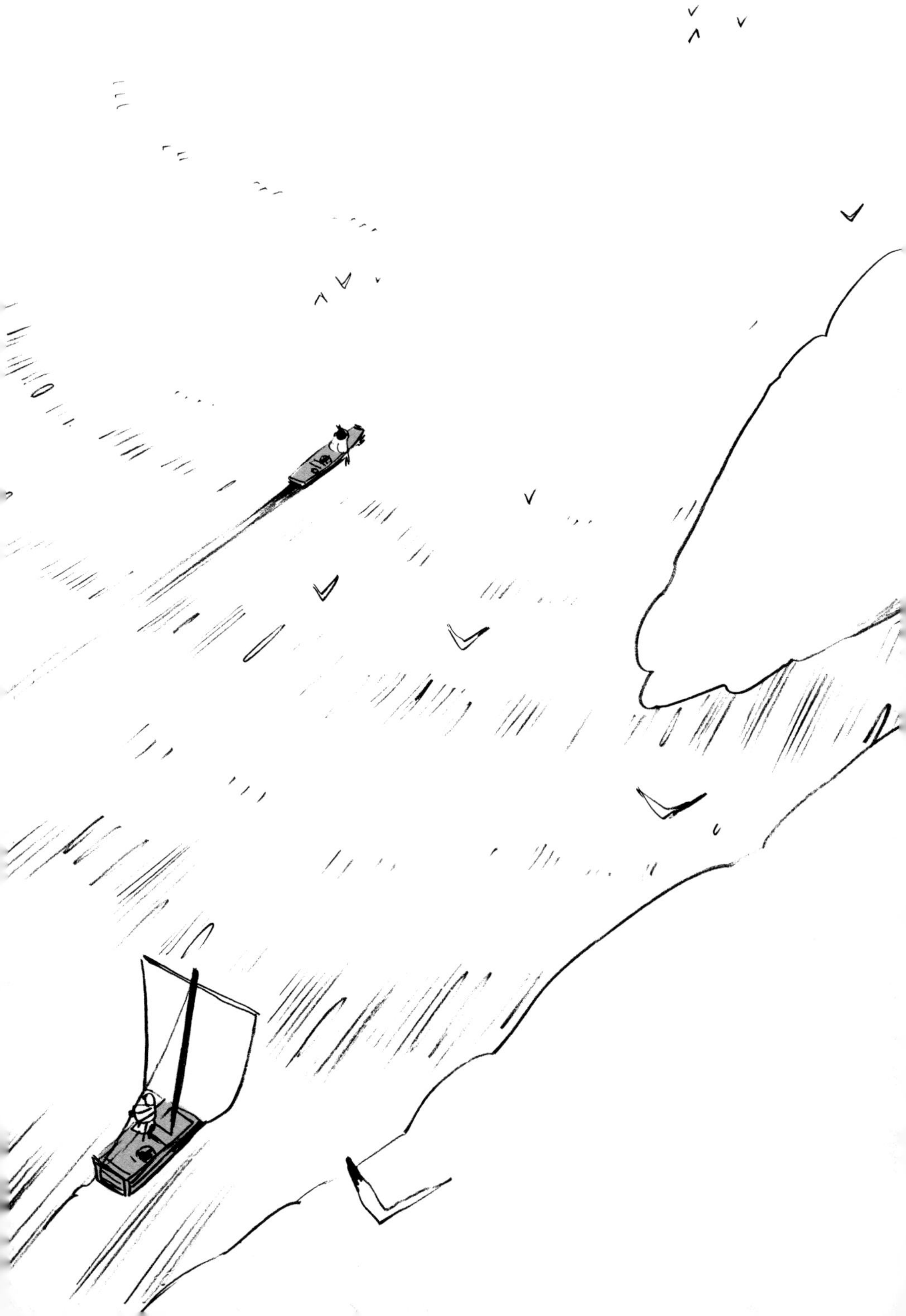

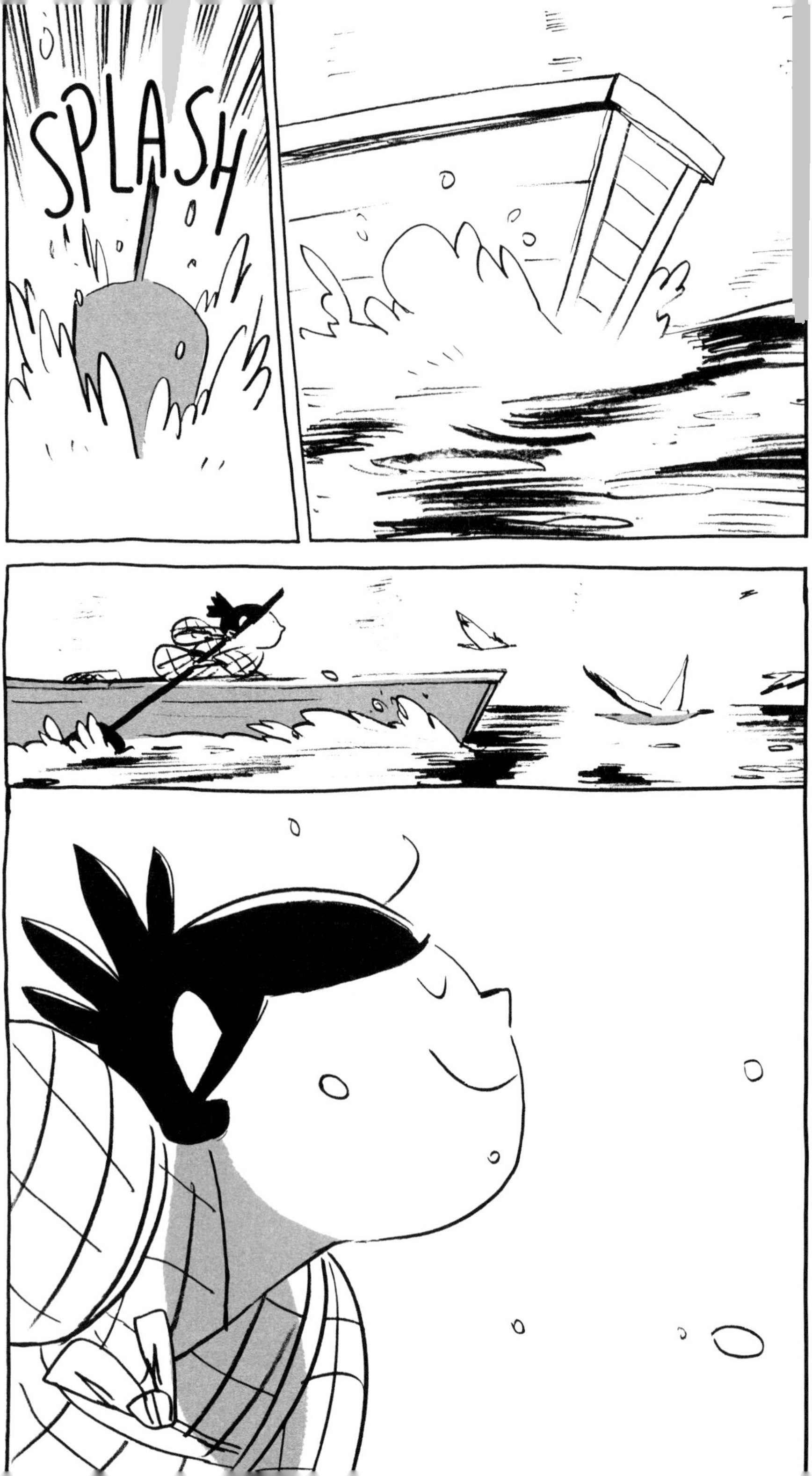
SPLASH

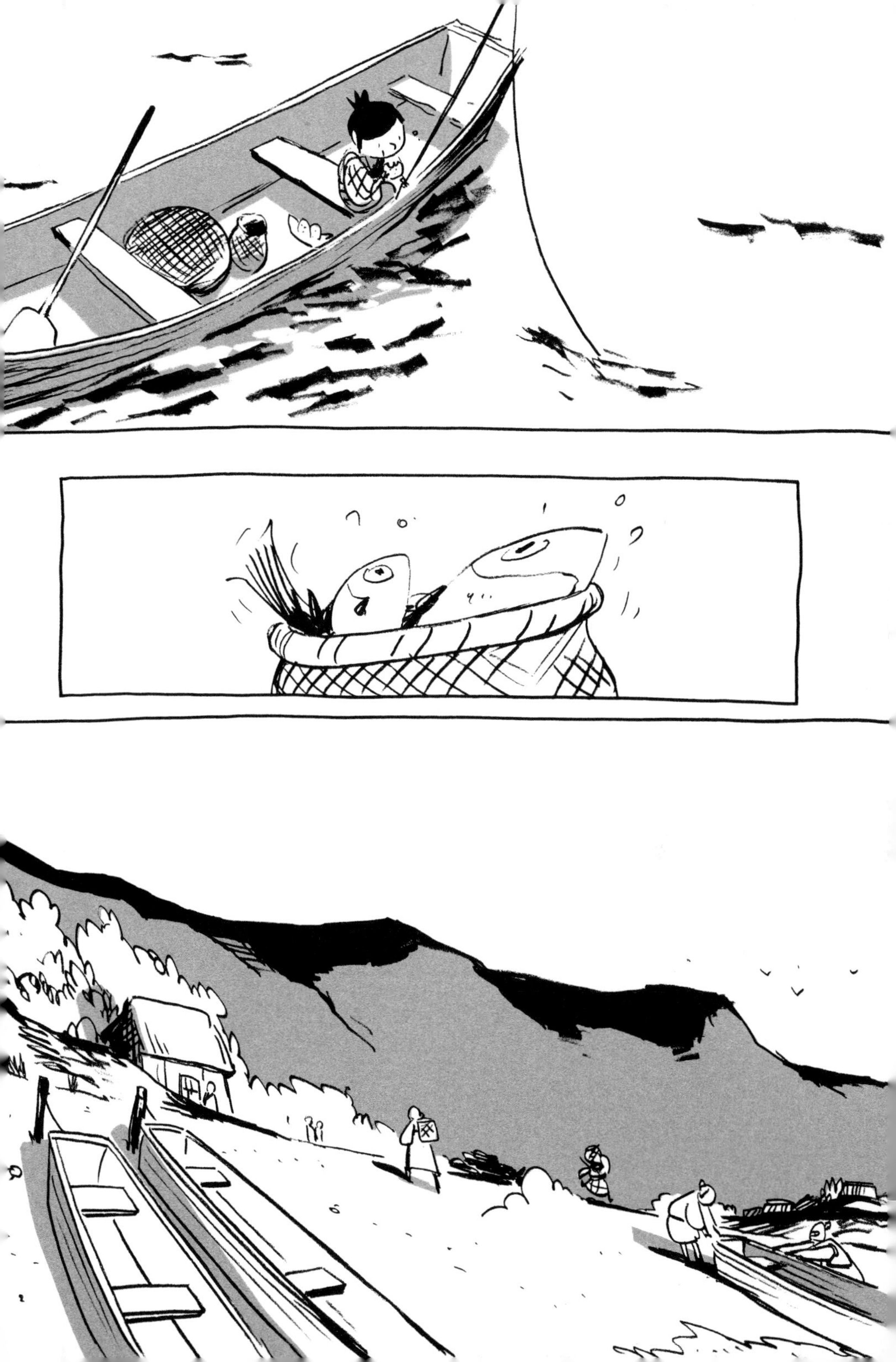

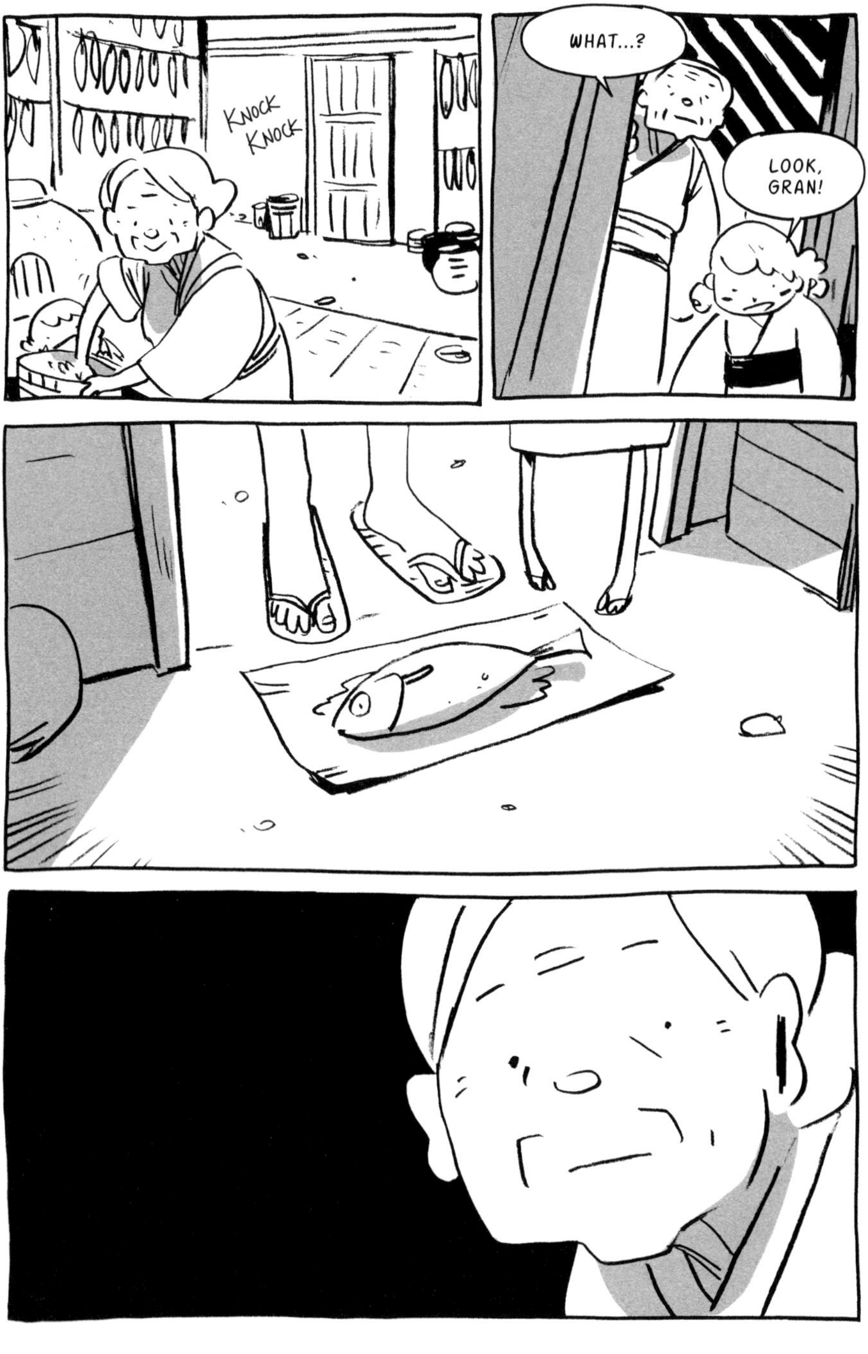
KNOCK
KNOCK
WHAT...?
LOOK, GRAN!

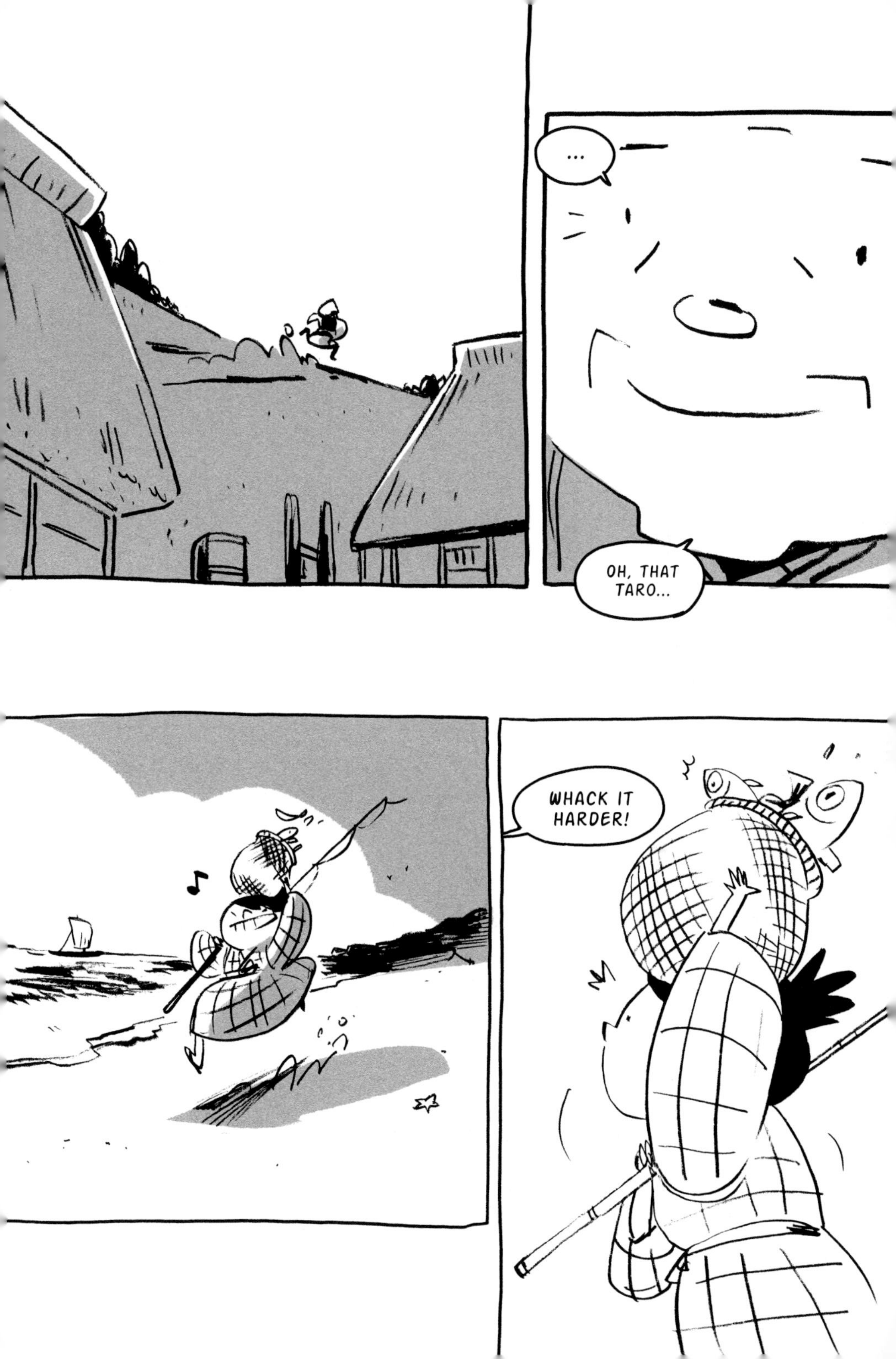
...
OH, THAT TARO...
WHACK IT HARDER!

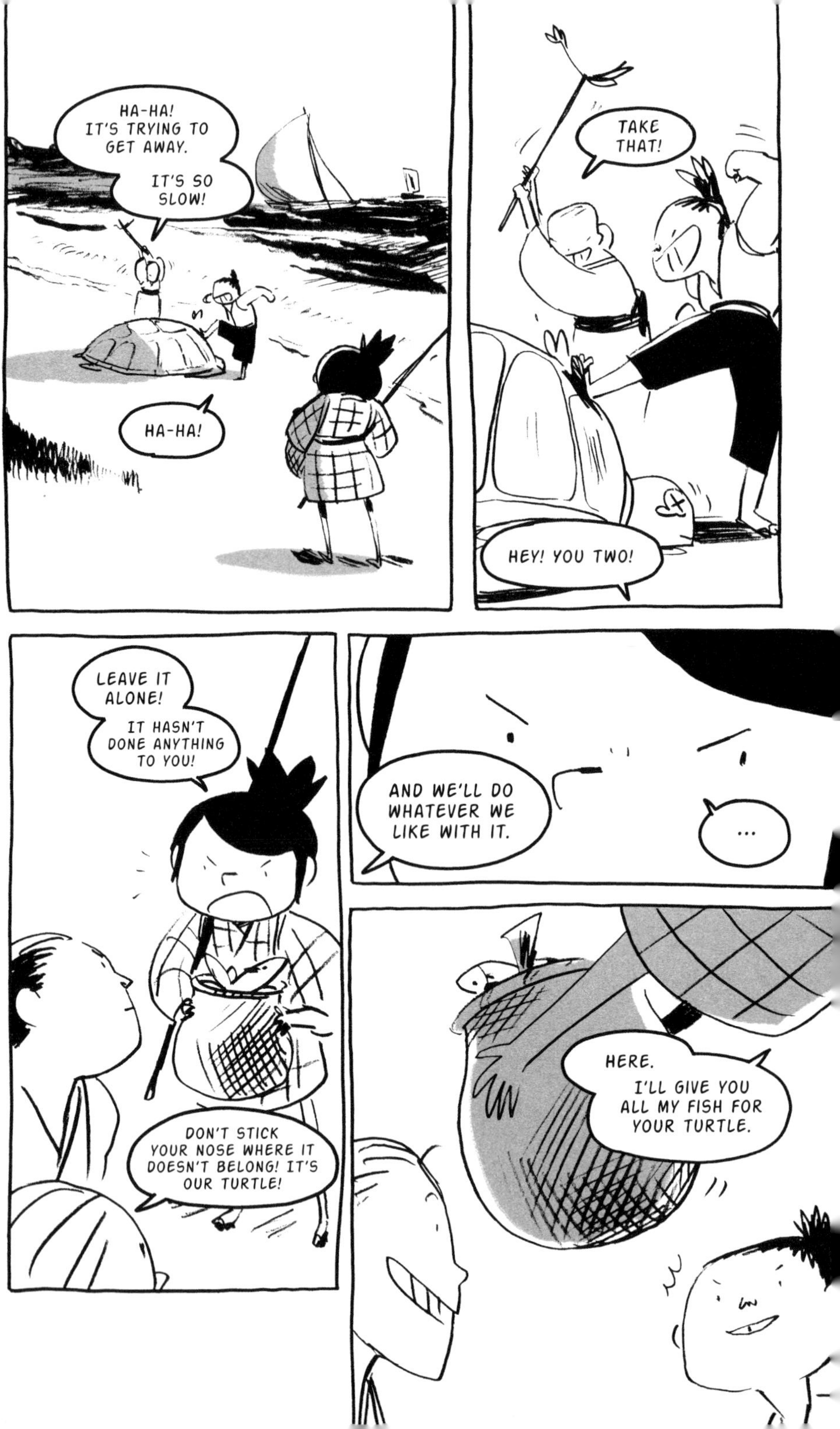
HA-HA! IT'S TRYING TO GET AWAY.
IT'S SO SLOW!
HA-HA!
TAKE THAT!
HEY! YOU TWO!
LEAVE IT ALONE!
IT HASN'T DONE ANYTHING TO YOU!
DON'T STICK YOUR NOSE WHERE IT DOESN'T BELONG! IT'S OUR TURTLE!
AND WE'LL DO WHATEVER WE LIKE WITH IT.
...
HERE.
I'LL GIVE YOU ALL MY FISH FOR YOUR TURTLE.

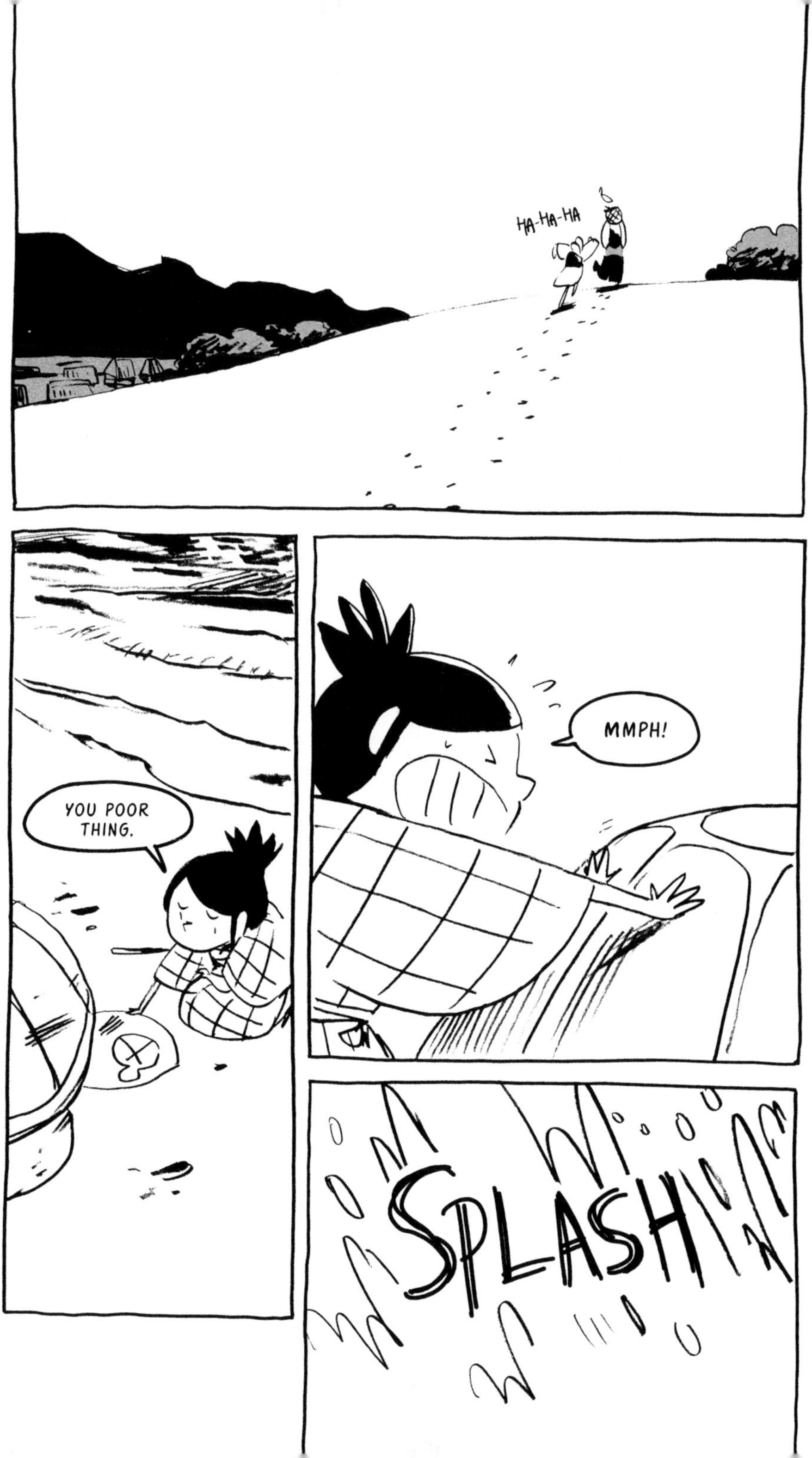
HA-HA-HA
YOU POOR THING.
MMPH!
SPLASH

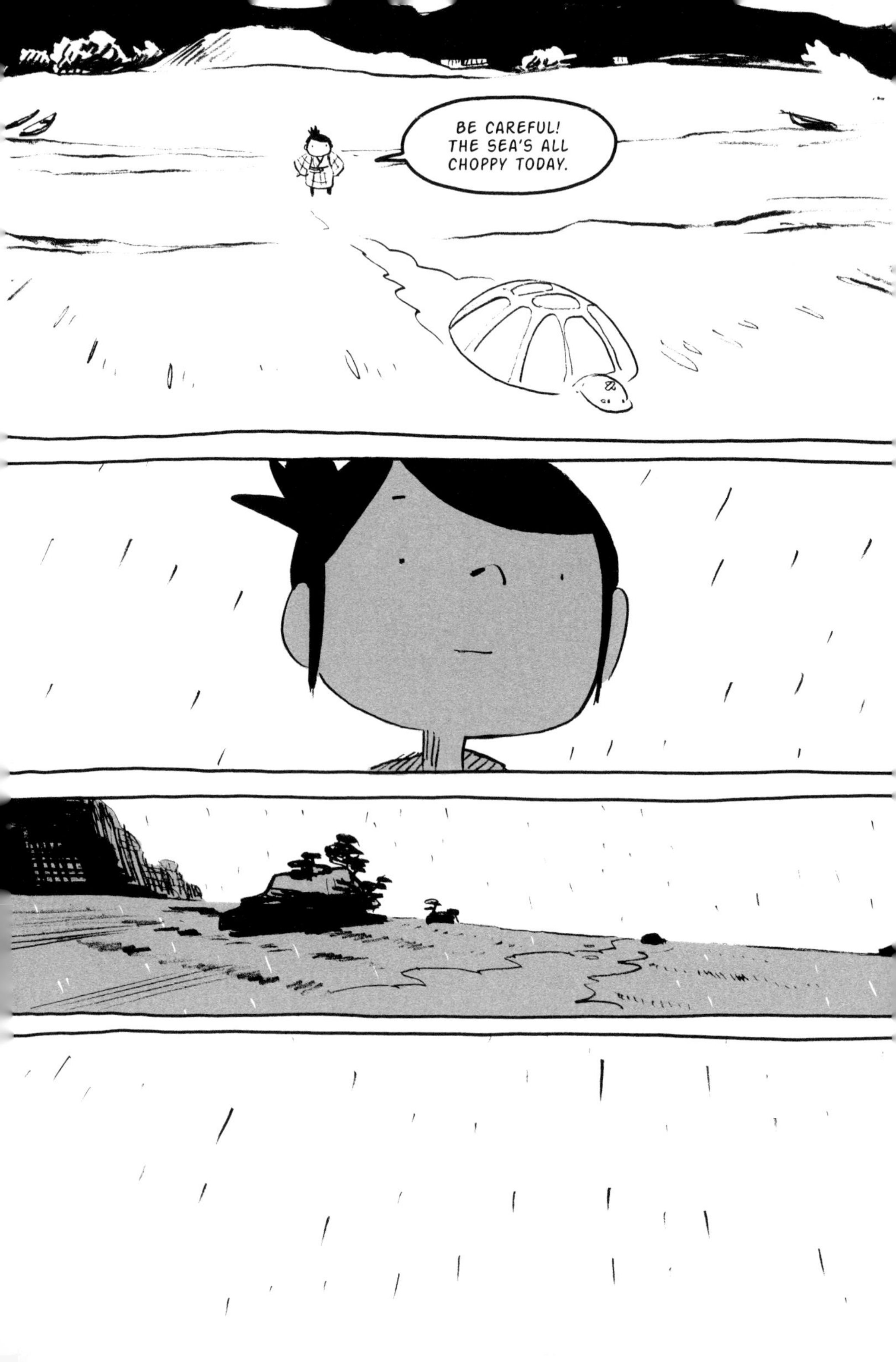
BE CAREFUL! THE SEA'S ALL CHOPPY TODAY.

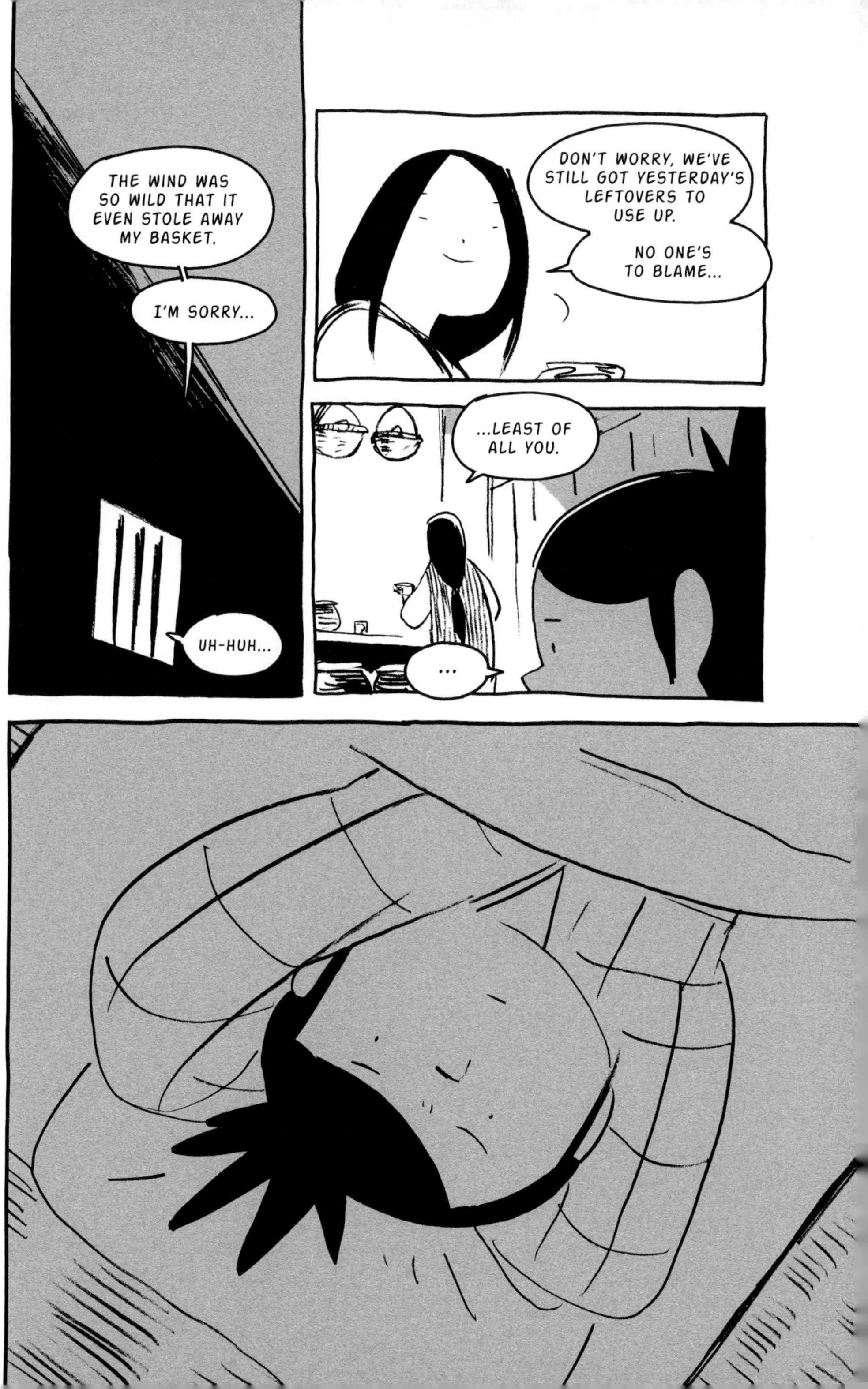
THE WIND WAS SO WILD THAT IT EVEN STOLE AWAY MY BASKET.
I'M SORRY...
UH-HUH...
DON'T WORRY, WE'VE STILL GOT YESTERDAY'S LEFTOVERS TO USE UP.
NO ONE'S TO BLAME...
...LEAST OF ALL YOU.
...

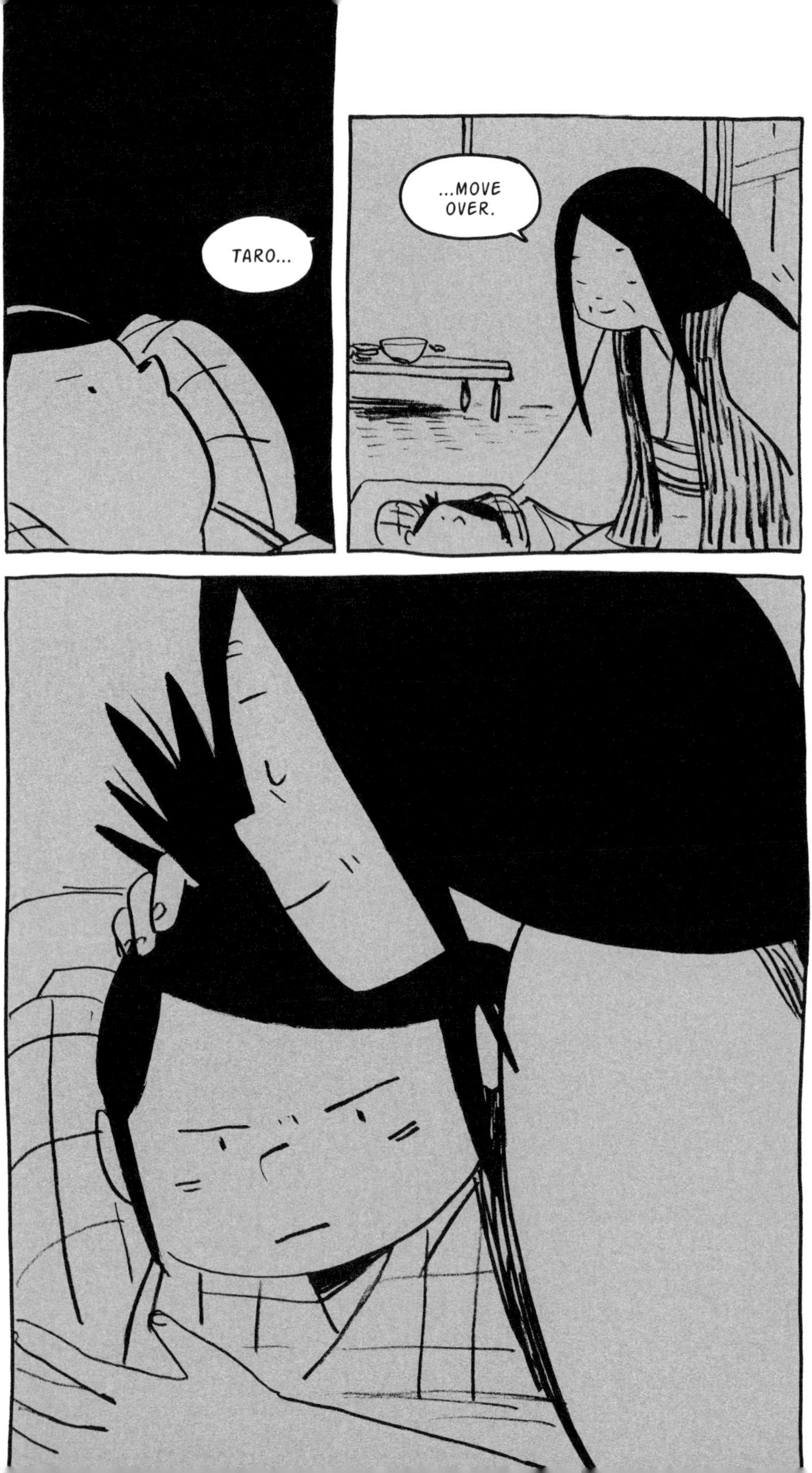
TARO...
...MOVE OVER.

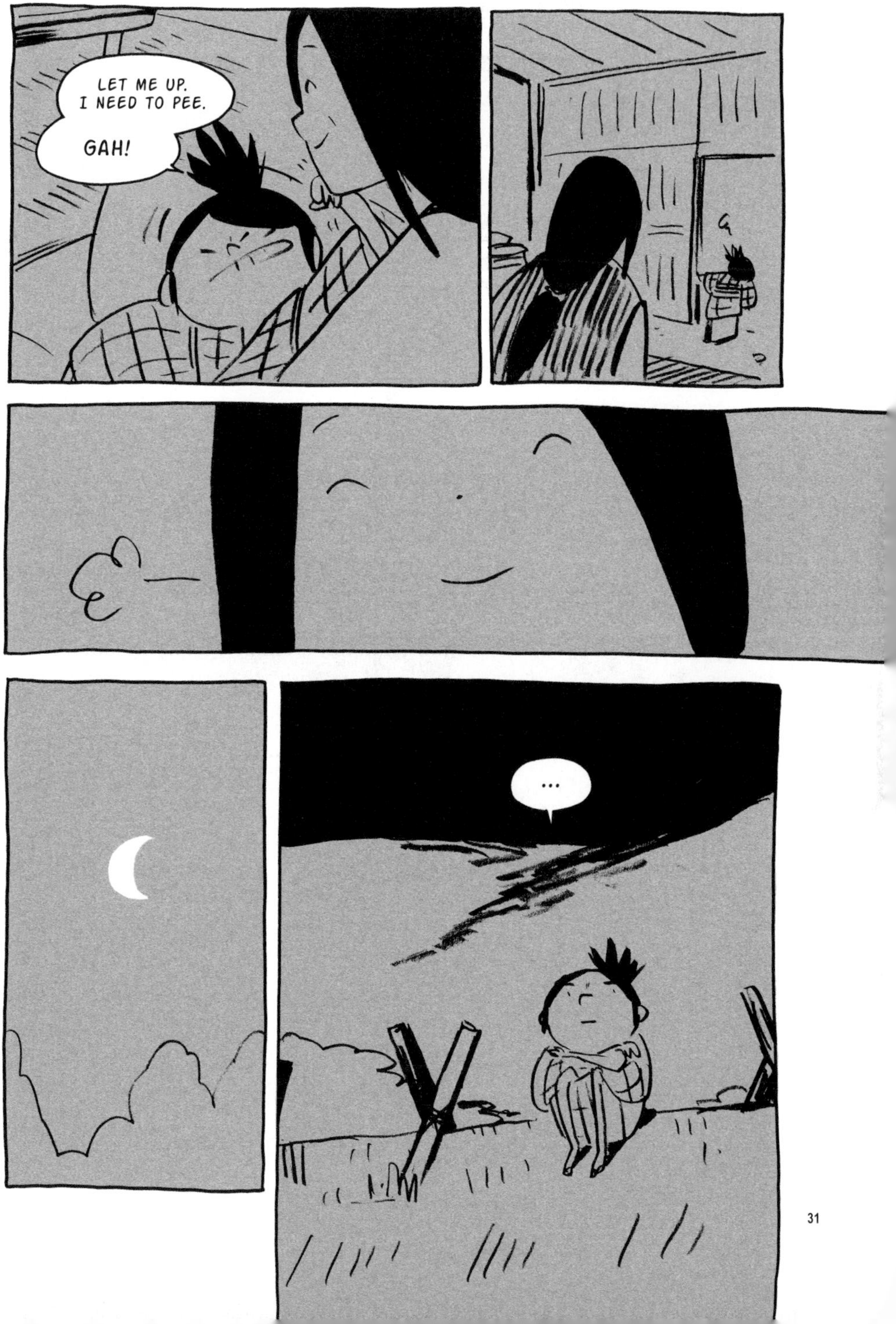
LET ME UP. I NEED TO PEE.
GAH!
...

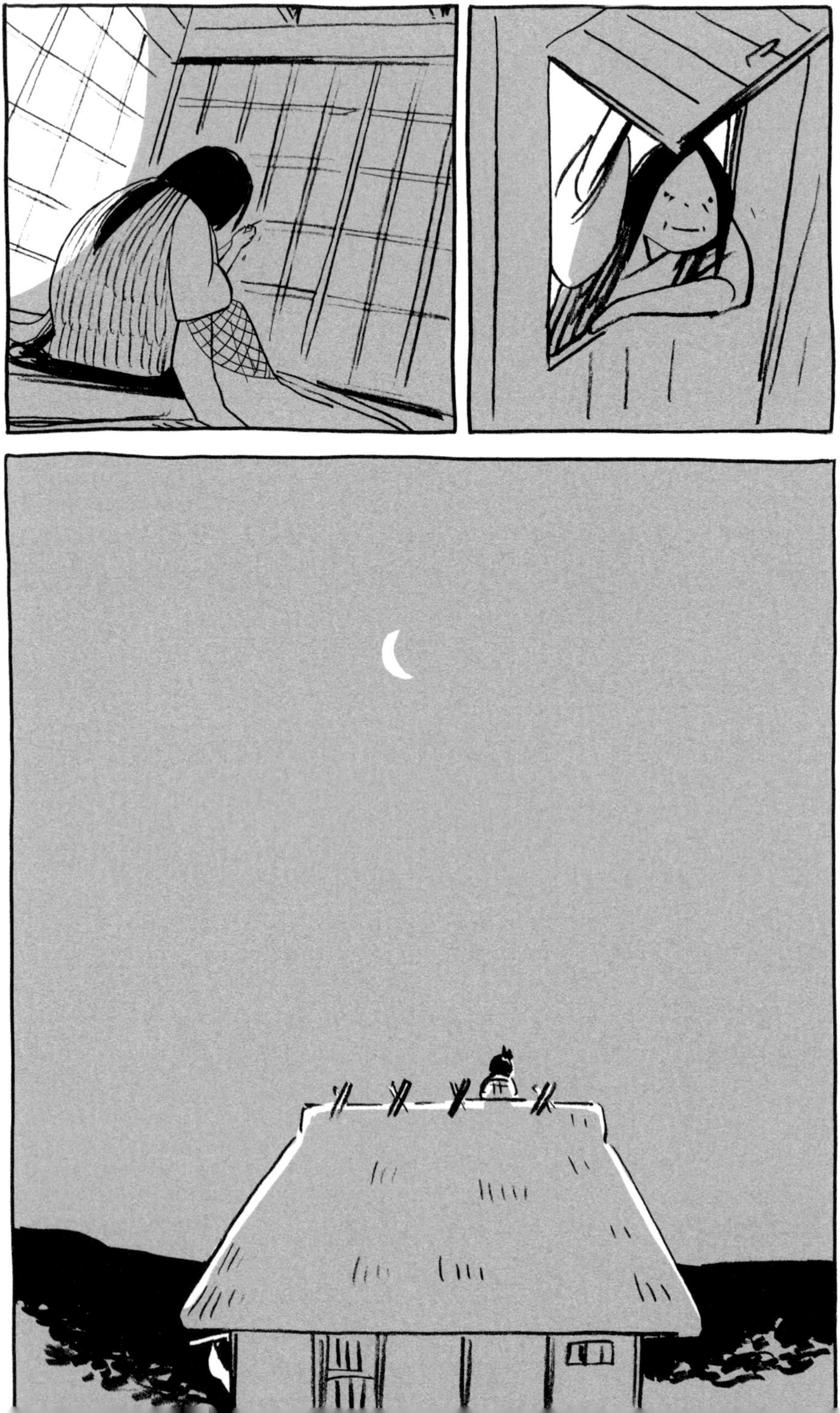

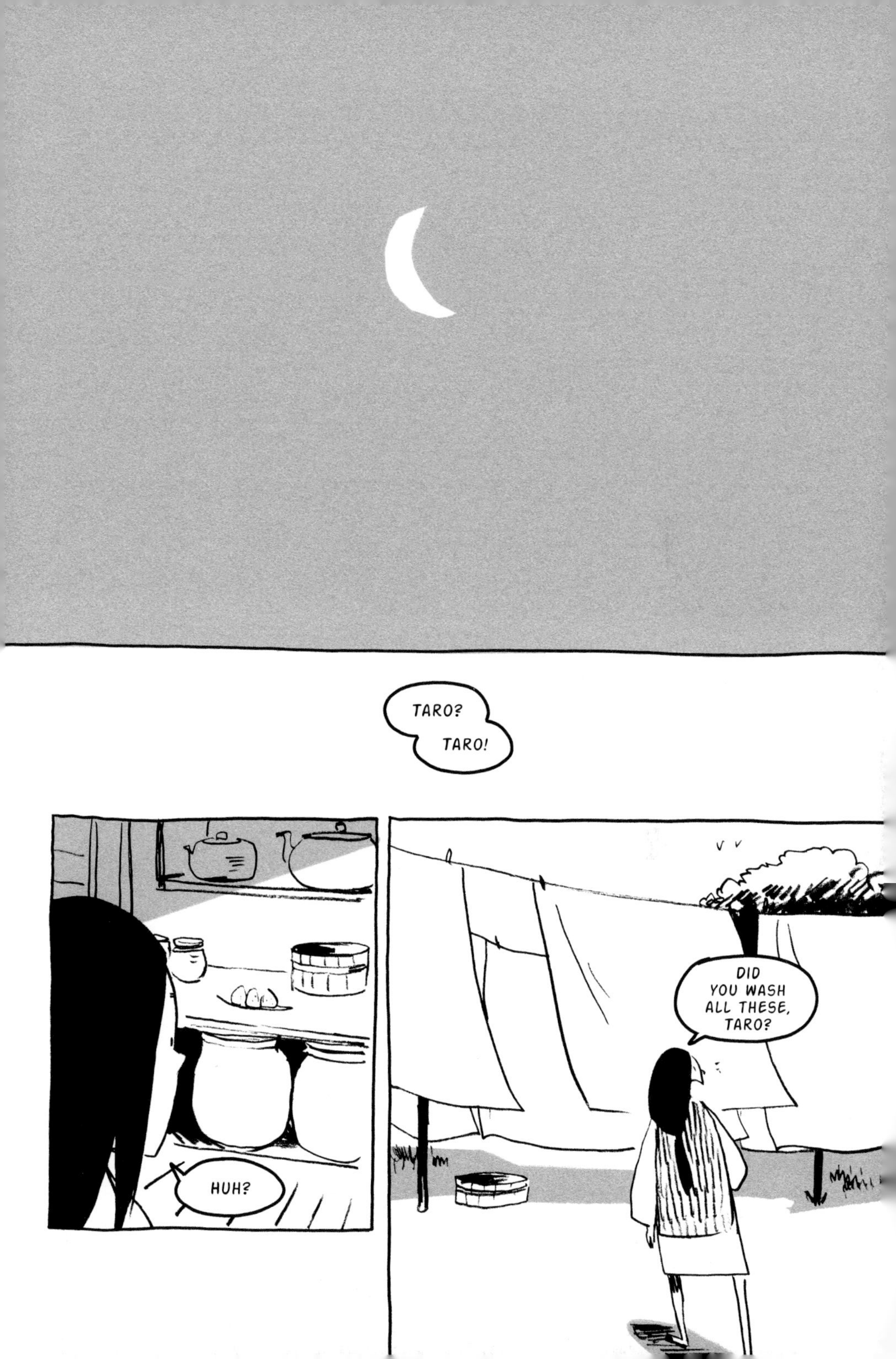
TARO?
TARO!
HUH?
DID YOU WASH ALL THESE, TARO?

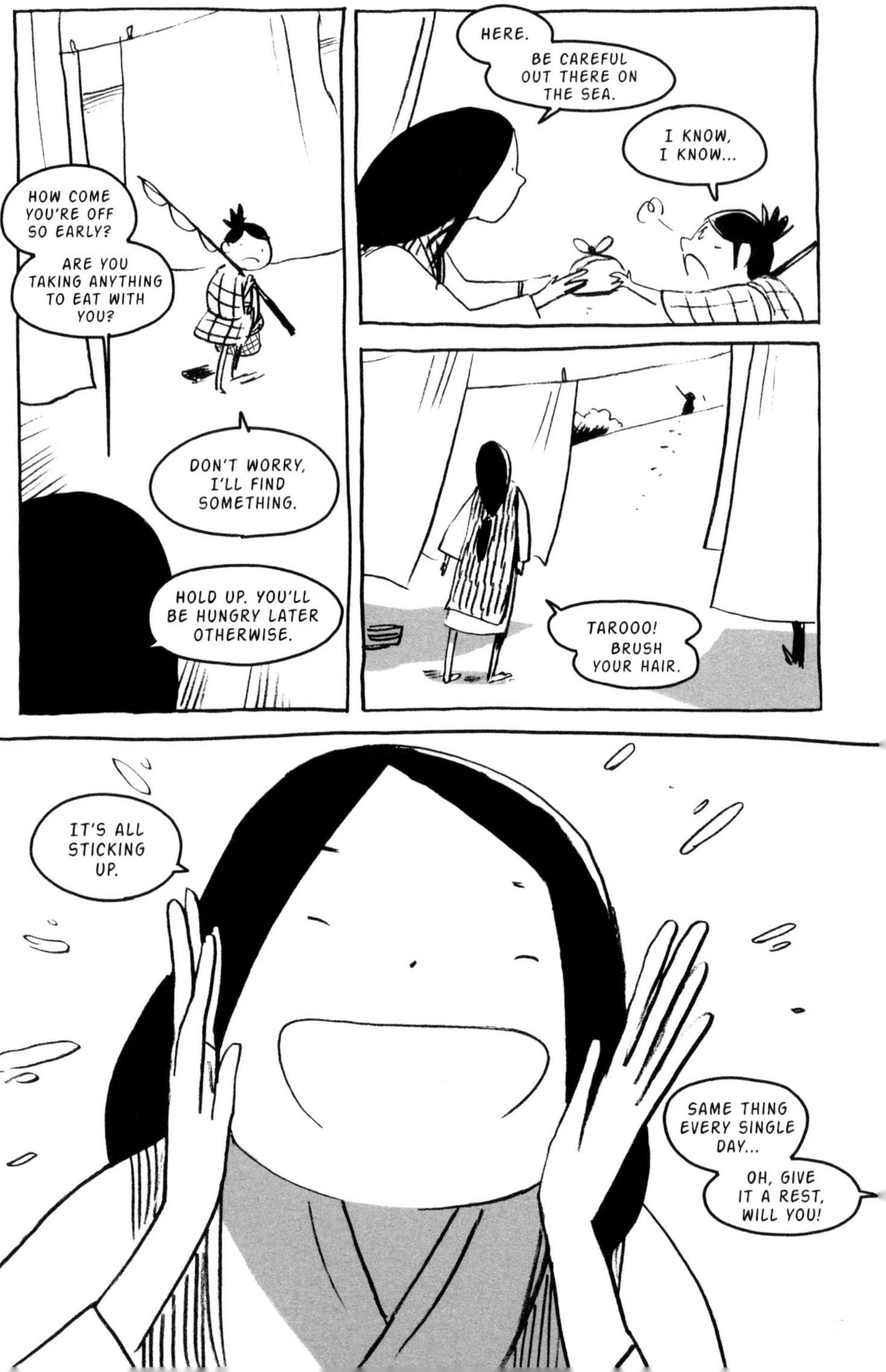
HOW COME YOU'RE OFF SO EARLY?
ARE YOU TAKING ANYTHING TO EAT WITH YOU?
DON'T WORRY, I'LL FIND SOMETHING.
HOLD UP. YOU'LL BE HUNGRY LATER OTHERWISE.
HERE.
BE CAREFUL OUT THERE ON THE SEA.
I KNOW, I KNOW...
TAROOO! BRUSH YOUR HAIR.
IT'S ALL STICKING UP.
SAME THING EVERY SINGLE DAY...
OH, GIVE IT A REST, WILL YOU!

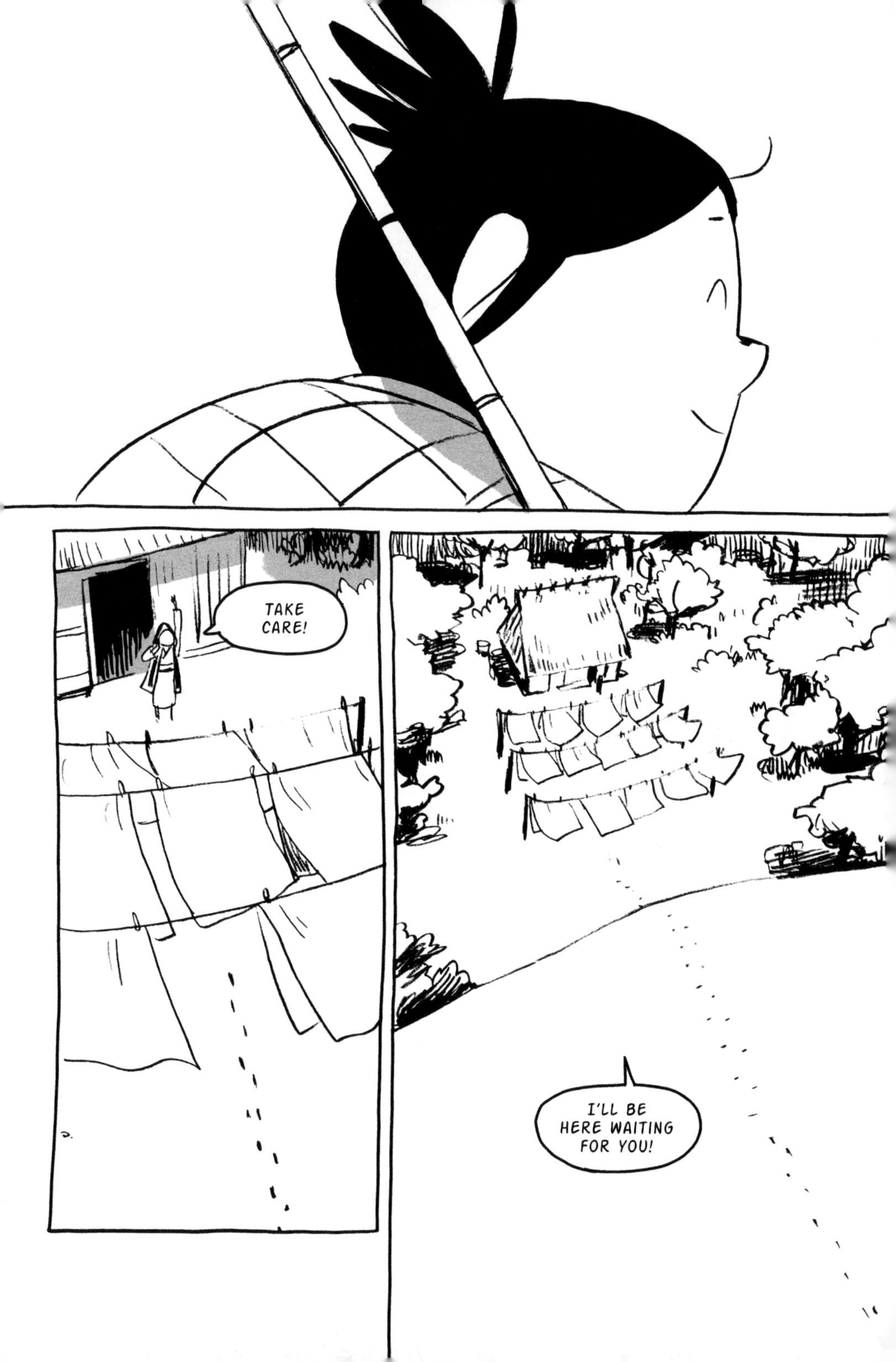
TAKE CARE!
I'LL BE HERE WAITING FOR YOU!

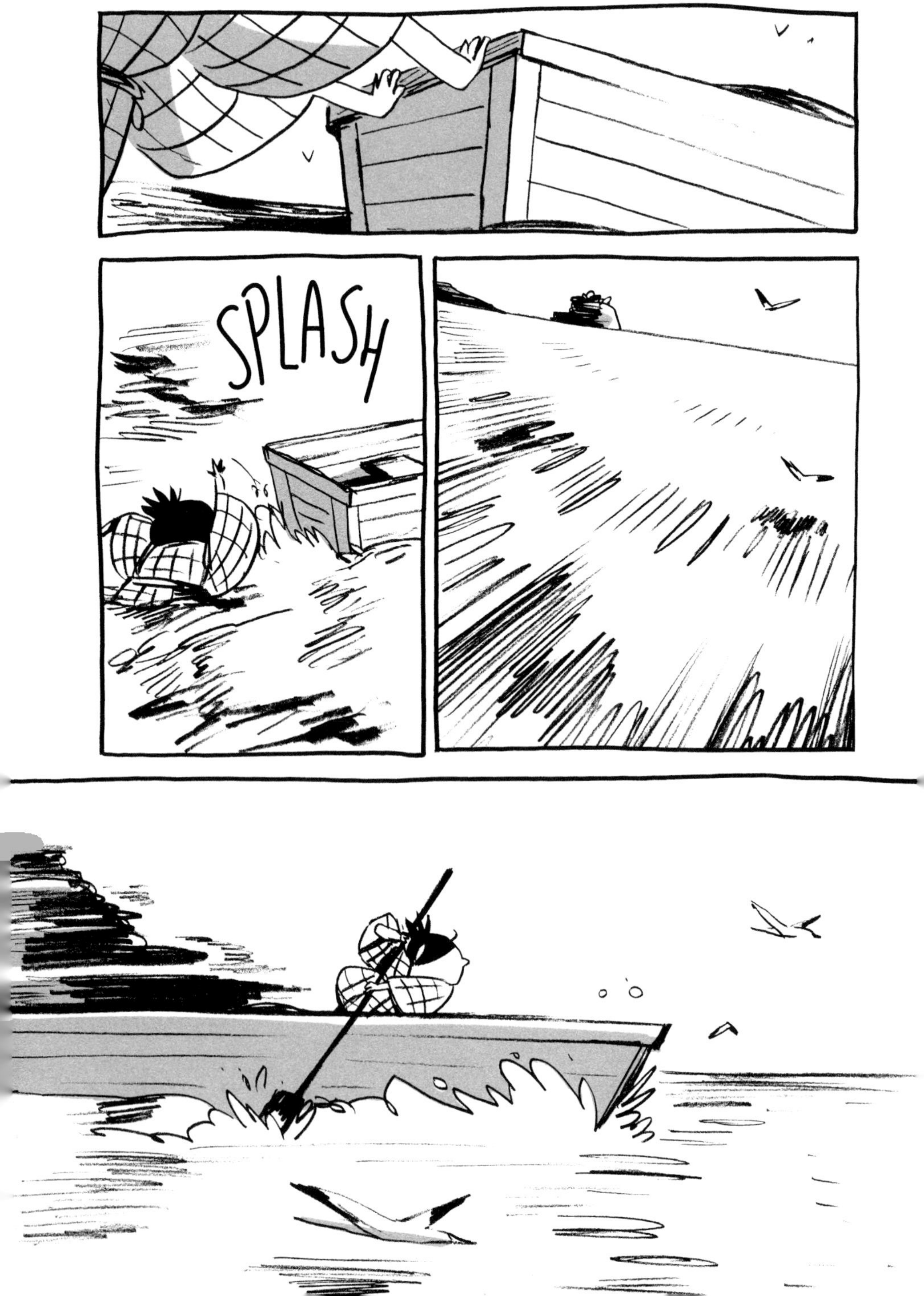
SPLASH

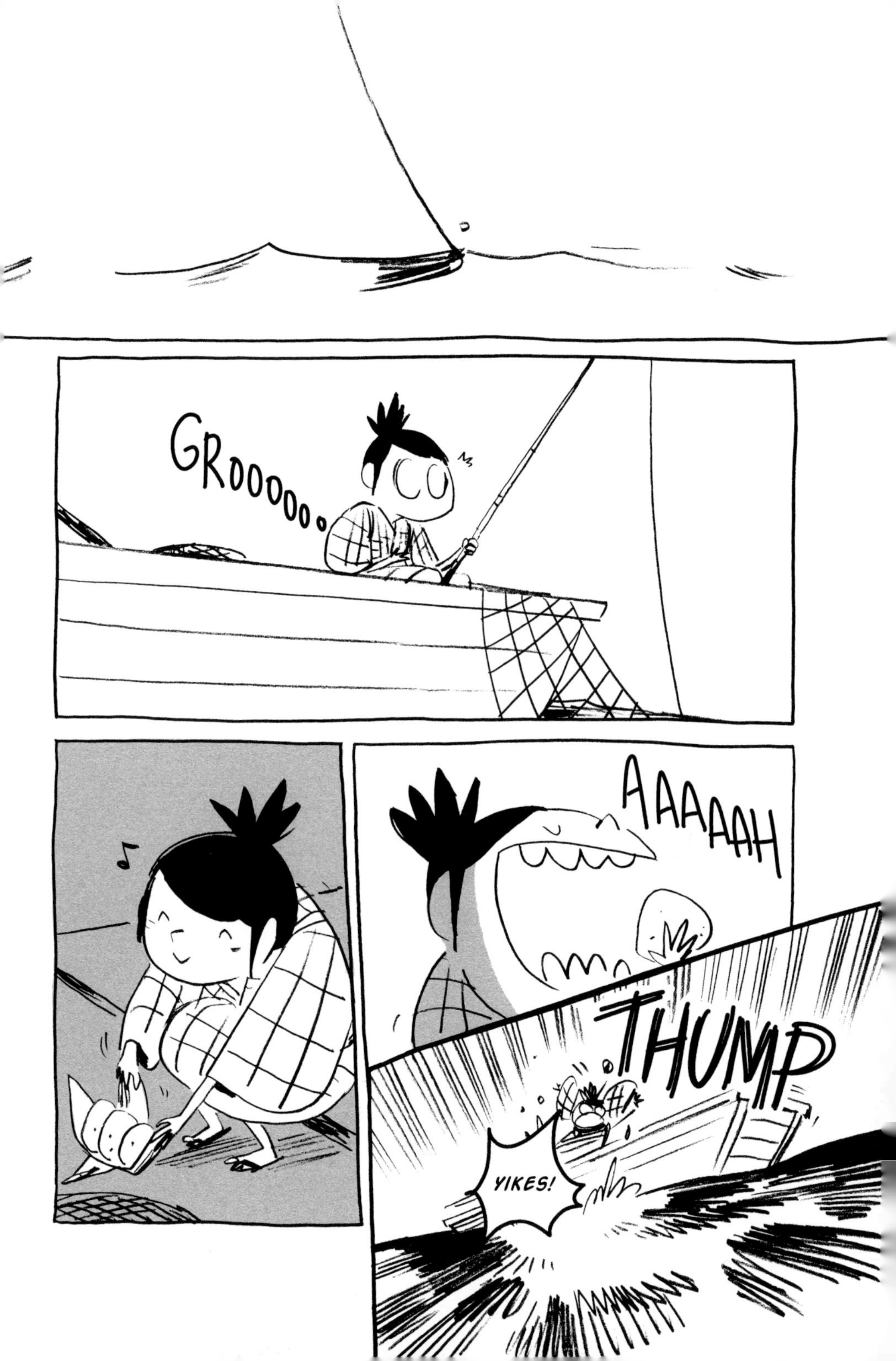
GROOOOOOo
AAAAAH
THUMP
YIKES!

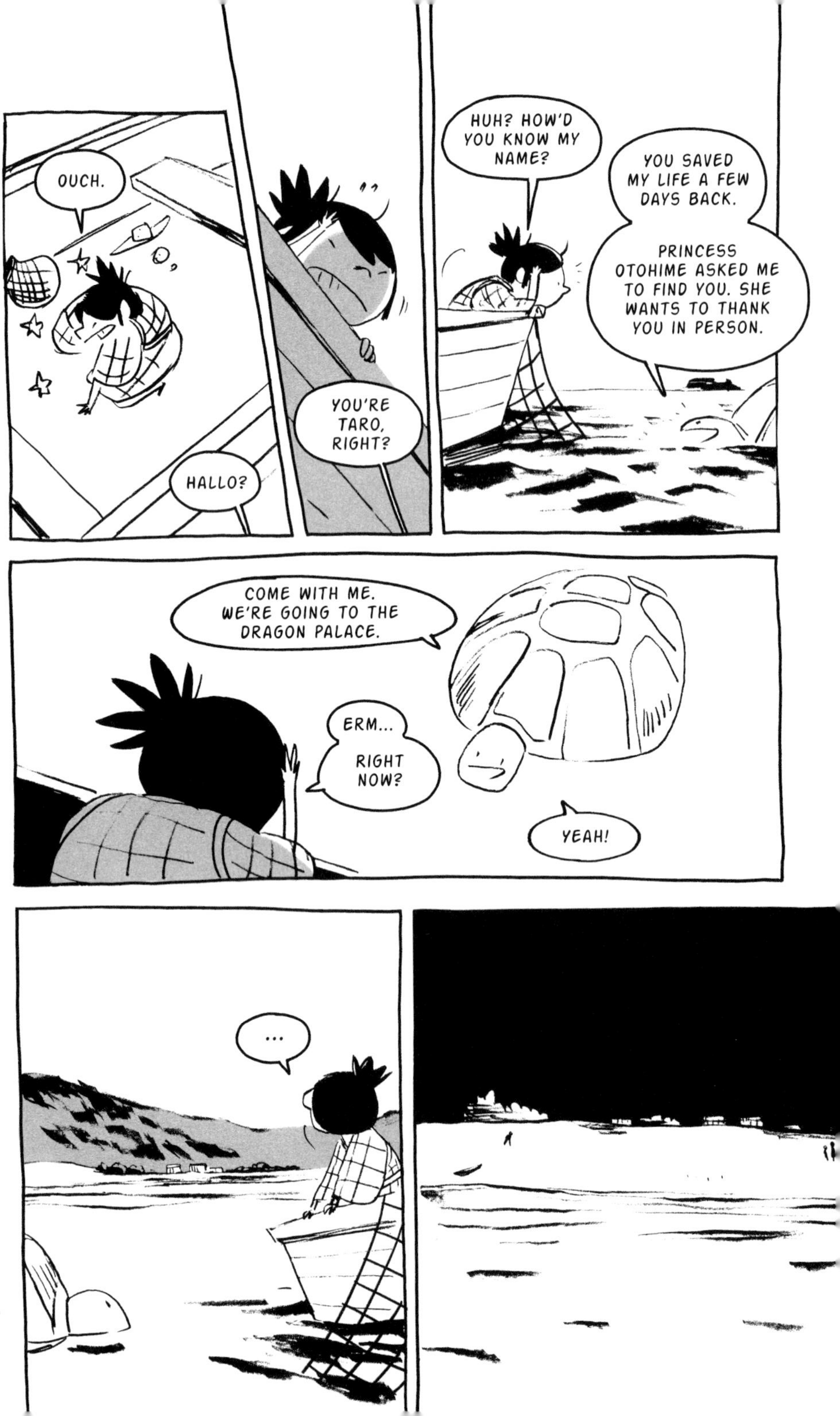
OUCH.
HALLO?
YOU'RE TARO, RIGHT?
HUH? HOW'D YOU KNOW MY NAME?
YOU SAVED MY LIFE A FEW DAYS BACK.
PRINCESS OTOHIME ASKED ME TO FIND YOU. SHE WANTS TO THANK YOU IN PERSON.
COME WITH ME. WE'RE GOING TO THE DRAGON PALACE.
ERM... RIGHT NOW?
YEAH!
...

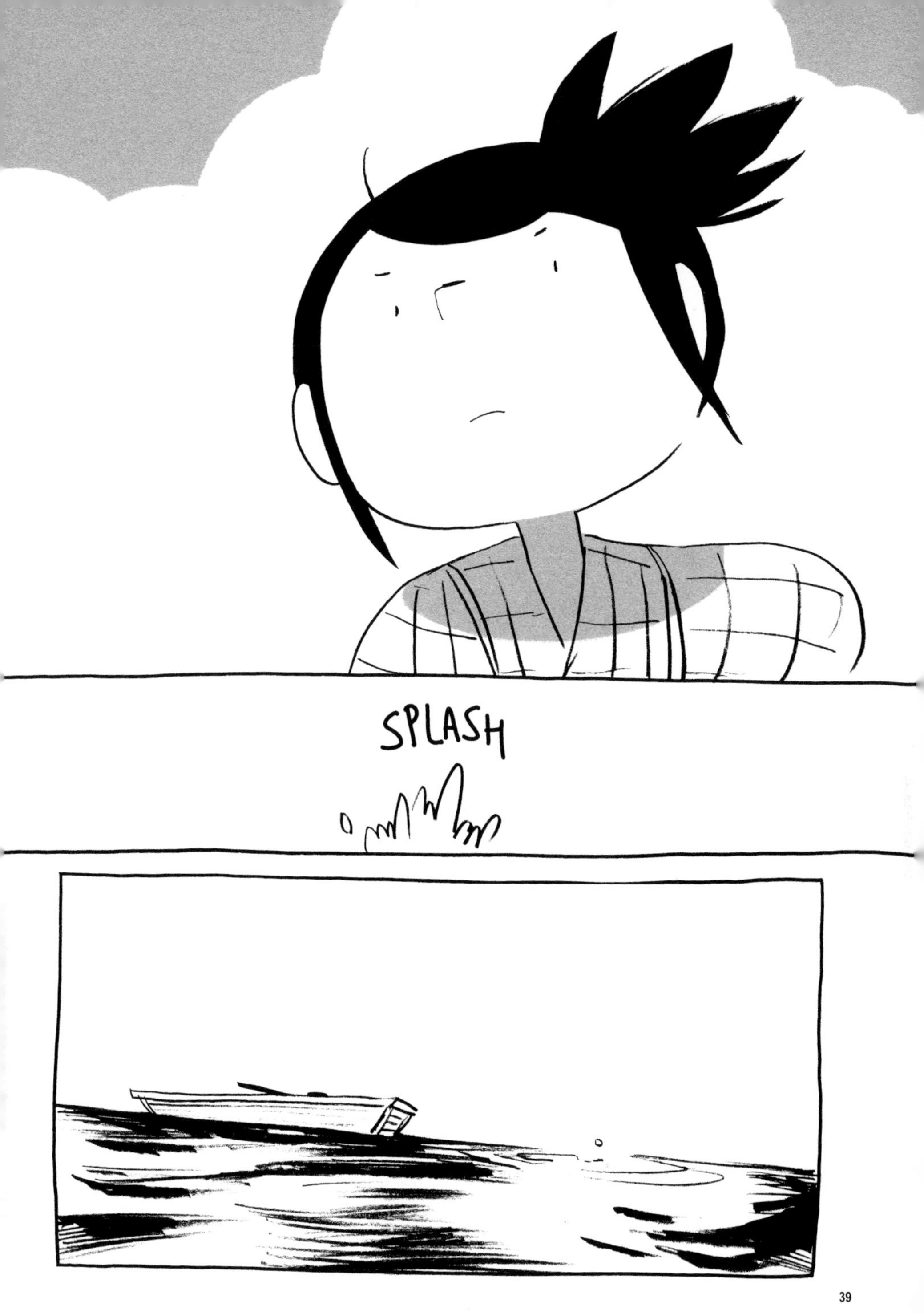
SPLASH

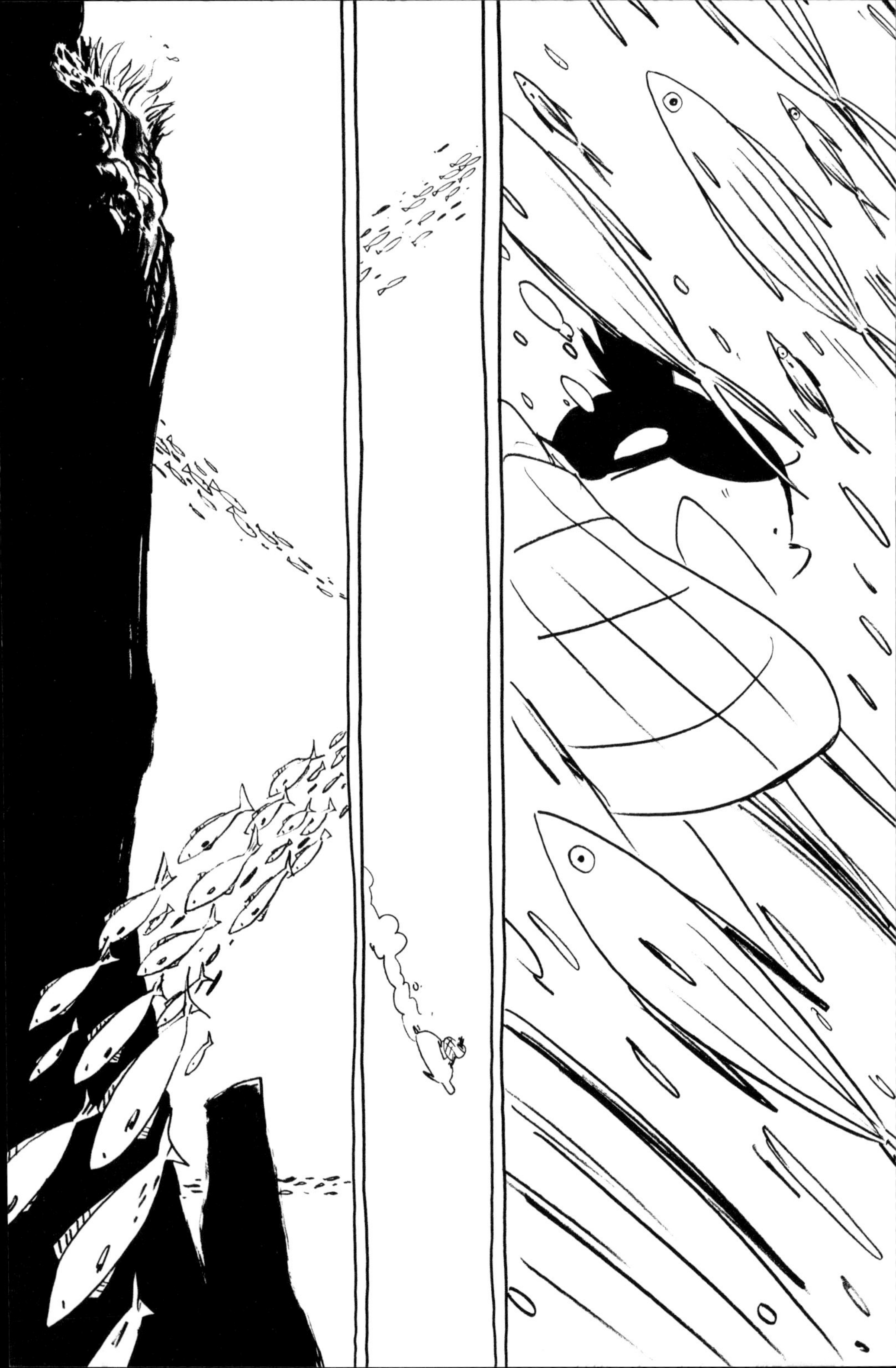

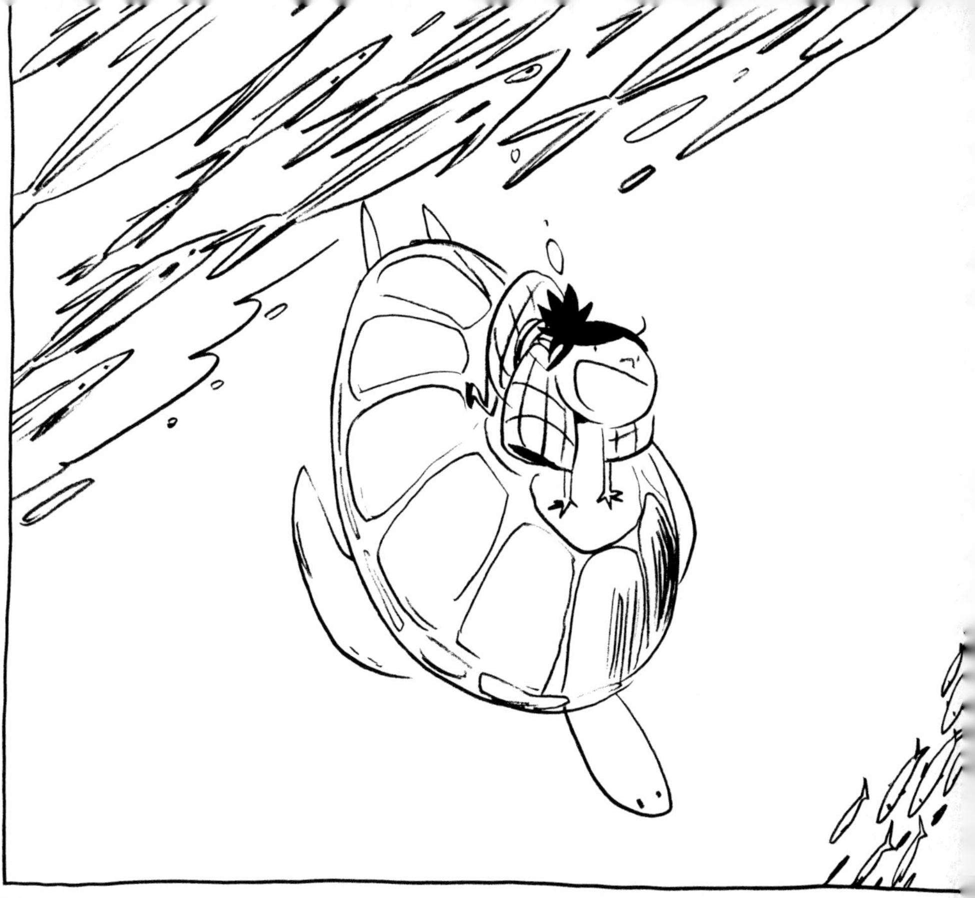

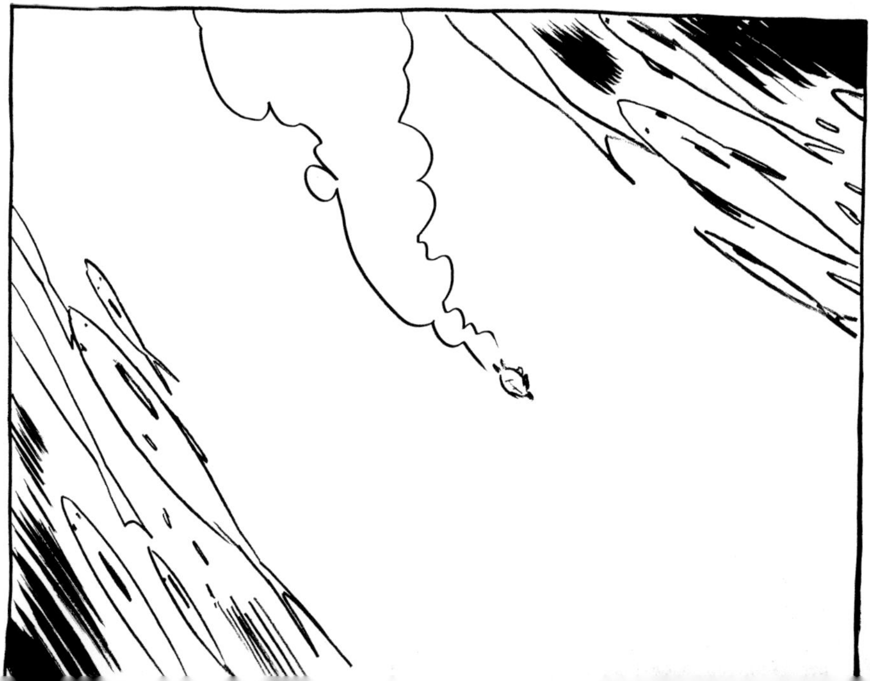

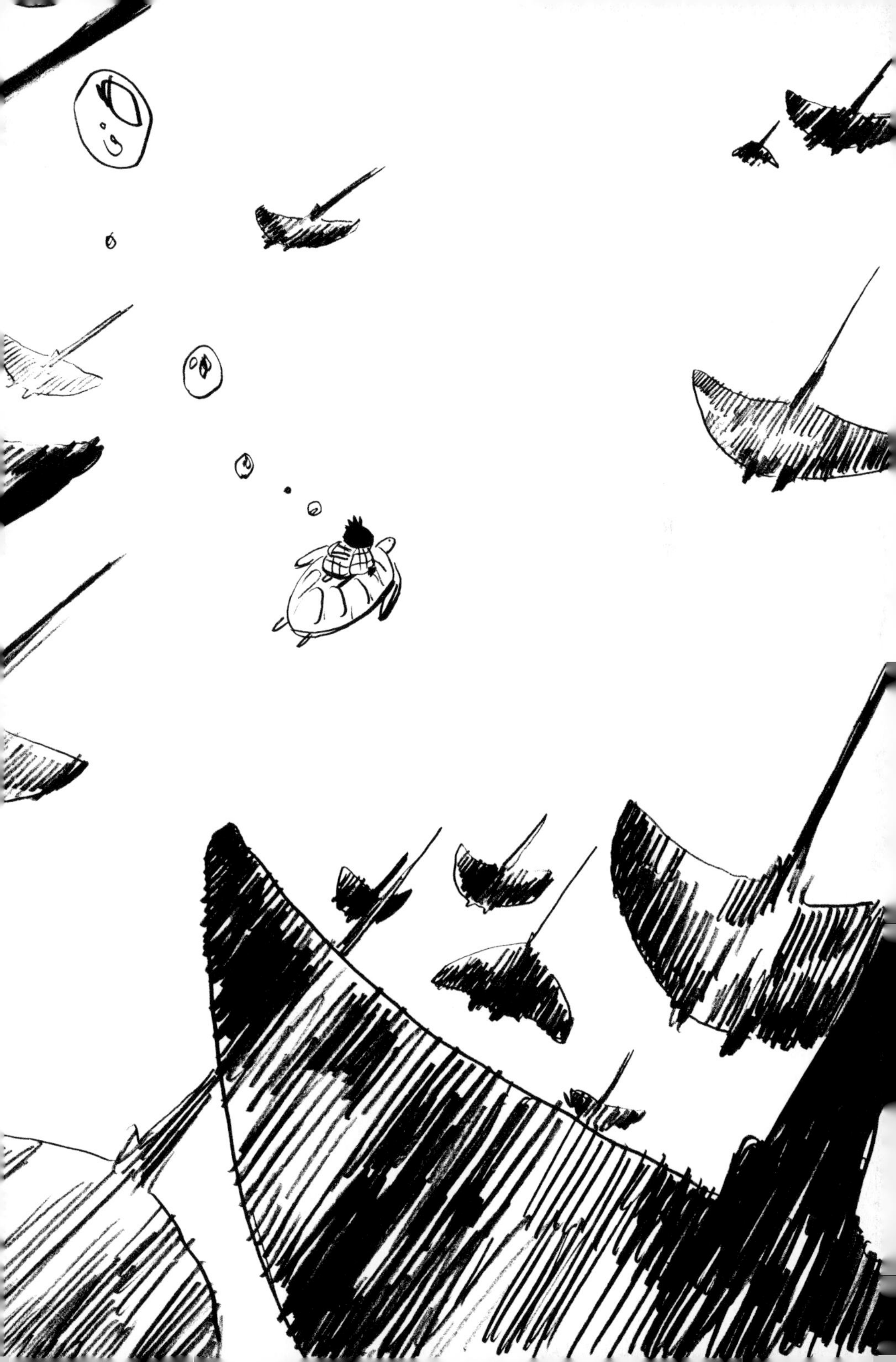

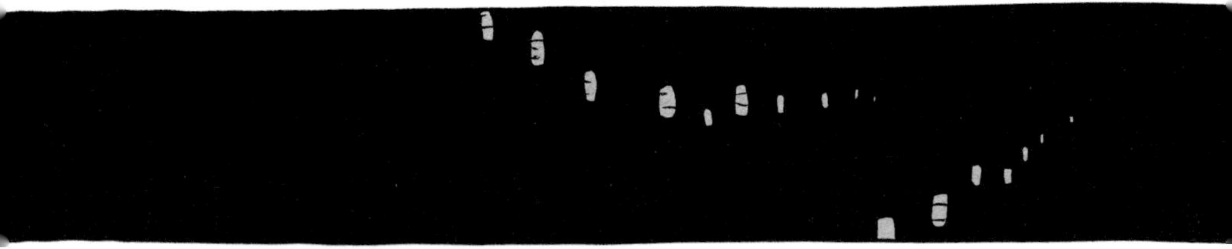

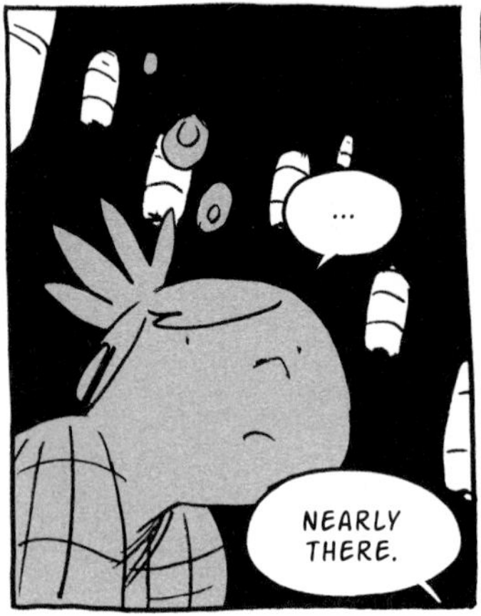
...
NEARLY THERE.

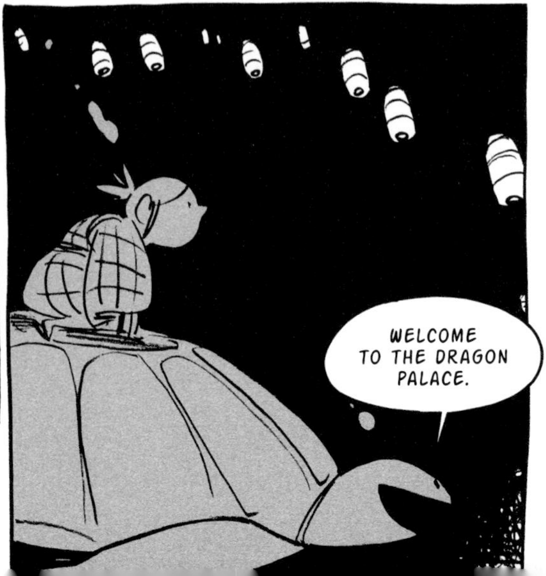
WELCOME TO THE DRAGON PALACE.

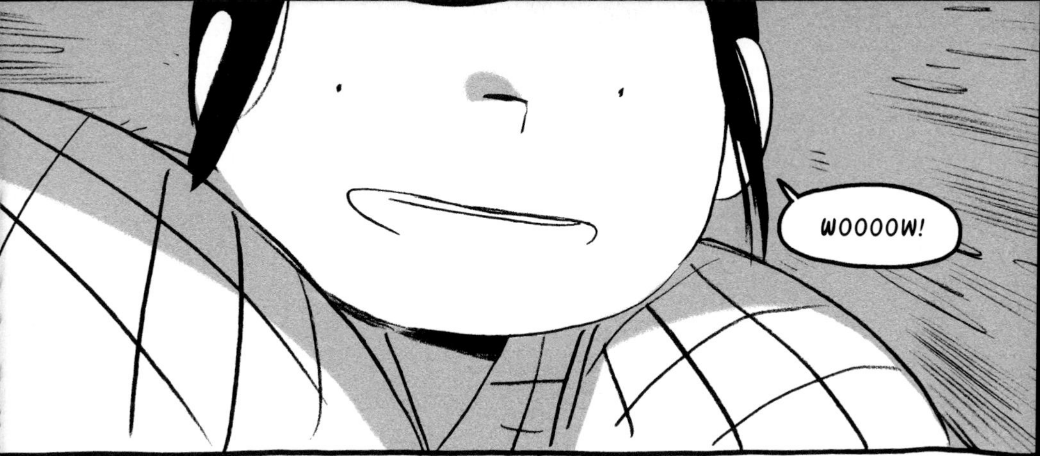
WOOOOW!
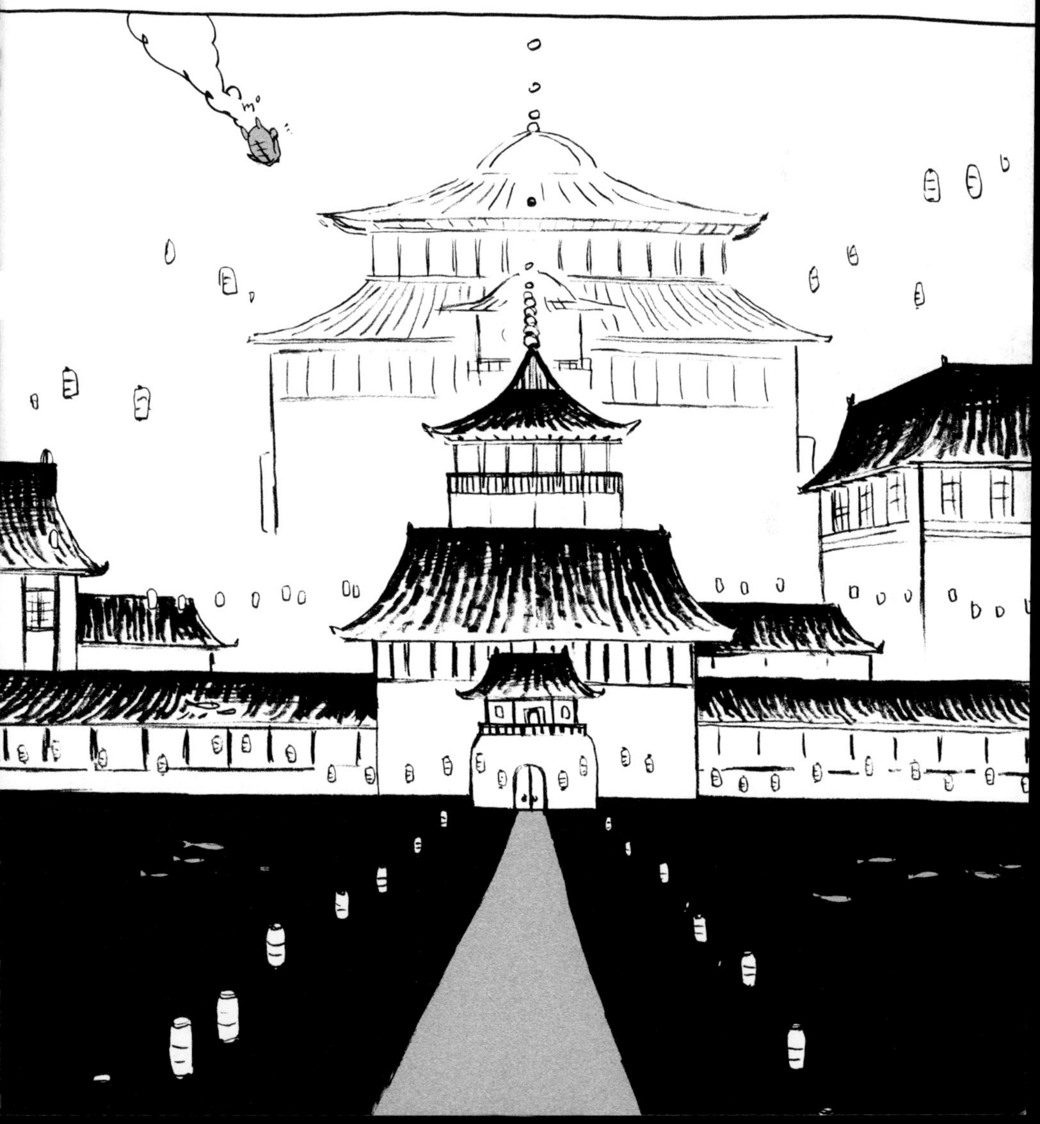

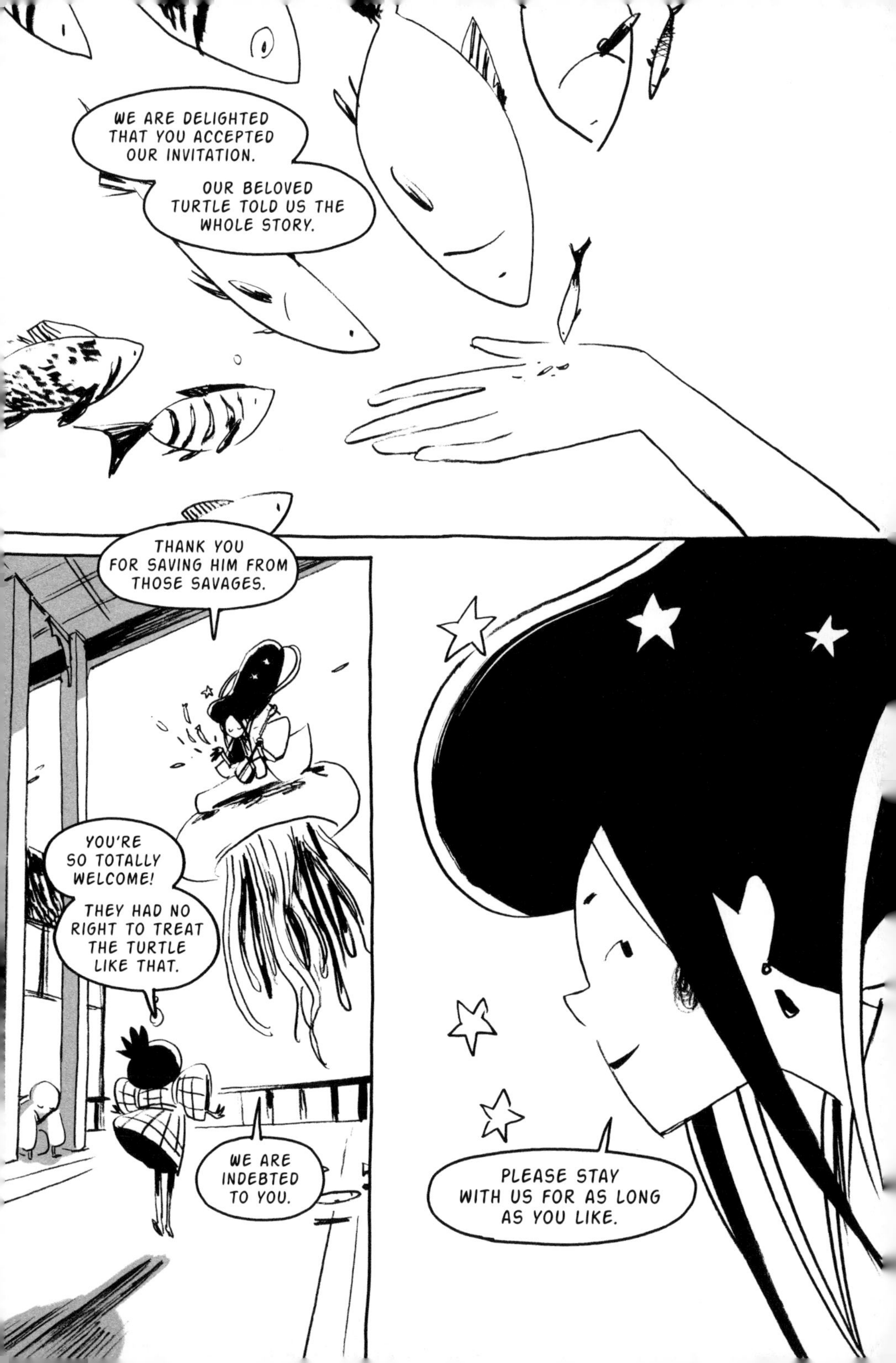
WE ARE DELIGHTED THAT YOU ACCEPTED OUR INVITATION.
OUR BELOVED TURTLE TOLD US THE WHOLE STORY.
THANK YOU FOR SAVING HIM FROM THOSE SAVAGES.
YOU'RE SO TOTALLY WELCOME!
THEY HAD NO RIGHT TO TREAT THE TURTLE LIKE THAT.
WE ARE INDEBTED TO YOU.
PLEASE STAY WITH US FOR AS LONG AS YOU LIKE.

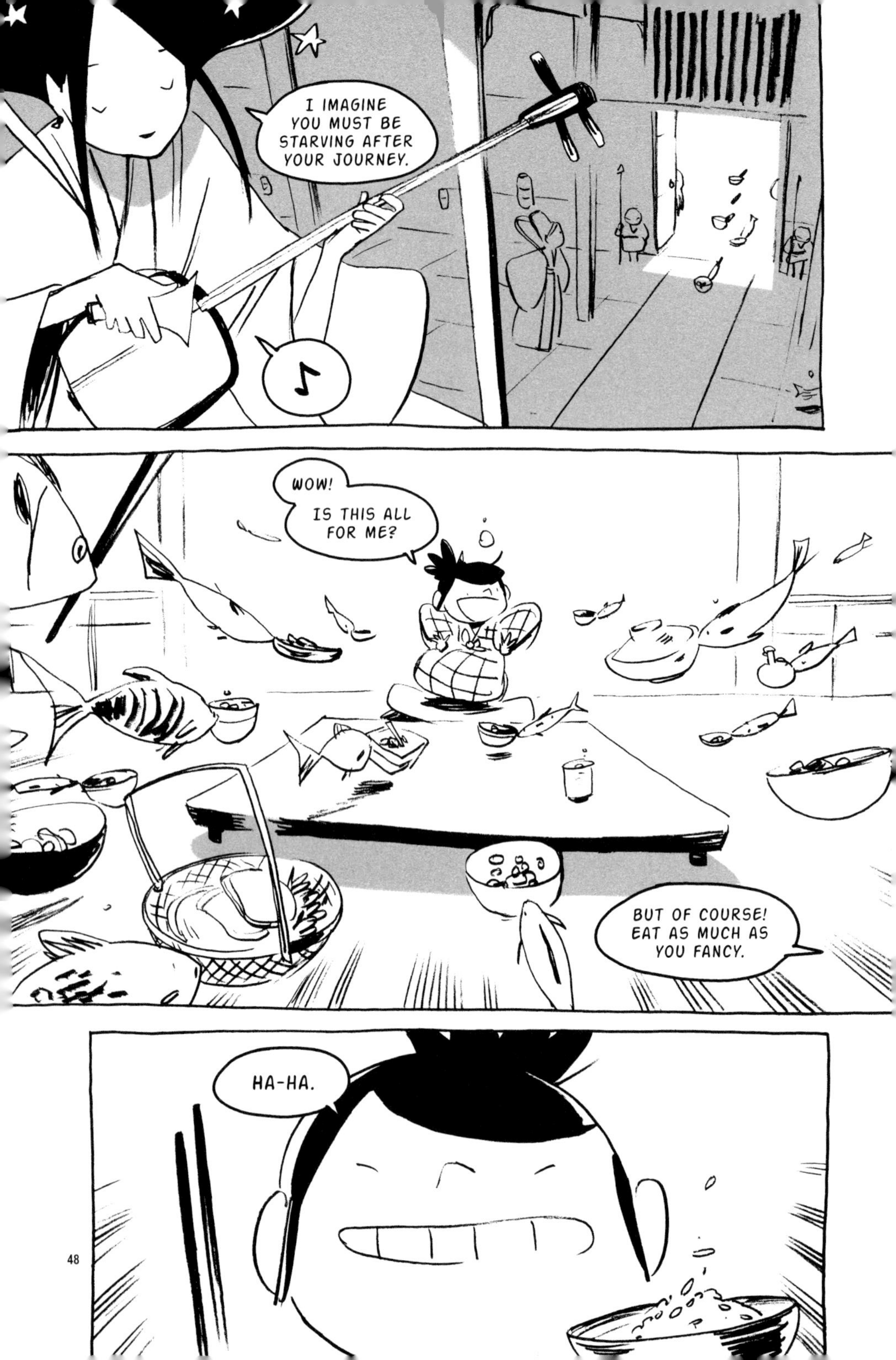
I IMAGINE YOU MUST BE STARVING AFTER YOUR JOURNEY.
♪
WOW!
IS THIS ALL FOR ME?
BUT OF COURSE! EAT AS MUCH AS YOU FANCY.
HA-HA.

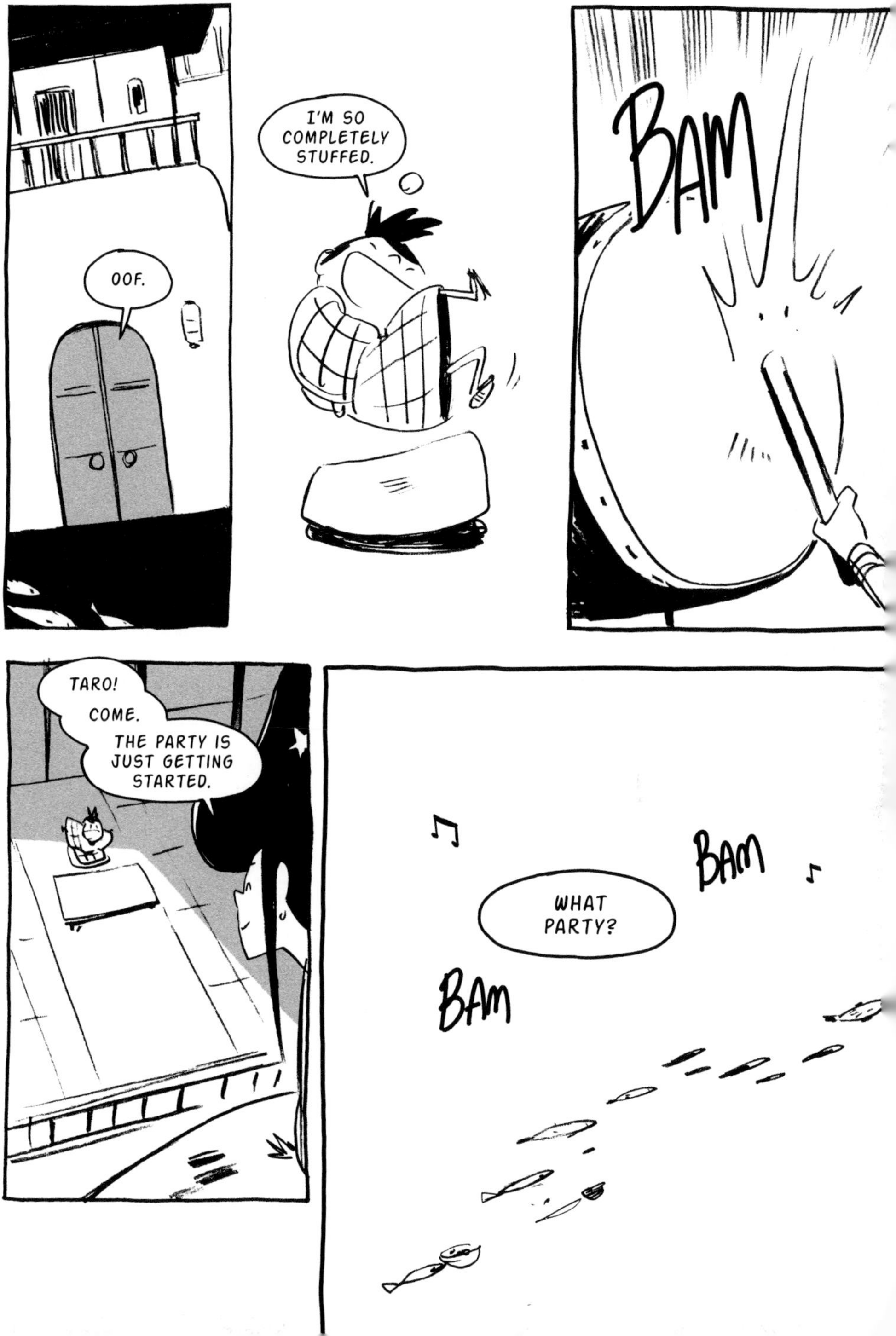

OOF.
I'M SO COMPLETELY STUFFED.
BAM
TARO!
COME.
THE PARTY IS JUST GETTING STARTED.
BAM
WHAT PARTY?
BAM

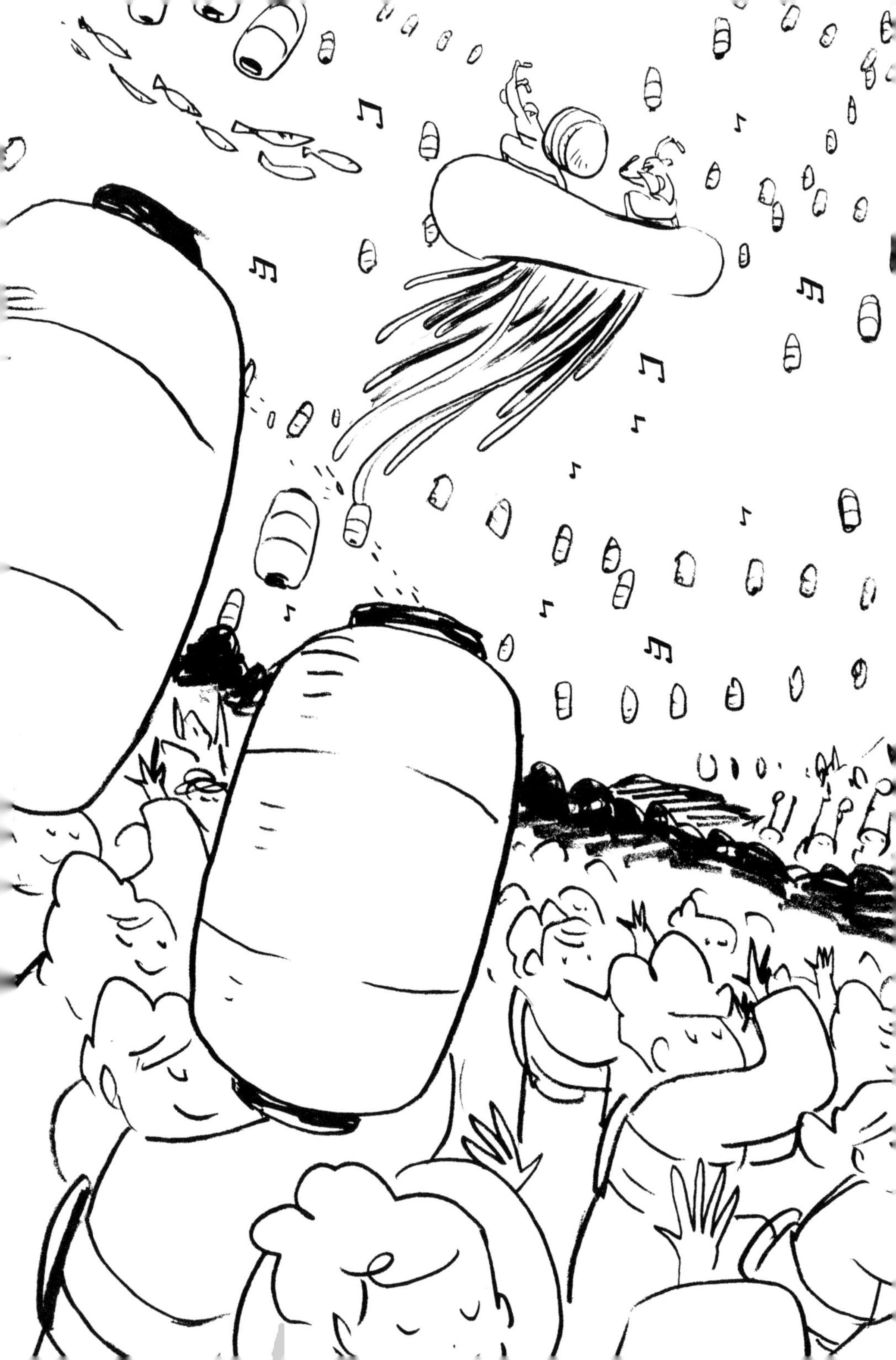

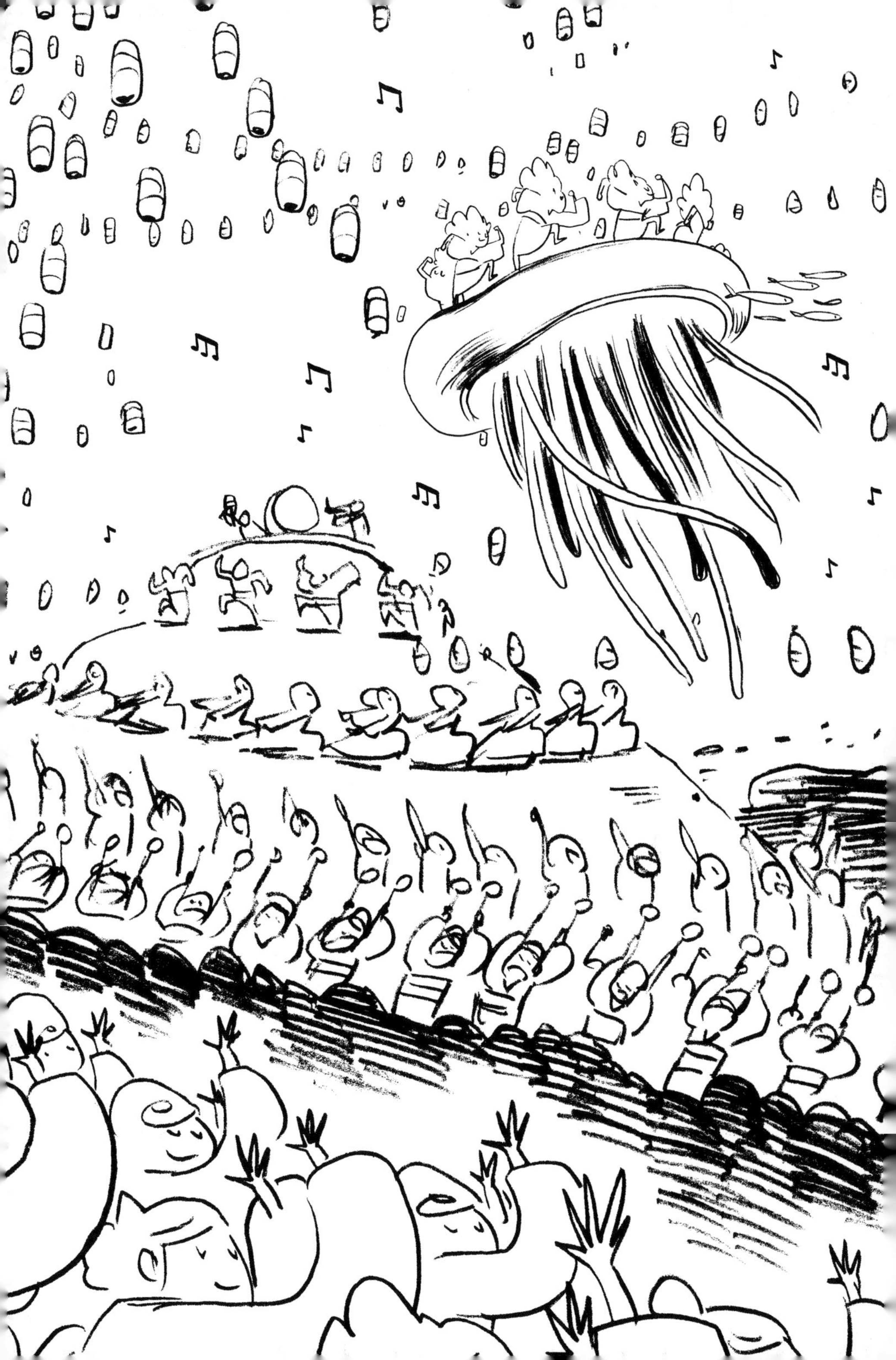

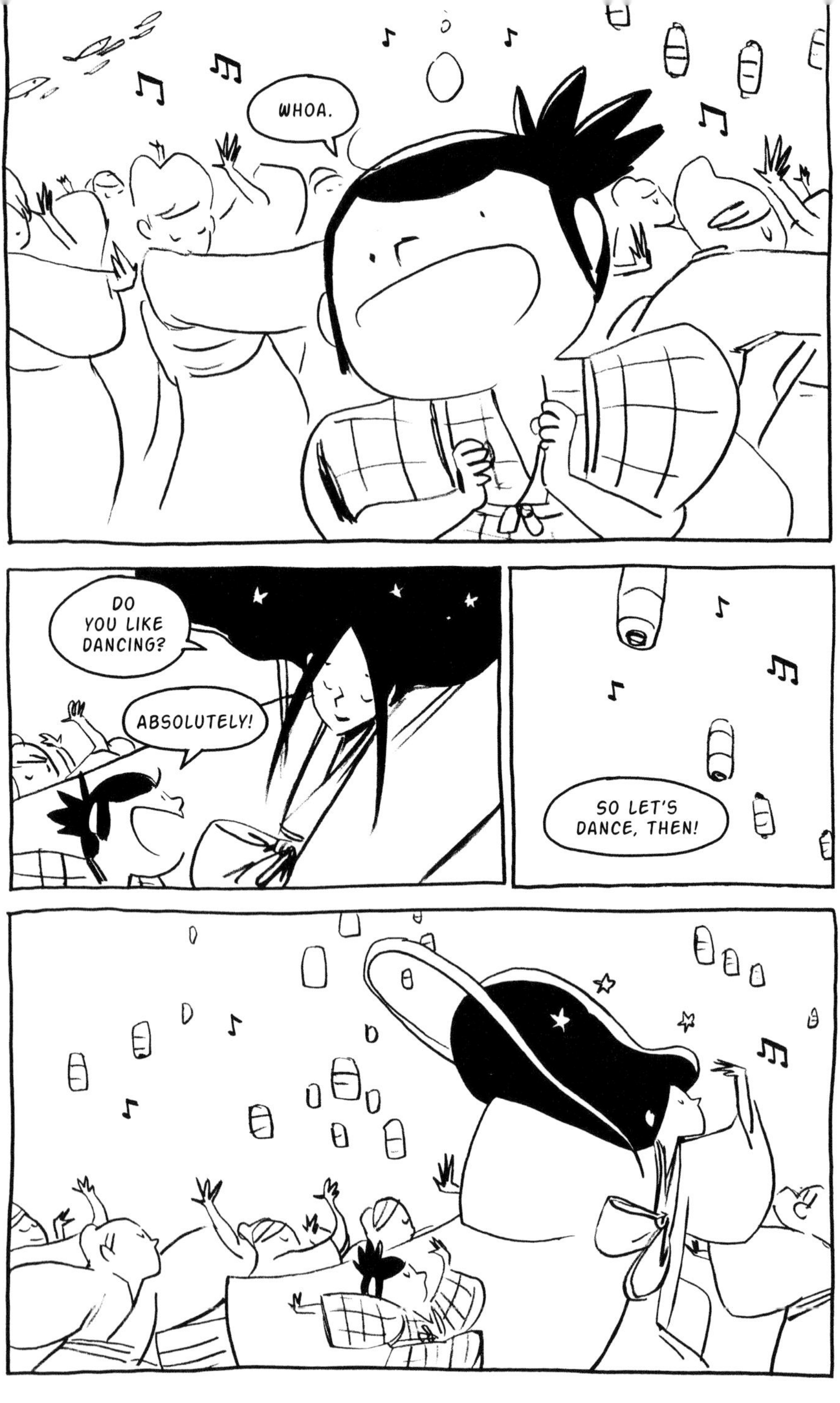

WHOA.
DO YOU LIKE DANCING?
ABSOLUTELY!
SO LET'S DANCE, THEN!

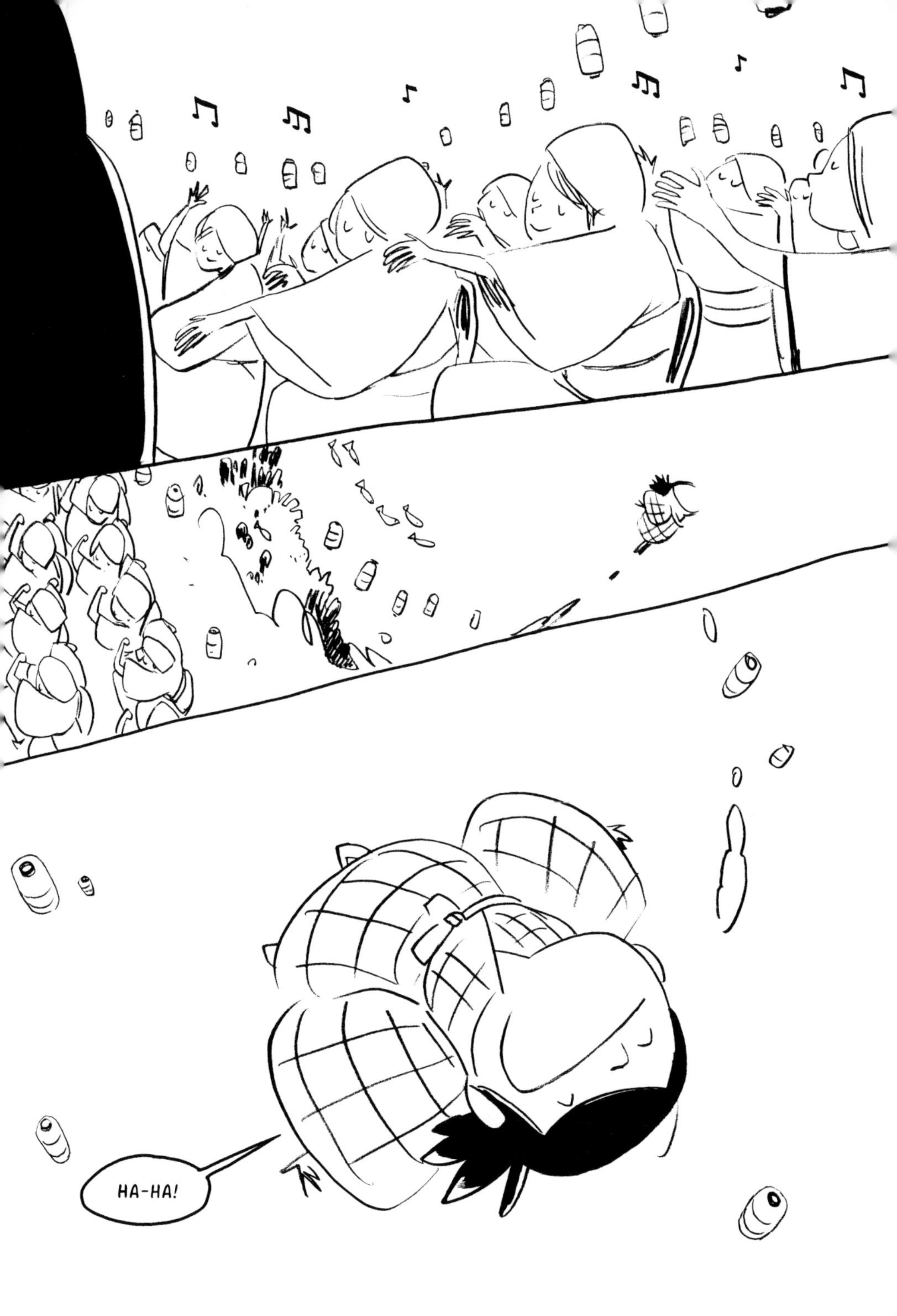
HA-HA!

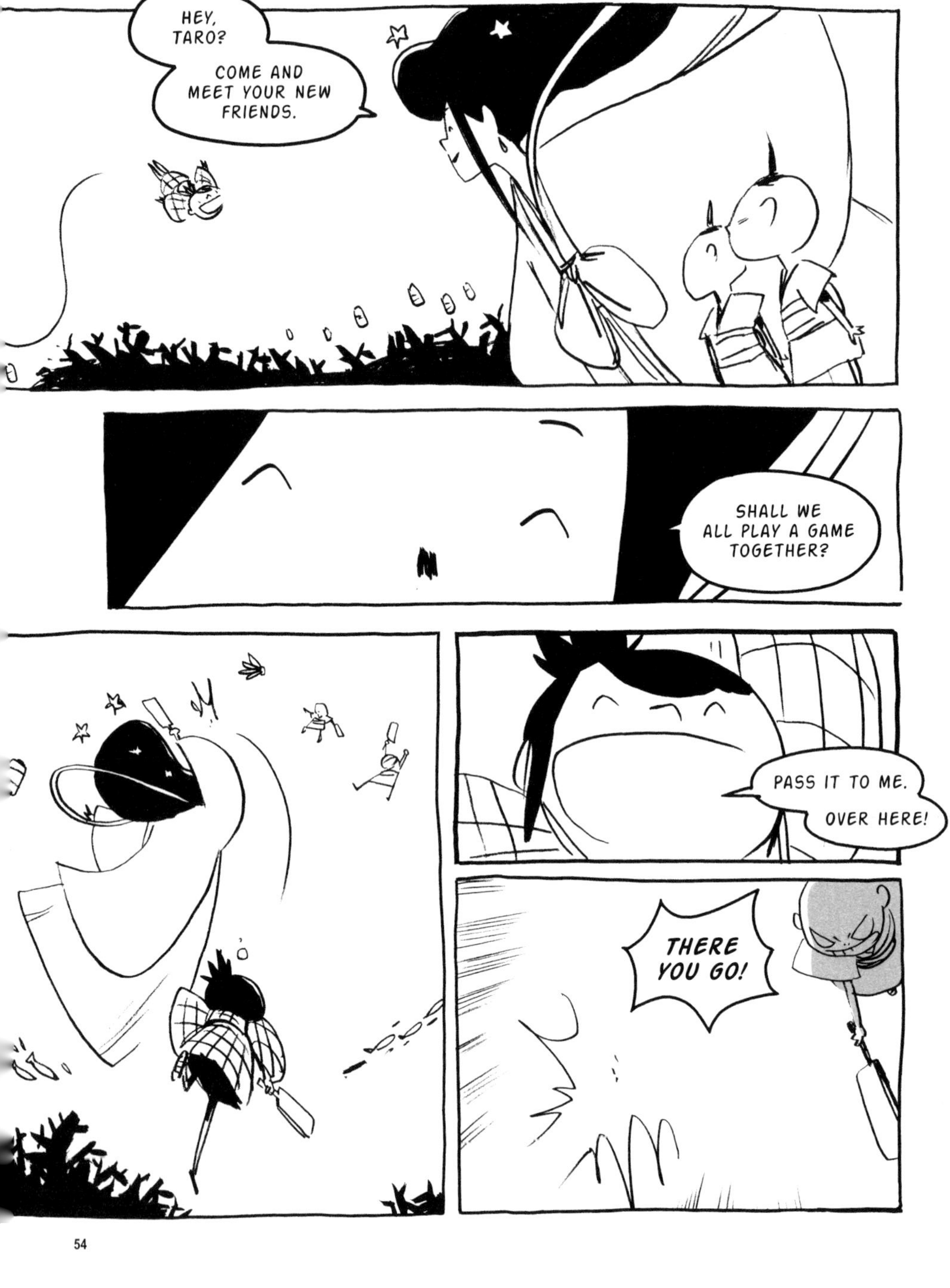
HEY, TARO?
COME AND MEET YOUR NEW FRIENDS.
SHALL WE ALL PLAY A GAME TOGETHER?
PASS IT TO ME.
OVER HERE!
THERE YOU GO!

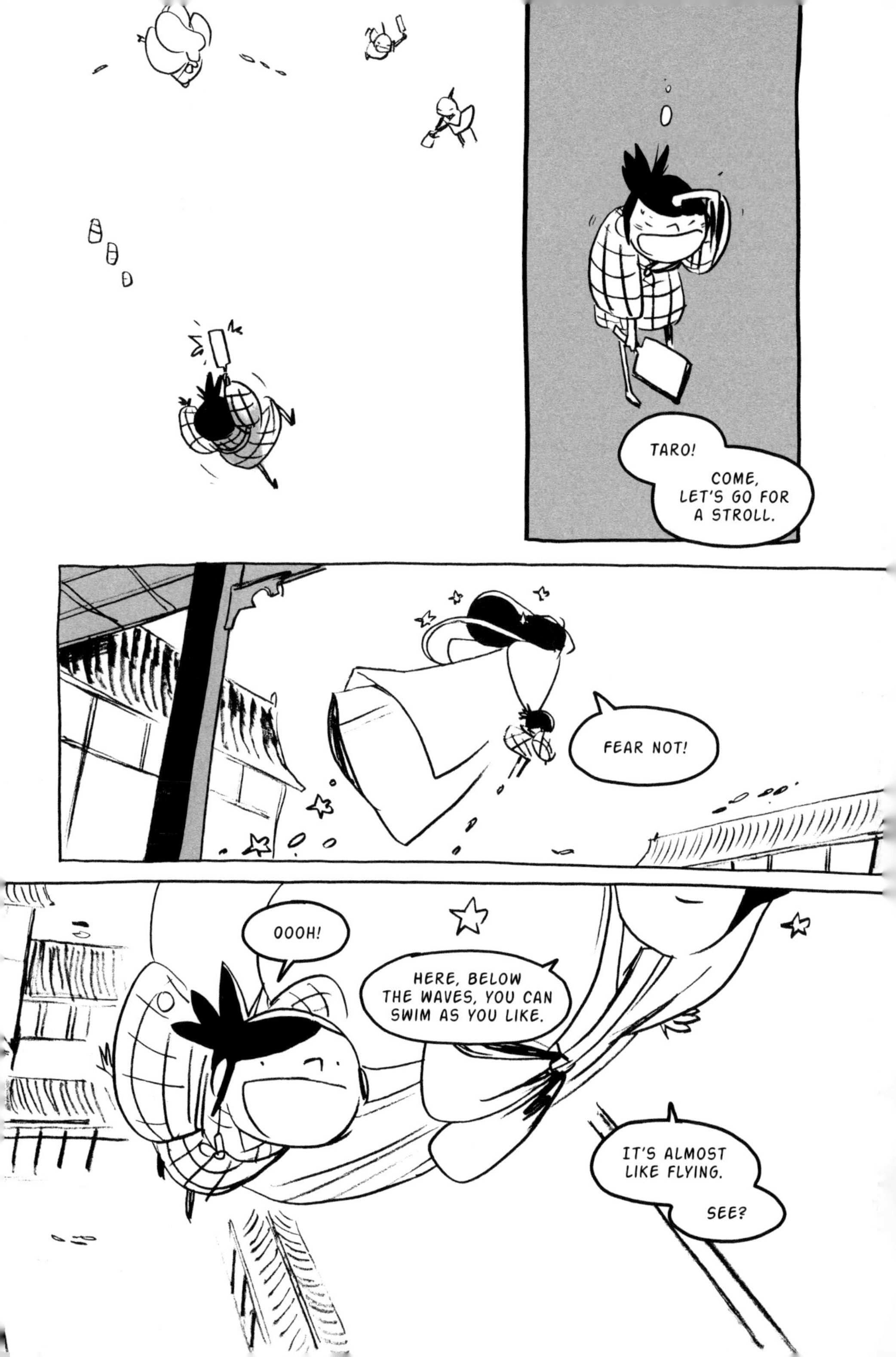
TARO!
COME, LET'S GO FOR A STROLL.
FEAR NOT!
OOOH!
HERE, BELOW THE WAVES, YOU CAN SWIM AS YOU LIKE.
IT'S ALMOST LIKE FLYING.
SEE?

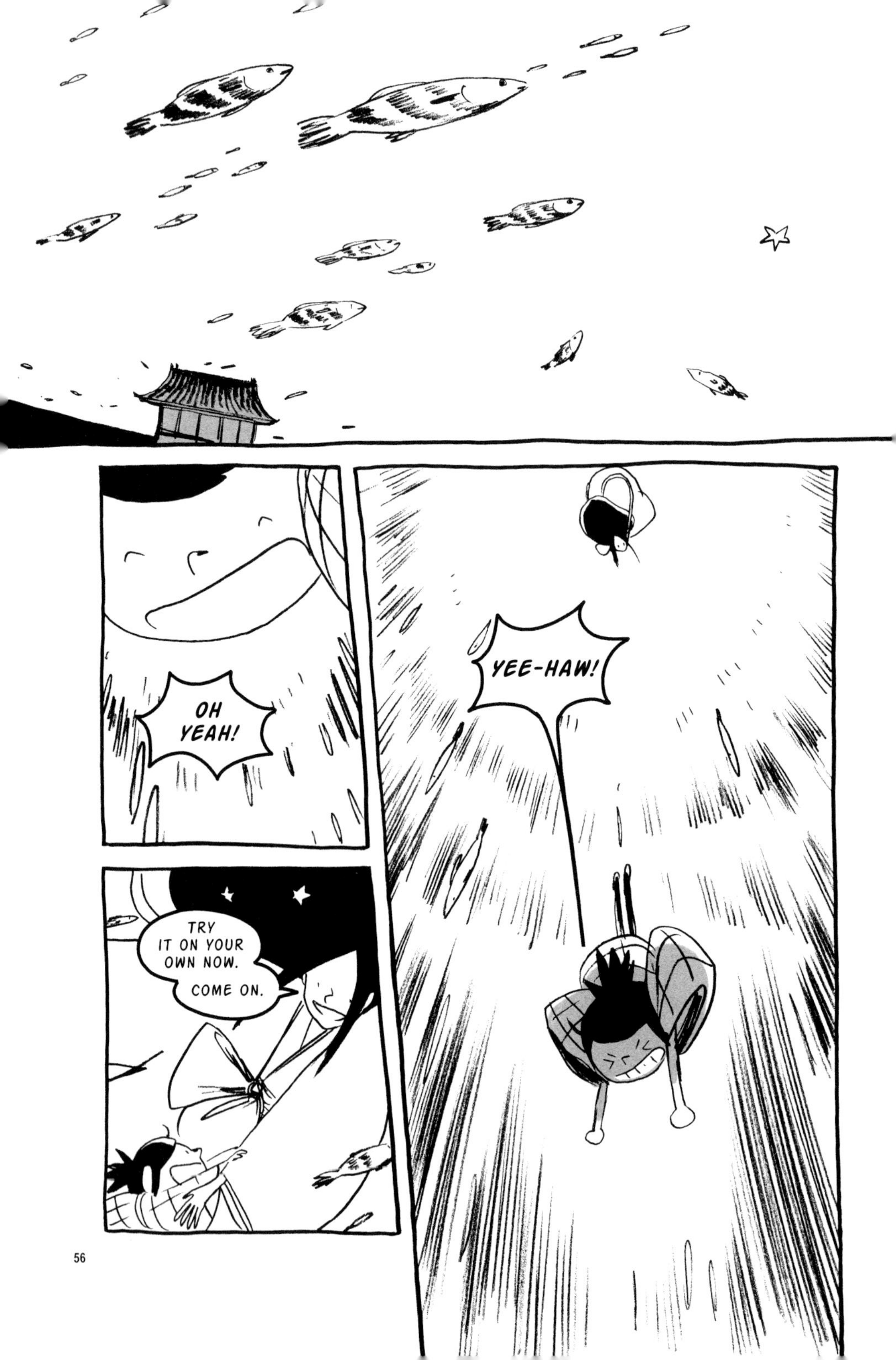
OH YEAH!
TRY IT ON YOUR OWN NOW. COME ON.
YEE-HAW!

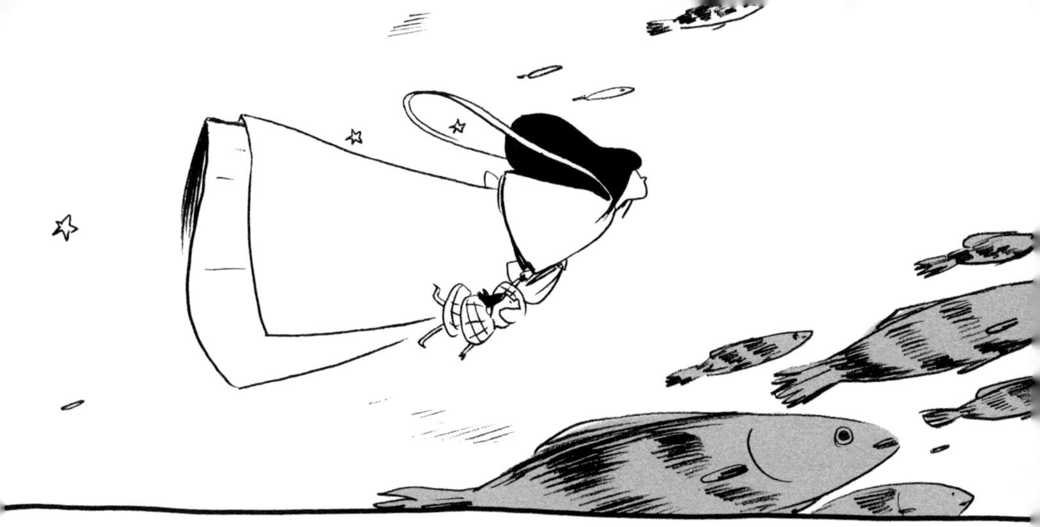

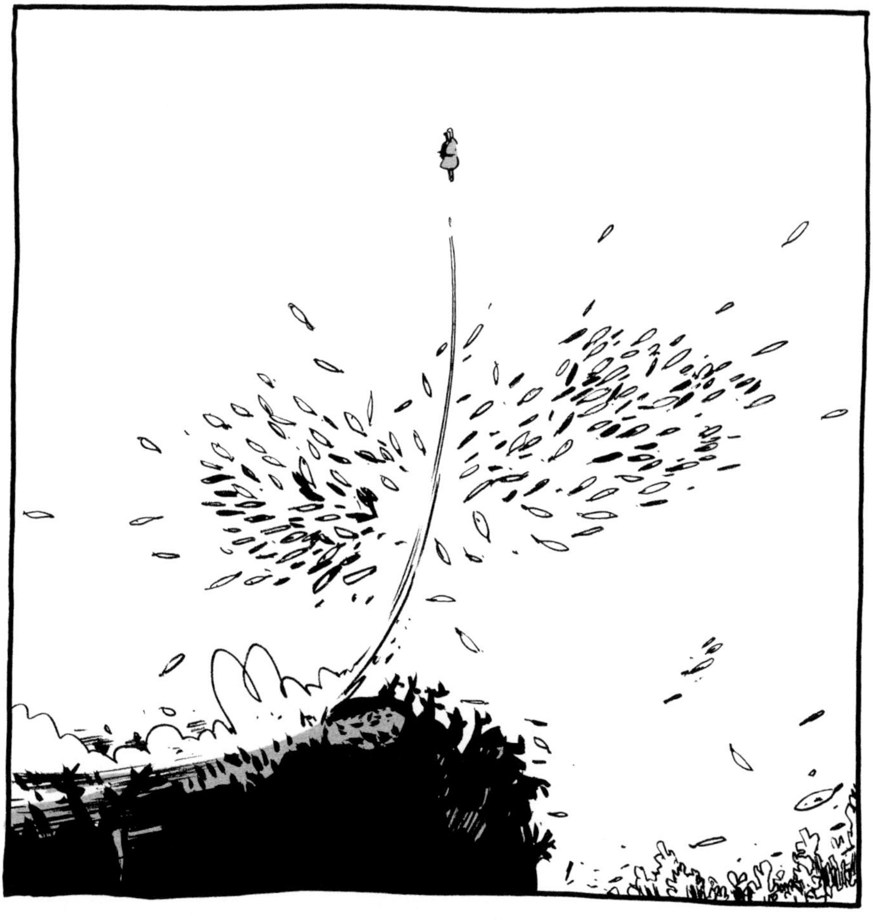

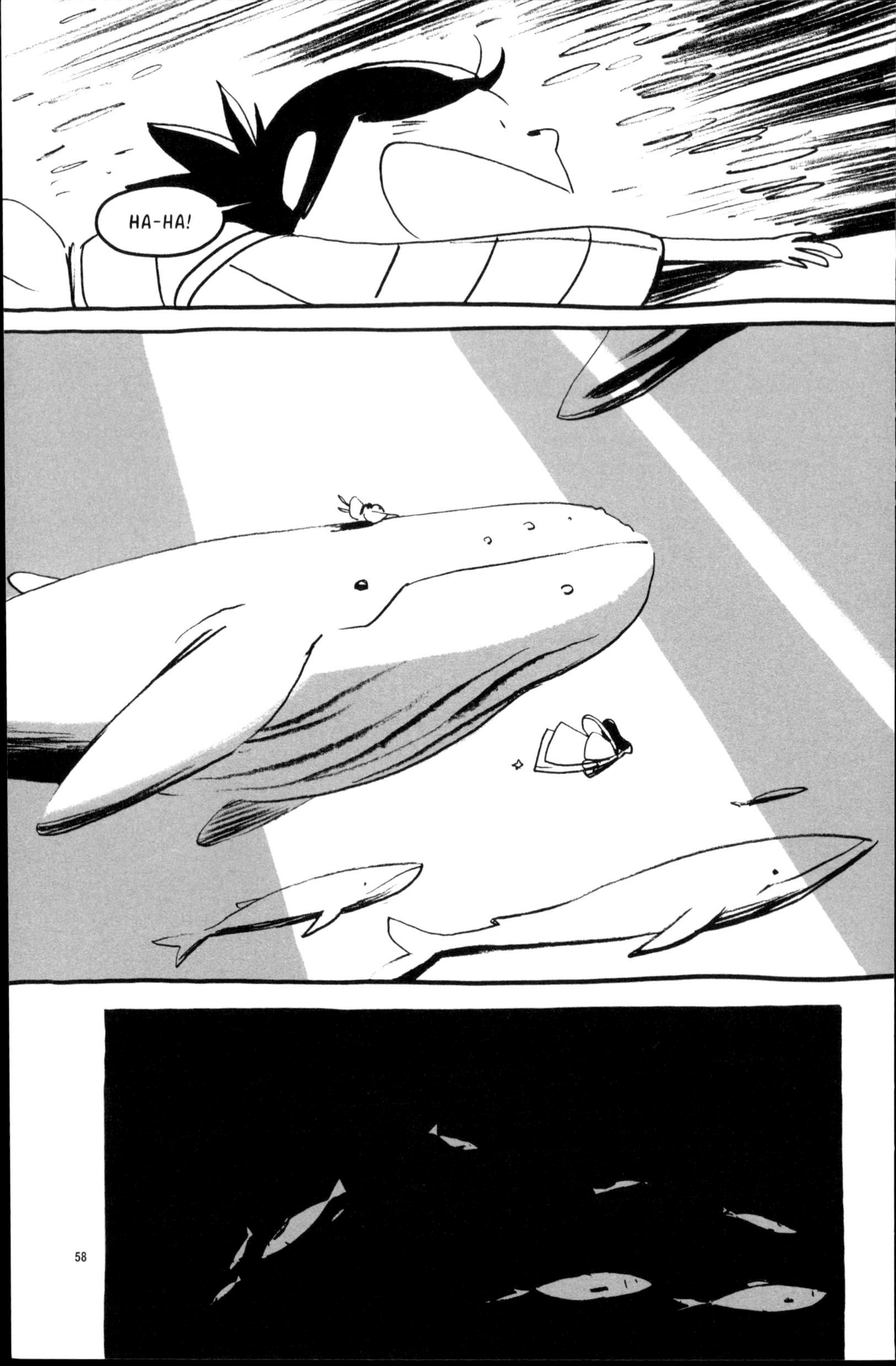
HA-HA!

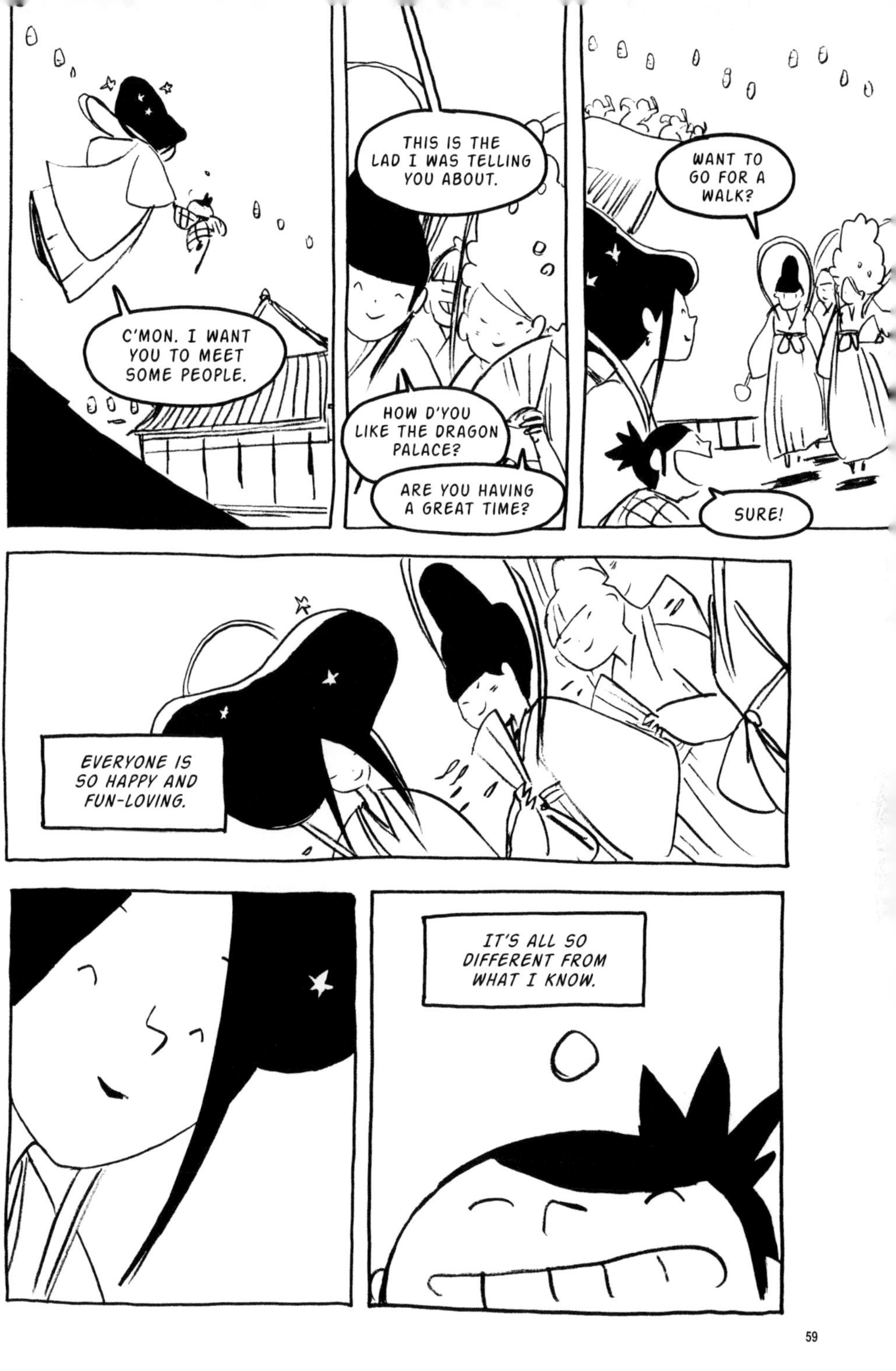
C'MON. I WANT YOU TO MEET SOME PEOPLE.
THIS IS THE LAD I WAS TELLING YOU ABOUT.
HOW D'YOU LIKE THE DRAGON PALACE?
ARE YOU HAVING A GREAT TIME?
WANT TO GO FOR A WALK?
SURE!
EVERYONE IS SO HAPPY AND FUN-LOVING.
IT'S ALL SO DIFFERENT FROM WHAT I KNOW.

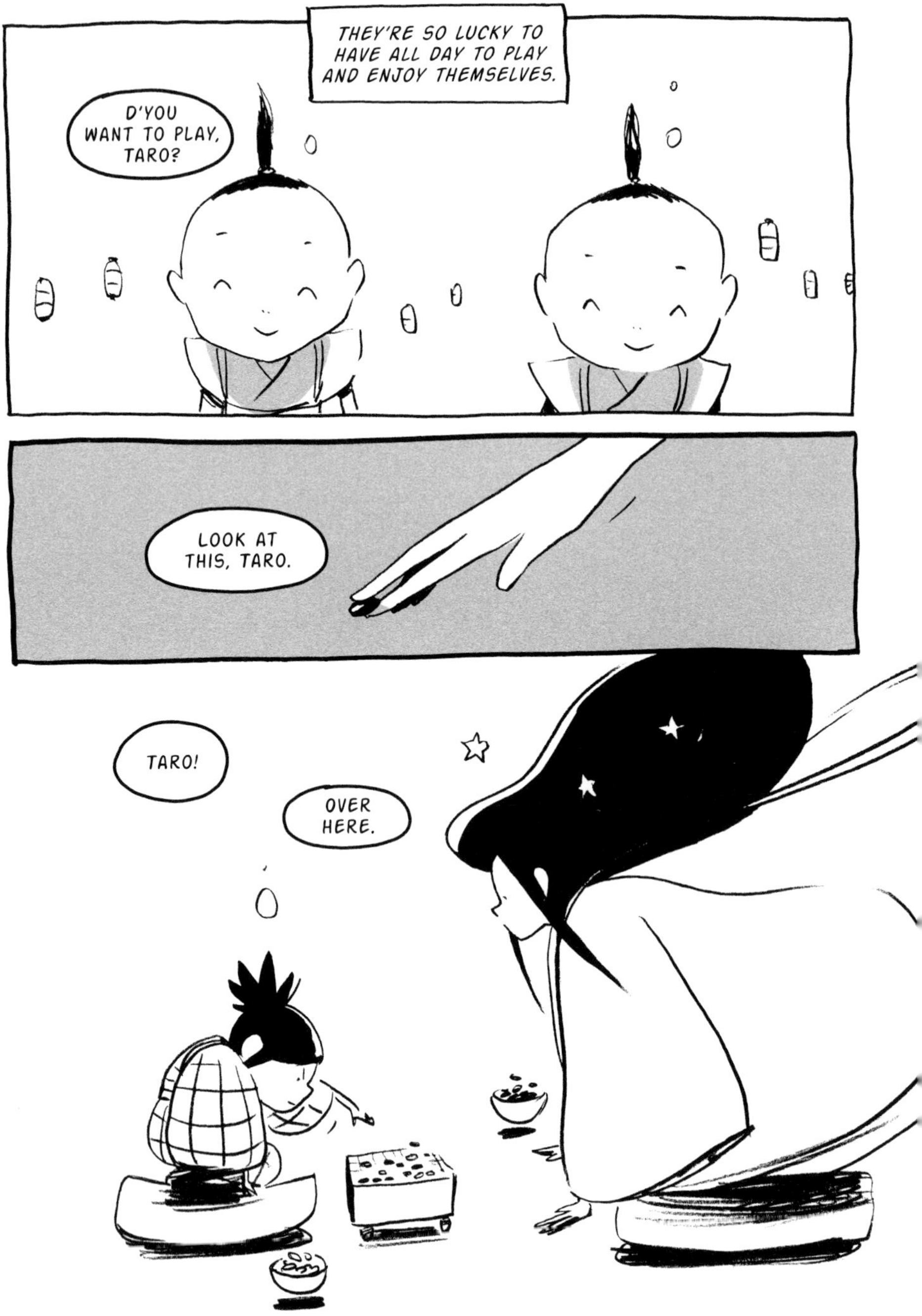
THEY'RE SO LUCKY TO HAVE ALL DAY TO PLAY AND ENJOY THEMSELVES.
D'YOU WANT TO PLAY, TARO?
LOOK AT THIS, TARO.
TARO!
OVER HERE.

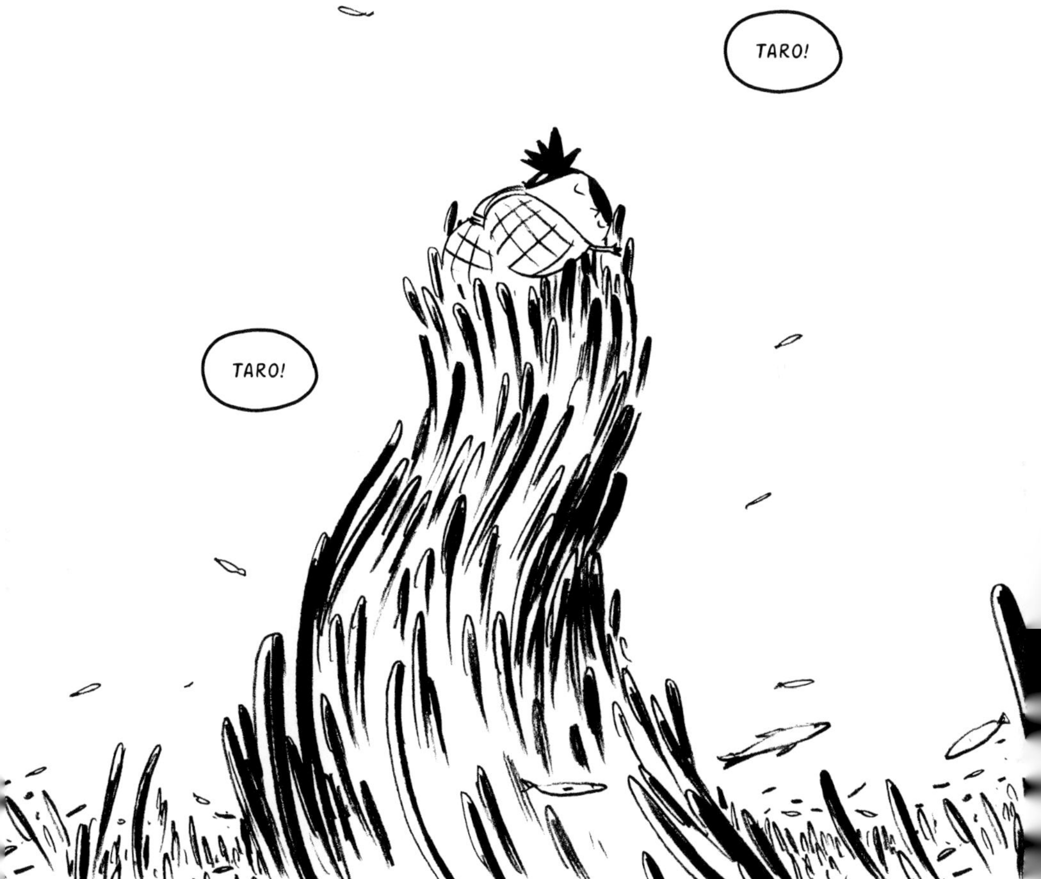
TARO!
TARO!
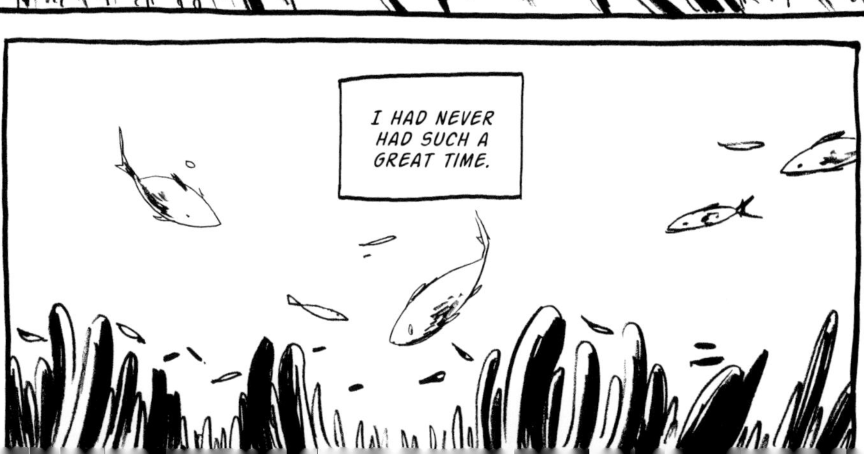
I HAD NEVER HAD SUCH A GREAT TIME.

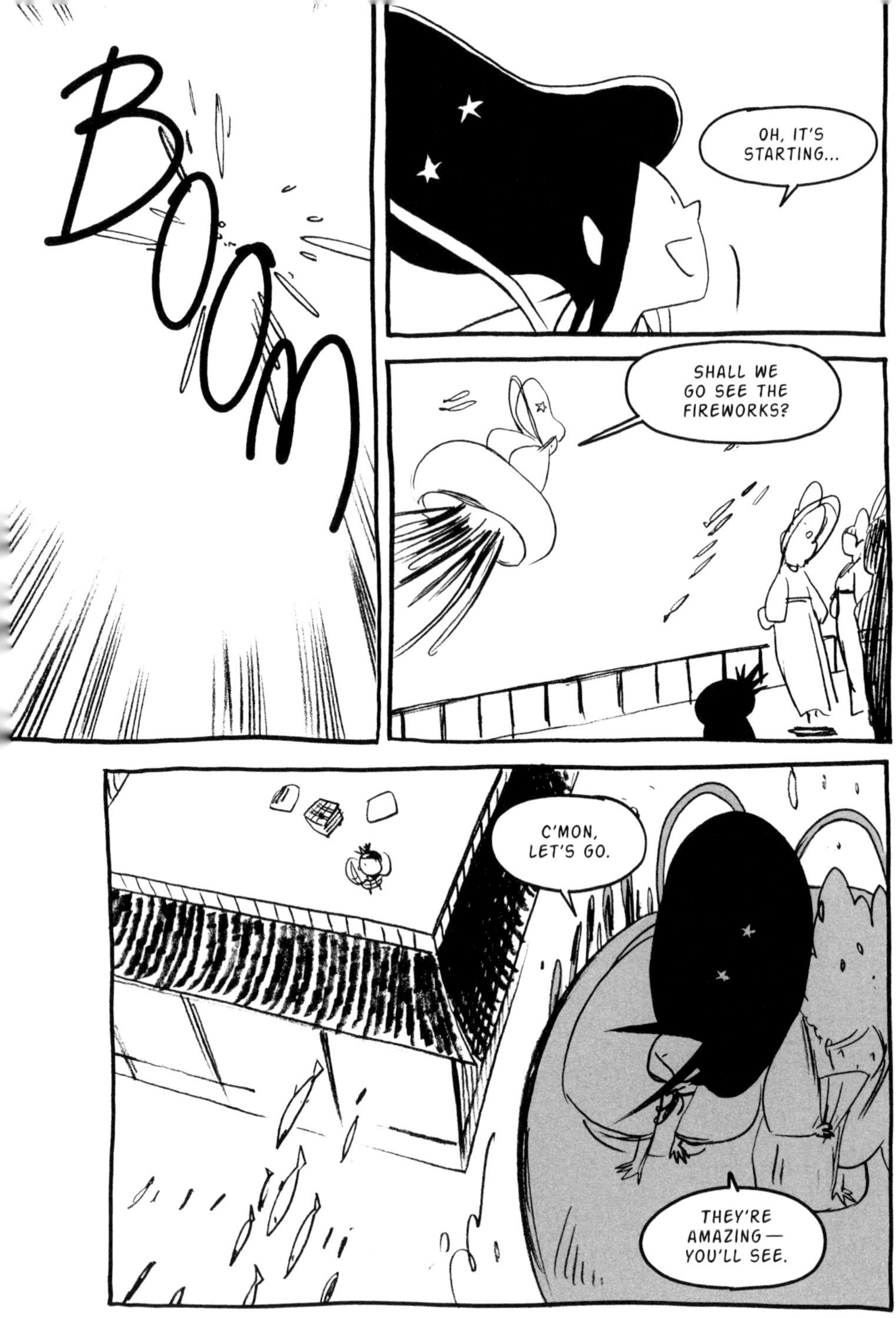
BOOM
OH, IT'S STARTING...
SHALL WE GO SEE THE FIREWORKS?
C'MON, LET'S GO.
THEY'RE AMAZING— YOU'LL SEE.

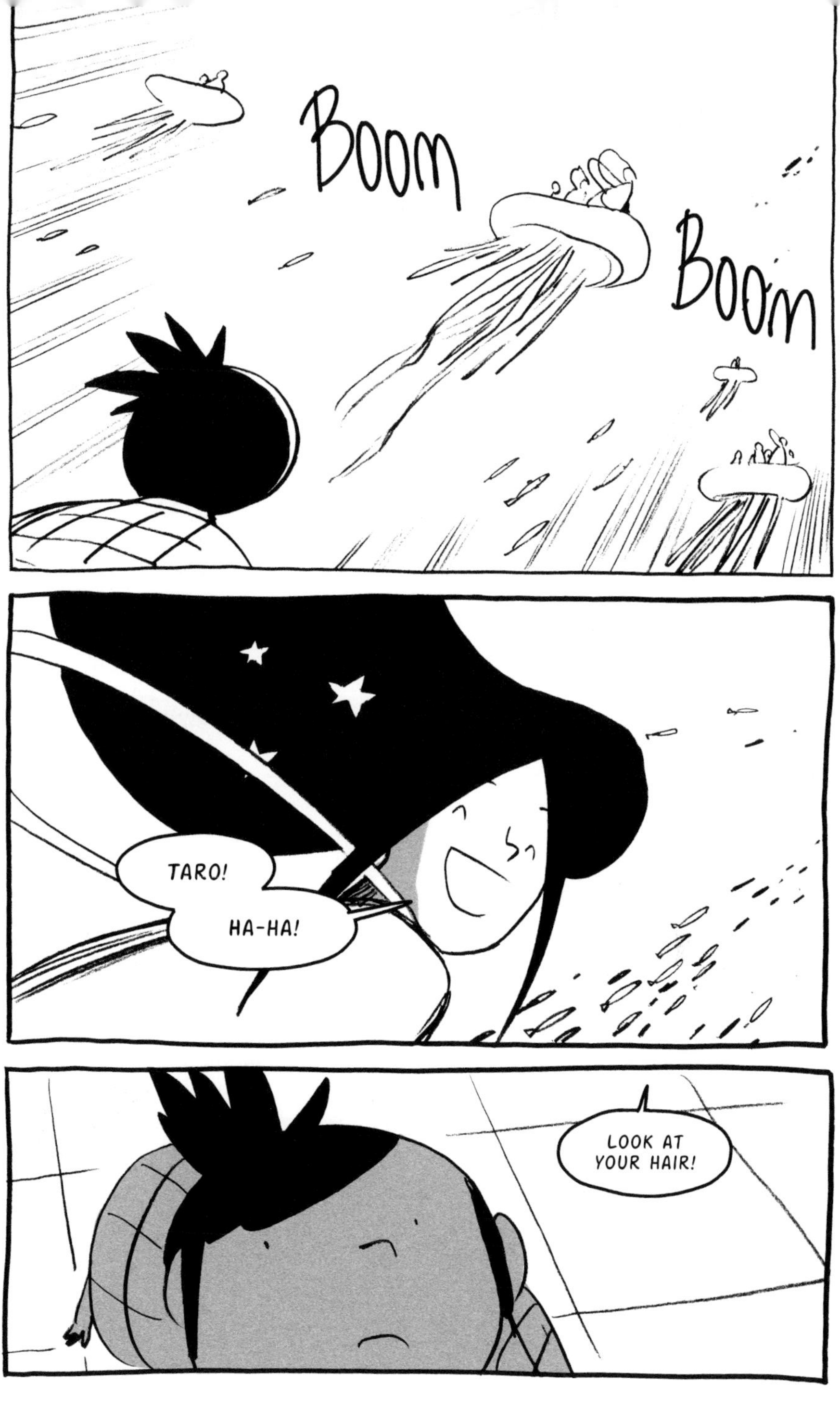
Boom
Boom
TARO!
HA-HA!
LOOK AT YOUR HAIR!

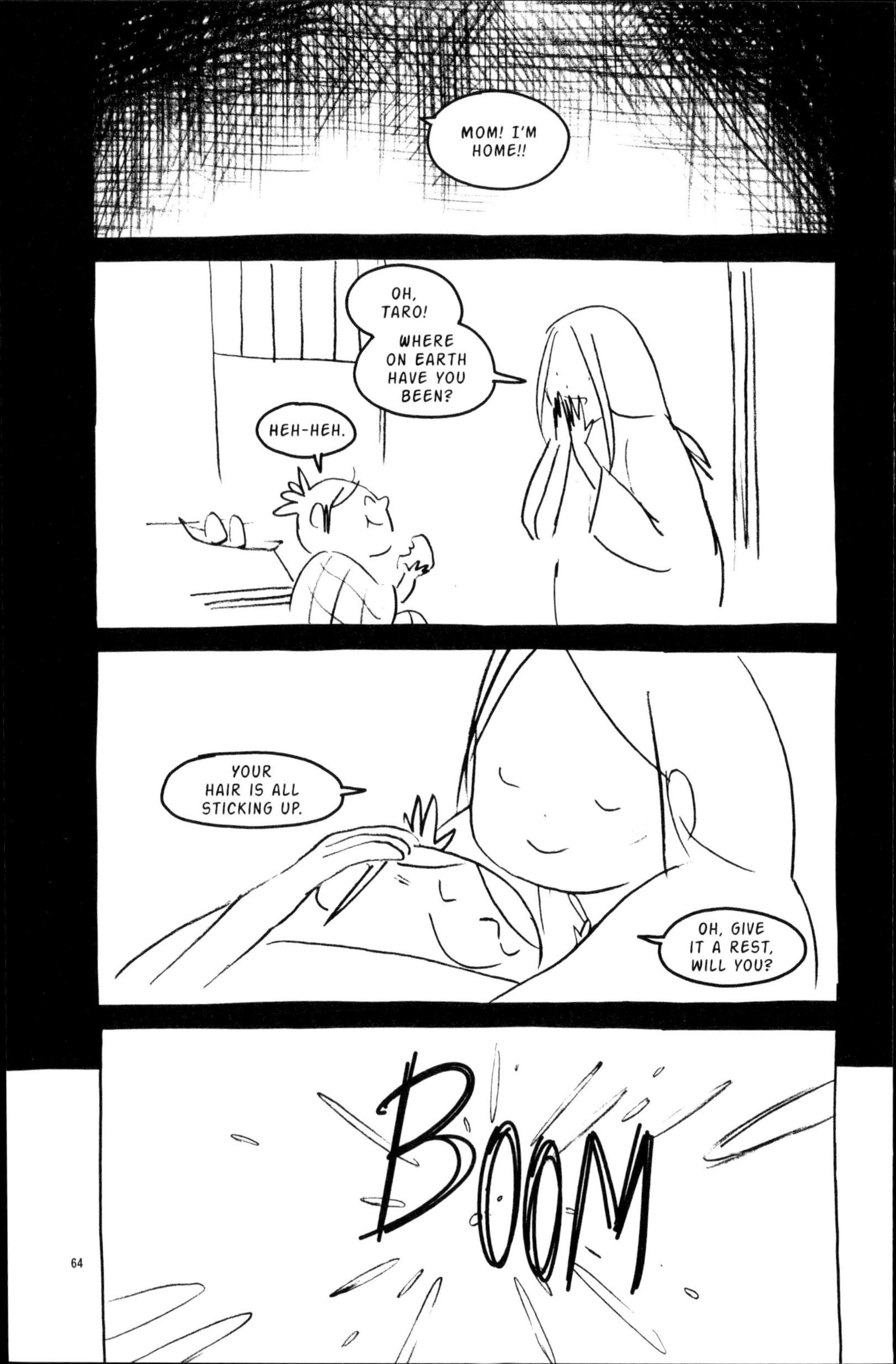
MOM! I'M HOME!!
OH, TARO!
WHERE ON EARTH HAVE YOU BEEN?
HEH-HEH.
YOUR HAIR IS ALL STICKING UP.
OH, GIVE IT A REST, WILL YOU?
BOOM

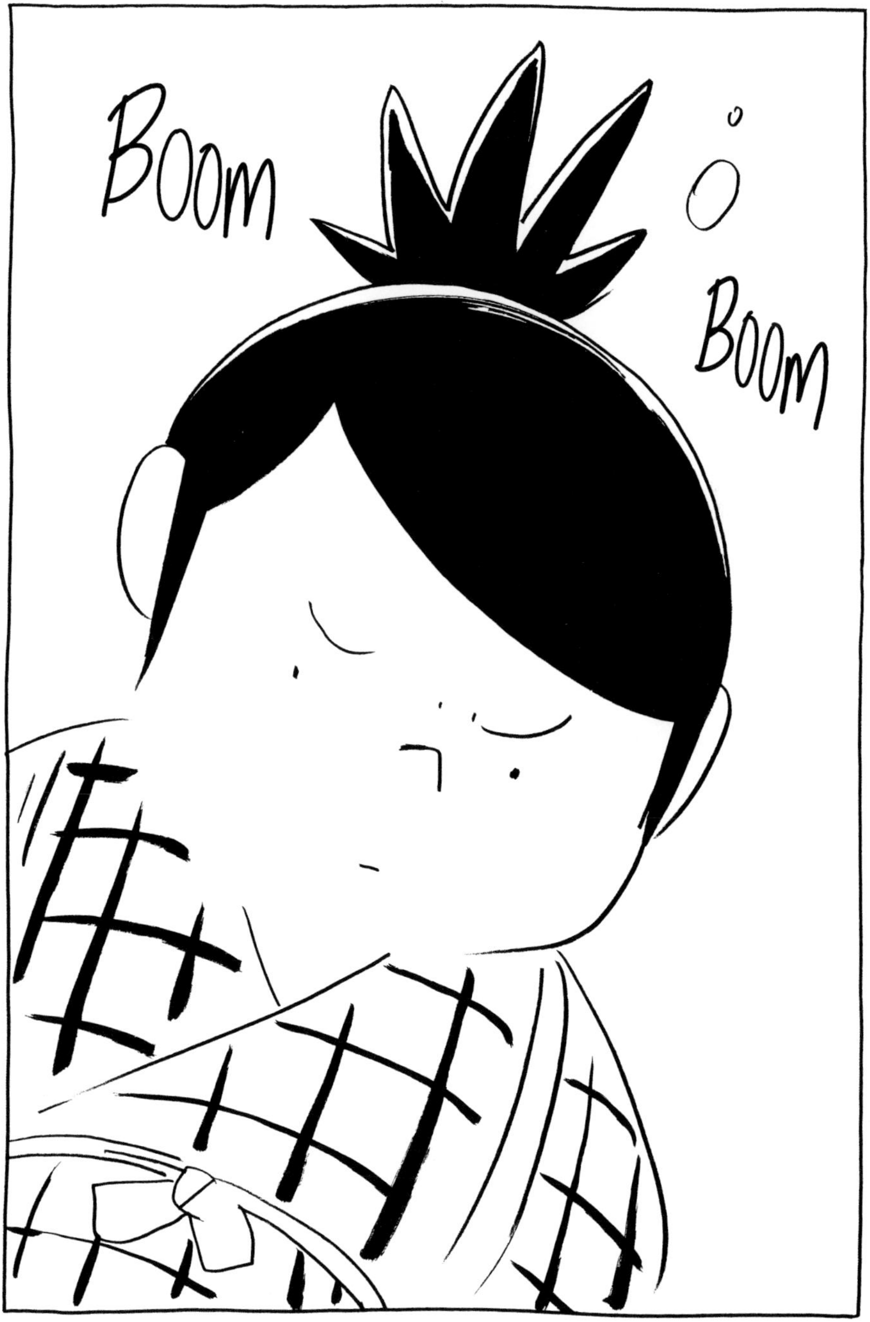
Boom
Boom

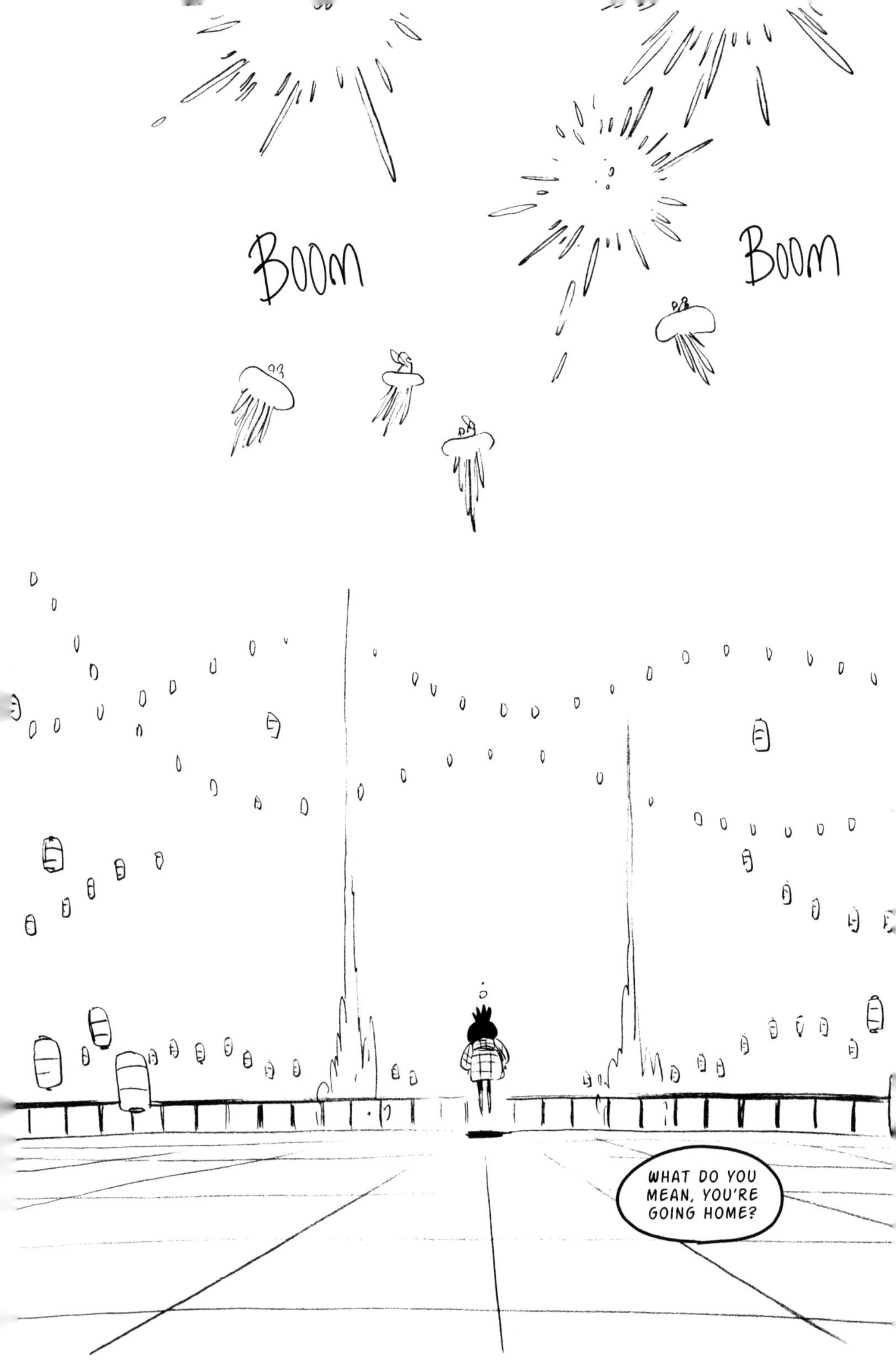

BOOM
BOOM
WHAT DO YOU MEAN, YOU'RE GOING HOME?

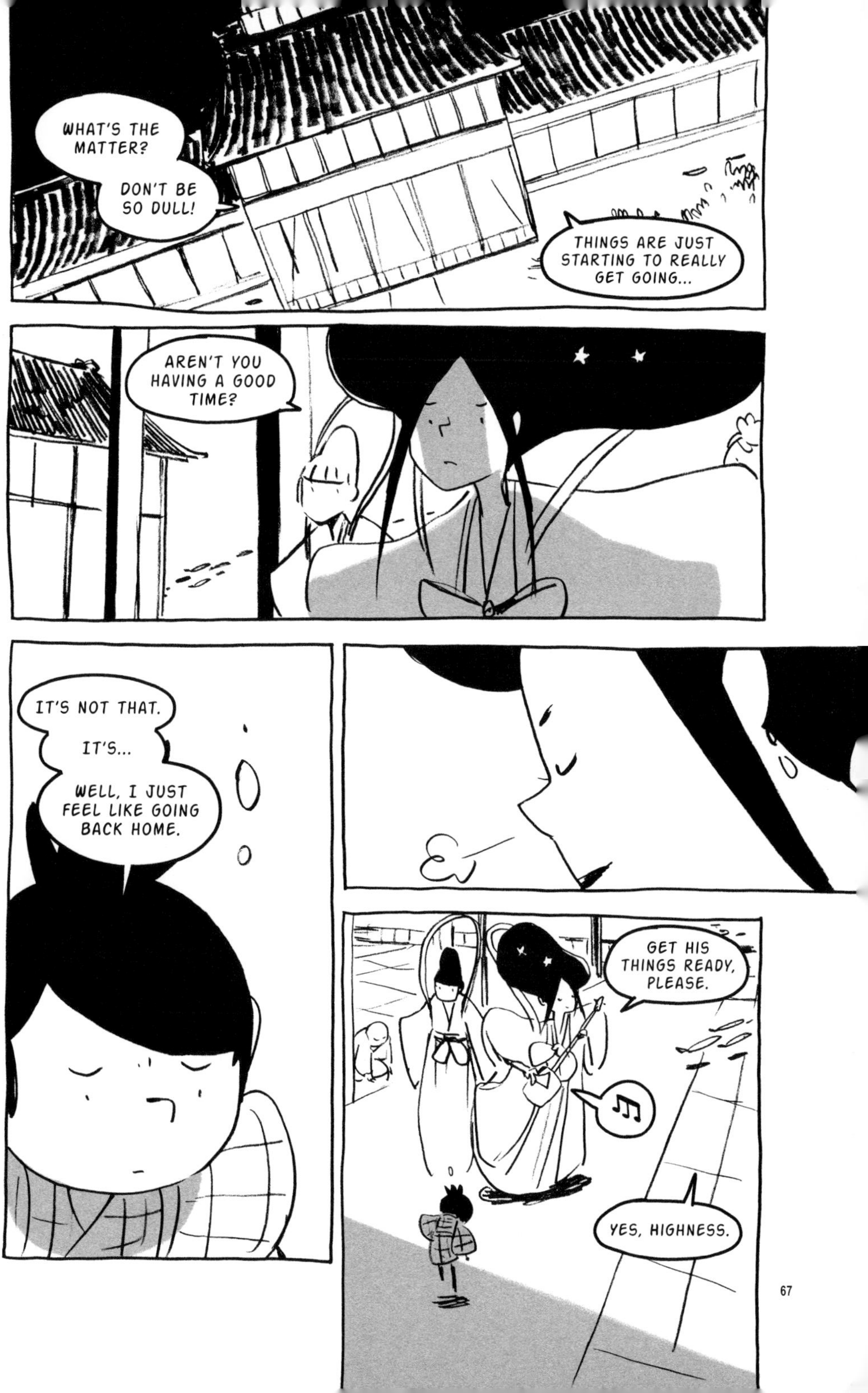
WHAT'S THE MATTER?
DON'T BE SO DULL!
THINGS ARE JUST STARTING TO REALLY GET GOING...
AREN'T YOU HAVING A GOOD TIME?
IT'S NOT THAT.
IT'S...
WELL, I JUST FEEL LIKE GOING BACK HOME.
GET HIS THINGS READY, PLEASE.
YES, HIGHNESS.

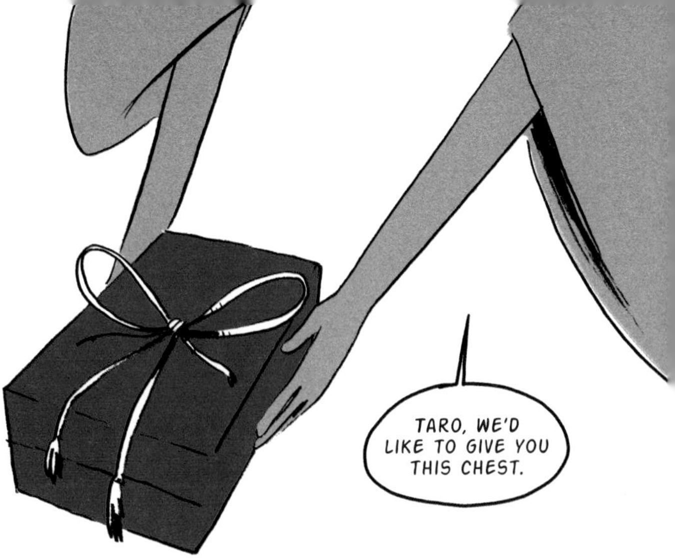
TARO, WE'D LIKE TO GIVE YOU THIS CHEST.

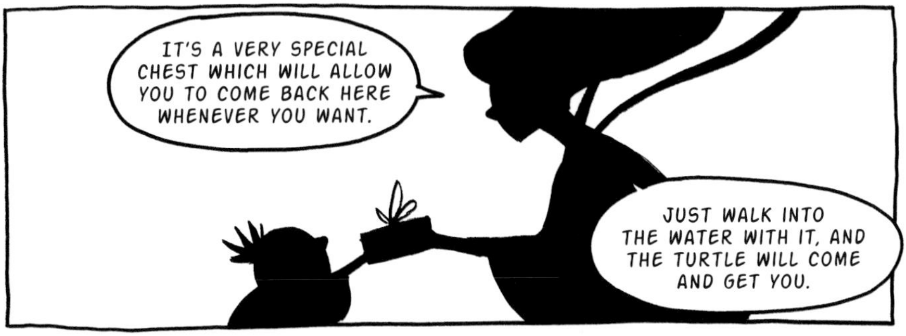
IT'S A VERY SPECIAL CHEST WHICH WILL ALLOW YOU TO COME BACK HERE WHENEVER YOU WANT.
JUST WALK INTO THE WATER WITH IT, AND THE TURTLE WILL COME AND GET YOU.

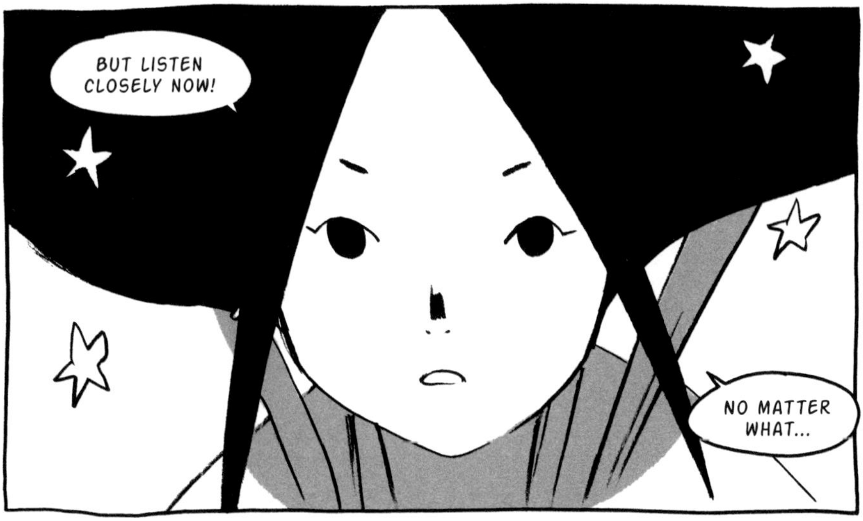
BUT LISTEN CLOSELY NOW!
NO MATTER WHAT...

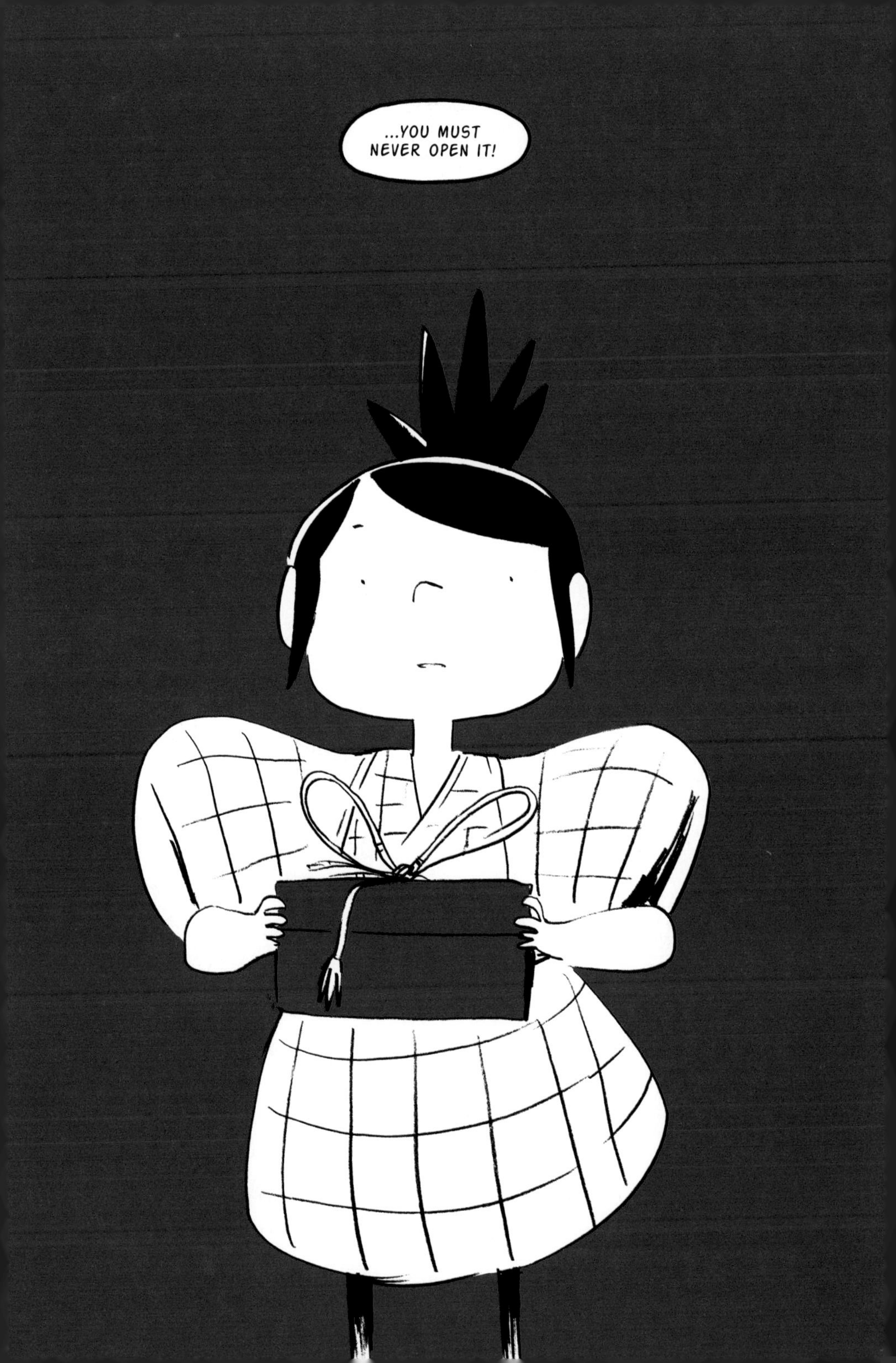
...YOU MUST NEVER OPEN IT!

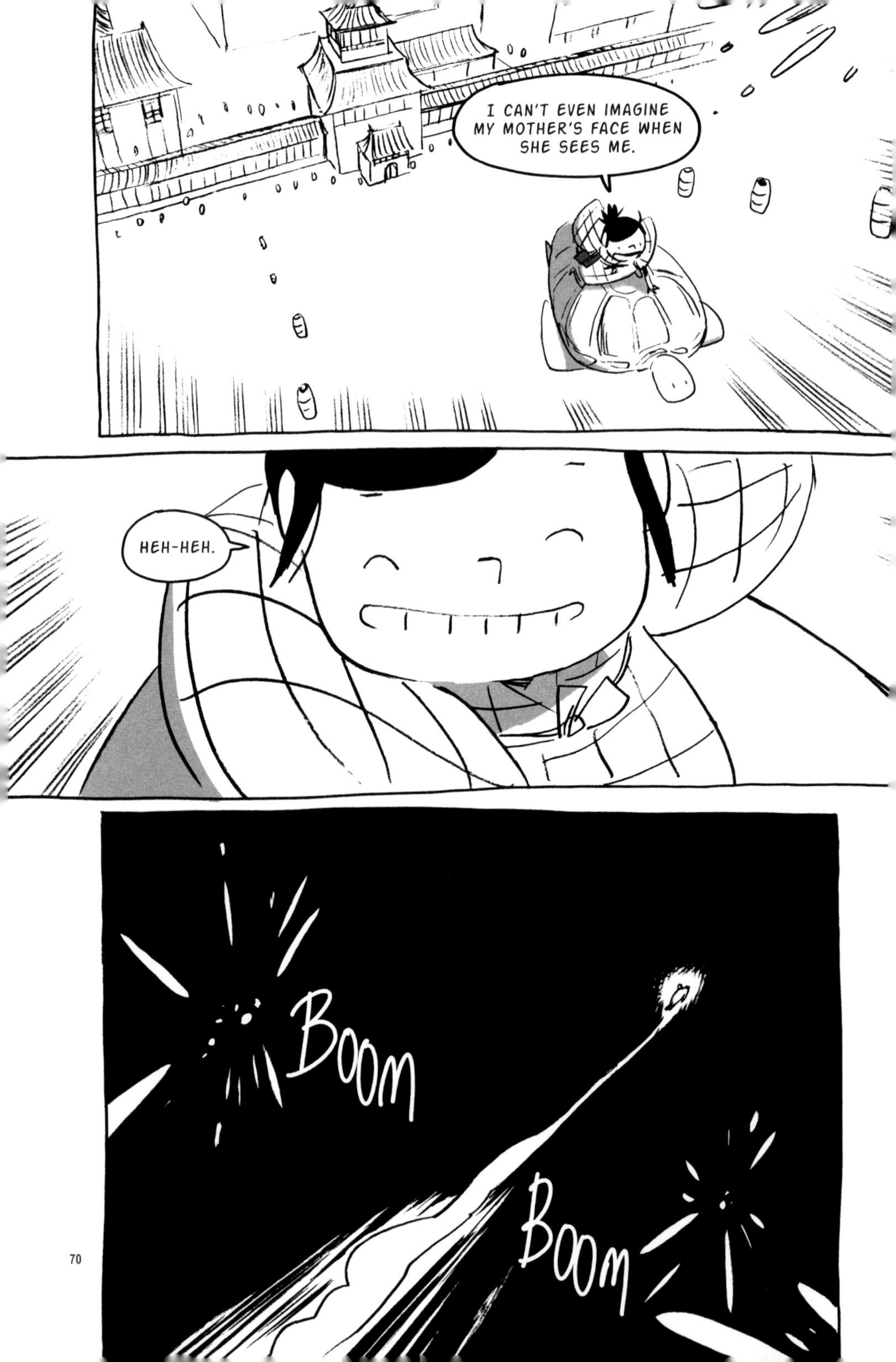

I CAN'T EVEN IMAGINE MY MOTHER'S FACE WHEN SHE SEES ME.
HEH-HEH.
Boom
Boom

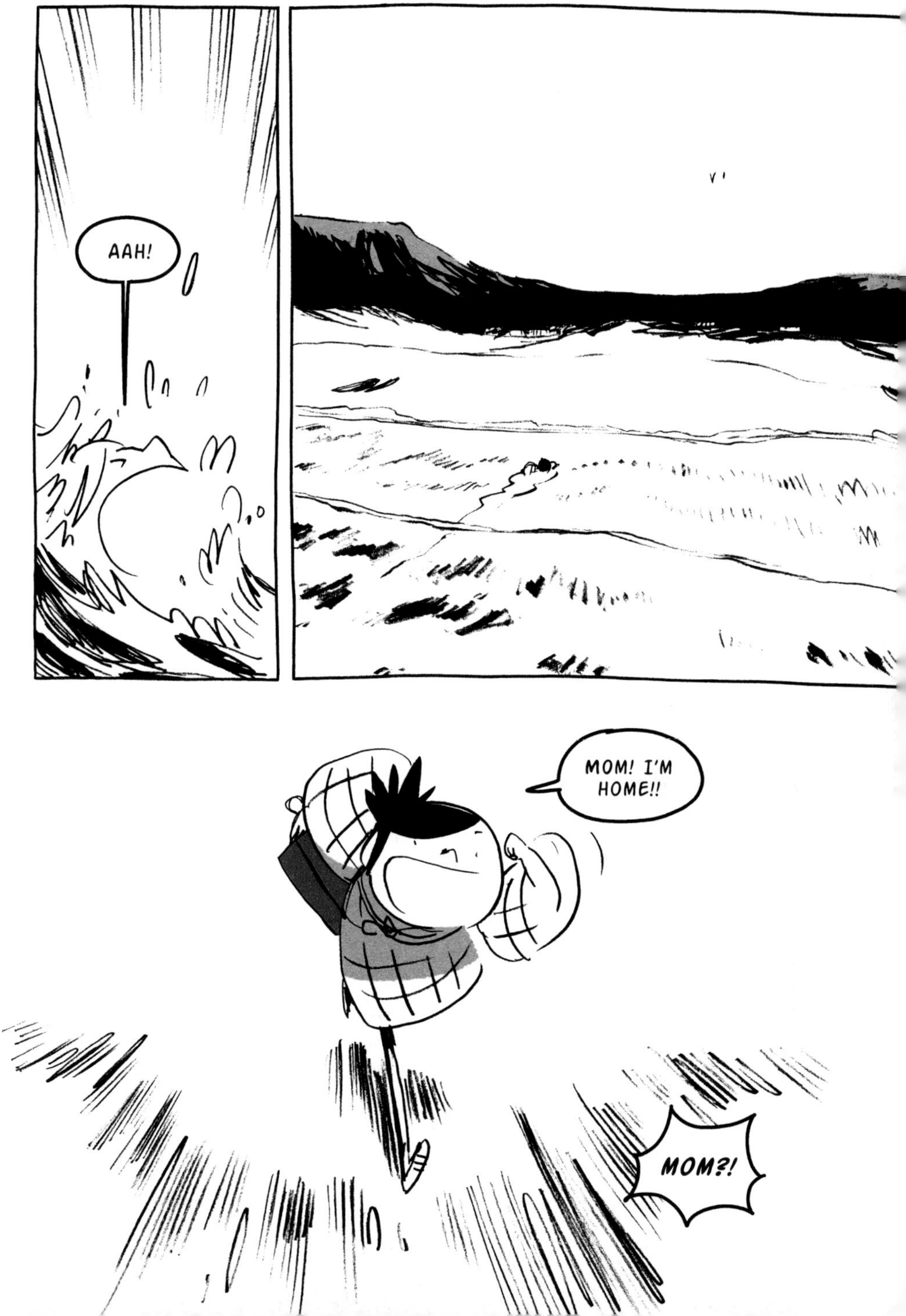
AAH!
MOM! I'M HOME!!
MOM?!

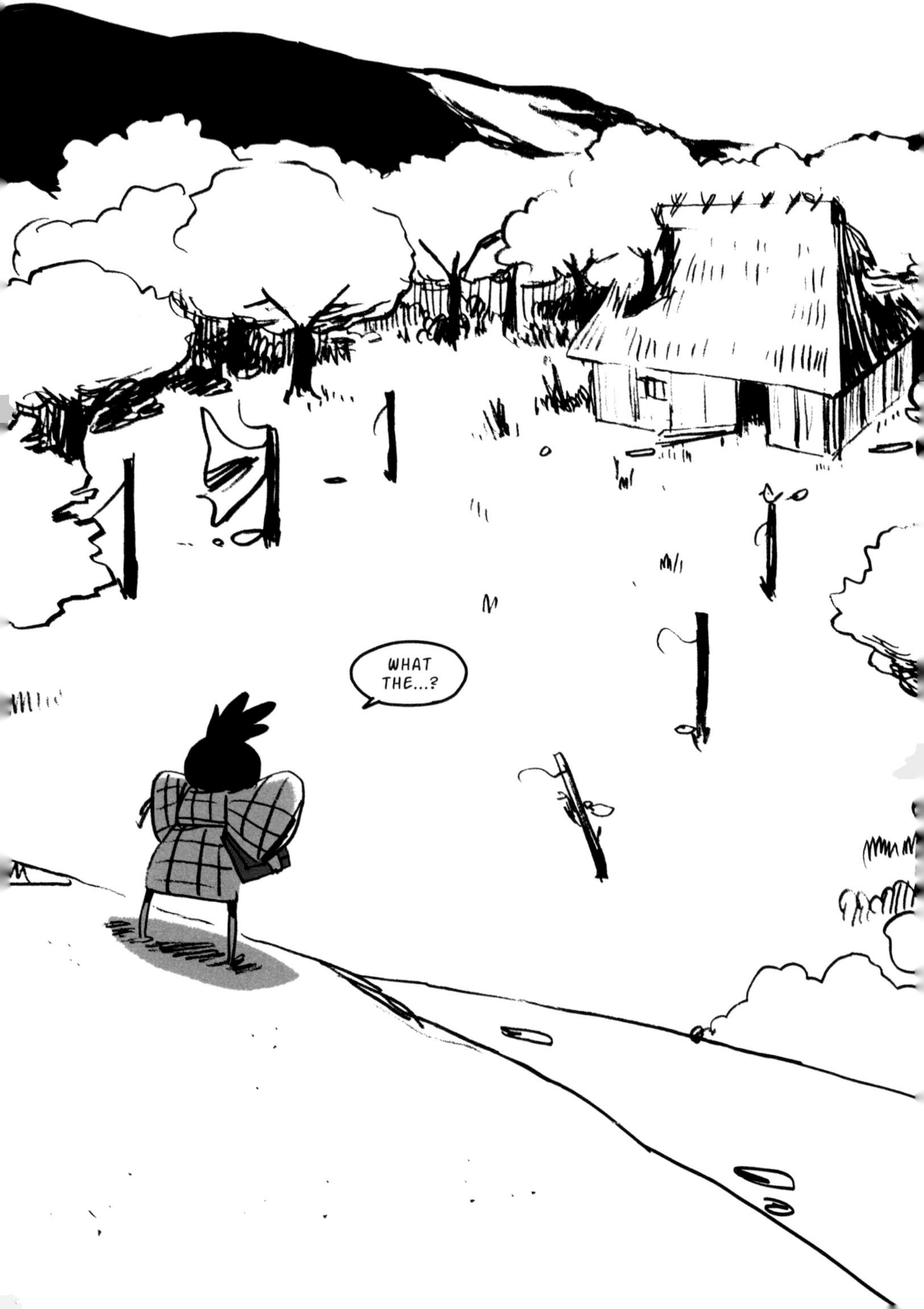
WHAT THE...?

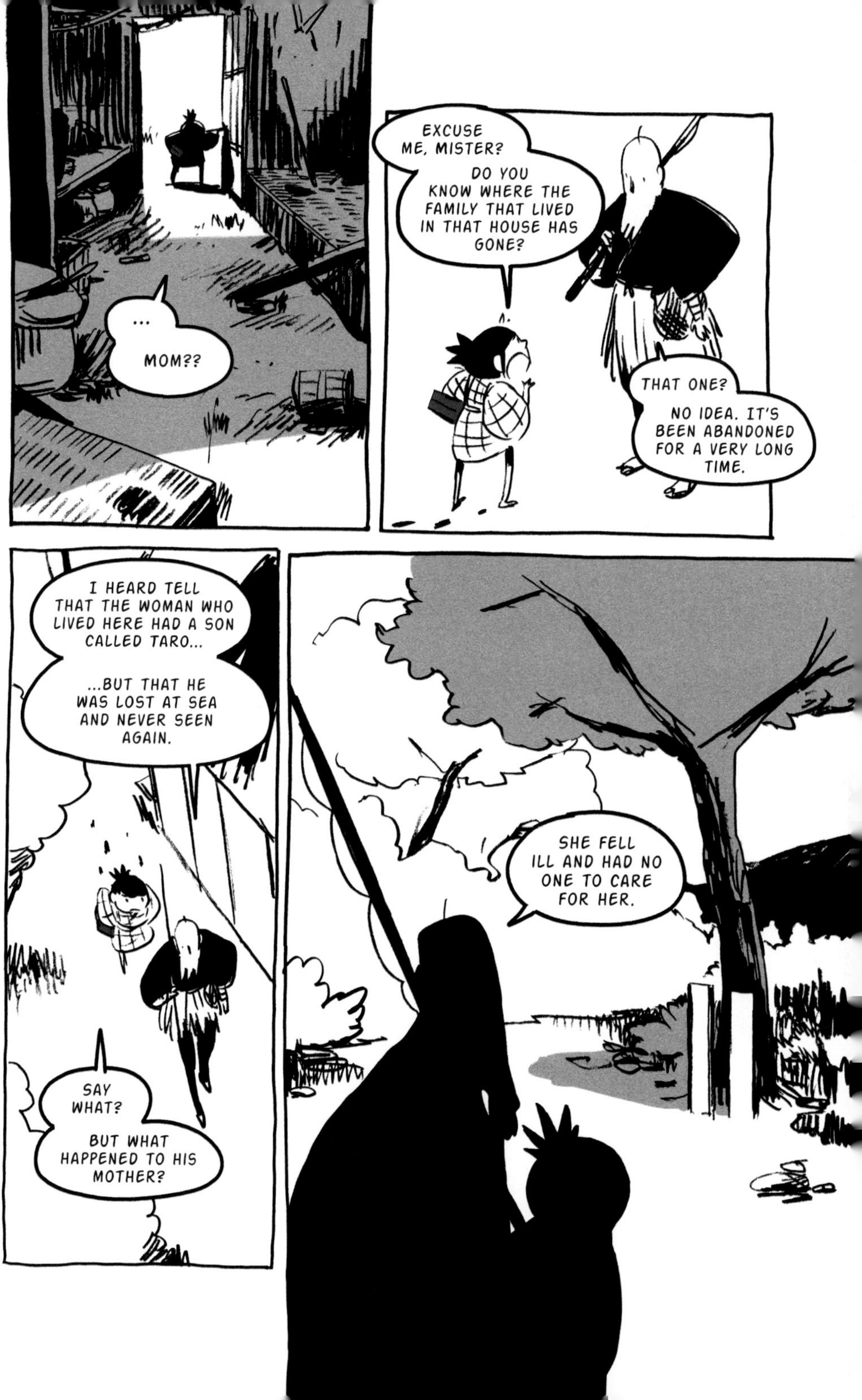
...
MOM??
EXCUSE ME, MISTER?
DO YOU KNOW WHERE THE FAMILY THAT LIVED IN THAT HOUSE HAS GONE?
THAT ONE?
NO IDEA. IT'S BEEN ABANDONED FOR A VERY LONG TIME.
I HEARD TELL THAT THE WOMAN WHO LIVED HERE HAD A SON CALLED TARO...
...BUT THAT HE WAS LOST AT SEA AND NEVER SEEN AGAIN.
SAY WHAT?
BUT WHAT HAPPENED TO HIS MOTHER?
SHE FELL ILL AND HAD NO ONE TO CARE FOR HER.

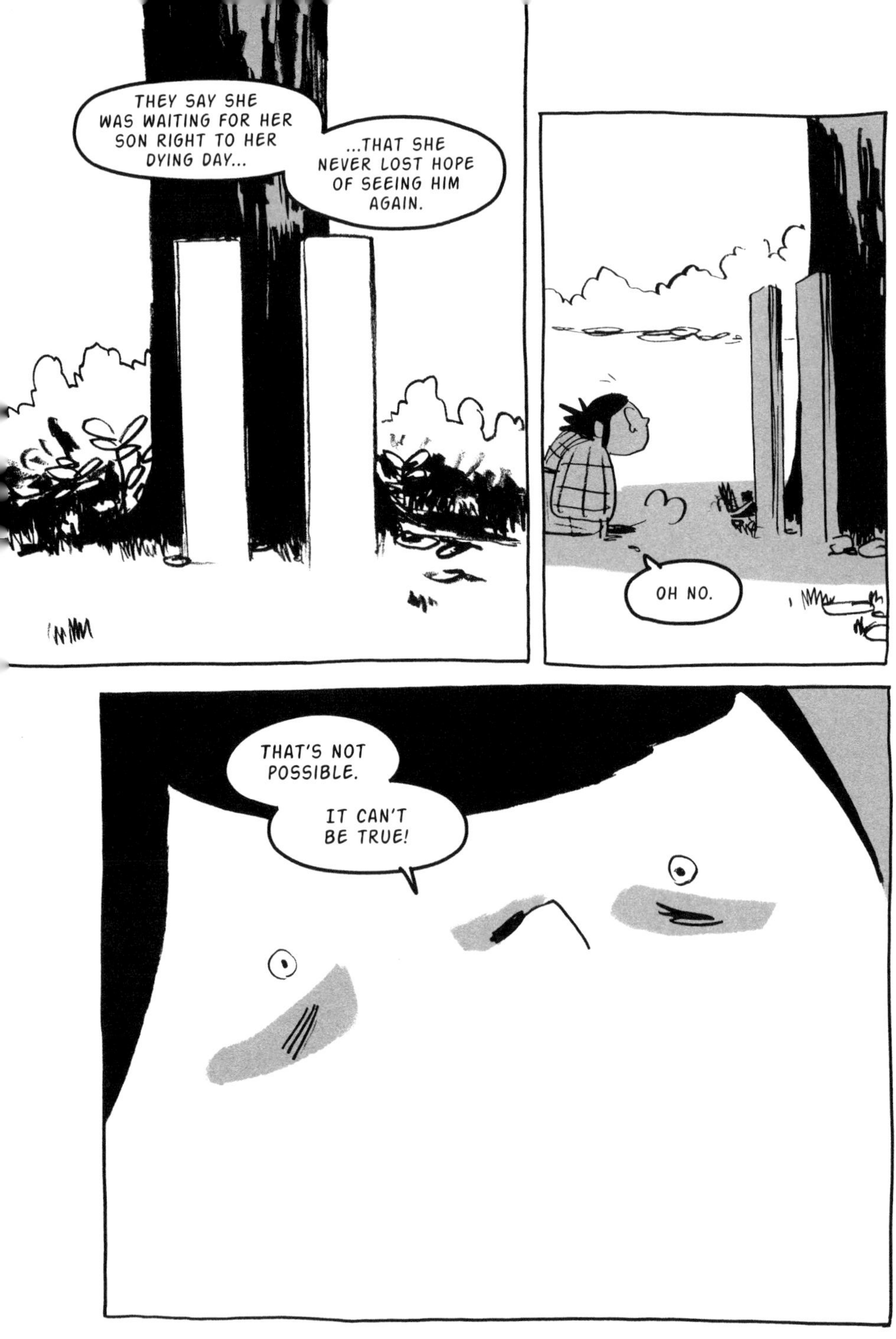
THEY SAY SHE WAS WAITING FOR HER SON RIGHT TO HER DYING DAY...
...THAT SHE NEVER LOST HOPE OF SEEING HIM AGAIN.
OH NO.
THAT'S NOT POSSIBLE.
IT CAN'T BE TRUE!

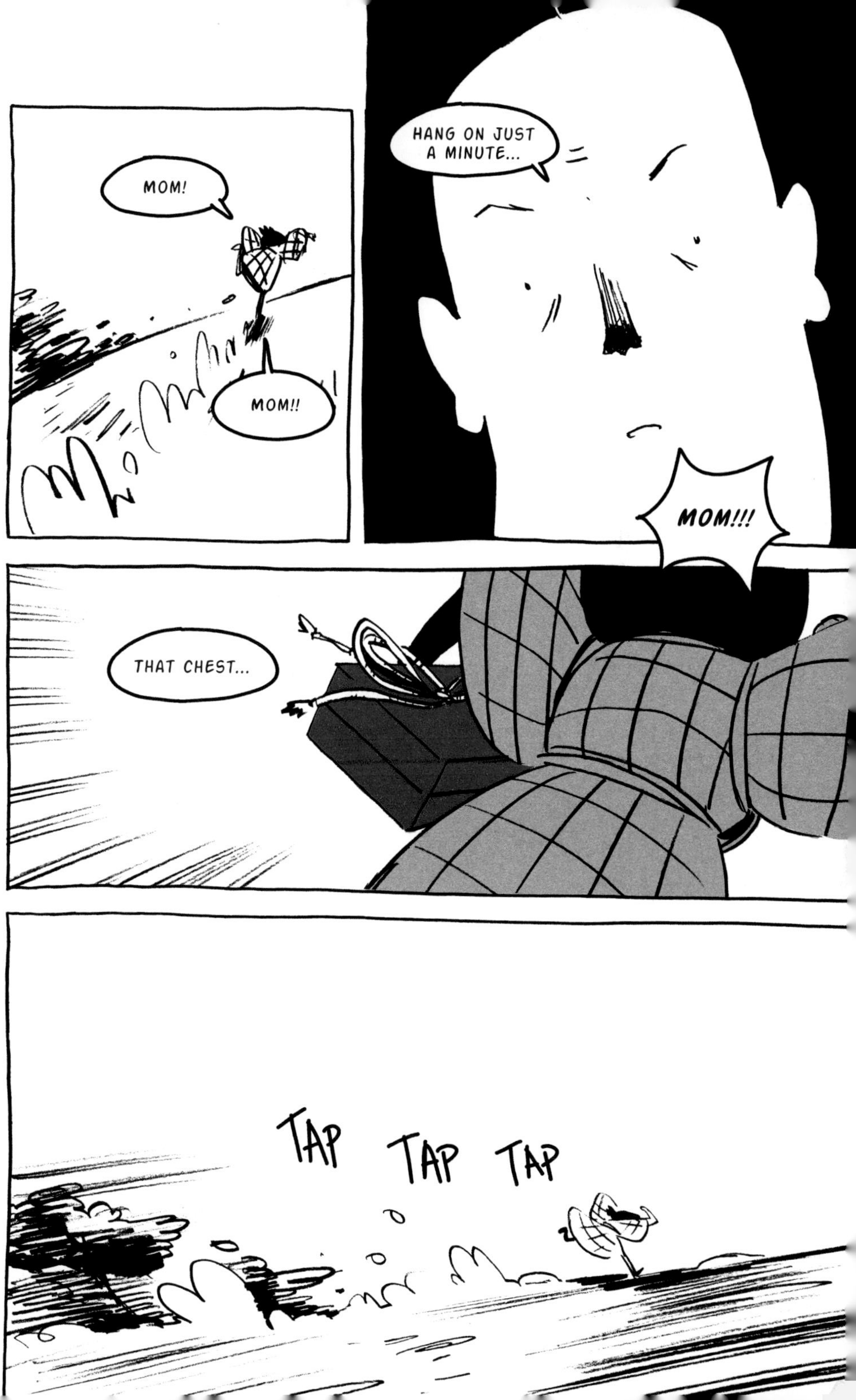
MOM!
MOM!!
HANG ON JUST A MINUTE...
MOM!!!
THAT CHEST...
TAP TAP TAP

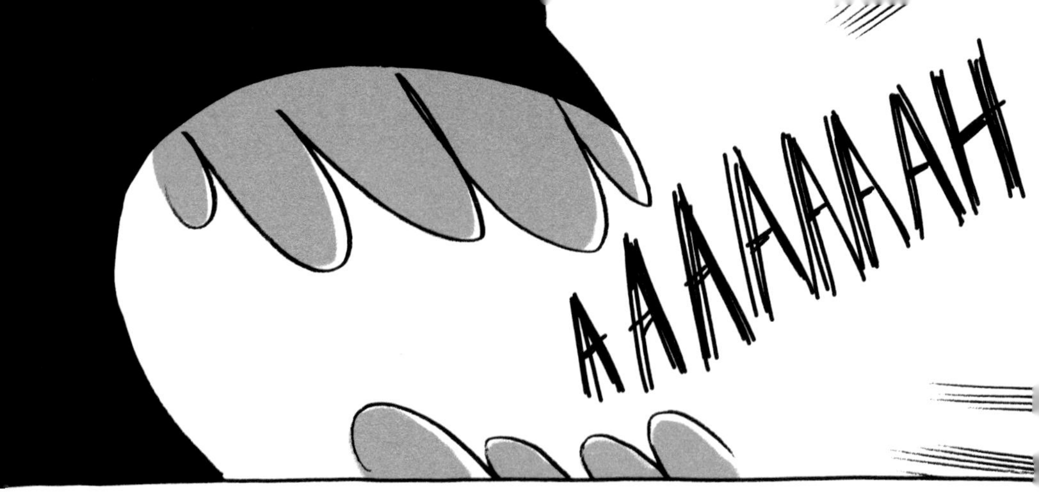
AAAAAAAAH

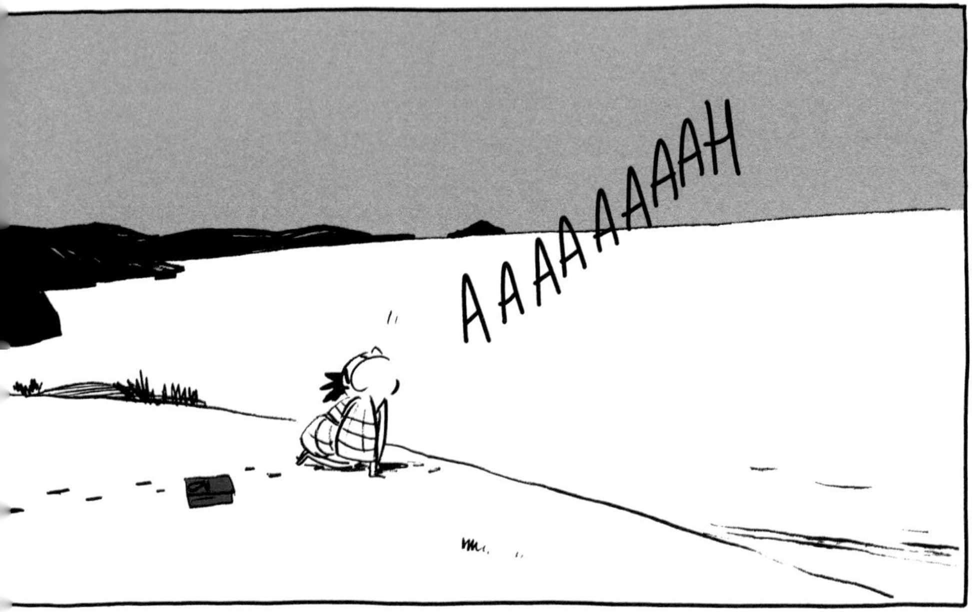
AAAAAAAAH

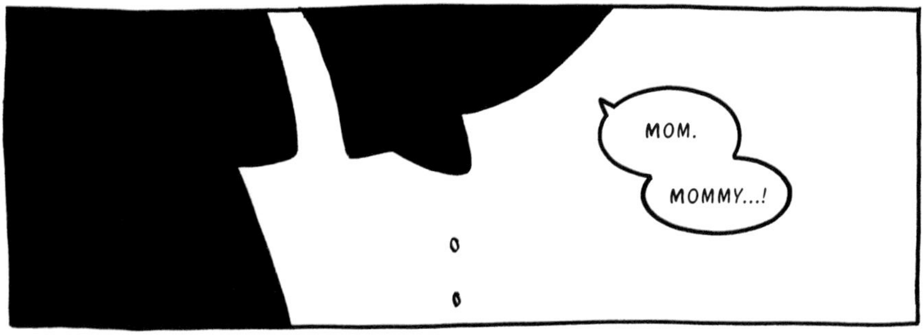
MOM.
MOMMY...!

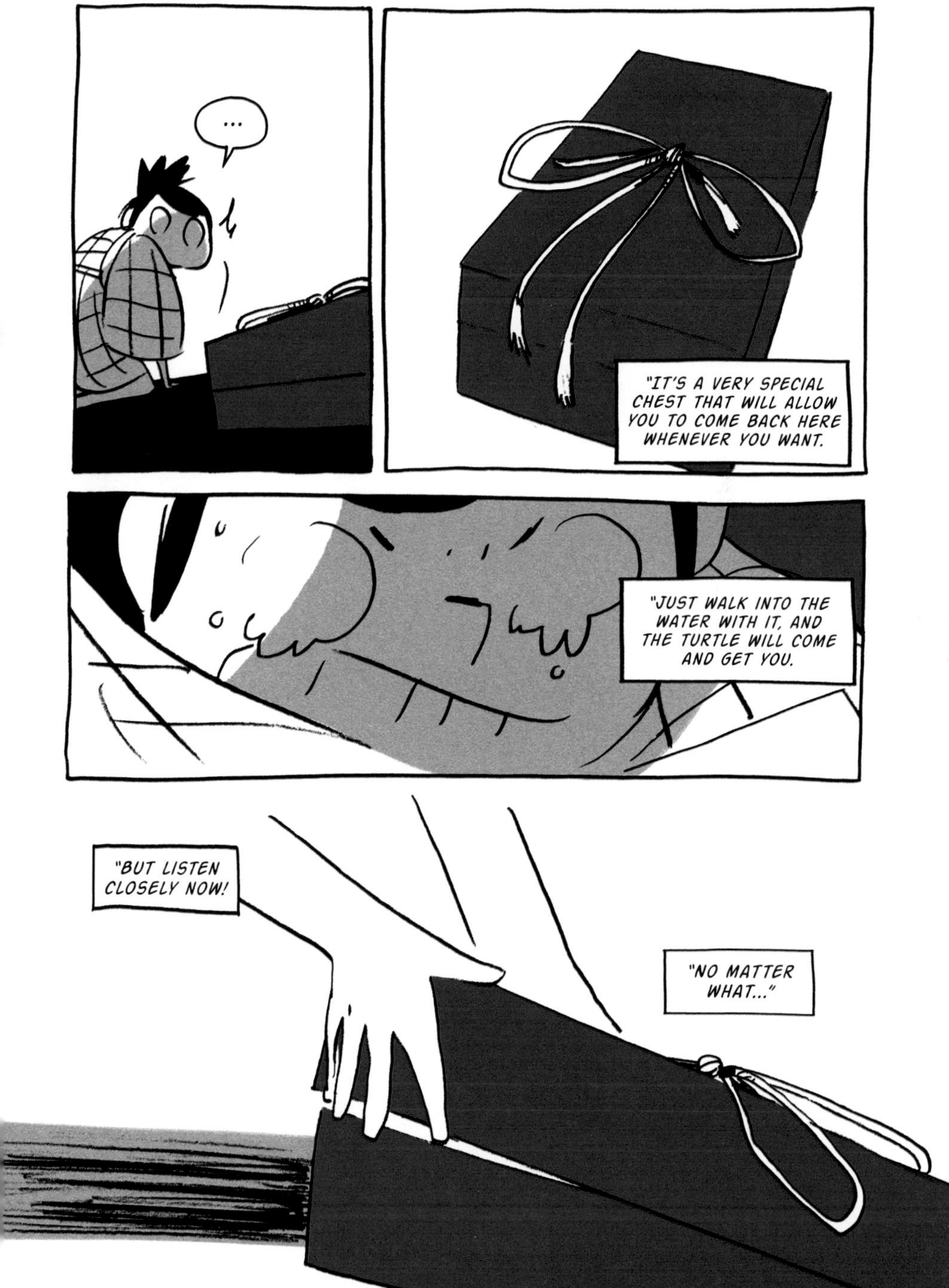
...
"IT'S A VERY SPECIAL CHEST THAT WILL ALLOW YOU TO COME BACK HERE WHENEVER YOU WANT.
"JUST WALK INTO THE WATER WITH IT, AND THE TURTLE WILL COME AND GET YOU.
"BUT LISTEN CLOSELY NOW!
"NO MATTER WHAT..."

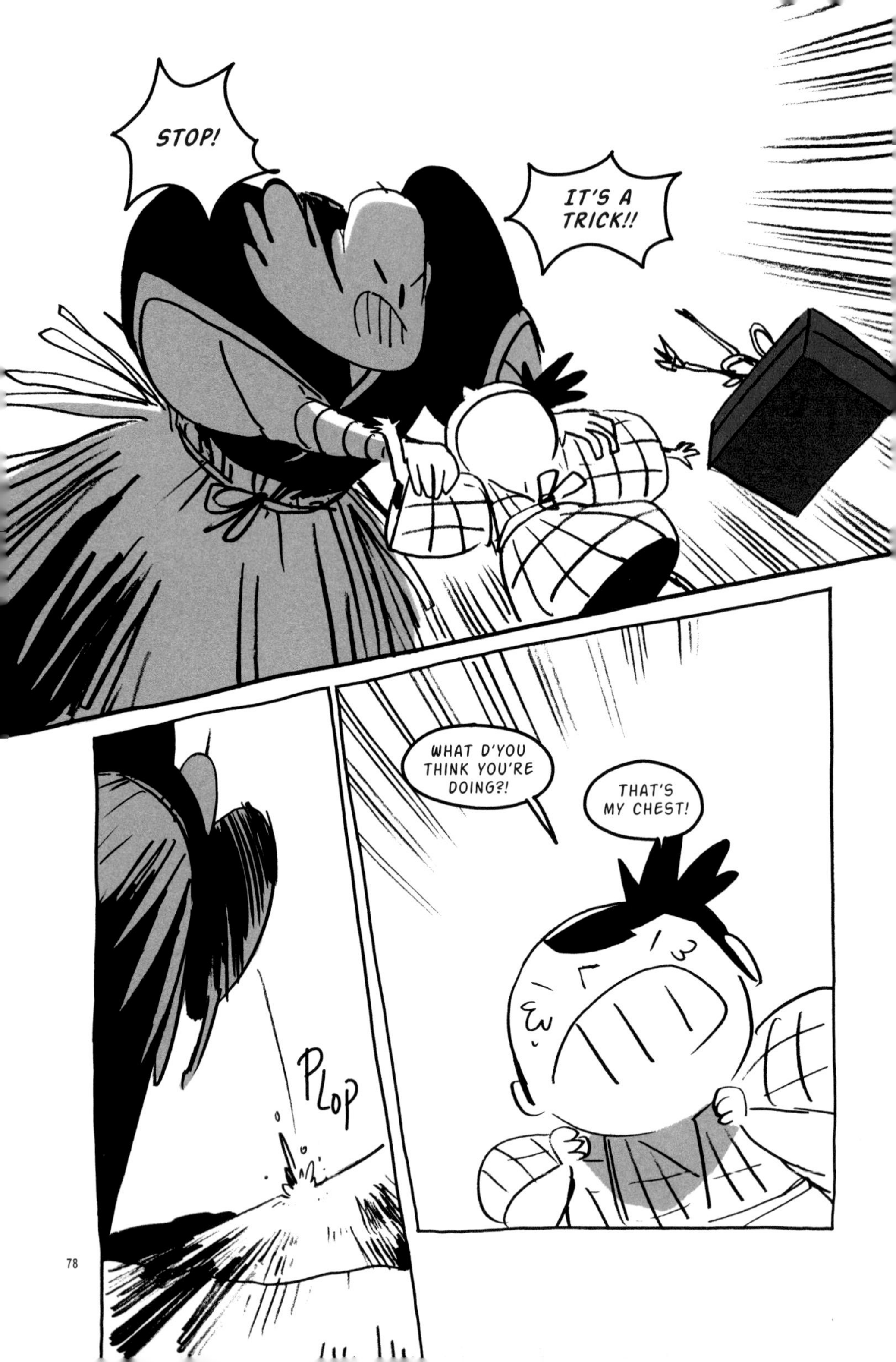
STOP!
IT'S A TRICK!!
WHAT D'YOU THINK YOU'RE DOING?!
THAT'S MY CHEST!
PLOP

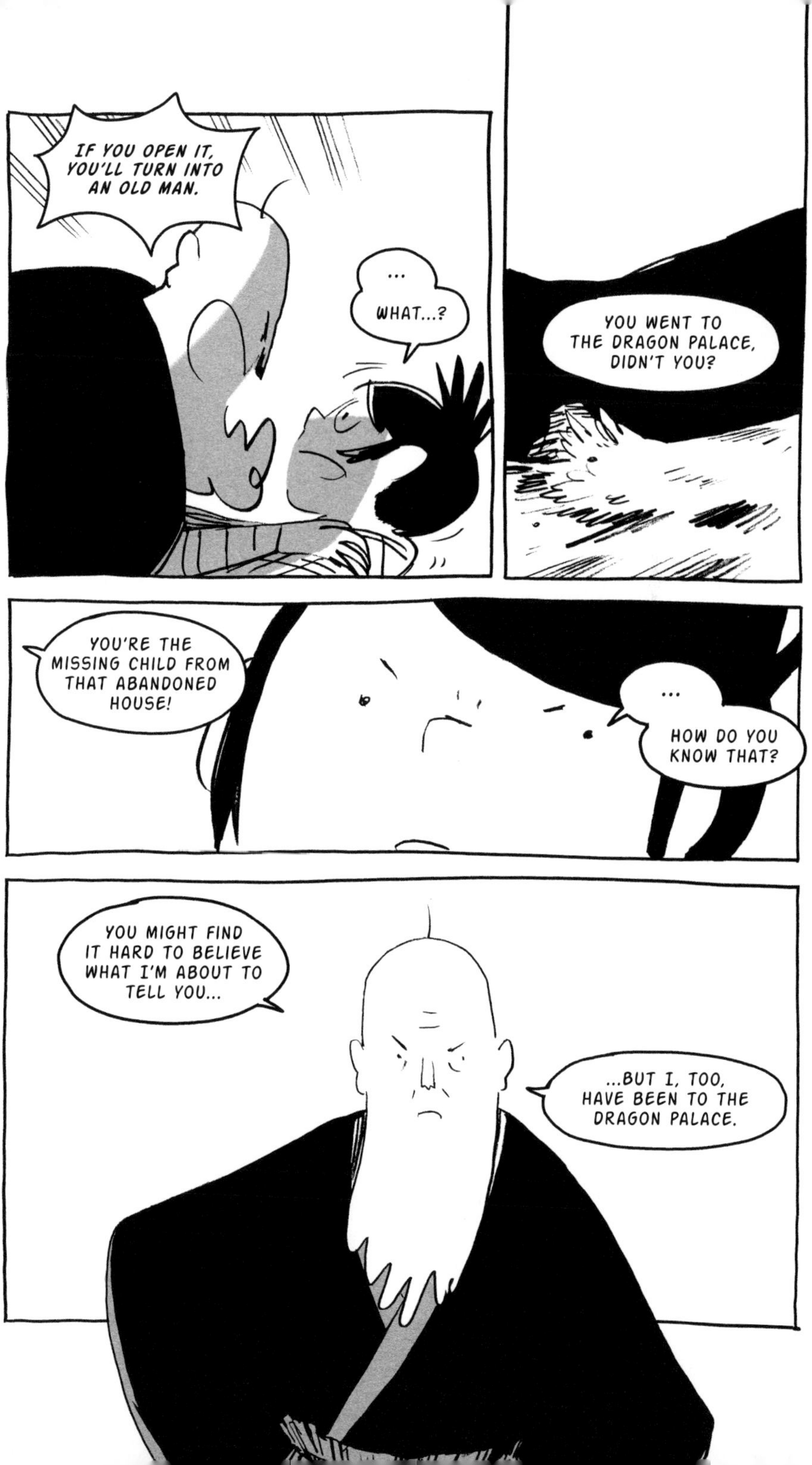
IF YOU OPEN IT, YOU'LL TURN INTO AN OLD MAN.
... WHAT...?
YOU WENT TO THE DRAGON PALACE, DIDN'T YOU?
YOU'RE THE MISSING CHILD FROM THAT ABANDONED HOUSE!
... HOW DO YOU KNOW THAT?
YOU MIGHT FIND IT HARD TO BELIEVE WHAT I'M ABOUT TO TELL YOU...
...BUT I, TOO, HAVE BEEN TO THE DRAGON PALACE.

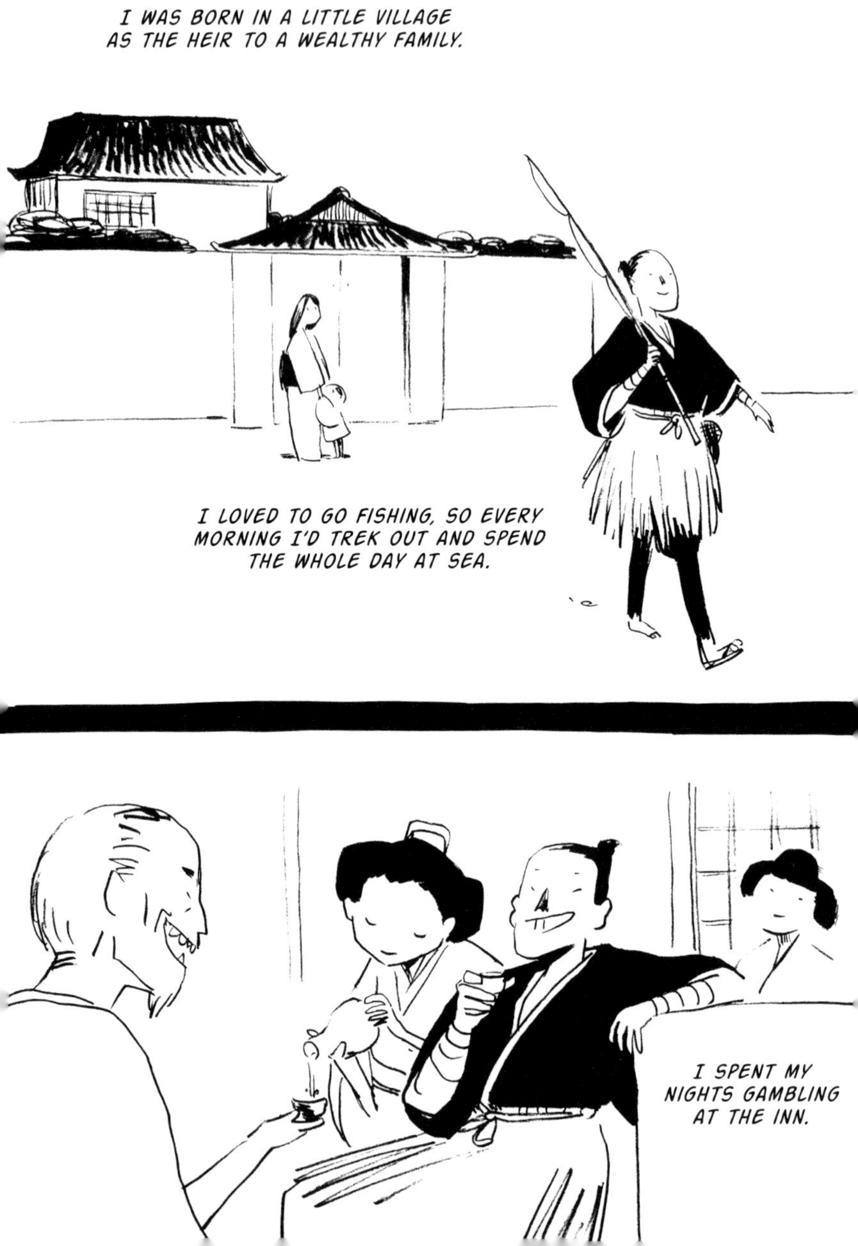
I WAS BORN IN A LITTLE VILLAGE AS THE HEIR TO A WEALTHY FAMILY.
I LOVED TO GO FISHING, SO EVERY MORNING I'D TREK OUT AND SPEND THE WHOLE DAY AT SEA.
I SPENT MY NIGHTS GAMBLING AT THE INN.

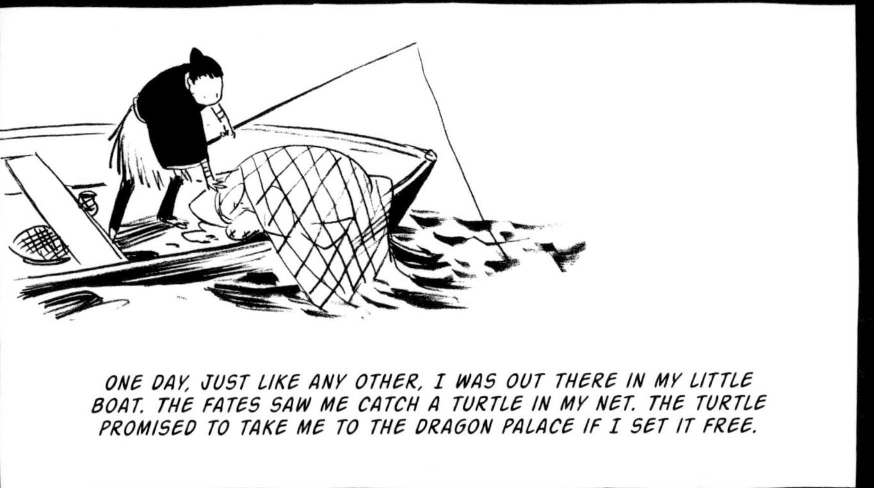
ONE DAY, JUST LIKE ANY OTHER, I WAS OUT THERE IN MY LITTLE BOAT. THE FATES SAW ME CATCH A TURTLE IN MY NET. THE TURTLE PROMISED TO TAKE ME TO THE DRAGON PALACE IF I SET IT FREE.

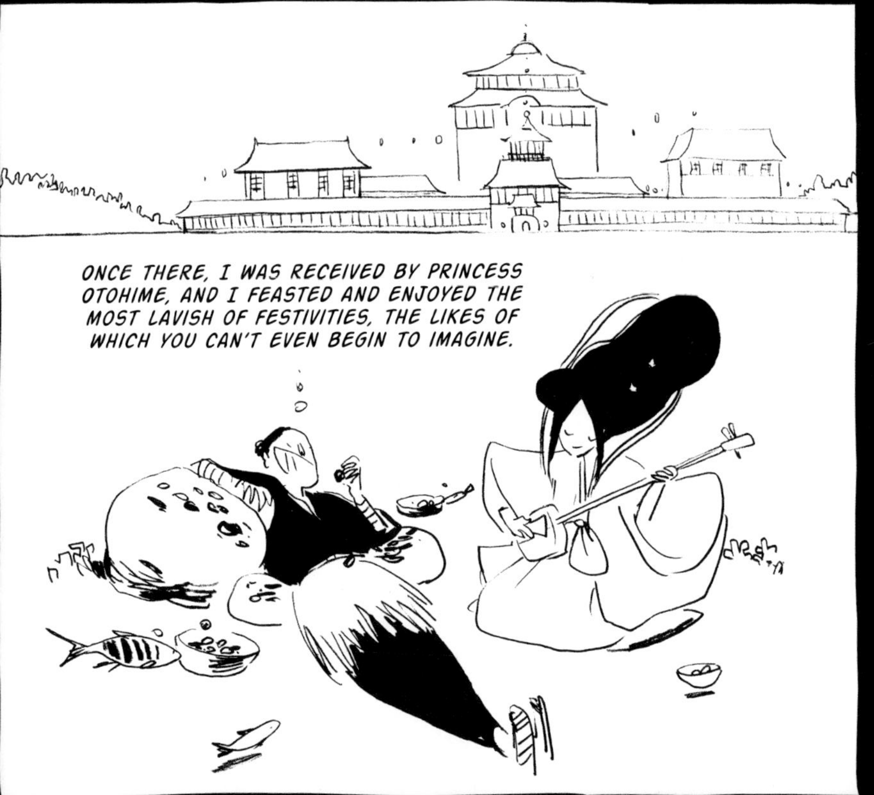
ONCE THERE, I WAS RECEIVED BY PRINCESS OTOHIME, AND I FEASTED AND ENJOYED THE MOST LAVISH OF FESTIVITIES, THE LIKES OF WHICH YOU CAN'T EVEN BEGIN TO IMAGINE.

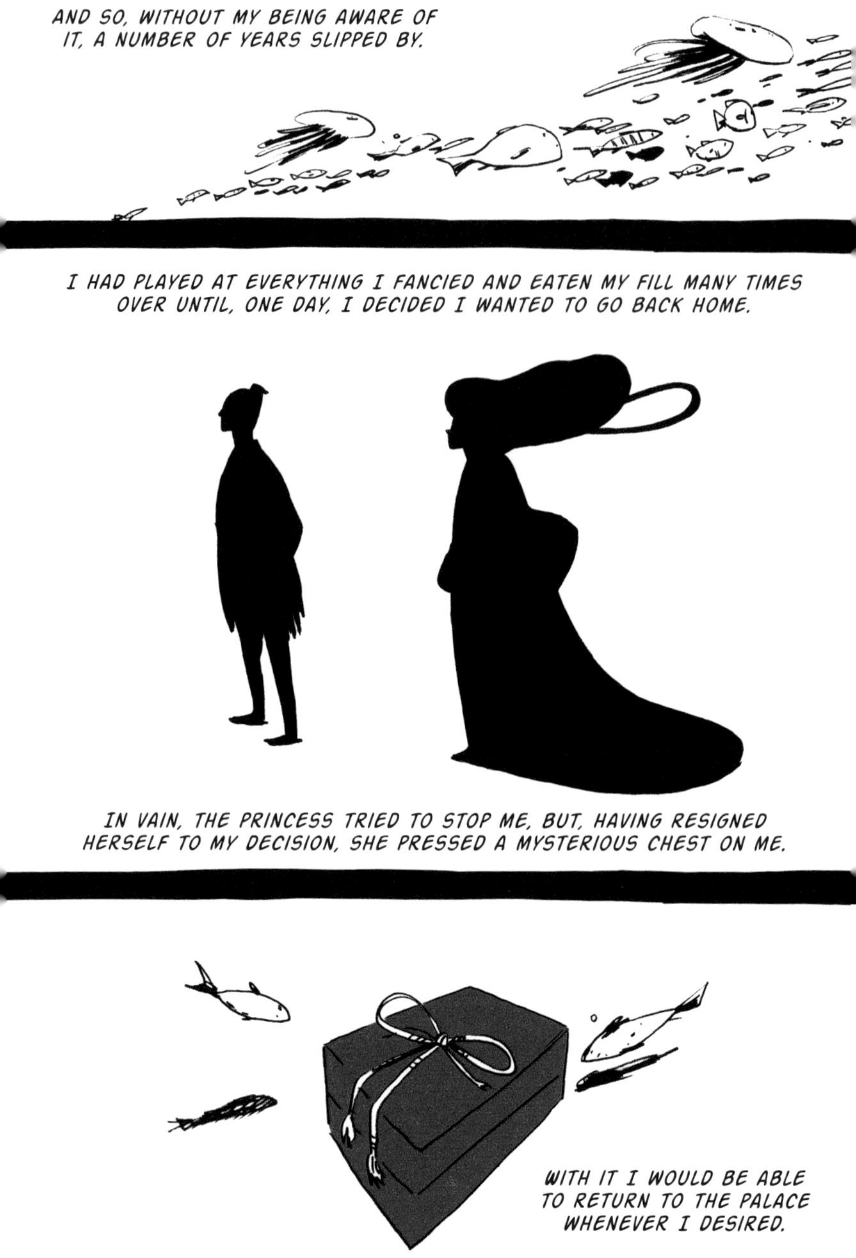
AND SO, WITHOUT MY BEING AWARE OF IT, A NUMBER OF YEARS SLIPPED BY.
I HAD PLAYED AT EVERYTHING I FANCIED AND EATEN MY FILL MANY TIMES OVER UNTIL, ONE DAY, I DECIDED I WANTED TO GO BACK HOME.
IN VAIN, THE PRINCESS TRIED TO STOP ME, BUT, HAVING RESIGNED HERSELF TO MY DECISION, SHE PRESSED A MYSTERIOUS CHEST ON ME.
WITH IT I WOULD BE ABLE TO RETURN TO THE PALACE WHENEVER I DESIRED.

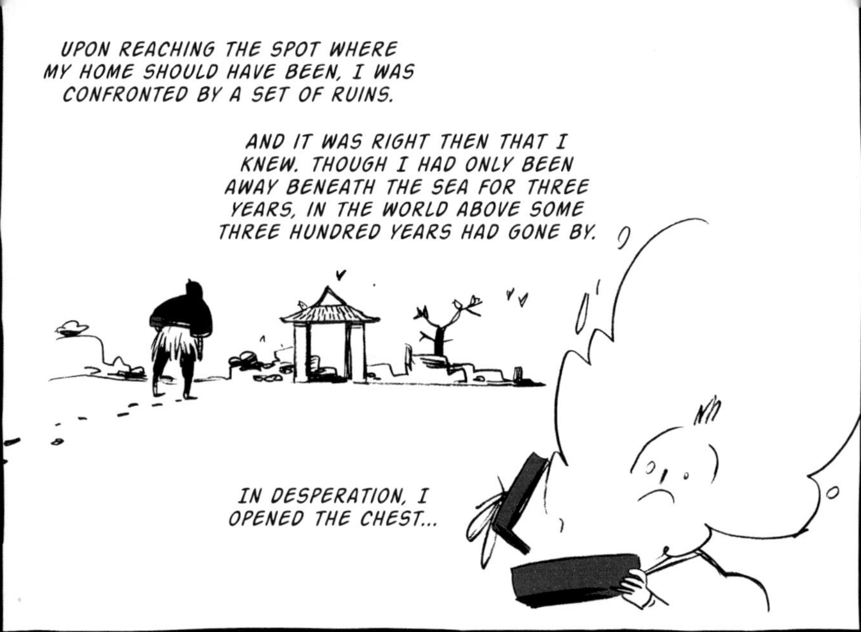
UPON REACHING THE SPOT WHERE MY HOME SHOULD HAVE BEEN, I WAS CONFRONTED BY A SET OF RUINS.
AND IT WAS RIGHT THEN THAT I KNEW. THOUGH I HAD ONLY BEEN AWAY BENEATH THE SEA FOR THREE YEARS, IN THE WORLD ABOVE SOME THREE HUNDRED YEARS HAD GONE BY.
IN DESPERATION, I OPENED THE CHEST...

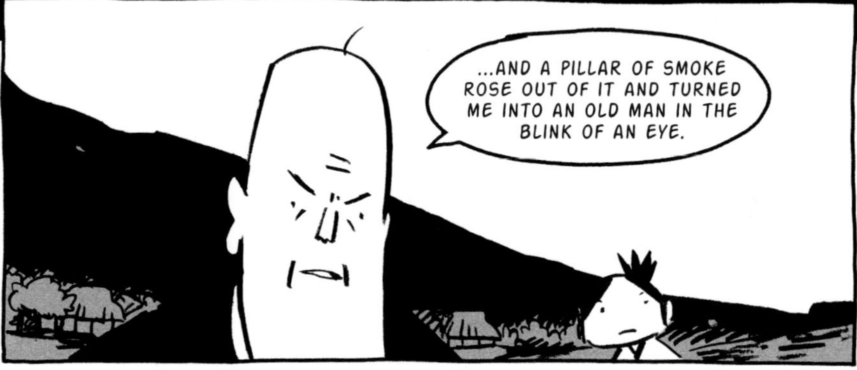
...AND A PILLAR OF SMOKE ROSE OUT OF IT AND TURNED ME INTO AN OLD MAN IN THE BLINK OF AN EYE.

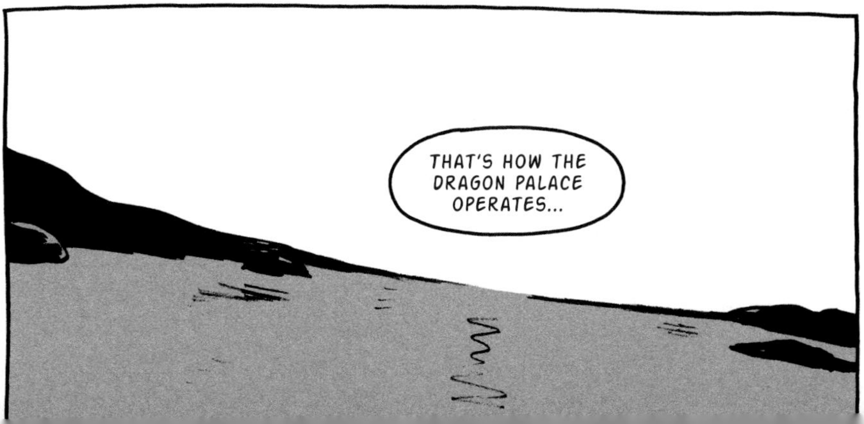
THAT'S HOW THE DRAGON PALACE OPERATES...

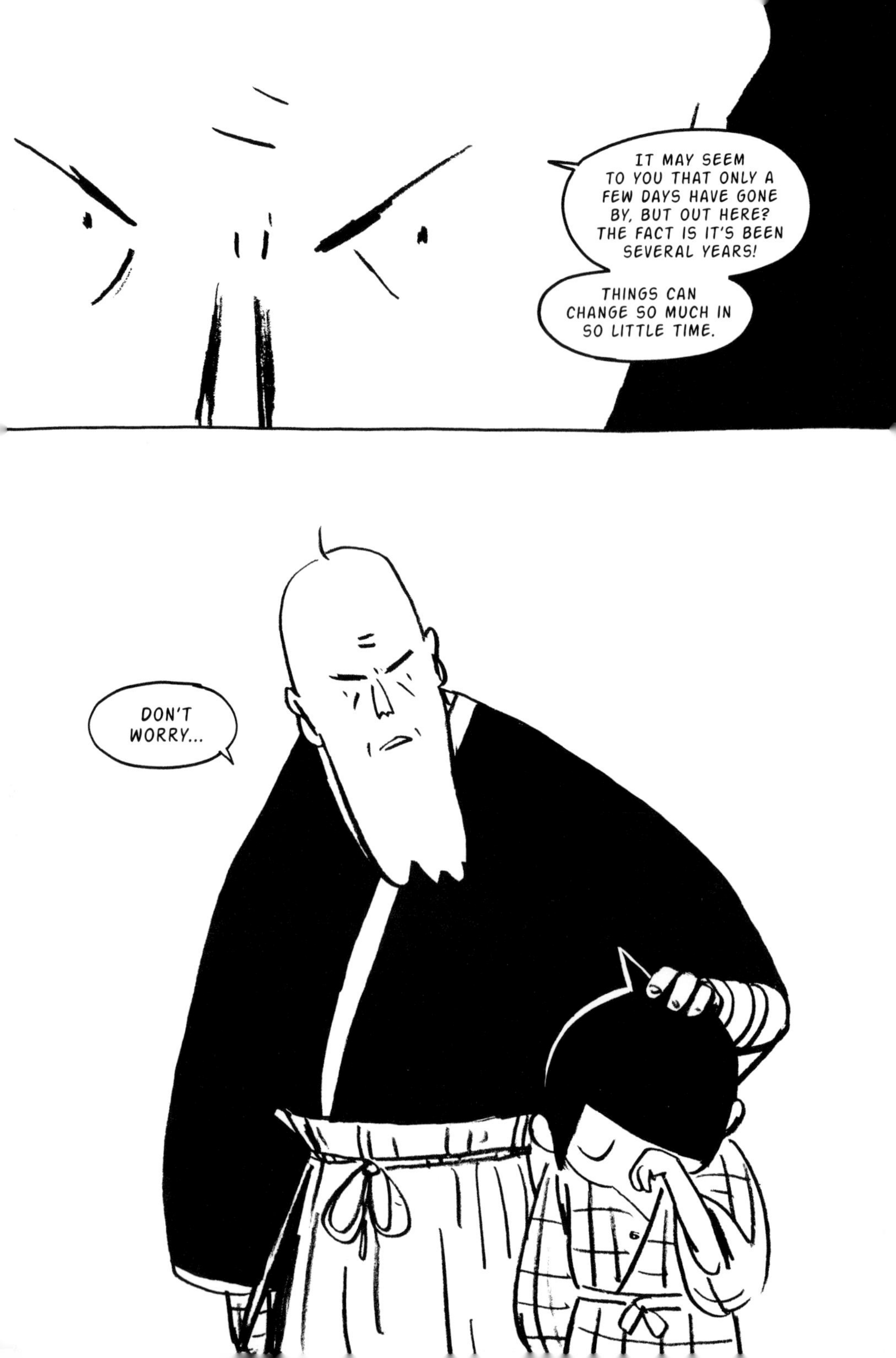
IT MAY SEEM TO YOU THAT ONLY A FEW DAYS HAVE GONE BY, BUT OUT HERE? THE FACT IS IT'S BEEN SEVERAL YEARS!
THINGS CAN CHANGE SO MUCH IN SO LITTLE TIME.
DON'T WORRY...

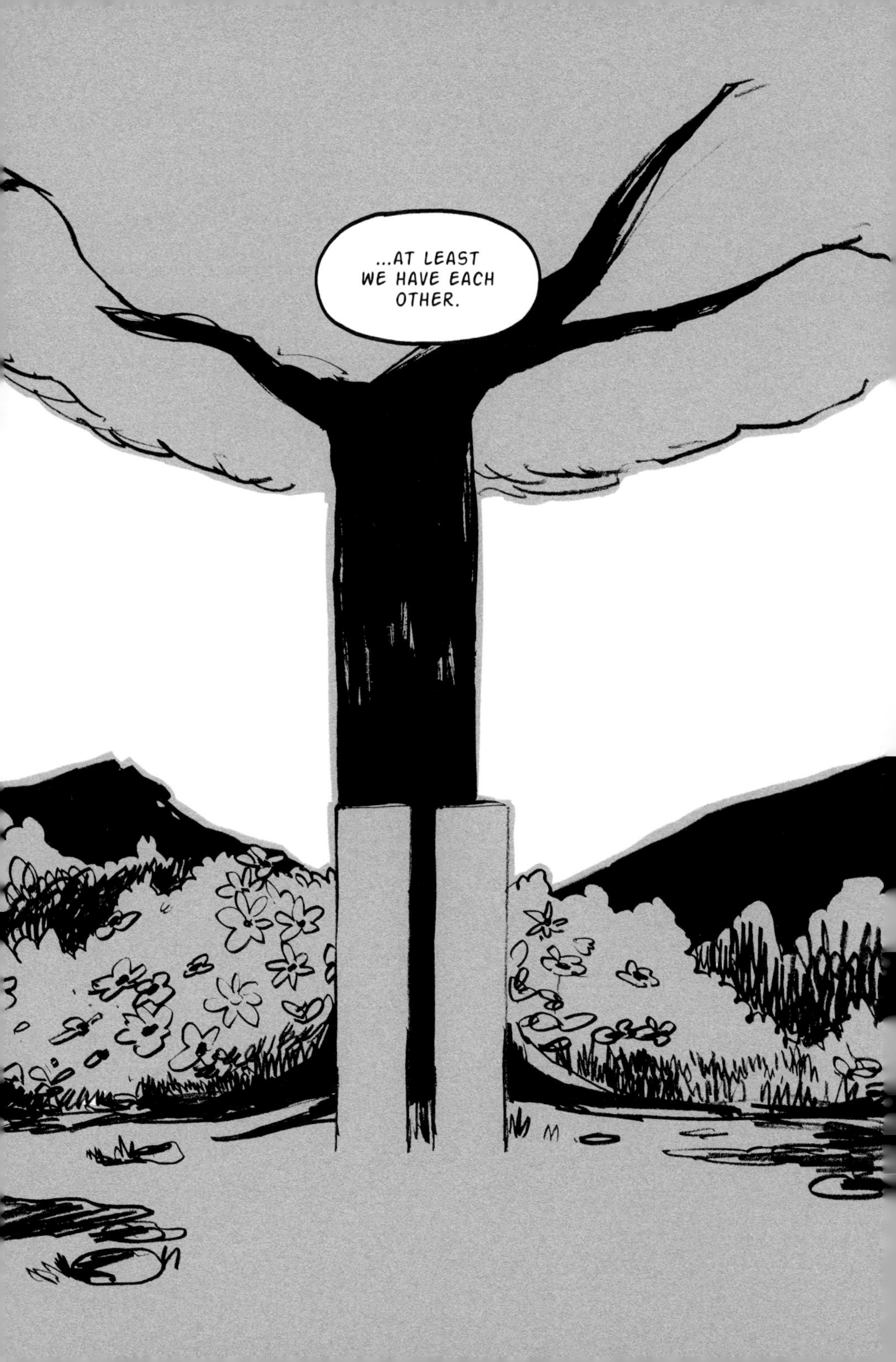
...AT LEAST WE HAVE EACH OTHER.

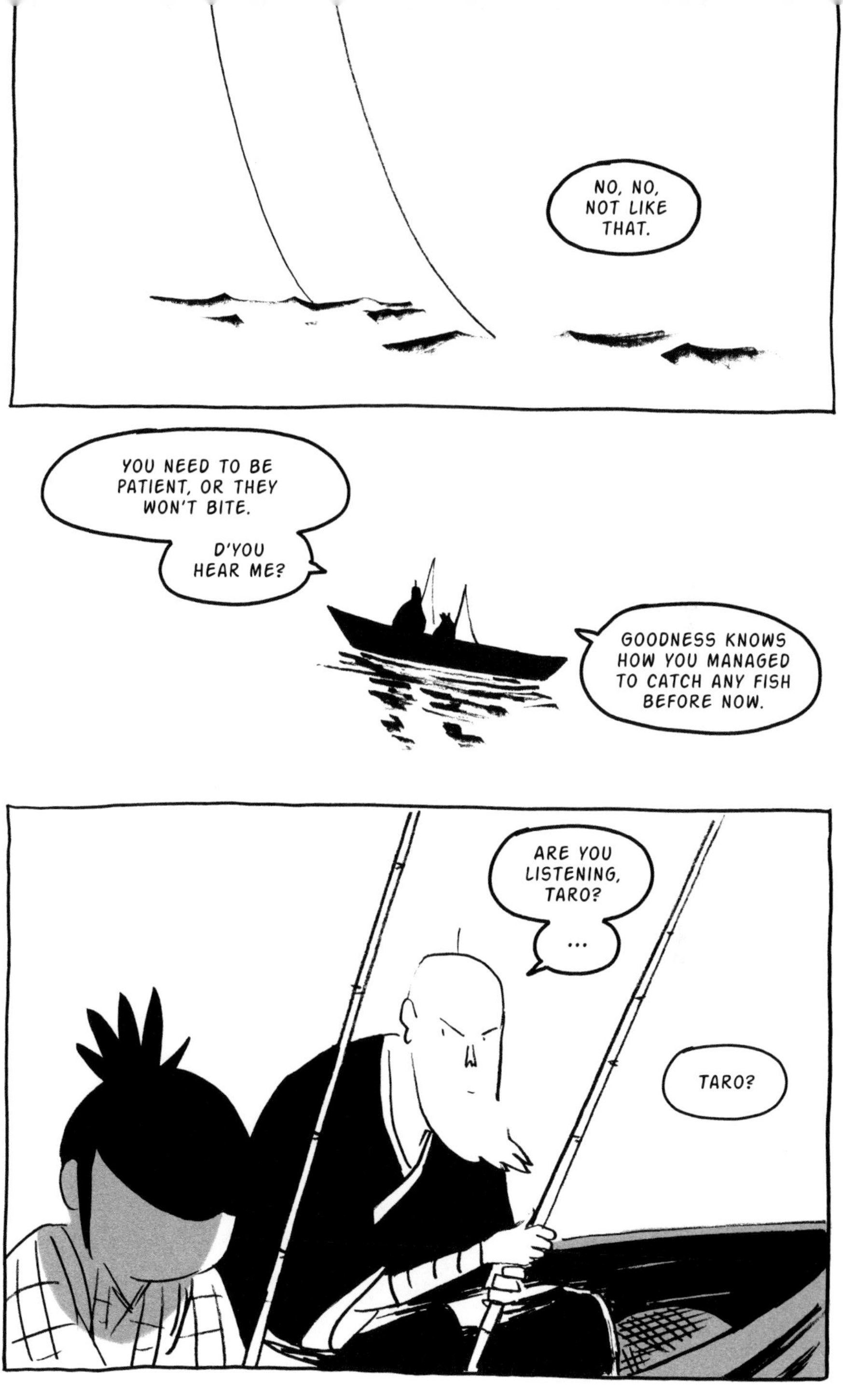
NO, NO, NOT LIKE THAT.
YOU NEED TO BE PATIENT, OR THEY WON'T BITE.
D'YOU HEAR ME?
GOODNESS KNOWS HOW YOU MANAGED TO CATCH ANY FISH BEFORE NOW.
ARE YOU LISTENING, TARO?
...
TARO?

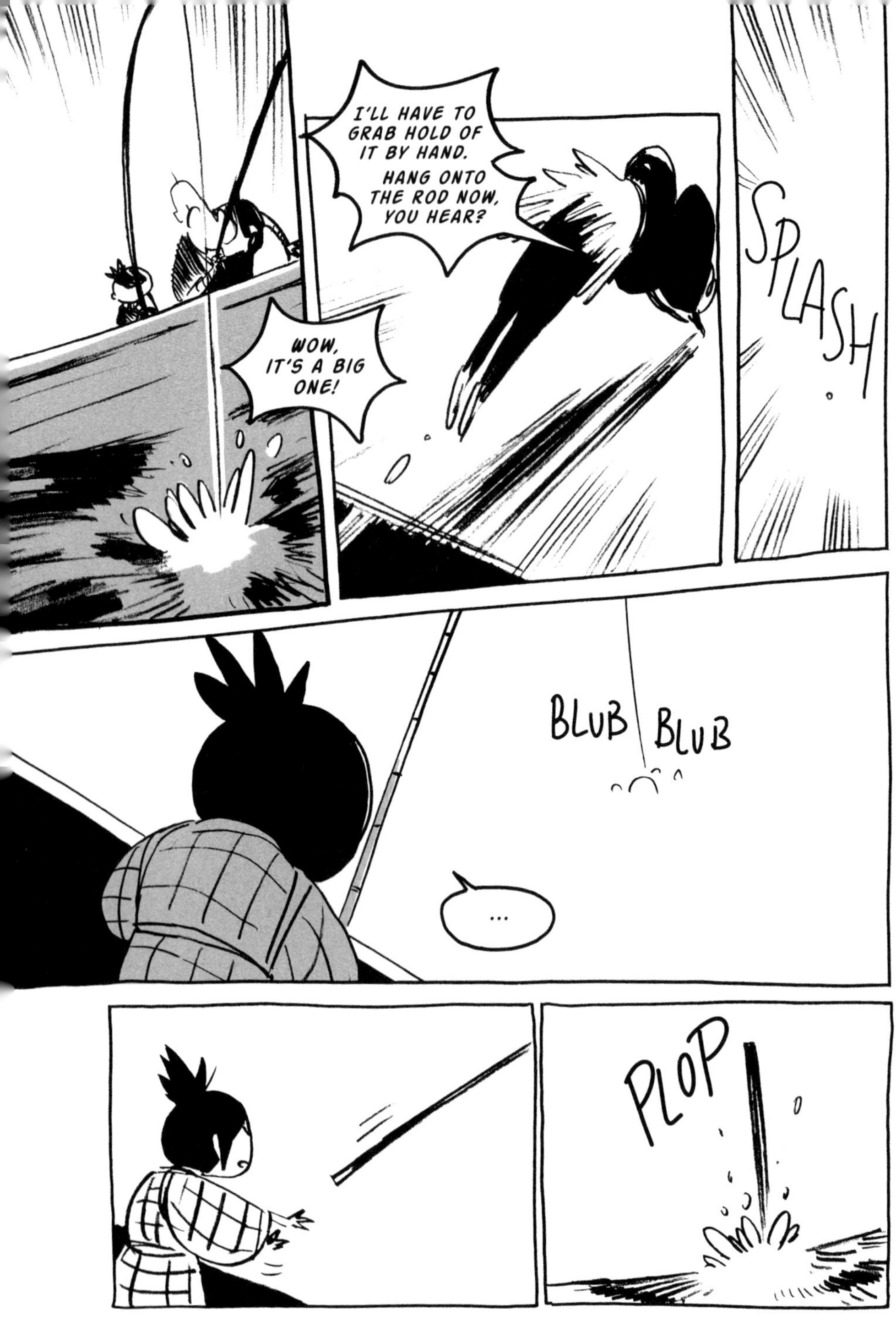
I'LL HAVE TO GRAB HOLD OF IT BY HAND.
HANG ONTO THE ROD NOW, YOU HEAR?
WOW, IT'S A BIG ONE!
SPLASH
BLUB BLUB
...
PLOP

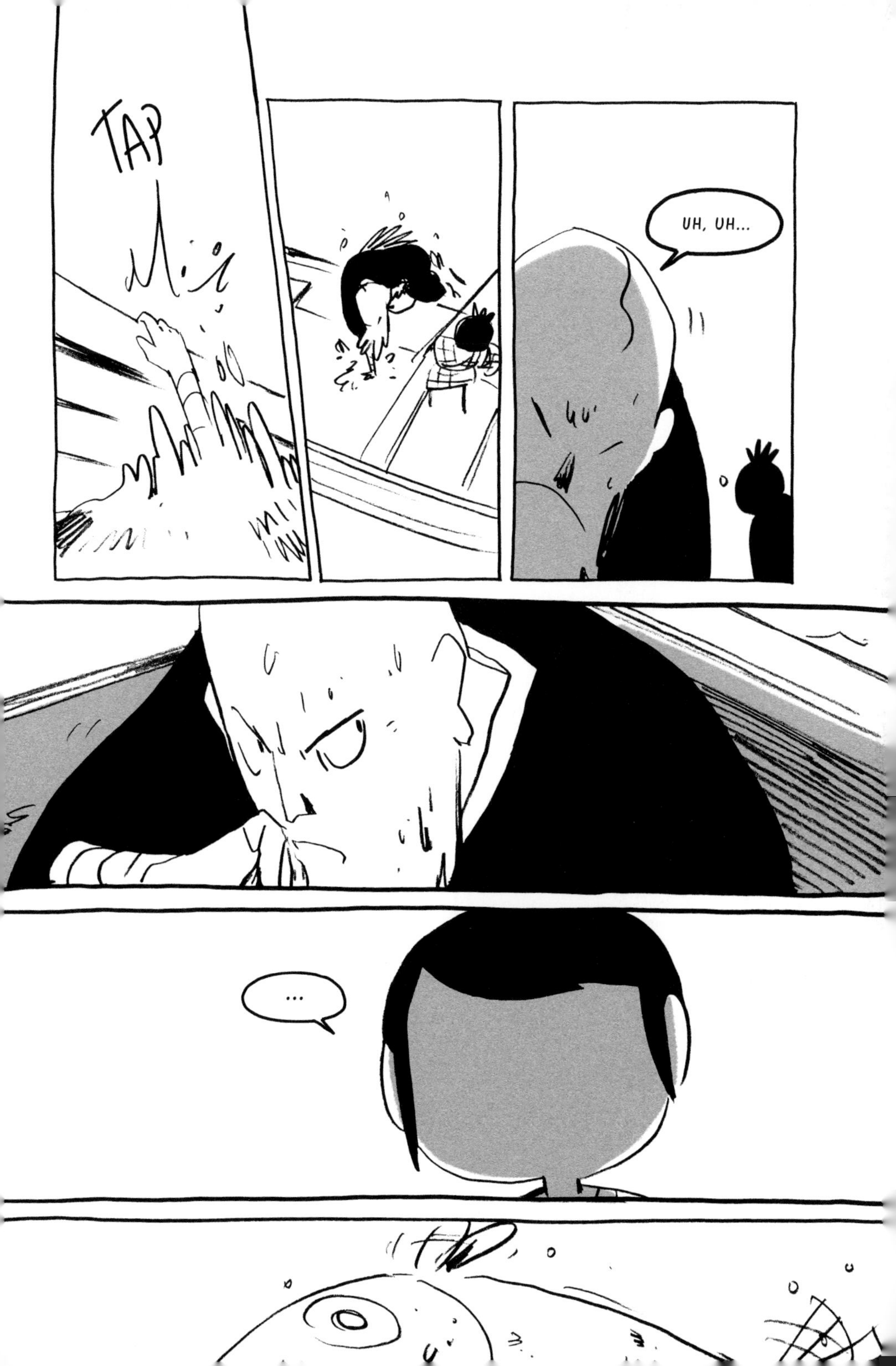
TAP
UH, UH...
...

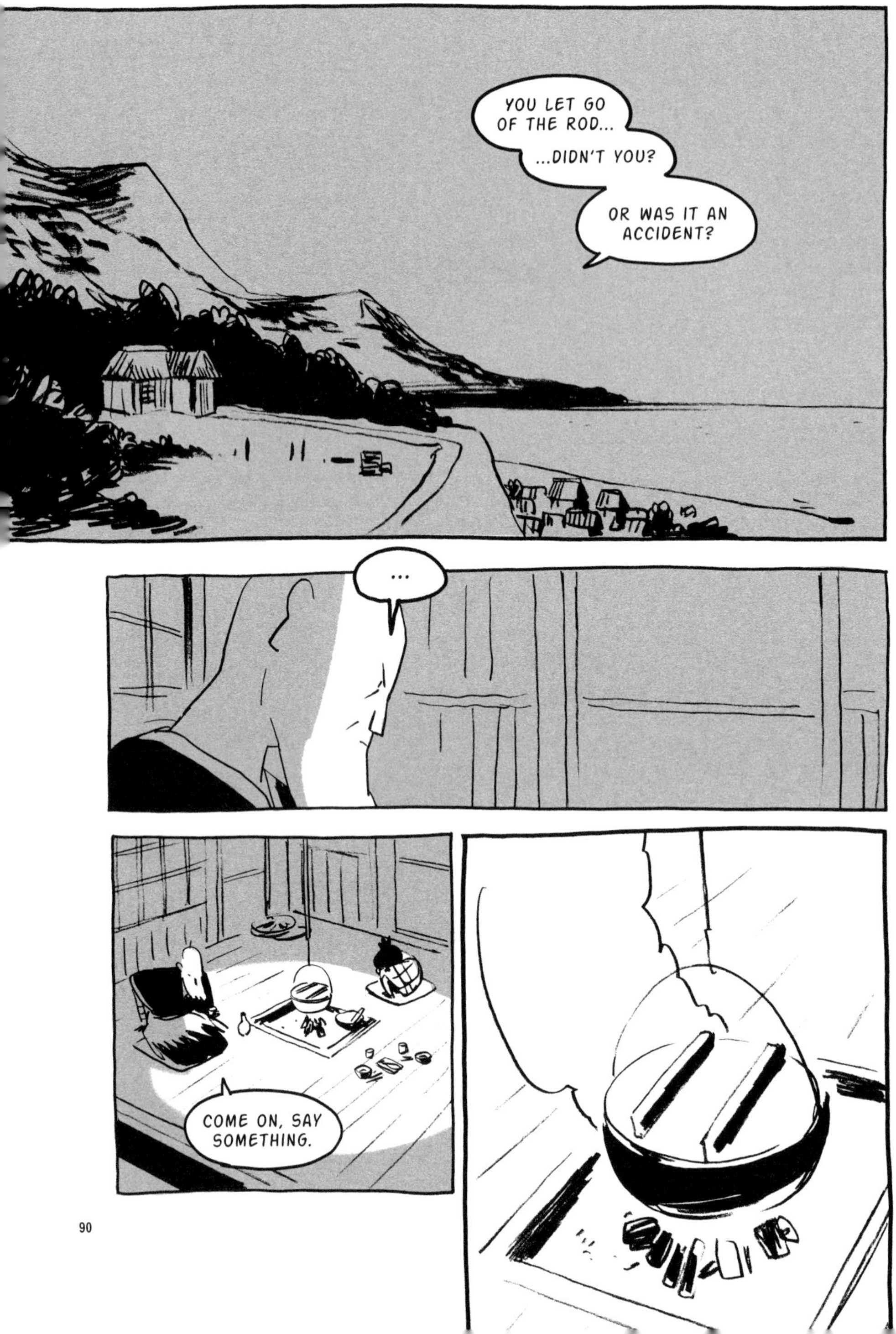
YOU LET GO OF THE ROD...
...DIDN'T YOU?
OR WAS IT AN ACCIDENT?
...
COME ON, SAY SOMETHING.

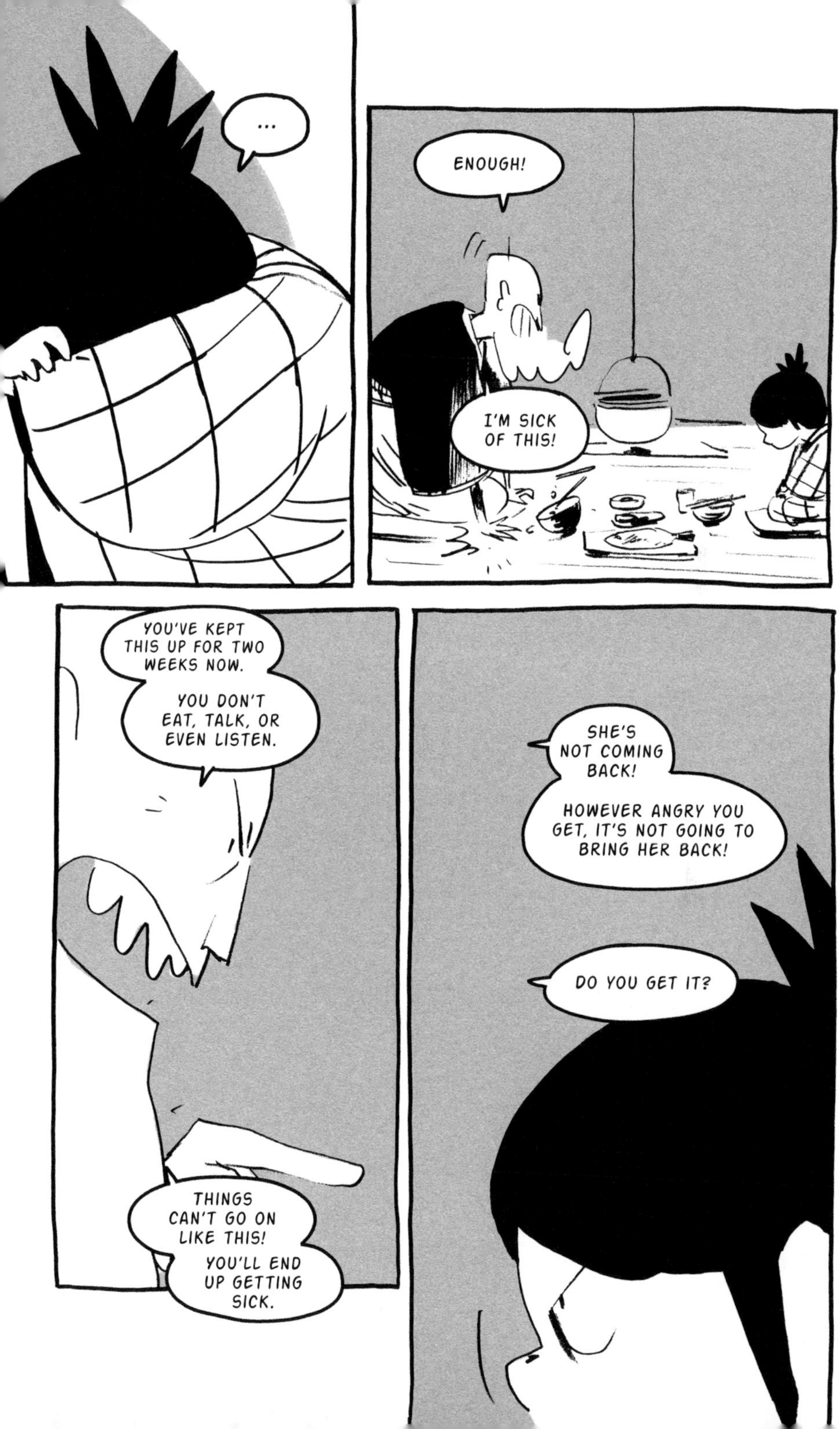
...
ENOUGH!
I'M SICK OF THIS!
YOU'VE KEPT THIS UP FOR TWO WEEKS NOW.
YOU DON'T EAT, TALK, OR EVEN LISTEN.
THINGS CAN'T GO ON LIKE THIS!
YOU'LL END UP GETTING SICK.
SHE'S NOT COMING BACK!
HOWEVER ANGRY YOU GET, IT'S NOT GOING TO BRING HER BACK!
DO YOU GET IT?

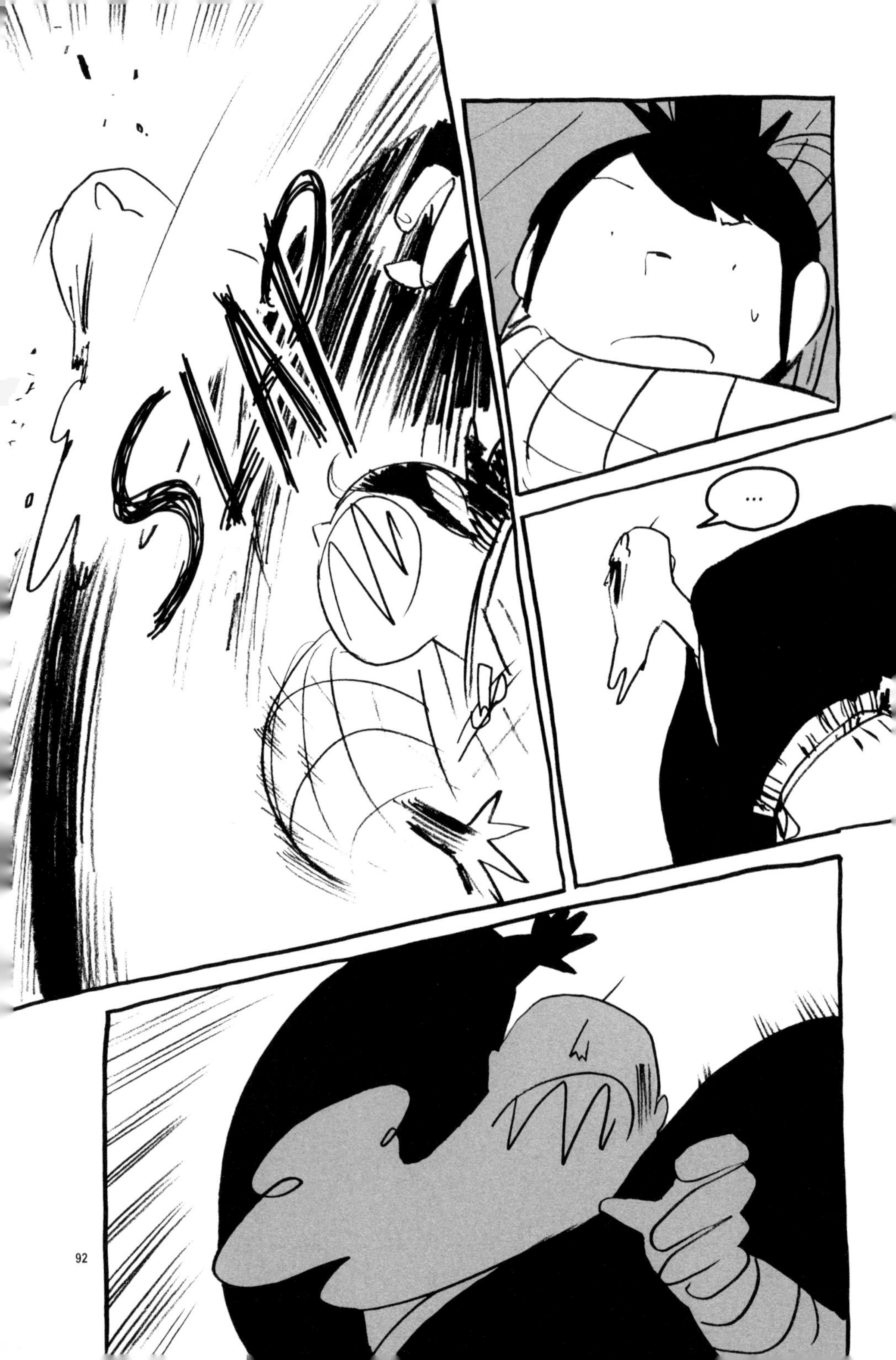
SLAP
...

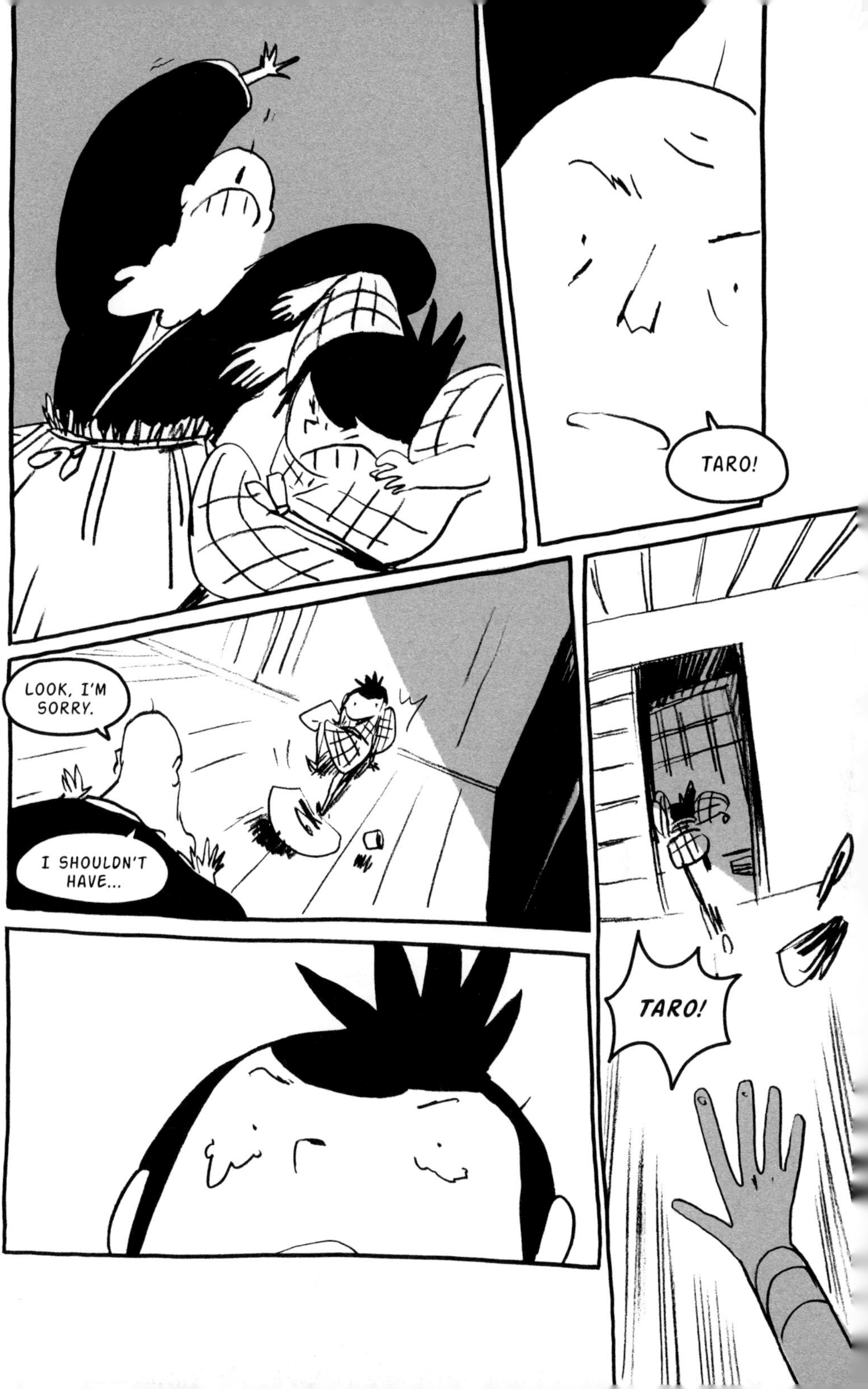
TARO!
LOOK, I'M SORRY.
I SHOULDN'T HAVE...
TARO!

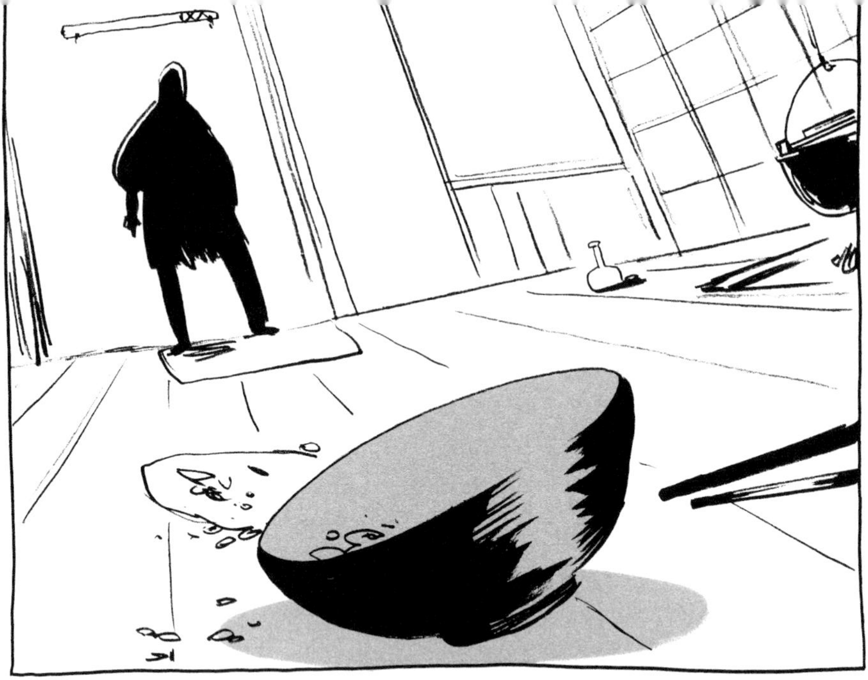

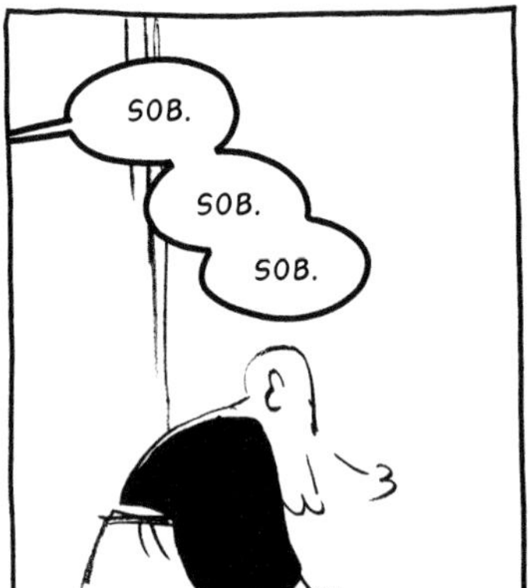
SOB.
SOB.
SOB.

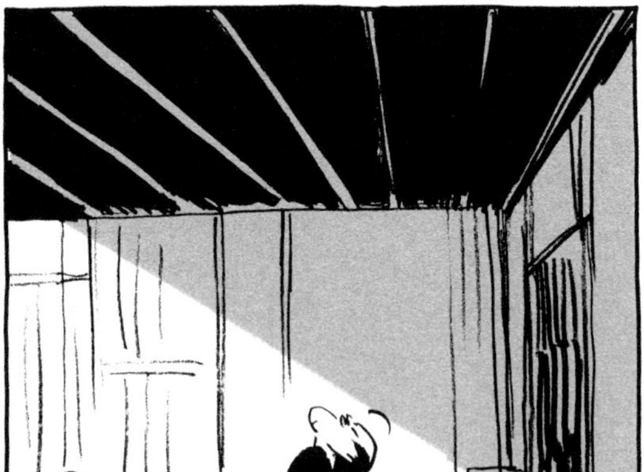

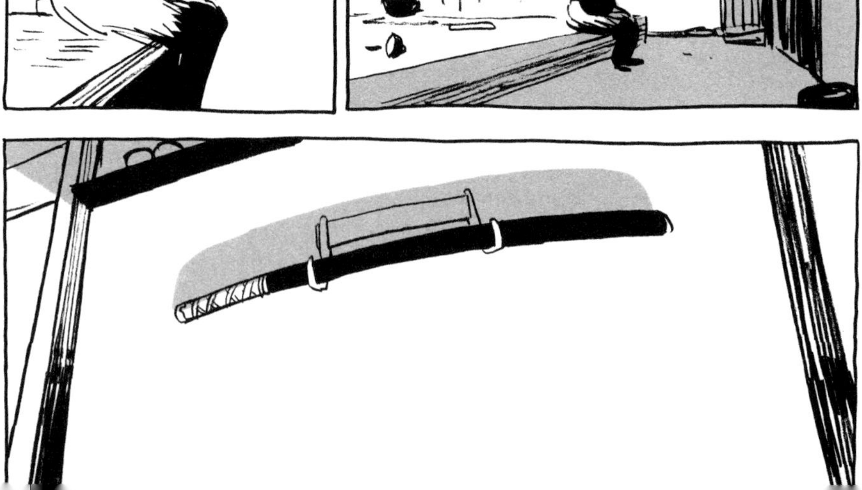

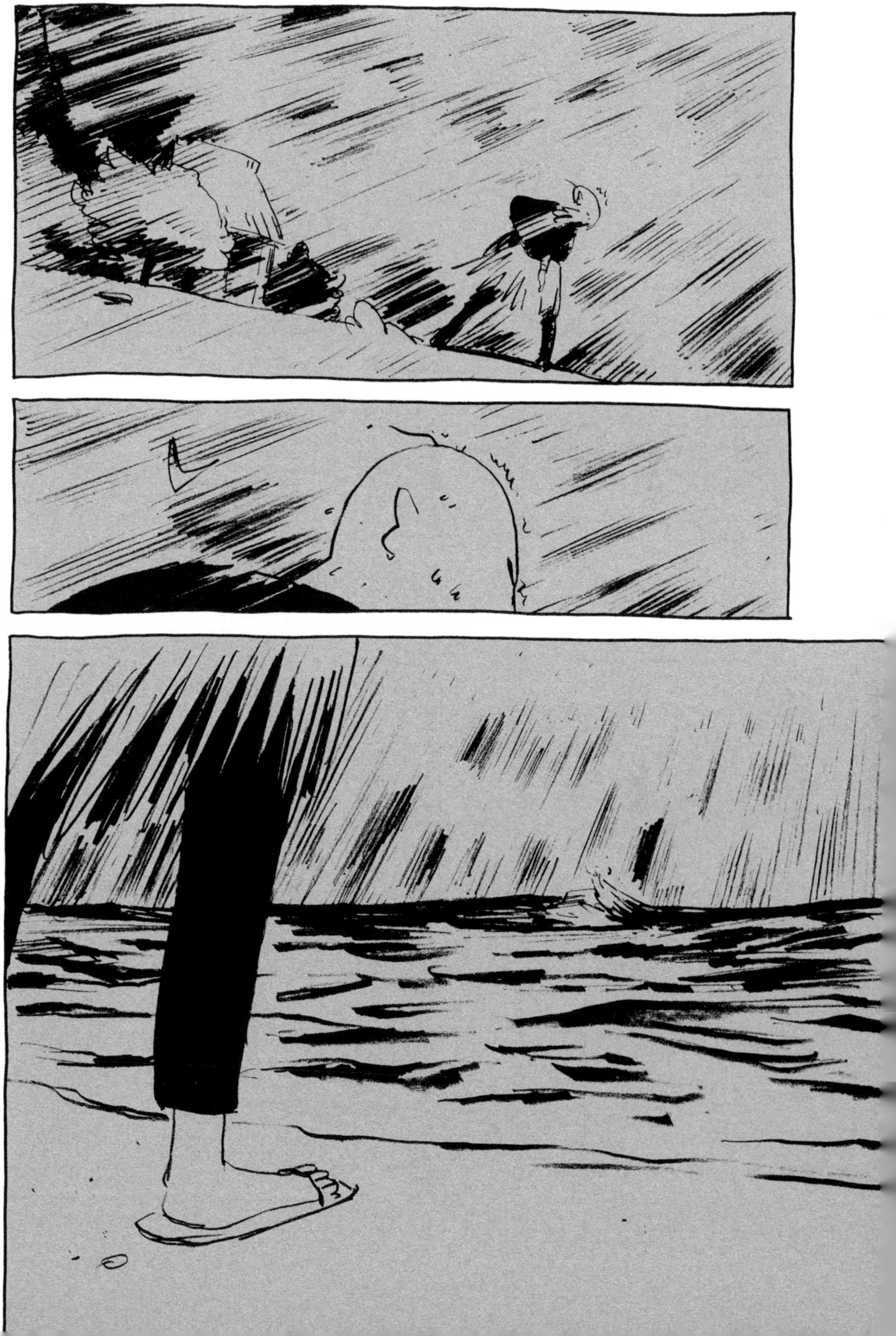

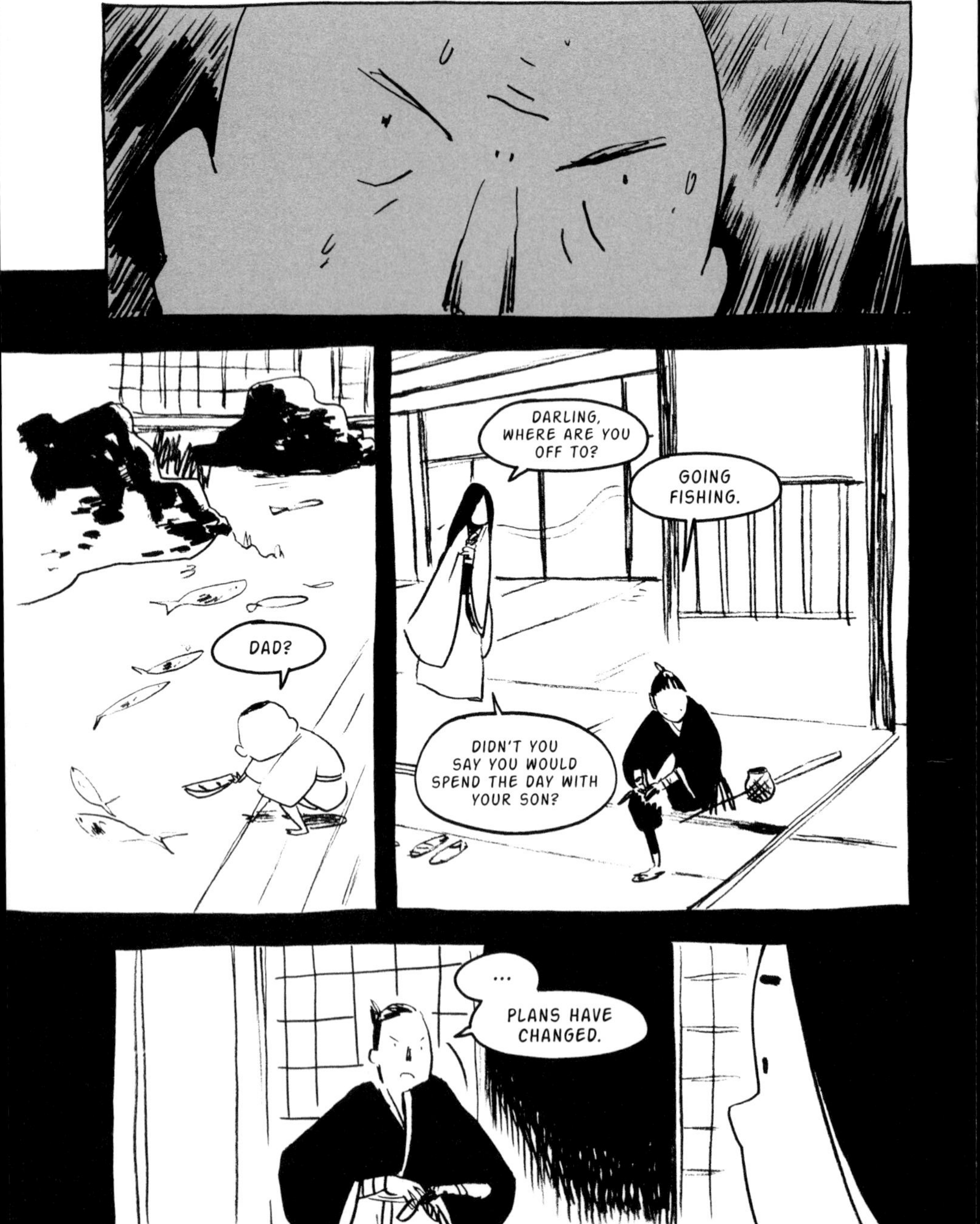
DAD?
DARLING, WHERE ARE YOU OFF TO?
GOING FISHING.
DIDN'T YOU SAY YOU WOULD SPEND THE DAY WITH YOUR SON?
...
PLANS HAVE CHANGED.

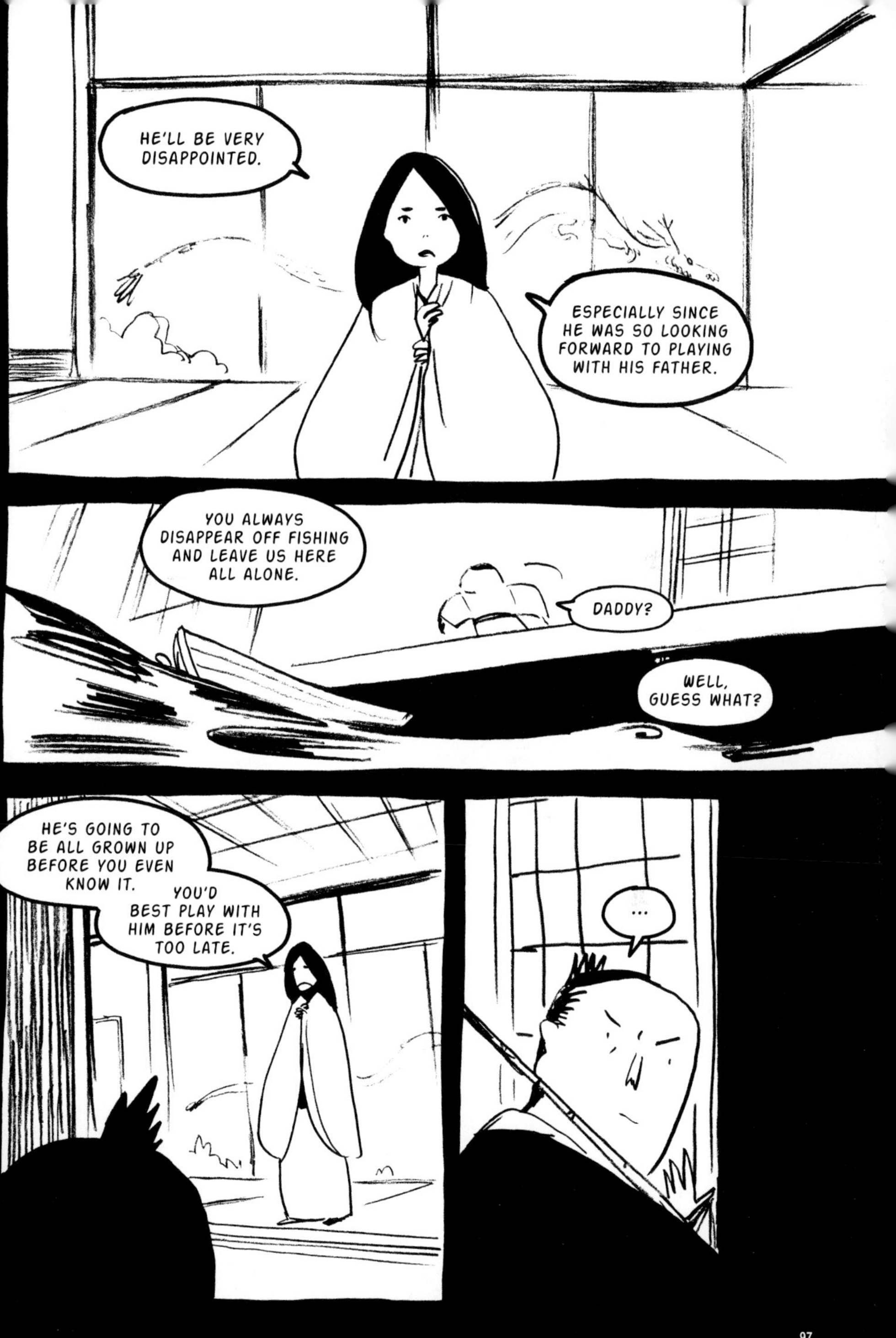
HE'LL BE VERY DISAPPOINTED.
ESPECIALLY SINCE HE WAS SO LOOKING FORWARD TO PLAYING WITH HIS FATHER.
YOU ALWAYS DISAPPEAR OFF FISHING AND LEAVE US HERE ALL ALONE.
DADDY?
WELL, GUESS WHAT?
HE'S GOING TO BE ALL GROWN UP BEFORE YOU EVEN KNOW IT.
YOU'D BEST PLAY WITH HIM BEFORE IT'S TOO LATE.
...

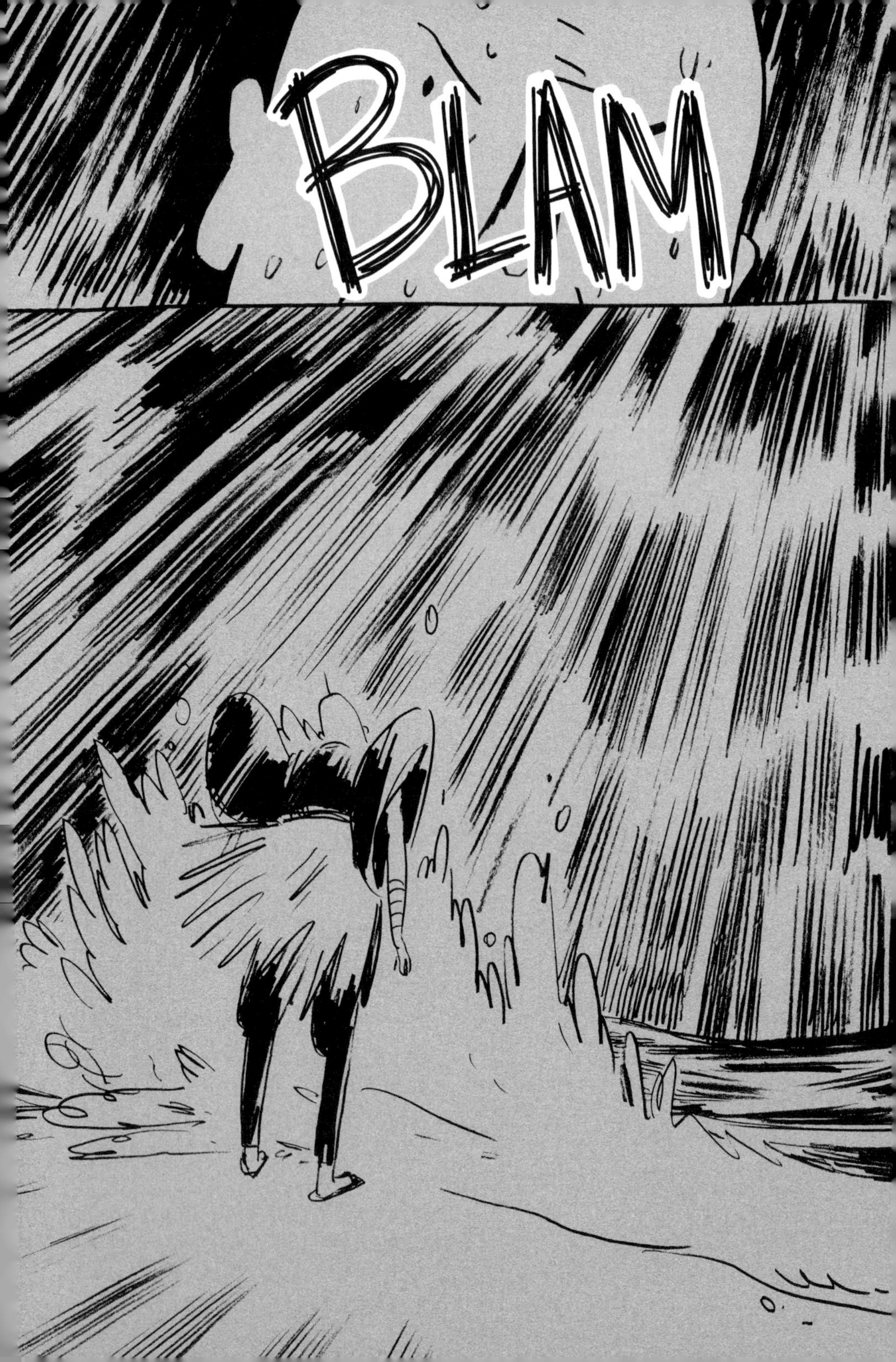
BLAM

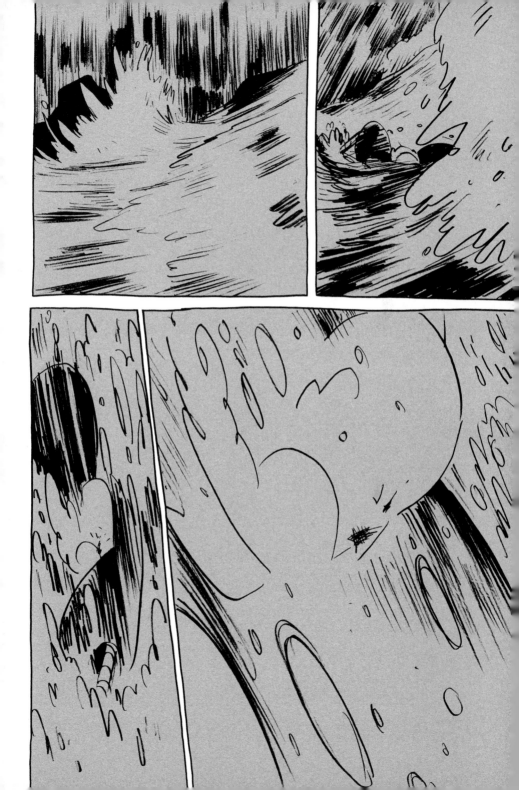

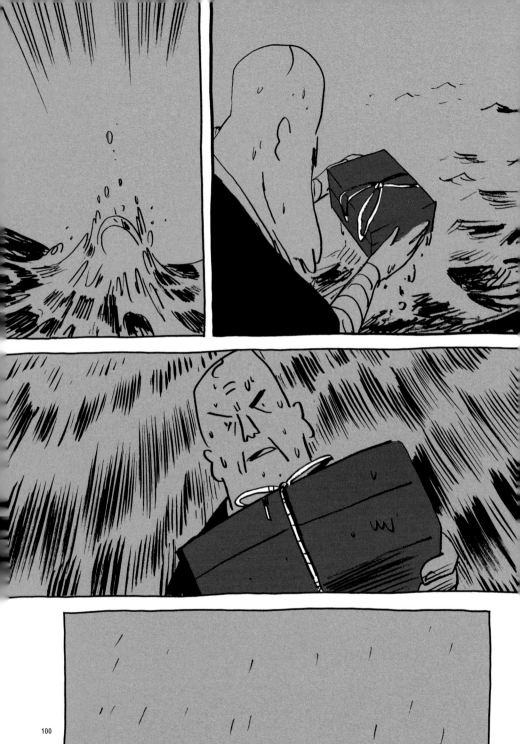

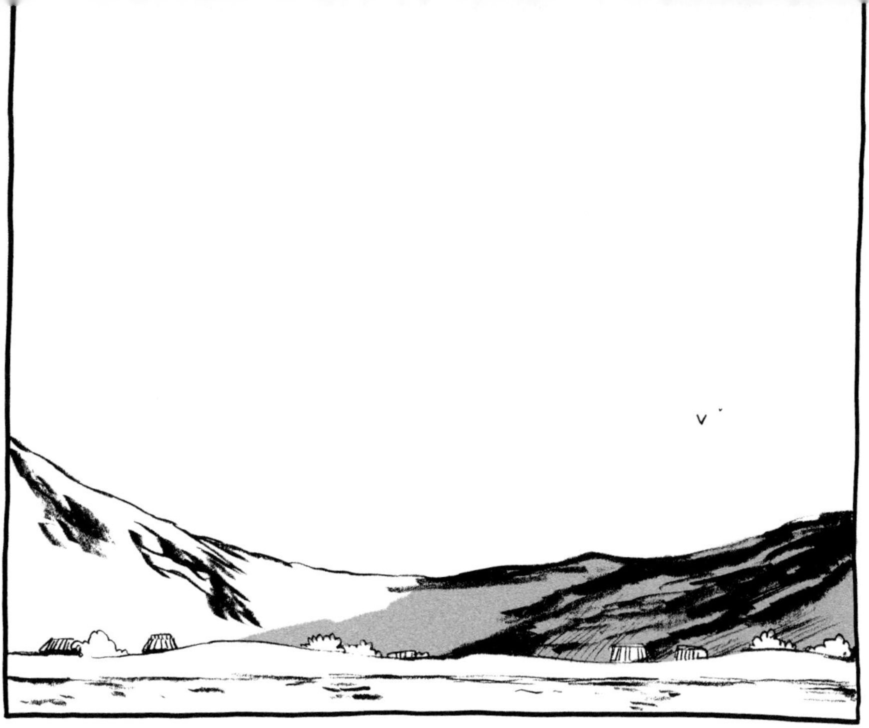

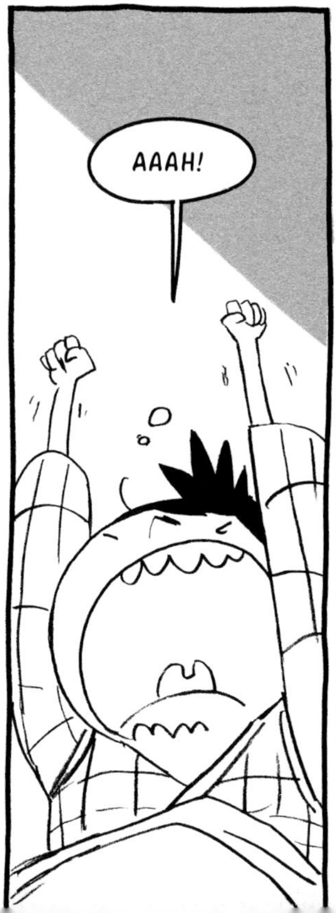
AAAH!

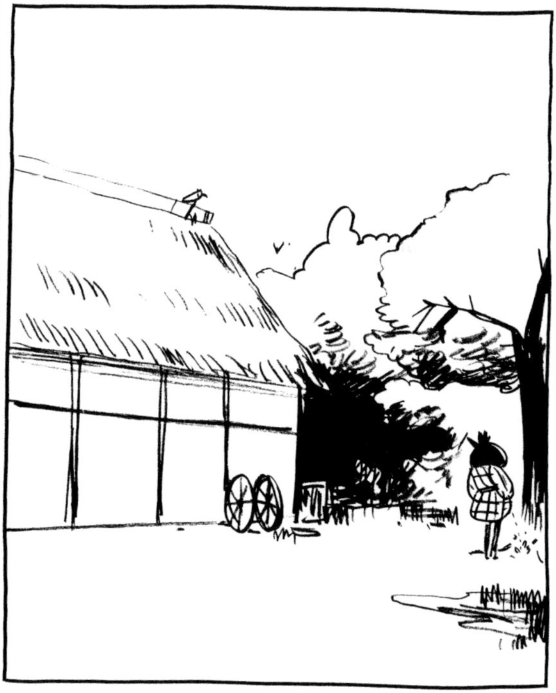

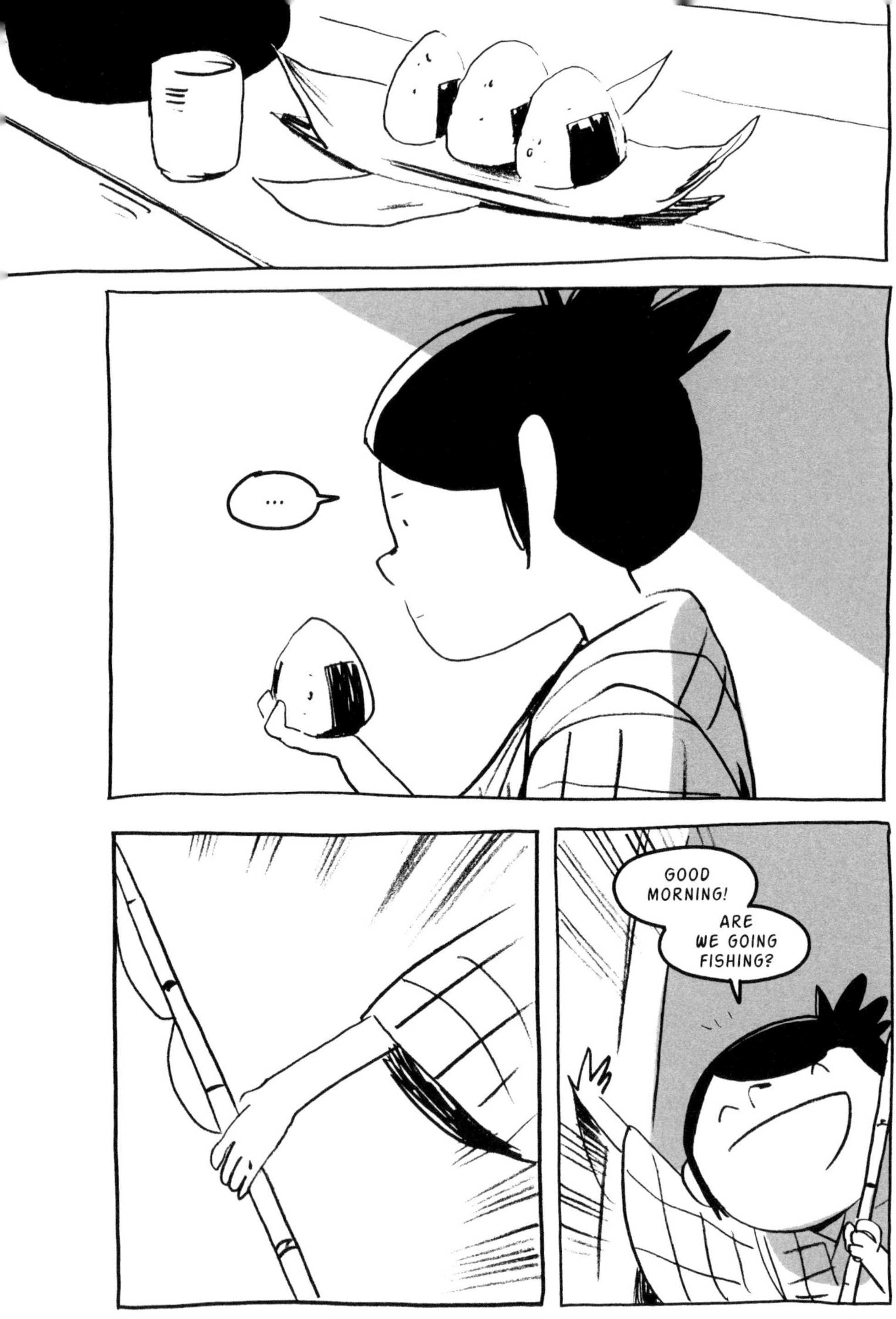
...
GOOD MORNING!
ARE WE GOING FISHING?

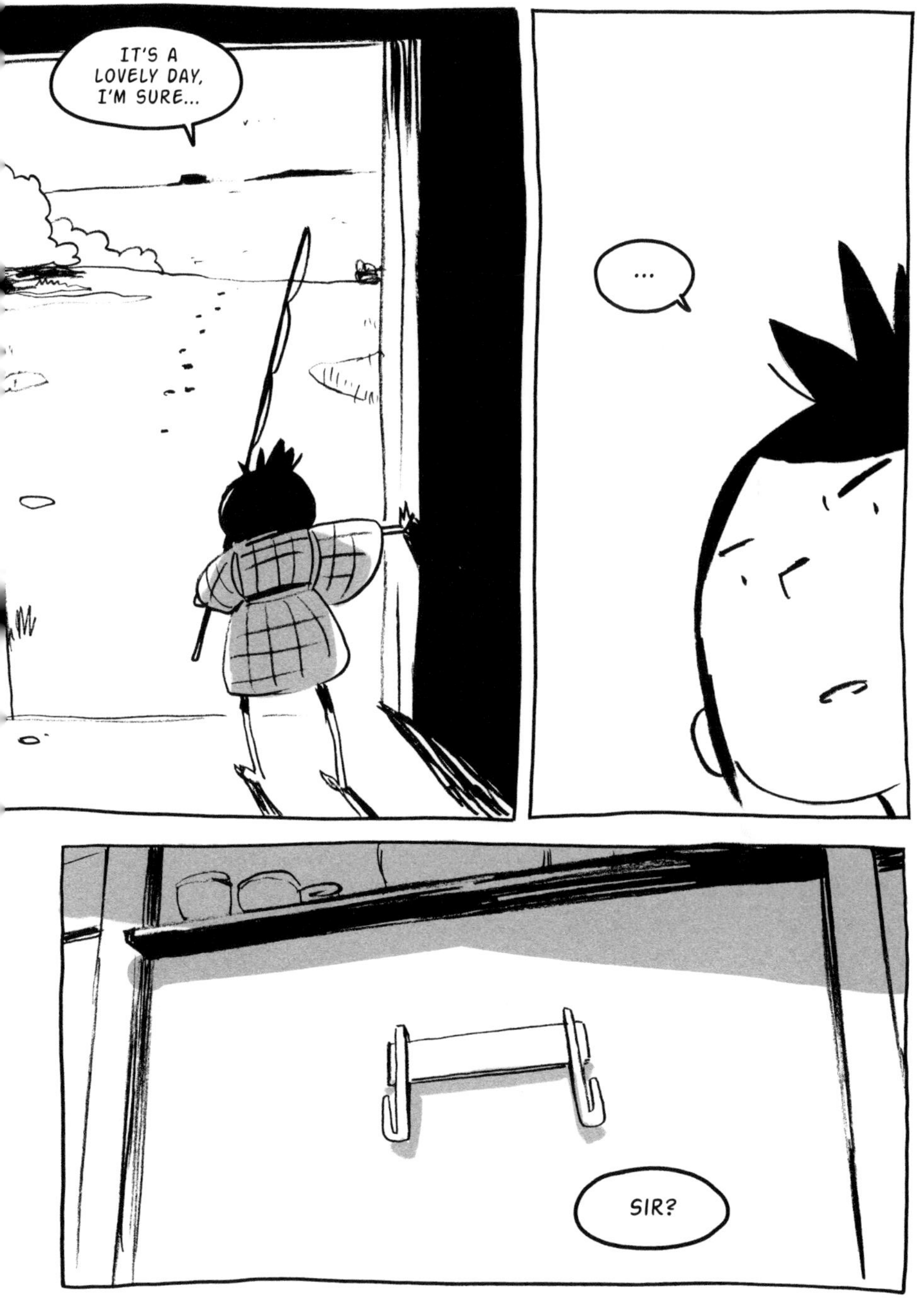
IT'S A LOVELY DAY, I'M SURE...
...
SIR?

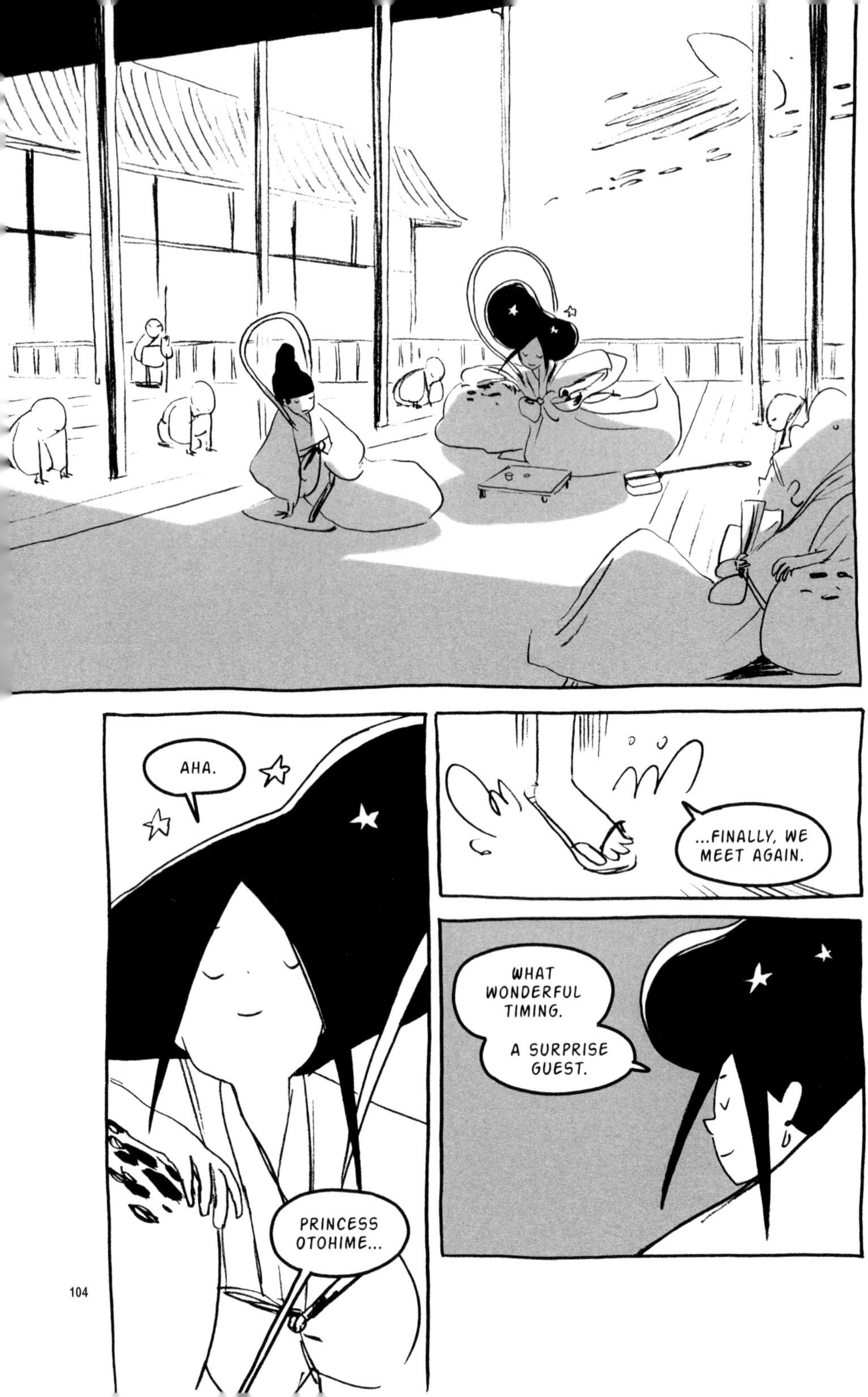
AHA.
...FINALLY, WE MEET AGAIN.
PRINCESS OTOHIME...
WHAT WONDERFUL TIMING.
A SURPRISE GUEST.

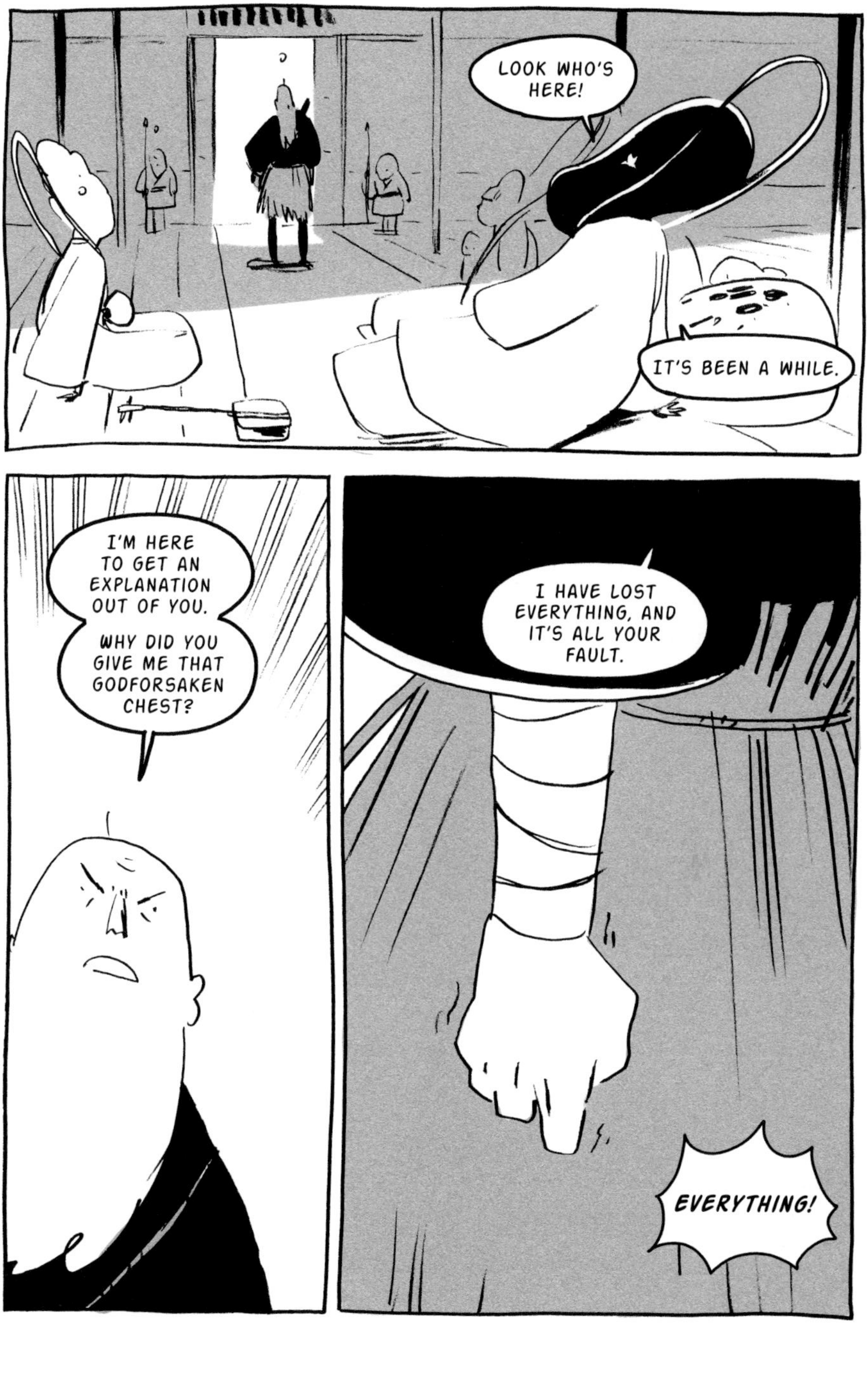
LOOK WHO'S HERE!
IT'S BEEN A WHILE.
I'M HERE TO GET AN EXPLANATION OUT OF YOU.
WHY DID YOU GIVE ME THAT GODFORSAKEN CHEST?
I HAVE LOST EVERYTHING, AND IT'S ALL YOUR FAULT.
EVERYTHING!

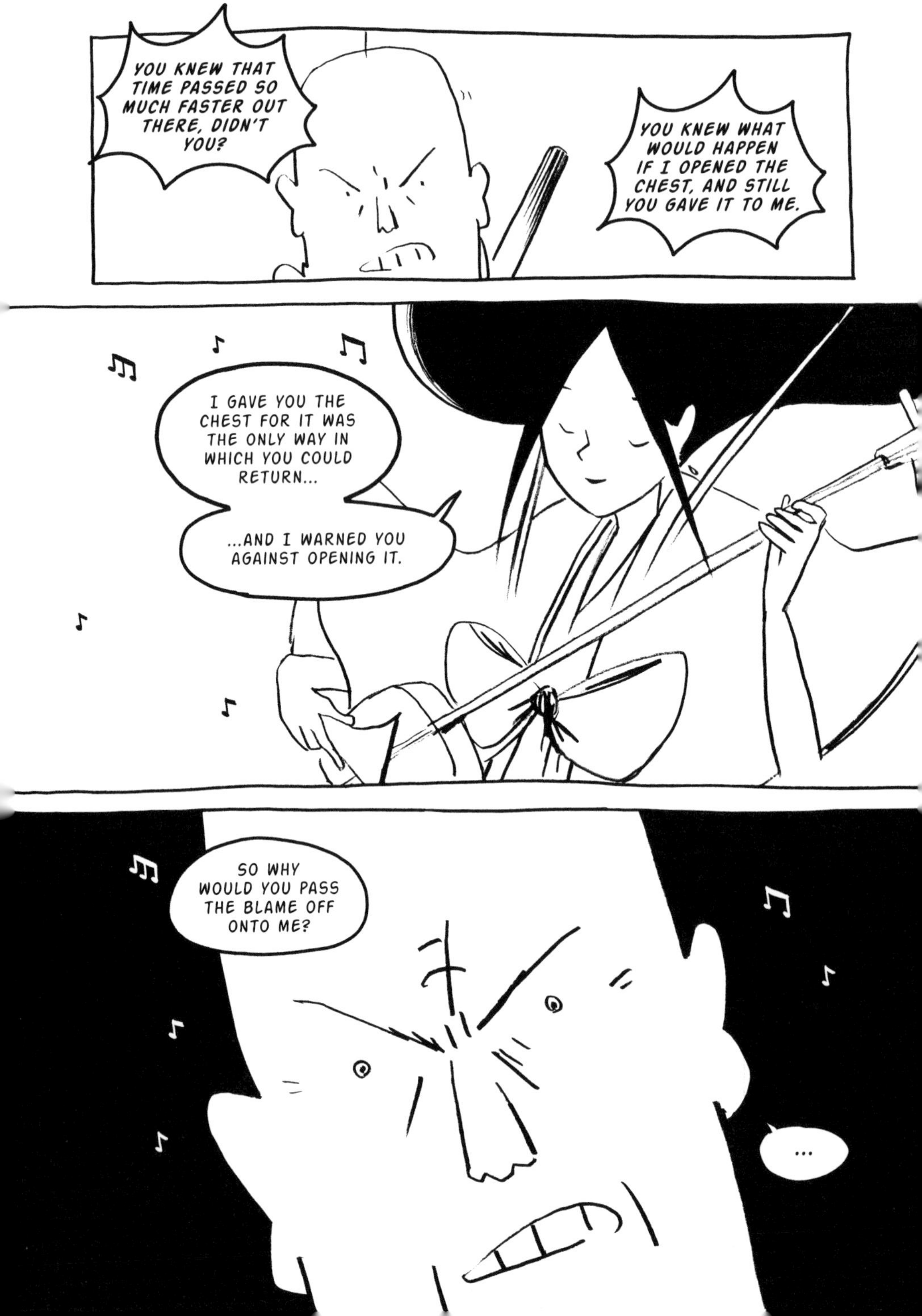

YOU KNEW THAT TIME PASSED SO MUCH FASTER OUT THERE, DIDN'T YOU?
YOU KNEW WHAT WOULD HAPPEN IF I OPENED THE CHEST, AND STILL YOU GAVE IT TO ME.
I GAVE YOU THE CHEST FOR IT WAS THE ONLY WAY IN WHICH YOU COULD RETURN...
...AND I WARNED YOU AGAINST OPENING IT.
SO WHY WOULD YOU PASS THE BLAME OFF ONTO ME?
...

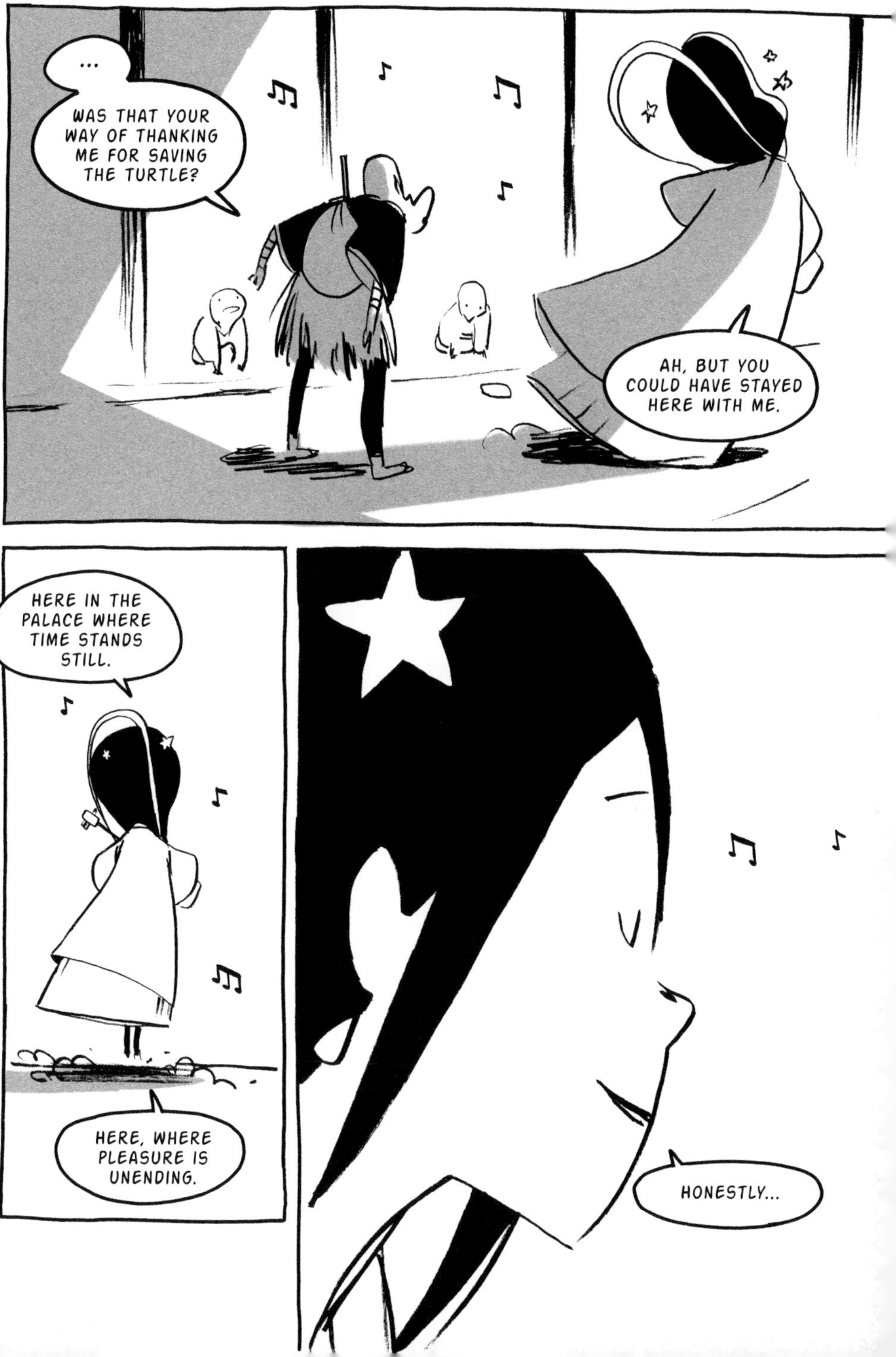
...
WAS THAT YOUR WAY OF THANKING ME FOR SAVING THE TURTLE?
AH, BUT YOU COULD HAVE STAYED HERE WITH ME.
HERE IN THE PALACE WHERE TIME STANDS STILL.
HERE, WHERE PLEASURE IS UNENDING.
HONESTLY...

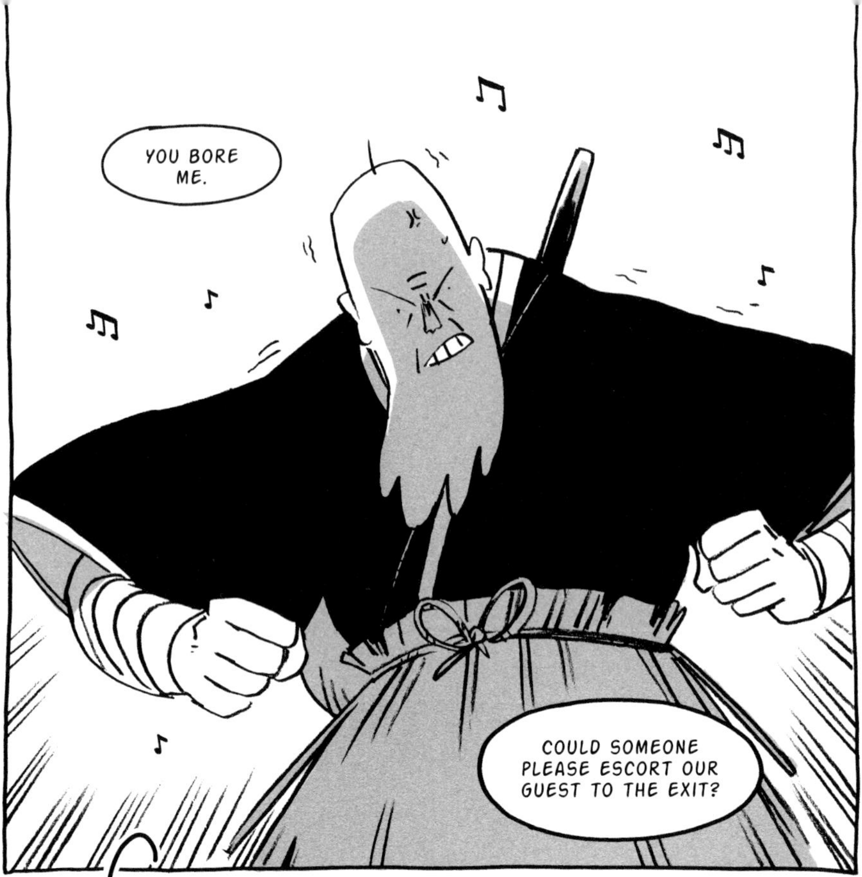
YOU BORE ME.
COULD SOMEONE PLEASE ESCORT OUR GUEST TO THE EXIT?

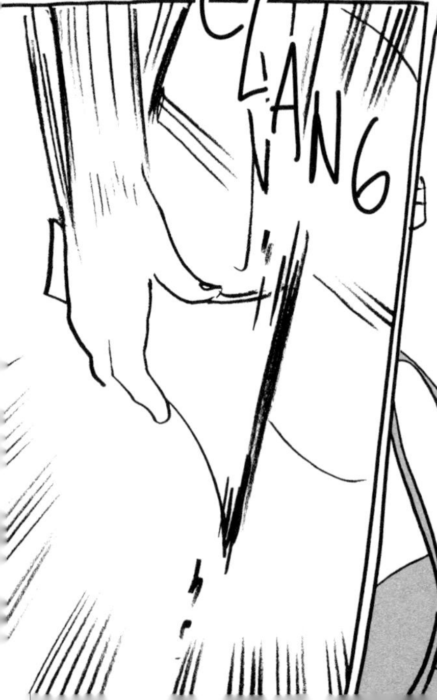
CLANG

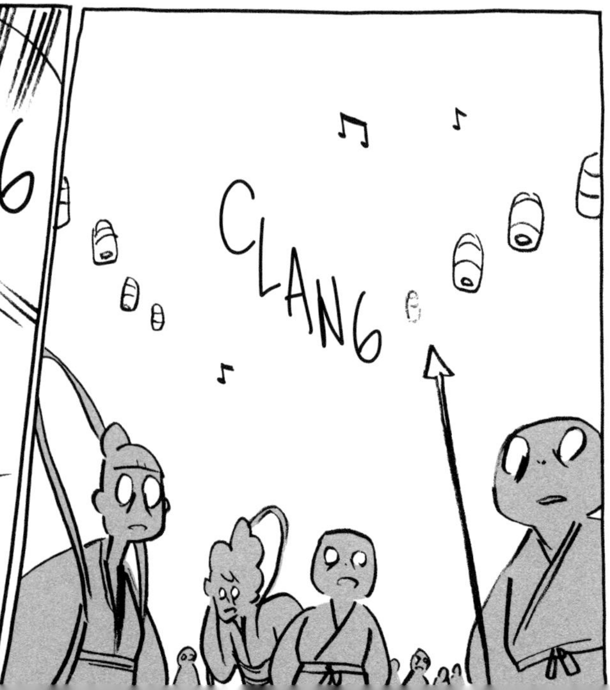
CLANG

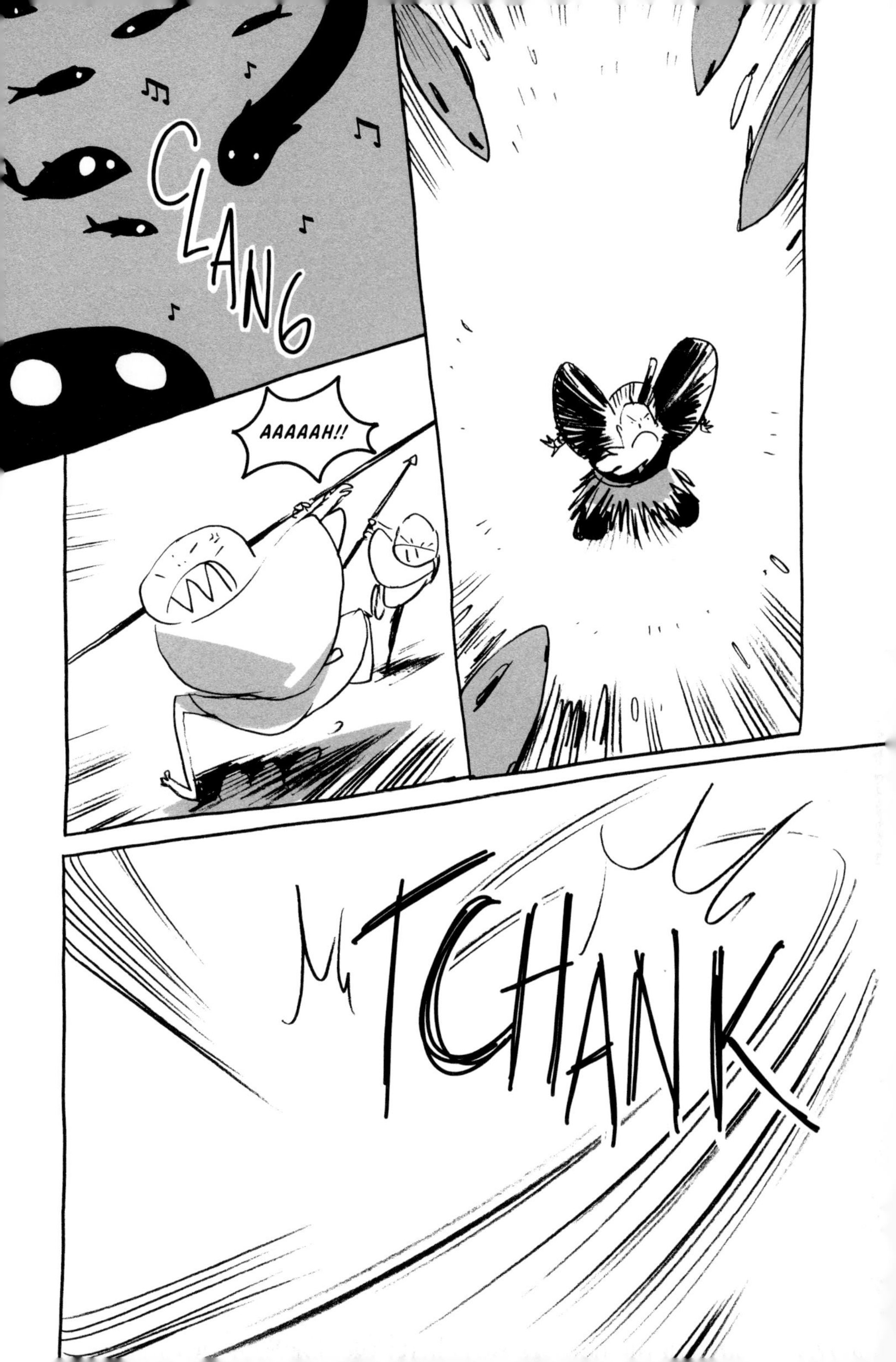
CLANG
AAAAAH!!
TCHANK

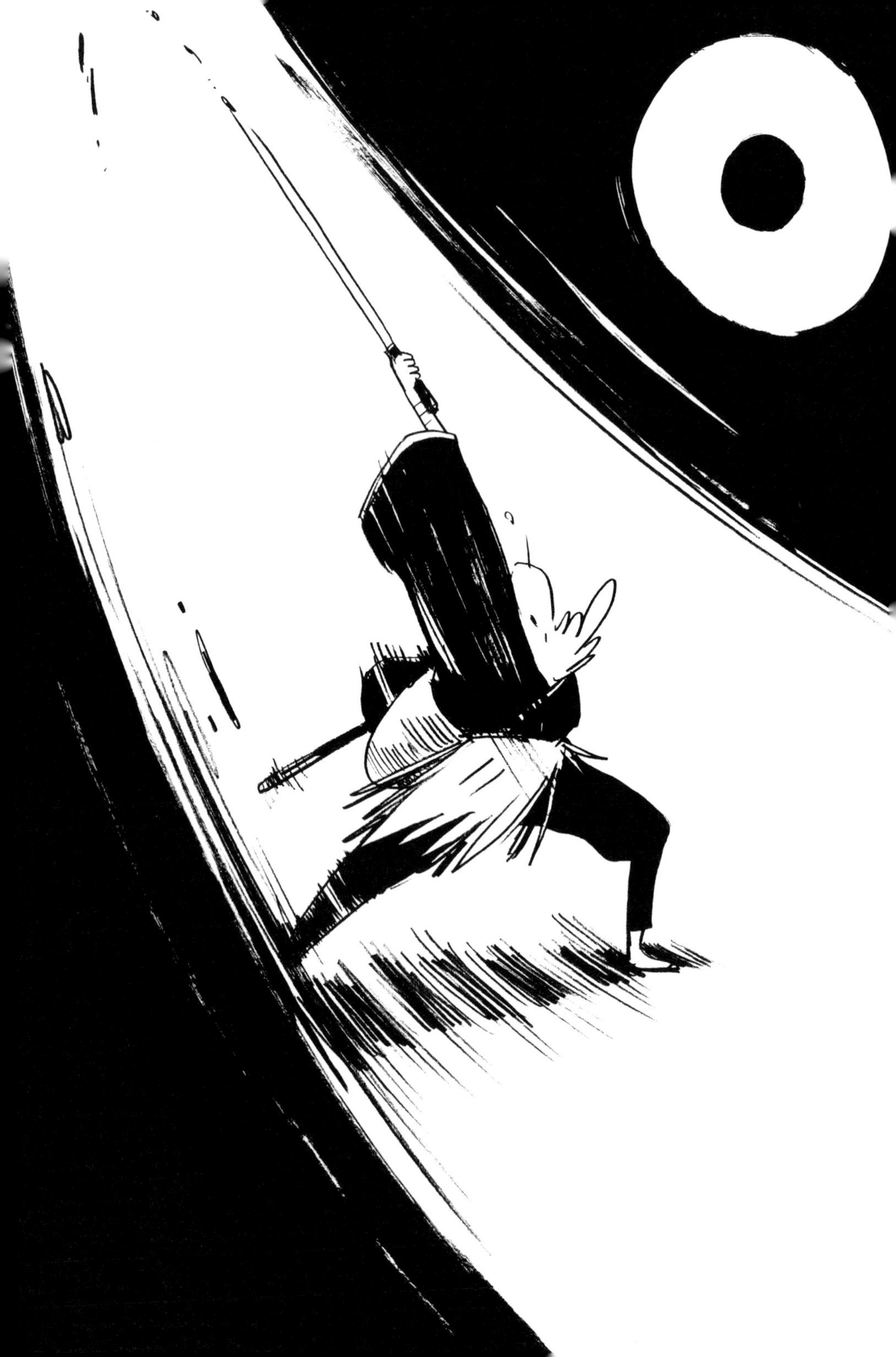

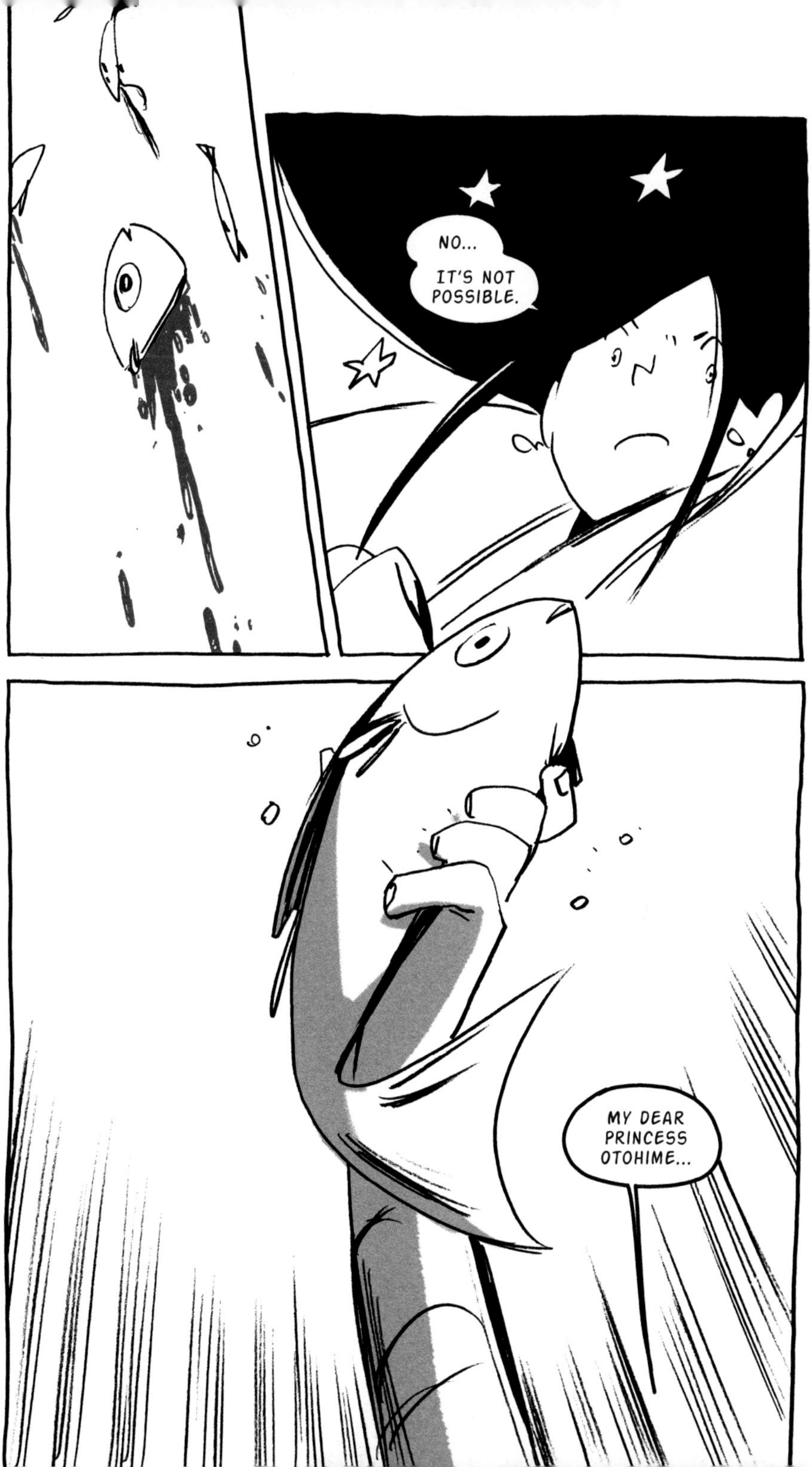
NO... IT'S NOT POSSIBLE.
MY DEAR PRINCESS OTOHIME...

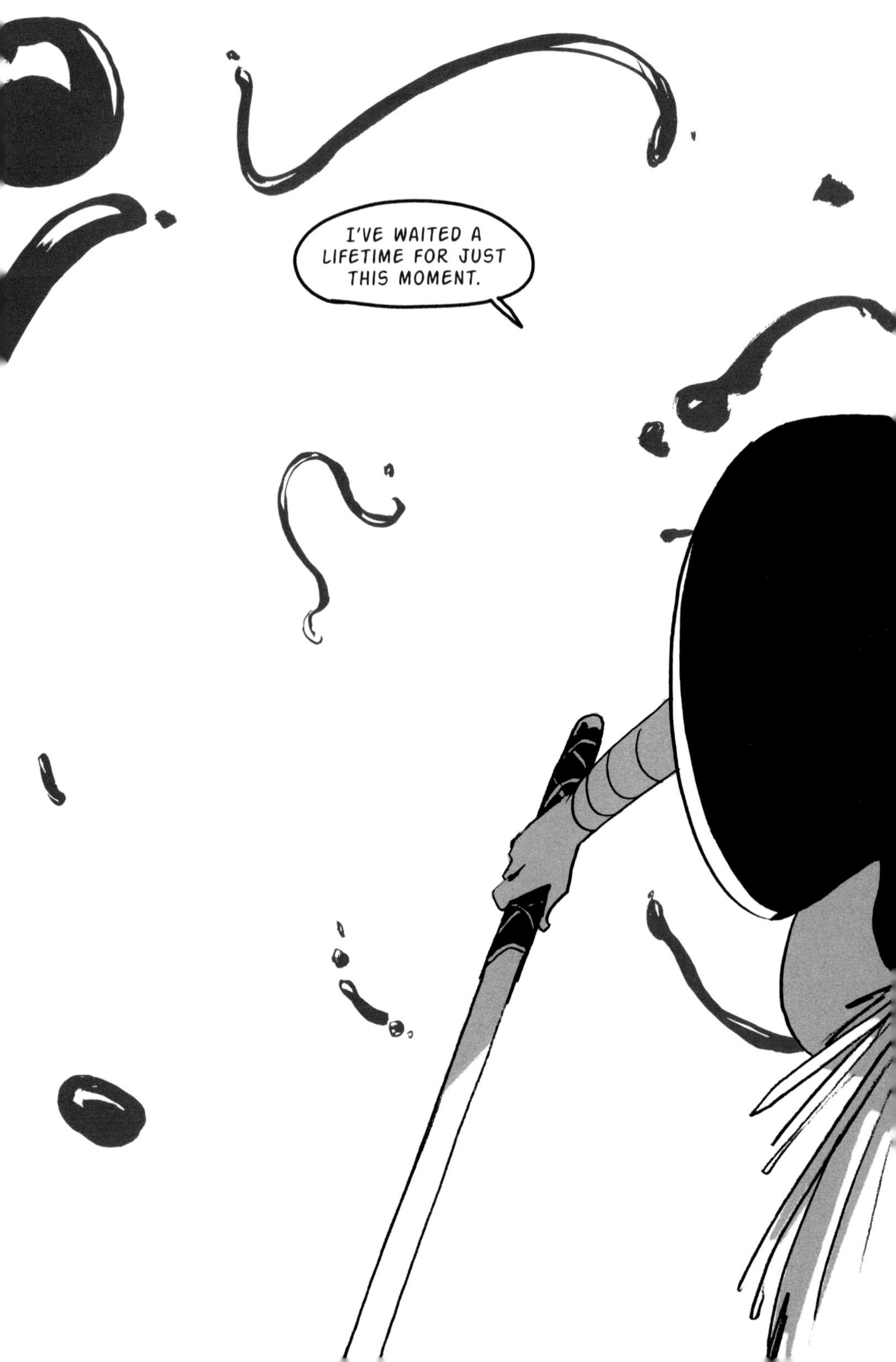
I'VE WAITED A LIFETIME FOR JUST THIS MOMENT.

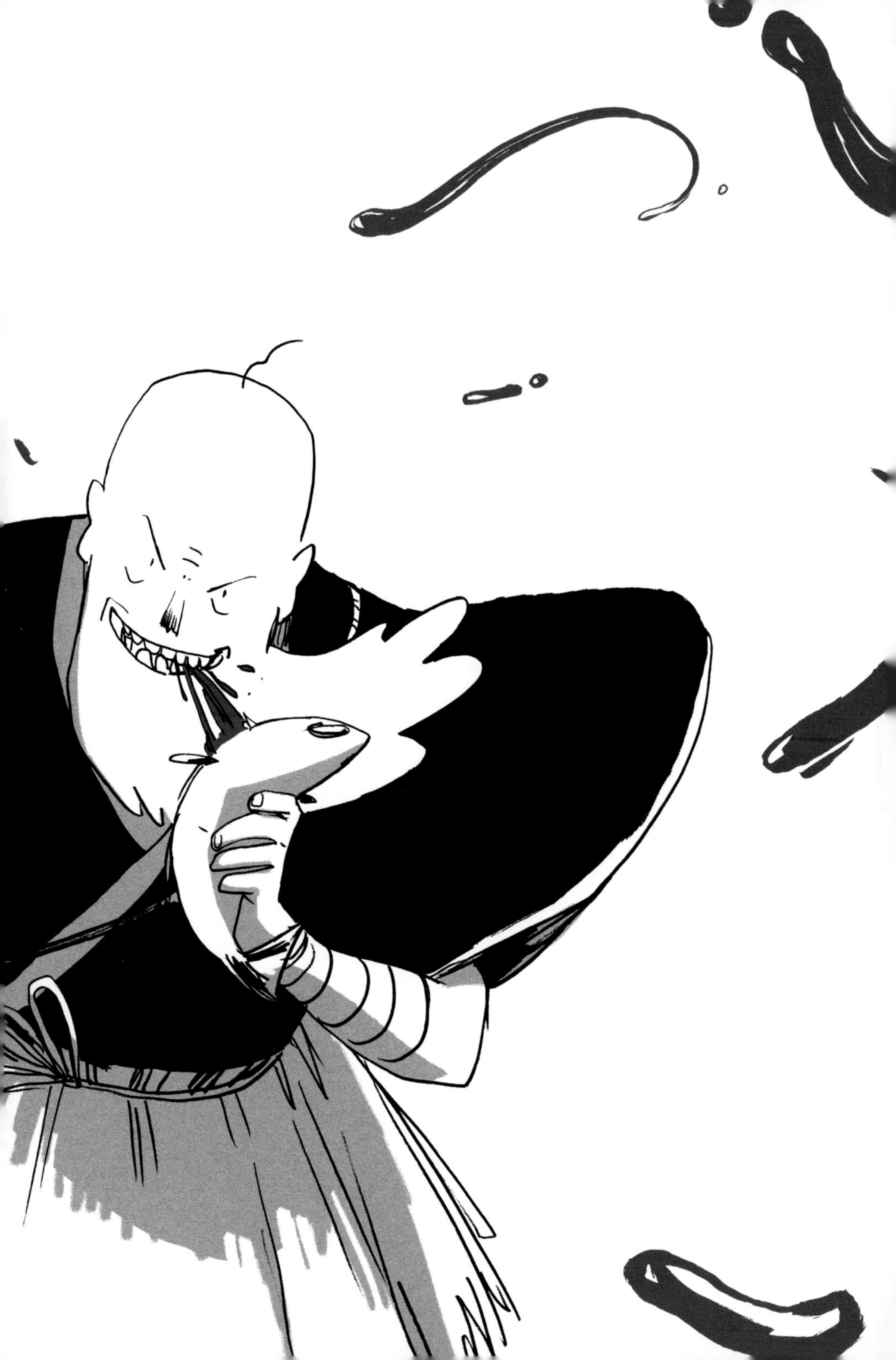

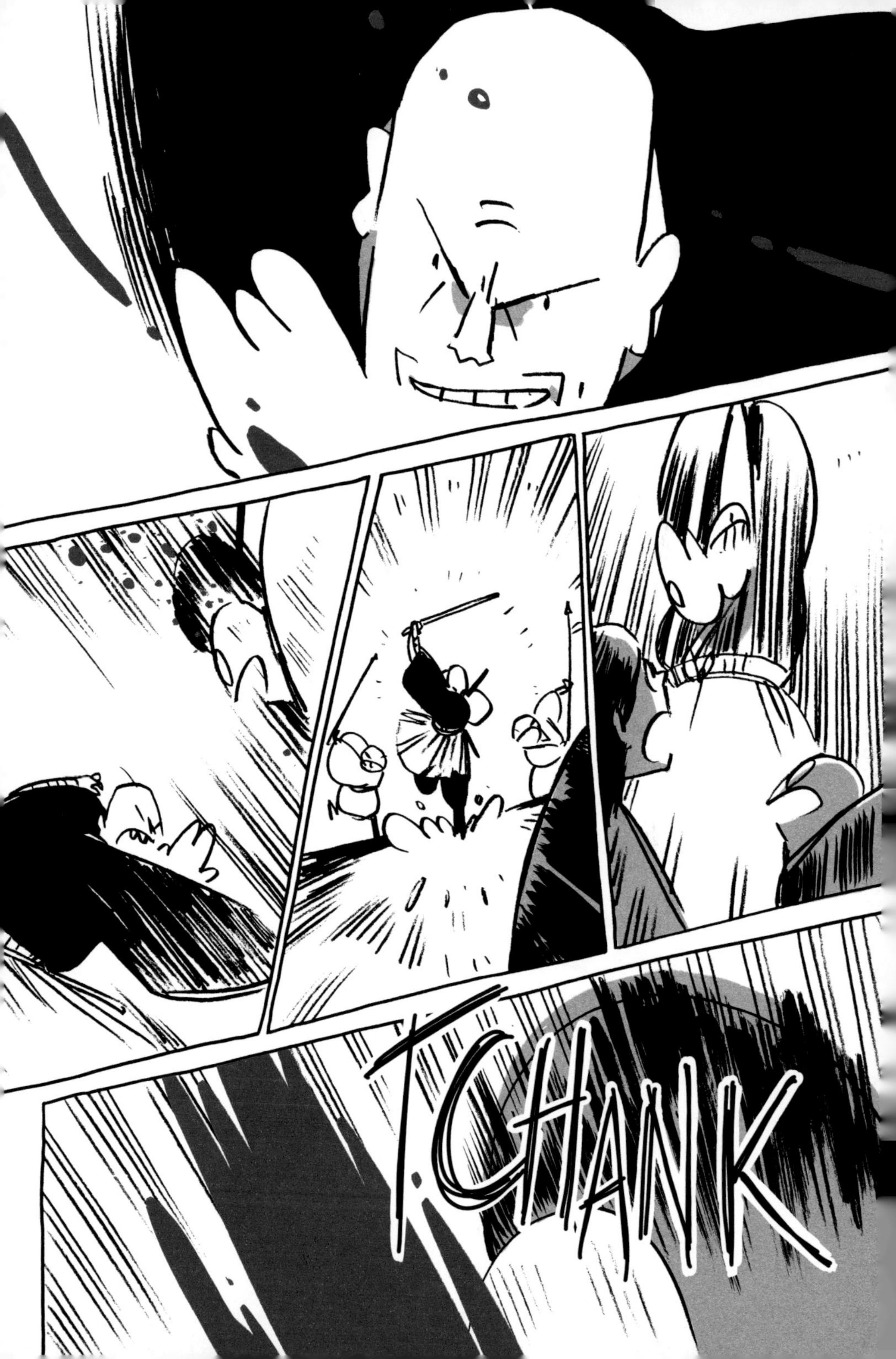

...
TCHANK

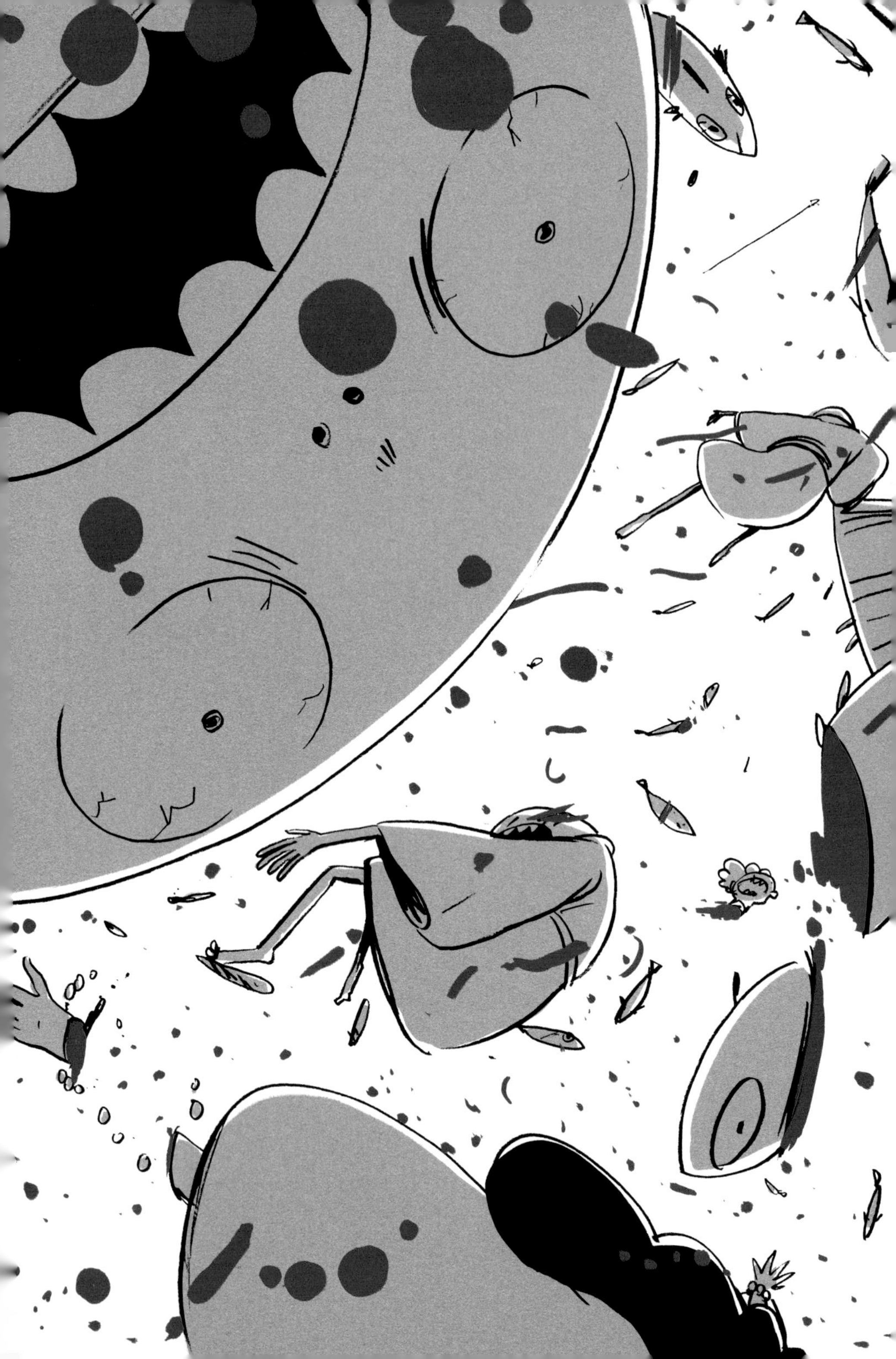

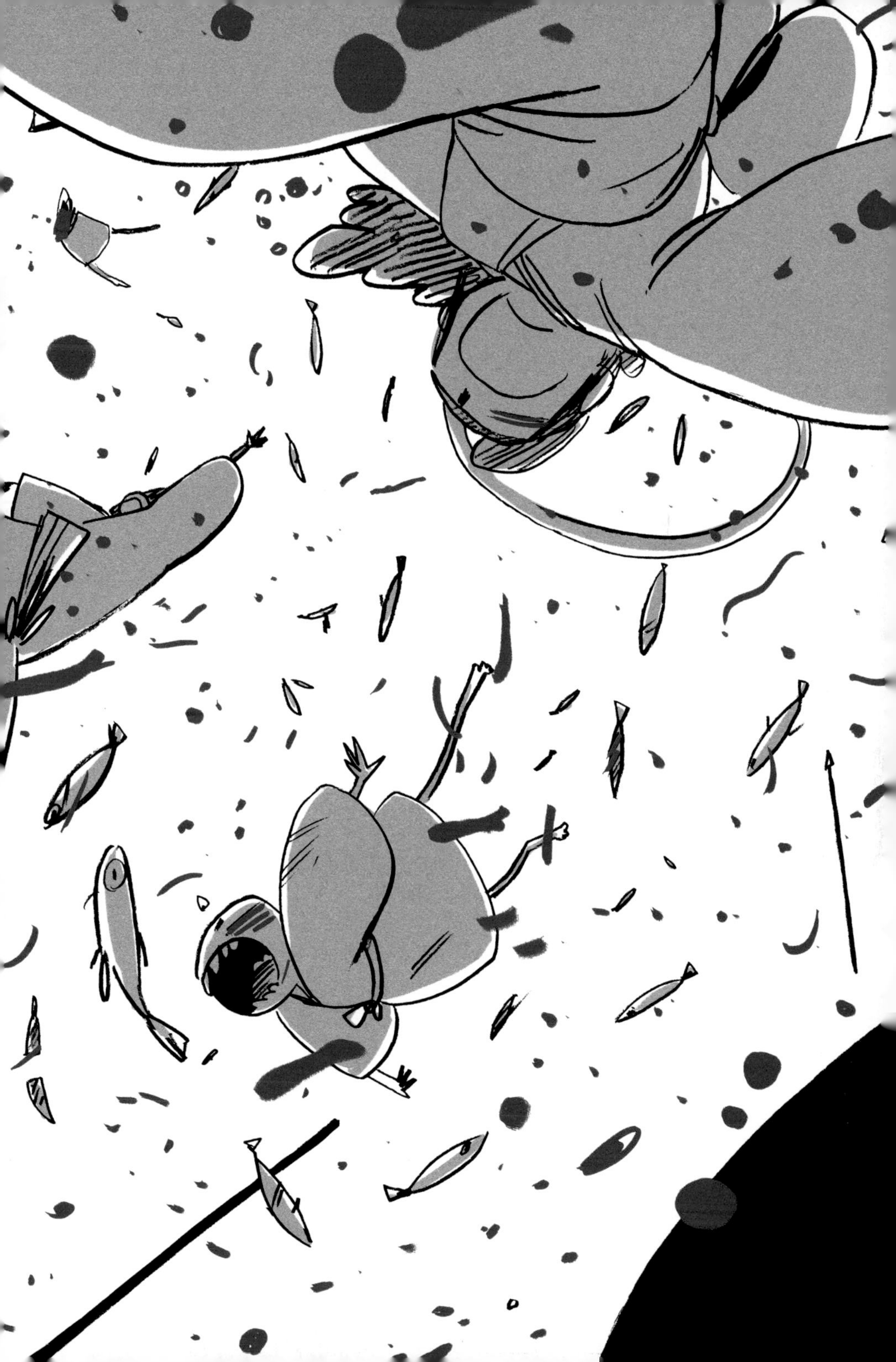

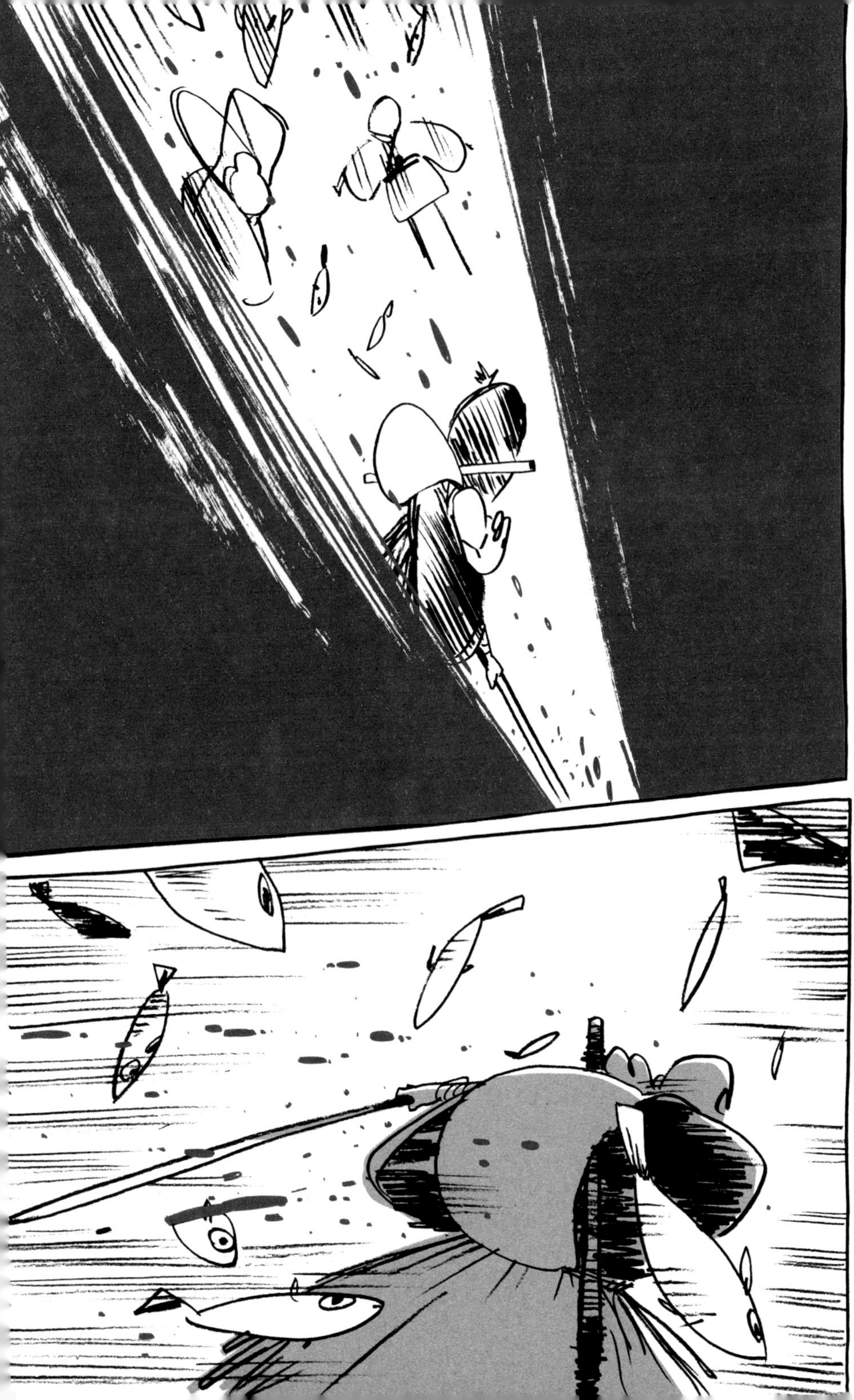

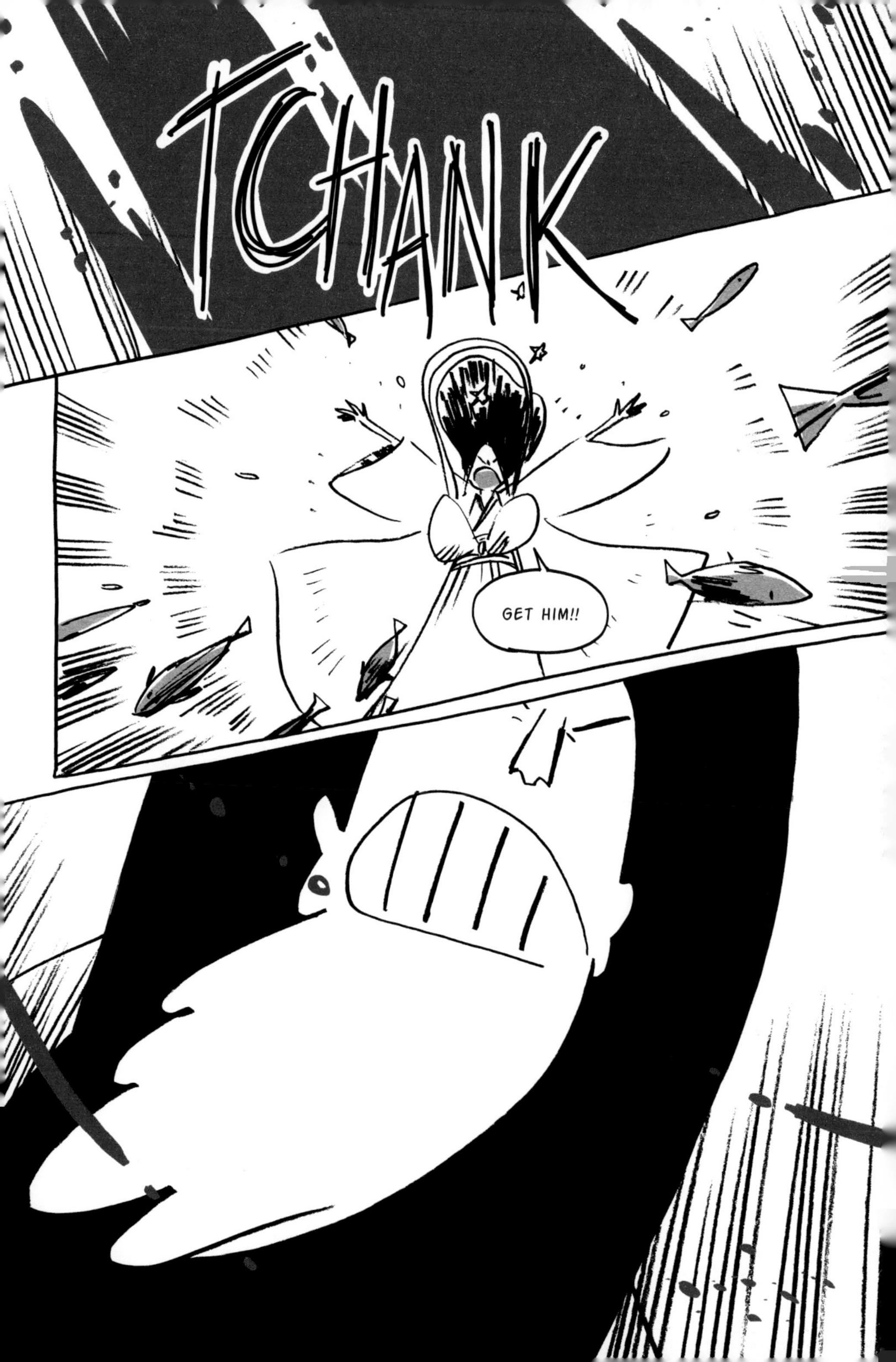
TCHANK
GET HIM!!

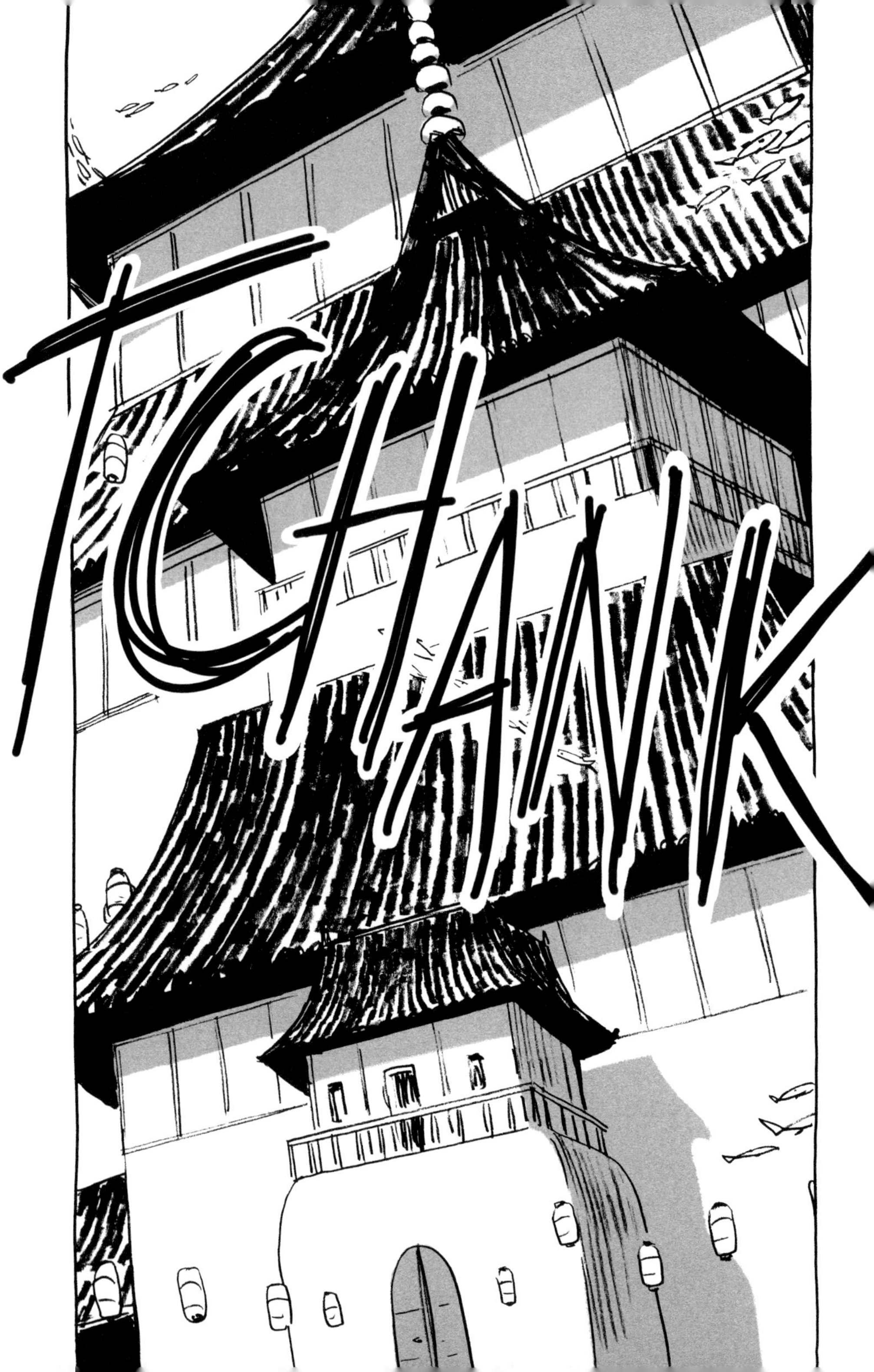
TCHANK

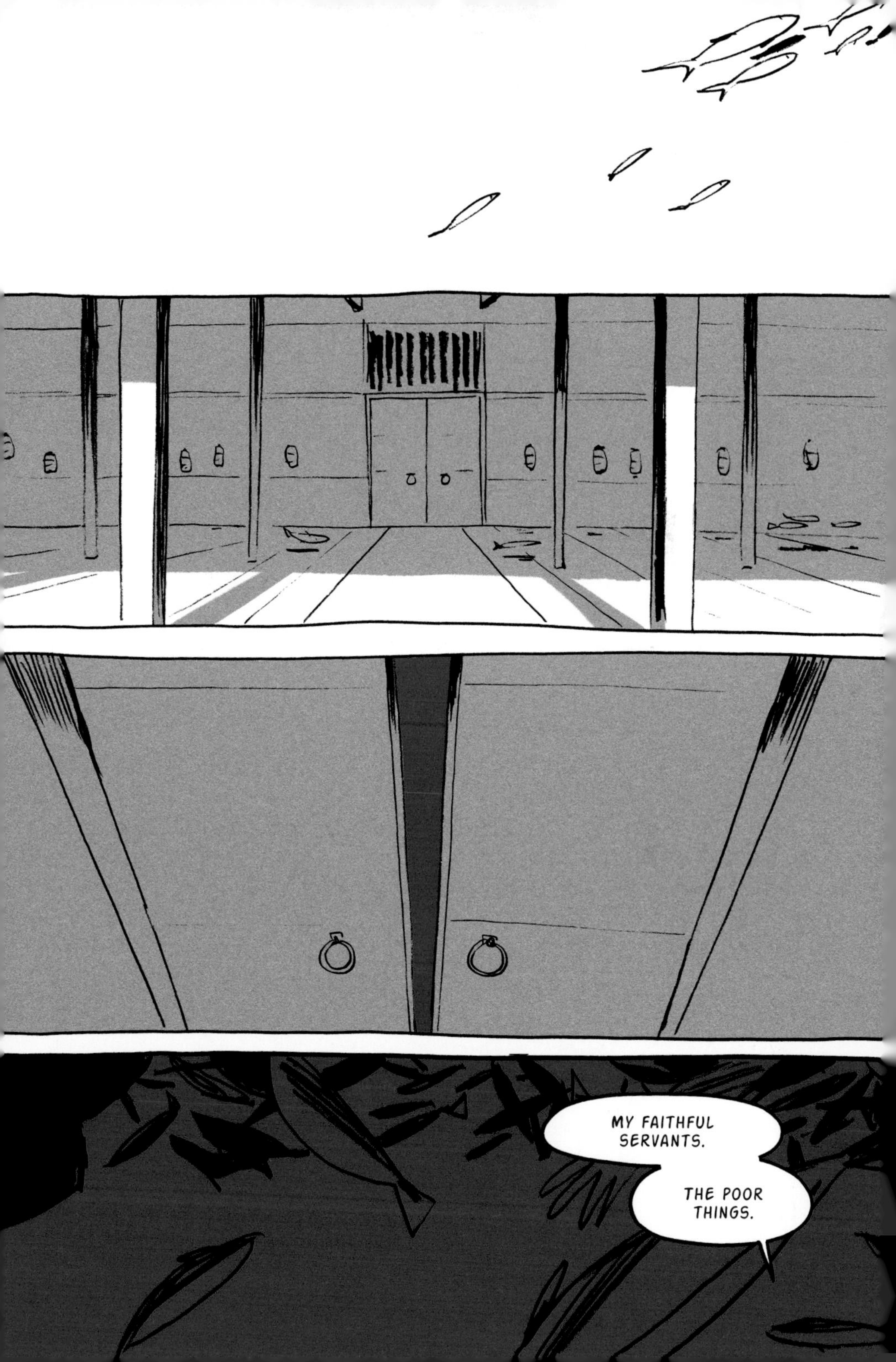
MY FAITHFUL SERVANTS.
THE POOR THINGS.

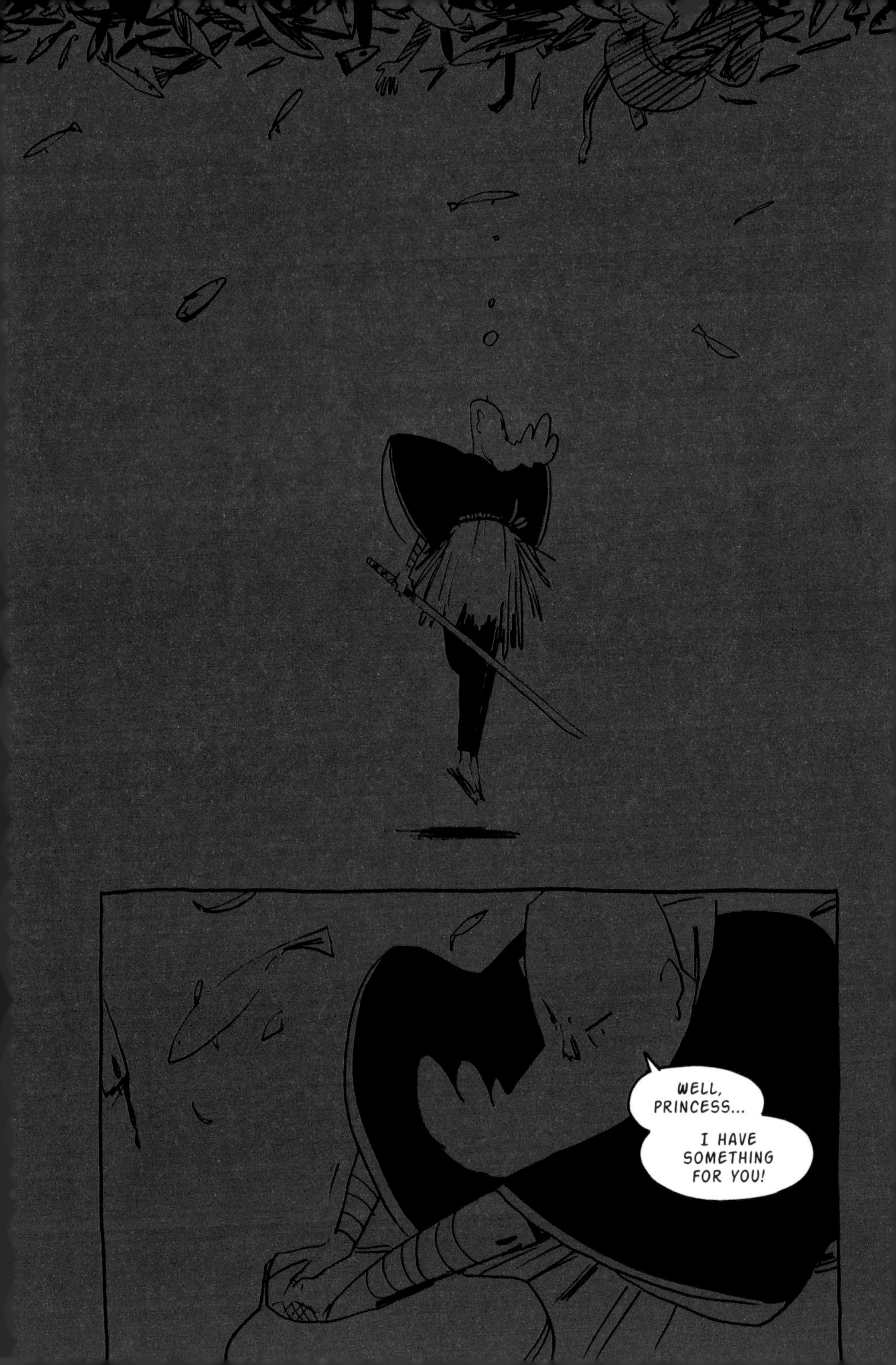
WELL, PRINCESS...
I HAVE SOMETHING FOR YOU!

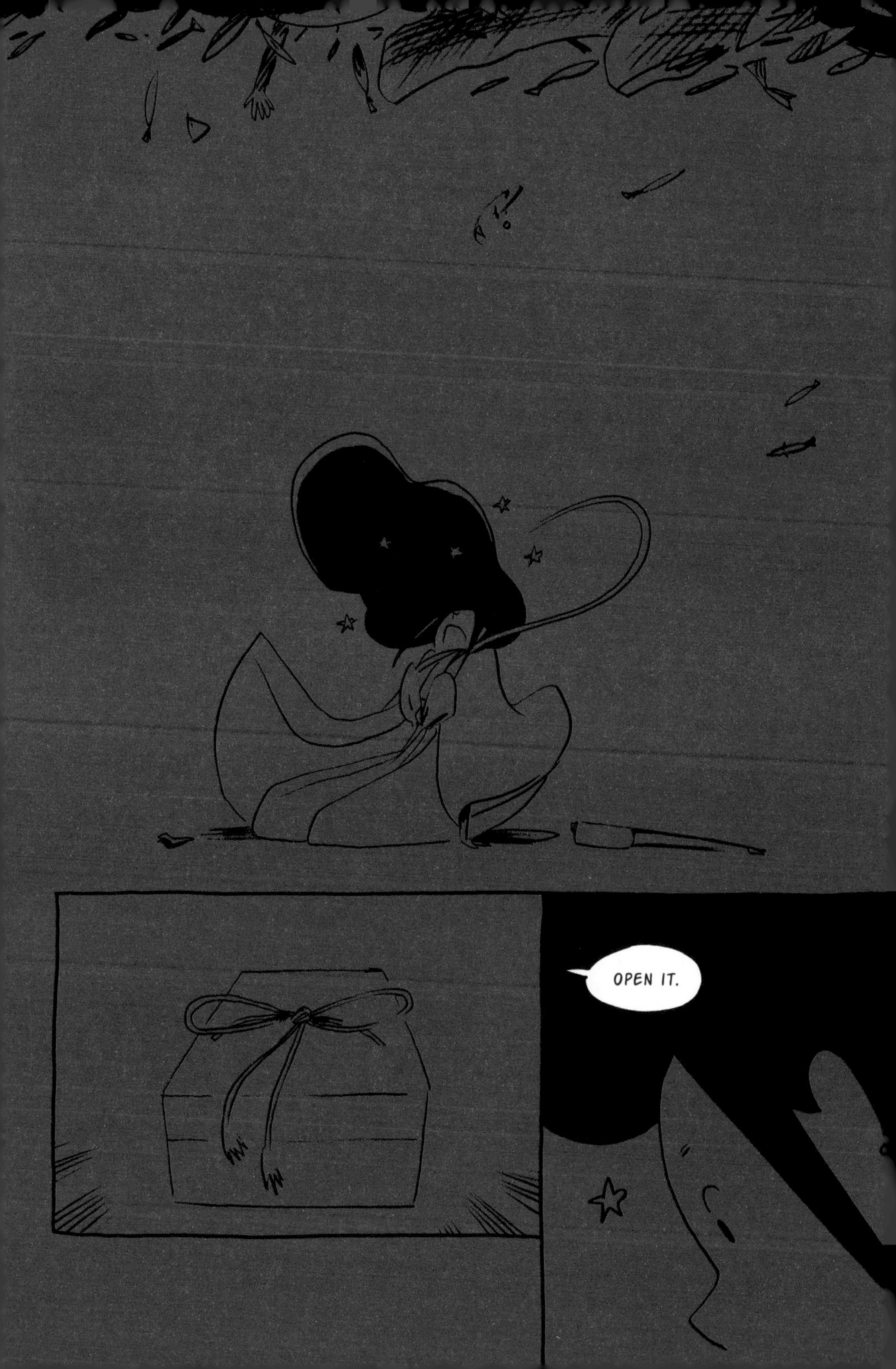
OPEN IT.

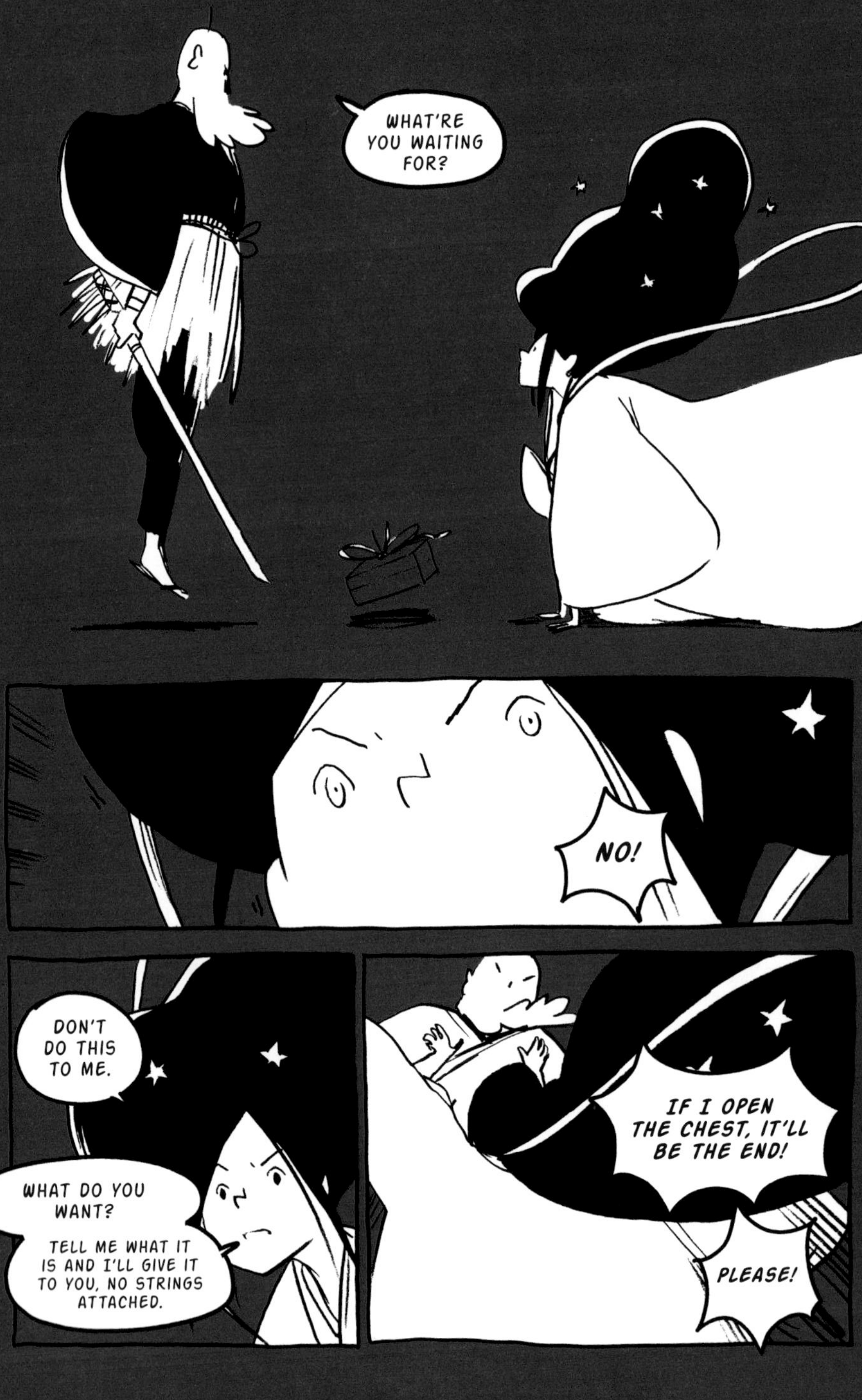
WHAT'RE YOU WAITING FOR?
NO!
DON'T DO THIS TO ME.
WHAT DO YOU WANT?
TELL ME WHAT IT IS AND I'LL GIVE IT TO YOU, NO STRINGS ATTACHED.
IF I OPEN THE CHEST, IT'LL BE THE END!
PLEASE!

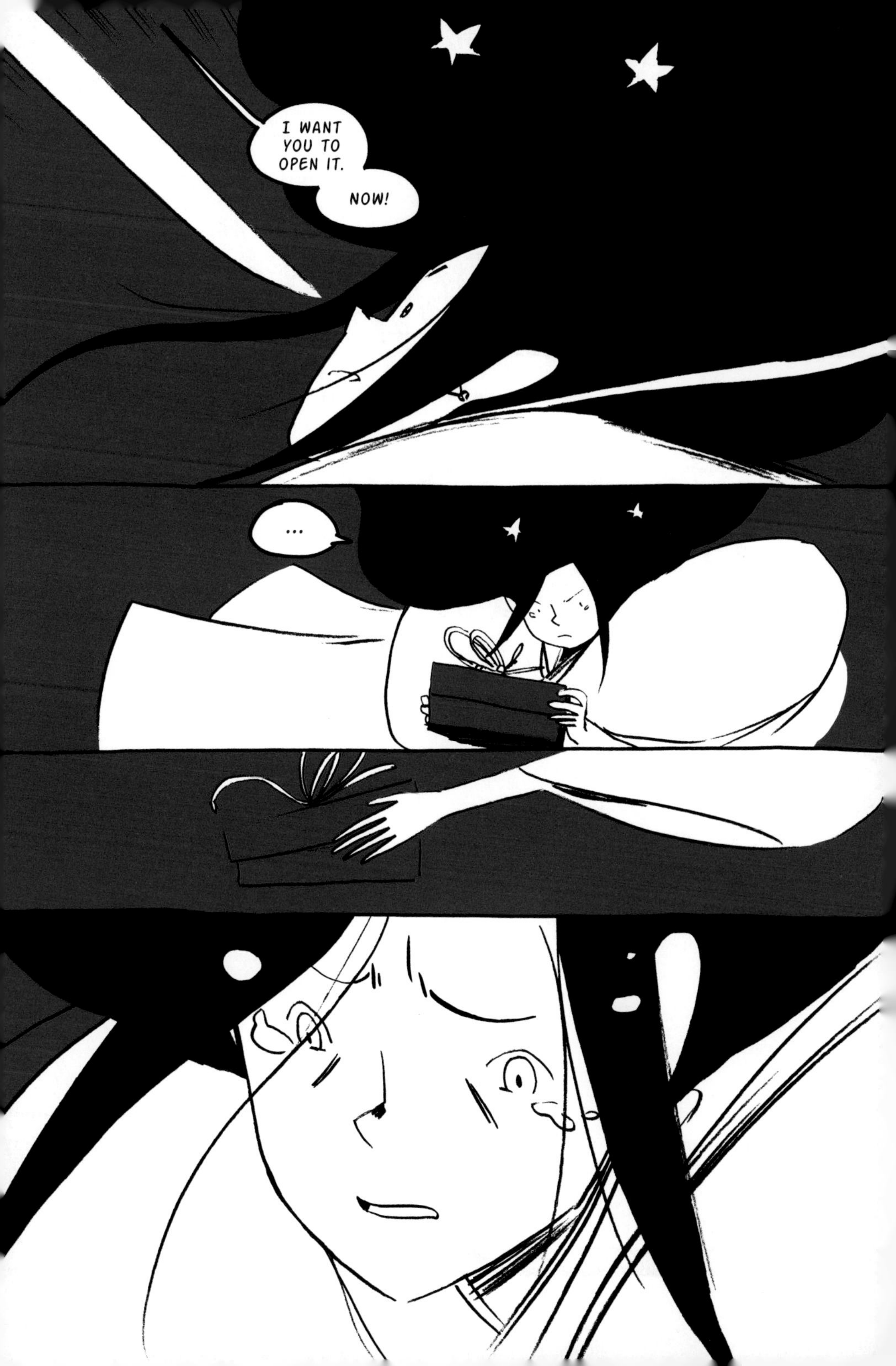
I WANT YOU TO OPEN IT.
NOW!
...

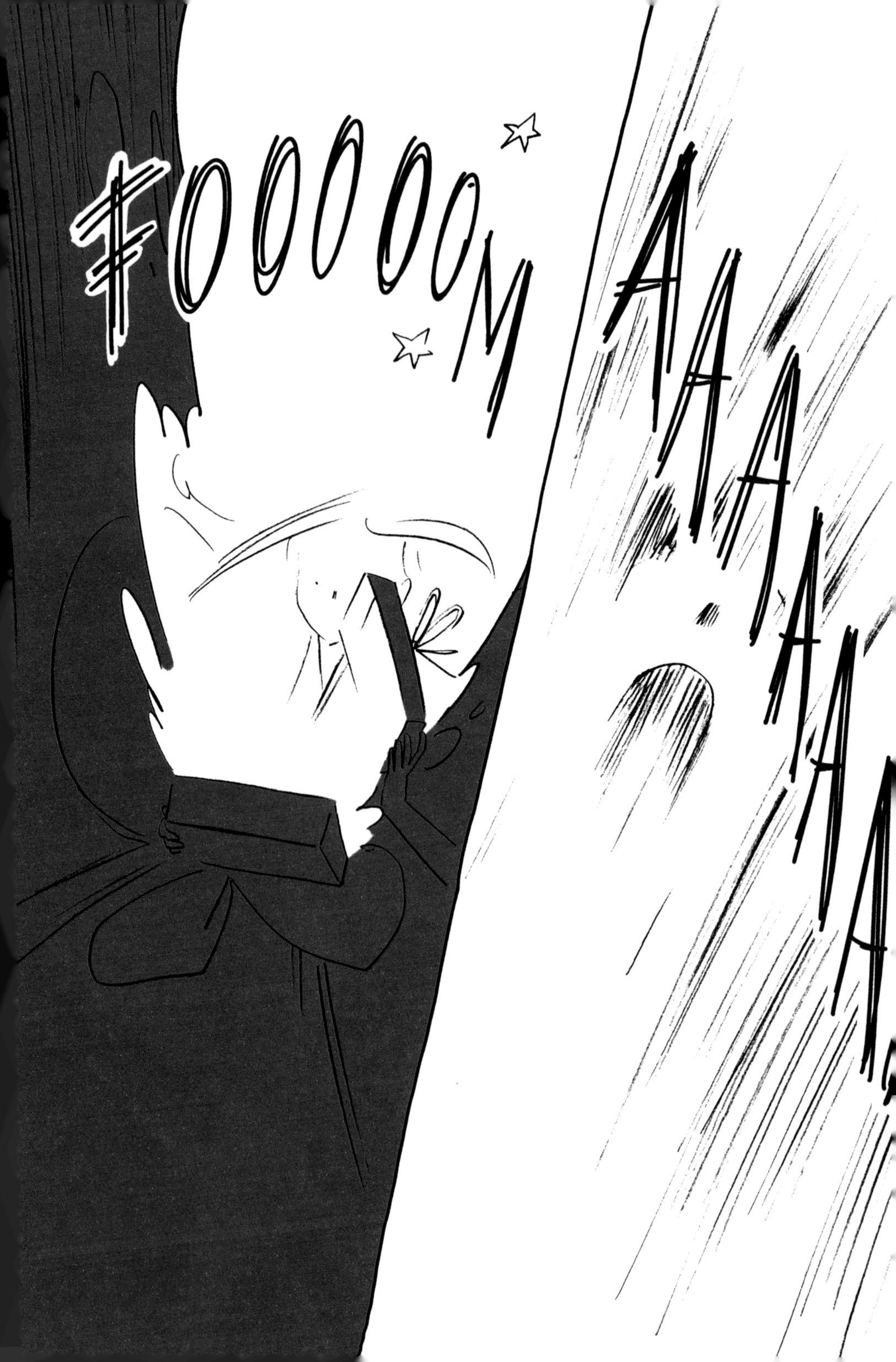
FOOOOOM
AAAAAAAA

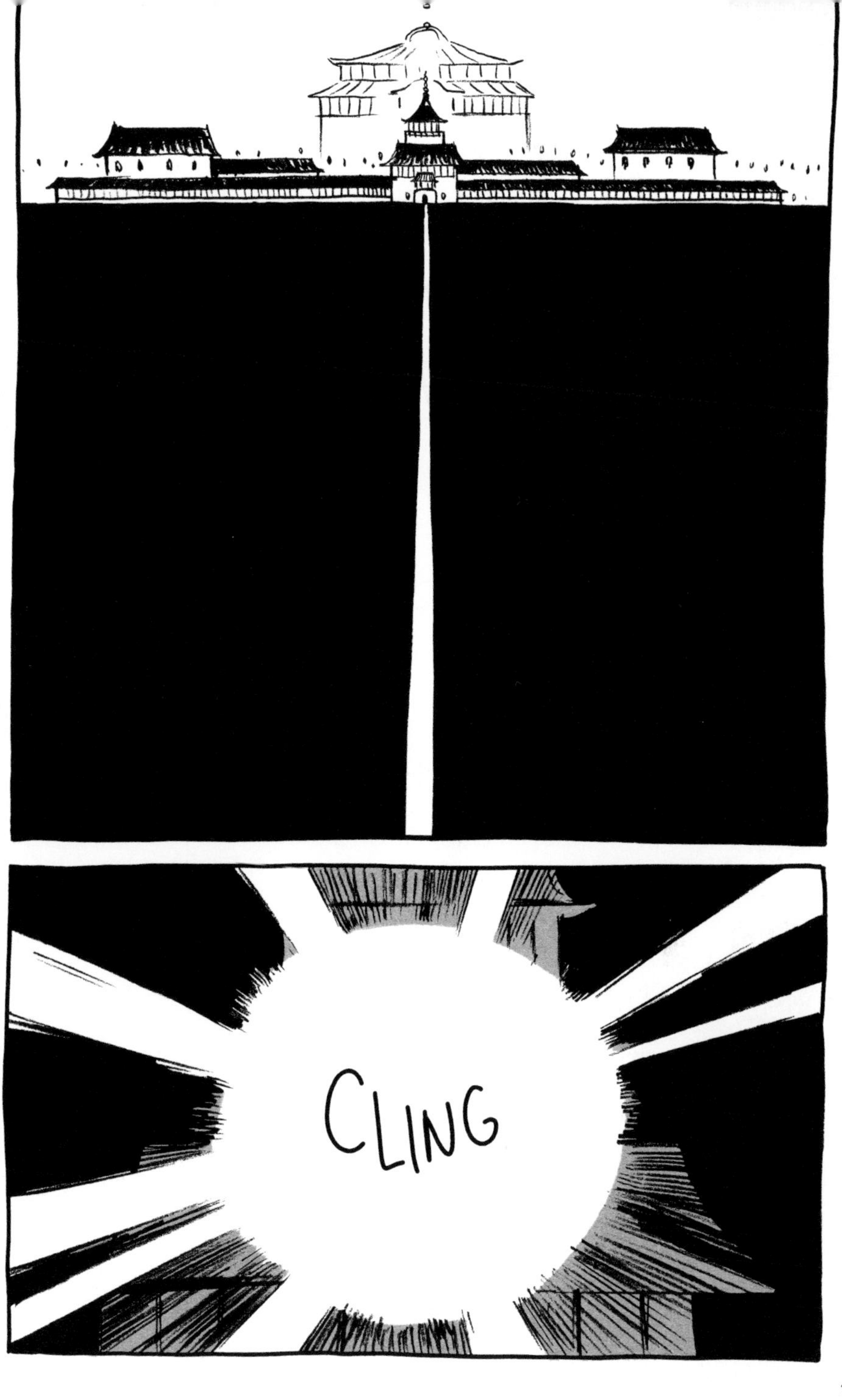
CLING

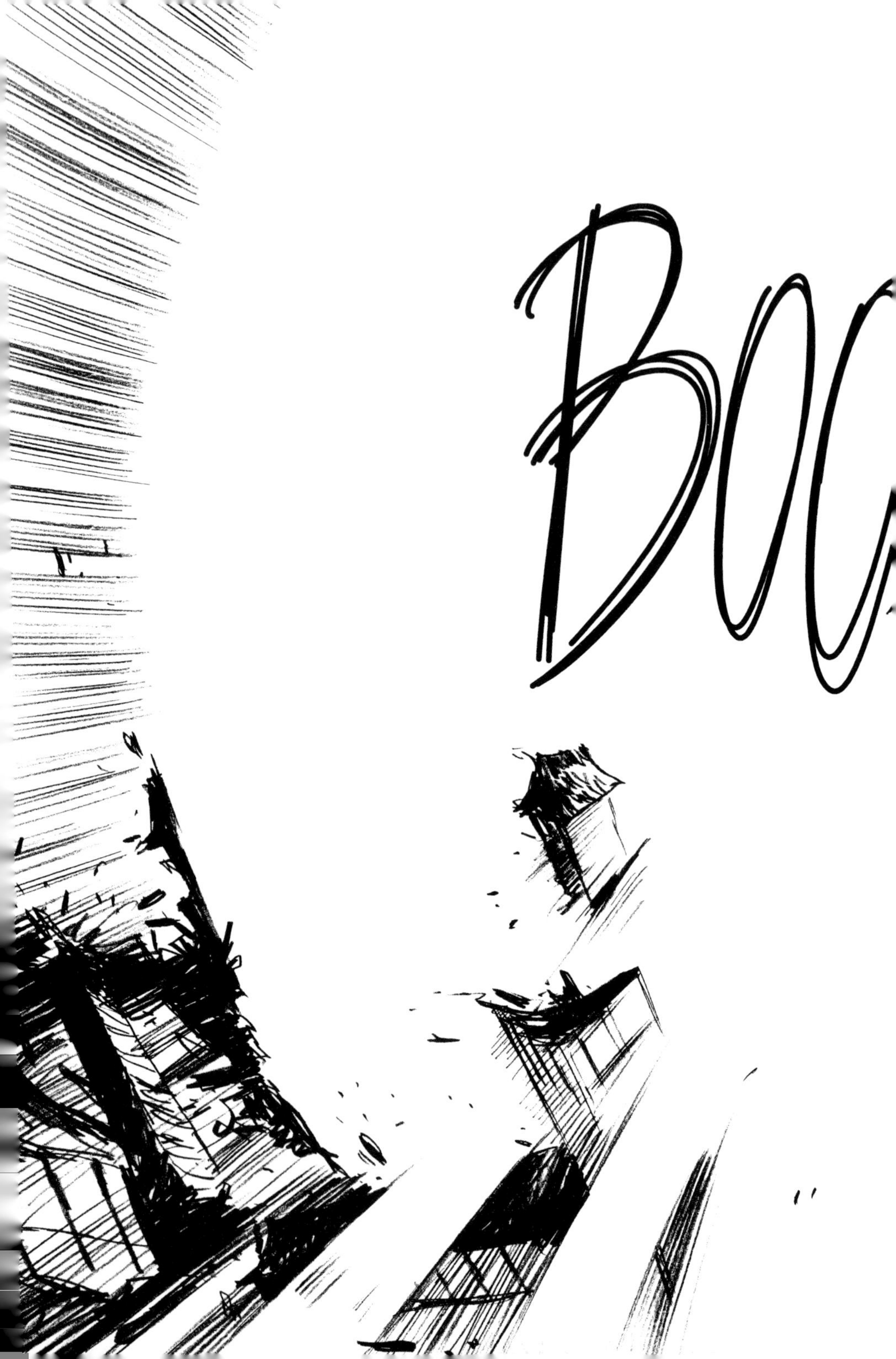

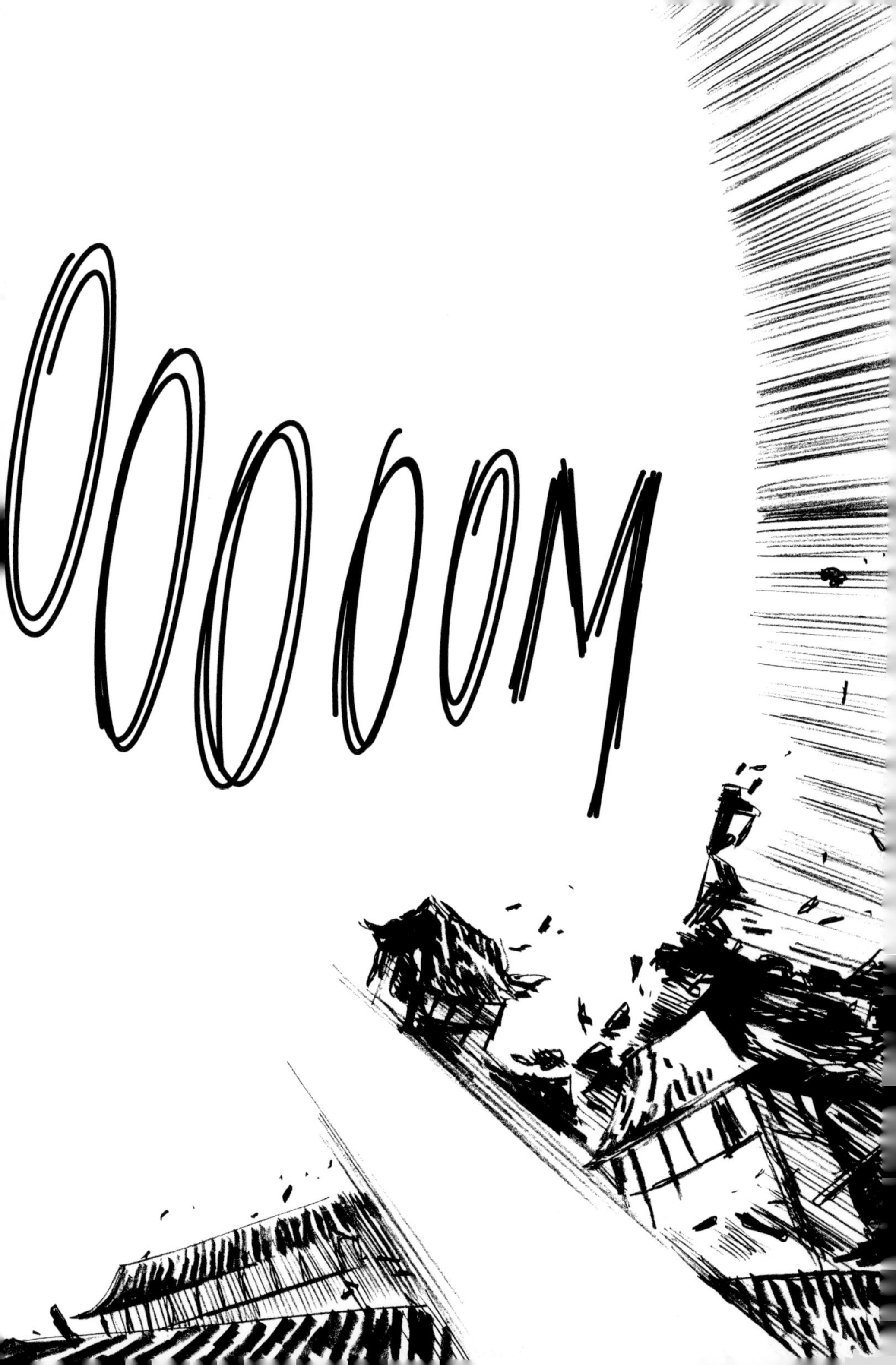
OOOOOM

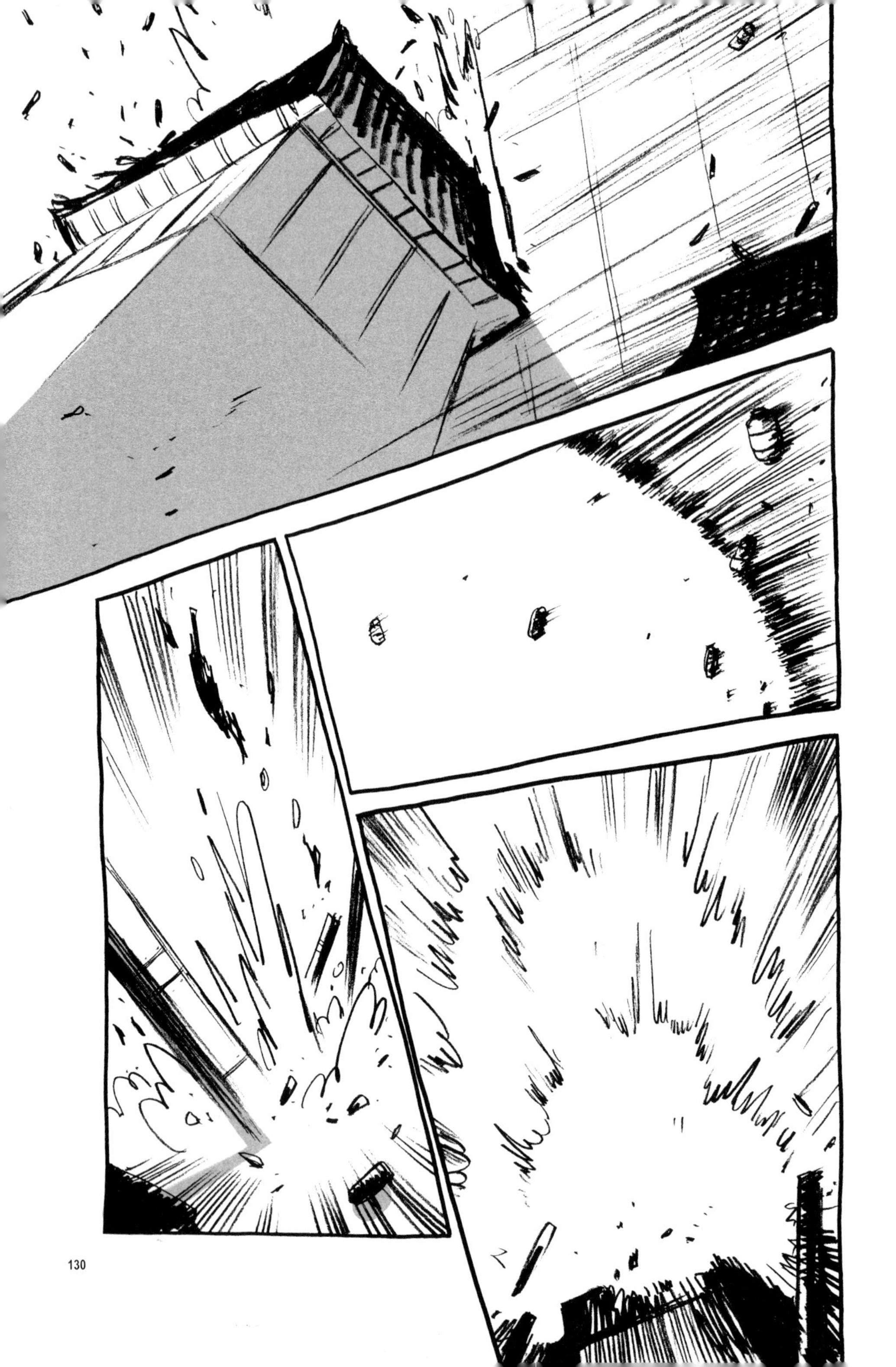

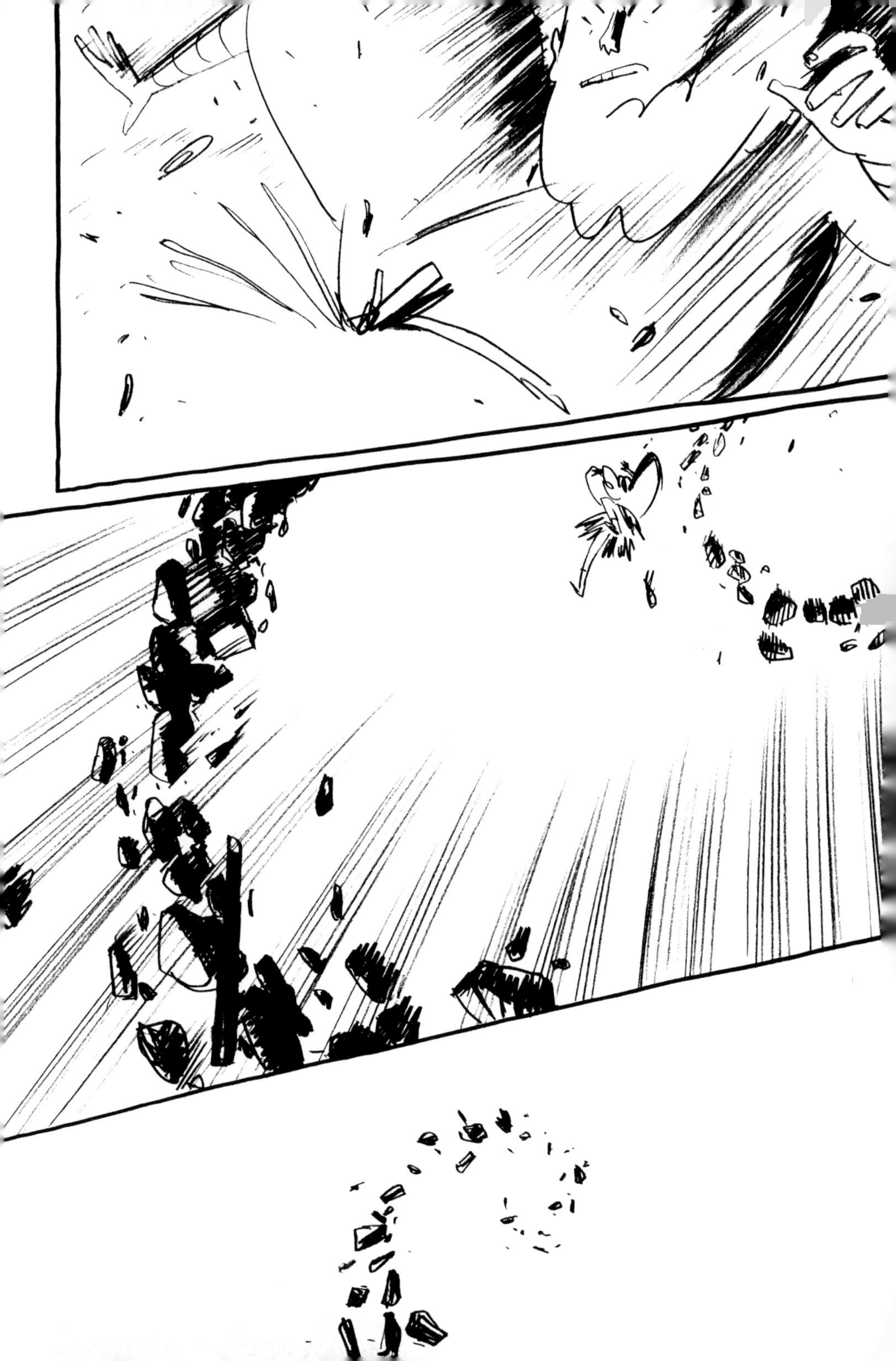

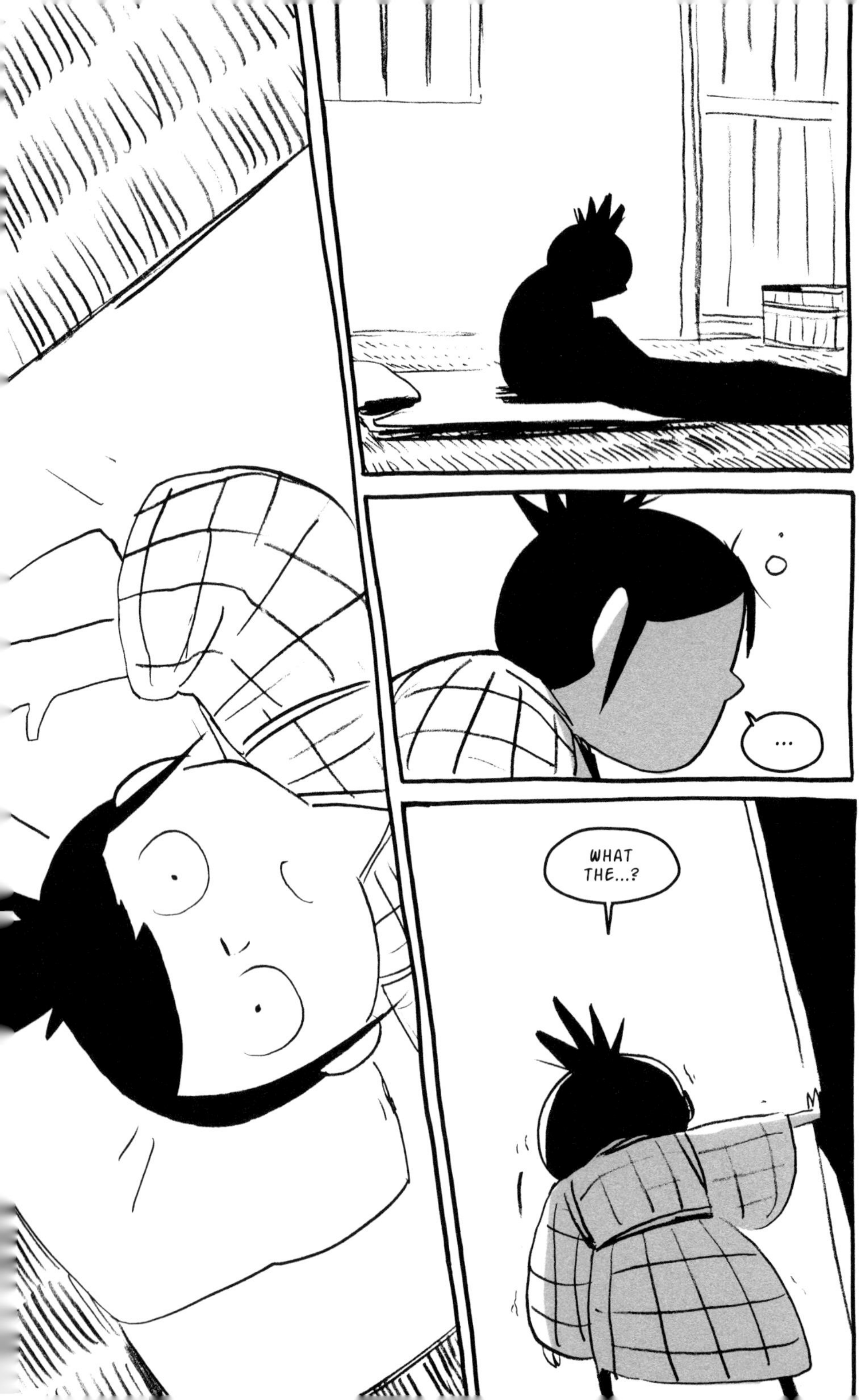
...
WHAT THE...?

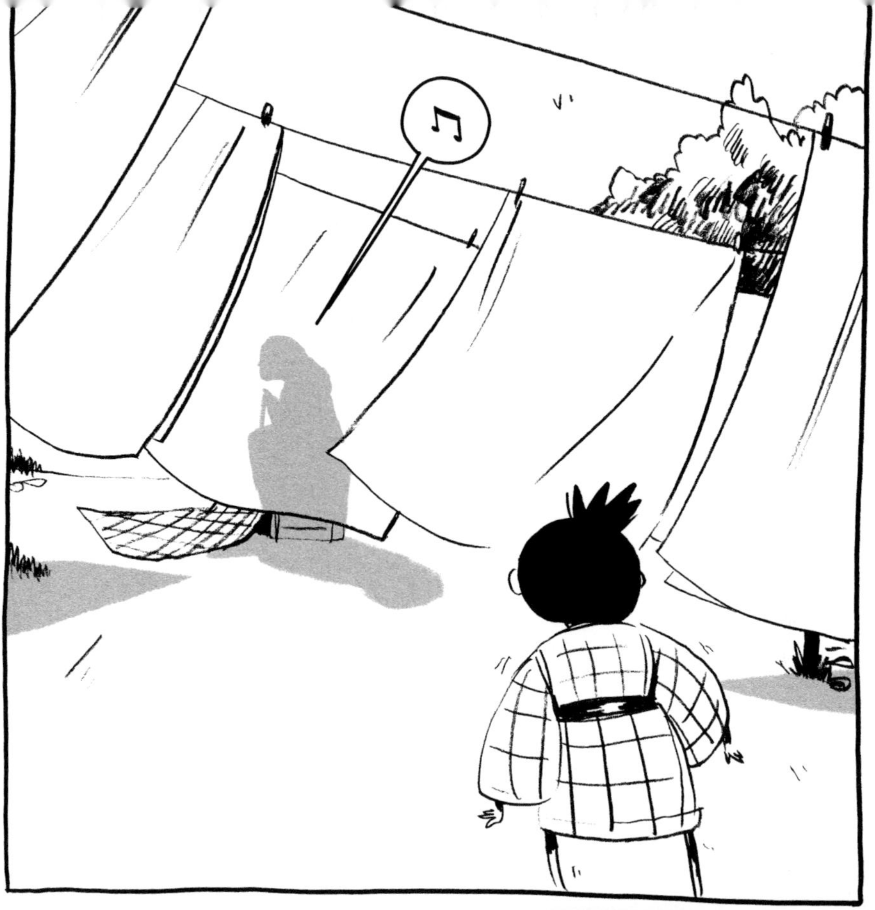
♫

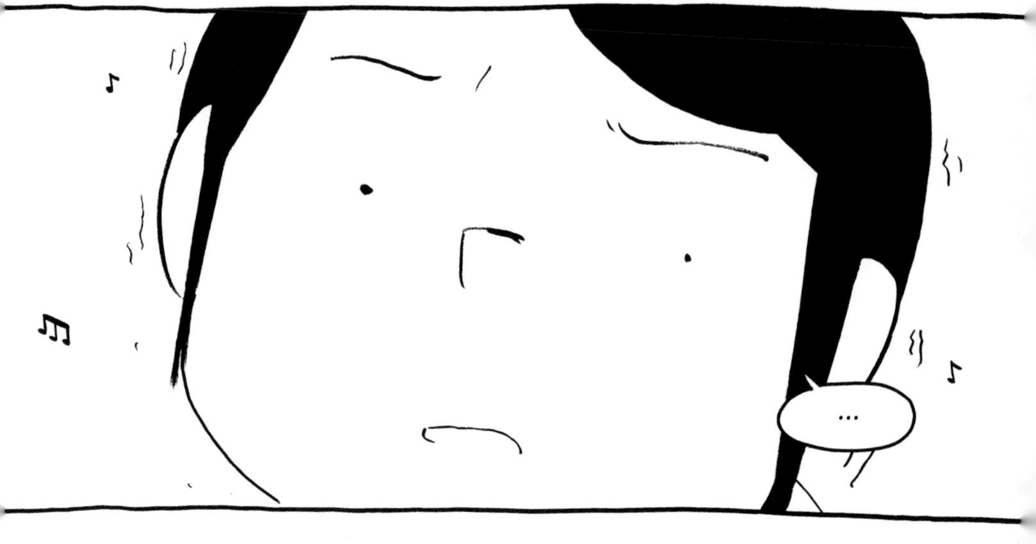
♪
♫
♪
...

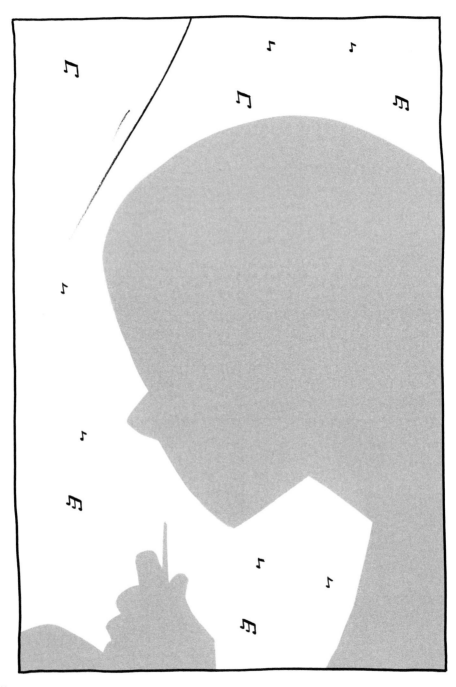

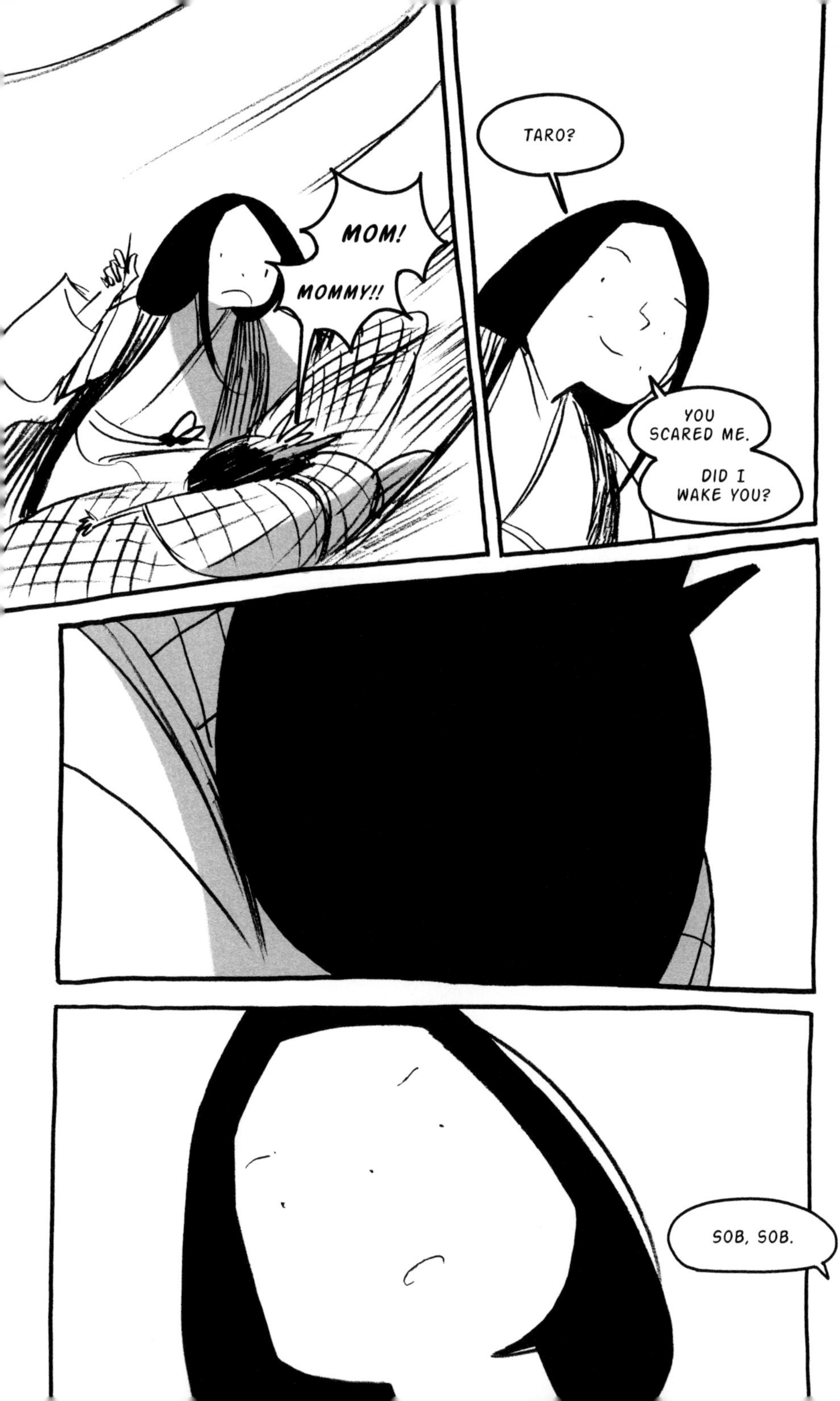
MOM!
MOMMY!!
TARO?
YOU SCARED ME.
DID I WAKE YOU?
SOB, SOB.

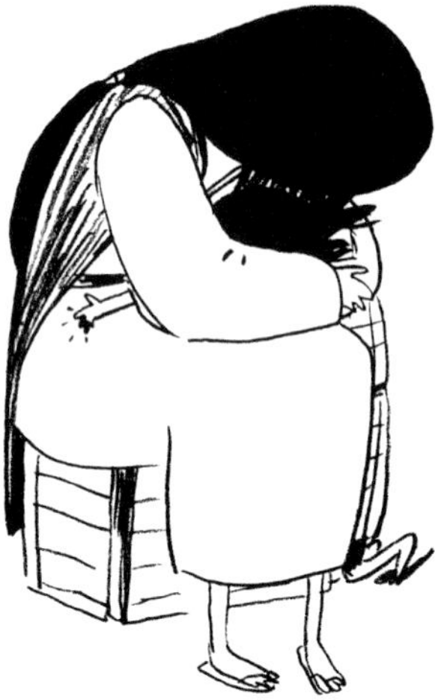

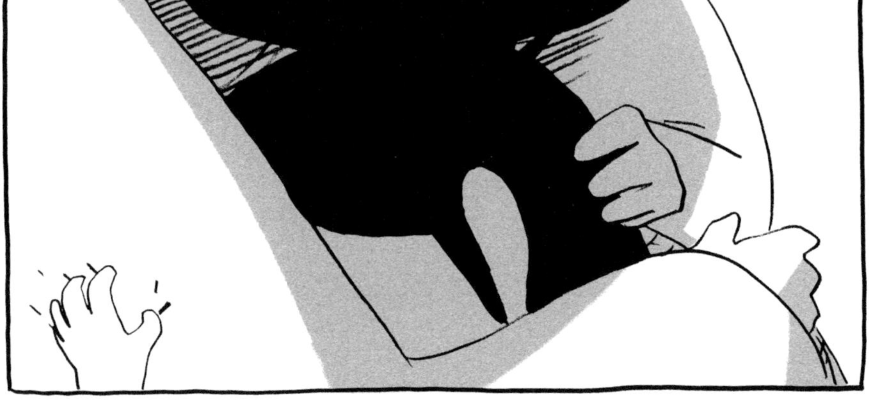

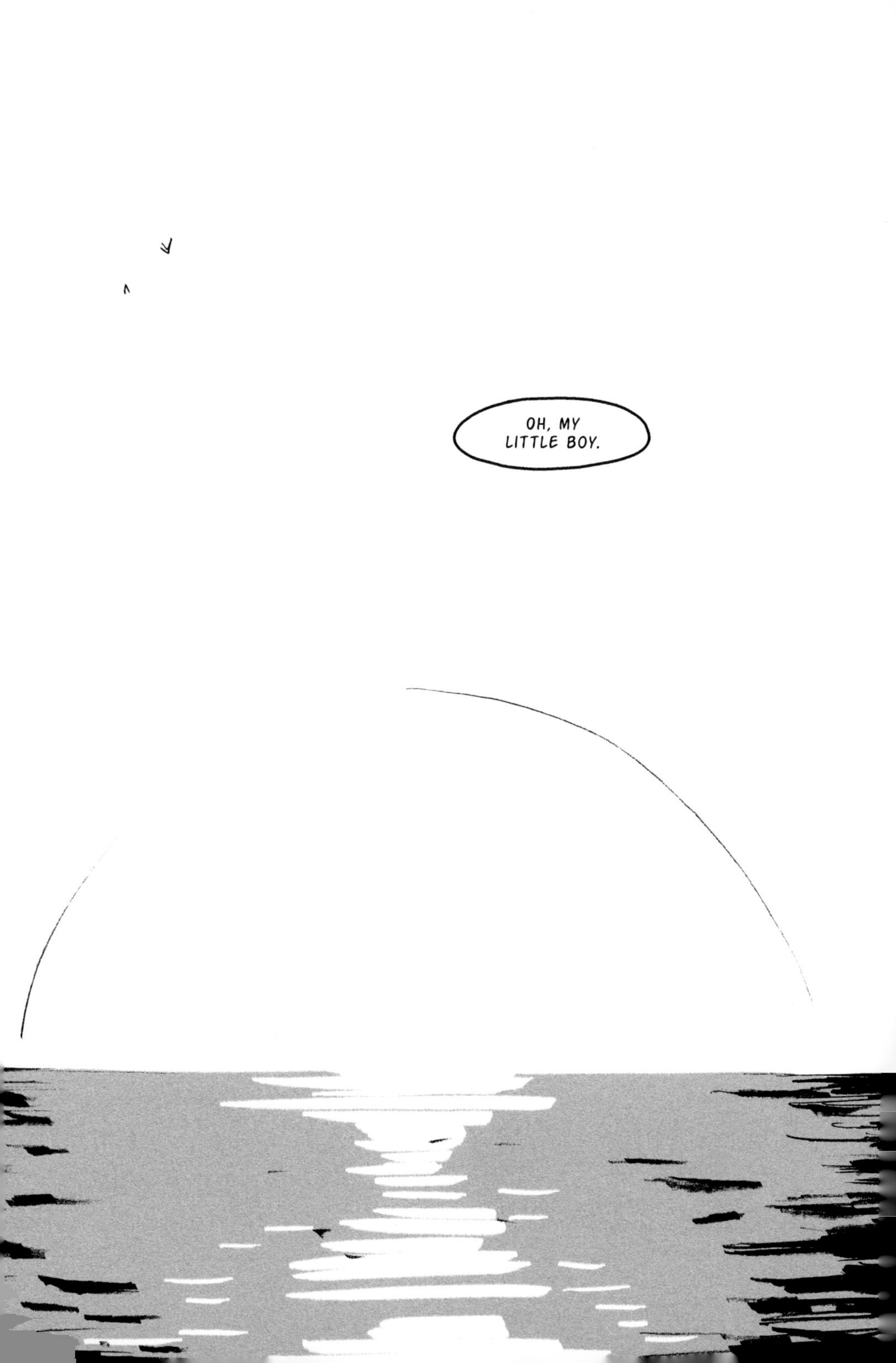
OH, MY
LITTLE BOY.

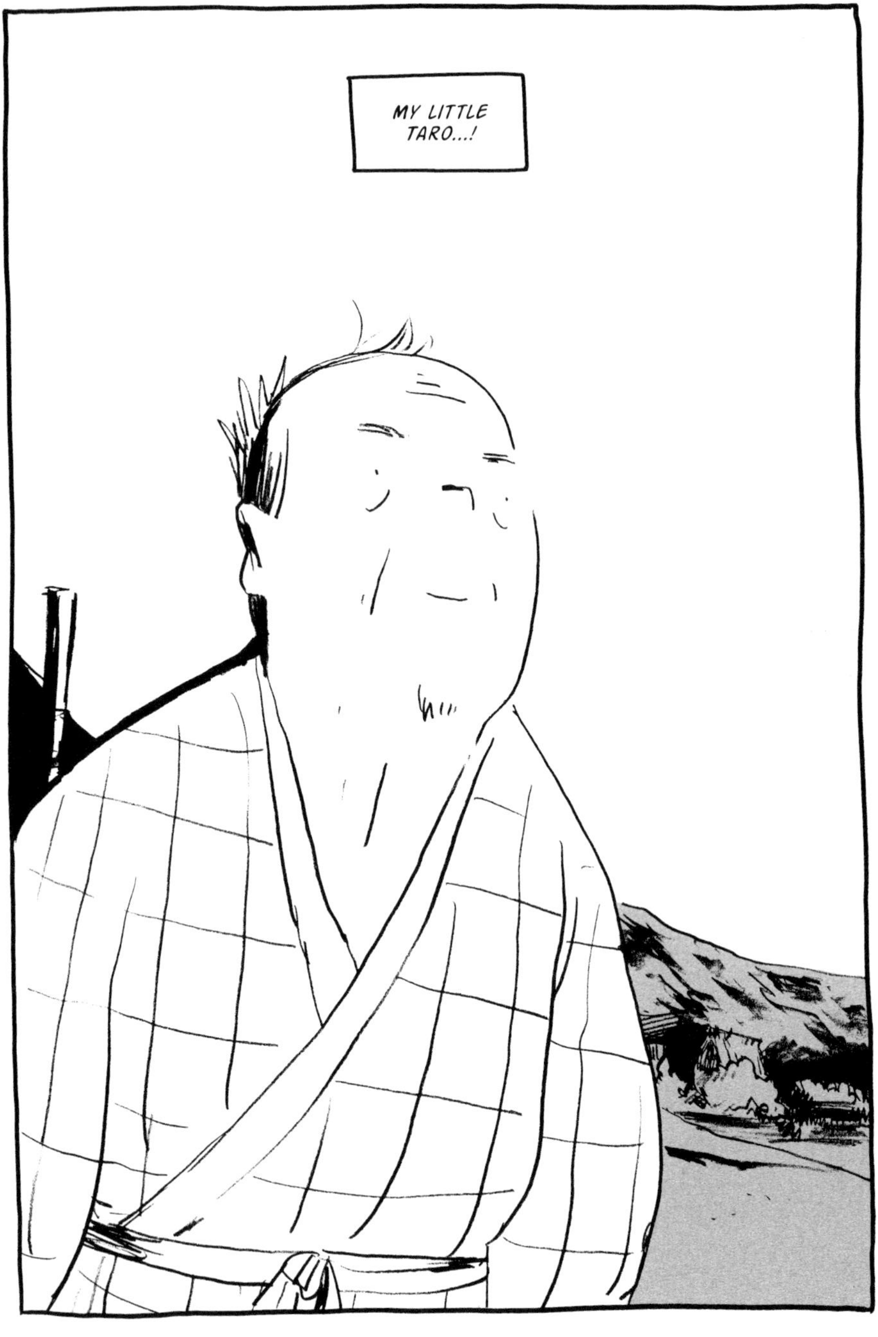
MY LITTLE TARO...!

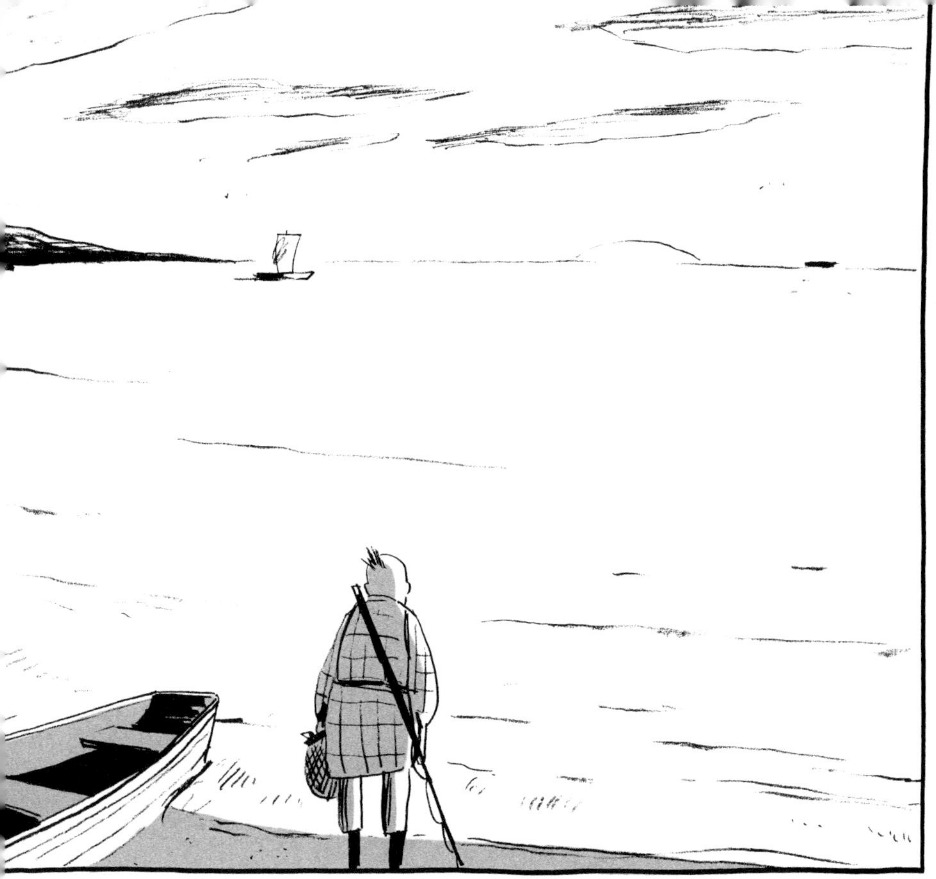

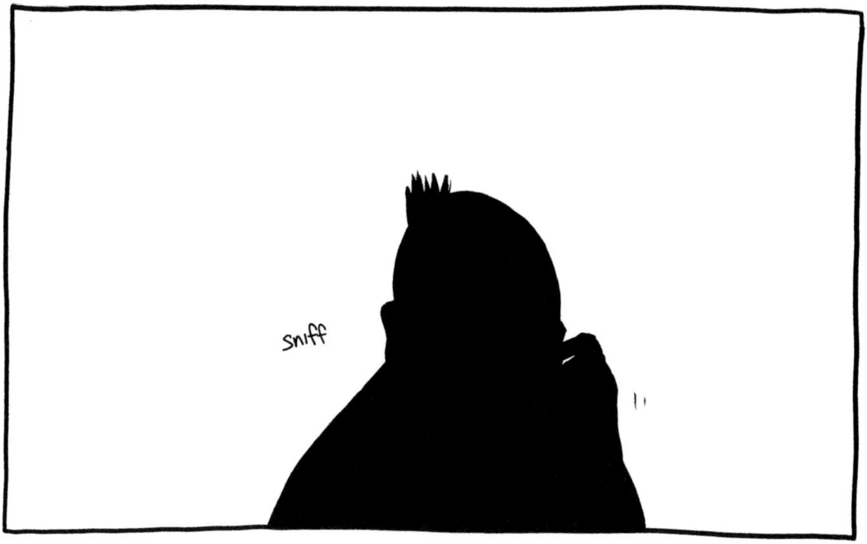
sniff

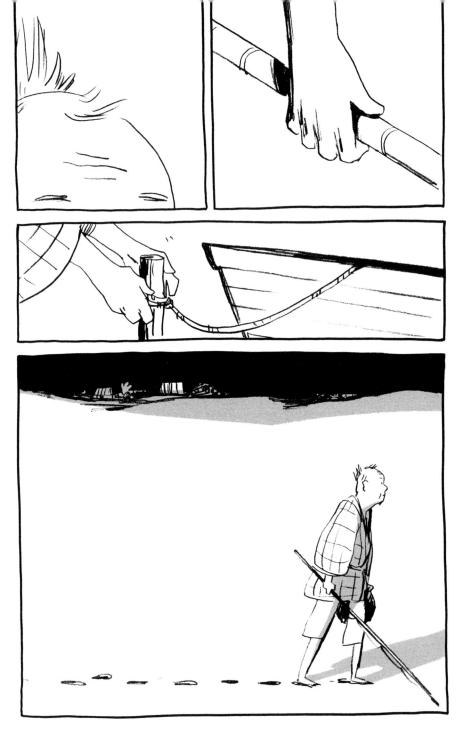

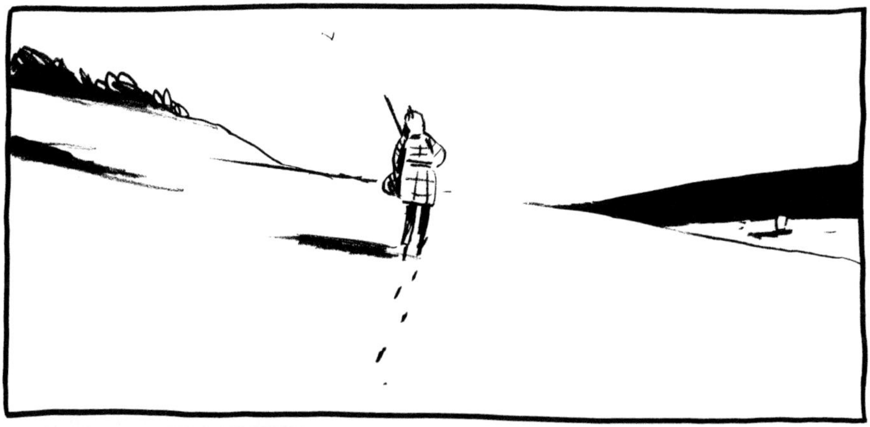

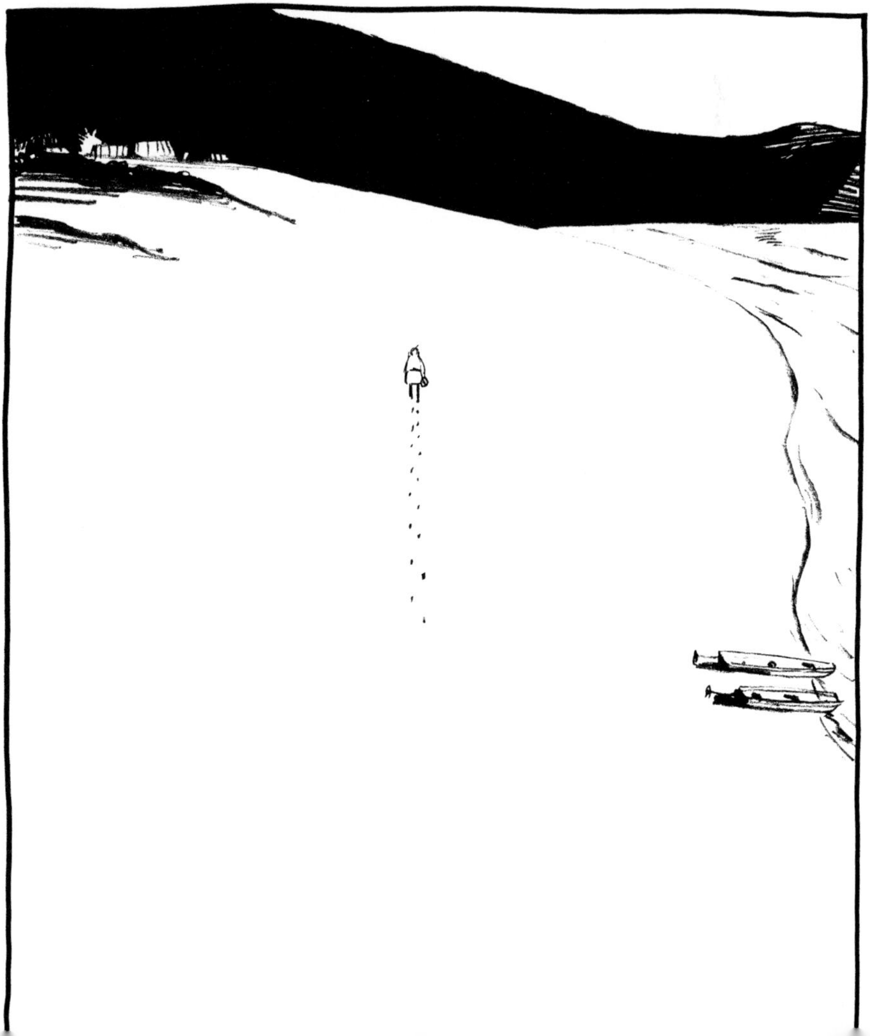

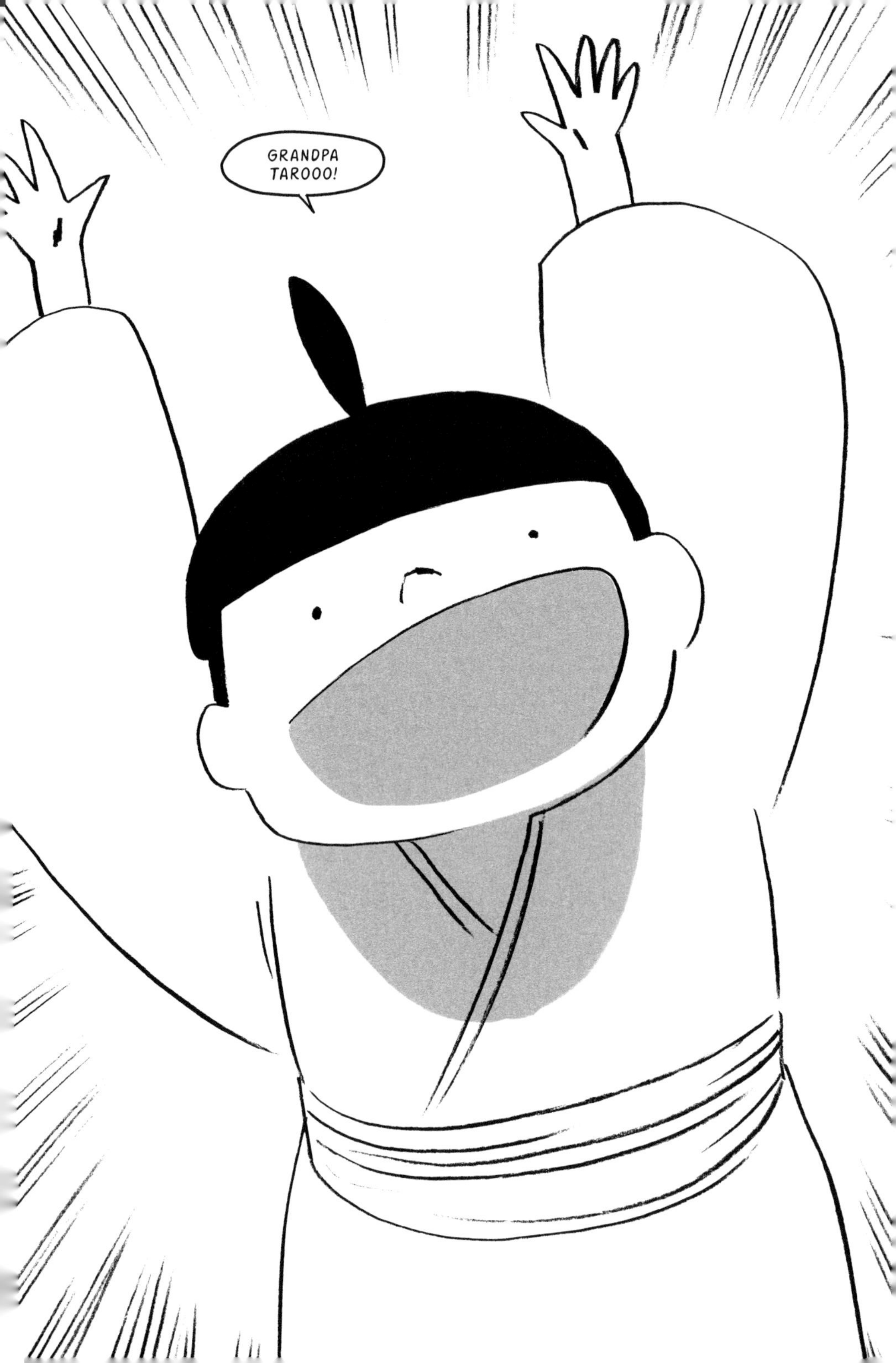
GRANDPA
TAROOO!

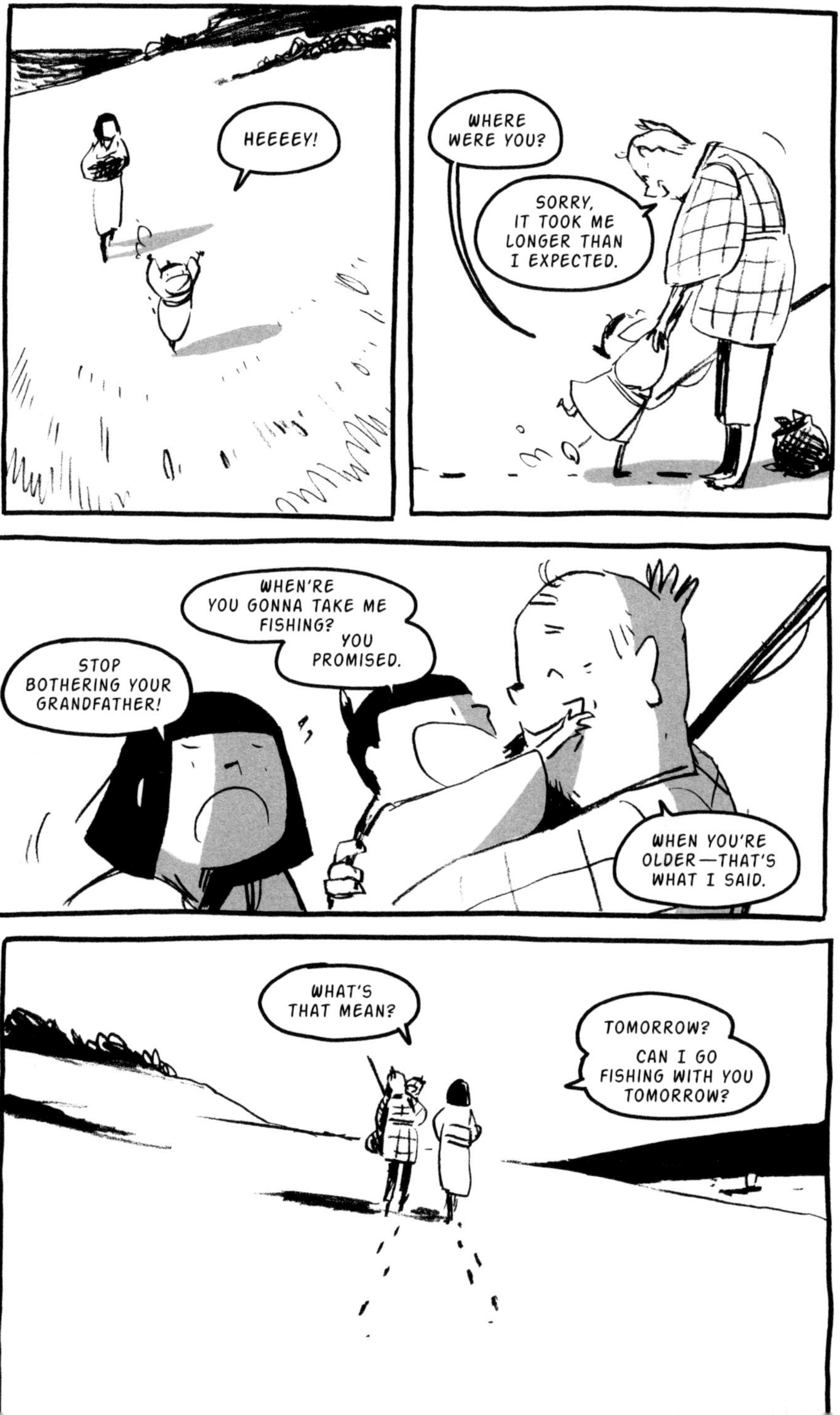
HEEEEY!
WHERE WERE YOU?
SORRY, IT TOOK ME LONGER THAN I EXPECTED.
WHEN'RE YOU GONNA TAKE ME FISHING?
YOU PROMISED.
STOP BOTHERING YOUR GRANDFATHER!
WHEN YOU'RE OLDER—THAT'S WHAT I SAID.
WHAT'S THAT MEAN?
TOMORROW?
CAN I GO FISHING WITH YOU TOMORROW?

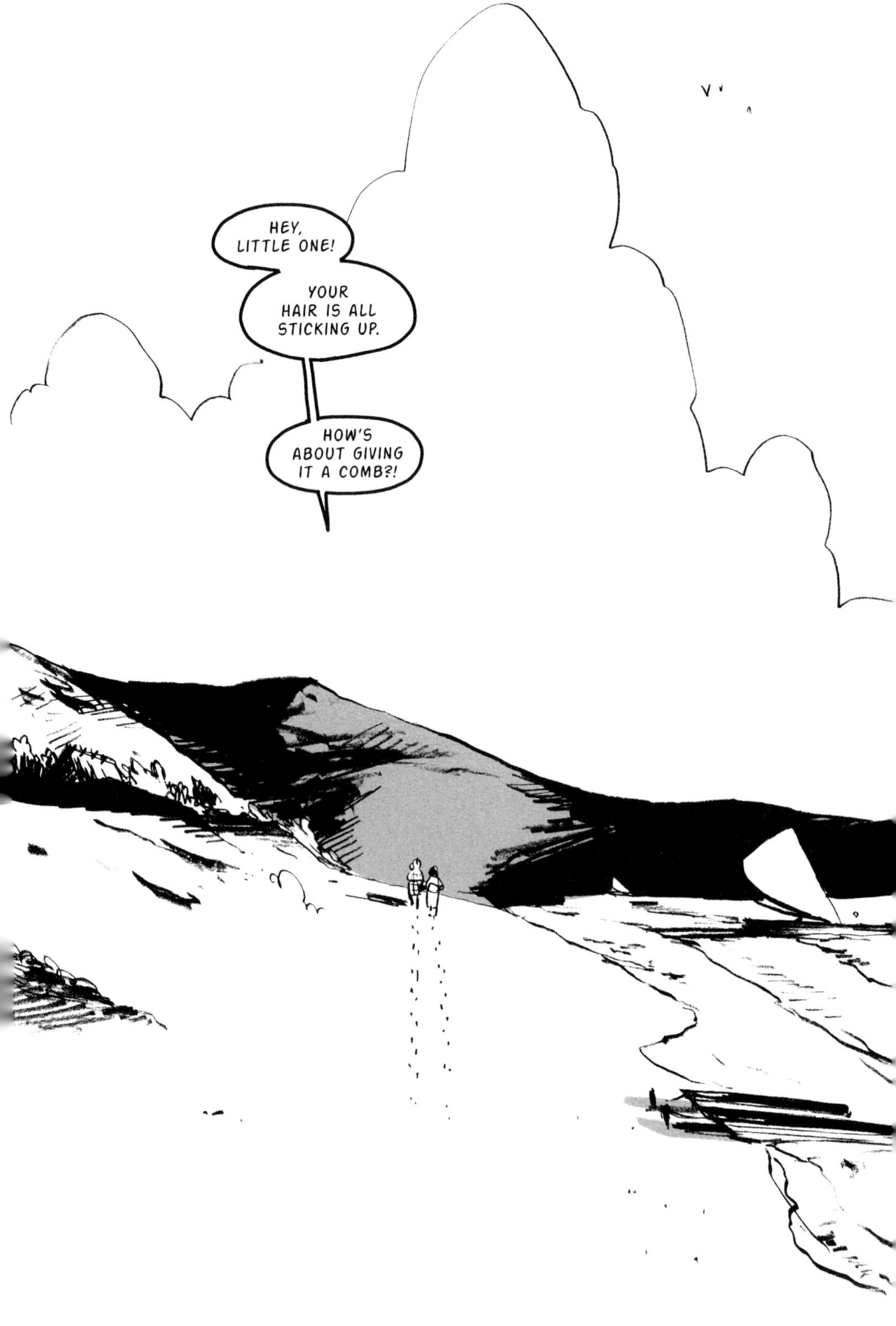
HEY, LITTLE ONE!
YOUR HAIR IS ALL STICKING UP.
HOW'S ABOUT GIVING IT A COMB?!

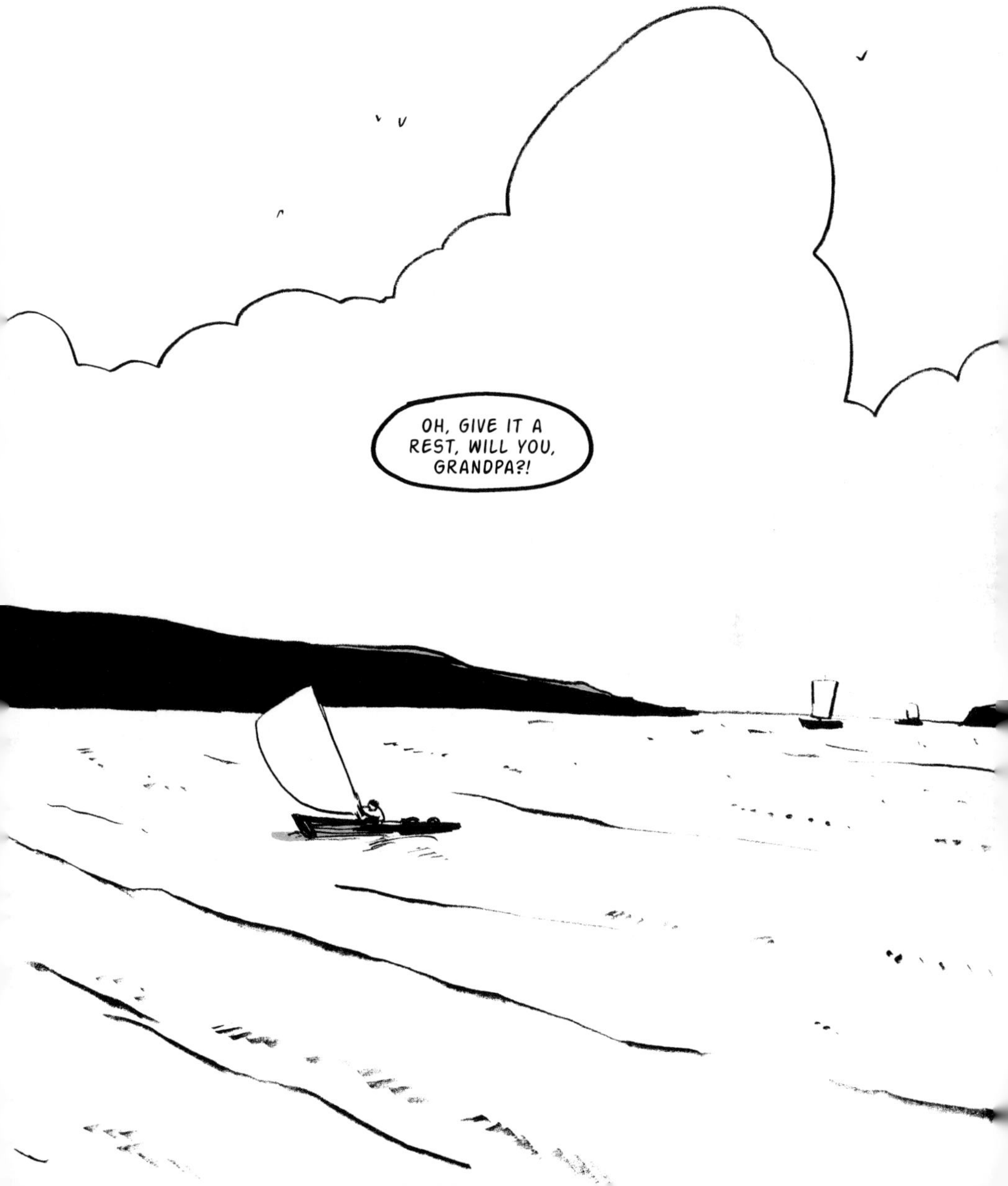
OH, GIVE IT A REST, WILL YOU, GRANDPA?!

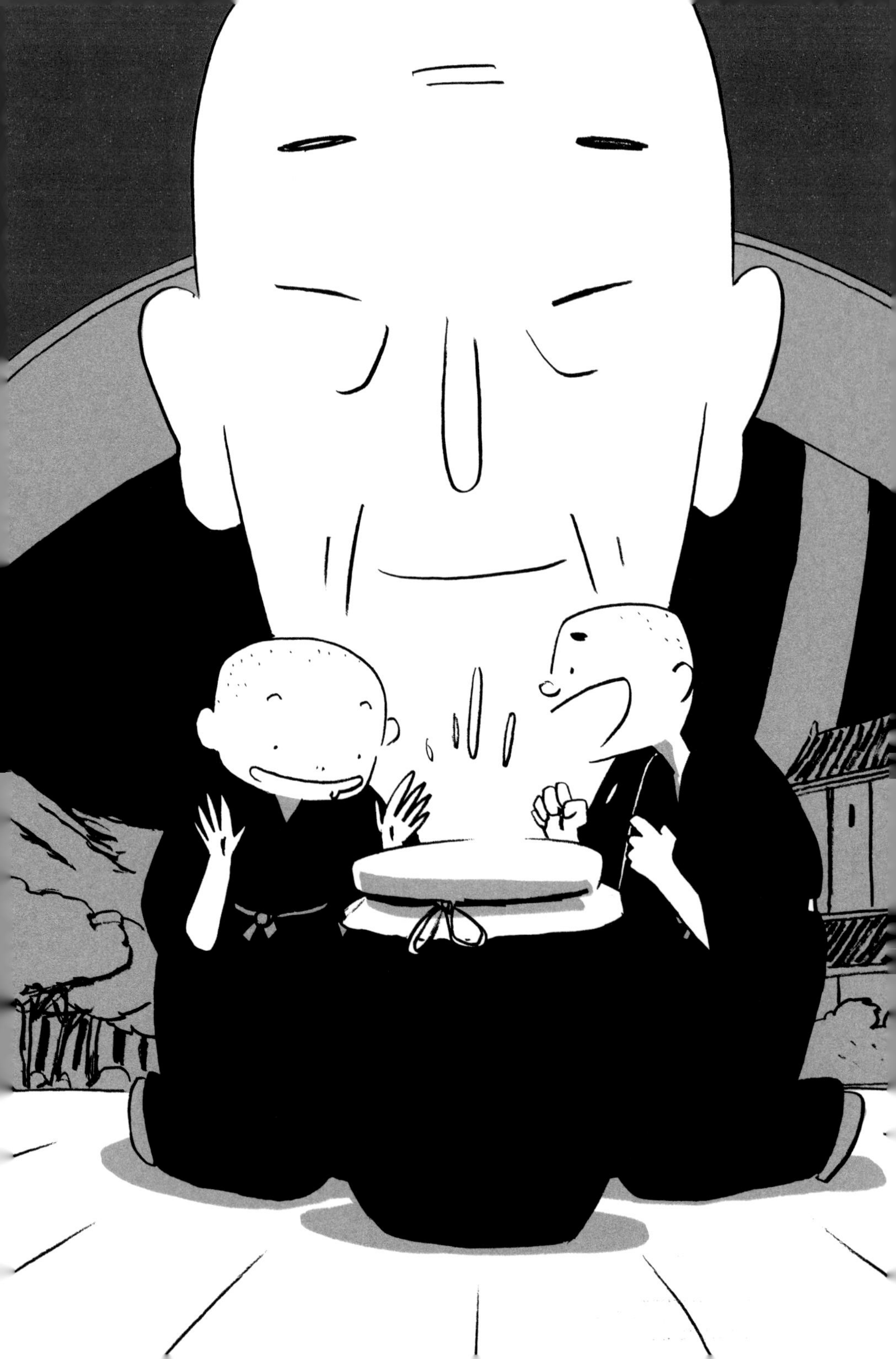

EMPTY

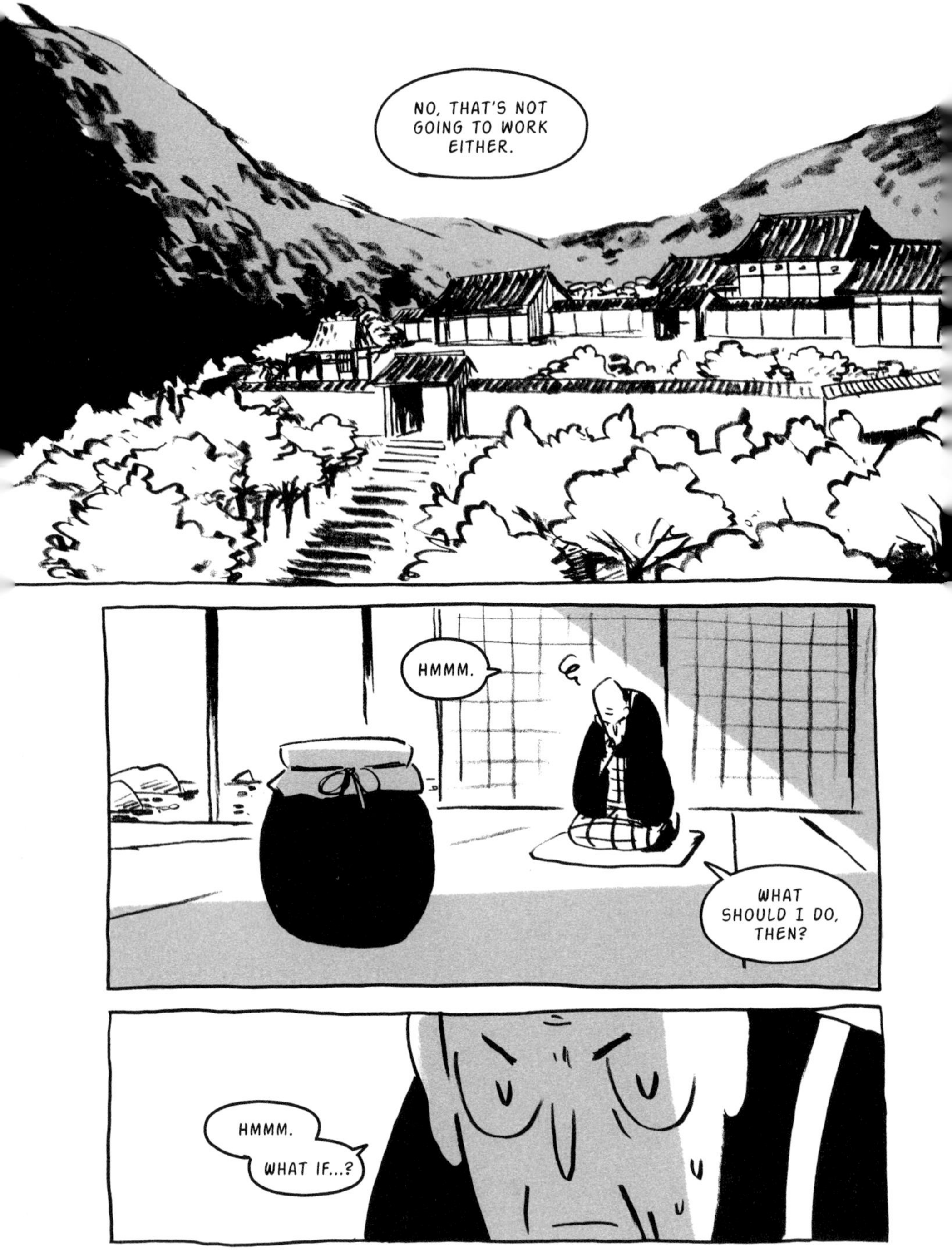
NO, THAT'S NOT GOING TO WORK EITHER.
HMMM.
WHAT SHOULD I DO, THEN?
HMMM.
WHAT IF...?

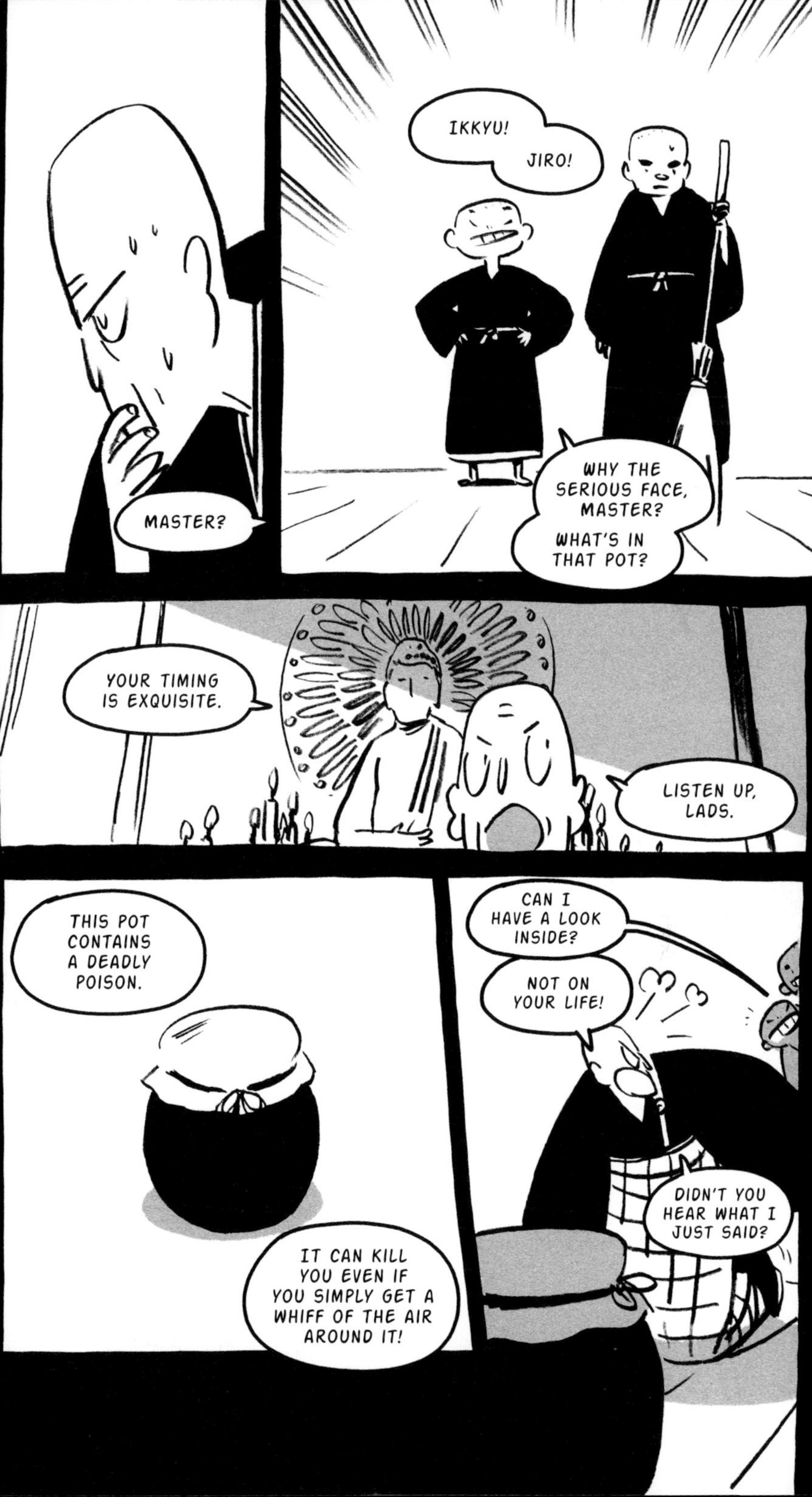
MASTER?
IKKYU!
JIRO!
WHY THE SERIOUS FACE, MASTER?
WHAT'S IN THAT POT?
YOUR TIMING IS EXQUISITE.
LISTEN UP, LADS.
THIS POT CONTAINS A DEADLY POISON.
IT CAN KILL YOU EVEN IF YOU SIMPLY GET A WHIFF OF THE AIR AROUND IT!
CAN I HAVE A LOOK INSIDE?
NOT ON YOUR LIFE!
DIDN'T YOU HEAR WHAT I JUST SAID?

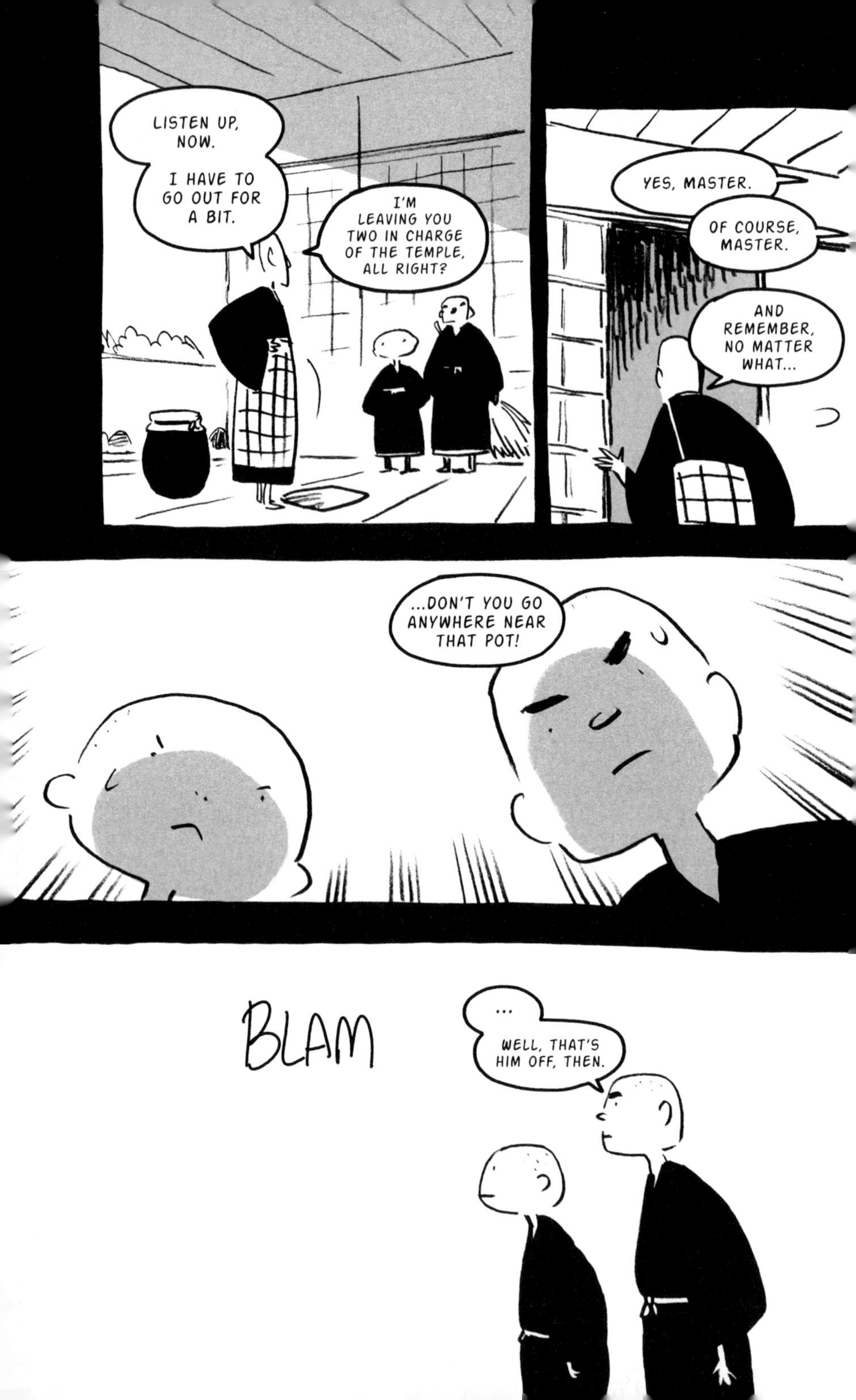
LISTEN UP, NOW.
I HAVE TO GO OUT FOR A BIT.
I'M LEAVING YOU TWO IN CHARGE OF THE TEMPLE, ALL RIGHT?
YES, MASTER.
OF COURSE, MASTER.
AND REMEMBER, NO MATTER WHAT...
...DON'T YOU GO ANYWHERE NEAR THAT POT!
BLAM
...
WELL, THAT'S HIM OFF, THEN.

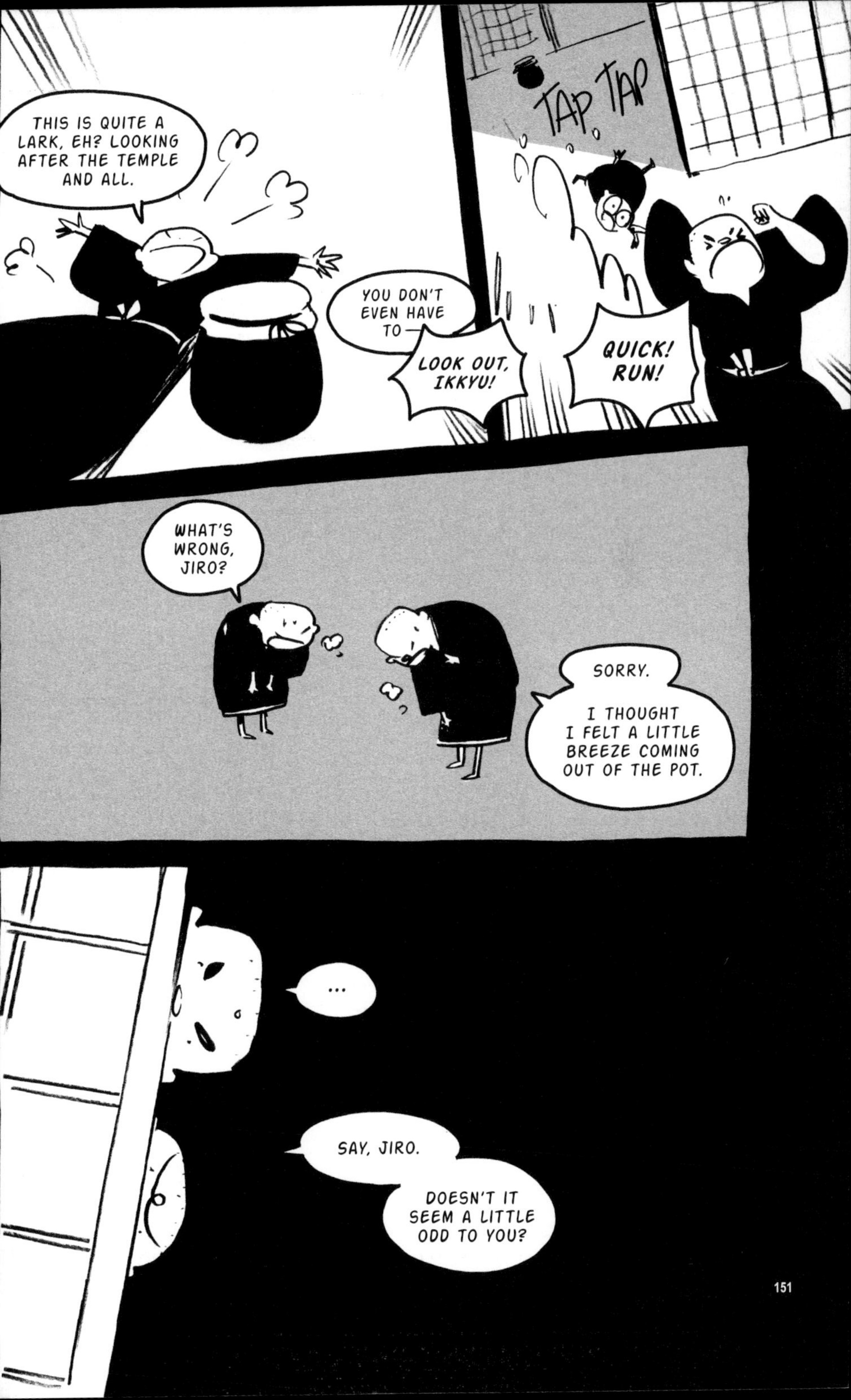
THIS IS QUITE A LARK, EH? LOOKING AFTER THE TEMPLE AND ALL.
YOU DON'T EVEN HAVE TO—
TAP TAP
LOOK OUT, IKKYU!
QUICK! RUN!
WHAT'S WRONG, JIRO?
SORRY.
I THOUGHT I FELT A LITTLE BREEZE COMING OUT OF THE POT.
...
SAY, JIRO.
DOESN'T IT SEEM A LITTLE ODD TO YOU?

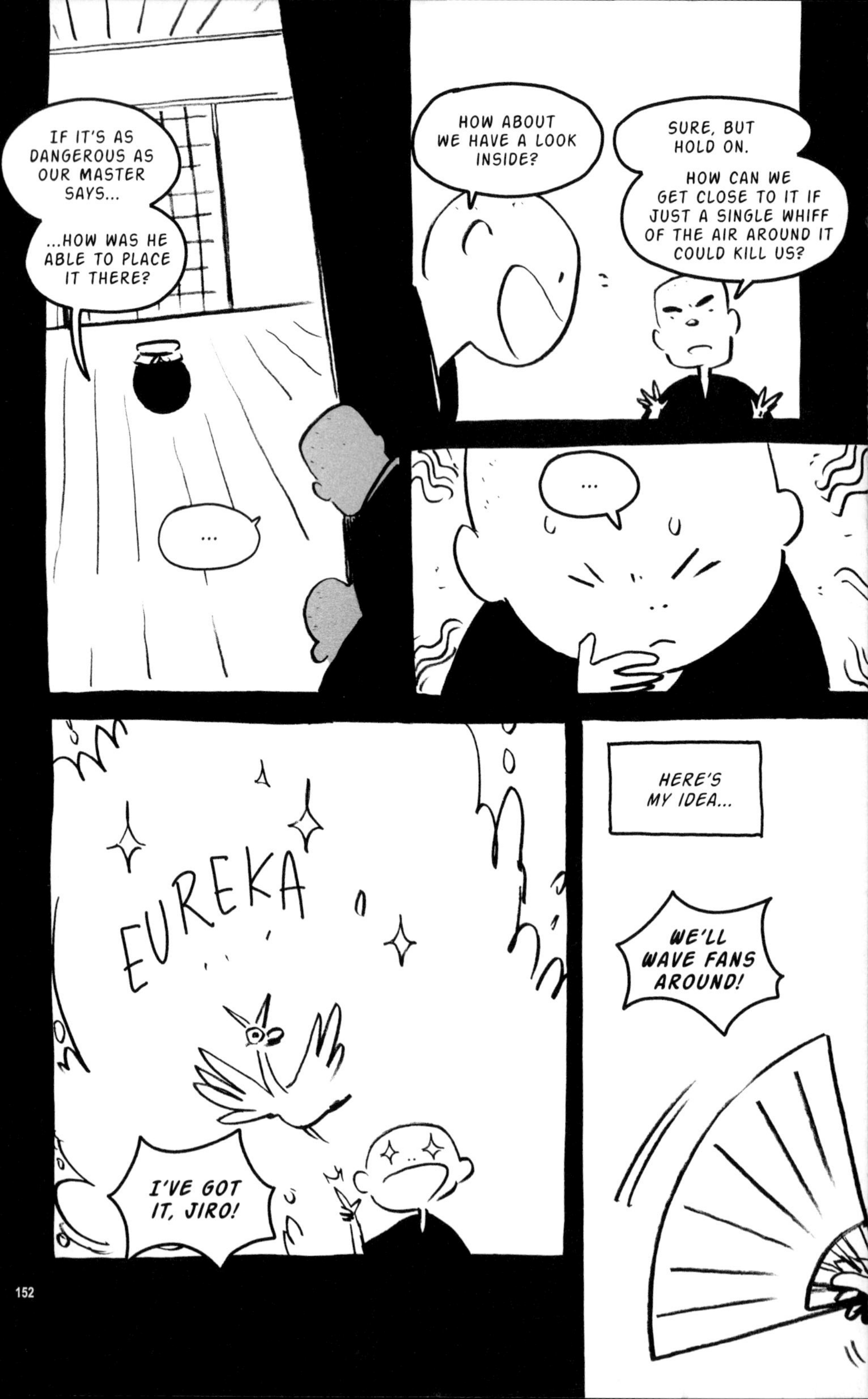
IF IT'S AS DANGEROUS AS OUR MASTER SAYS...
...HOW WAS HE ABLE TO PLACE IT THERE?
...
HOW ABOUT WE HAVE A LOOK INSIDE?
SURE, BUT HOLD ON.
HOW CAN WE GET CLOSE TO IT IF JUST A SINGLE WHIFF OF THE AIR AROUND IT COULD KILL US?
...
EUREKA
I'VE GOT IT, JIRO!
HERE'S MY IDEA...
WE'LL WAVE FANS AROUND!

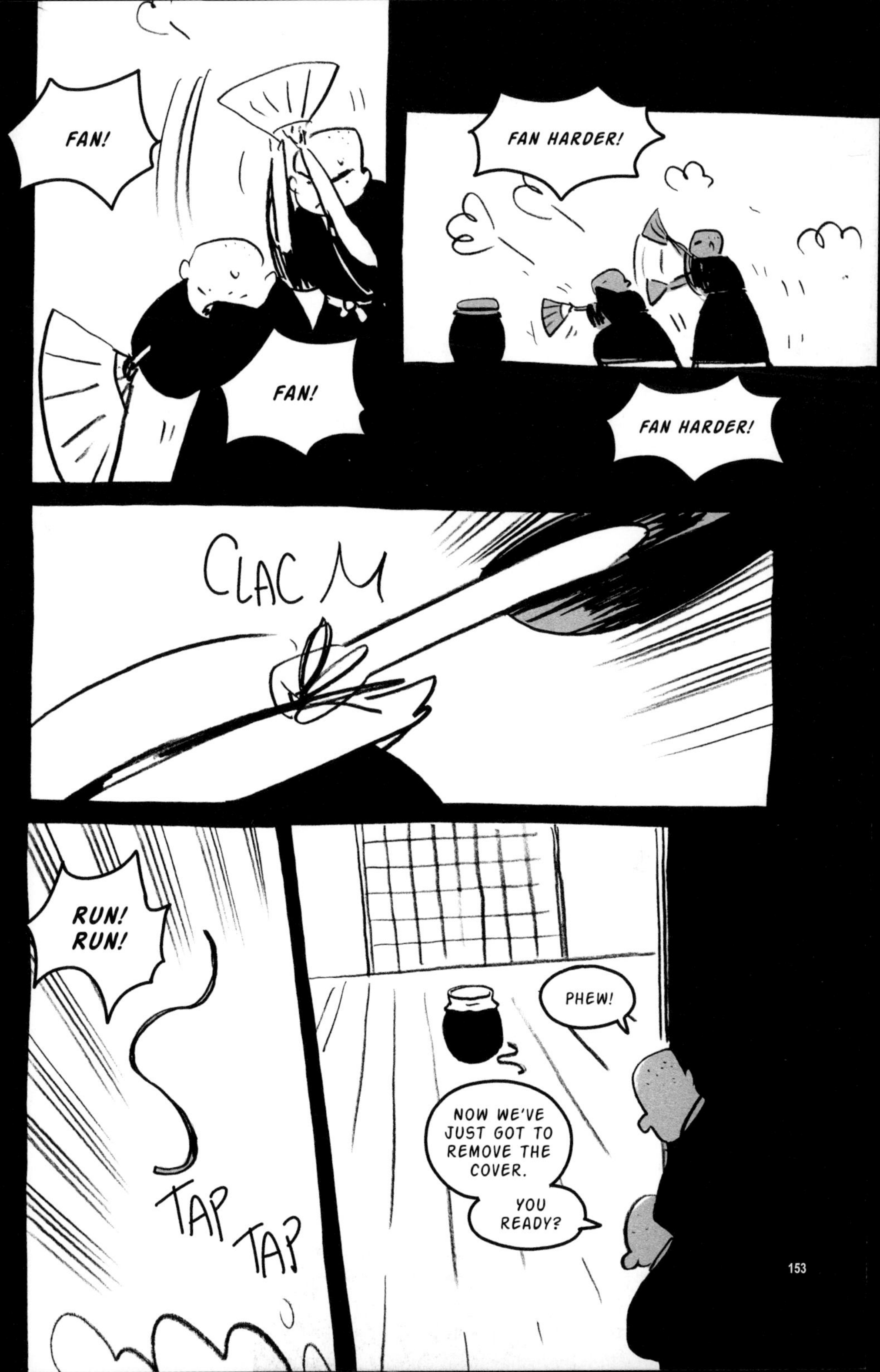
FAN!
FAN HARDER!
FAN!
FAN HARDER!
CLAC
RUN!
RUN!
TAP
TAP
PHEW!
NOW WE'VE JUST GOT TO REMOVE THE COVER.
YOU READY?

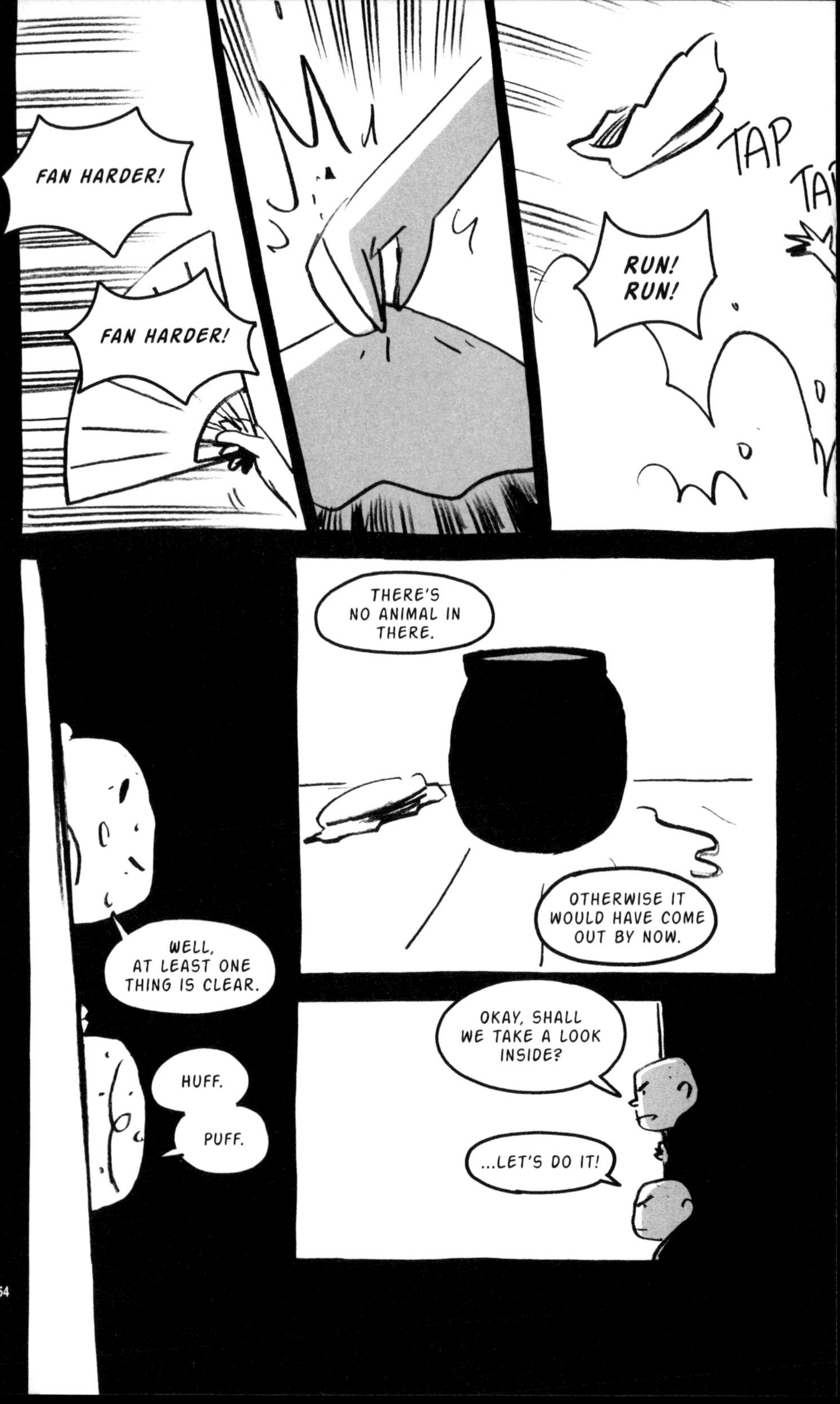
FAN HARDER!
FAN HARDER!
TAP
RUN! RUN!
THERE'S NO ANIMAL IN THERE.
OTHERWISE IT WOULD HAVE COME OUT BY NOW.
WELL, AT LEAST ONE THING IS CLEAR.
OKAY, SHALL WE TAKE A LOOK INSIDE?
HUFF.
PUFF.
...LET'S DO IT!

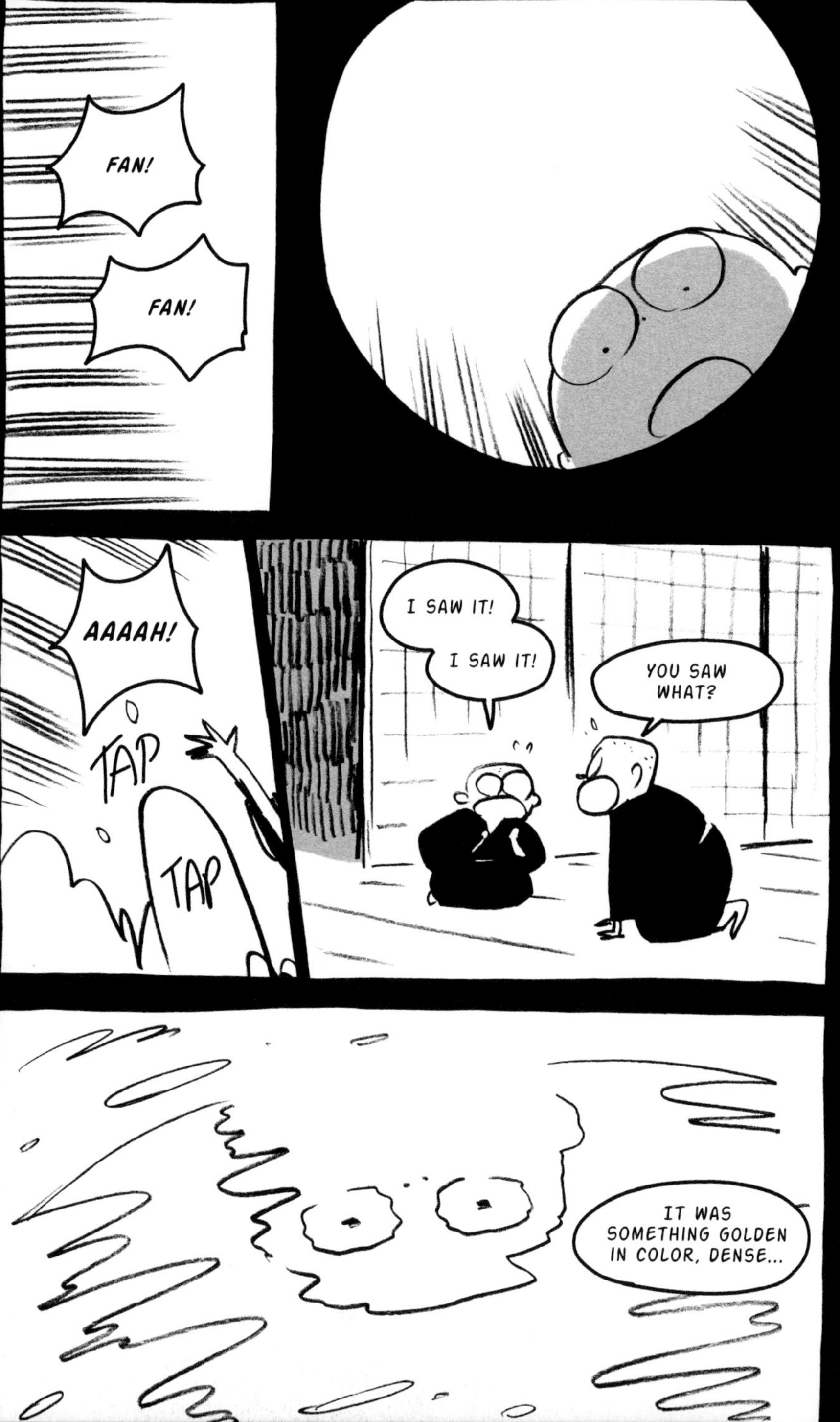
FAN!
FAN!
AAAAH!
TAP
TAP
I SAW IT!
I SAW IT!
YOU SAW WHAT?
IT WAS SOMETHING GOLDEN IN COLOR, DENSE...

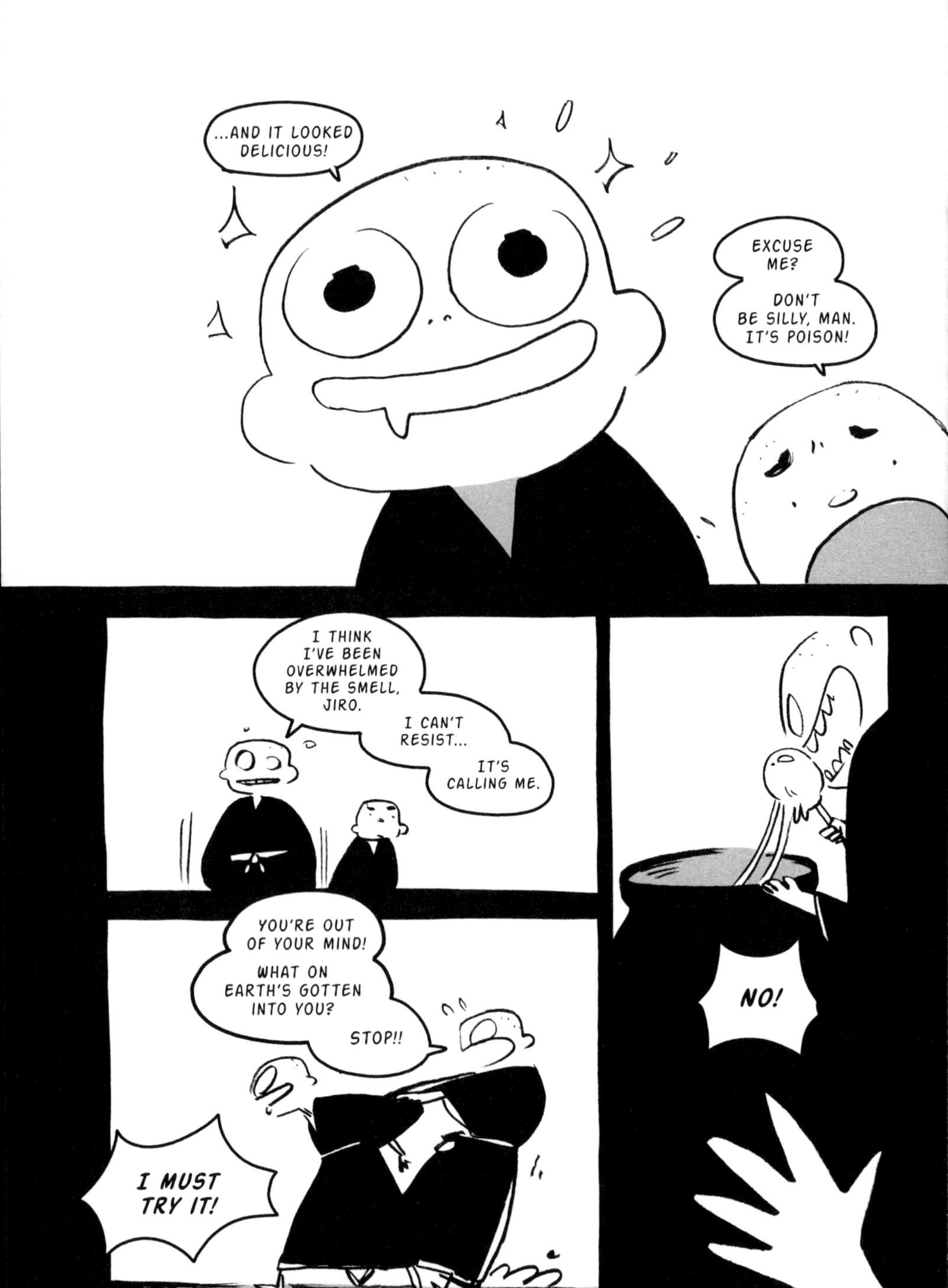
...AND IT LOOKED DELICIOUS!
EXCUSE ME?
DON'T BE SILLY, MAN. IT'S POISON!
I THINK I'VE BEEN OVERWHELMED BY THE SMELL, JIRO.
I CAN'T RESIST...
IT'S CALLING ME.
YOU'RE OUT OF YOUR MIND!
WHAT ON EARTH'S GOTTEN INTO YOU?
STOP!!
I MUST TRY IT!
NO!

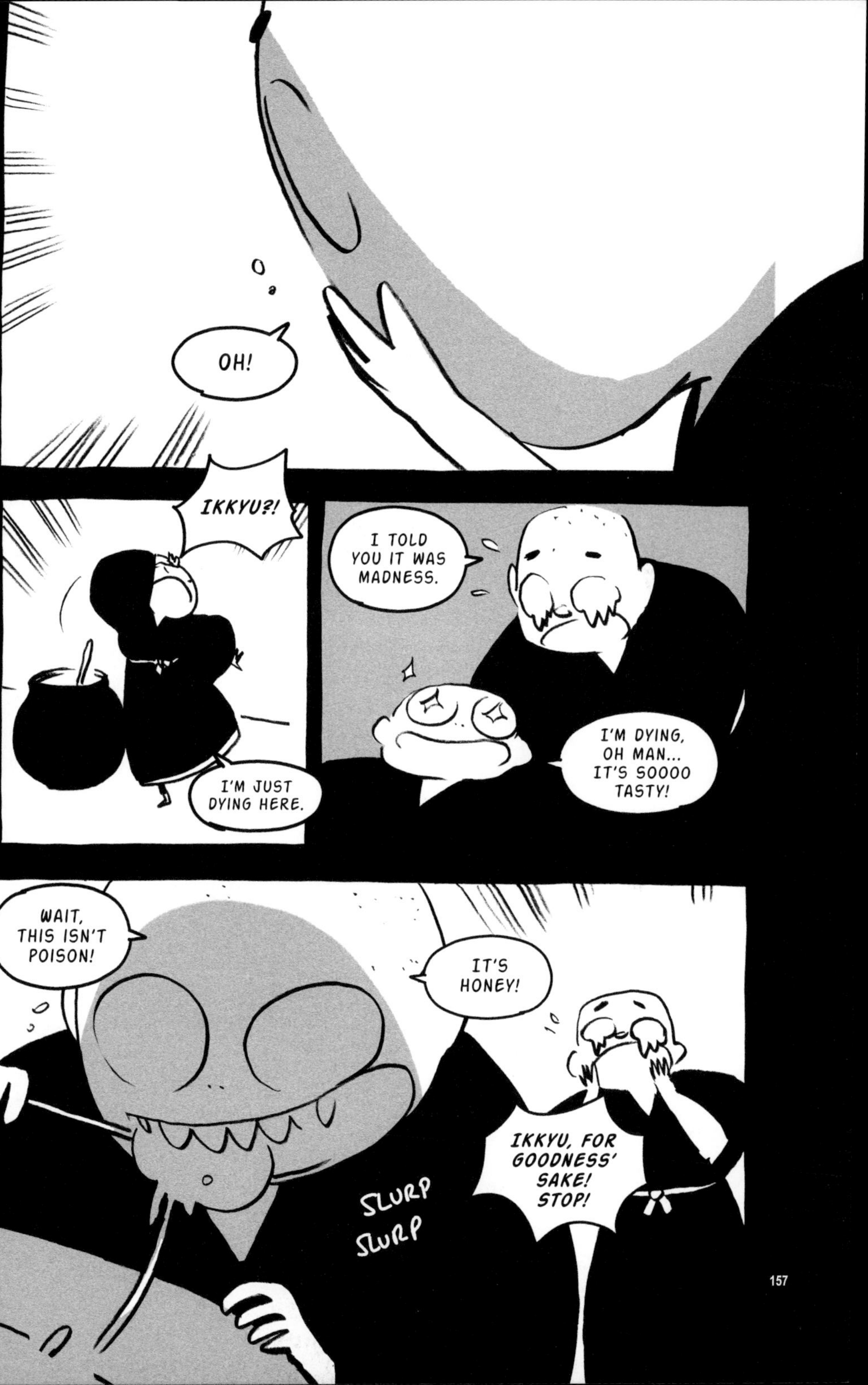
OH!
IKKYU?!
I'M JUST DYING HERE.
I TOLD YOU IT WAS MADNESS.
I'M DYING, OH MAN... IT'S SOOOO TASTY!
WAIT, THIS ISN'T POISON!
IT'S HONEY!
SLURP SLURP
IKKYU, FOR GOODNESS' SAKE! STOP!

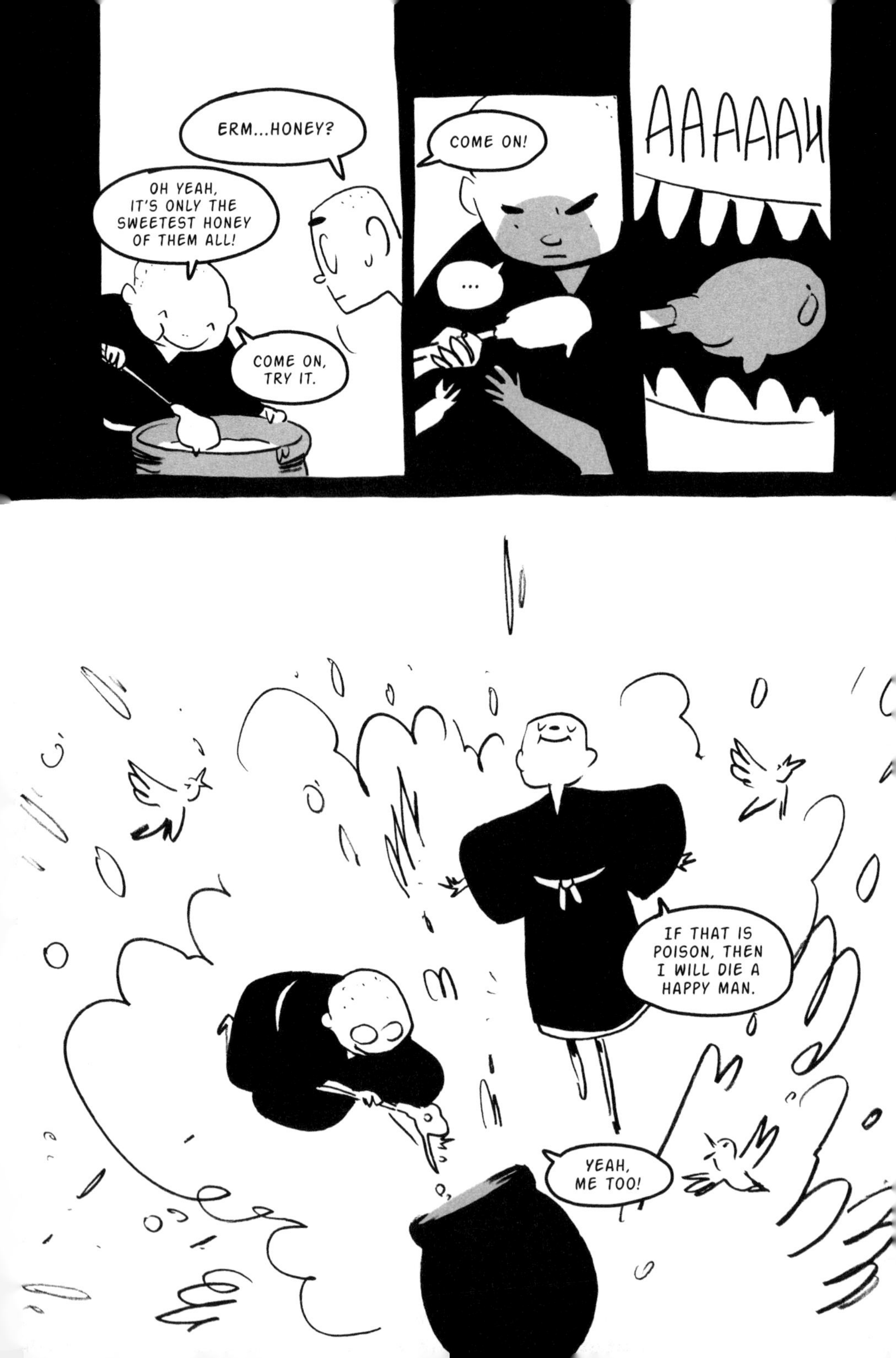
ERM...HONEY?
OH YEAH, IT'S ONLY THE SWEETEST HONEY OF THEM ALL!
COME ON, TRY IT.
COME ON!
...
AAAAAH
IF THAT IS POISON, THEN I WILL DIE A HAPPY MAN.
YEAH, ME TOO!

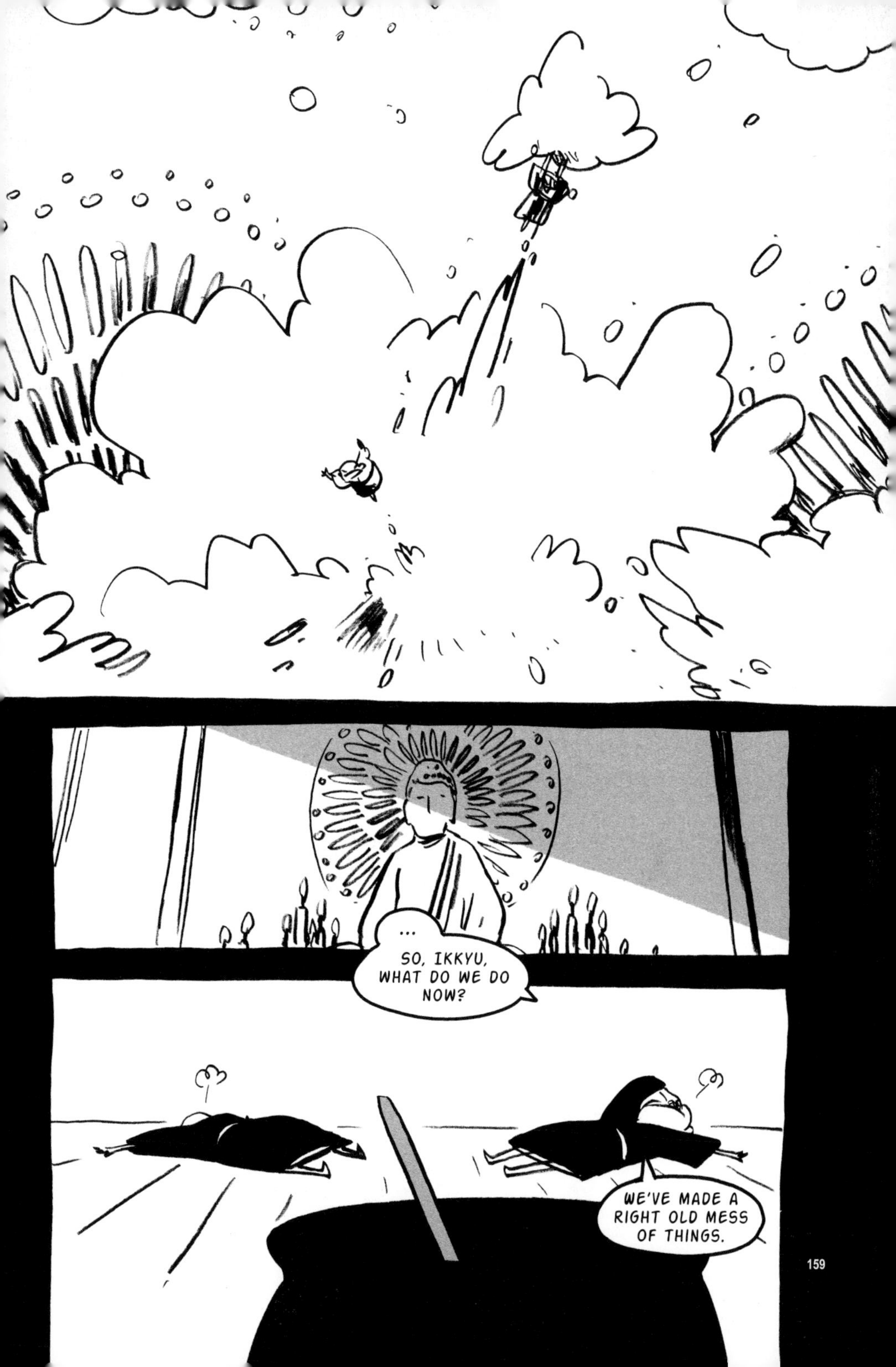
...
SO, IKKYU, WHAT DO WE DO NOW?
WE'VE MADE A RIGHT OLD MESS OF THINGS.

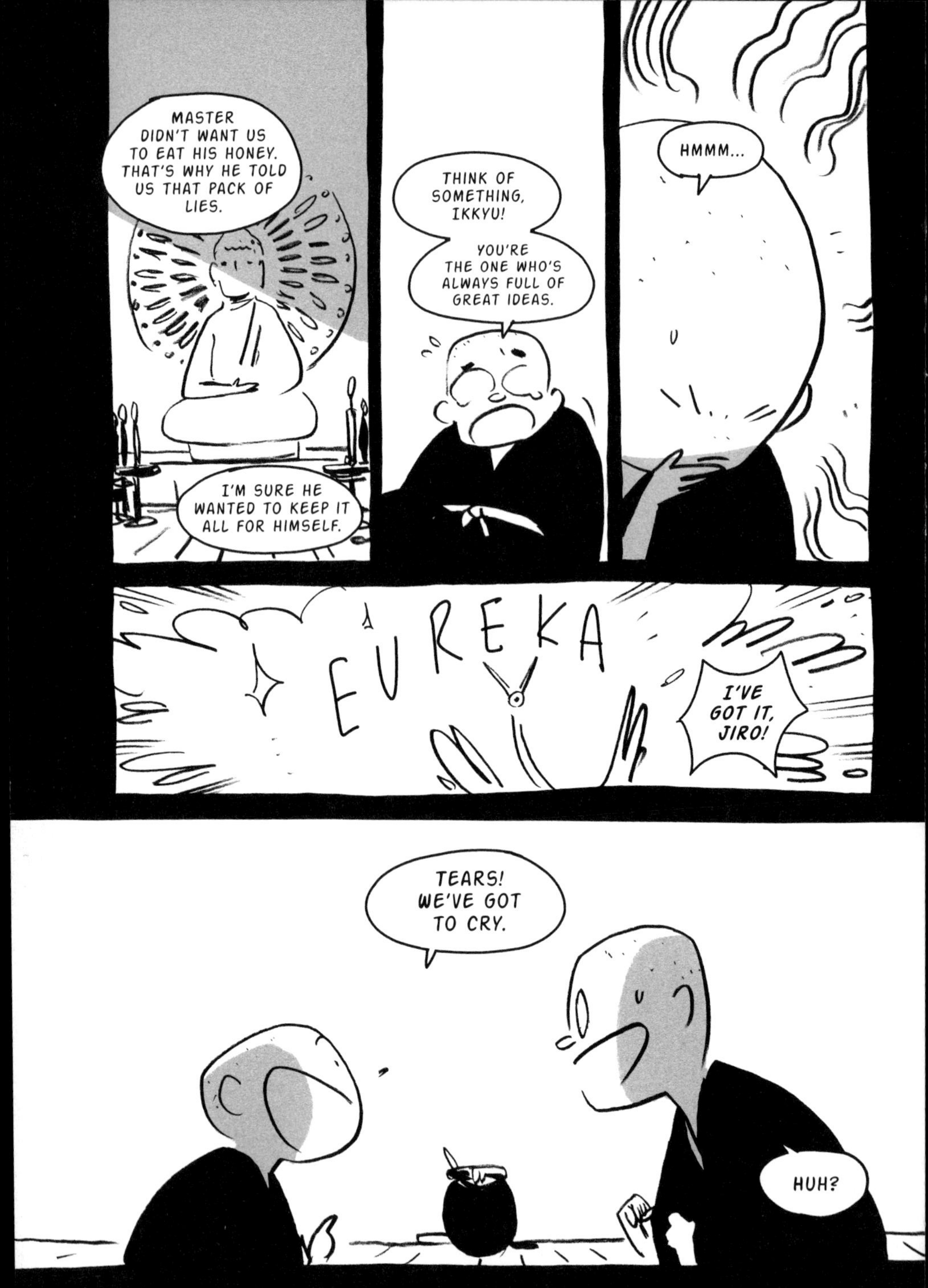
MASTER DIDN'T WANT US TO EAT HIS HONEY. THAT'S WHY HE TOLD US THAT PACK OF LIES.
I'M SURE HE WANTED TO KEEP IT ALL FOR HIMSELF.
THINK OF SOMETHING, IKKYU!
YOU'RE THE ONE WHO'S ALWAYS FULL OF GREAT IDEAS.
HMMM...
EUREKA
I'VE GOT IT, JIRO!
TEARS! WE'VE GOT TO CRY.
HUH?

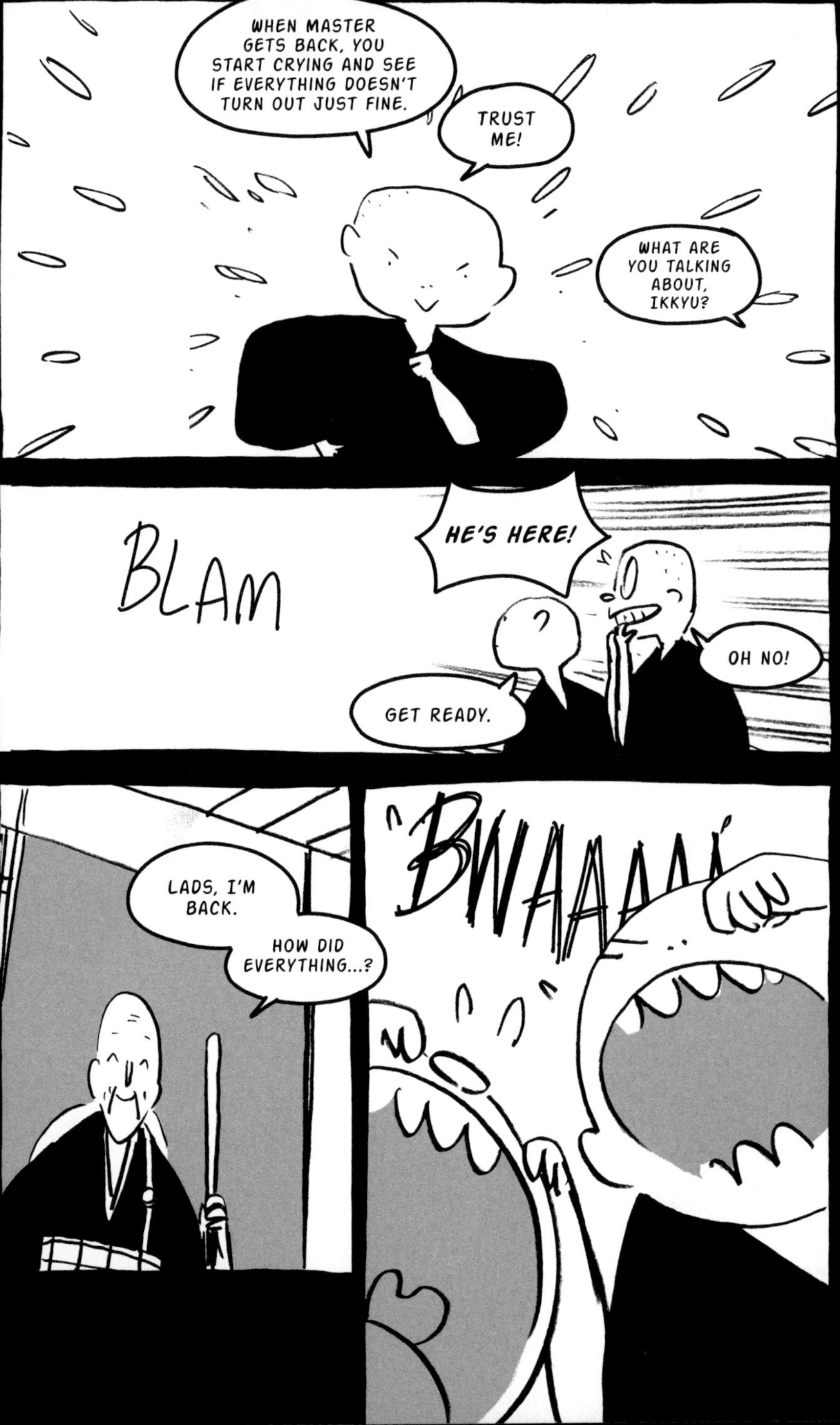
WHEN MASTER GETS BACK, YOU START CRYING AND SEE IF EVERYTHING DOESN'T TURN OUT JUST FINE.
TRUST ME!
WHAT ARE YOU TALKING ABOUT, IKKYU?
BLAM
HE'S HERE!
OH NO!
GET READY.
LADS, I'M BACK.
HOW DID EVERYTHING...?
BWAAAA

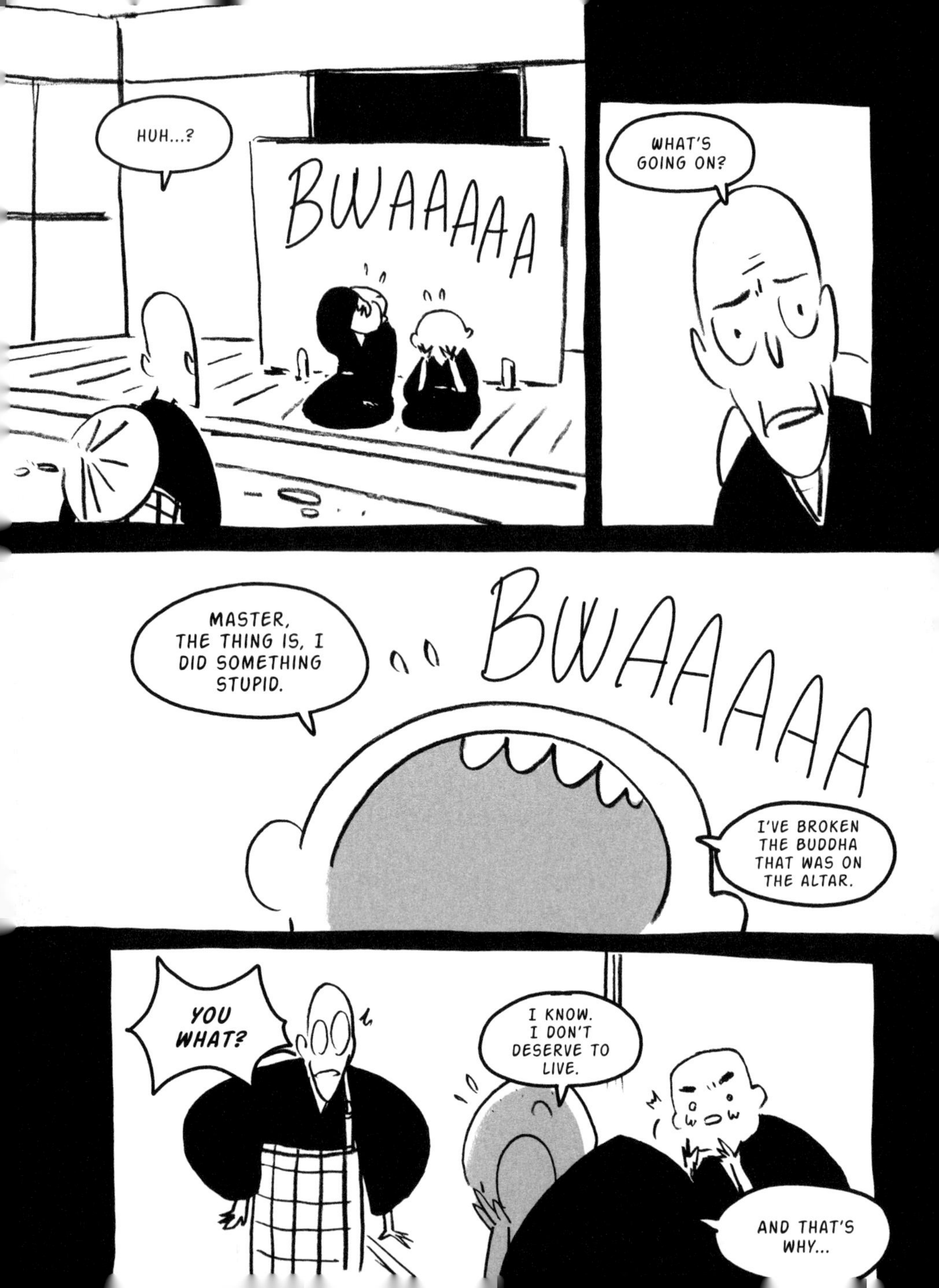
HUH...?
BWAAAAAA
WHAT'S GOING ON?
MASTER, THE THING IS, I DID SOMETHING STUPID.
BWAAAAAA
I'VE BROKEN THE BUDDHA THAT WAS ON THE ALTAR.
YOU WHAT?
I KNOW. I DON'T DESERVE TO LIVE.
AND THAT'S WHY...

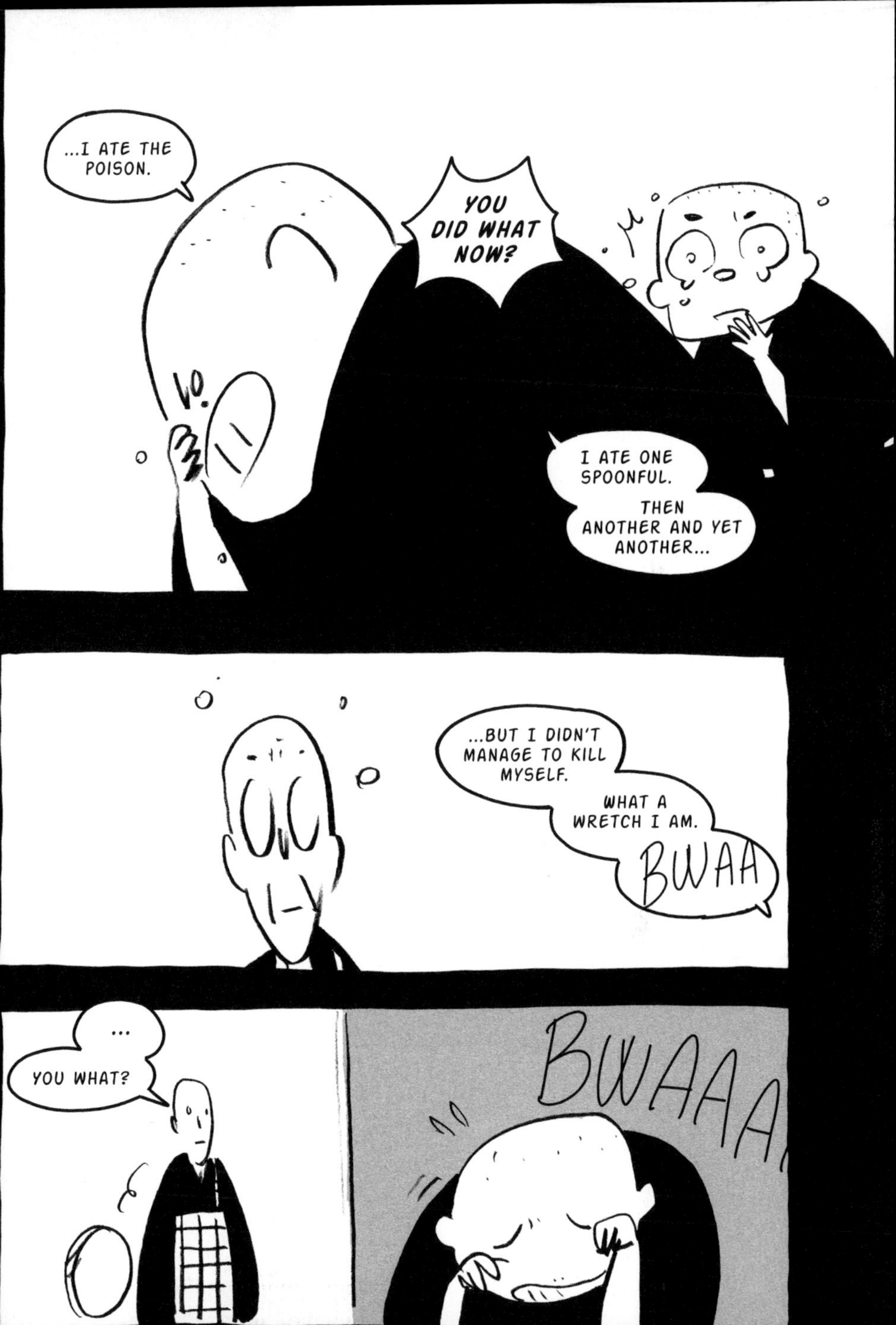
...I ATE THE POISON.
YOU DID WHAT NOW?
I ATE ONE SPOONFUL.
THEN ANOTHER AND YET ANOTHER...
...BUT I DIDN'T MANAGE TO KILL MYSELF.
WHAT A WRETCH I AM.
BWAA
...
YOU WHAT?
BWAAA

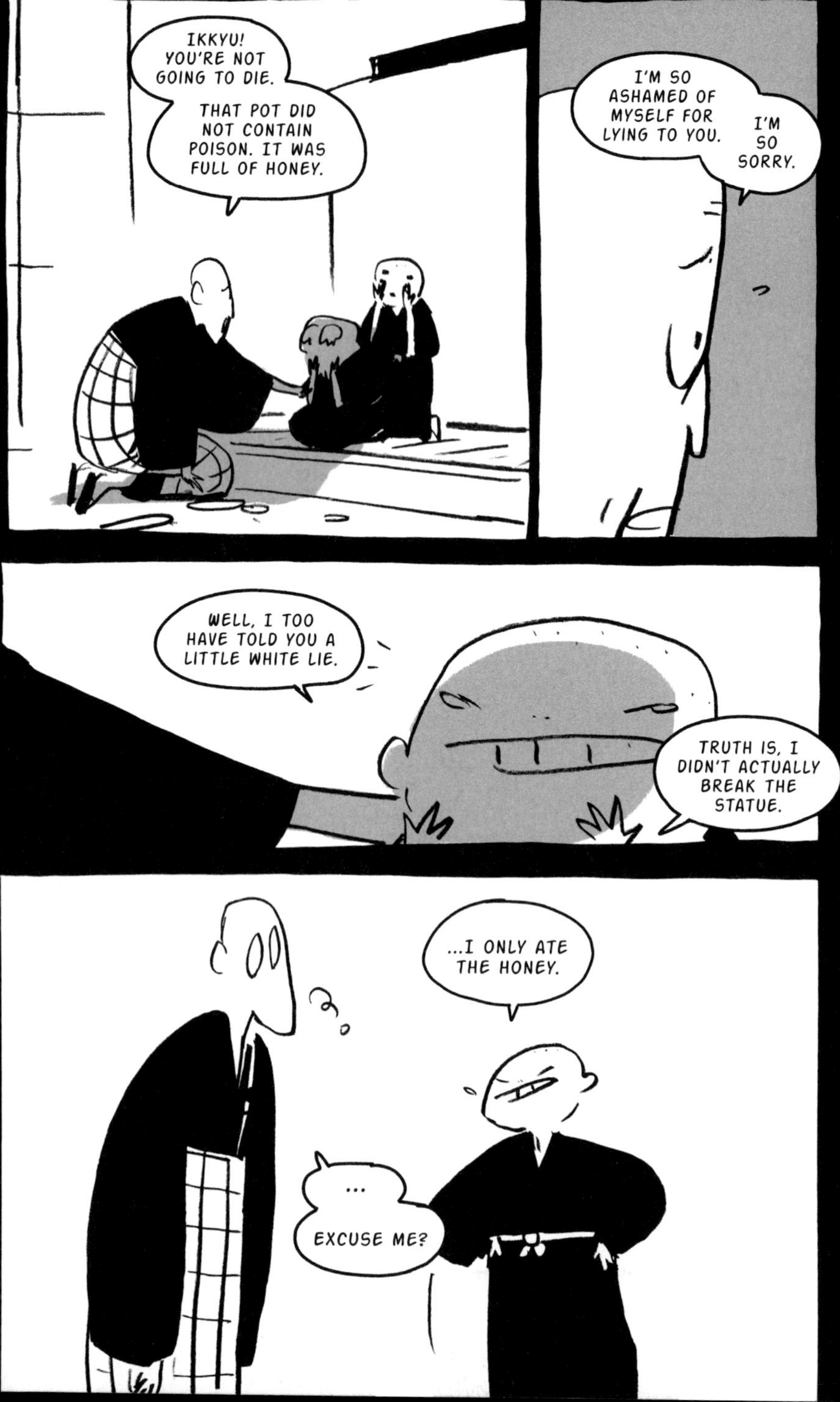
IKKYU! YOU'RE NOT GOING TO DIE.
THAT POT DID NOT CONTAIN POISON. IT WAS FULL OF HONEY.
I'M SO ASHAMED OF MYSELF FOR LYING TO YOU.
I'M SO SORRY.
WELL, I TOO HAVE TOLD YOU A LITTLE WHITE LIE.
TRUTH IS, I DIDN'T ACTUALLY BREAK THE STATUE.
...I ONLY ATE THE HONEY.
...
EXCUSE ME?

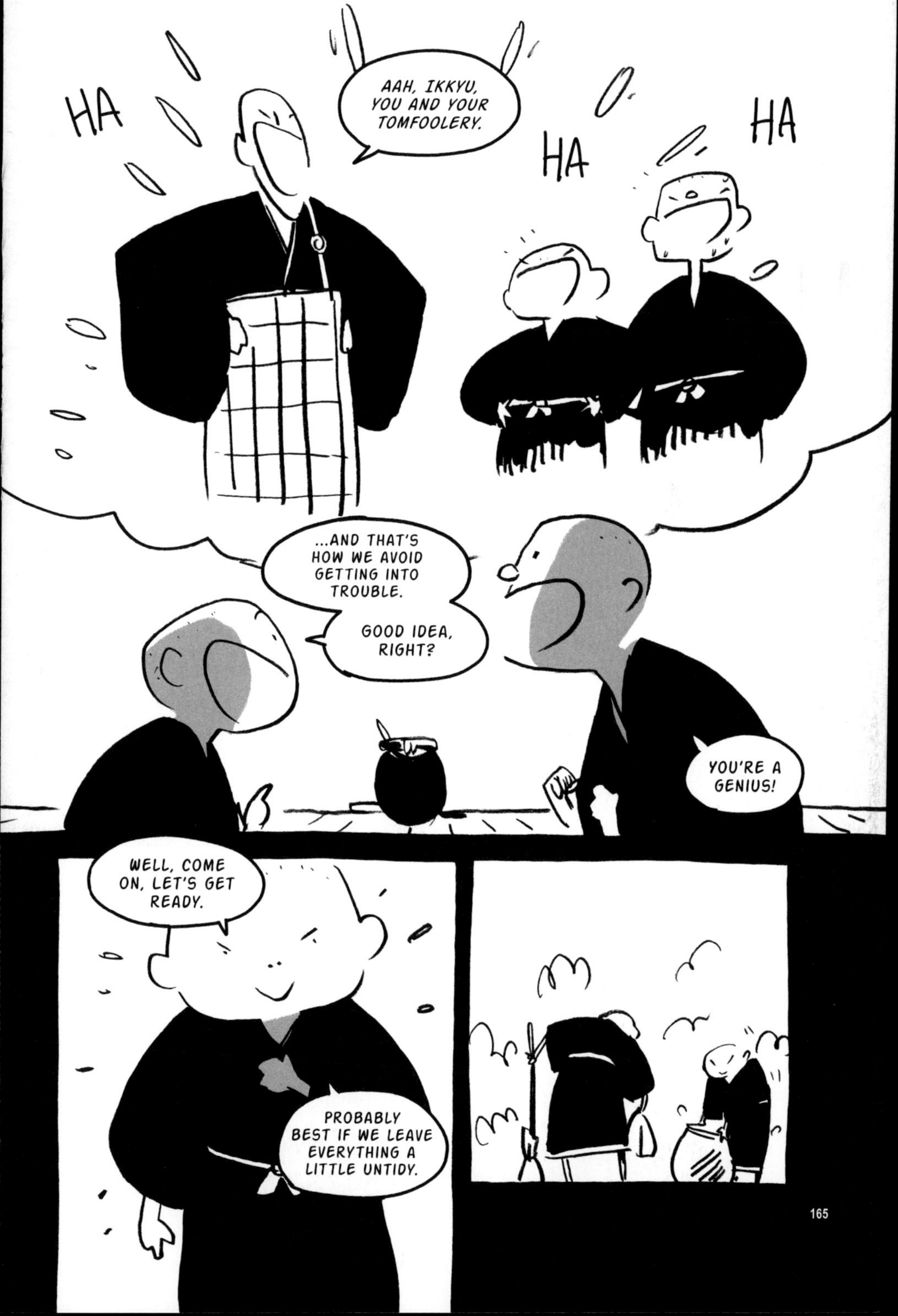
HA
AAH, IKKYU, YOU AND YOUR TOMFOOLERY.
HA
HA
...AND THAT'S HOW WE AVOID GETTING INTO TROUBLE.
GOOD IDEA, RIGHT?
YOU'RE A GENIUS!
WELL, COME ON, LET'S GET READY.
PROBABLY BEST IF WE LEAVE EVERYTHING A LITTLE UNTIDY.

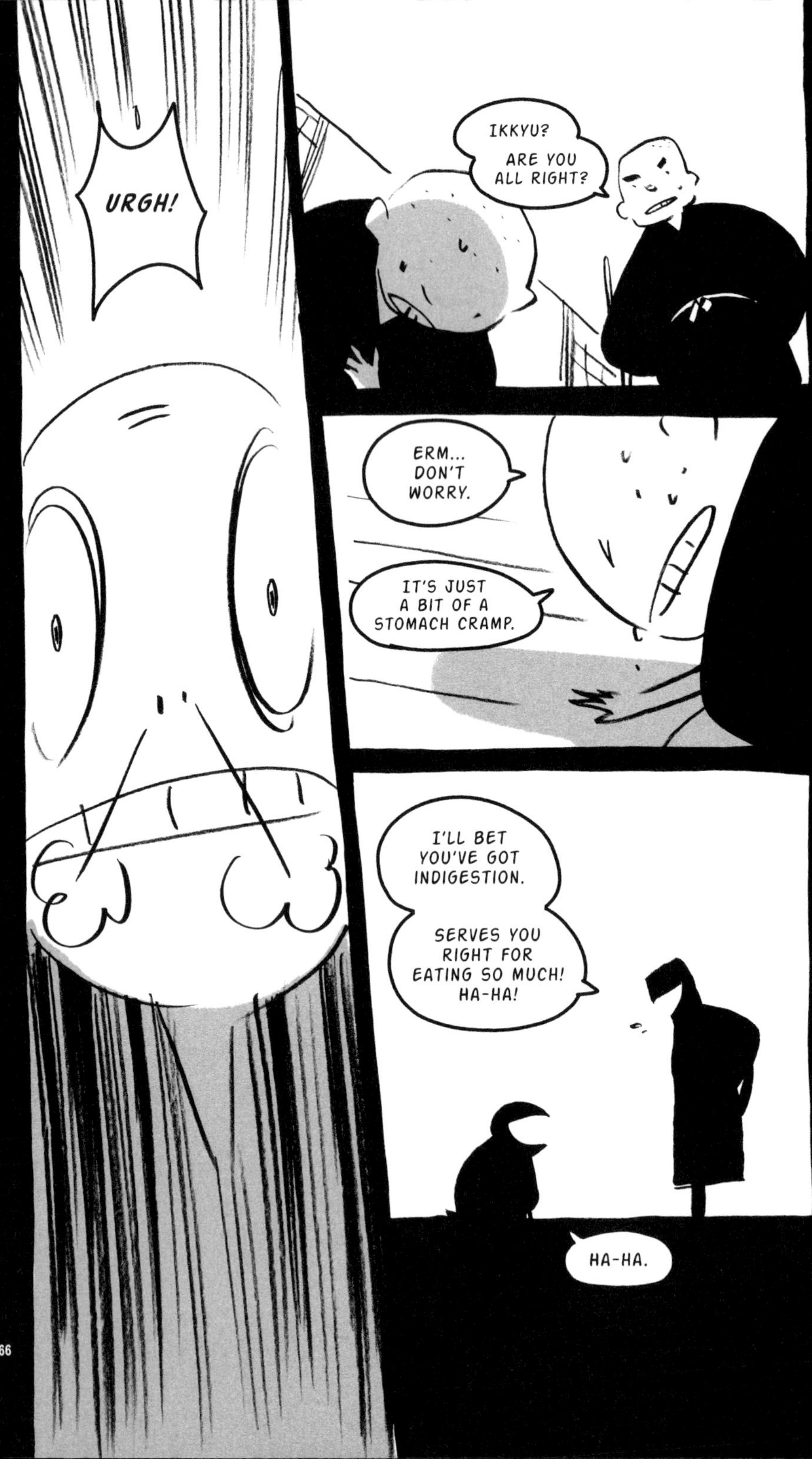
URGH!
IKKYU?
ARE YOU ALL RIGHT?
ERM... DON'T WORRY.
IT'S JUST A BIT OF A STOMACH CRAMP.
I'LL BET YOU'VE GOT INDIGESTION.
SERVES YOU RIGHT FOR EATING SO MUCH! HA-HA!
HA-HA.

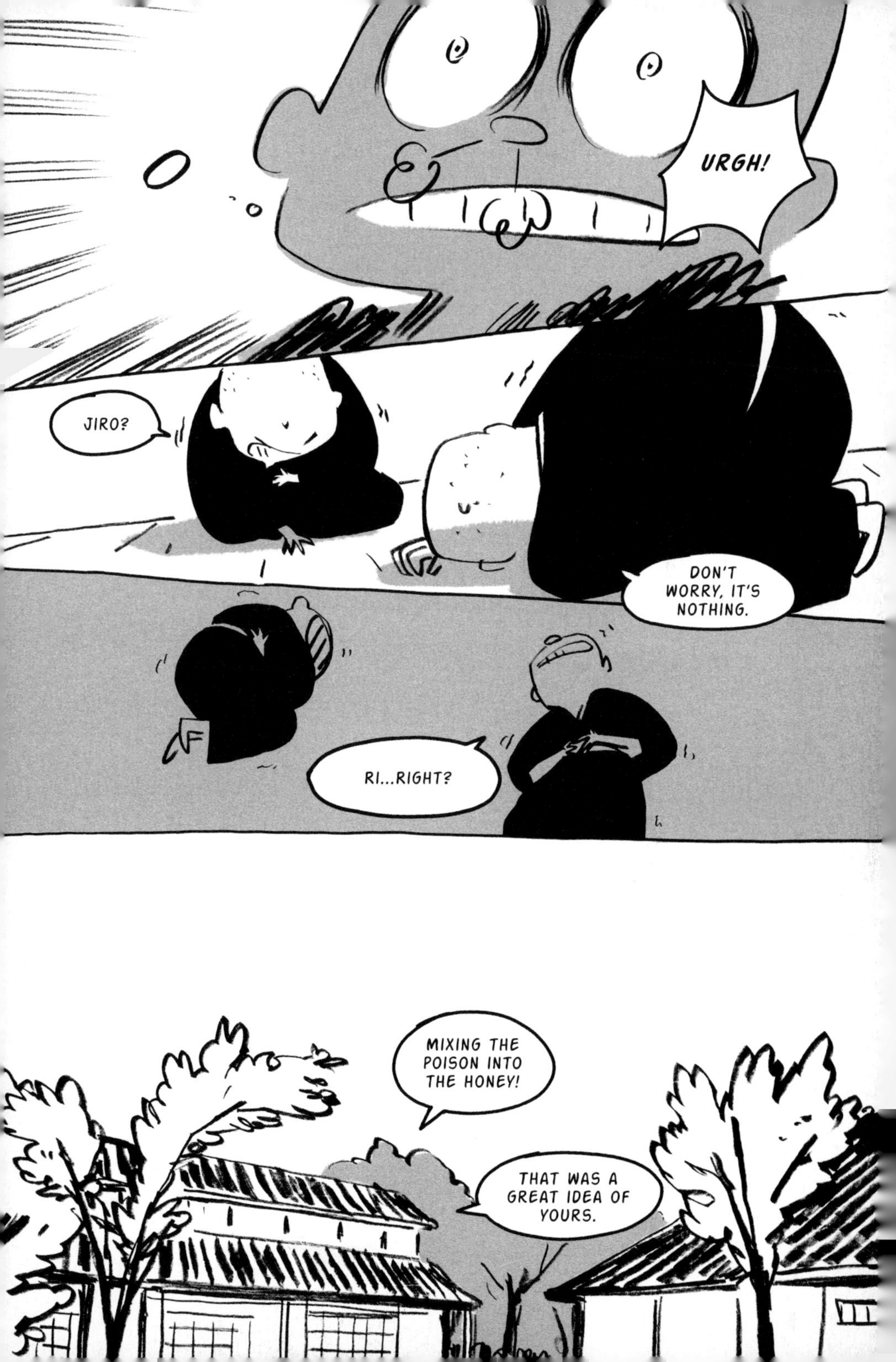
URGH!
JIRO?
DON'T WORRY, IT'S NOTHING.
RI...RIGHT?
MIXING THE POISON INTO THE HONEY!
THAT WAS A GREAT IDEA OF YOURS.

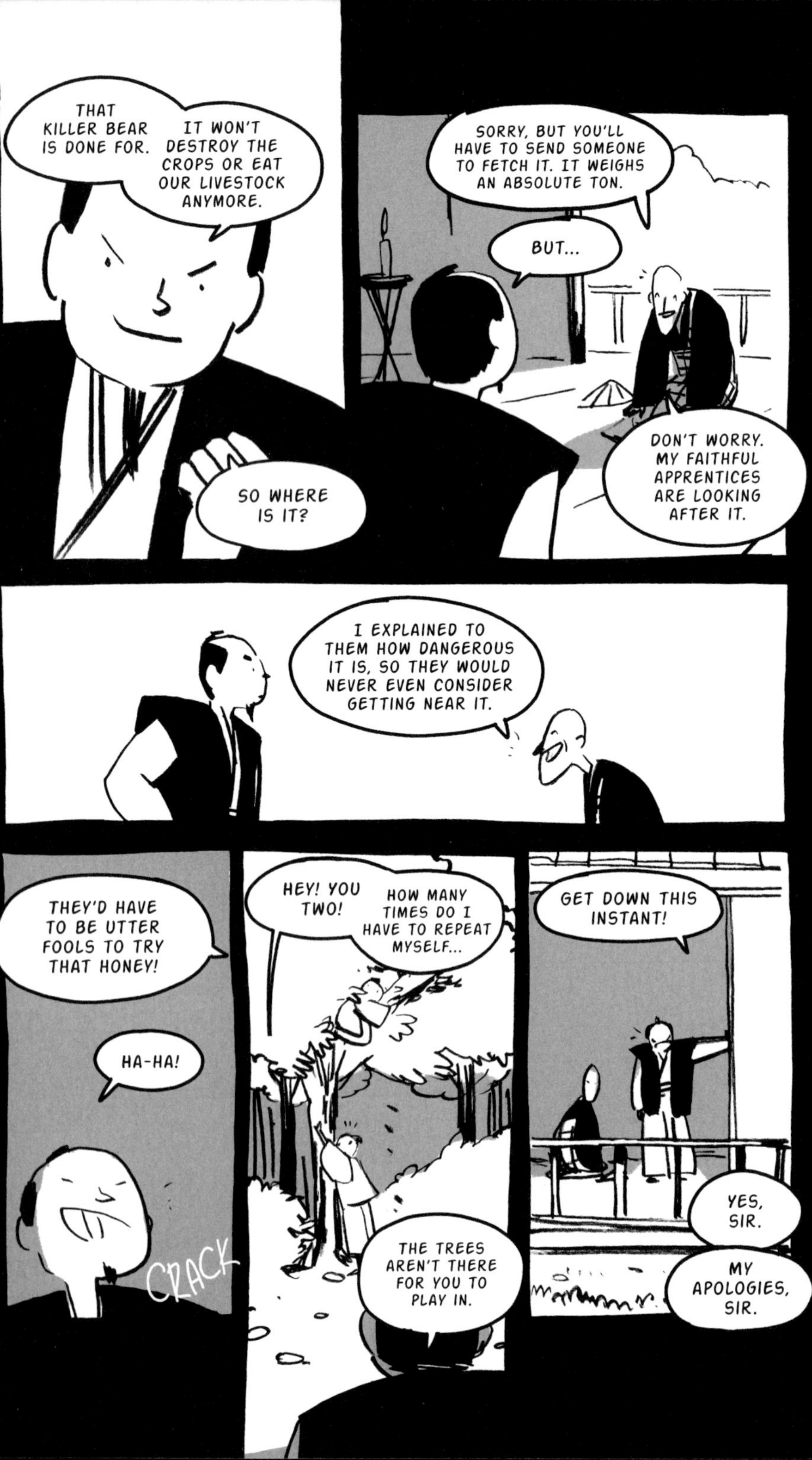
THAT KILLER BEAR IS DONE FOR.
IT WON'T DESTROY THE CROPS OR EAT OUR LIVESTOCK ANYMORE.
SO WHERE IS IT?
SORRY, BUT YOU'LL HAVE TO SEND SOMEONE TO FETCH IT. IT WEIGHS AN ABSOLUTE TON.
BUT...
DON'T WORRY. MY FAITHFUL APPRENTICES ARE LOOKING AFTER IT.
I EXPLAINED TO THEM HOW DANGEROUS IT IS, SO THEY WOULD NEVER EVEN CONSIDER GETTING NEAR IT.
THEY'D HAVE TO BE UTTER FOOLS TO TRY THAT HONEY!
HA-HA!
CRACK
HEY! YOU TWO!
HOW MANY TIMES DO I HAVE TO REPEAT MYSELF...
THE TREES AREN'T THERE FOR YOU TO PLAY IN.
GET DOWN THIS INSTANT!
YES, SIR.
MY APOLOGIES, SIR.

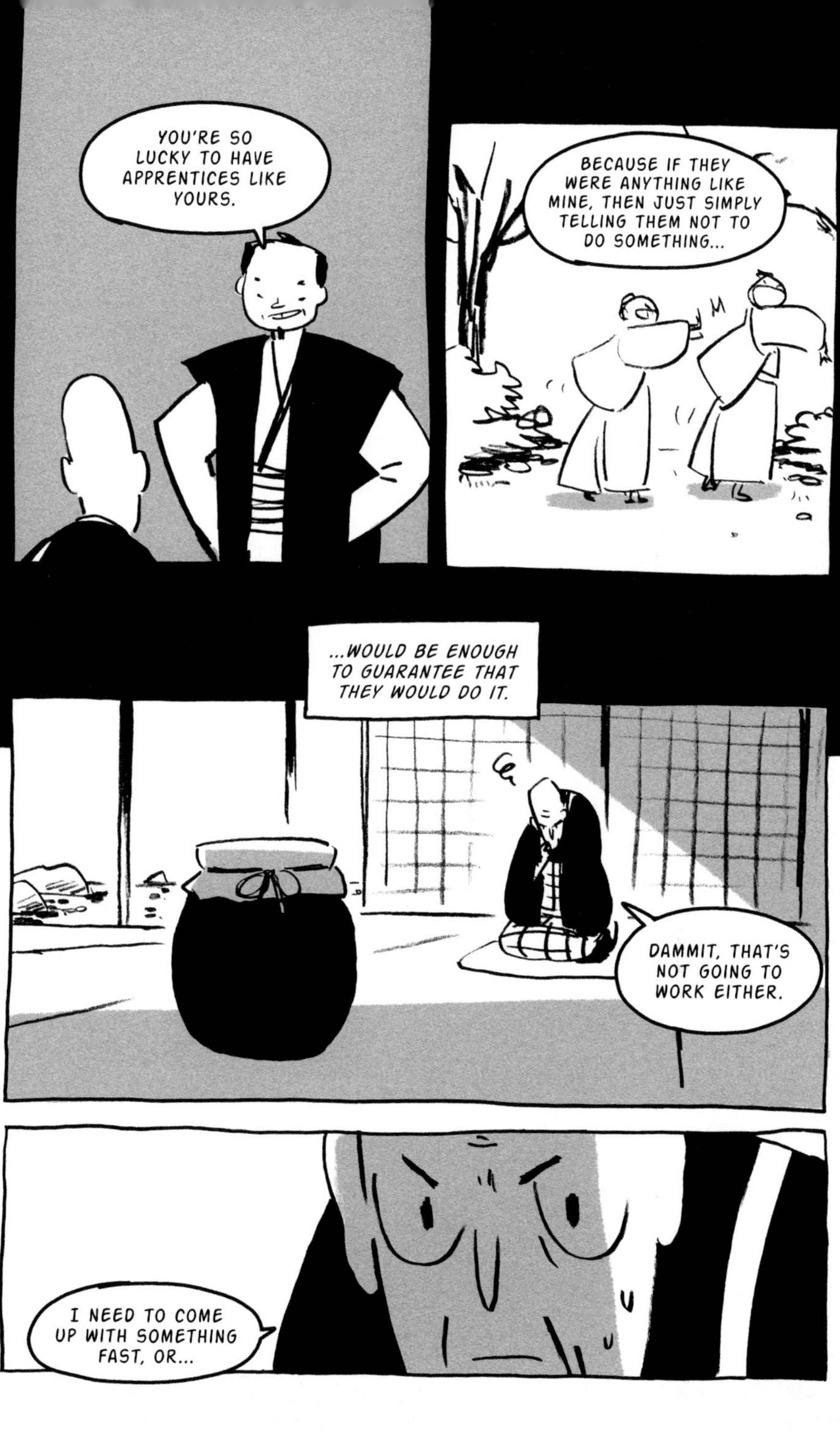
YOU'RE SO LUCKY TO HAVE APPRENTICES LIKE YOURS.
BECAUSE IF THEY WERE ANYTHING LIKE MINE, THEN JUST SIMPLY TELLING THEM NOT TO DO SOMETHING...
...WOULD BE ENOUGH TO GUARANTEE THAT THEY WOULD DO IT.
DAMMIT, THAT'S NOT GOING TO WORK EITHER.
I NEED TO COME UP WITH SOMETHING FAST, OR...

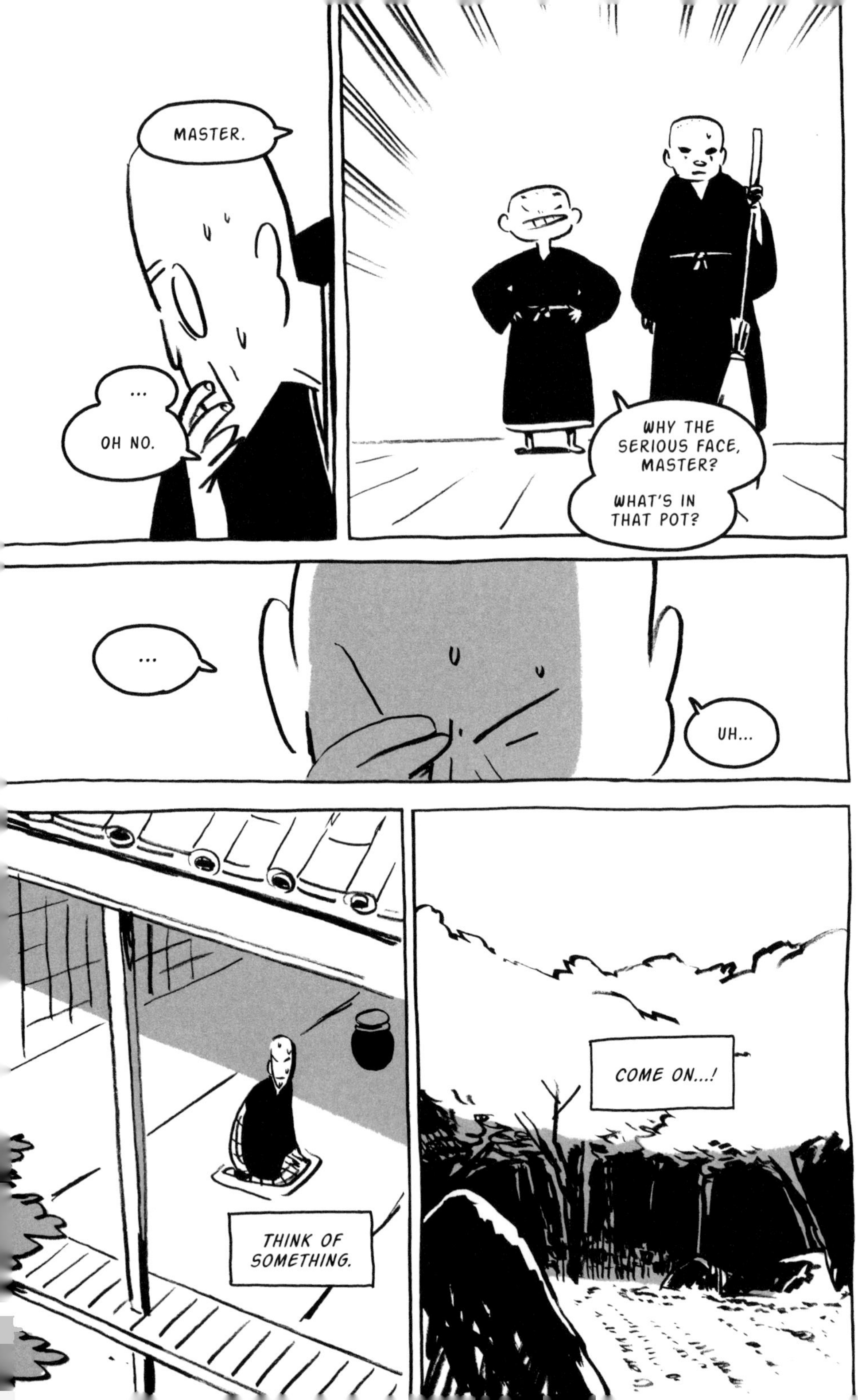
MASTER.
...
OH NO.
WHY THE SERIOUS FACE, MASTER?
WHAT'S IN THAT POT?
...
UH...
THINK OF SOMETHING.
COME ON...!

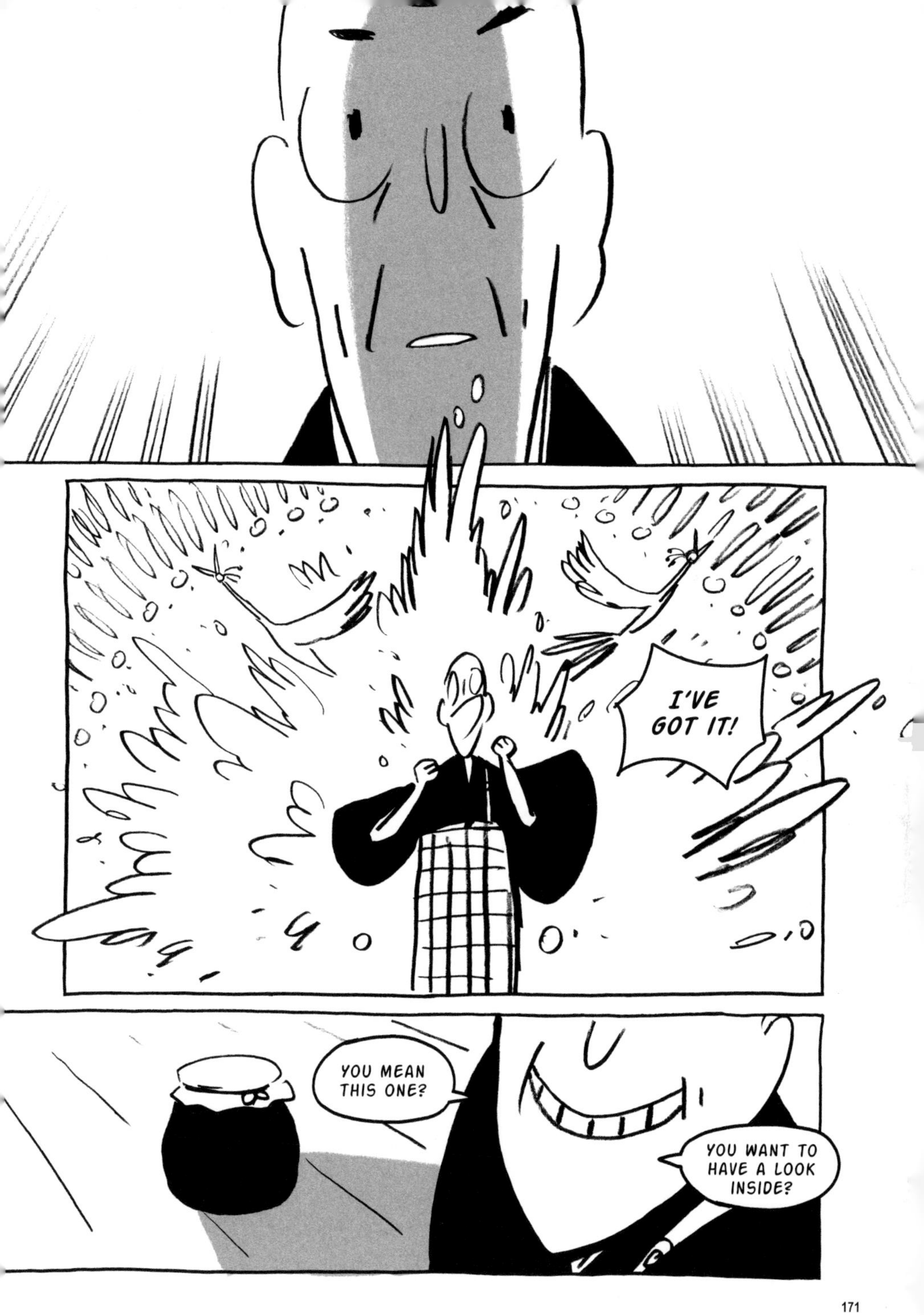
I'VE GOT IT!
YOU MEAN THIS ONE?
YOU WANT TO HAVE A LOOK INSIDE?

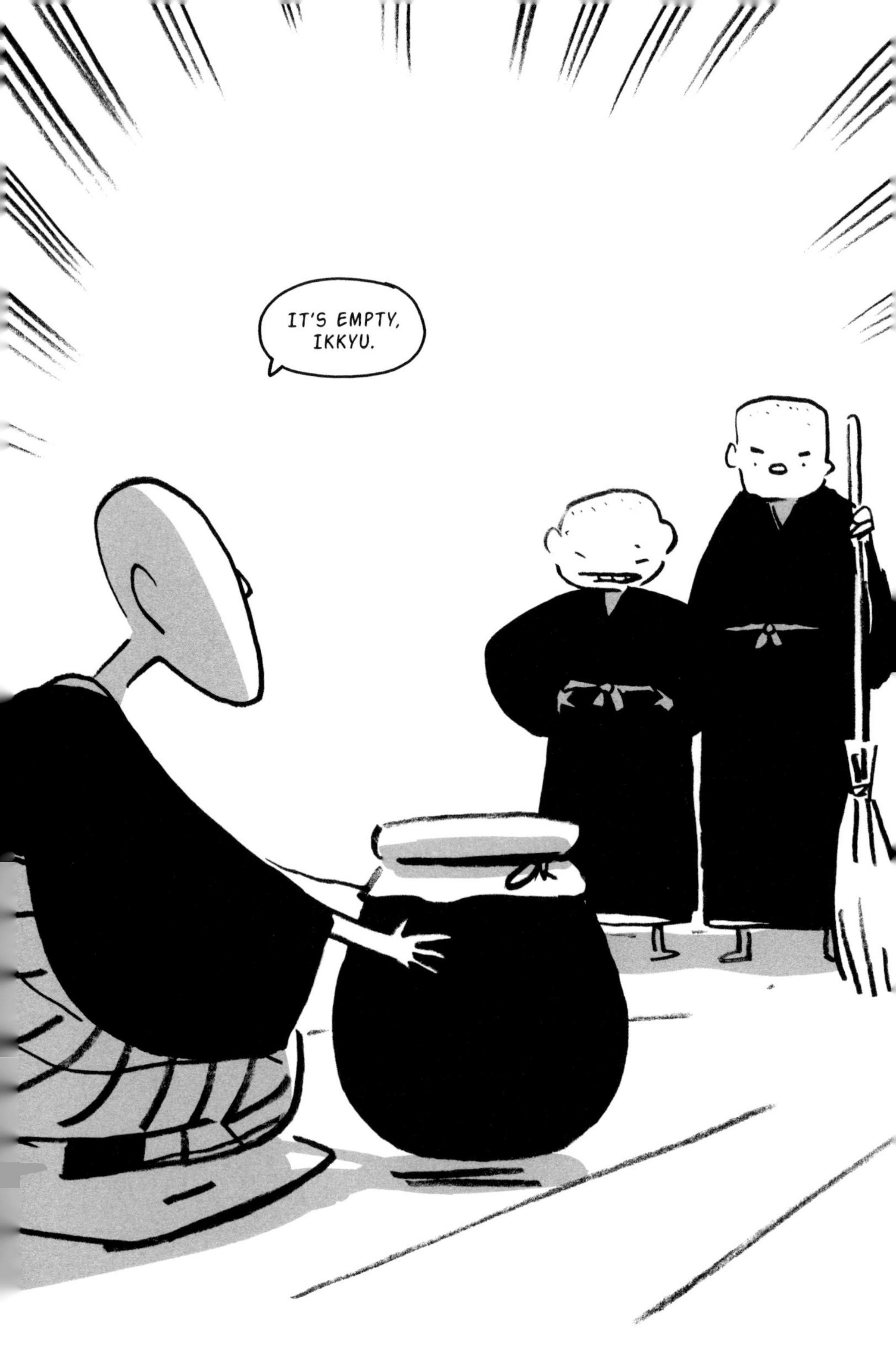
IT'S EMPTY, IKKYU.

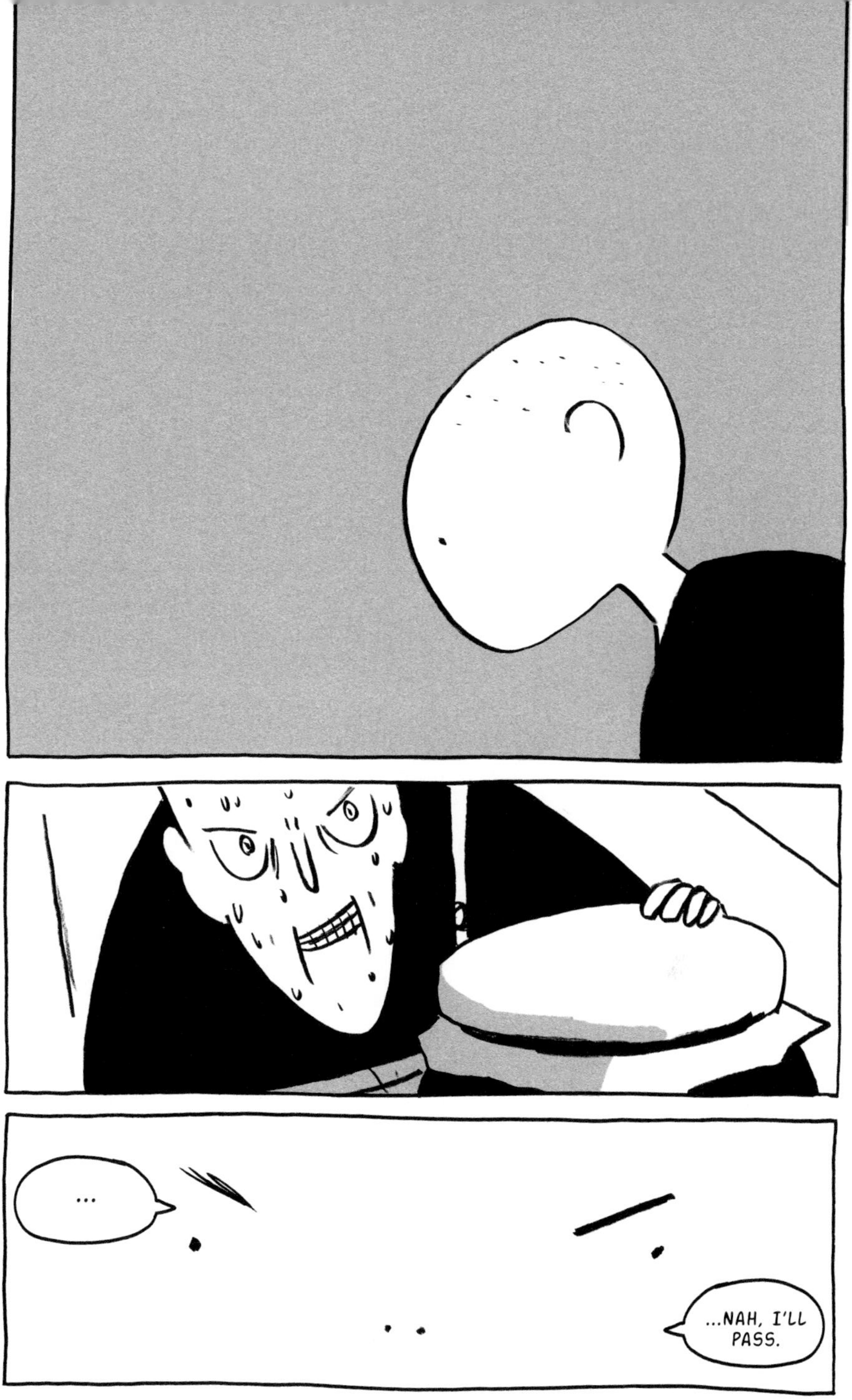
...
...NAH, I'LL PASS.

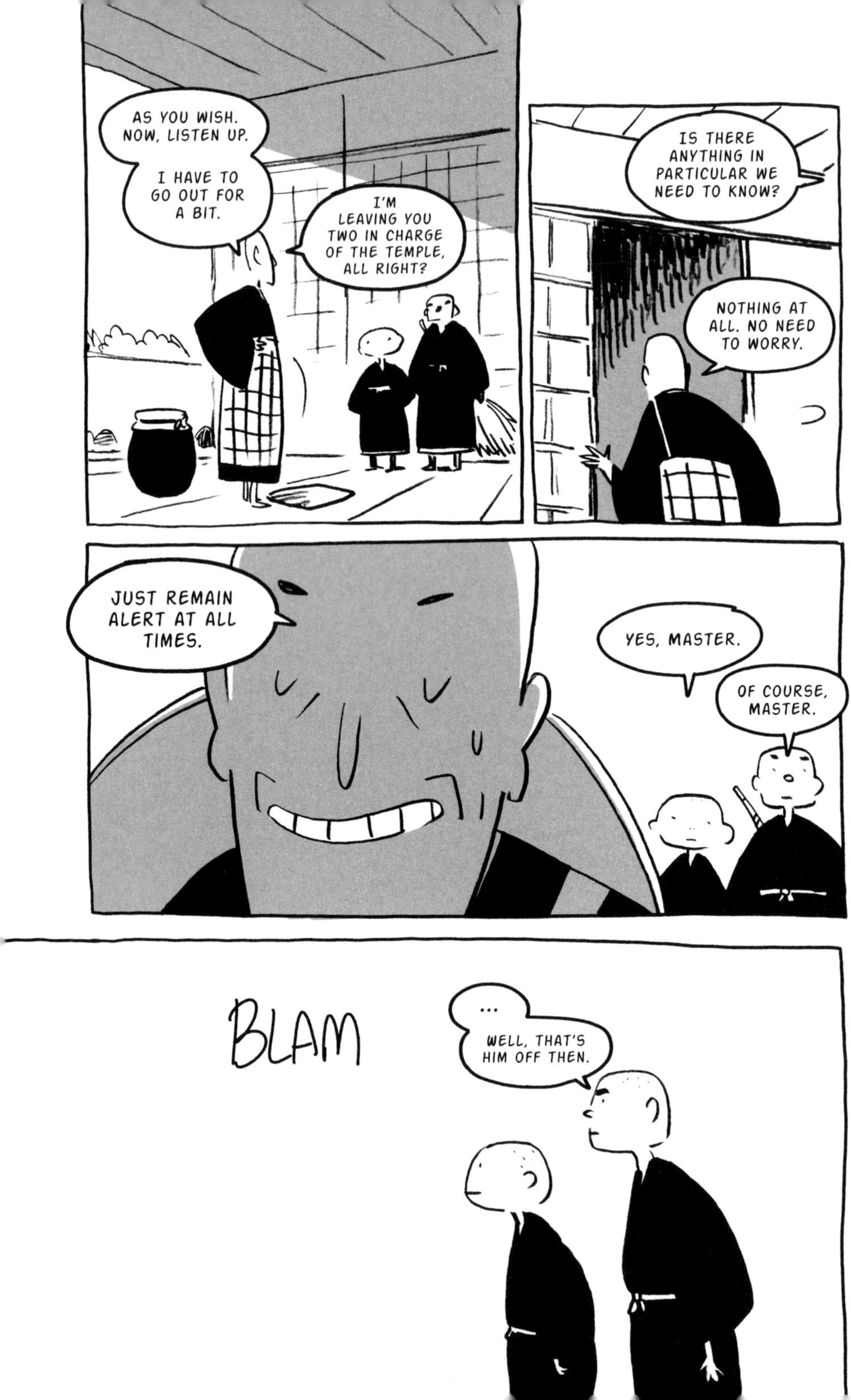
AS YOU WISH. NOW, LISTEN UP.
I HAVE TO GO OUT FOR A BIT.
I'M LEAVING YOU TWO IN CHARGE OF THE TEMPLE, ALL RIGHT?
IS THERE ANYTHING IN PARTICULAR WE NEED TO KNOW?
NOTHING AT ALL. NO NEED TO WORRY.
JUST REMAIN ALERT AT ALL TIMES.
YES, MASTER.
OF COURSE, MASTER.
BLAM
...
WELL, THAT'S HIM OFF THEN.

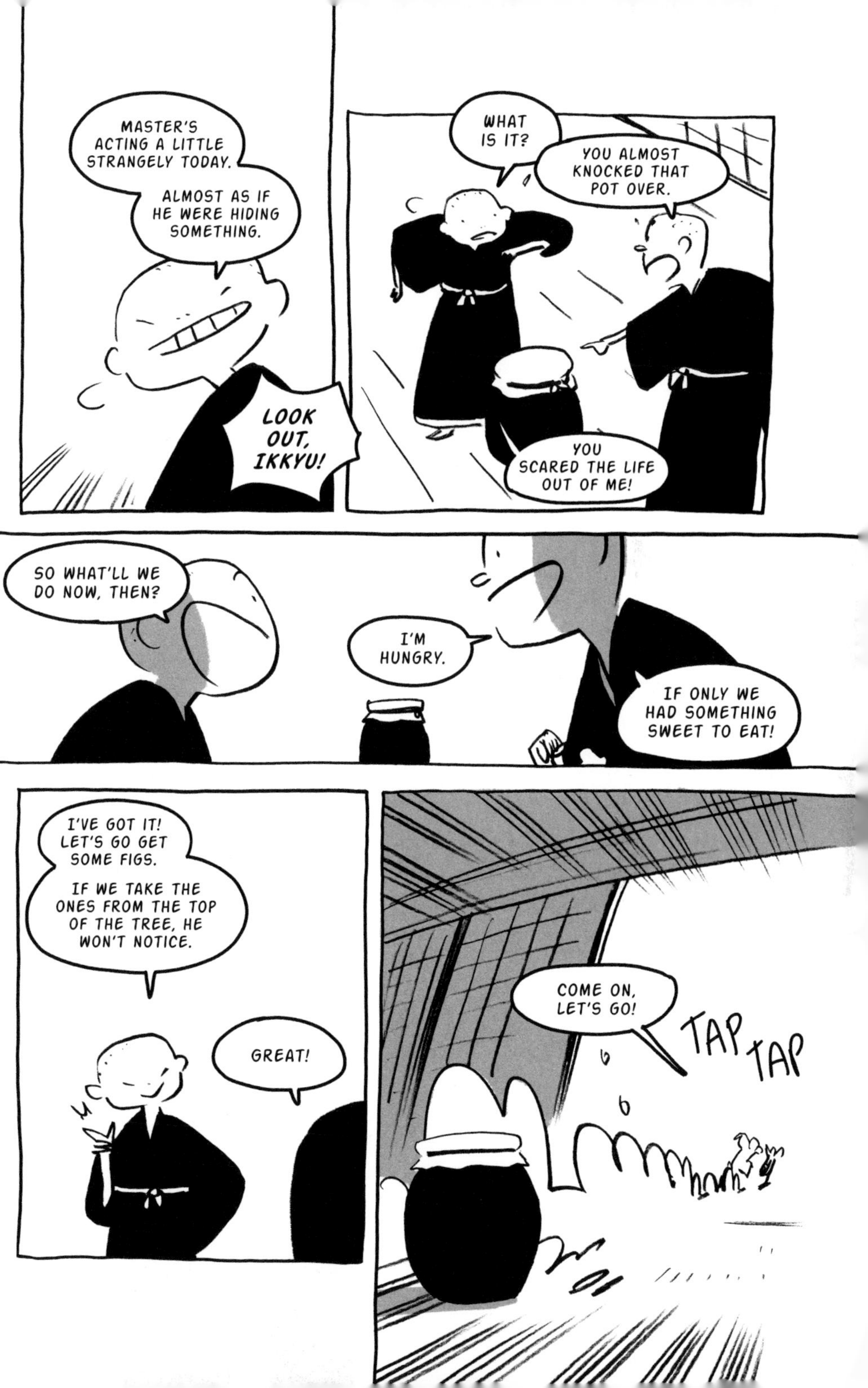
MASTER'S ACTING A LITTLE STRANGELY TODAY.
ALMOST AS IF HE WERE HIDING SOMETHING.
LOOK OUT, IKKYU!
WHAT IS IT?
YOU ALMOST KNOCKED THAT POT OVER.
YOU SCARED THE LIFE OUT OF ME!
SO WHAT'LL WE DO NOW, THEN?
I'M HUNGRY.
IF ONLY WE HAD SOMETHING SWEET TO EAT!
I'VE GOT IT! LET'S GO GET SOME FIGS.
IF WE TAKE THE ONES FROM THE TOP OF THE TREE, HE WON'T NOTICE.
GREAT!
COME ON, LET'S GO!
TAP TAP

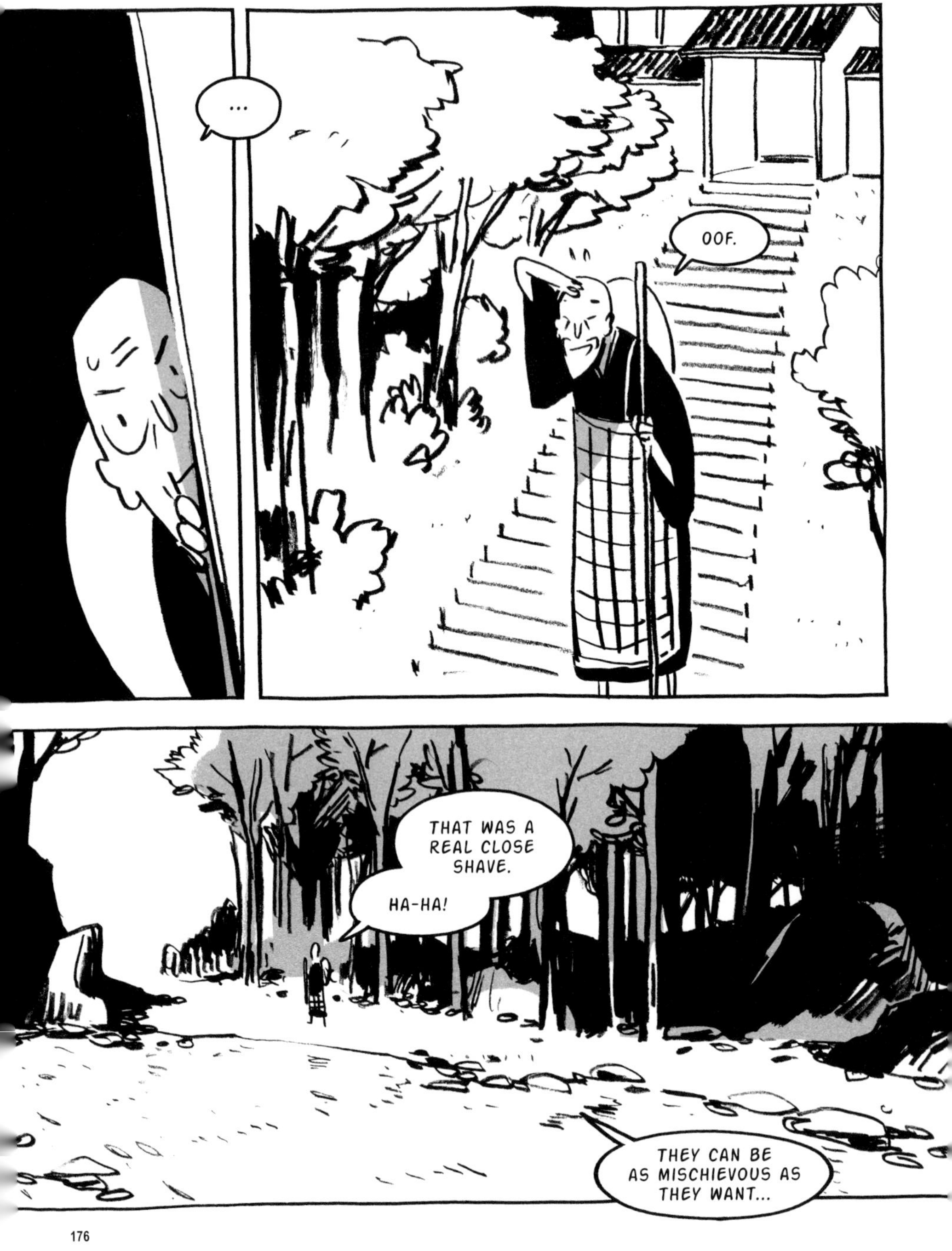
...
OOF.
THAT WAS A REAL CLOSE SHAVE.
HA-HA!
THEY CAN BE AS MISCHIEVOUS AS THEY WANT...

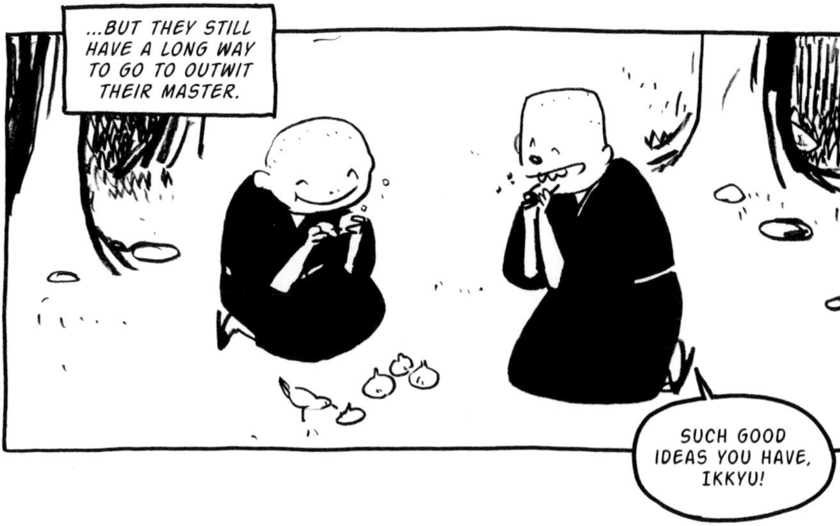
...BUT THEY STILL HAVE A LONG WAY TO GO TO OUTWIT THEIR MASTER.
SUCH GOOD IDEAS YOU HAVE, IKKYU!

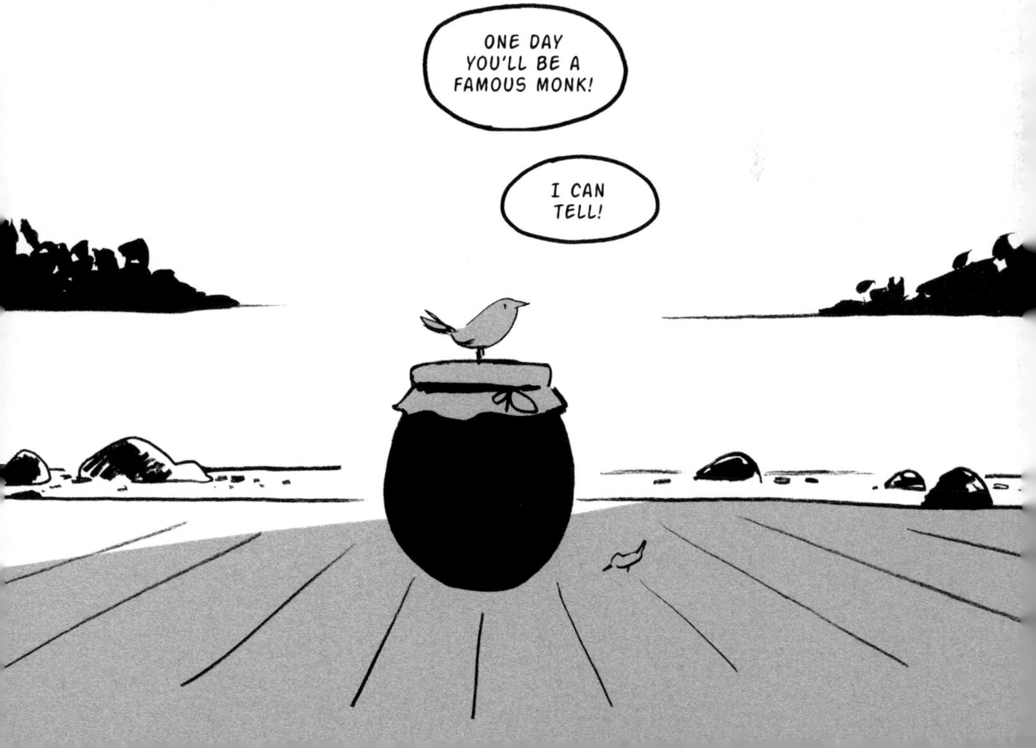
ONE DAY YOU'LL BE A FAMOUS MONK!
I CAN TELL!

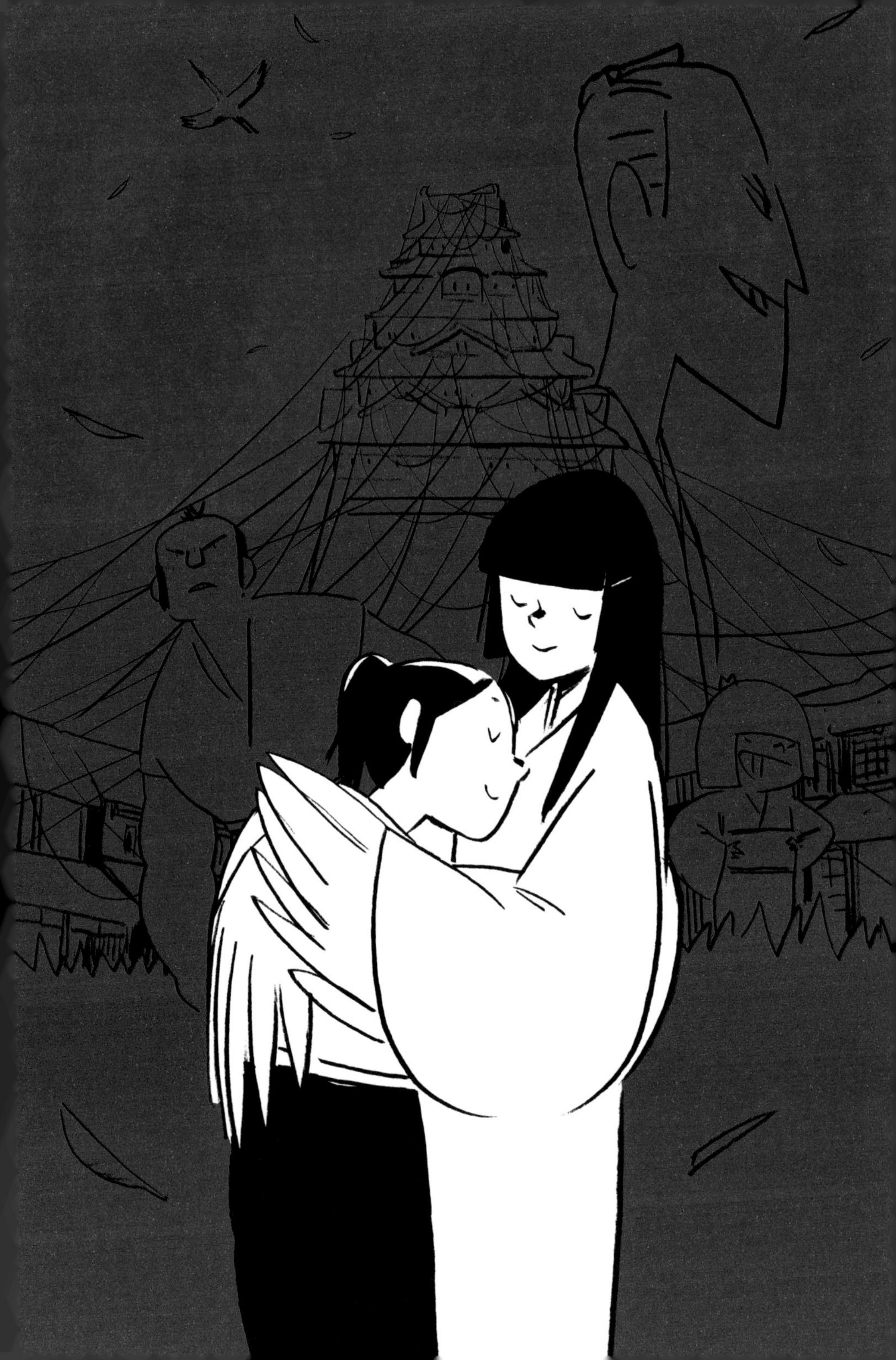

THE PROMISE

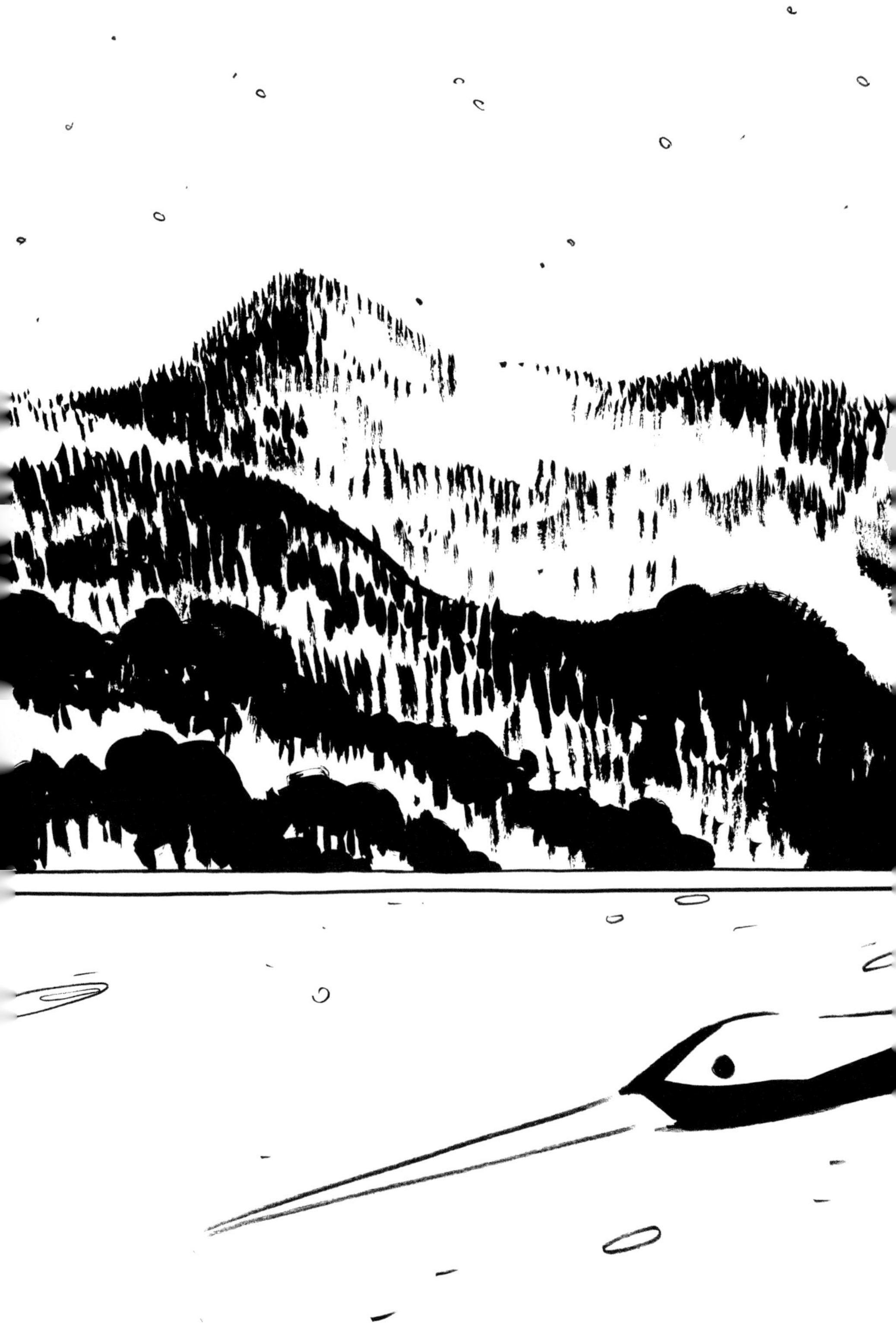

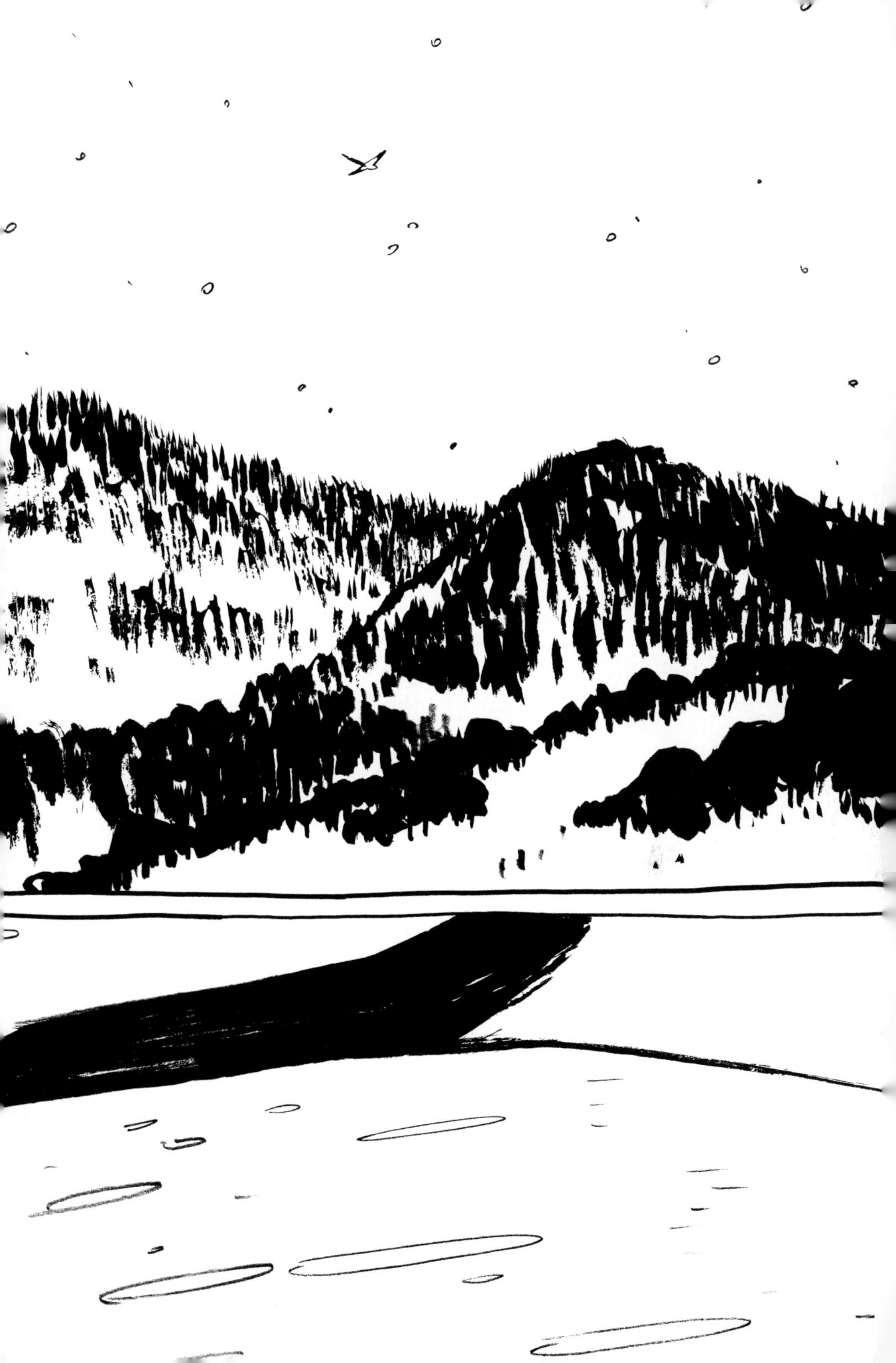

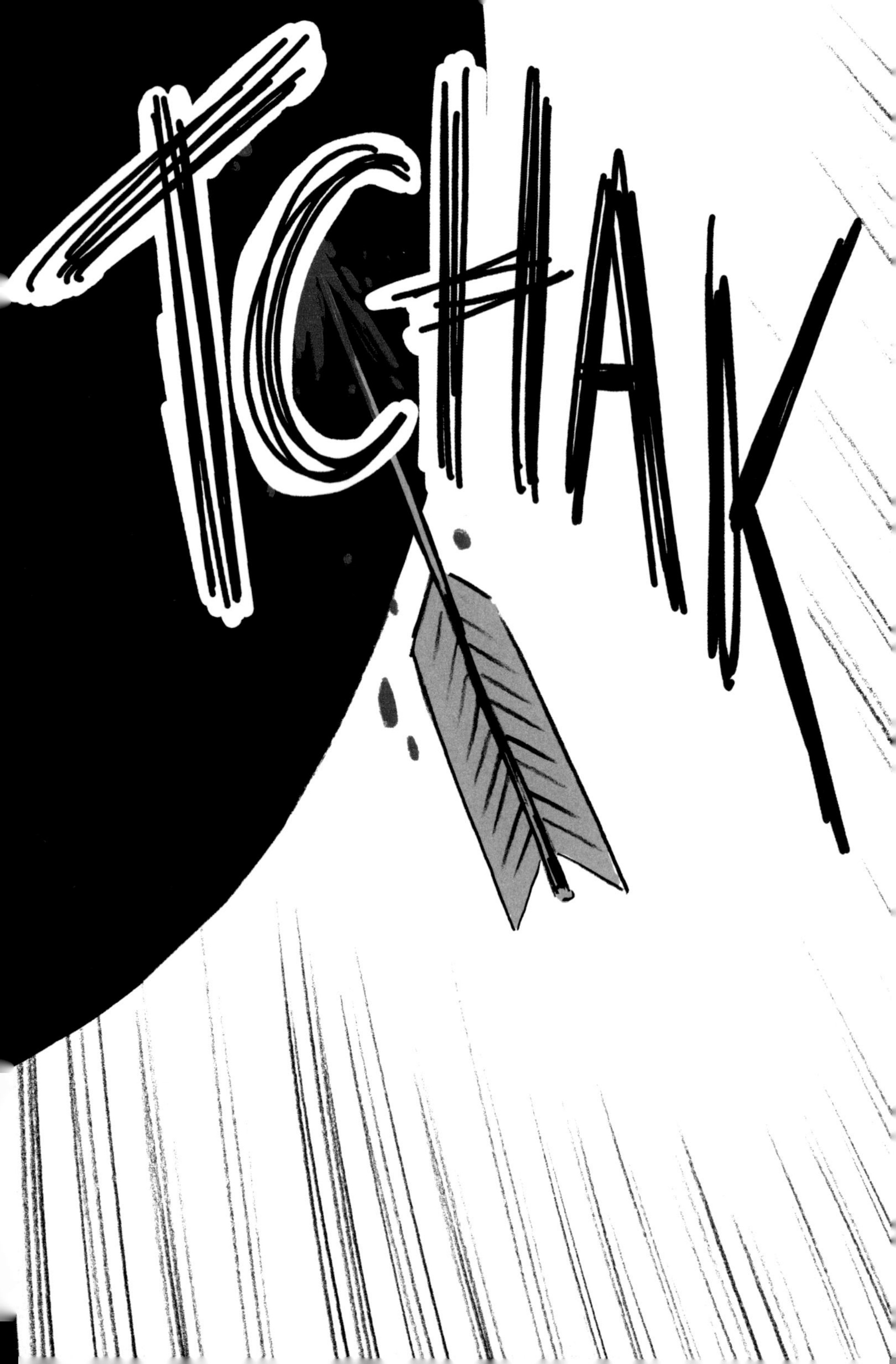
TCHAK

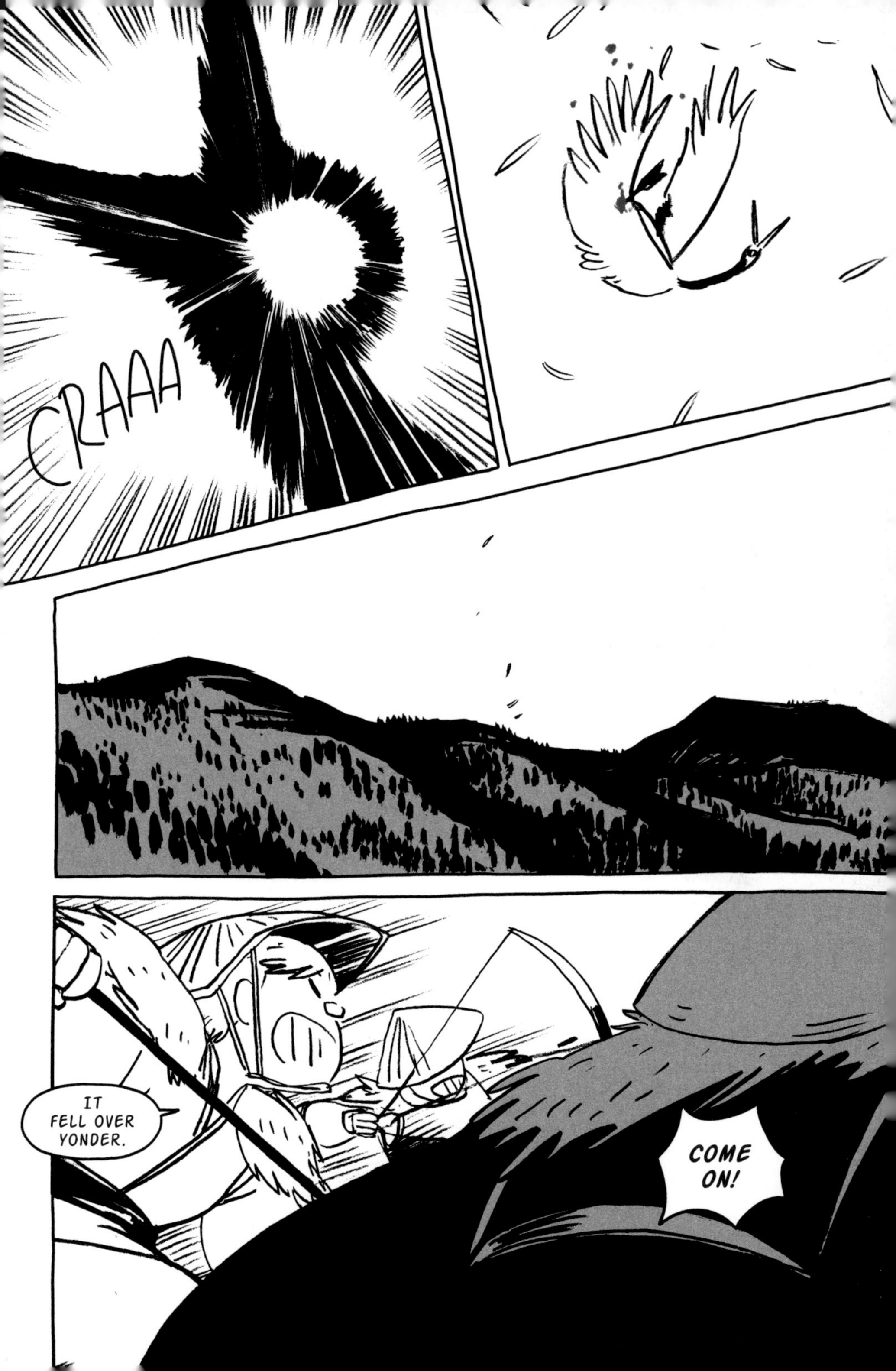
CRAAA
IT FELL OVER YONDER.
COME ON!

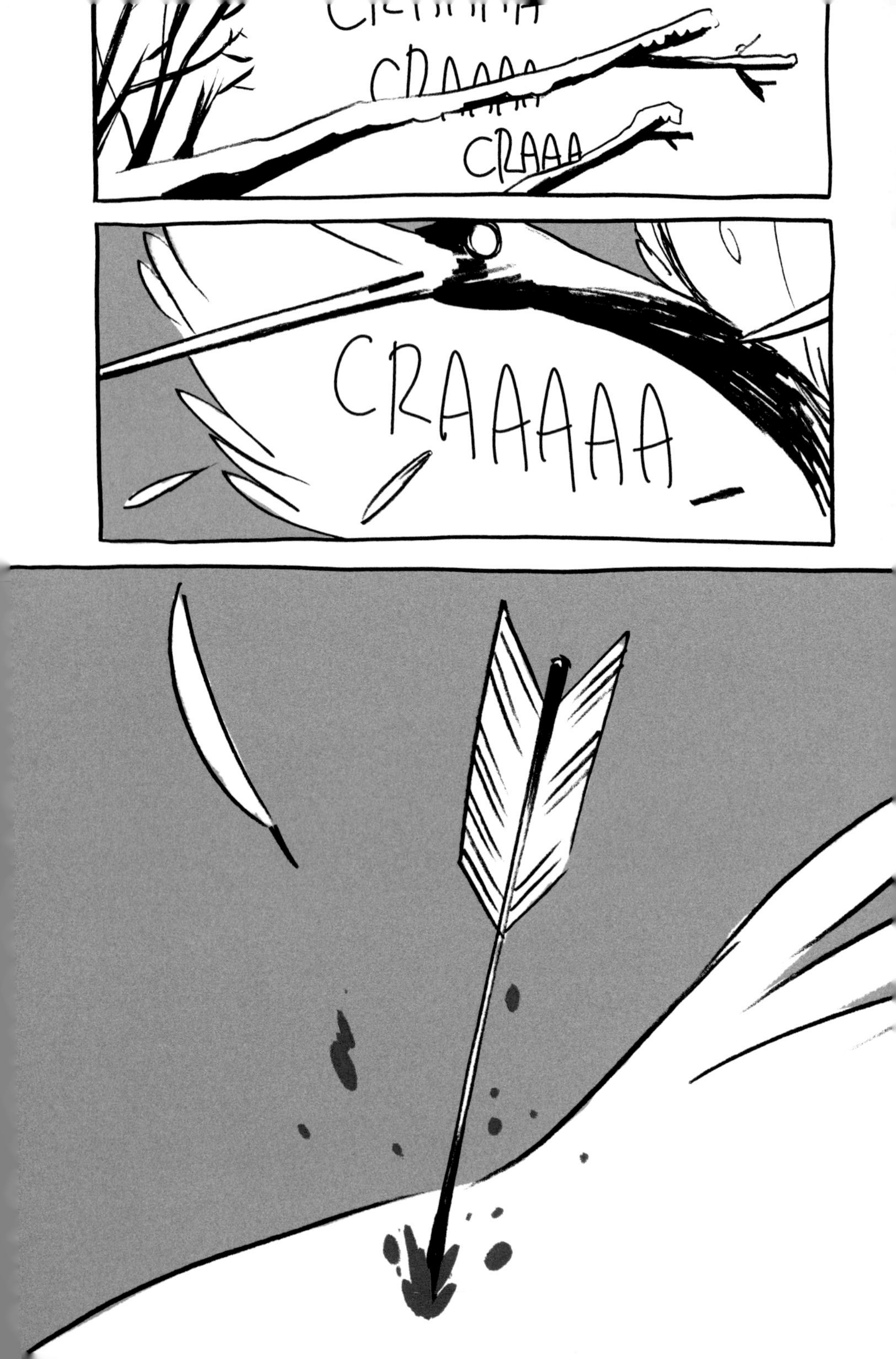
CRAAA
CRAAAAA

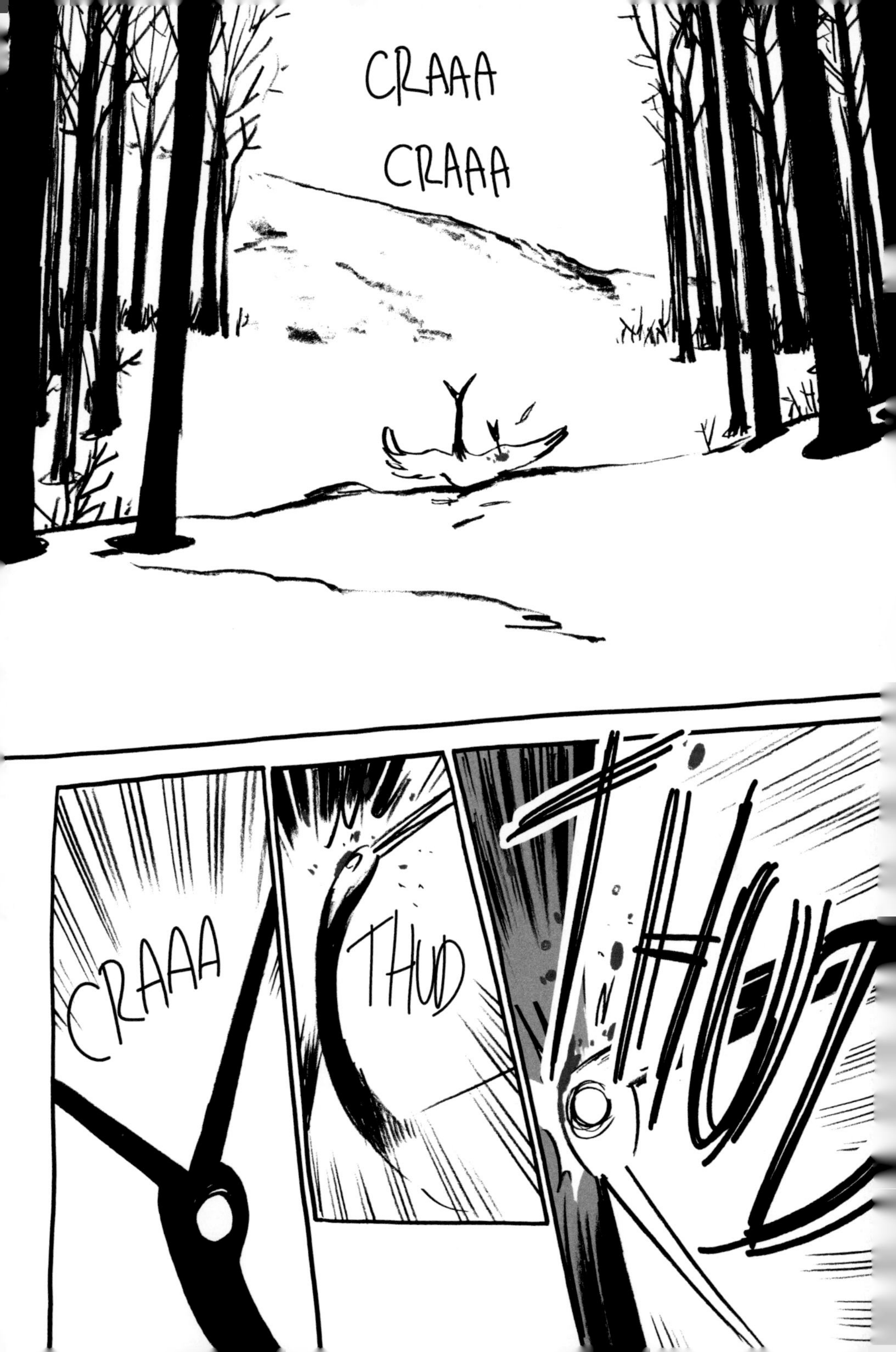
CRAAA
CRAAA
CRAAA
THUD
THOK

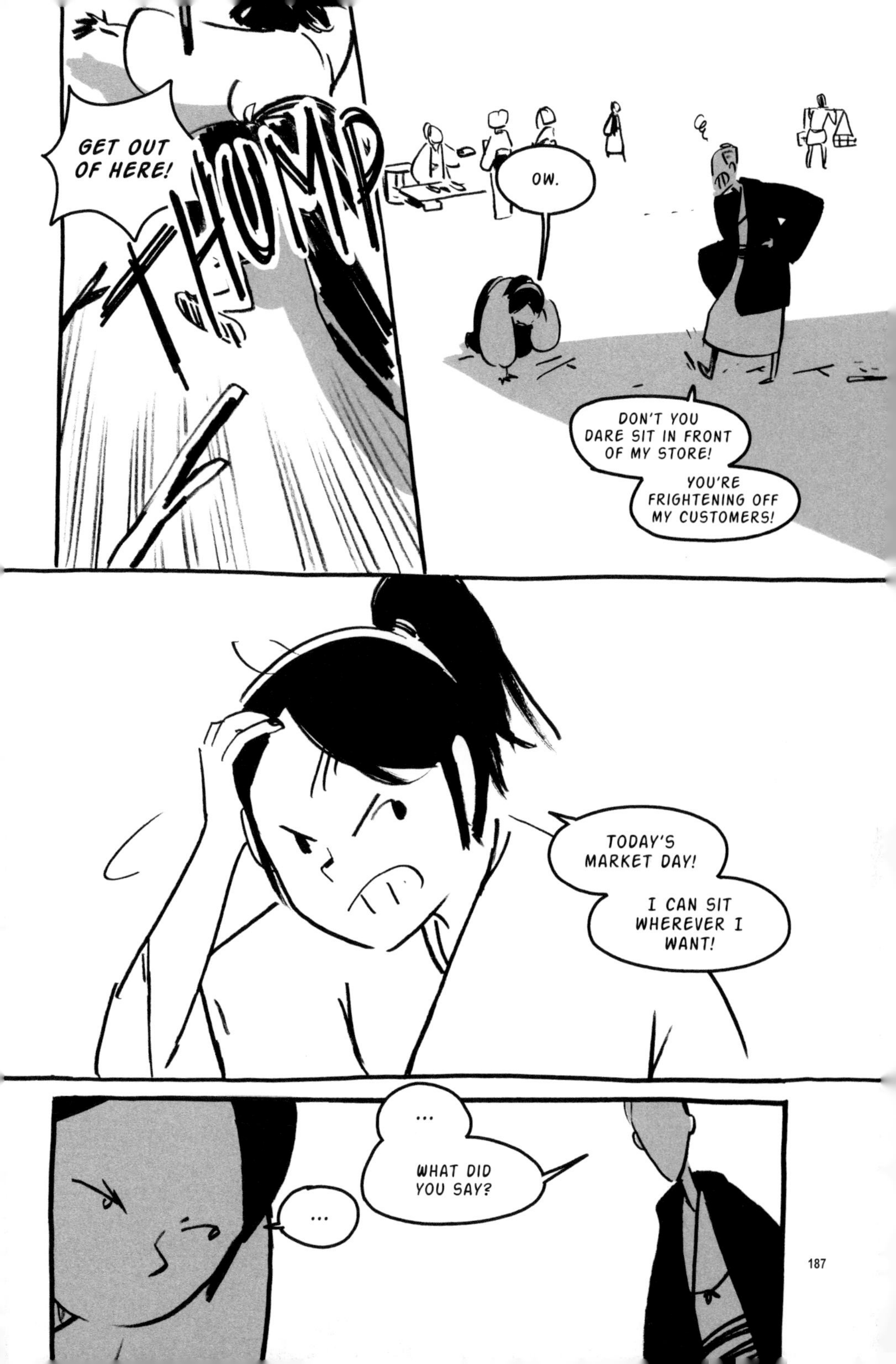
GET OUT OF HERE!
THOMP
OW.
DON'T YOU DARE SIT IN FRONT OF MY STORE!
YOU'RE FRIGHTENING OFF MY CUSTOMERS!
TODAY'S MARKET DAY!
I CAN SIT WHEREVER I WANT!
...
WHAT DID YOU SAY?
...

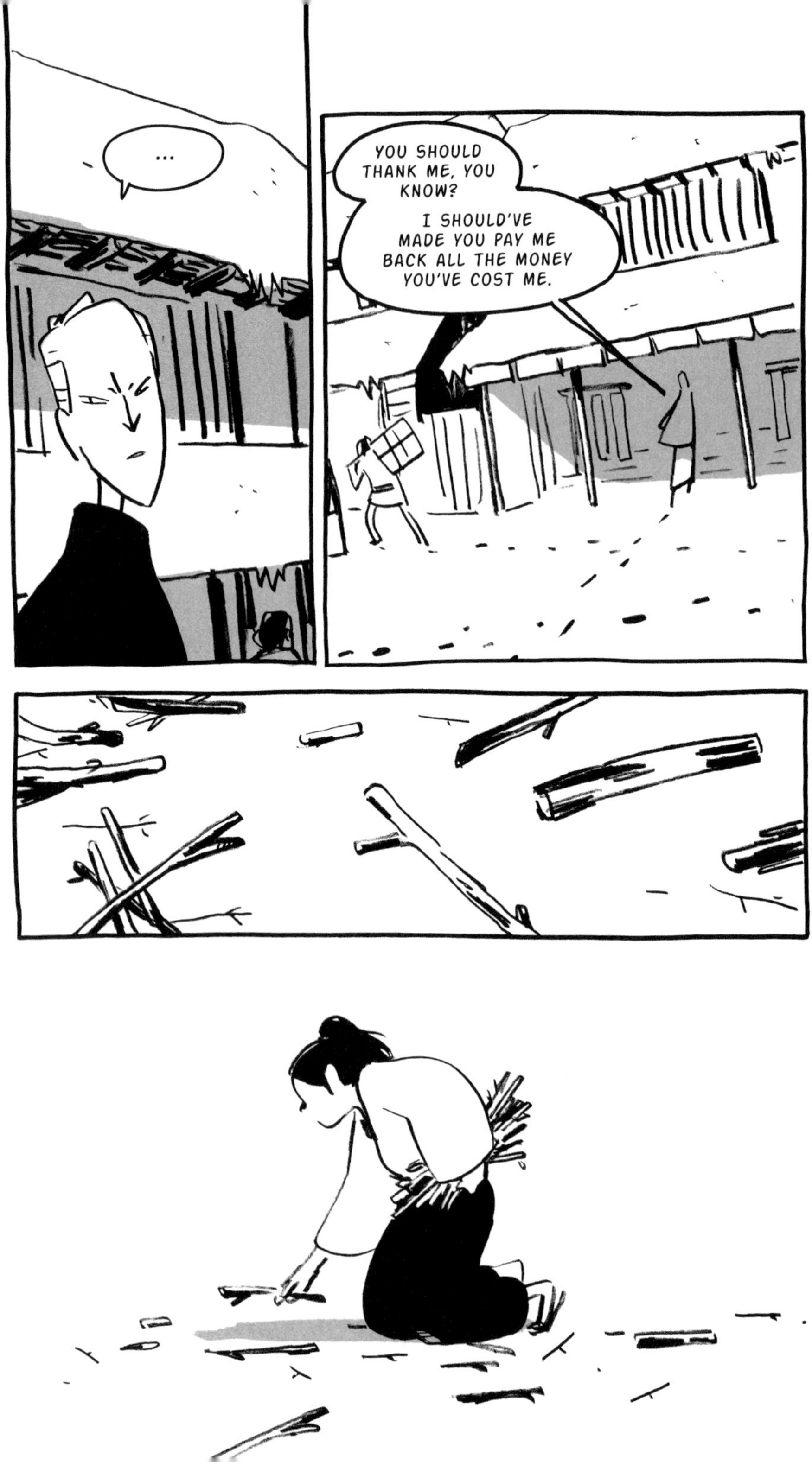
...
YOU SHOULD THANK ME, YOU KNOW?
I SHOULD'VE MADE YOU PAY ME BACK ALL THE MONEY YOU'VE COST ME.

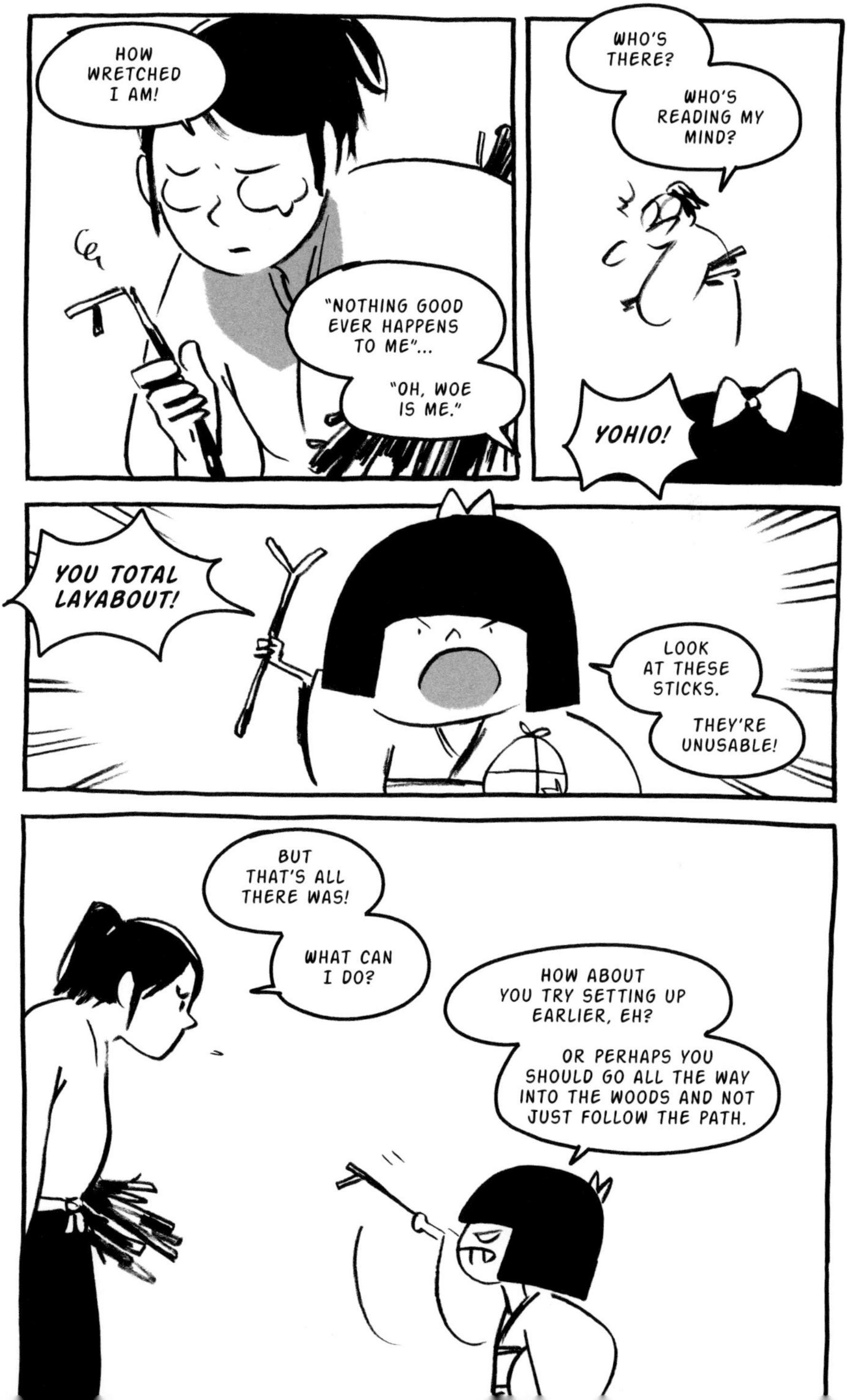
HOW WRETCHED I AM!
"NOTHING GOOD EVER HAPPENS TO ME"...
"OH, WOE IS ME."
WHO'S THERE?
WHO'S READING MY MIND?
YOHIO!
YOU TOTAL LAYABOUT!
LOOK AT THESE STICKS.
THEY'RE UNUSABLE!
BUT THAT'S ALL THERE WAS!
WHAT CAN I DO?
HOW ABOUT YOU TRY SETTING UP EARLIER, EH?
OR PERHAPS YOU SHOULD GO ALL THE WAY INTO THE WOODS AND NOT JUST FOLLOW THE PATH.

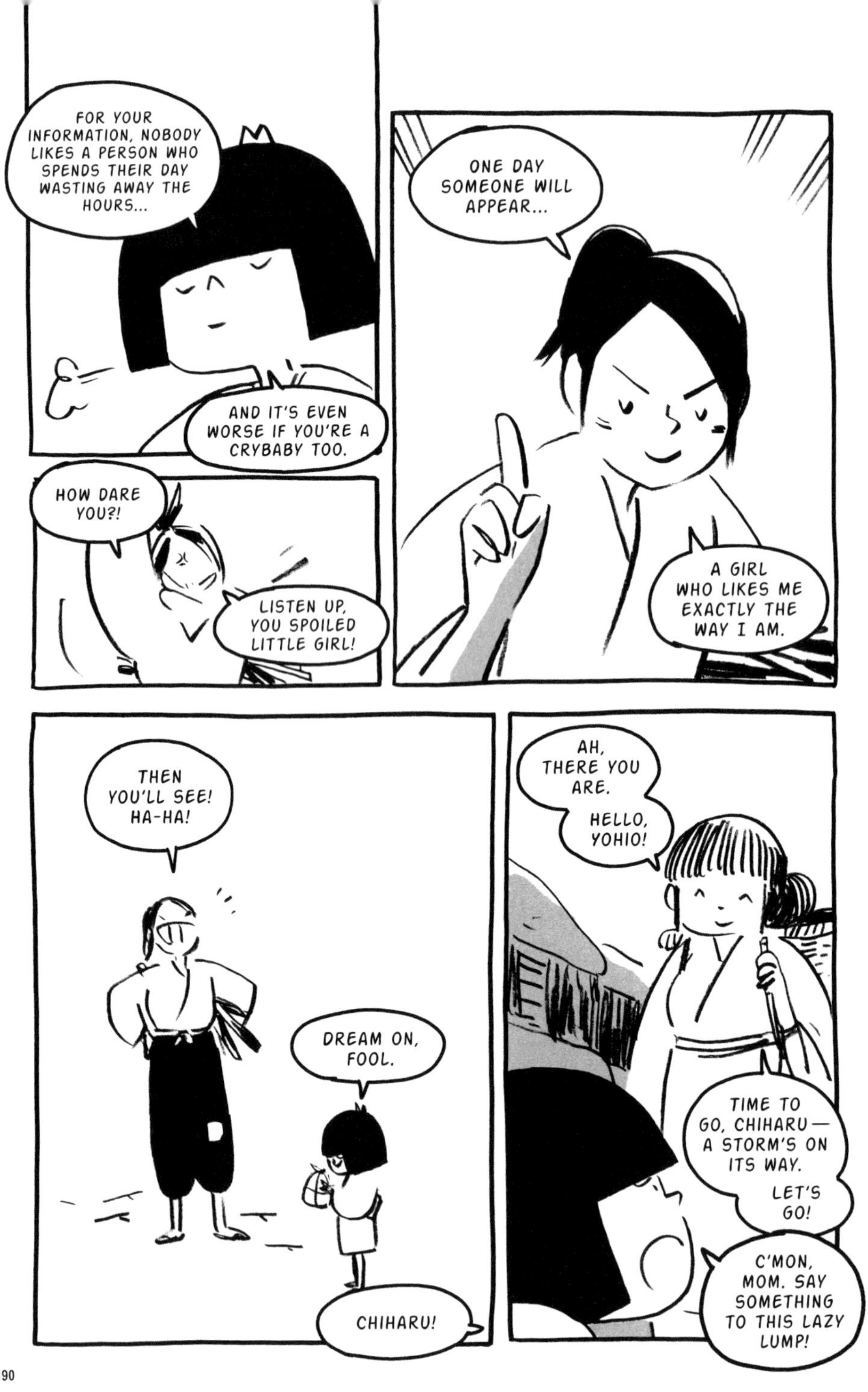

FOR YOUR INFORMATION, NOBODY LIKES A PERSON WHO SPENDS THEIR DAY WASTING AWAY THE HOURS...
AND IT'S EVEN WORSE IF YOU'RE A CRYBABY TOO.
HOW DARE YOU?!
LISTEN UP, YOU SPOILED LITTLE GIRL!
ONE DAY SOMEONE WILL APPEAR...
A GIRL WHO LIKES ME EXACTLY THE WAY I AM.
THEN YOU'LL SEE! HA-HA!
DREAM ON, FOOL.
CHIHARU!
AH, THERE YOU ARE.
HELLO, YOHIO!
TIME TO GO, CHIHARU—A STORM'S ON ITS WAY.
LET'S GO!
C'MON, MOM. SAY SOMETHING TO THIS LAZY LUMP!

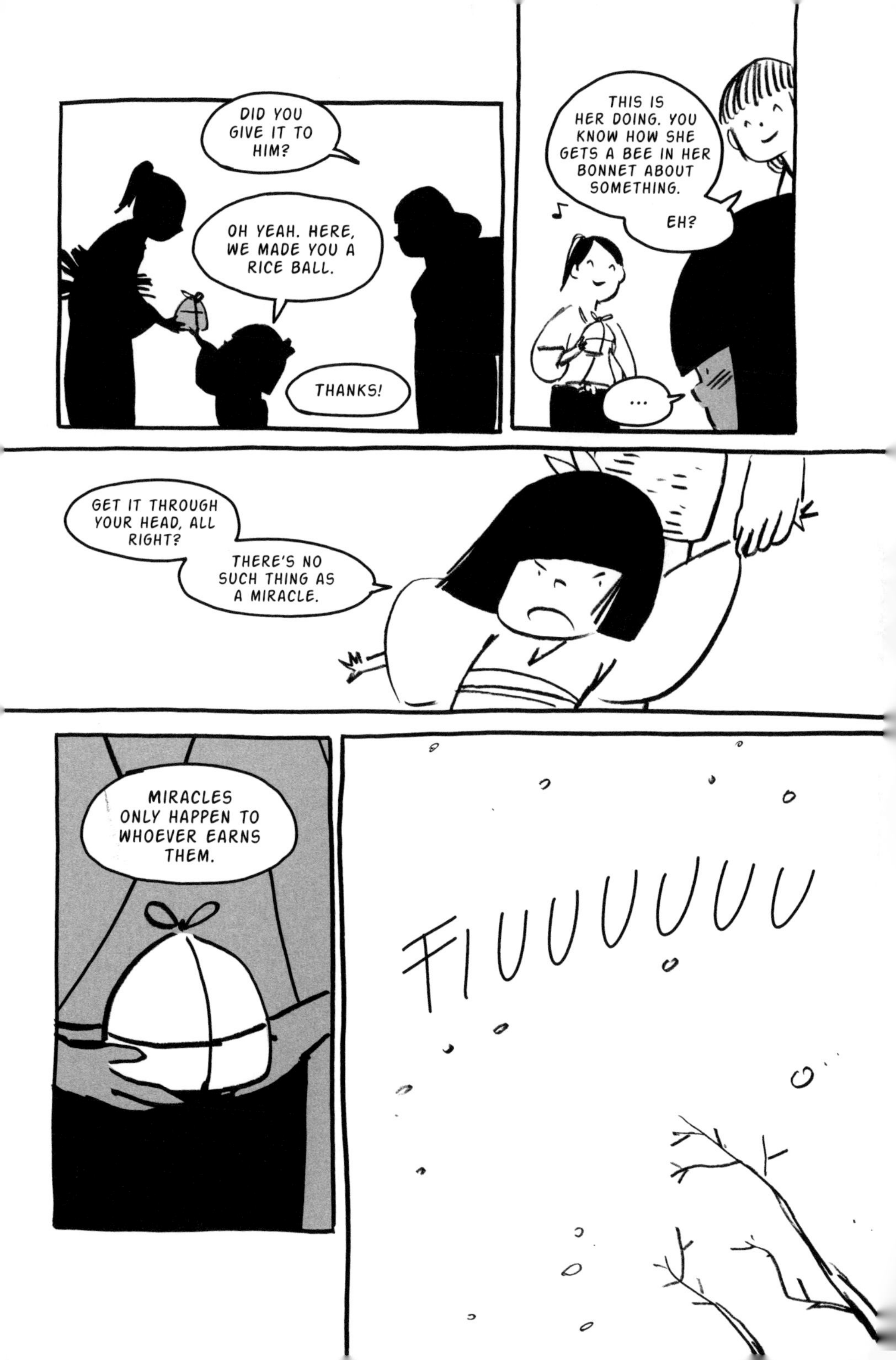
DID YOU GIVE IT TO HIM?
OH YEAH. HERE, WE MADE YOU A RICE BALL.
THANKS!
THIS IS HER DOING. YOU KNOW HOW SHE GETS A BEE IN HER BONNET ABOUT SOMETHING.
EH?
...
GET IT THROUGH YOUR HEAD, ALL RIGHT?
THERE'S NO SUCH THING AS A MIRACLE.
MIRACLES ONLY HAPPEN TO WHOEVER EARNS THEM.
FIUUUUUU

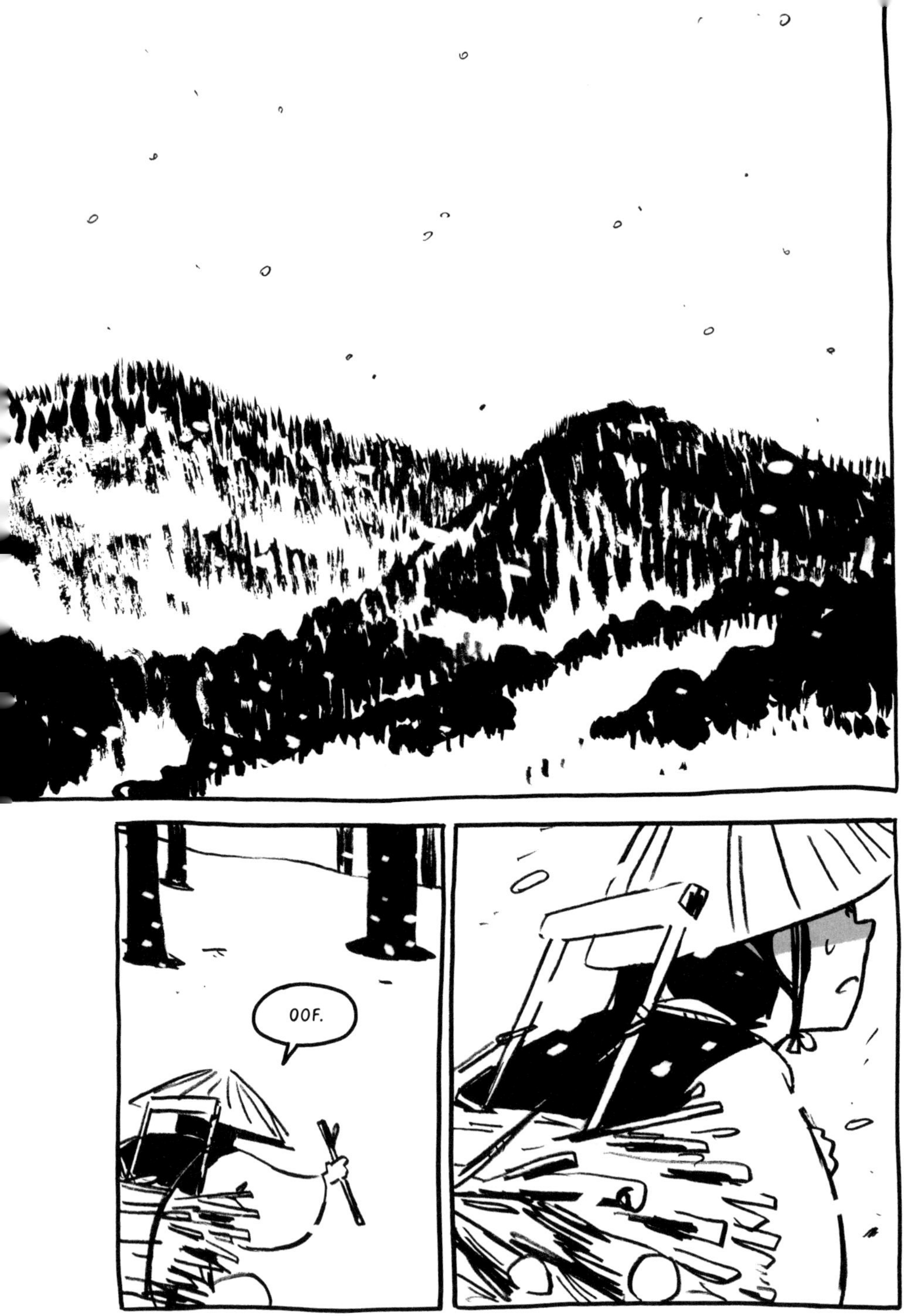
OOF.

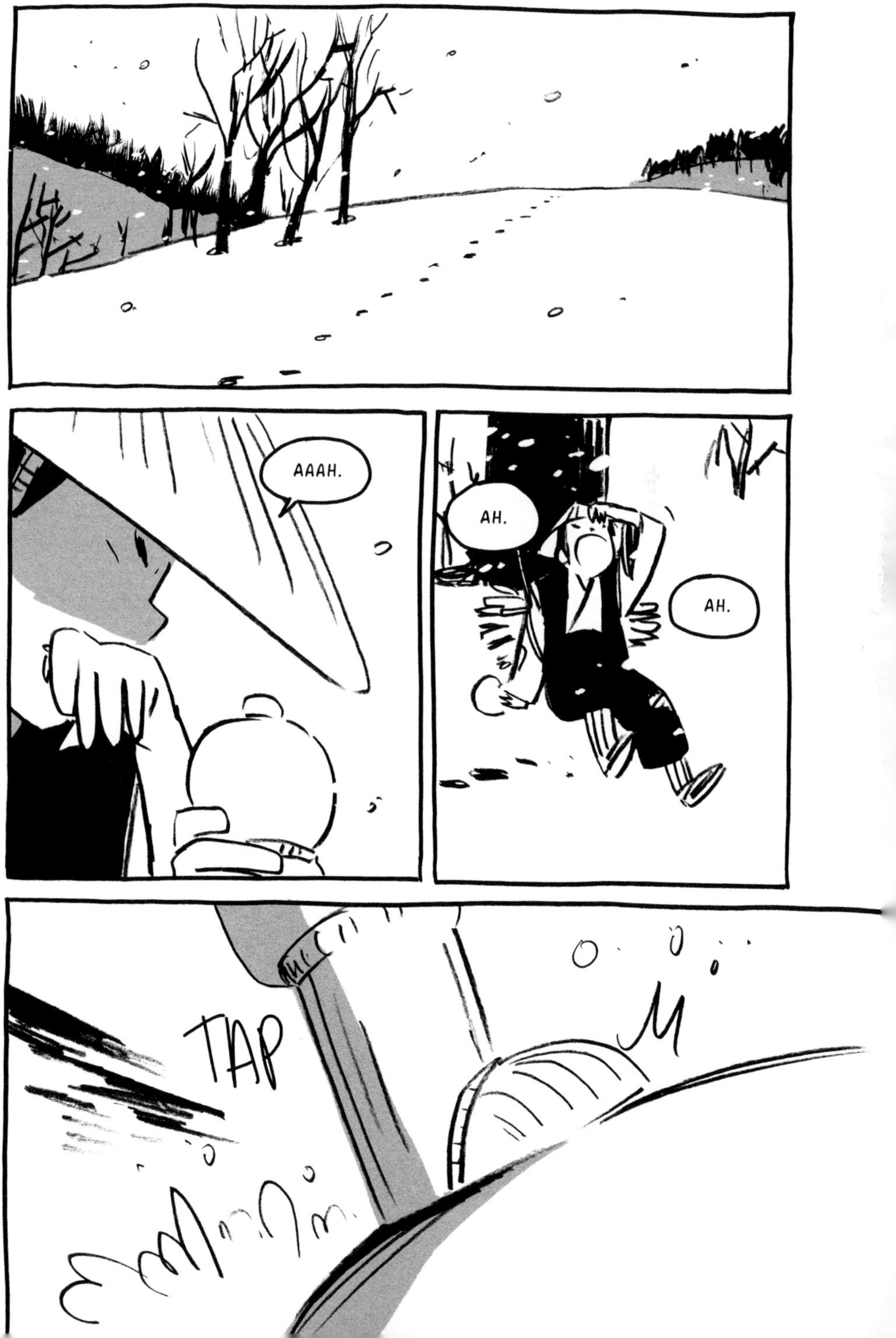
AAAH.
AH.
AH.
TAP

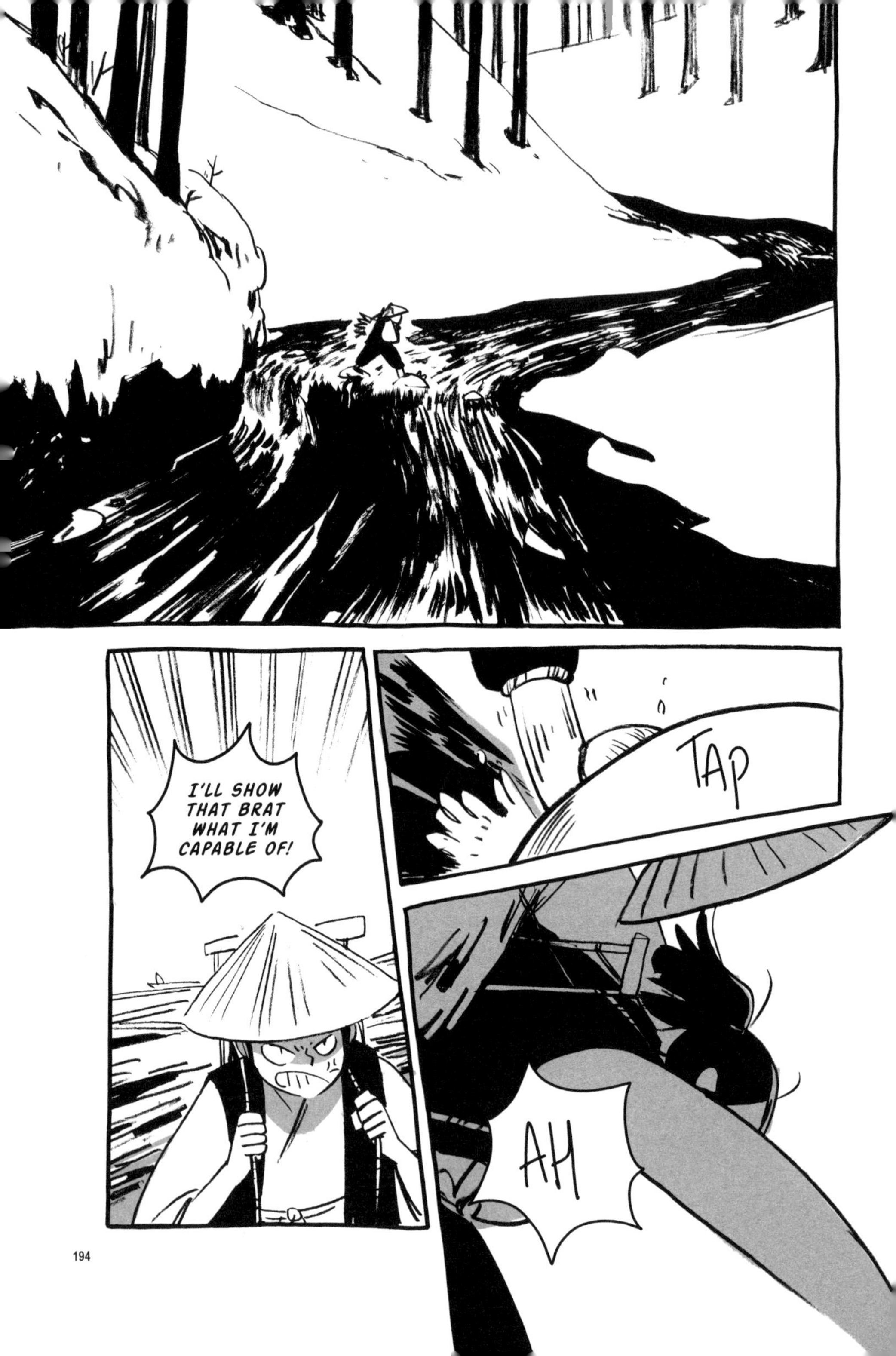

I'LL SHOW THAT BRAT WHAT I'M CAPABLE OF!
TAP
AH

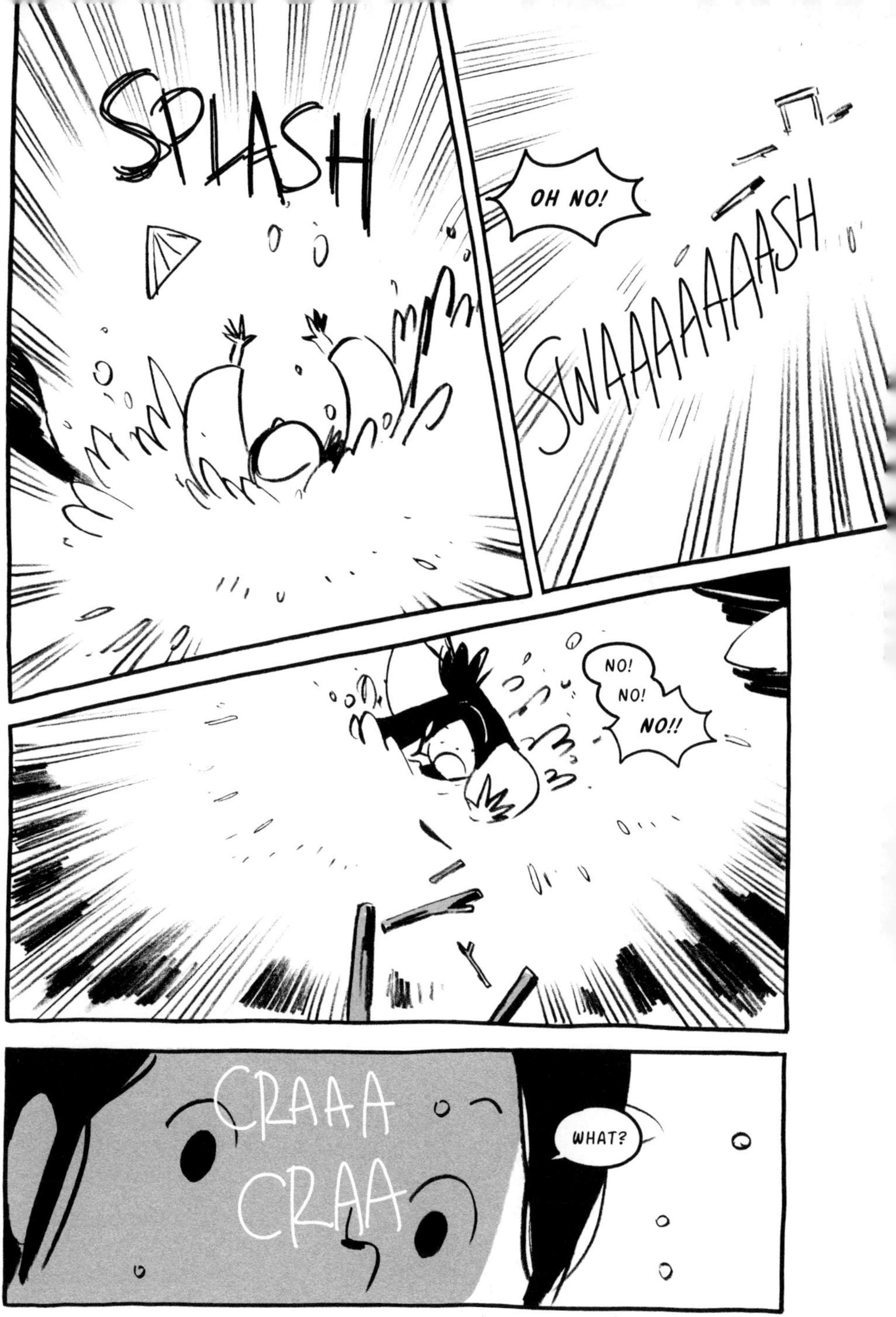
SPLASH
OH NO!
SWAAAAAAASH
NO!
NO!
NO!!
CRAAA
CRAA
WHAT?

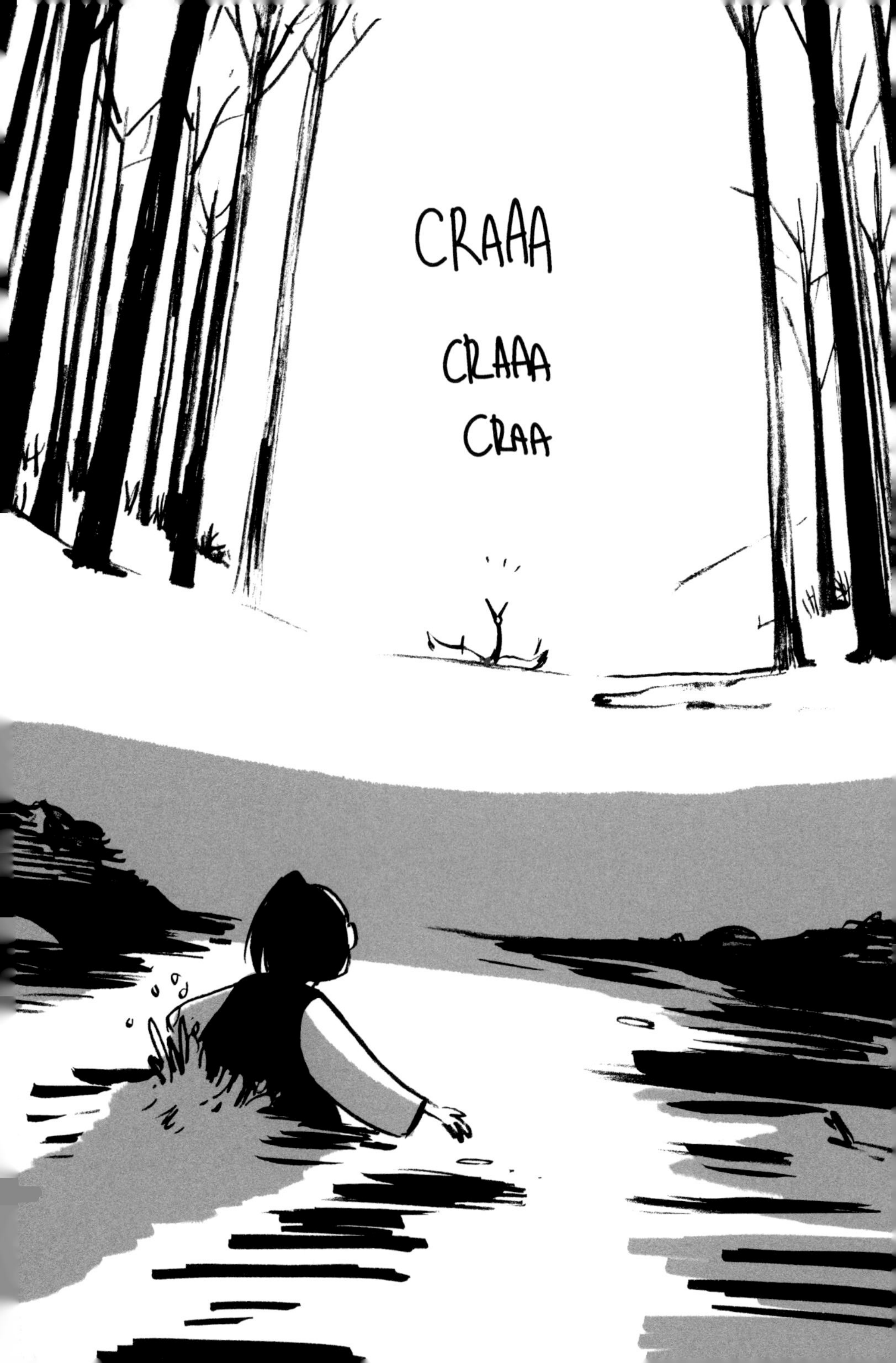
CRAAA
CRAAA
CRAA

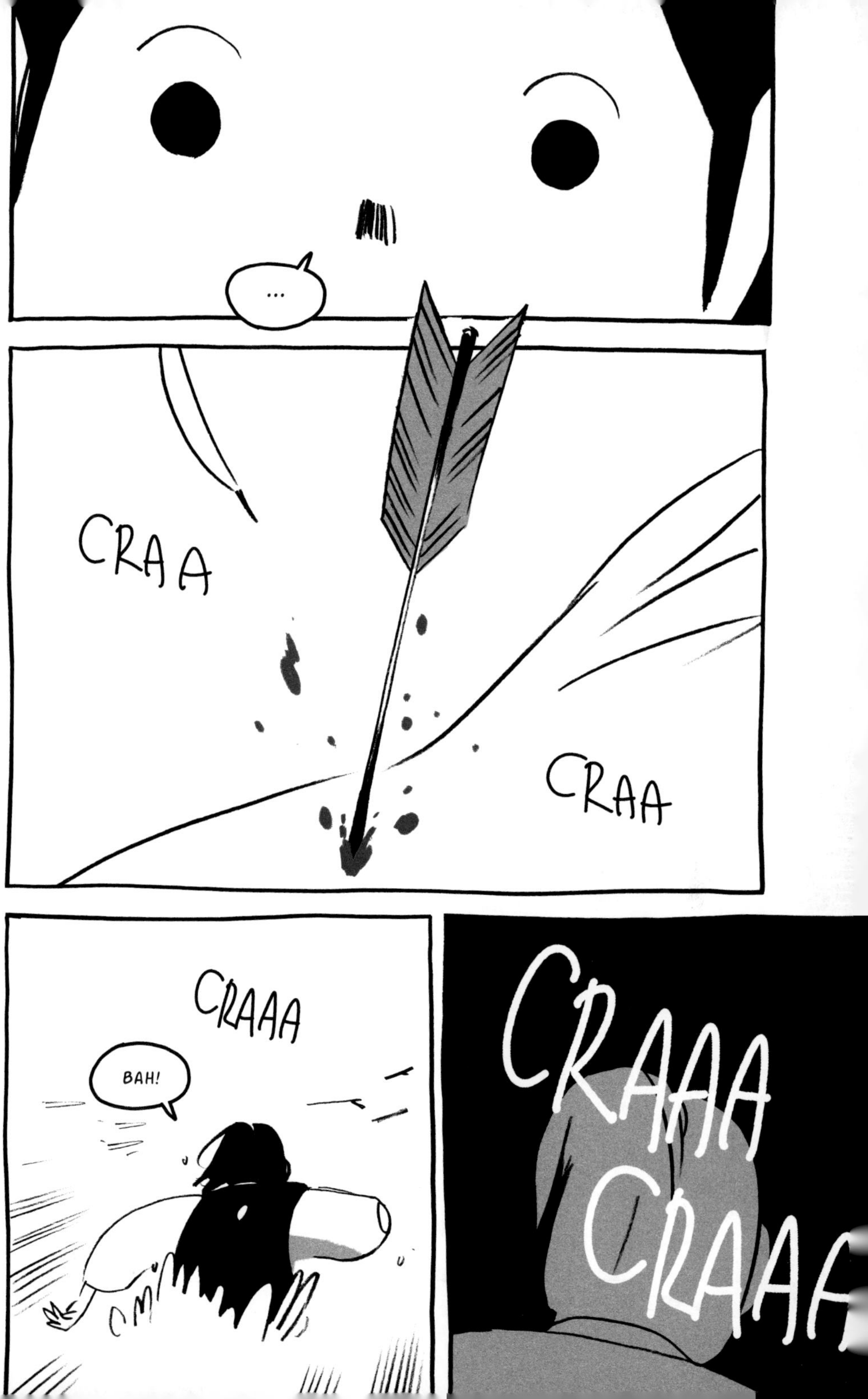
...
CRAA
CRAA
CRAAA
BAH!
CRAAA
CRAAA

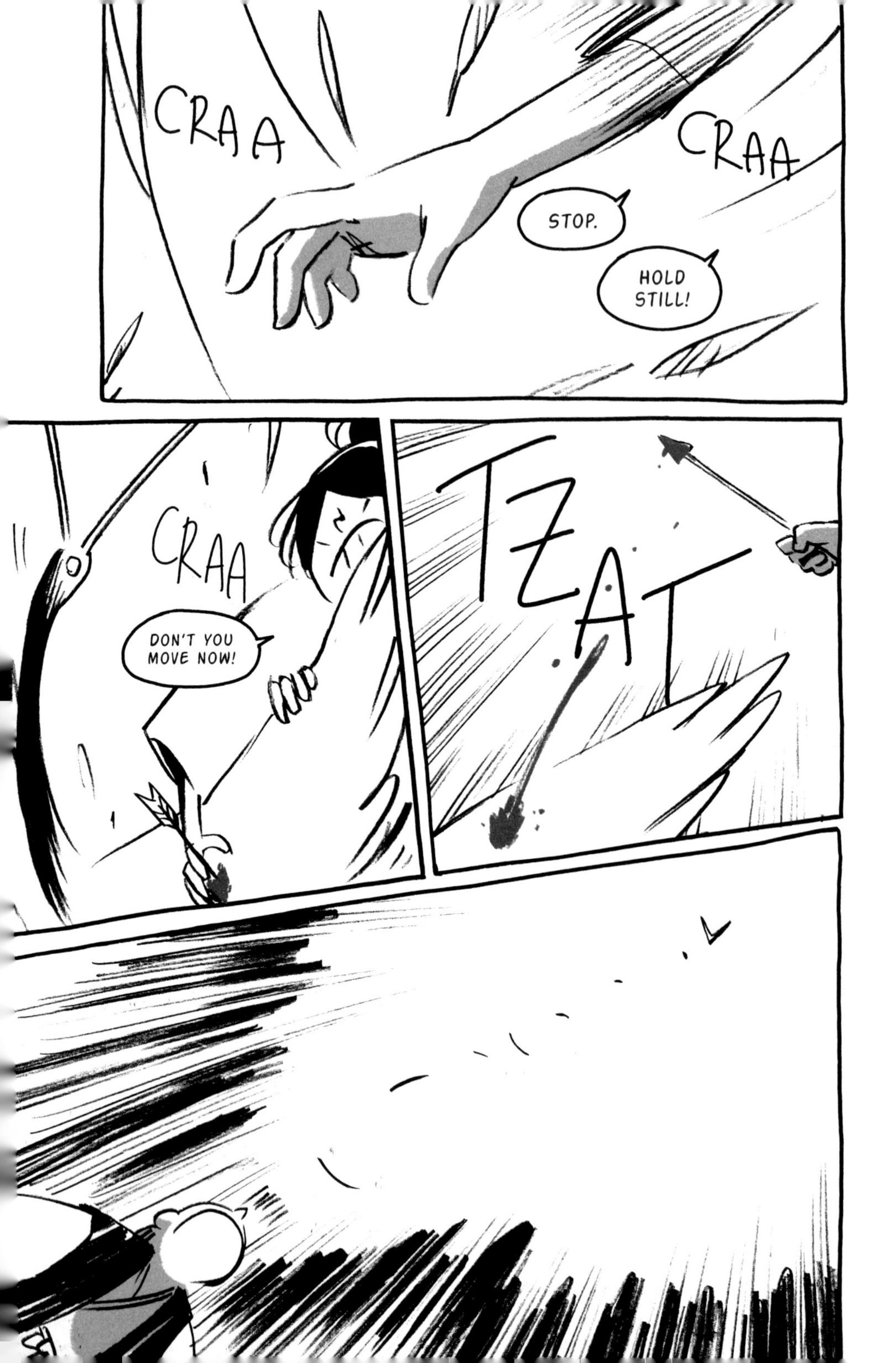
CRAA
CRAA
STOP.
HOLD STILL!
CRAA
DON'T YOU MOVE NOW!
TZAT

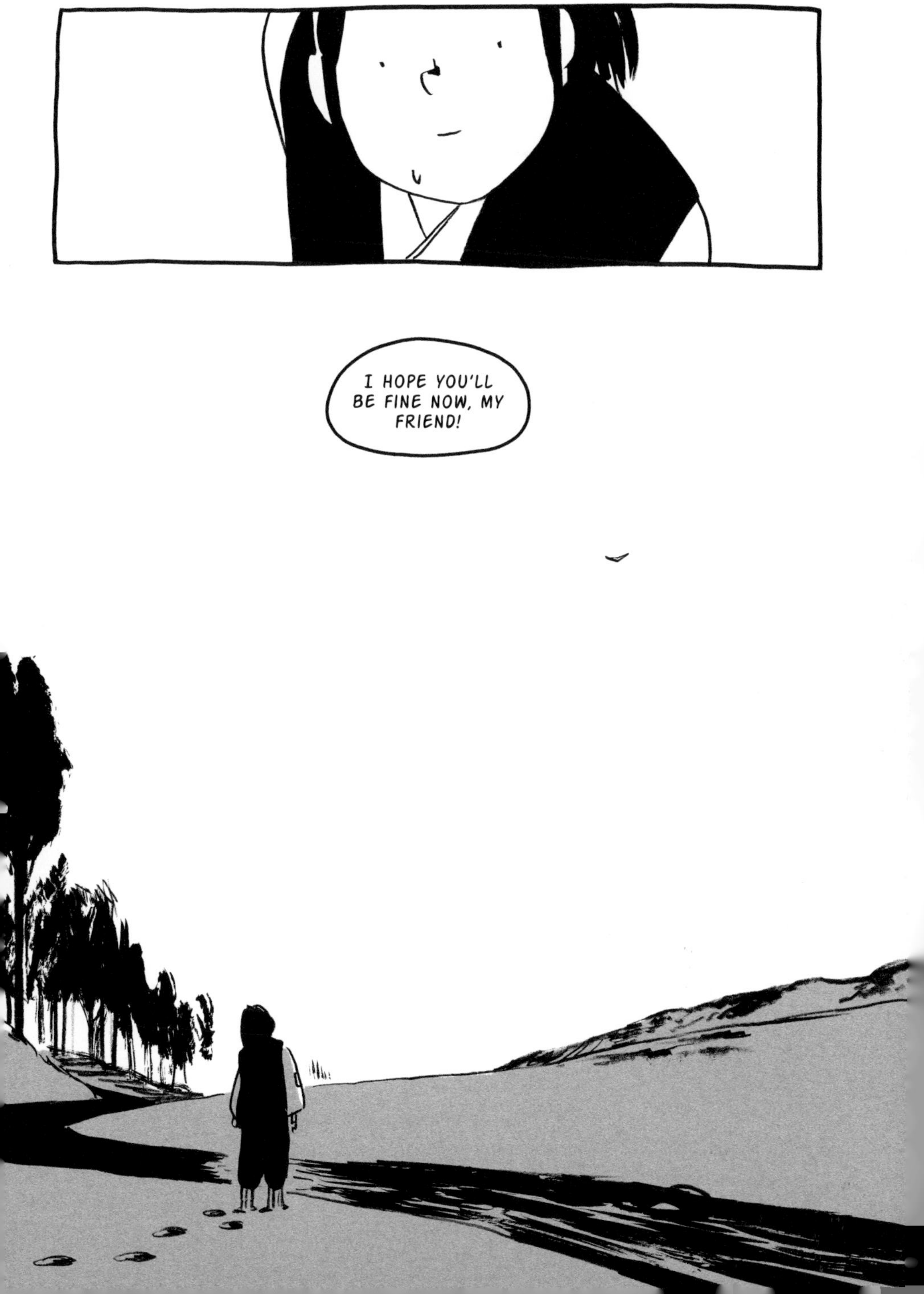
I HOPE YOU'LL BE FINE NOW, MY FRIEND!

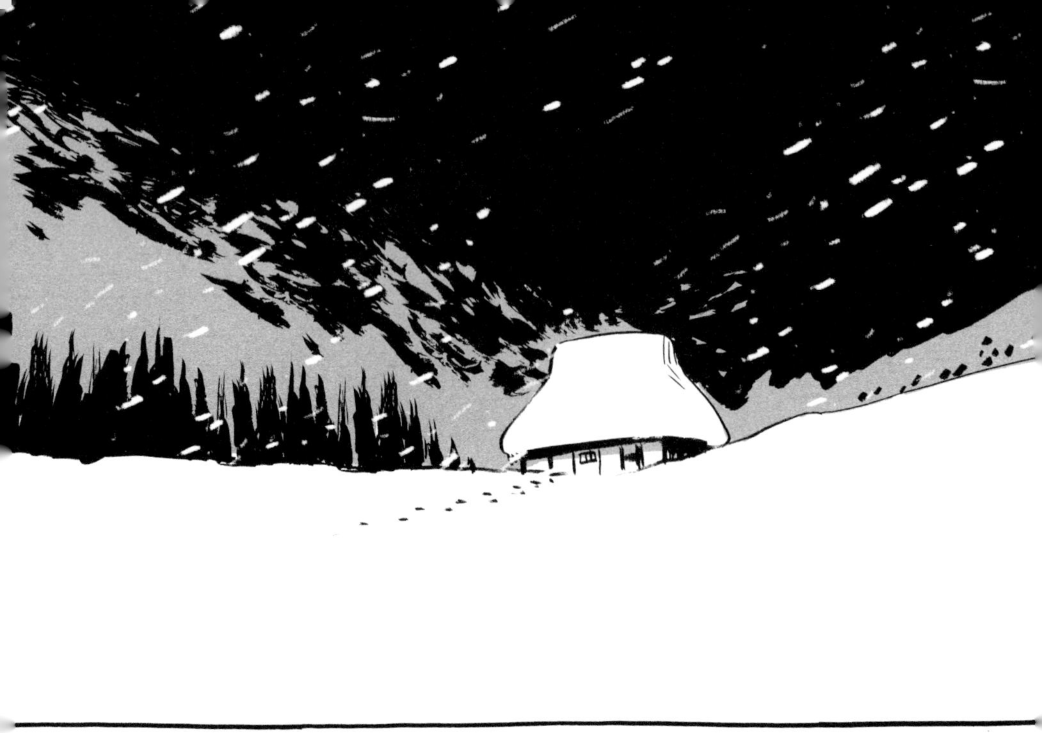

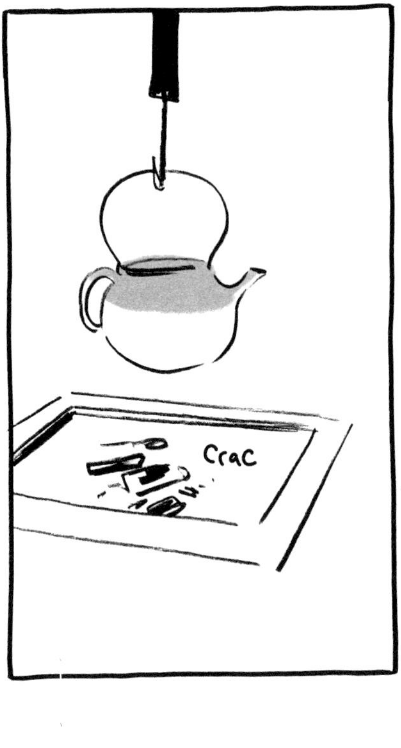
Crac

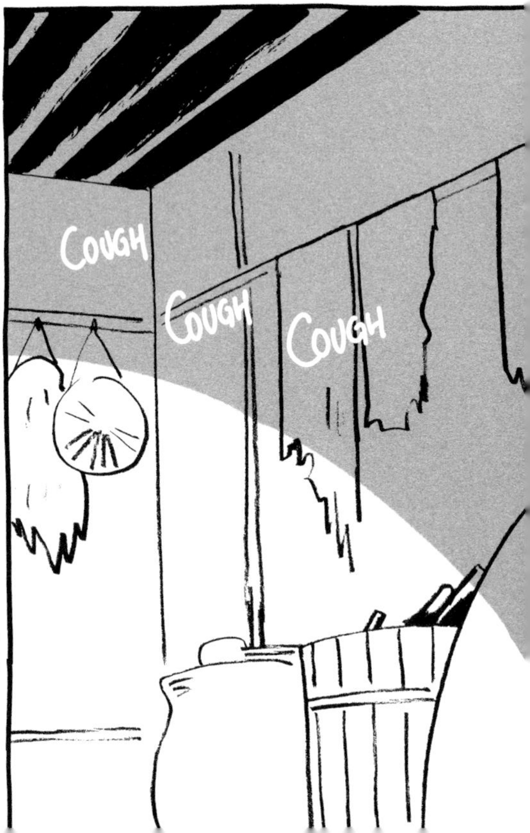
COUGH
COUGH
COUGH

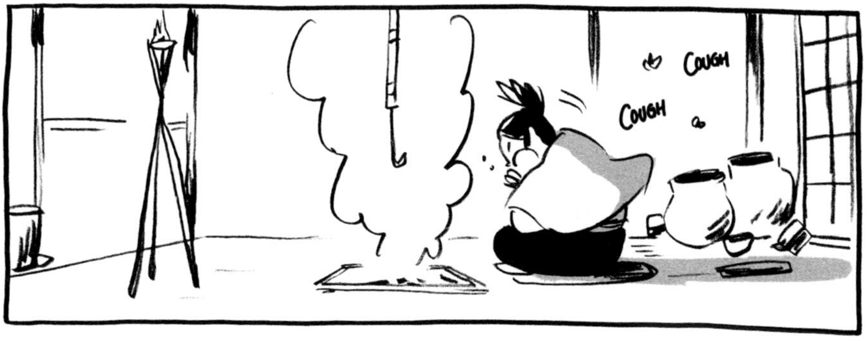
COUGH
COUGH

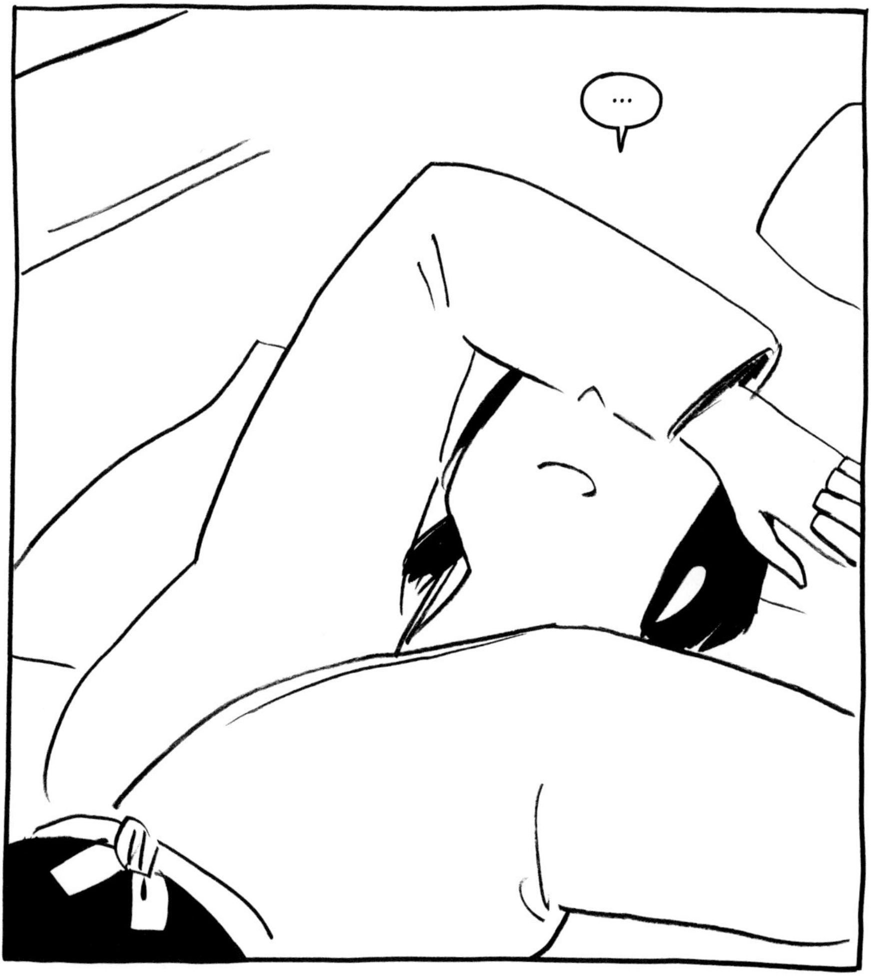
...

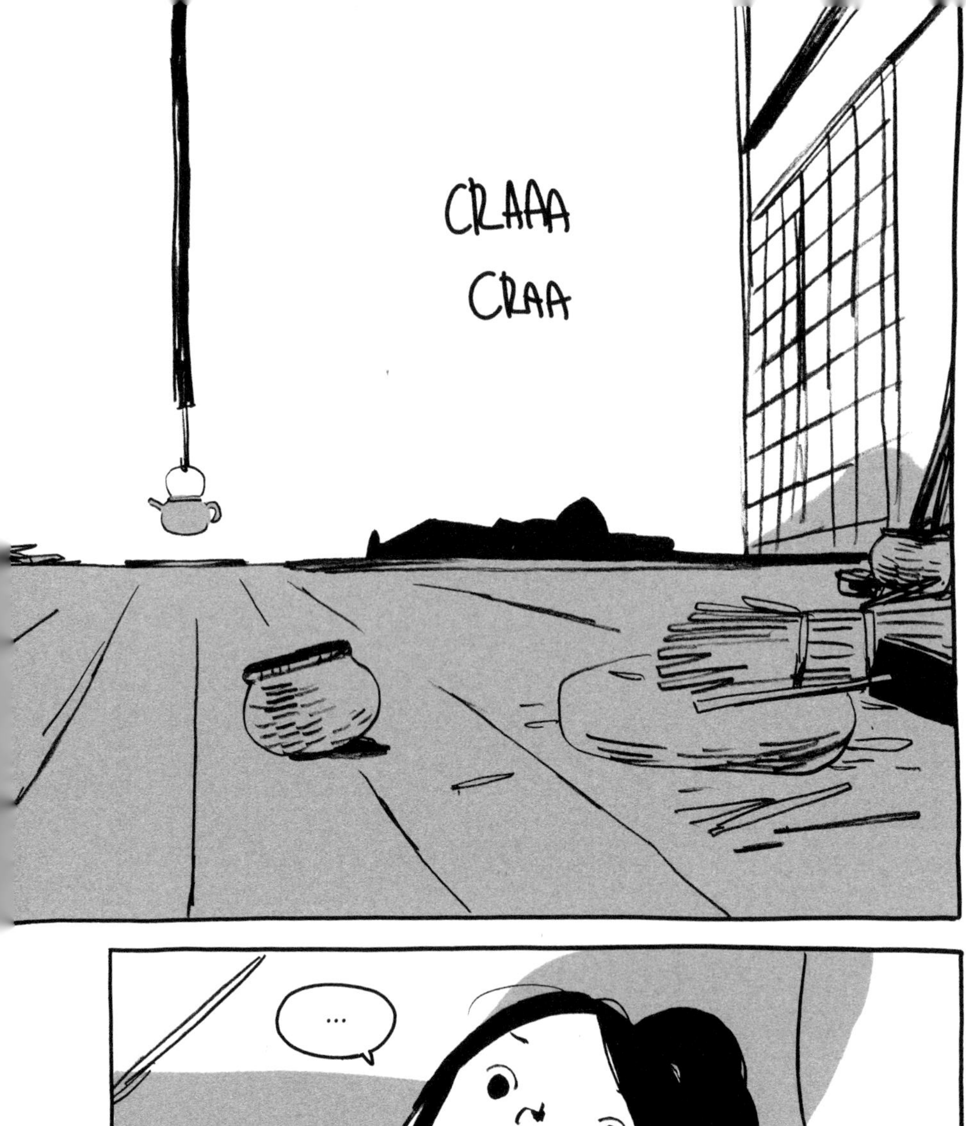
CRAAA
CRAA

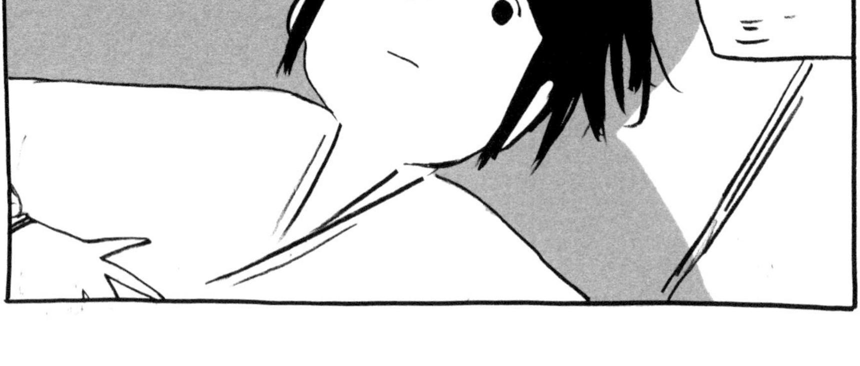
...

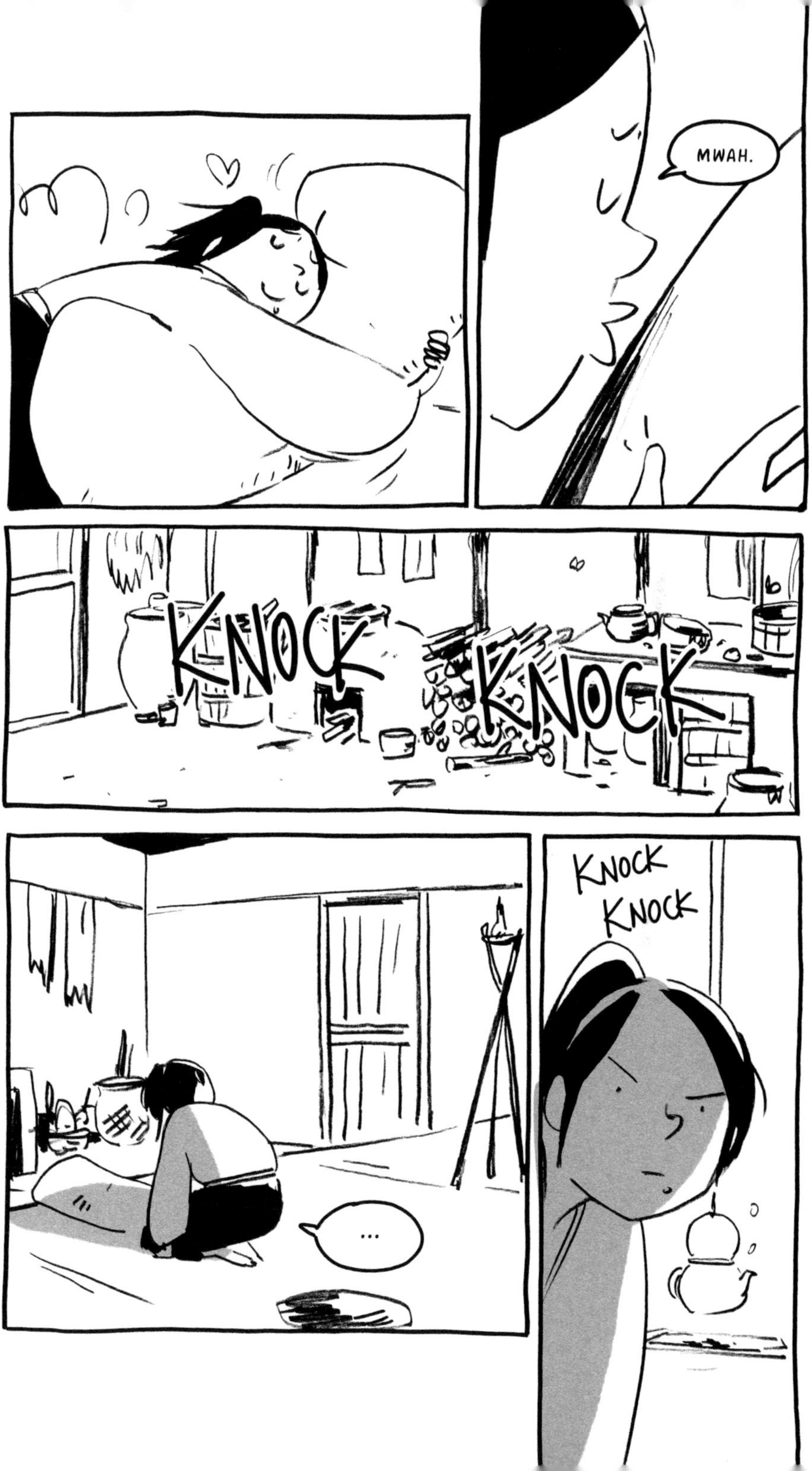
MWAH.
KNOCK
KNOCK
...
KNOCK
KNOCK

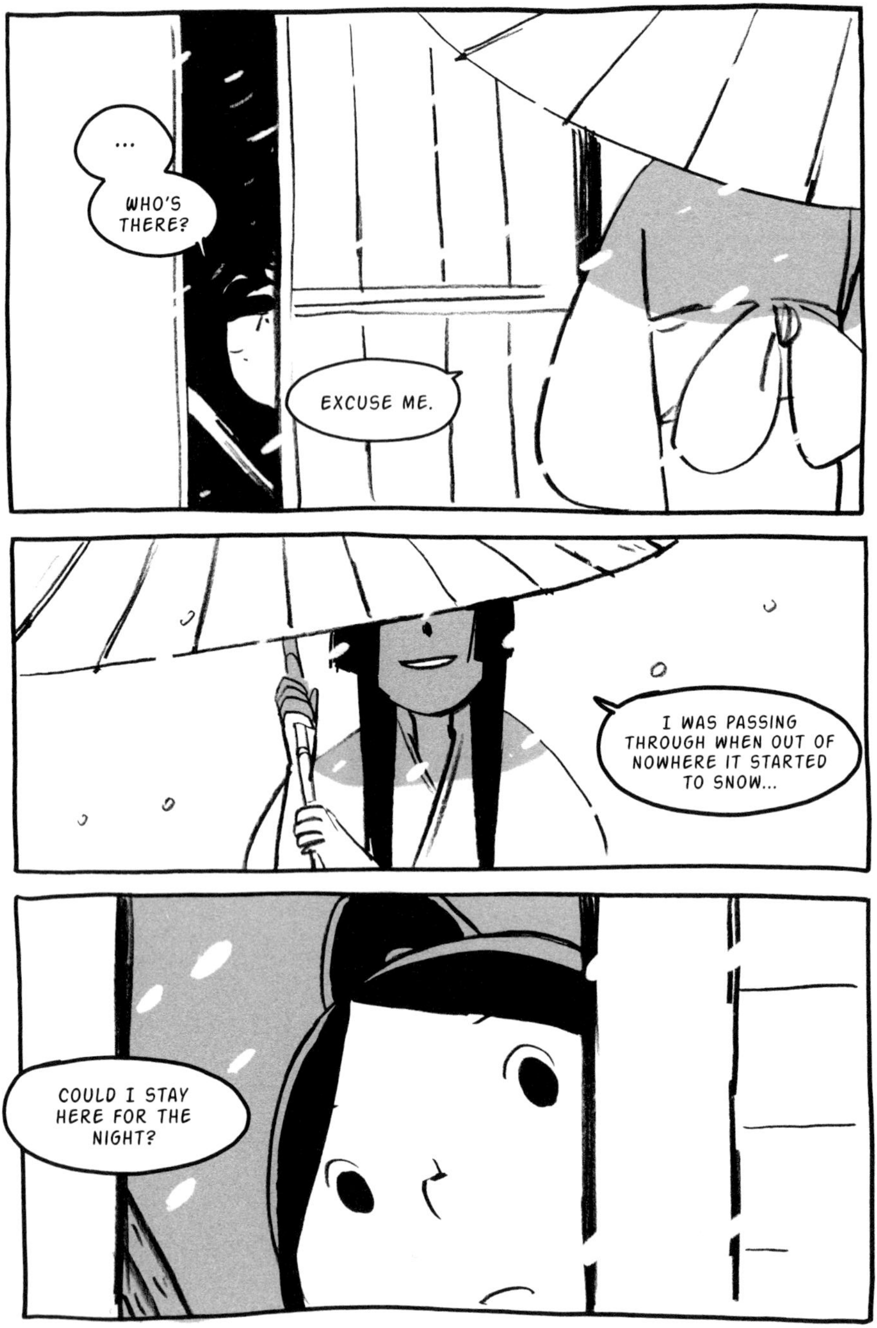
...
WHO'S THERE?
EXCUSE ME.
I WAS PASSING THROUGH WHEN OUT OF NOWHERE IT STARTED TO SNOW...
COULD I STAY HERE FOR THE NIGHT?

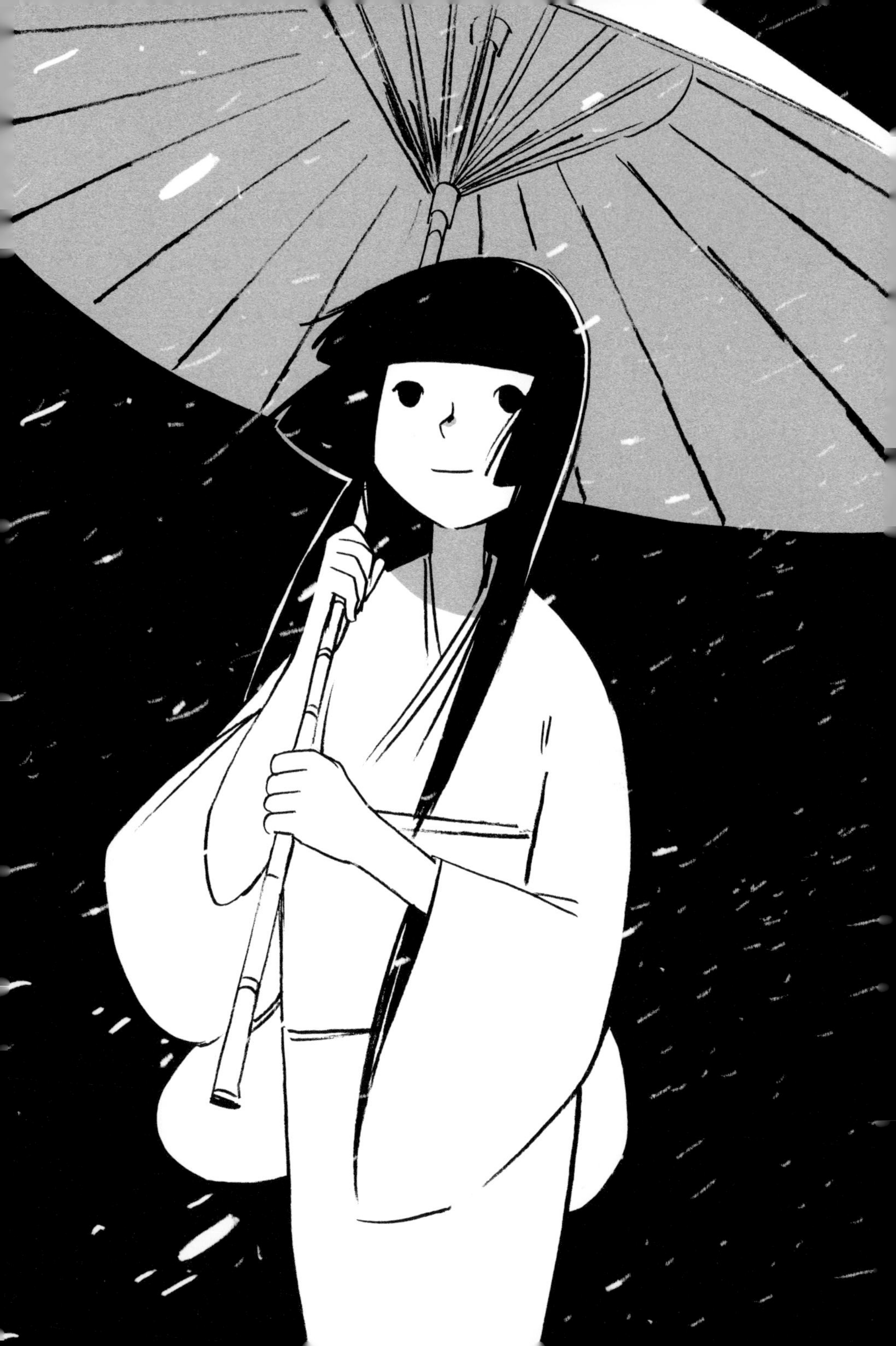

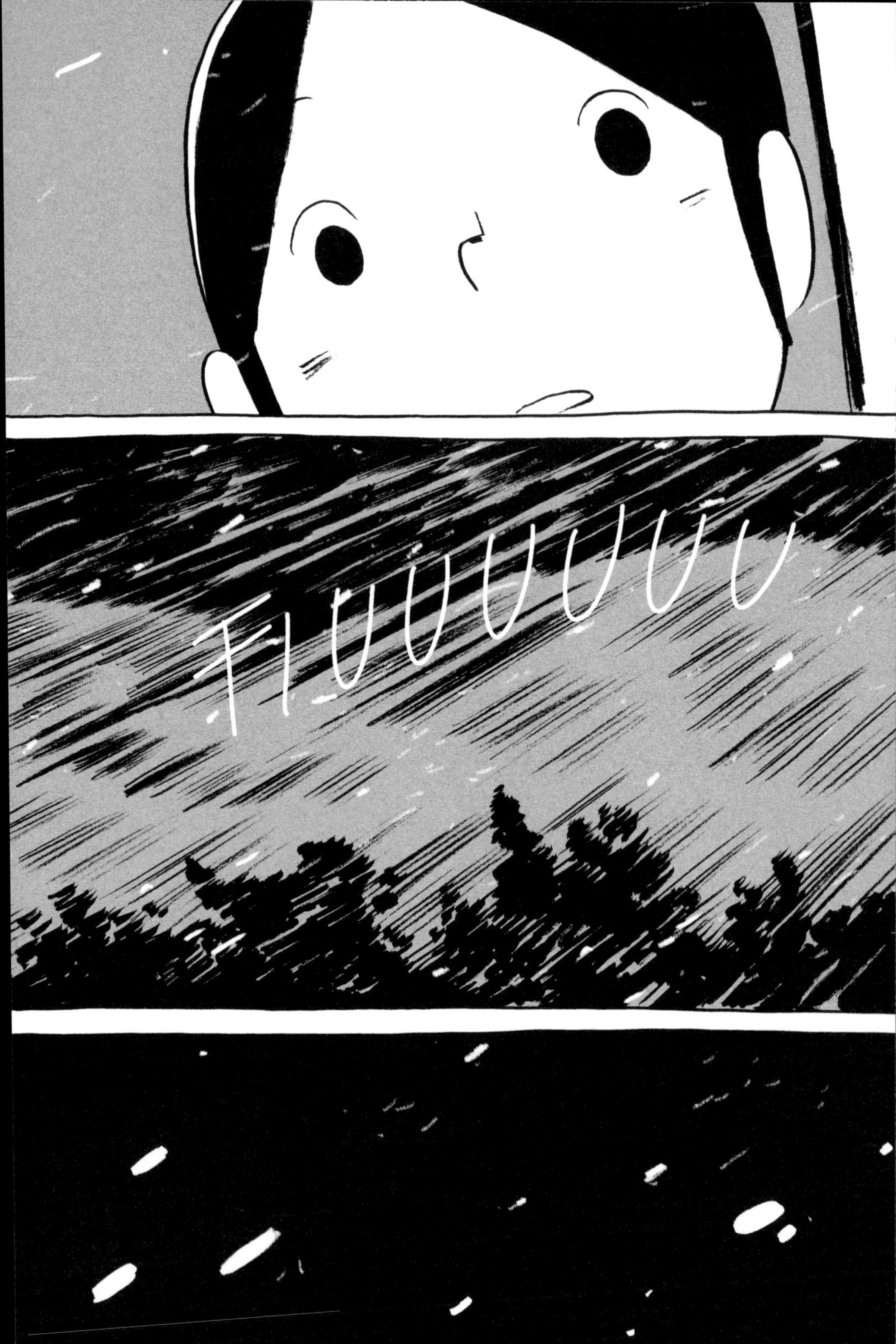
FIUUUUUUU

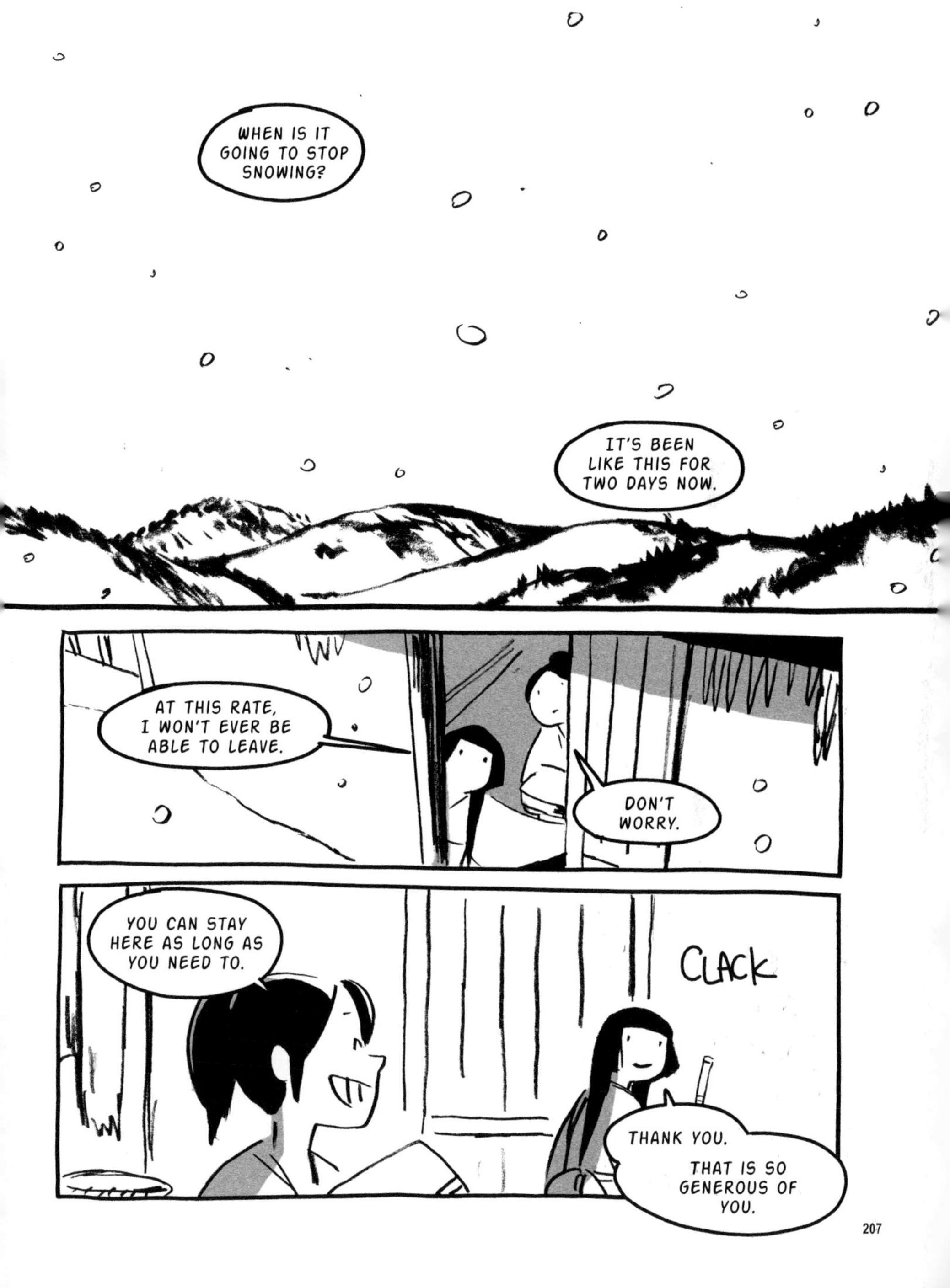
WHEN IS IT GOING TO STOP SNOWING?
IT'S BEEN LIKE THIS FOR TWO DAYS NOW.
AT THIS RATE, I WON'T EVER BE ABLE TO LEAVE.
DON'T WORRY.
YOU CAN STAY HERE AS LONG AS YOU NEED TO.
CLACK
THANK YOU.
THAT IS SO GENEROUS OF YOU.

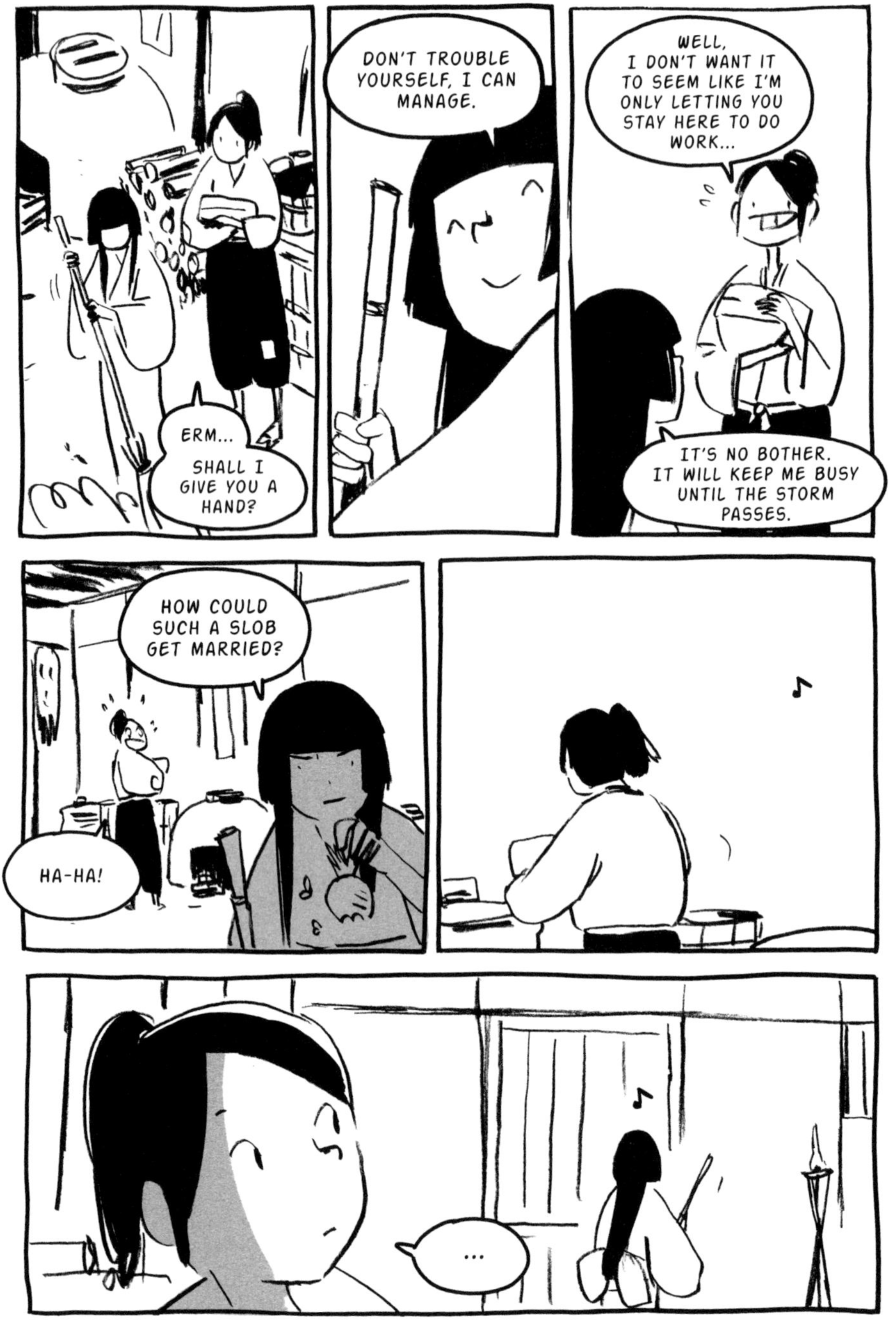
ERM... SHALL I GIVE YOU A HAND?
DON'T TROUBLE YOURSELF, I CAN MANAGE.
WELL, I DON'T WANT IT TO SEEM LIKE I'M ONLY LETTING YOU STAY HERE TO DO WORK...
IT'S NO BOTHER. IT WILL KEEP ME BUSY UNTIL THE STORM PASSES.
HOW COULD SUCH A SLOB GET MARRIED?
HA-HA!
...

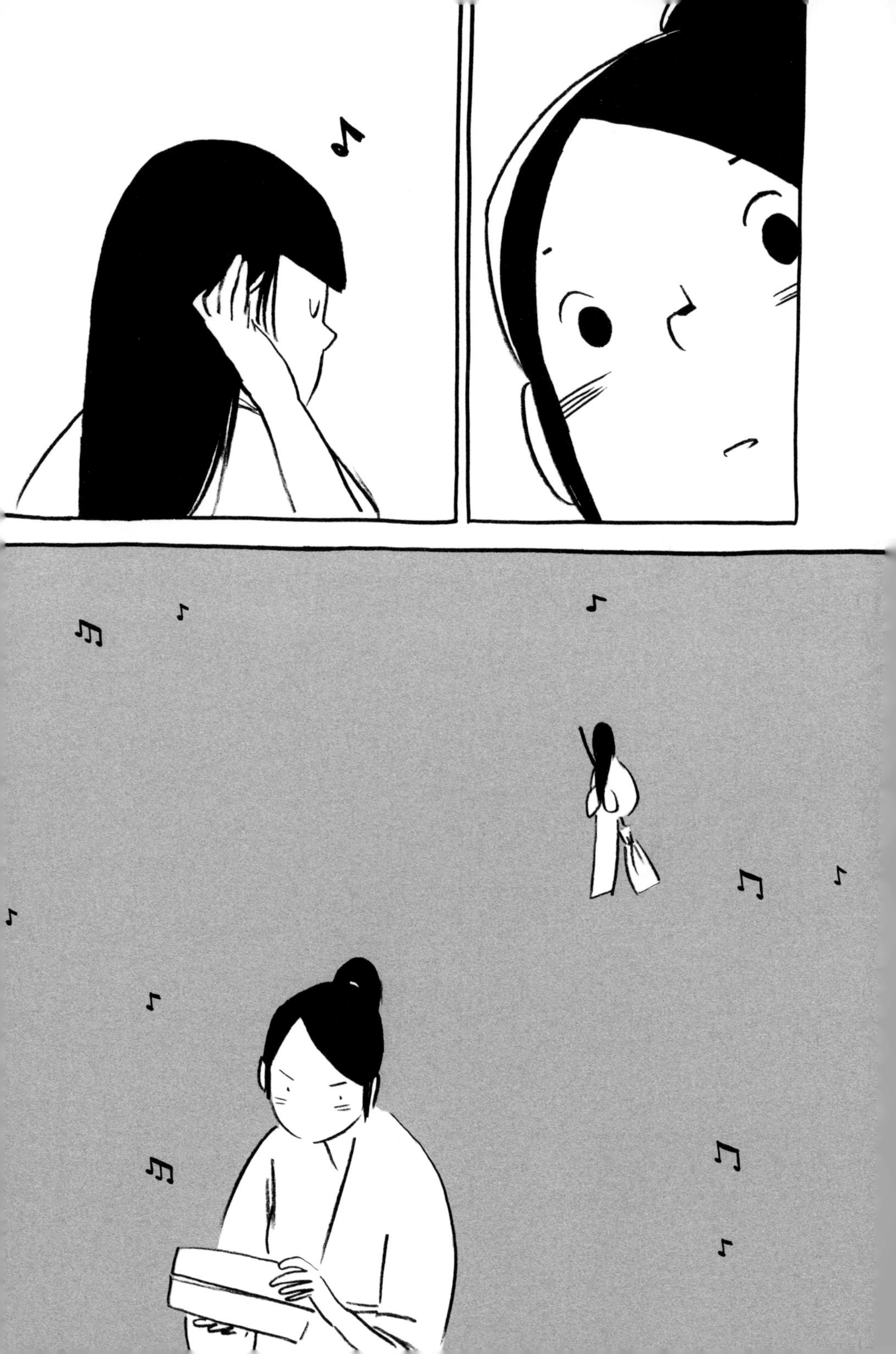

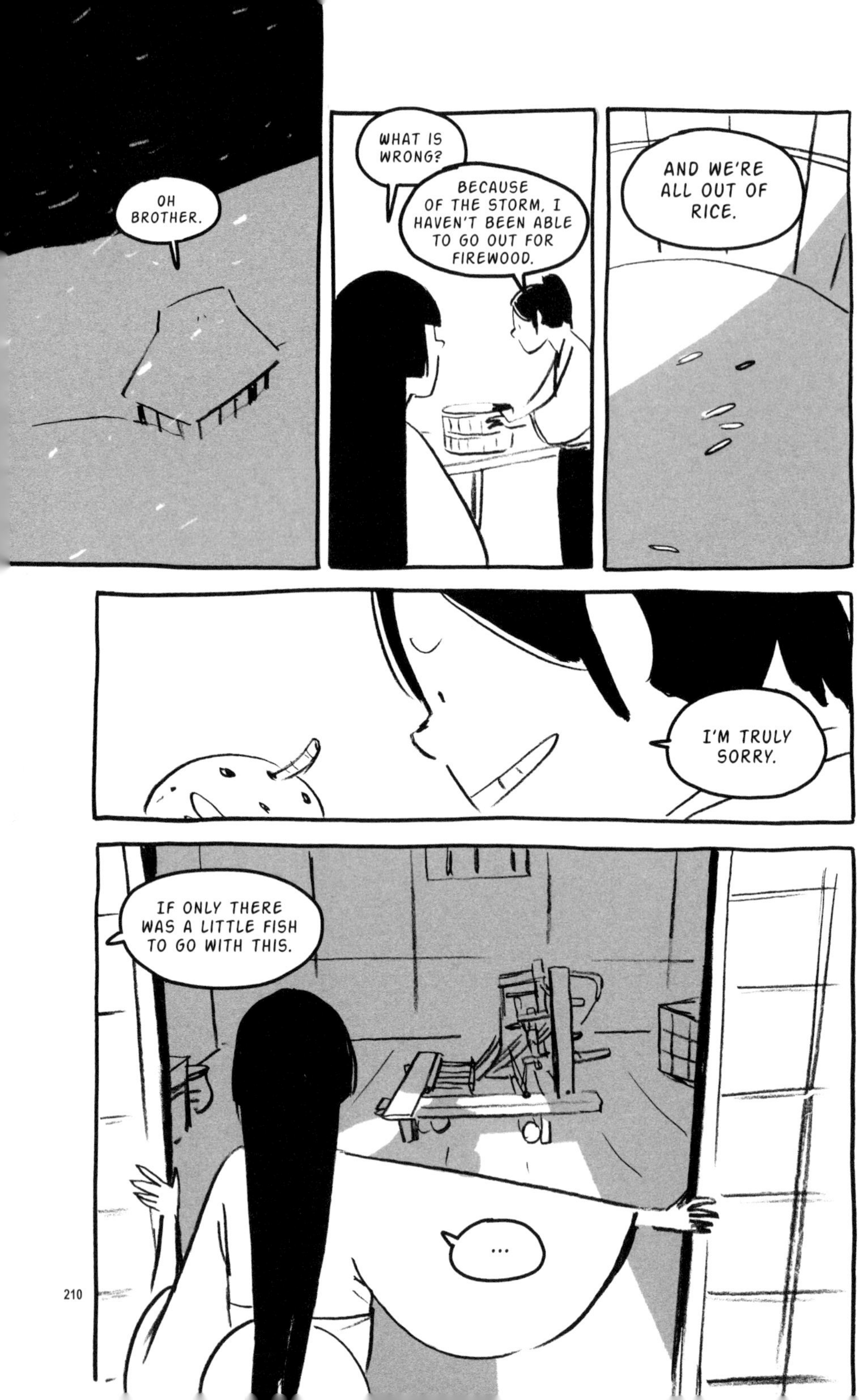
OH BROTHER.
WHAT IS WRONG?
BECAUSE OF THE STORM, I HAVEN'T BEEN ABLE TO GO OUT FOR FIREWOOD.
AND WE'RE ALL OUT OF RICE.
I'M TRULY SORRY.
IF ONLY THERE WAS A LITTLE FISH TO GO WITH THIS.
...

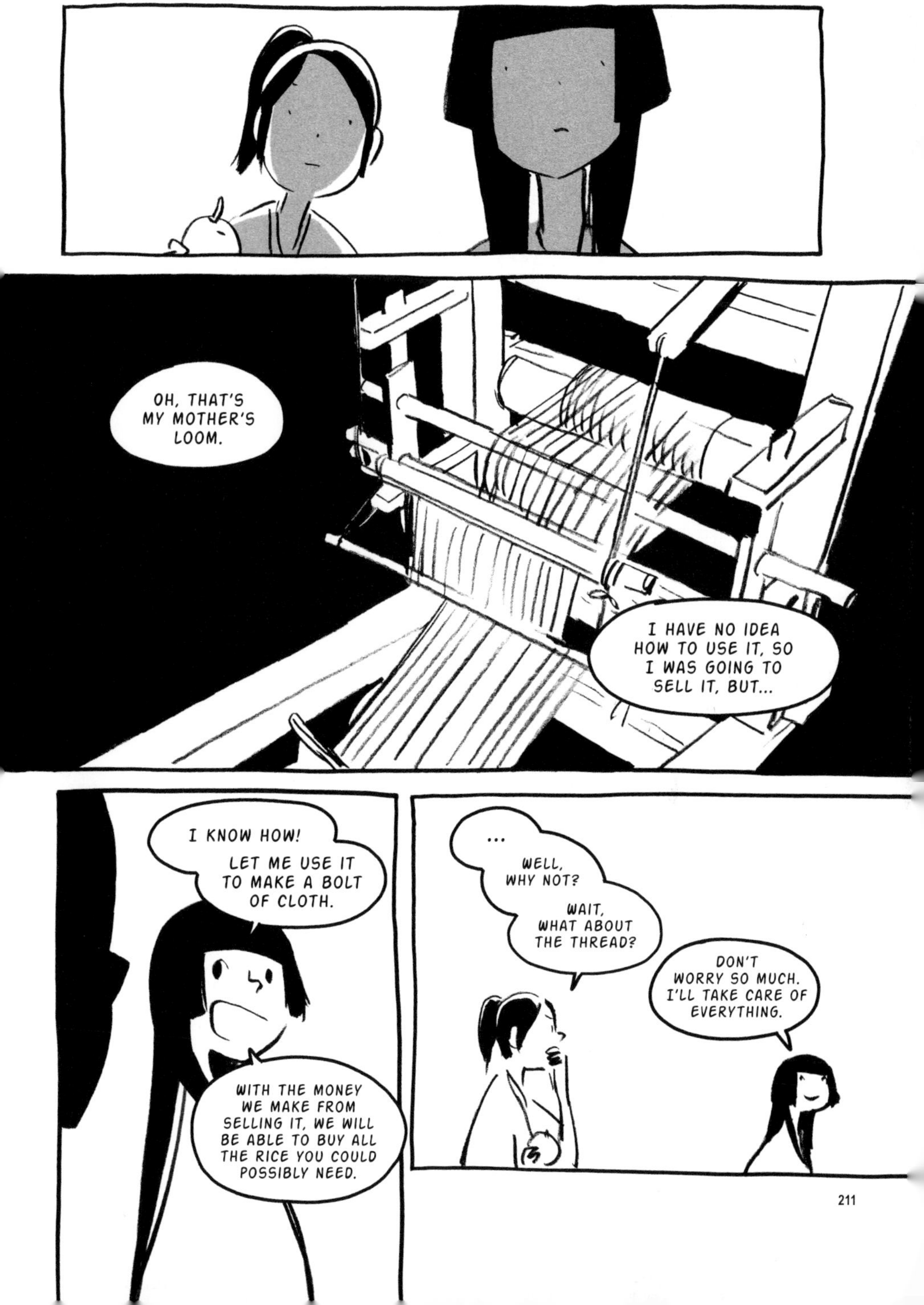
OH, THAT'S MY MOTHER'S LOOM.
I HAVE NO IDEA HOW TO USE IT, SO I WAS GOING TO SELL IT, BUT...
I KNOW HOW!
LET ME USE IT TO MAKE A BOLT OF CLOTH.
WITH THE MONEY WE MAKE FROM SELLING IT, WE WILL BE ABLE TO BUY ALL THE RICE YOU COULD POSSIBLY NEED.
...
WELL, WHY NOT?
WAIT, WHAT ABOUT THE THREAD?
DON'T WORRY SO MUCH. I'LL TAKE CARE OF EVERYTHING.

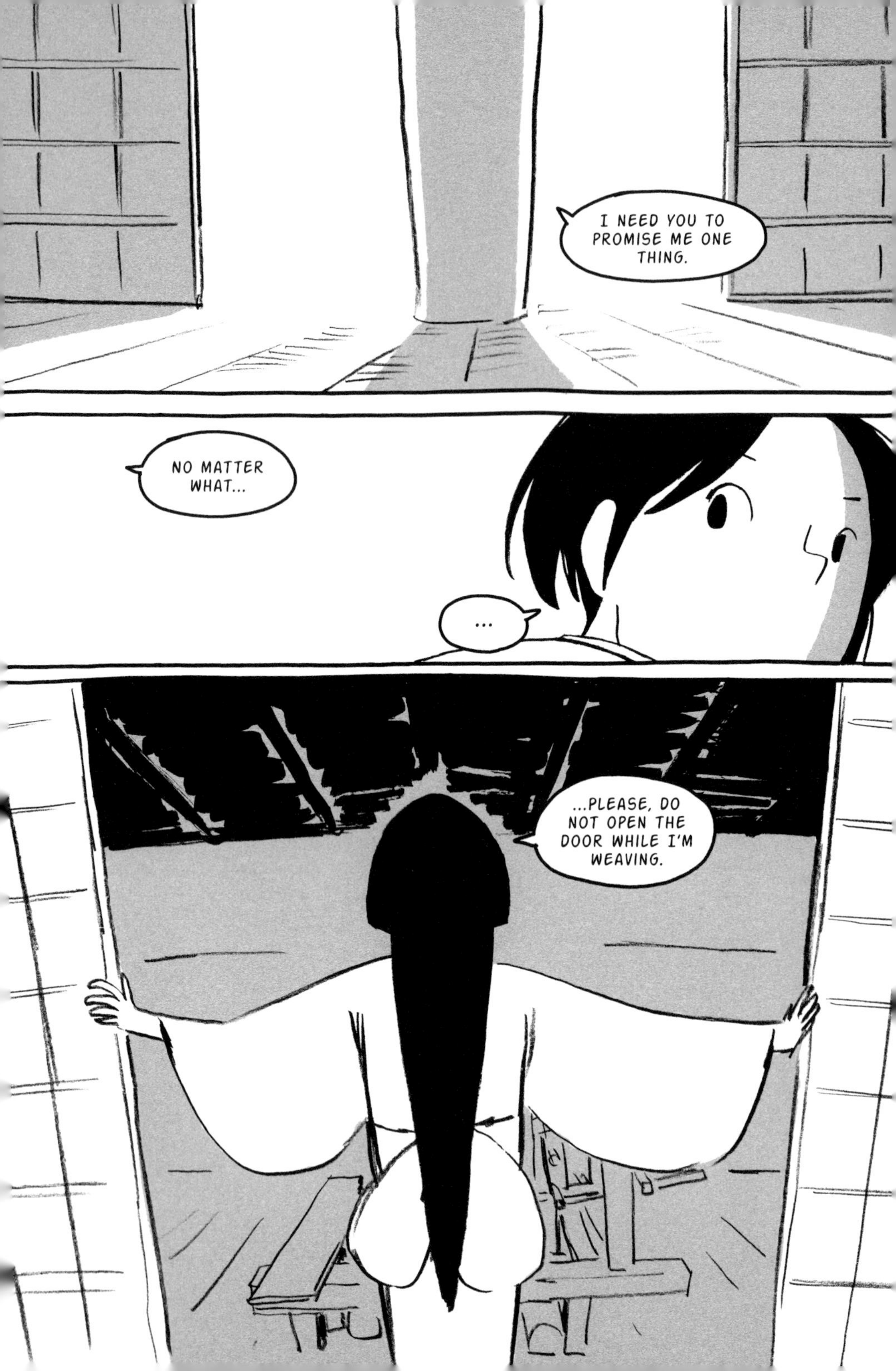
I NEED YOU TO PROMISE ME ONE THING.
NO MATTER WHAT...
...
...PLEASE, DO NOT OPEN THE DOOR WHILE I'M WEAVING.

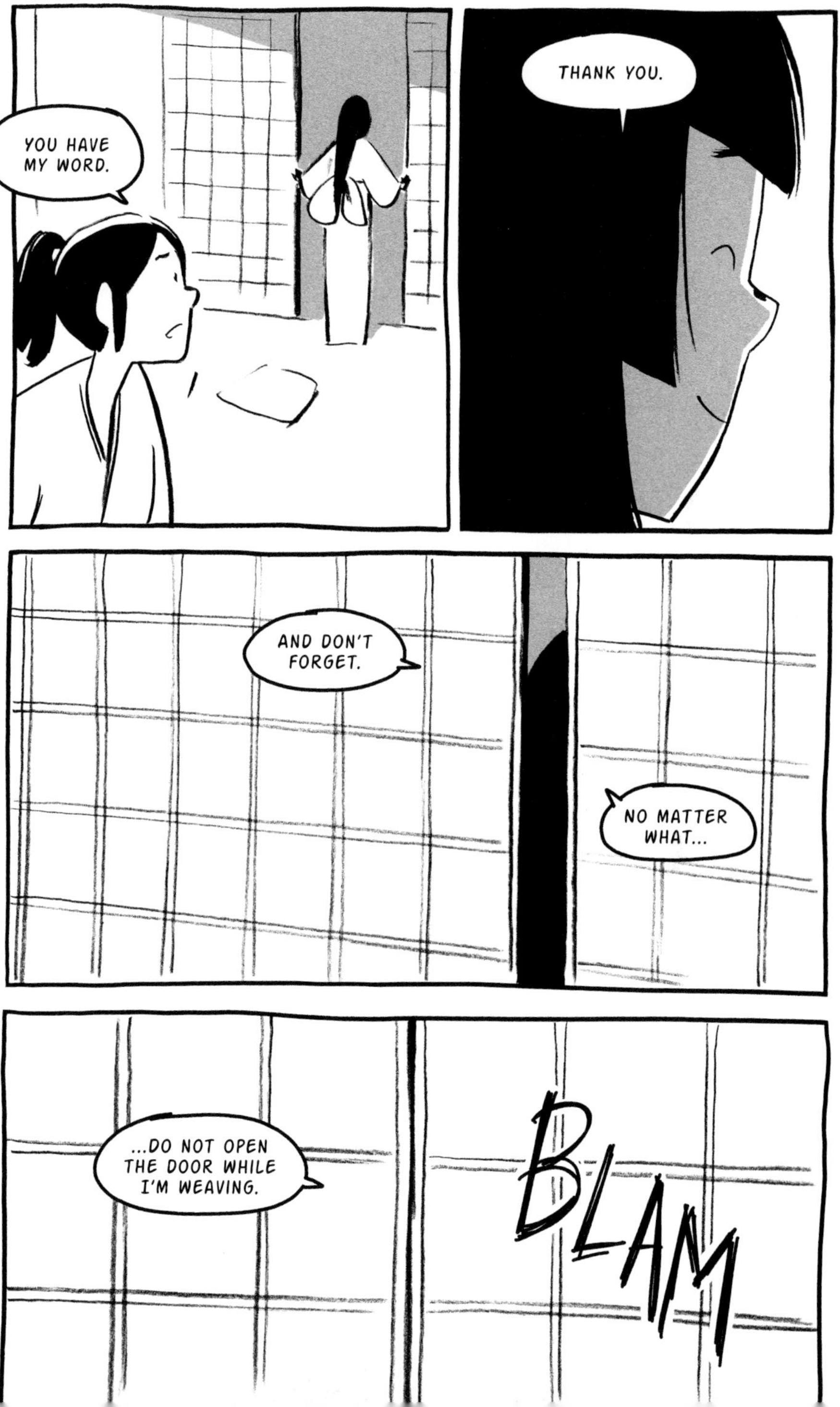
YOU HAVE MY WORD.
THANK YOU.
AND DON'T FORGET.
NO MATTER WHAT...
...DO NOT OPEN THE DOOR WHILE I'M WEAVING.
BLAM

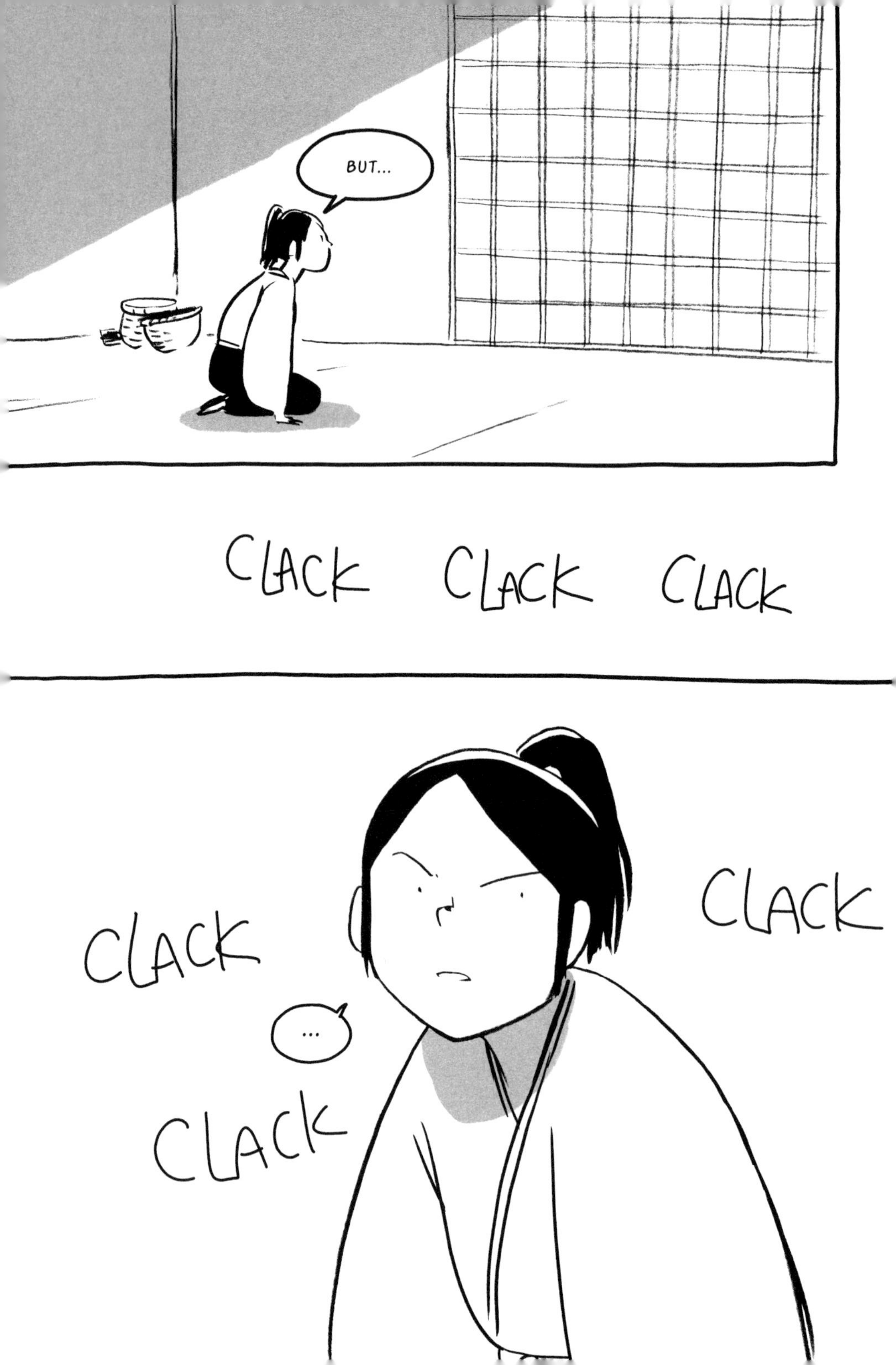
BUT...
CLACK CLACK CLACK
CLACK
CLACK
...
CLACK

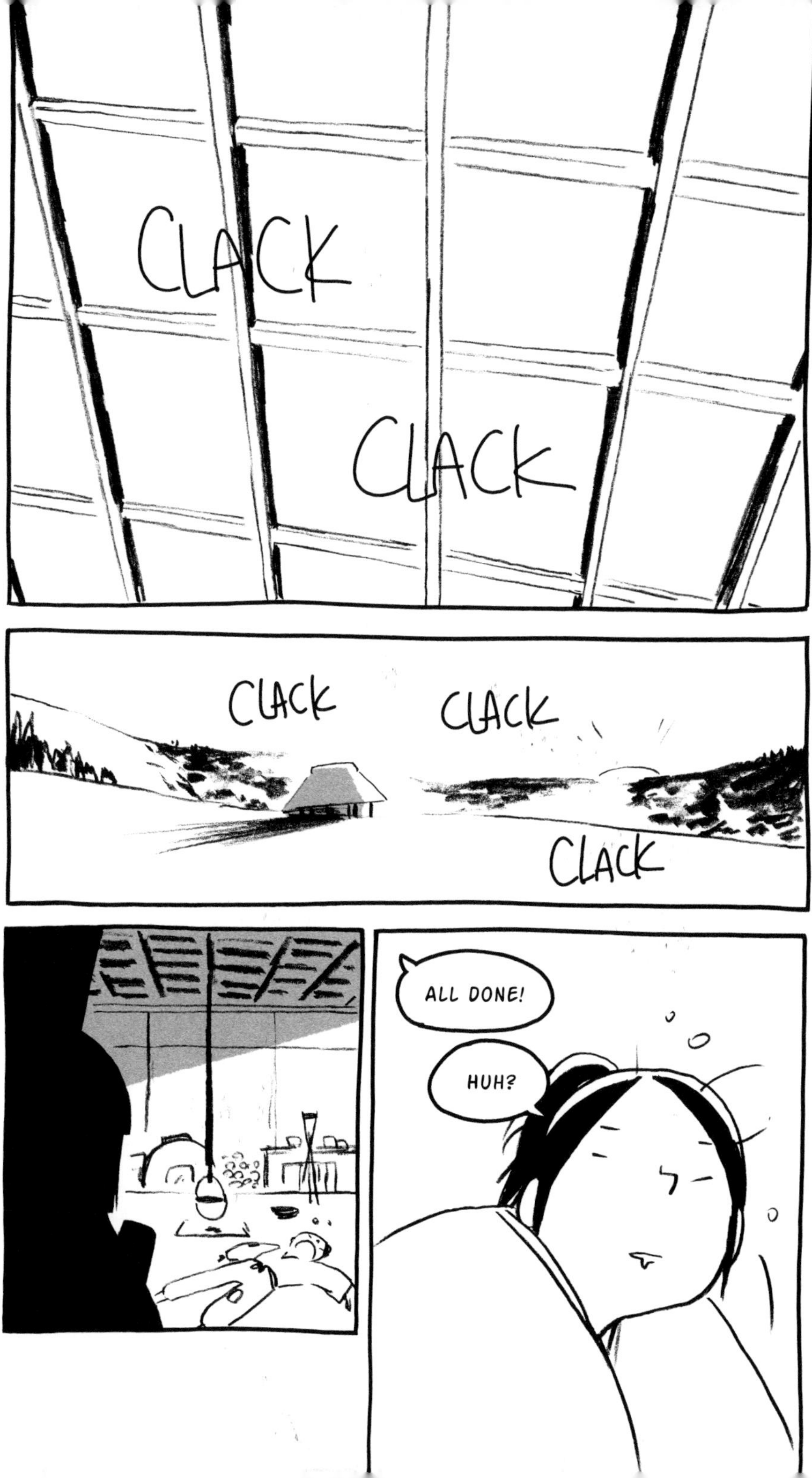
CLACK
CLACK
CLACK
CLACK
CLACK
ALL DONE!
HUH?

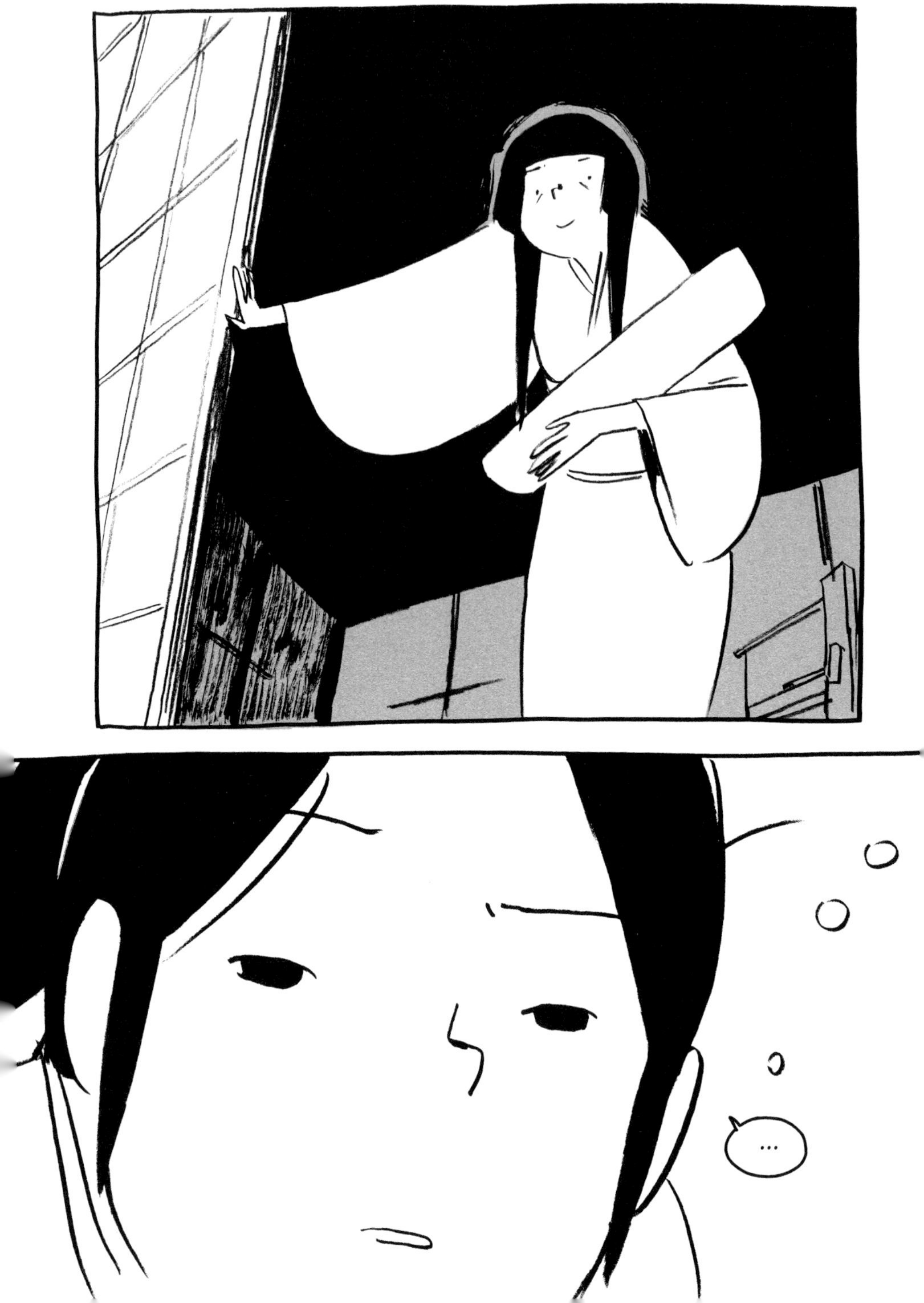
...

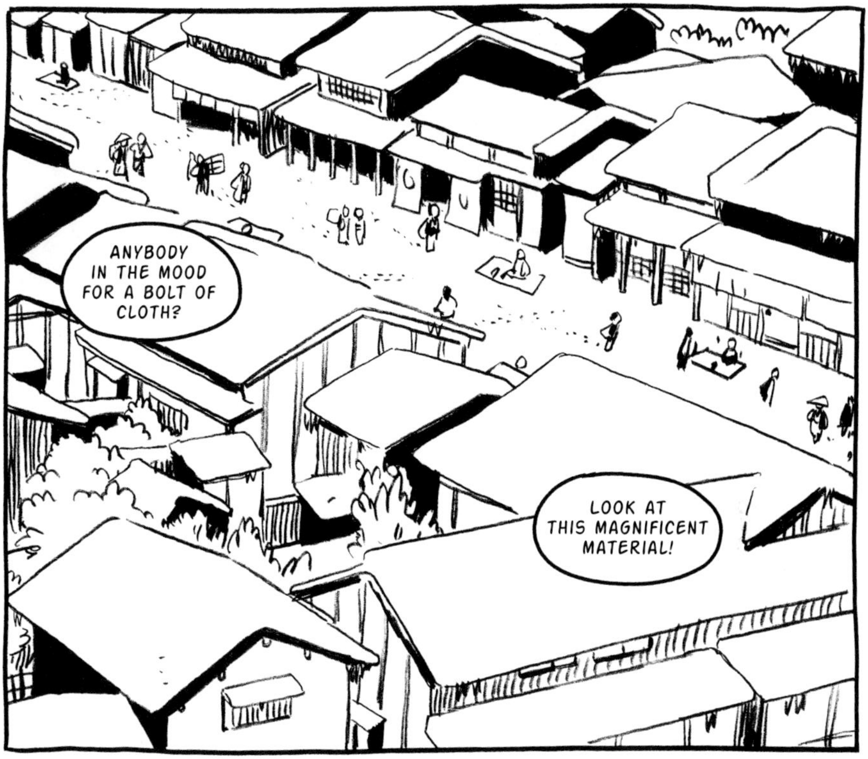
ANYBODY IN THE MOOD FOR A BOLT OF CLOTH?
LOOK AT THIS MAGNIFICENT MATERIAL!

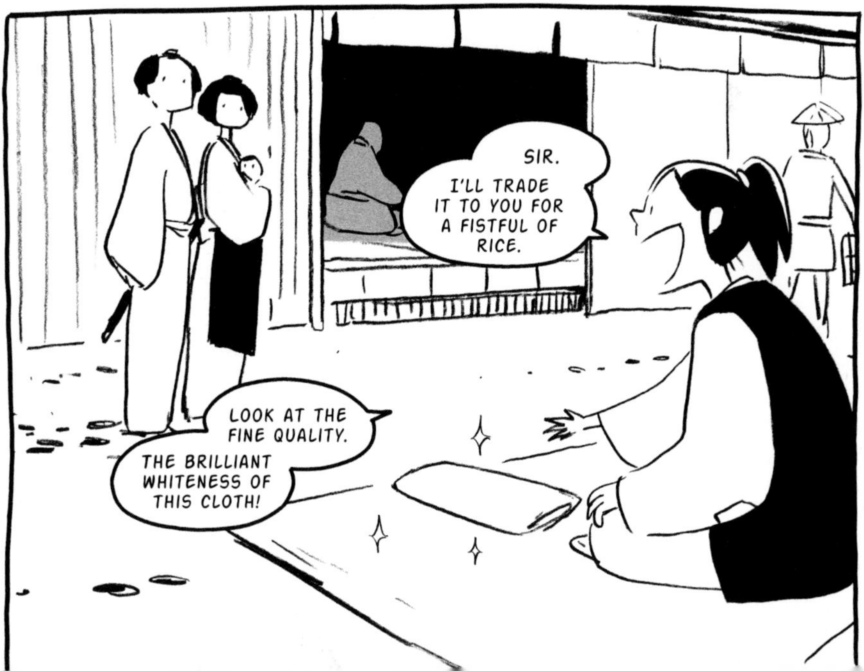
SIR.
I'LL TRADE IT TO YOU FOR A FISTFUL OF RICE.
LOOK AT THE FINE QUALITY.
THE BRILLIANT WHITENESS OF THIS CLOTH!

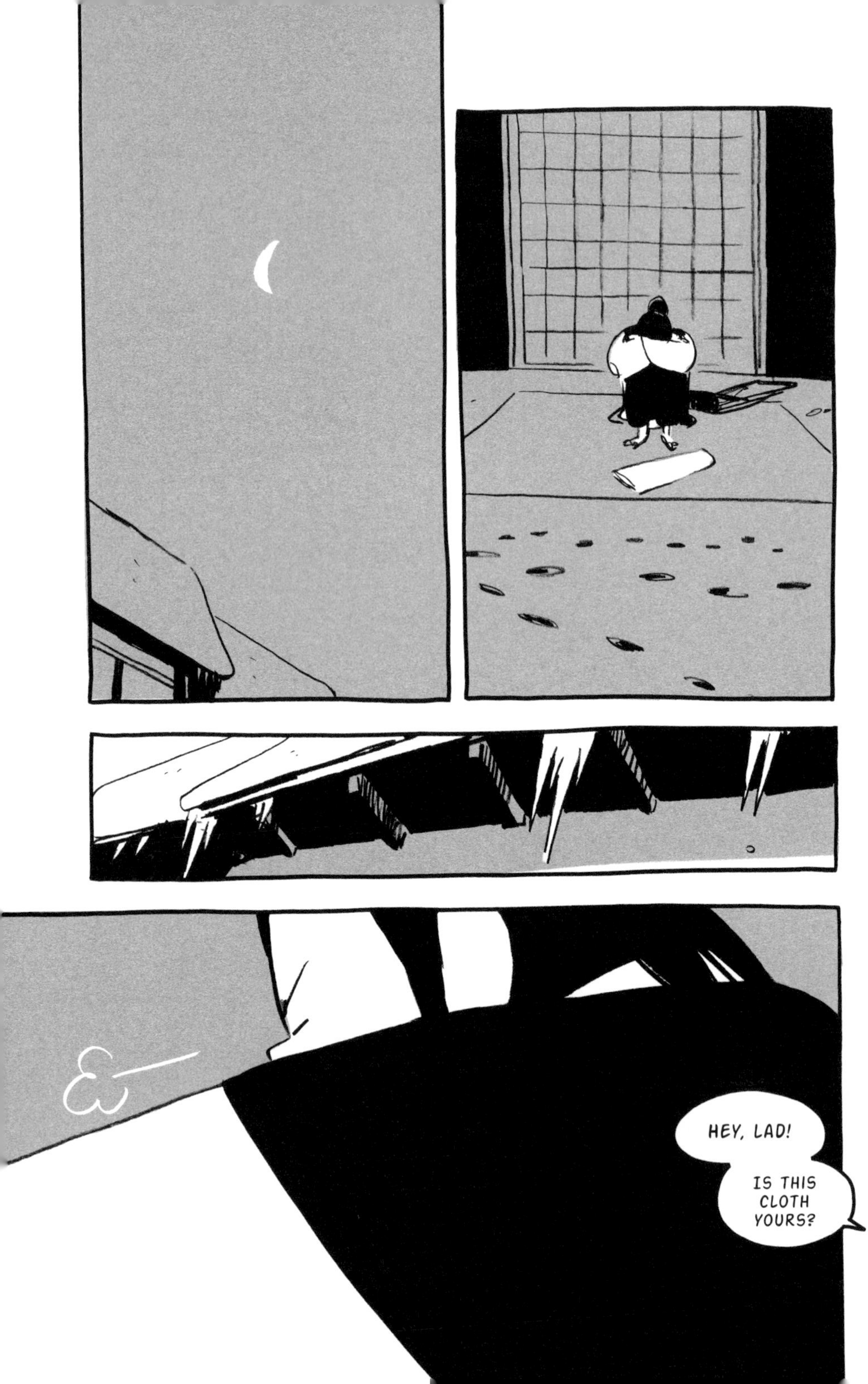
HEY, LAD!
IS THIS CLOTH YOURS?

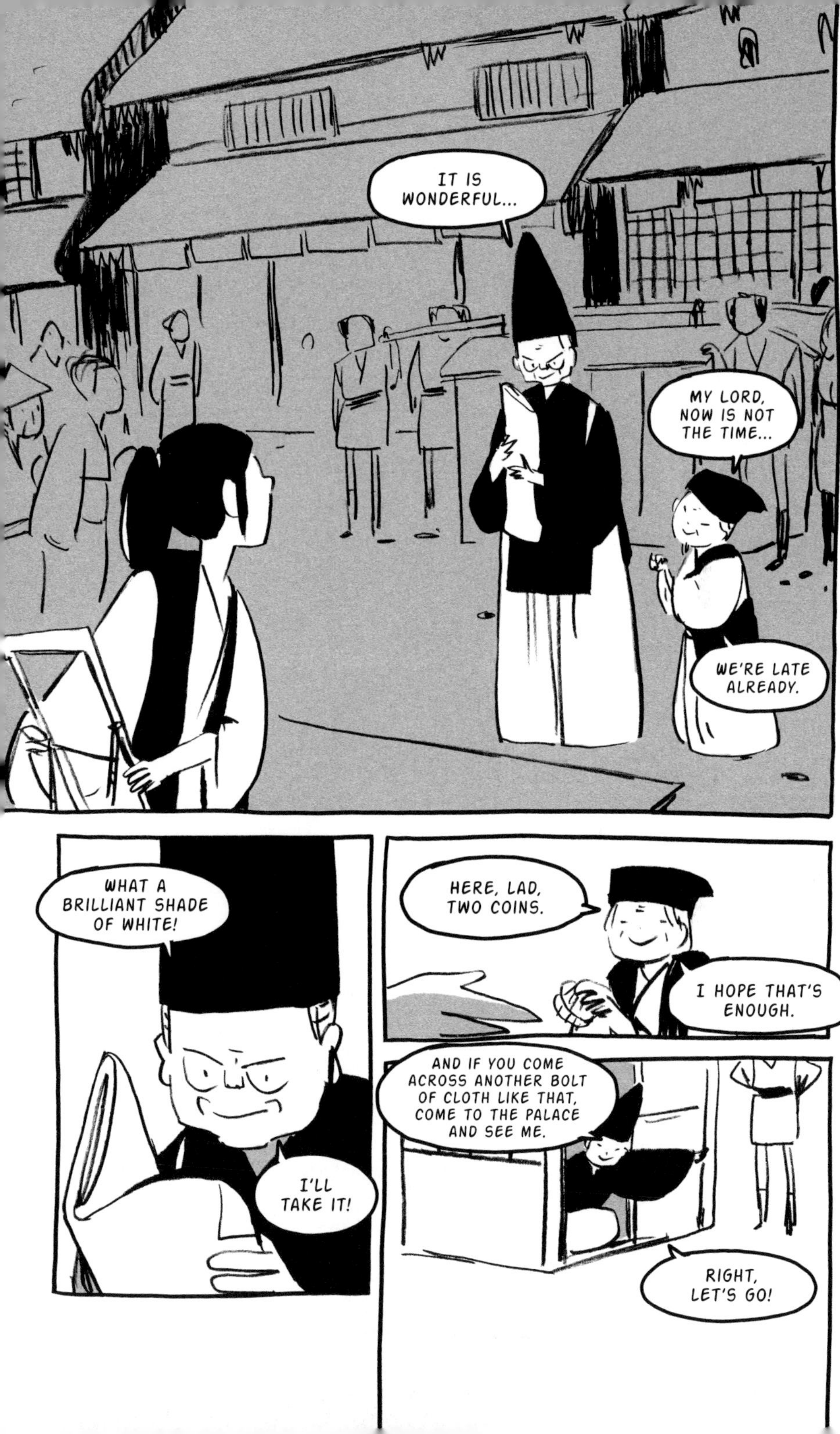
IT IS WONDERFUL...
MY LORD, NOW IS NOT THE TIME...
WE'RE LATE ALREADY.
WHAT A BRILLIANT SHADE OF WHITE!
I'LL TAKE IT!
HERE, LAD, TWO COINS.
I HOPE THAT'S ENOUGH.
AND IF YOU COME ACROSS ANOTHER BOLT OF CLOTH LIKE THAT, COME TO THE PALACE AND SEE ME.
RIGHT, LET'S GO!

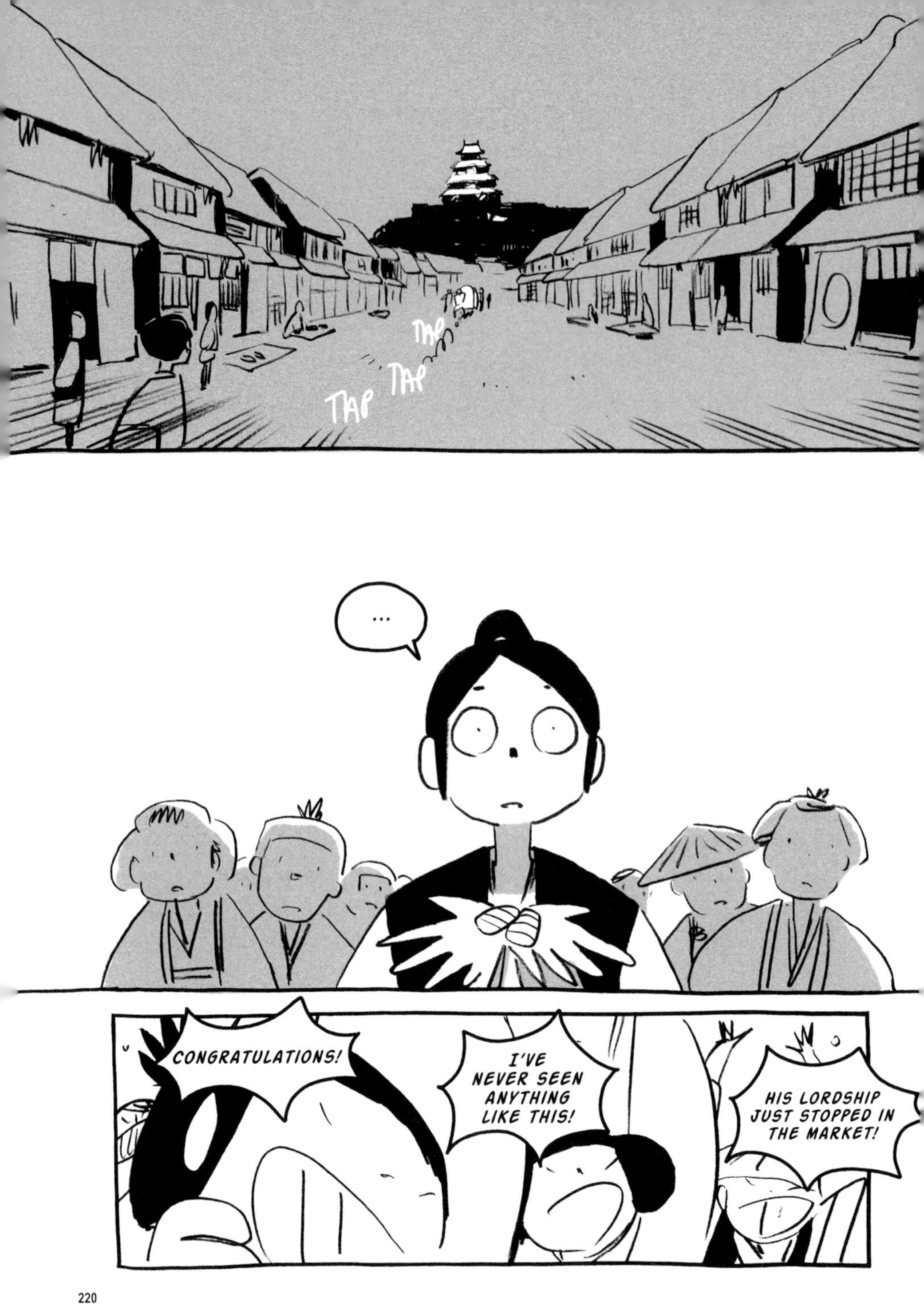
TAP
TAP
TAP
...
CONGRATULATIONS!
I'VE NEVER SEEN ANYTHING LIKE THIS!
HIS LORDSHIP JUST STOPPED IN THE MARKET!

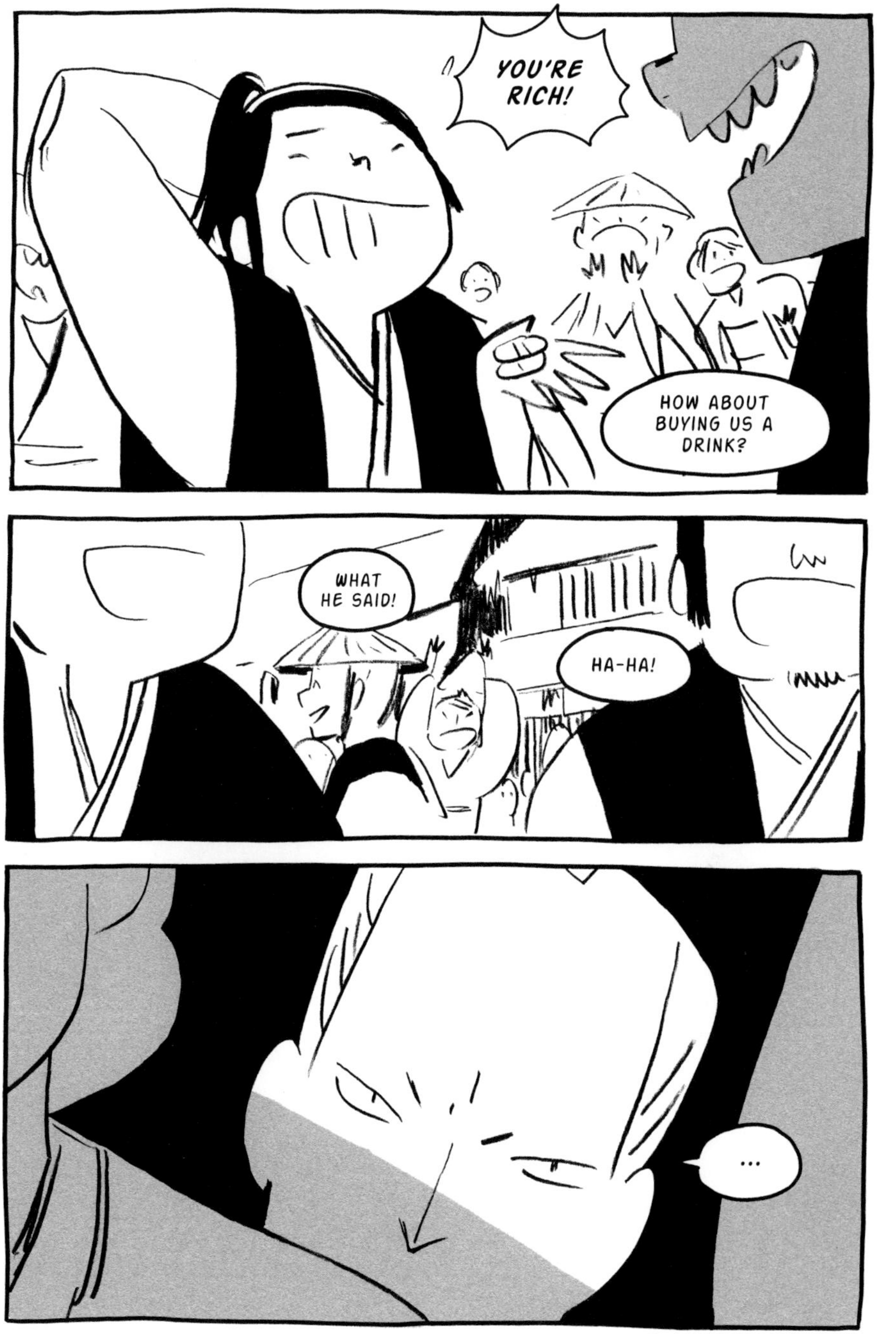
YOU'RE RICH!
HOW ABOUT BUYING US A DRINK?
WHAT HE SAID!
HA-HA!
...

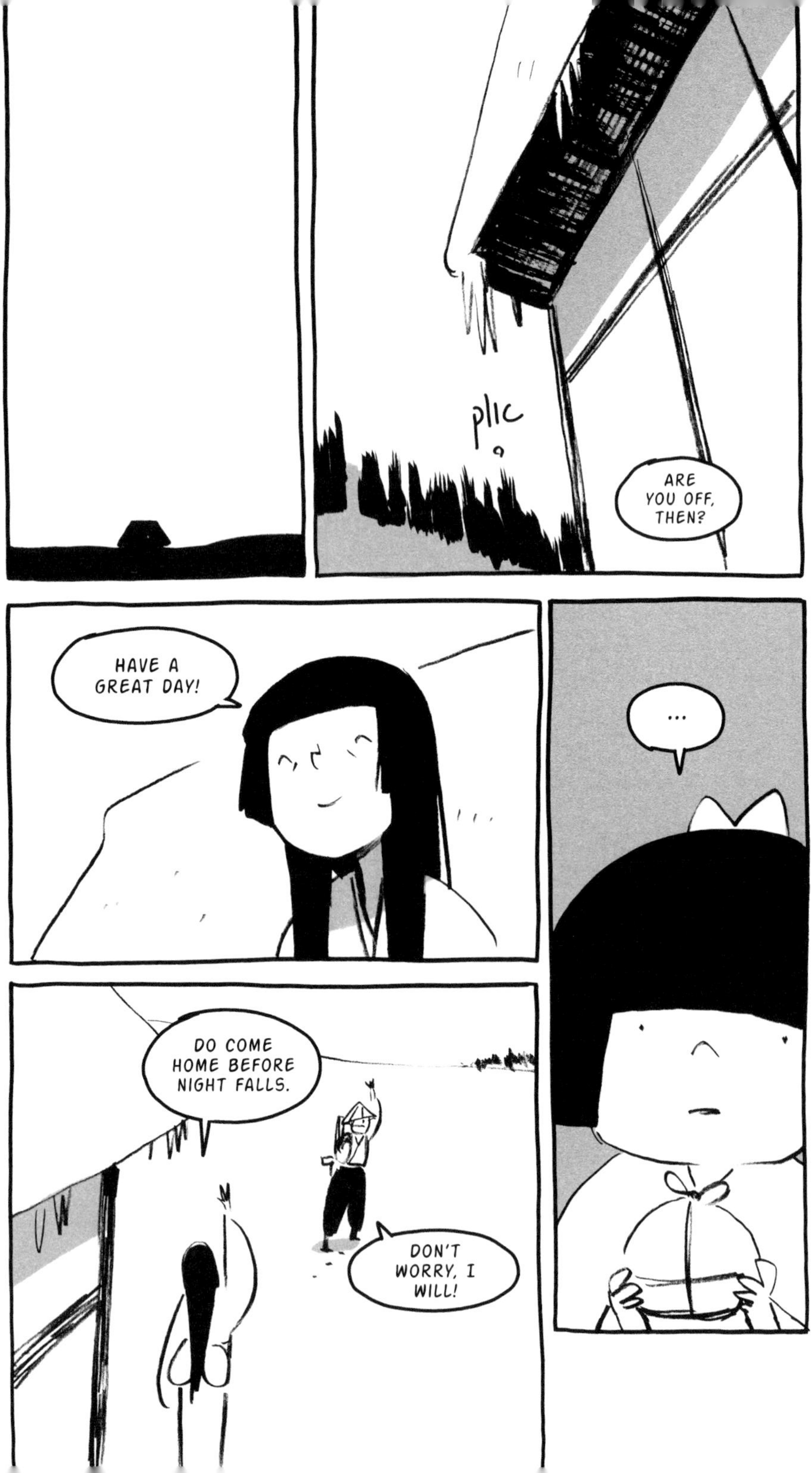
plic
ARE YOU OFF, THEN?
HAVE A GREAT DAY!
...
DO COME HOME BEFORE NIGHT FALLS.
DON'T WORRY, I WILL!

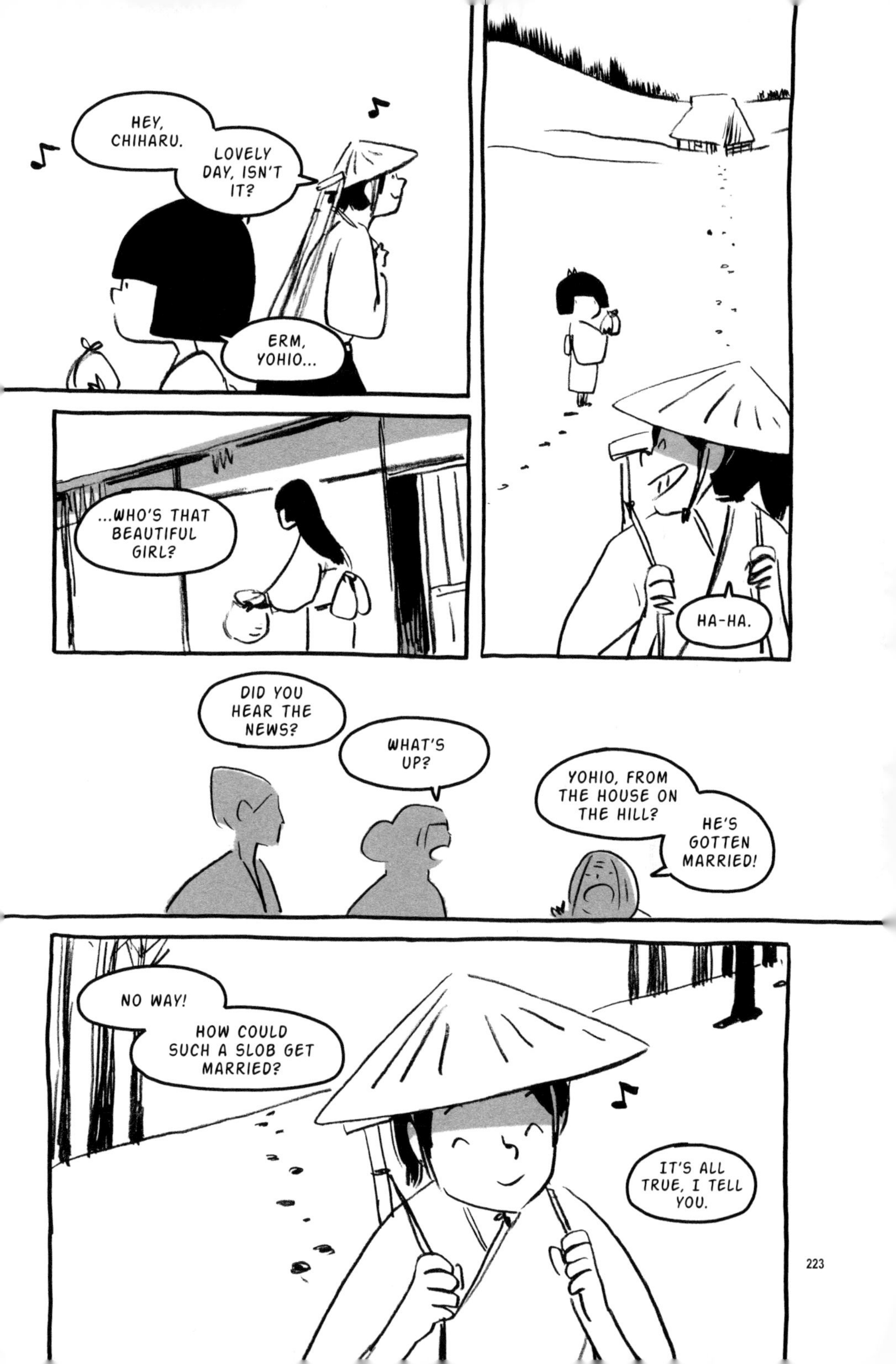
HEY, CHIHARU.
LOVELY DAY, ISN'T IT?
ERM, YOHIO...
...WHO'S THAT BEAUTIFUL GIRL?
HA-HA.
DID YOU HEAR THE NEWS?
WHAT'S UP?
YOHIO, FROM THE HOUSE ON THE HILL?
HE'S GOTTEN MARRIED!
NO WAY!
HOW COULD SUCH A SLOB GET MARRIED?
IT'S ALL TRUE, I TELL YOU.

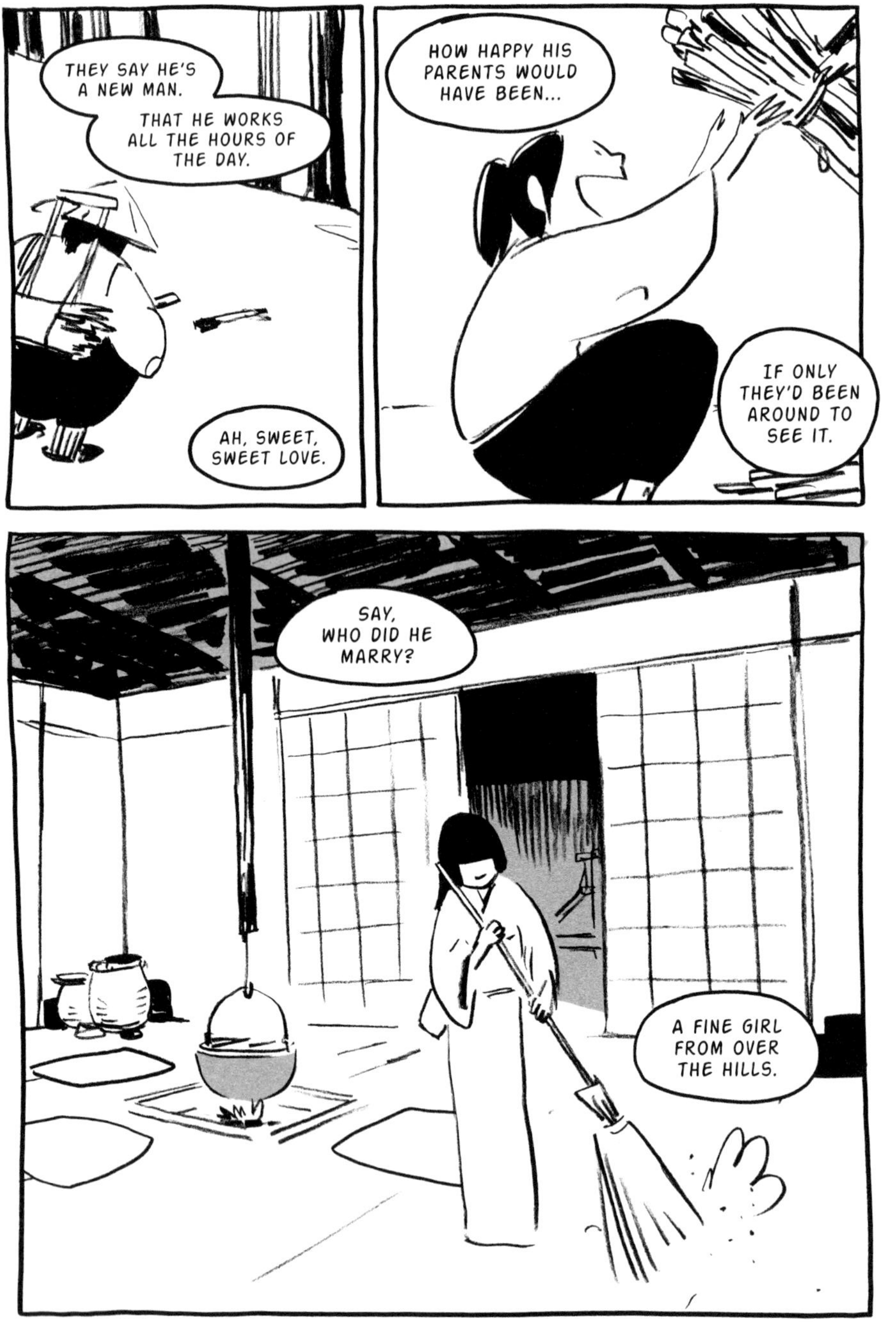
THEY SAY HE'S A NEW MAN.
THAT HE WORKS ALL THE HOURS OF THE DAY.
AH, SWEET, SWEET LOVE.
HOW HAPPY HIS PARENTS WOULD HAVE BEEN...
IF ONLY THEY'D BEEN AROUND TO SEE IT.
SAY, WHO DID HE MARRY?
A FINE GIRL FROM OVER THE HILLS.

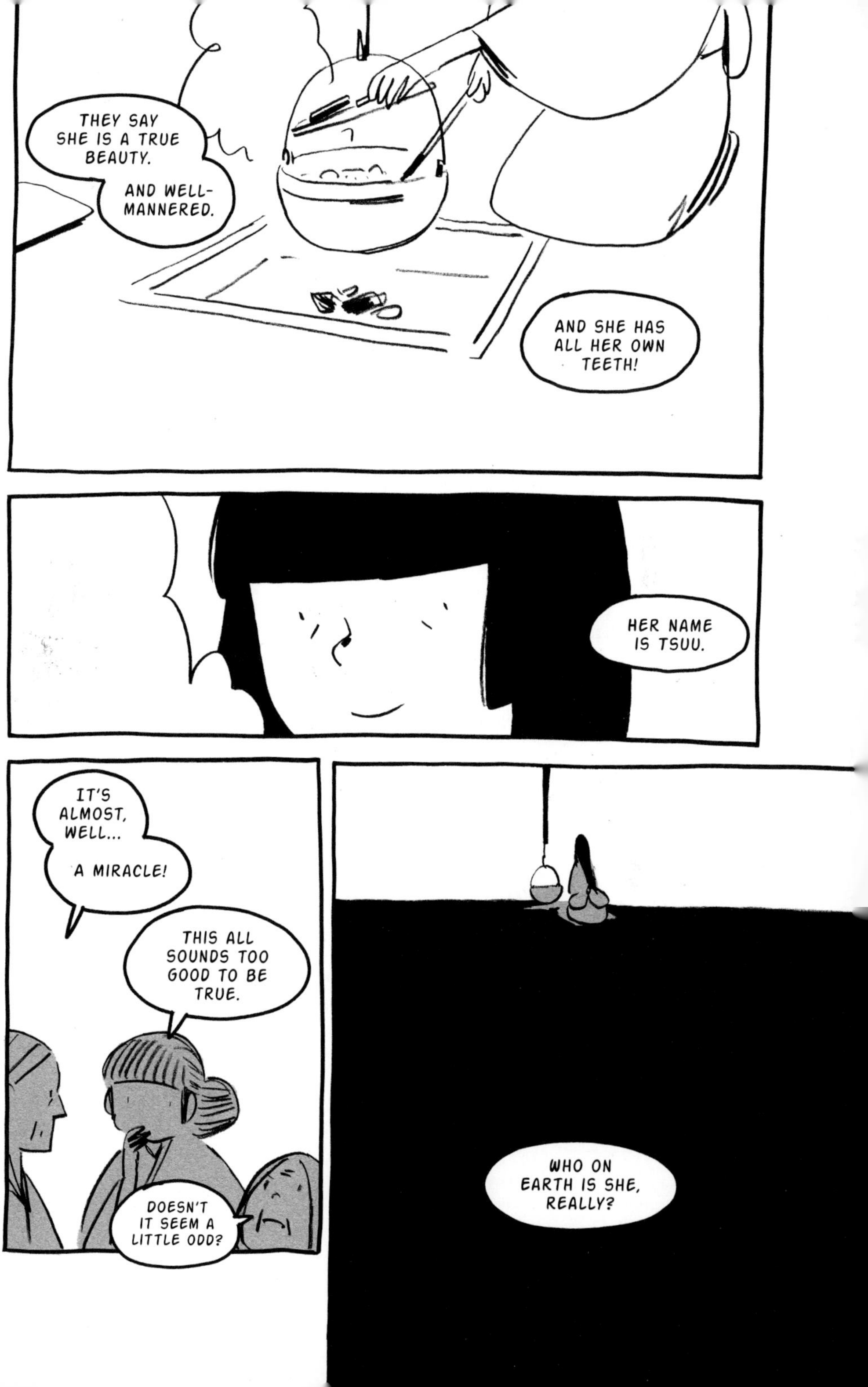
THEY SAY SHE IS A TRUE BEAUTY.
AND WELL-MANNERED.
AND SHE HAS ALL HER OWN TEETH!
HER NAME IS TSUU.
IT'S ALMOST, WELL...
A MIRACLE!
THIS ALL SOUNDS TOO GOOD TO BE TRUE.
DOESN'T IT SEEM A LITTLE ODD?
WHO ON EARTH IS SHE, REALLY?

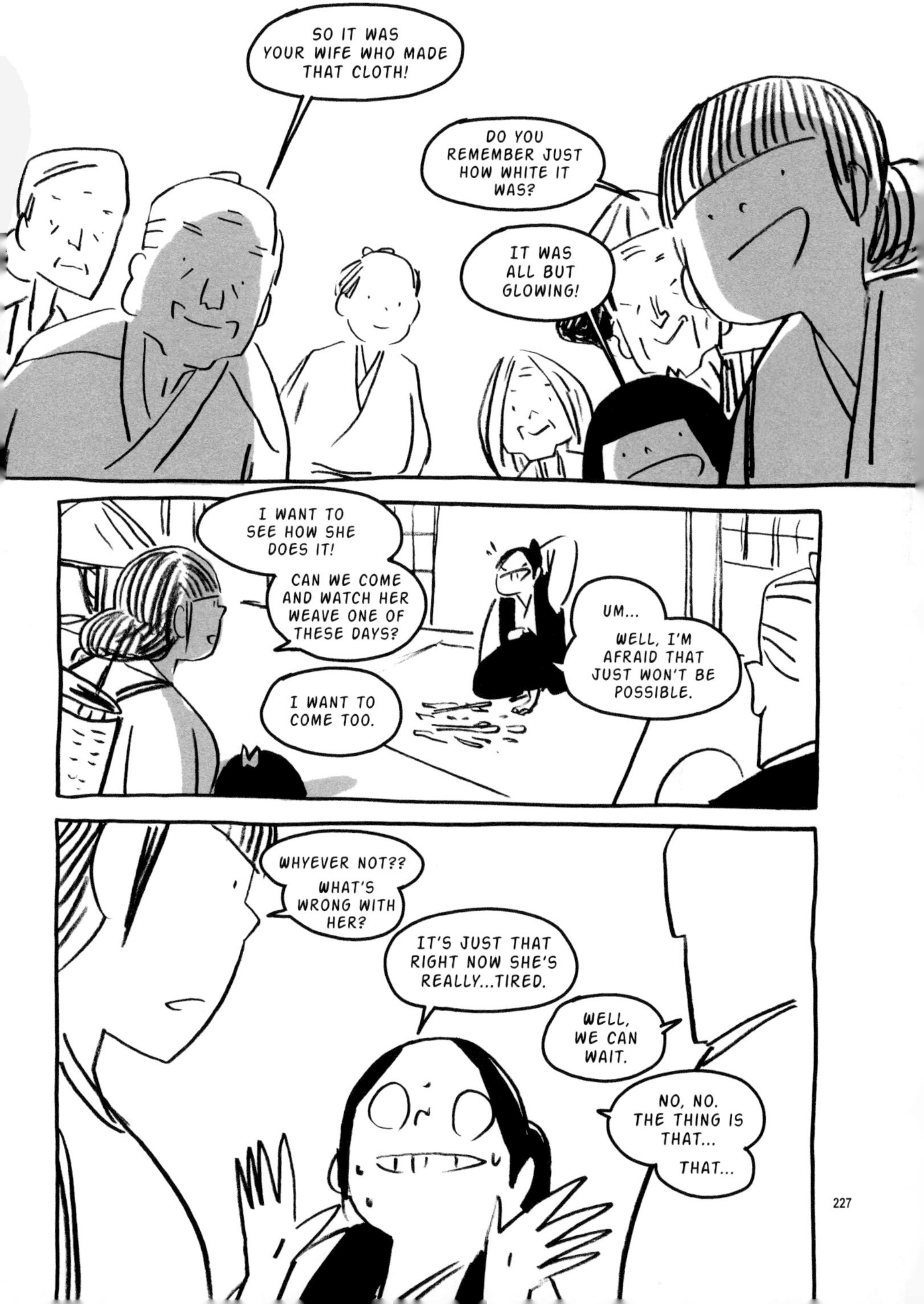

SO IT WAS YOUR WIFE WHO MADE THAT CLOTH!
DO YOU REMEMBER JUST HOW WHITE IT WAS?
IT WAS ALL BUT GLOWING!
I WANT TO SEE HOW SHE DOES IT!
CAN WE COME AND WATCH HER WEAVE ONE OF THESE DAYS?
I WANT TO COME TOO.
UM...
WELL, I'M AFRAID THAT JUST WON'T BE POSSIBLE.
WHYEVER NOT??
WHAT'S WRONG WITH HER?
IT'S JUST THAT RIGHT NOW SHE'S REALLY...TIRED.
WELL, WE CAN WAIT.
NO, NO. THE THING IS THAT...
THAT...

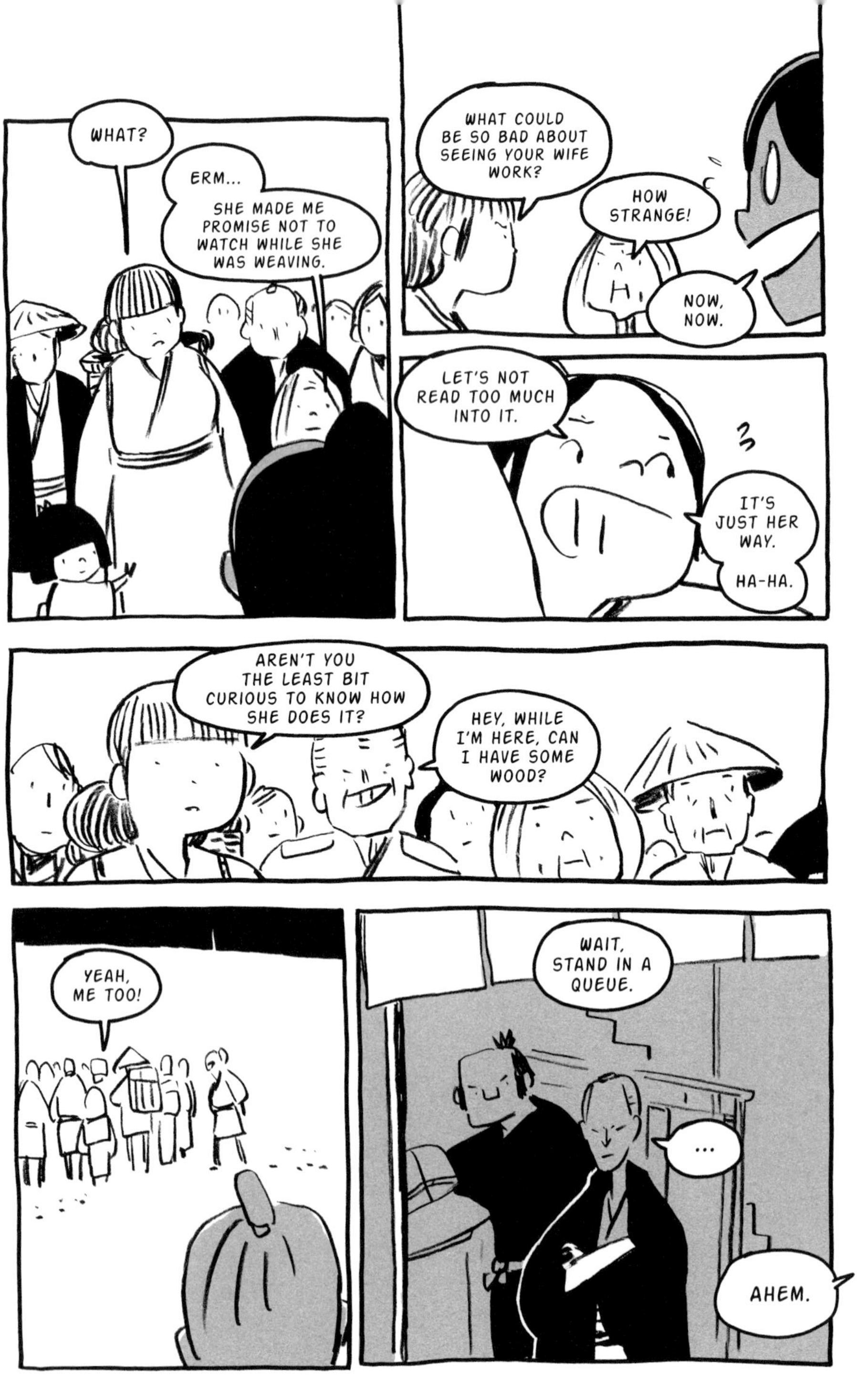
WHAT?
ERM...
SHE MADE ME PROMISE NOT TO WATCH WHILE SHE WAS WEAVING.
WHAT COULD BE SO BAD ABOUT SEEING YOUR WIFE WORK?
HOW STRANGE!
NOW, NOW.
LET'S NOT READ TOO MUCH INTO IT.
IT'S JUST HER WAY.
HA-HA.
AREN'T YOU THE LEAST BIT CURIOUS TO KNOW HOW SHE DOES IT?
HEY, WHILE I'M HERE, CAN I HAVE SOME WOOD?
YEAH, ME TOO!
WAIT, STAND IN A QUEUE.
...
AHEM.

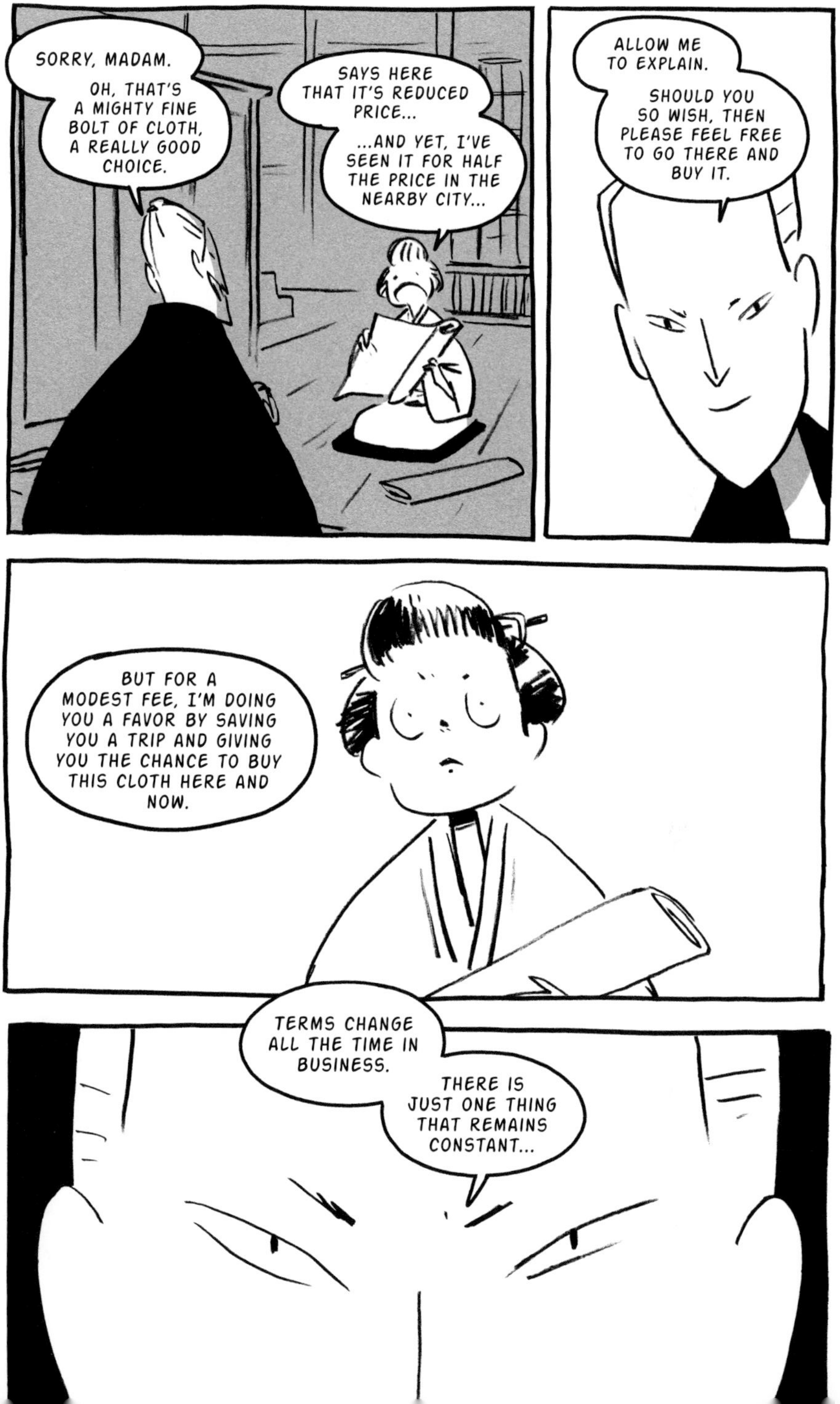
SORRY, MADAM.
OH, THAT'S A MIGHTY FINE BOLT OF CLOTH, A REALLY GOOD CHOICE.
SAYS HERE THAT IT'S REDUCED PRICE...
...AND YET, I'VE SEEN IT FOR HALF THE PRICE IN THE NEARBY CITY...
ALLOW ME TO EXPLAIN.
SHOULD YOU SO WISH, THEN PLEASE FEEL FREE TO GO THERE AND BUY IT.
BUT FOR A MODEST FEE, I'M DOING YOU A FAVOR BY SAVING YOU A TRIP AND GIVING YOU THE CHANCE TO BUY THIS CLOTH HERE AND NOW.
TERMS CHANGE ALL THE TIME IN BUSINESS.
THERE IS JUST ONE THING THAT REMAINS CONSTANT...

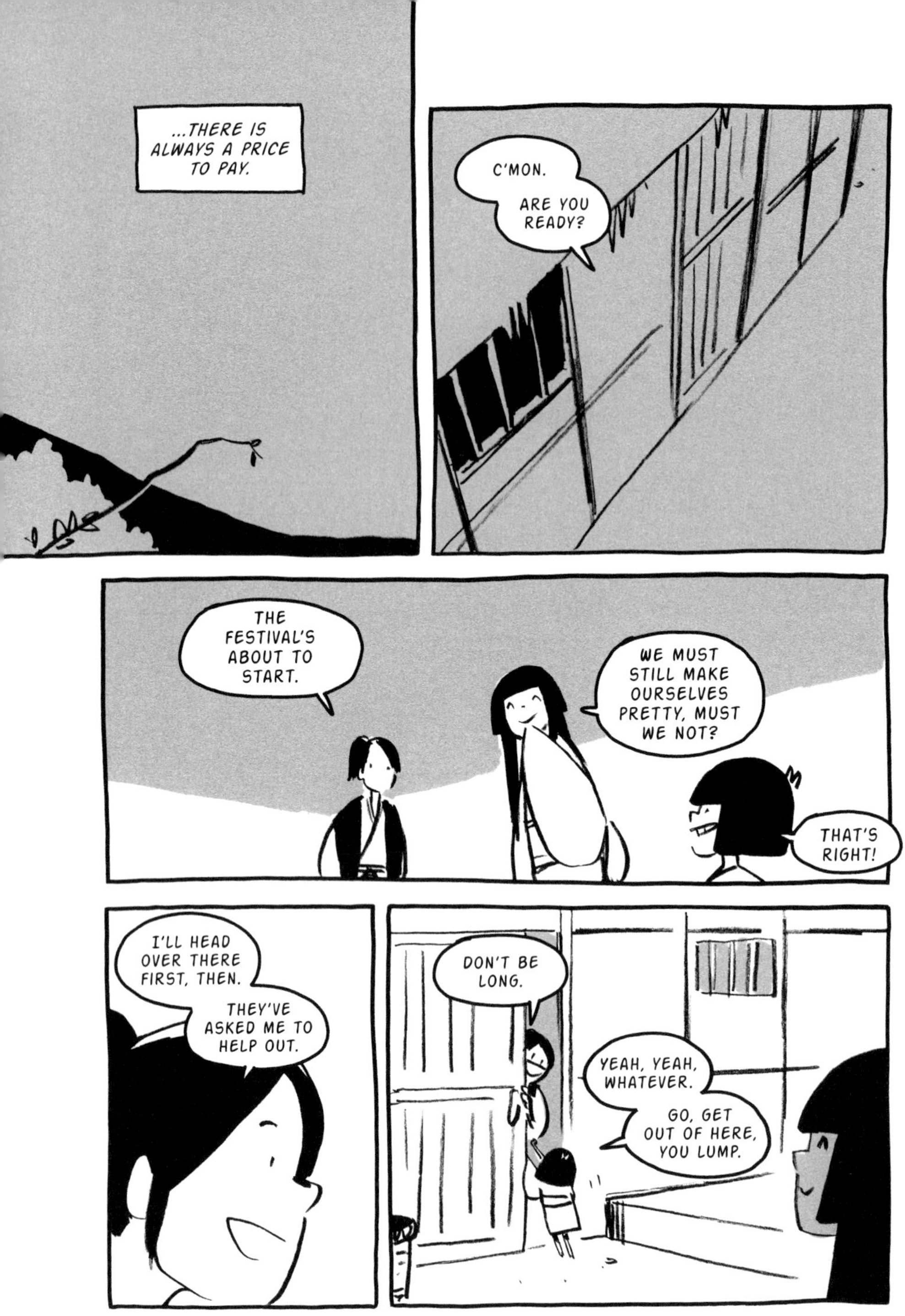
...THERE IS ALWAYS A PRICE TO PAY.
C'MON.
ARE YOU READY?
THE FESTIVAL'S ABOUT TO START.
WE MUST STILL MAKE OURSELVES PRETTY, MUST WE NOT?
THAT'S RIGHT!
I'LL HEAD OVER THERE FIRST, THEN.
THEY'VE ASKED ME TO HELP OUT.
DON'T BE LONG.
YEAH, YEAH, WHATEVER.
GO, GET OUT OF HERE, YOU LUMP.

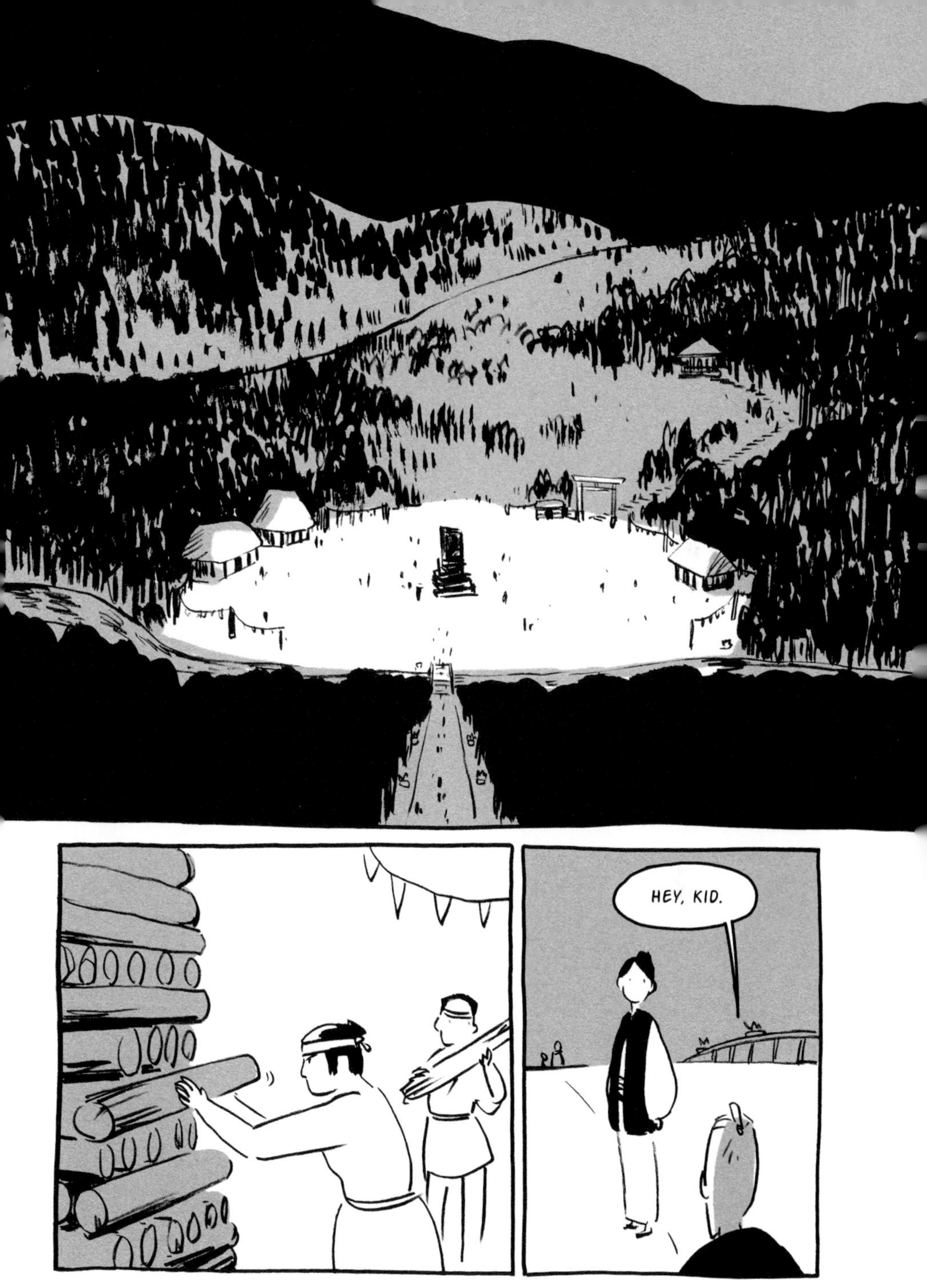
HEY, KID.

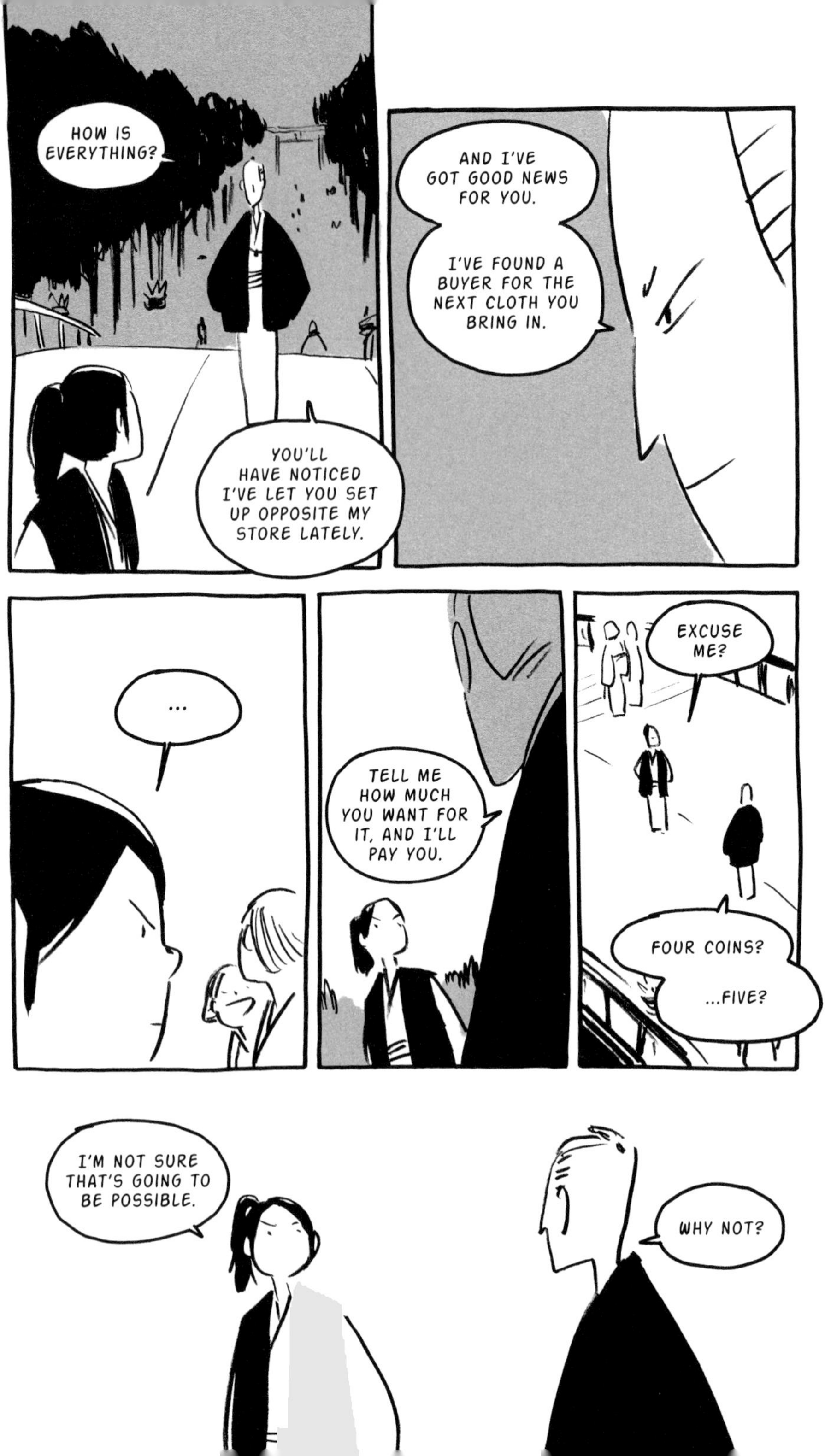
HOW IS EVERYTHING?
YOU'LL HAVE NOTICED I'VE LET YOU SET UP OPPOSITE MY STORE LATELY.
AND I'VE GOT GOOD NEWS FOR YOU.
I'VE FOUND A BUYER FOR THE NEXT CLOTH YOU BRING IN.
...
TELL ME HOW MUCH YOU WANT FOR IT, AND I'LL PAY YOU.
EXCUSE ME?
FOUR COINS?
...FIVE?
I'M NOT SURE THAT'S GOING TO BE POSSIBLE.
WHY NOT?

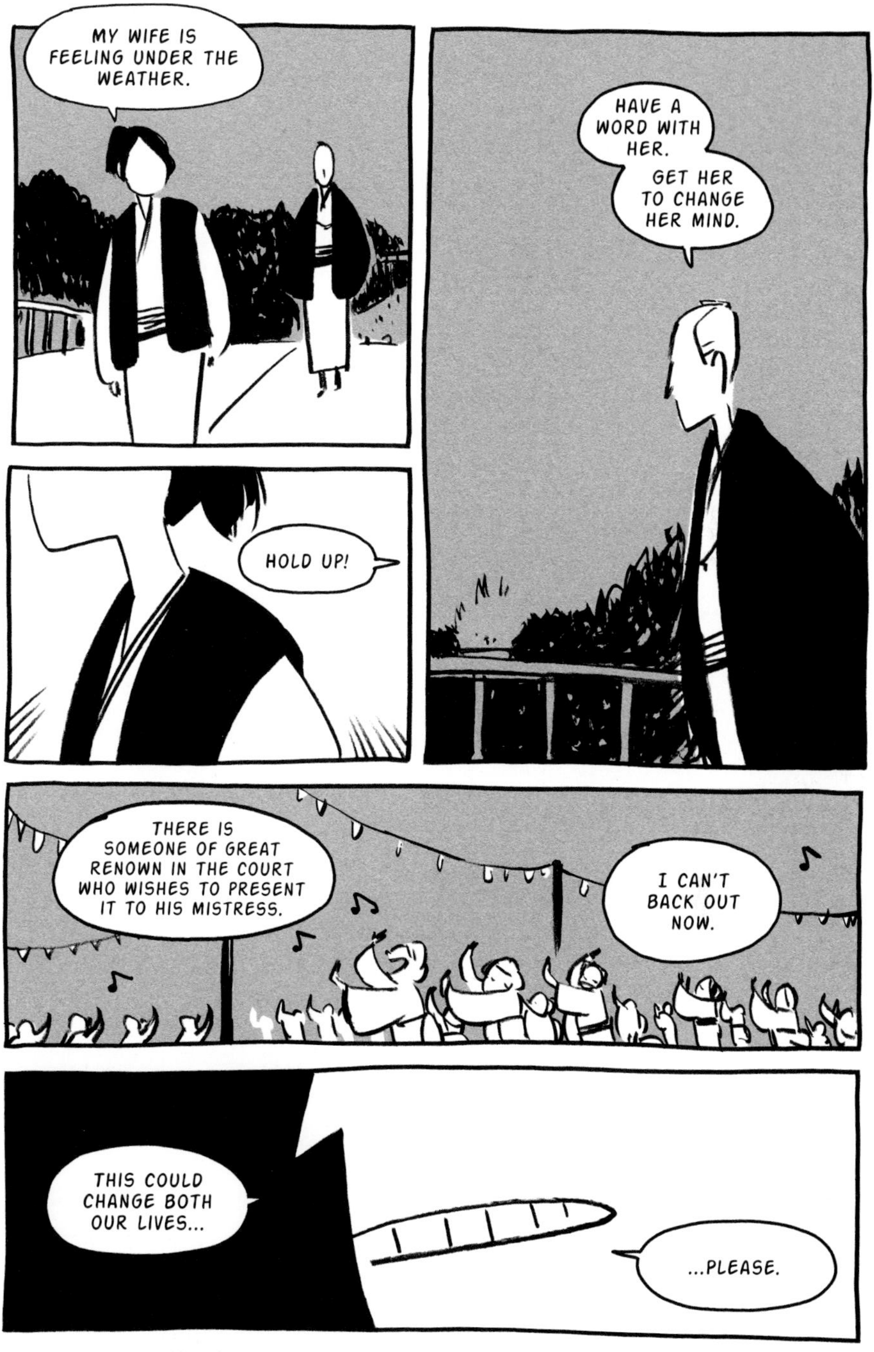
MY WIFE IS FEELING UNDER THE WEATHER.
HAVE A WORD WITH HER.
GET HER TO CHANGE HER MIND.
HOLD UP!
THERE IS SOMEONE OF GREAT RENOWN IN THE COURT WHO WISHES TO PRESENT IT TO HIS MISTRESS.
I CAN'T BACK OUT NOW.
THIS COULD CHANGE BOTH OUR LIVES...
...PLEASE.

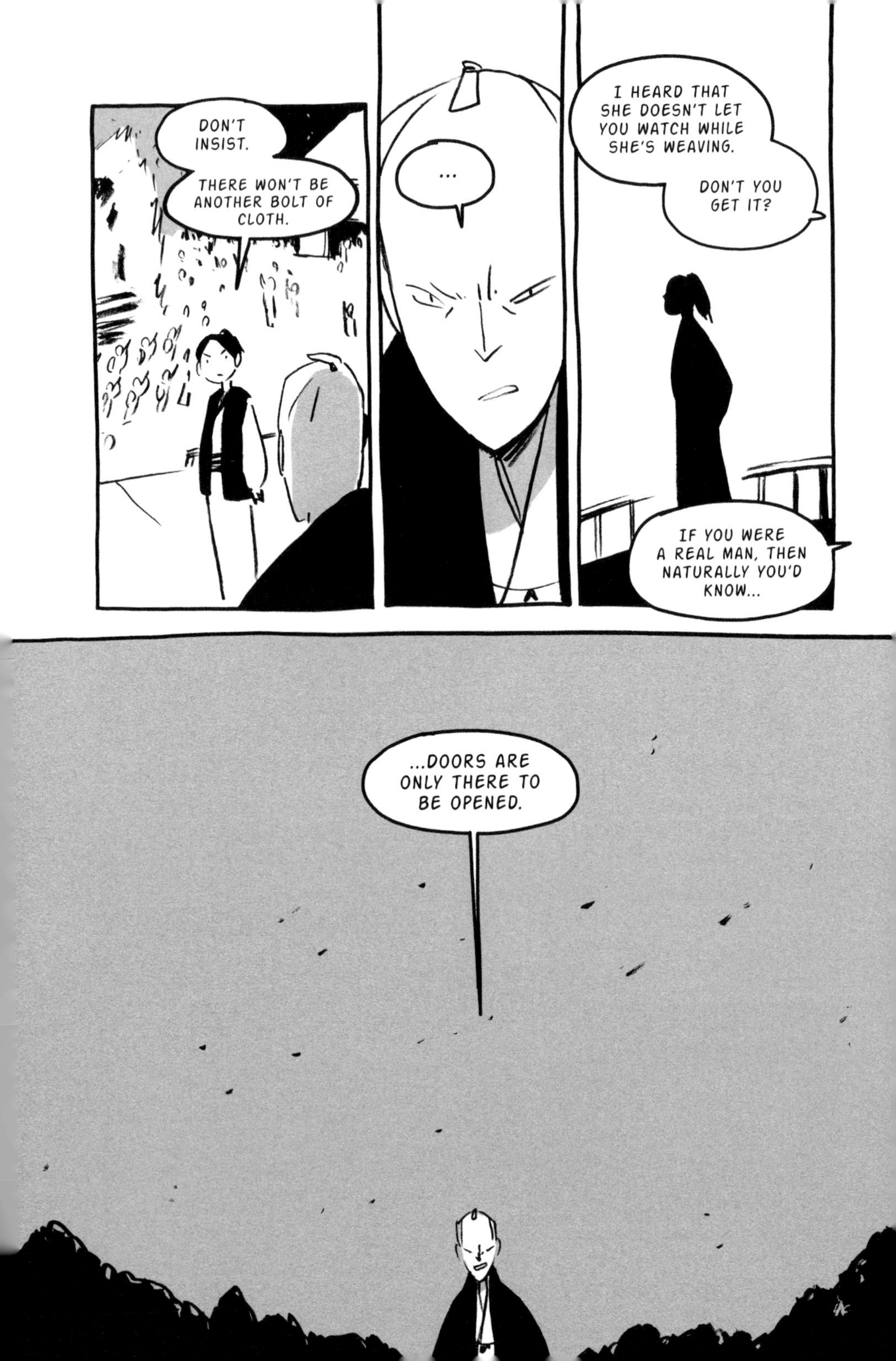
DON'T INSIST.
THERE WON'T BE ANOTHER BOLT OF CLOTH.
...
I HEARD THAT SHE DOESN'T LET YOU WATCH WHILE SHE'S WEAVING.
DON'T YOU GET IT?
IF YOU WERE A REAL MAN, THEN NATURALLY YOU'D KNOW...
...DOORS ARE ONLY THERE TO BE OPENED.

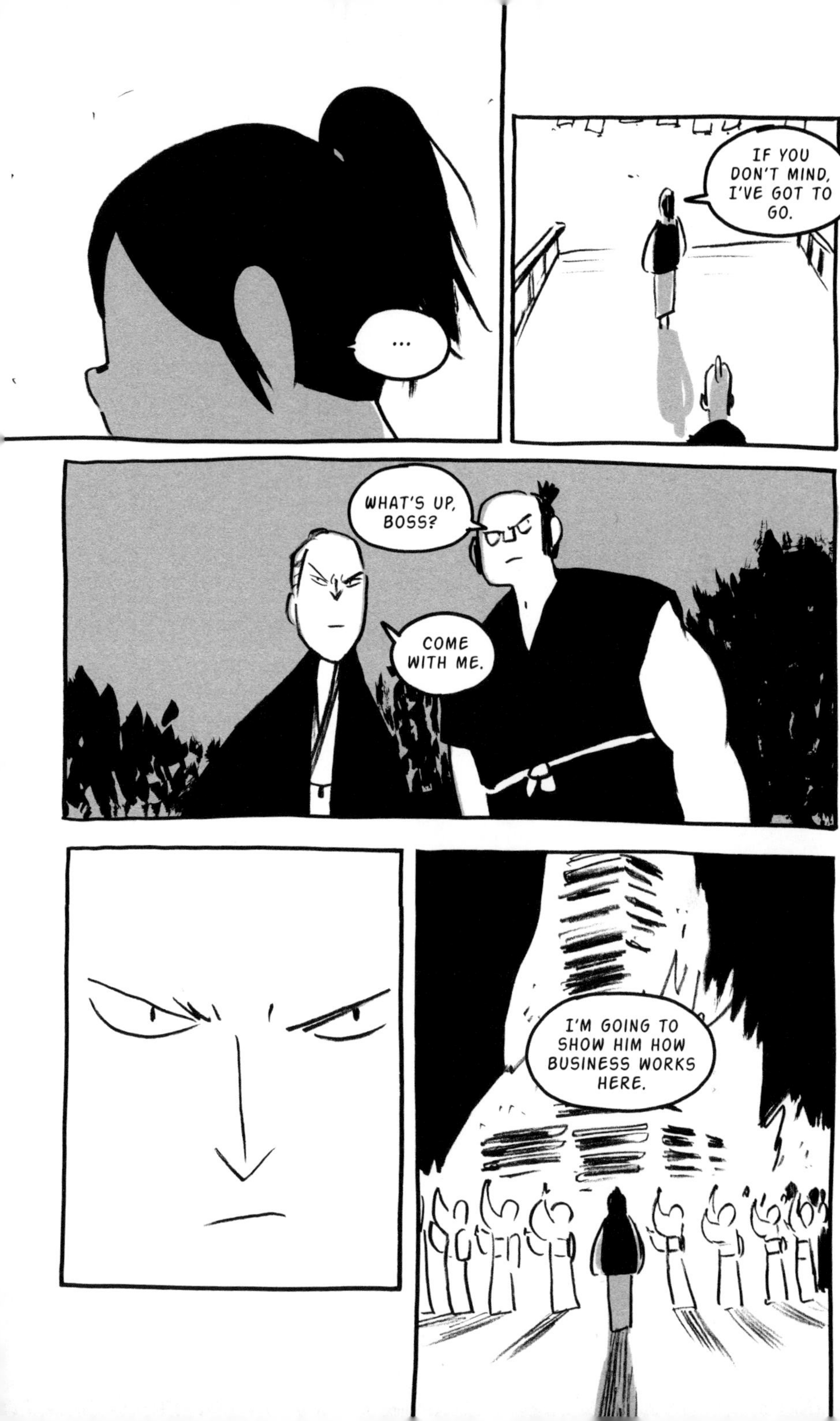
...
IF YOU DON'T MIND, I'VE GOT TO GO.
WHAT'S UP, BOSS?
COME WITH ME.
I'M GOING TO SHOW HIM HOW BUSINESS WORKS HERE.

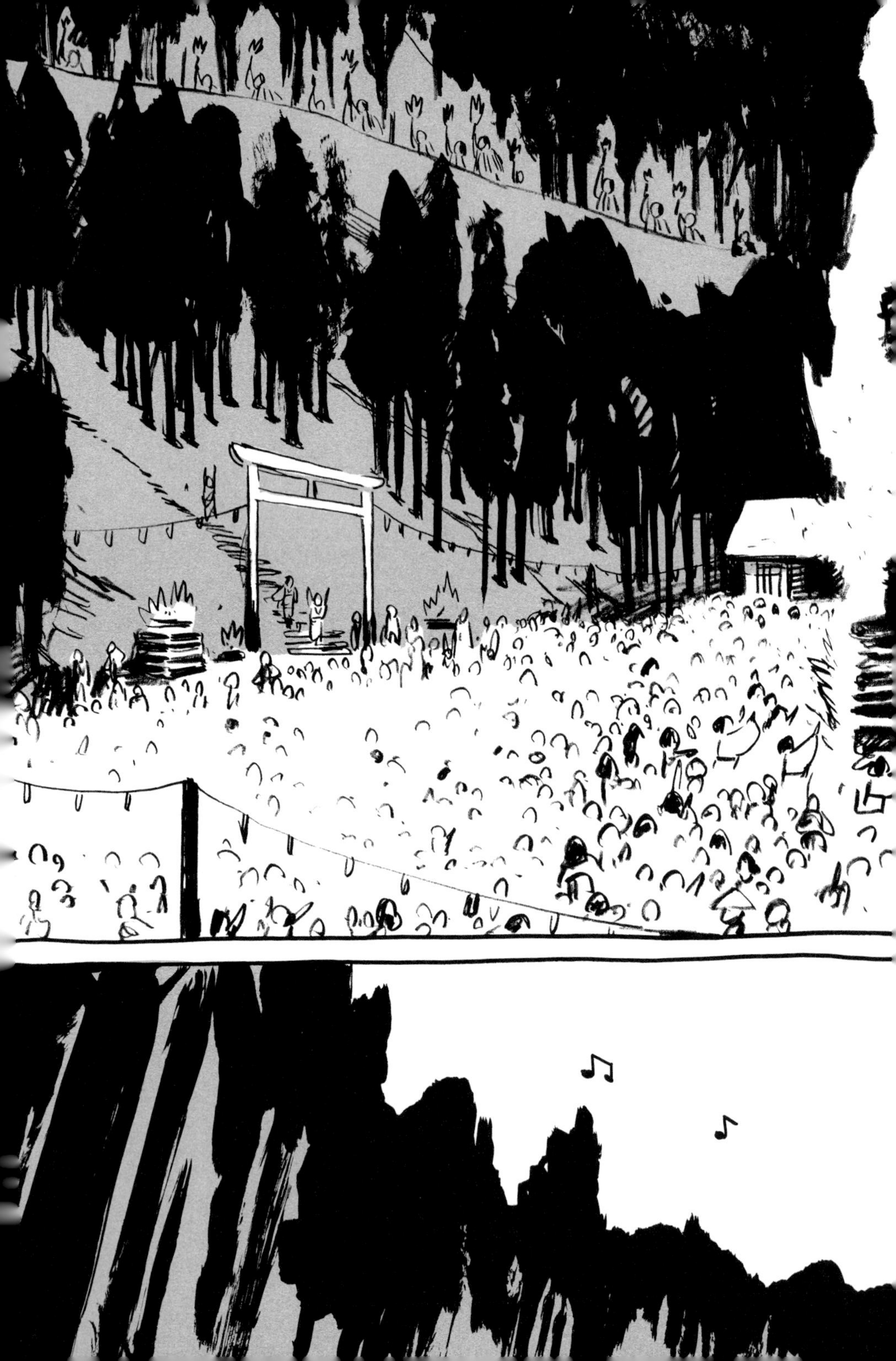

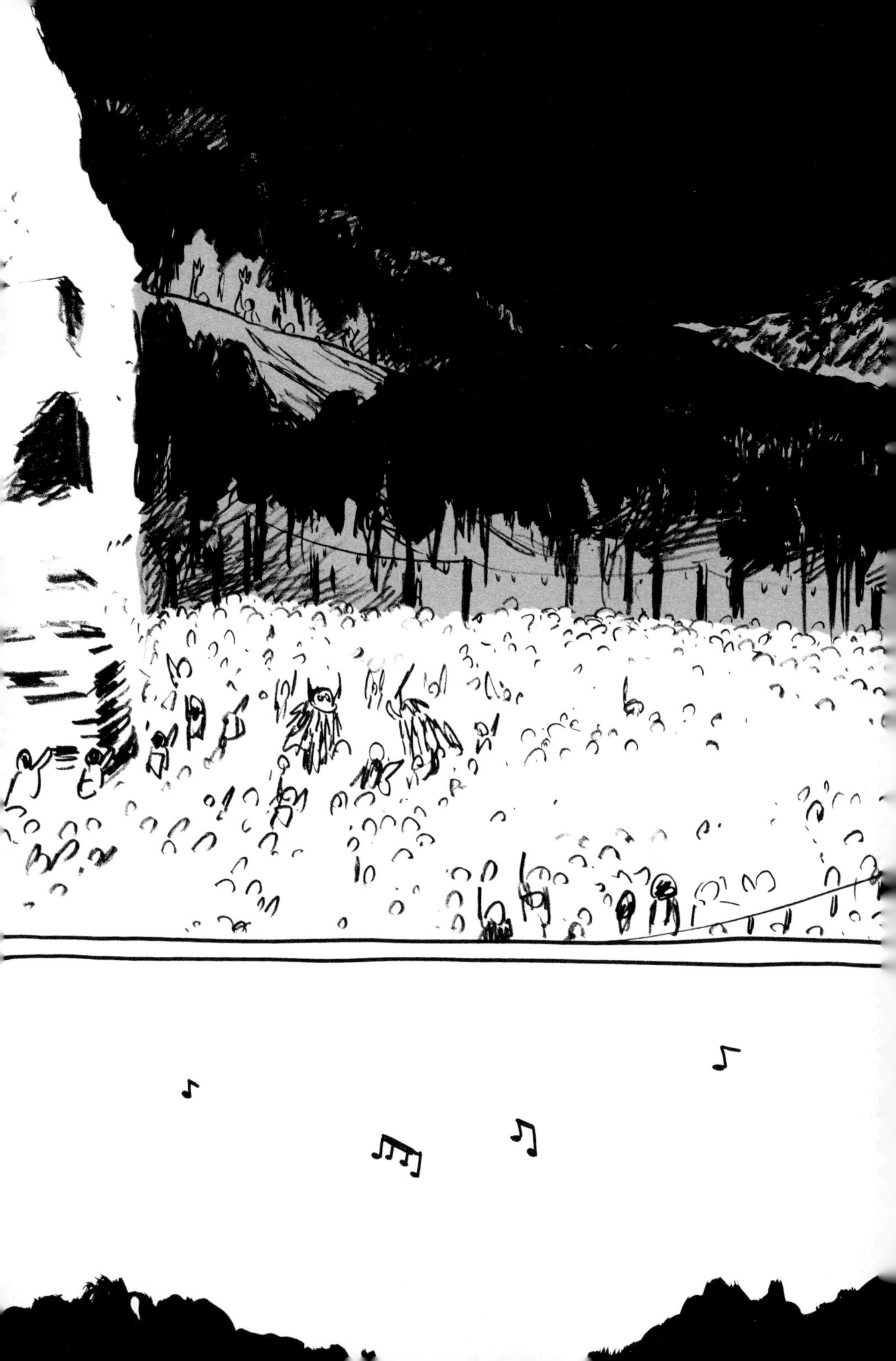

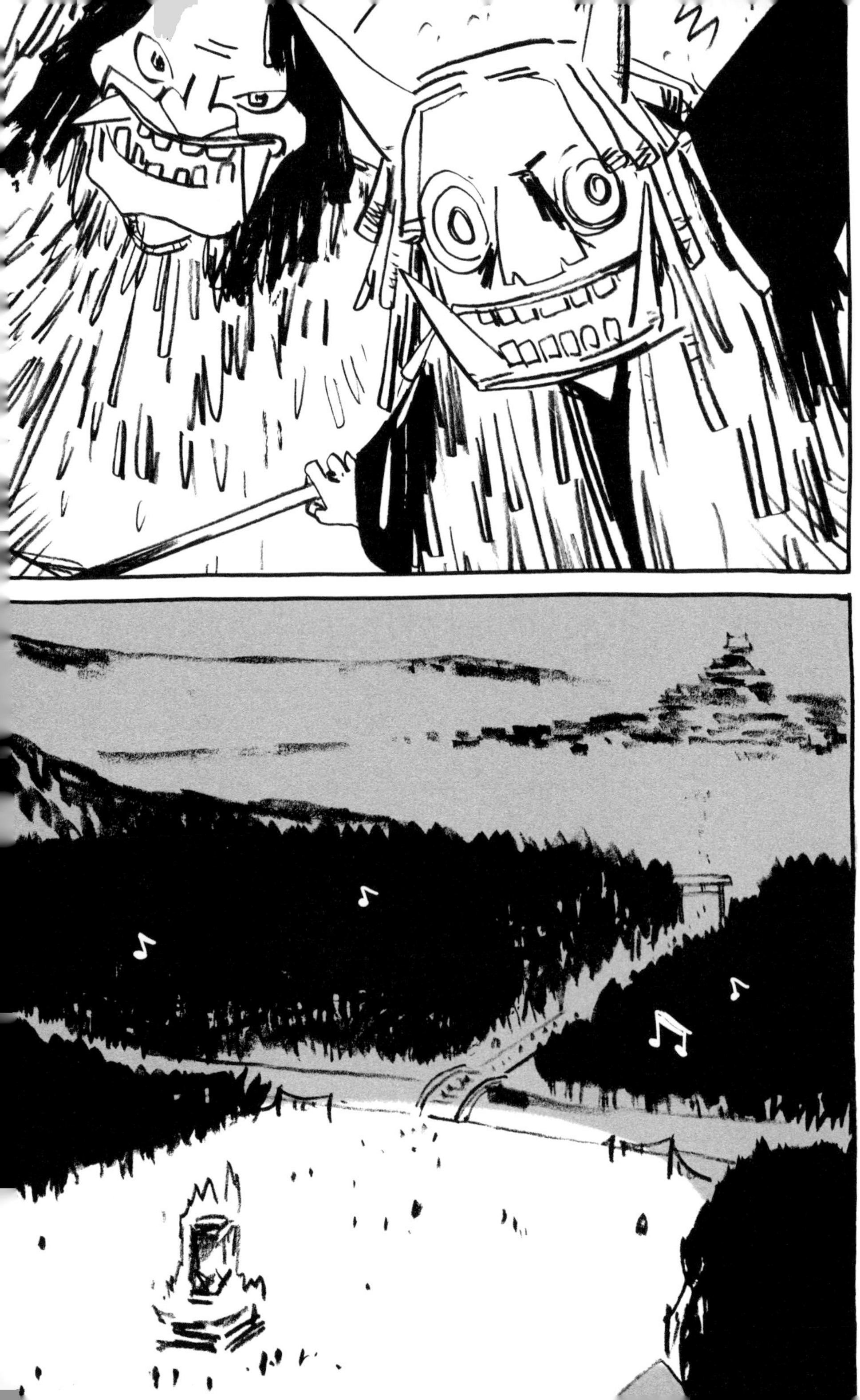

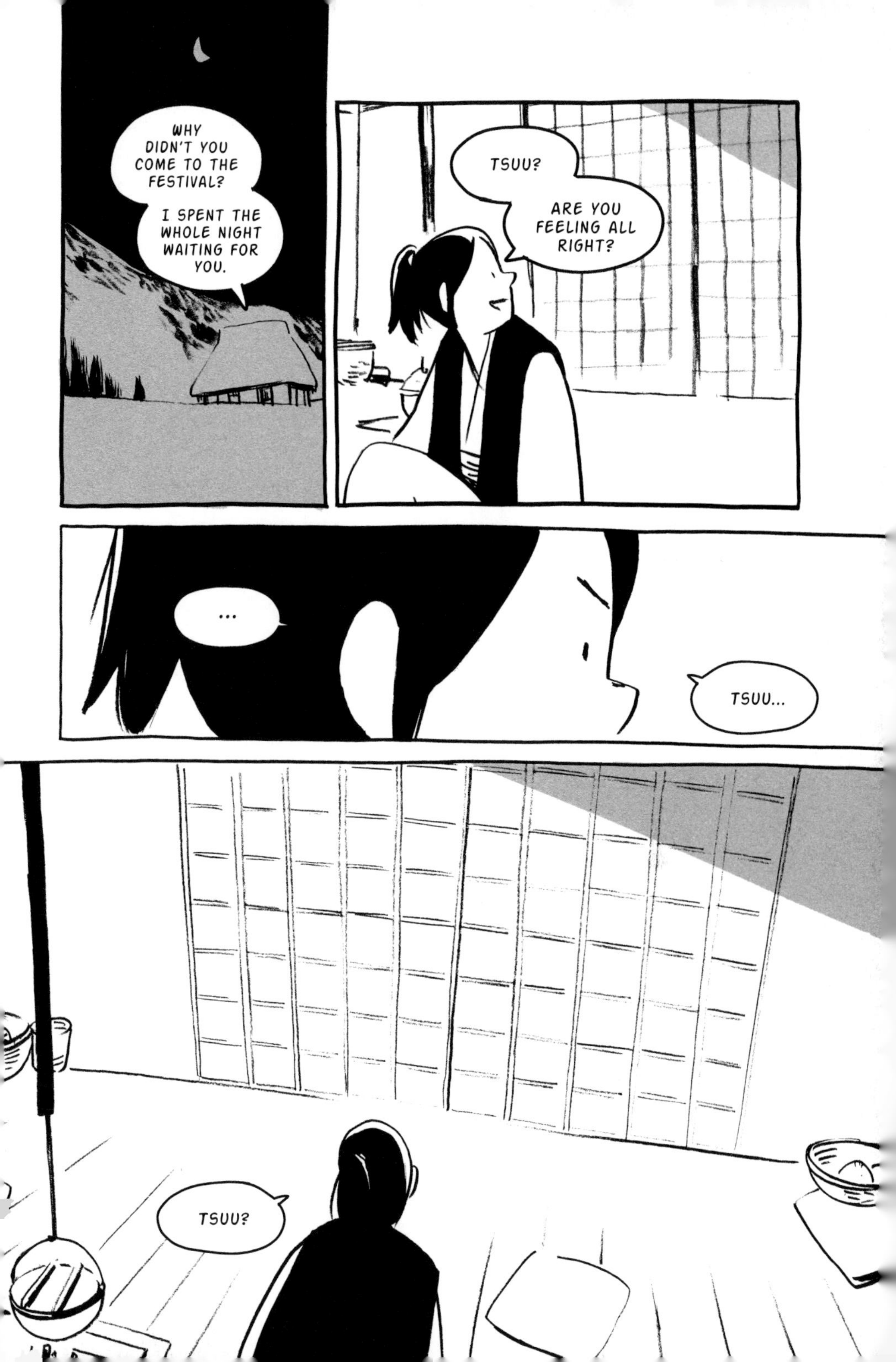
WHY DIDN'T YOU COME TO THE FESTIVAL?
I SPENT THE WHOLE NIGHT WAITING FOR YOU.
TSUU?
ARE YOU FEELING ALL RIGHT?
...
TSUU...
TSUU?

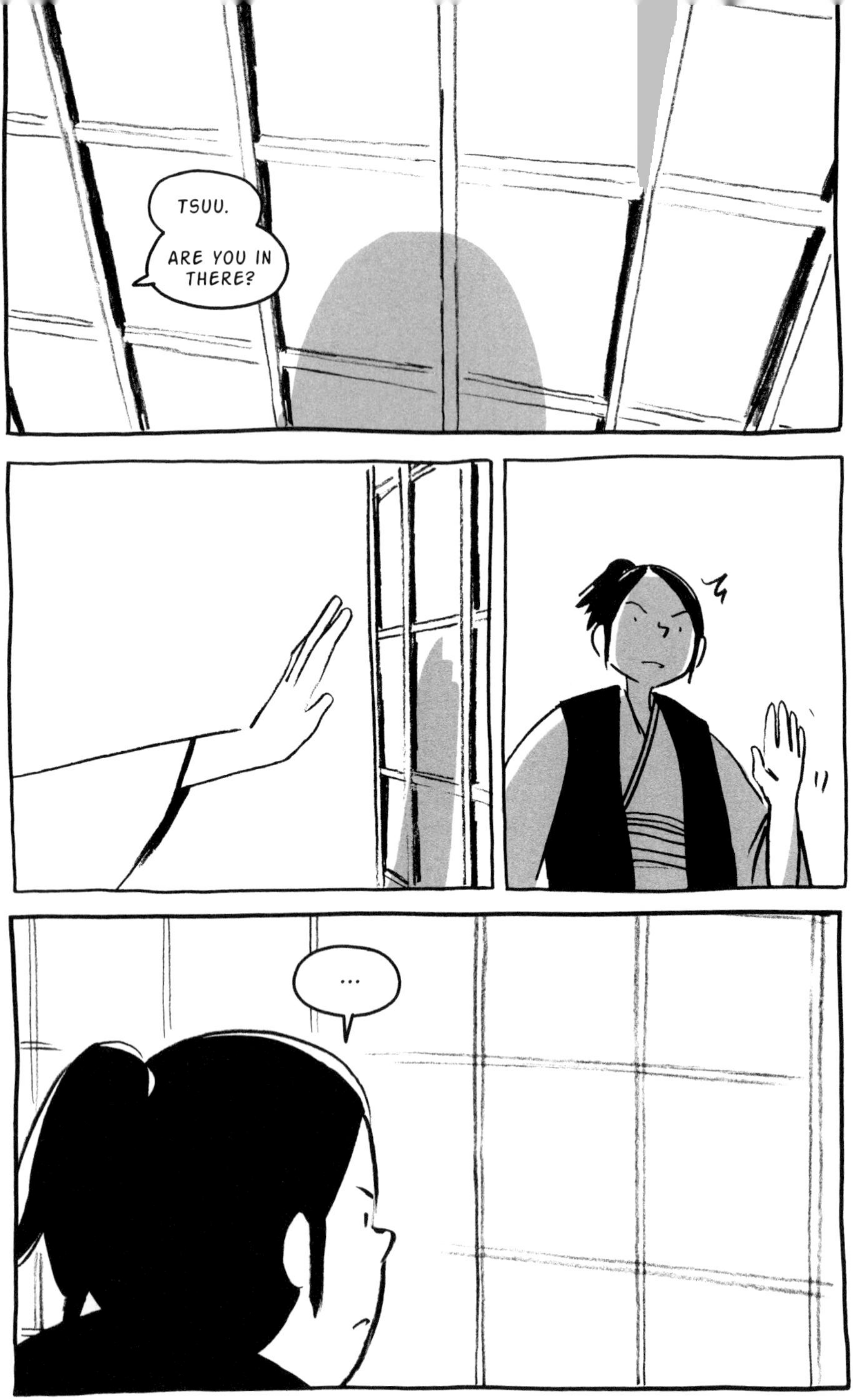
TSUU.
ARE YOU IN THERE?
...

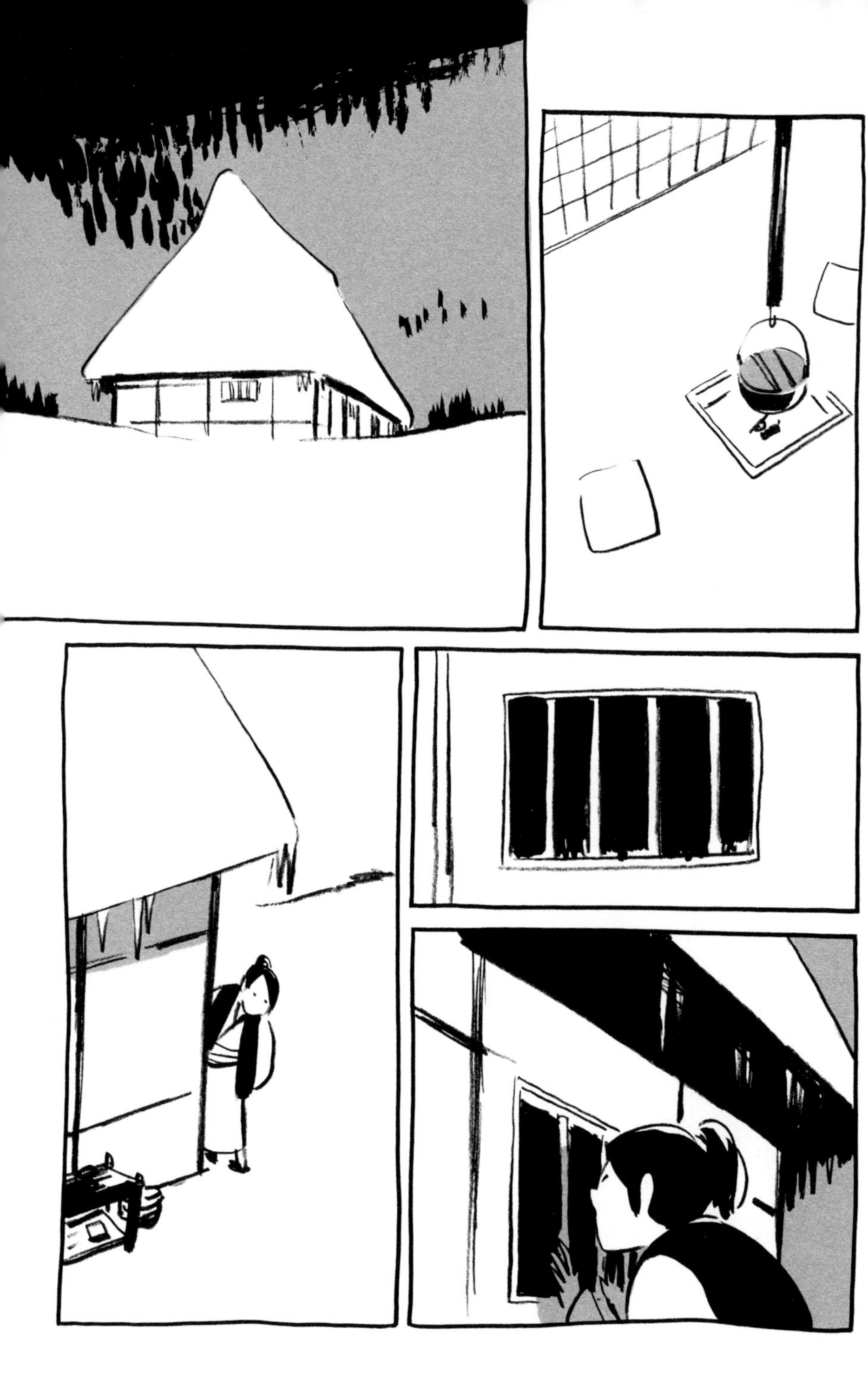

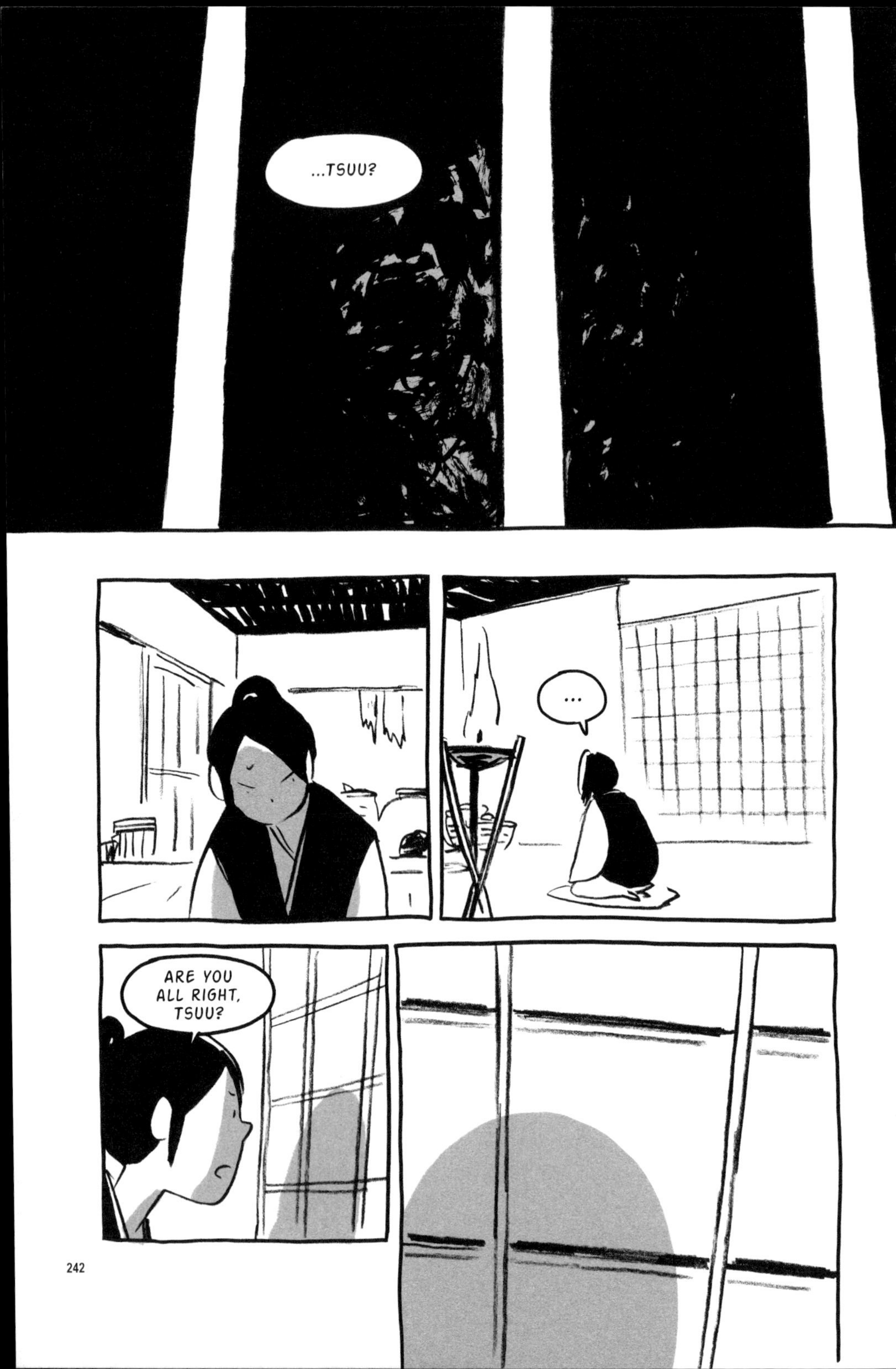
...TSUU?
...
ARE YOU ALL RIGHT, TSUU?

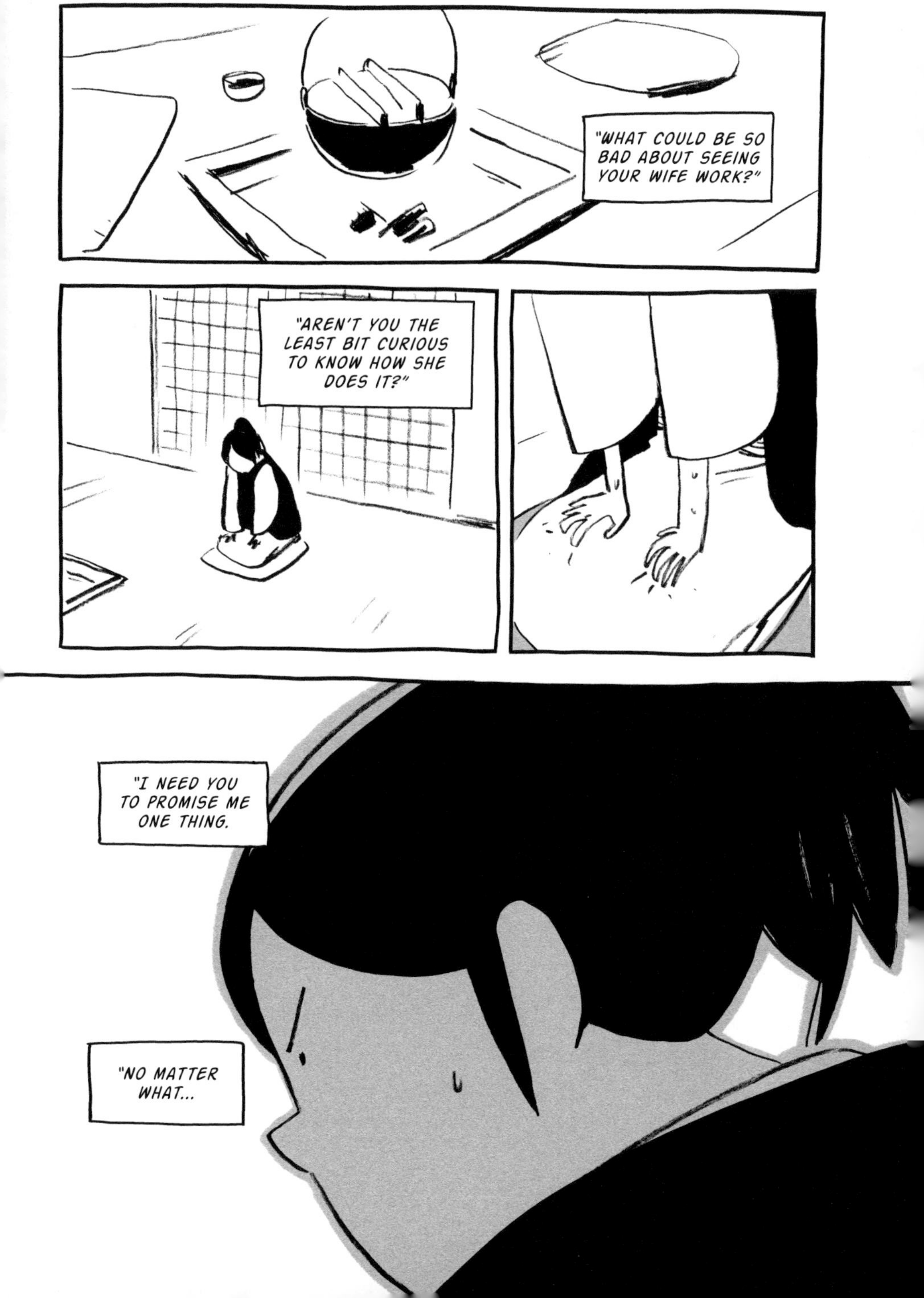
"WHAT COULD BE SO BAD ABOUT SEEING YOUR WIFE WORK?"
"AREN'T YOU THE LEAST BIT CURIOUS TO KNOW HOW SHE DOES IT?"
"I NEED YOU TO PROMISE ME ONE THING.
"NO MATTER WHAT...

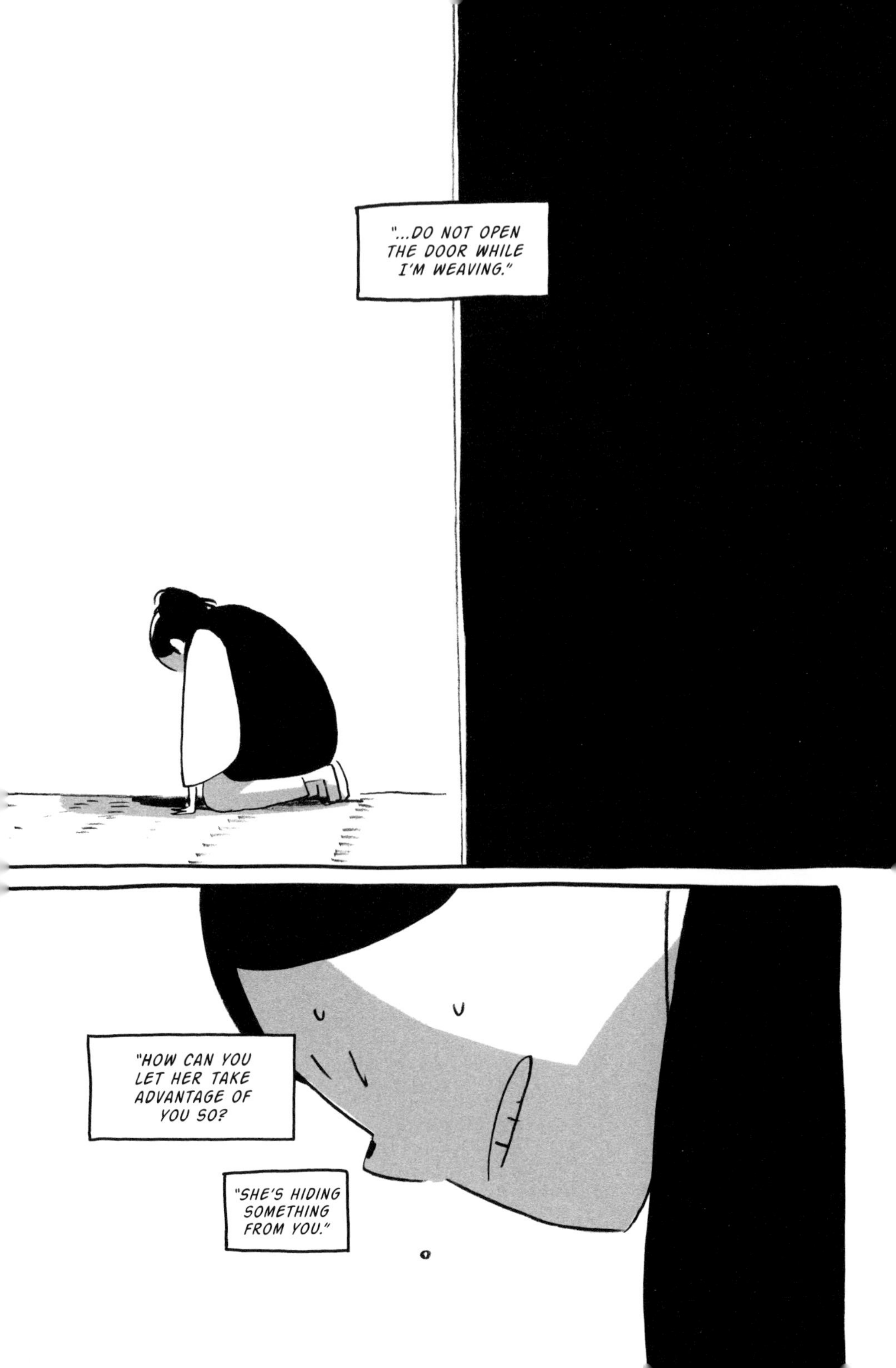
"...DO NOT OPEN THE DOOR WHILE I'M WEAVING."
"HOW CAN YOU LET HER TAKE ADVANTAGE OF YOU SO?
"SHE'S HIDING SOMETHING FROM YOU."

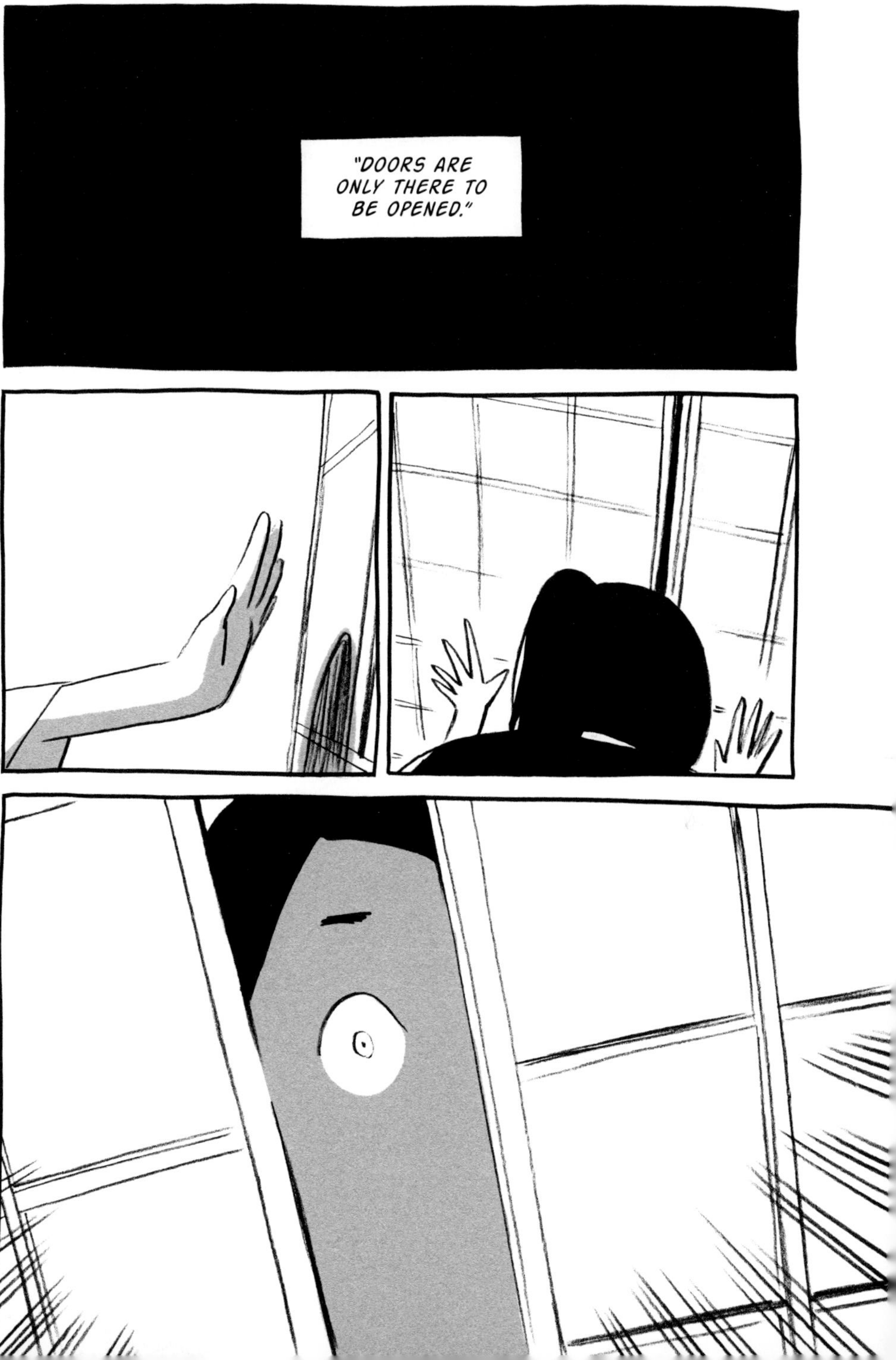
"DOORS ARE ONLY THERE TO BE OPENED."

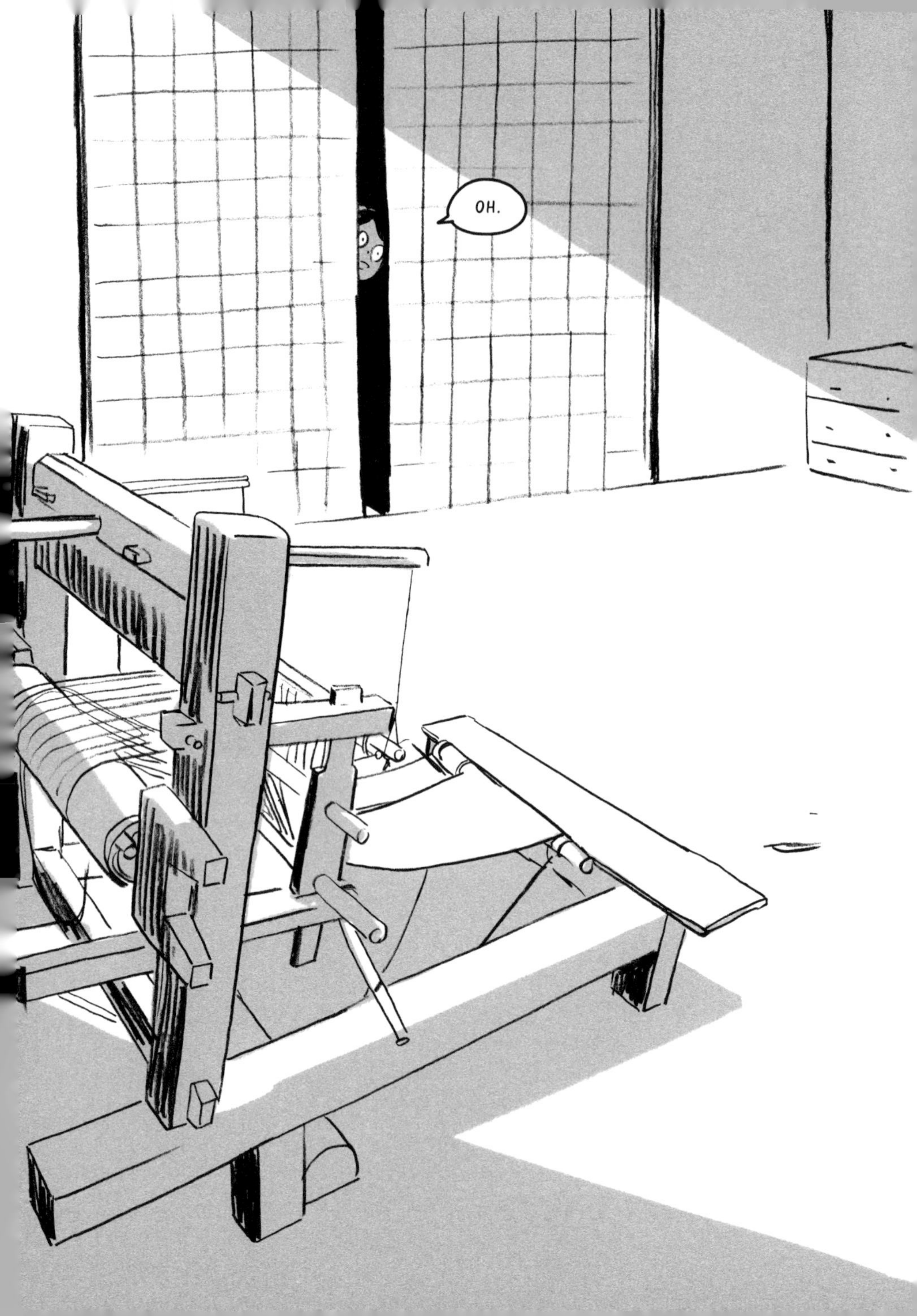
OH.

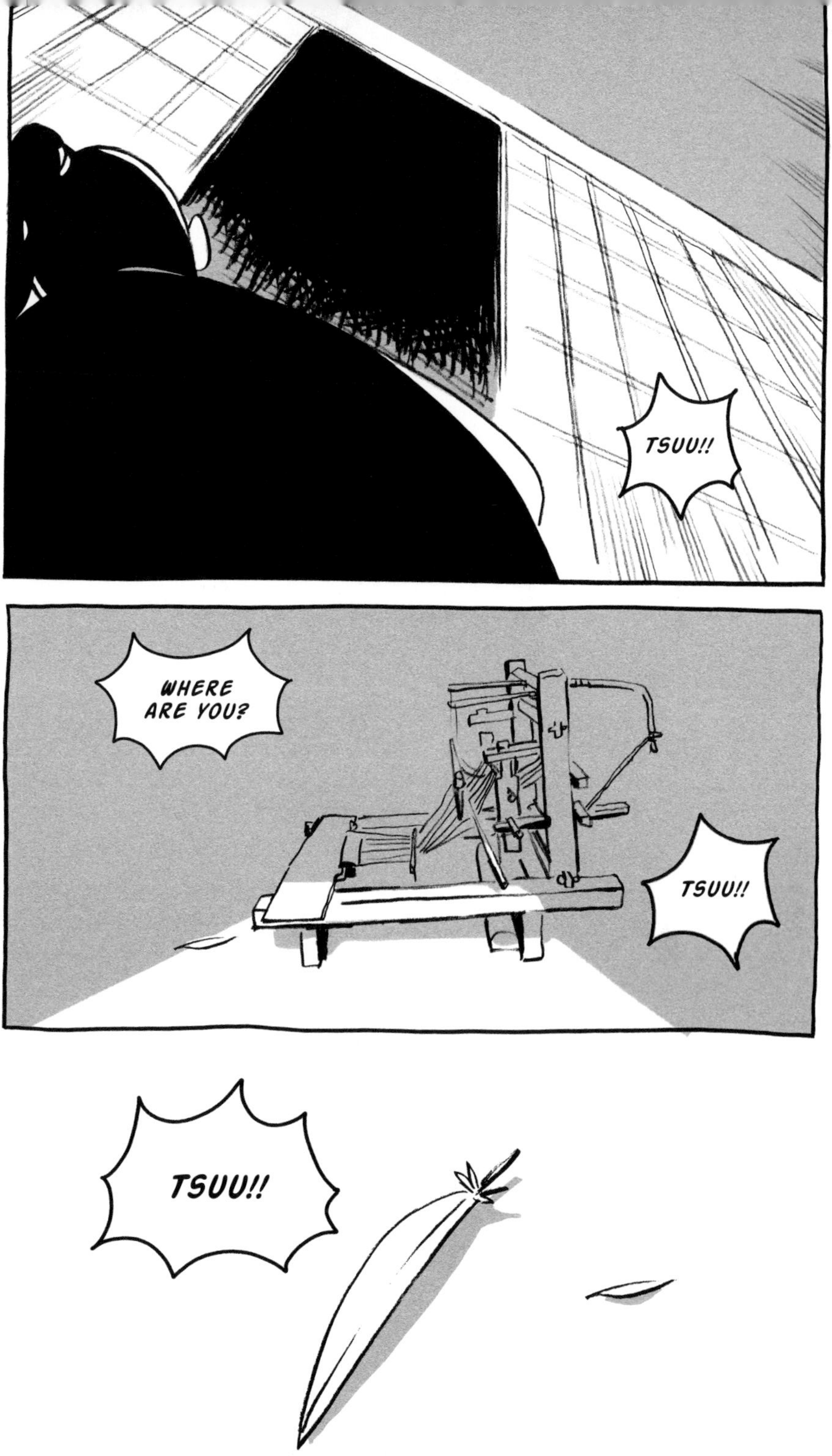
TSUU!!
WHERE ARE YOU?
TSUU!!
TSUU!!

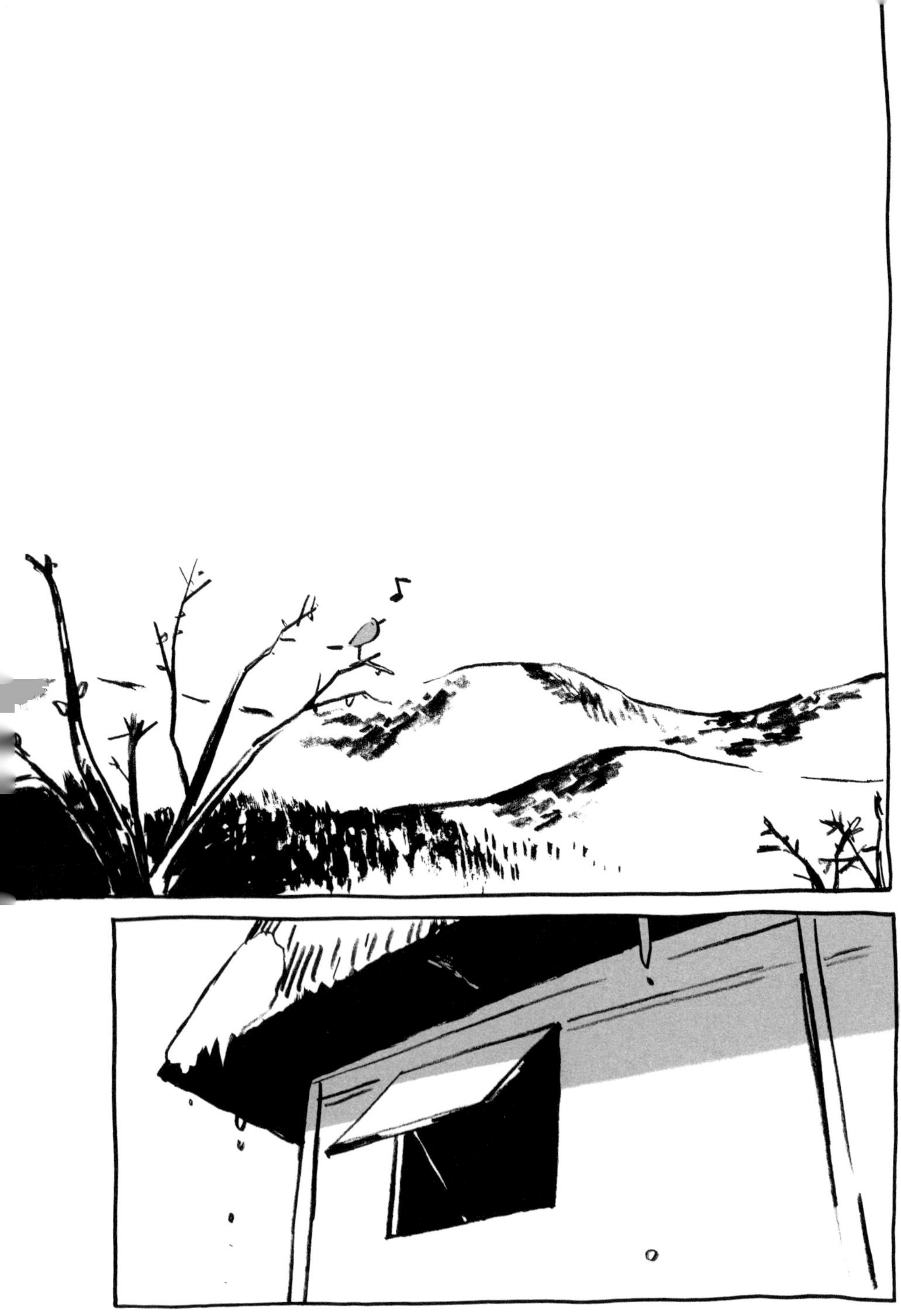

WHAT DID I DO WRONG?
WE COULD HAVE LIVED HAPPILY EVER AFTER.

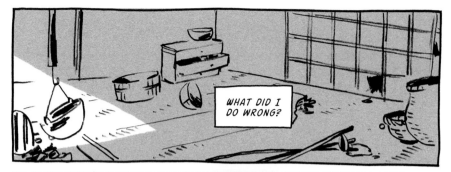

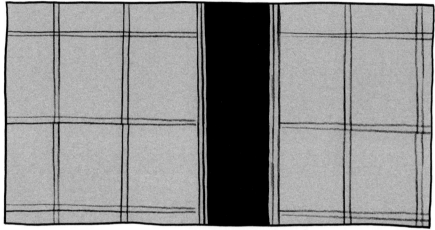

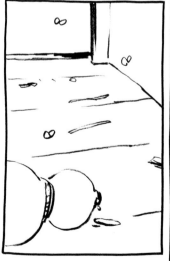

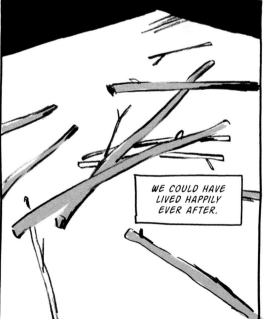

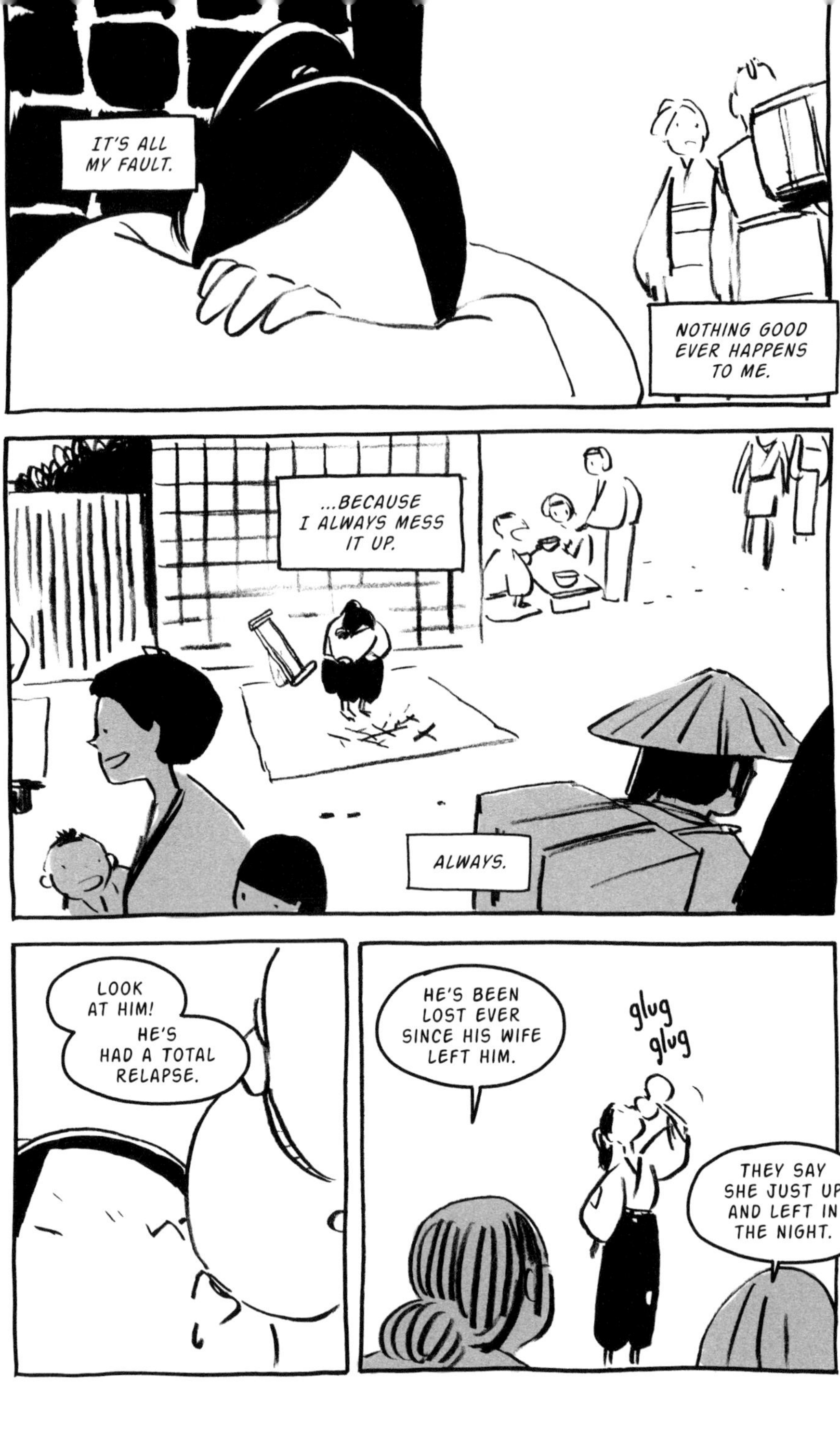
IT'S ALL MY FAULT.
NOTHING GOOD EVER HAPPENS TO ME.
...BECAUSE I ALWAYS MESS IT UP.
ALWAYS.
LOOK AT HIM!
HE'S HAD A TOTAL RELAPSE.
HE'S BEEN LOST EVER SINCE HIS WIFE LEFT HIM.
glug glug
THEY SAY SHE JUST UP AND LEFT IN THE NIGHT.

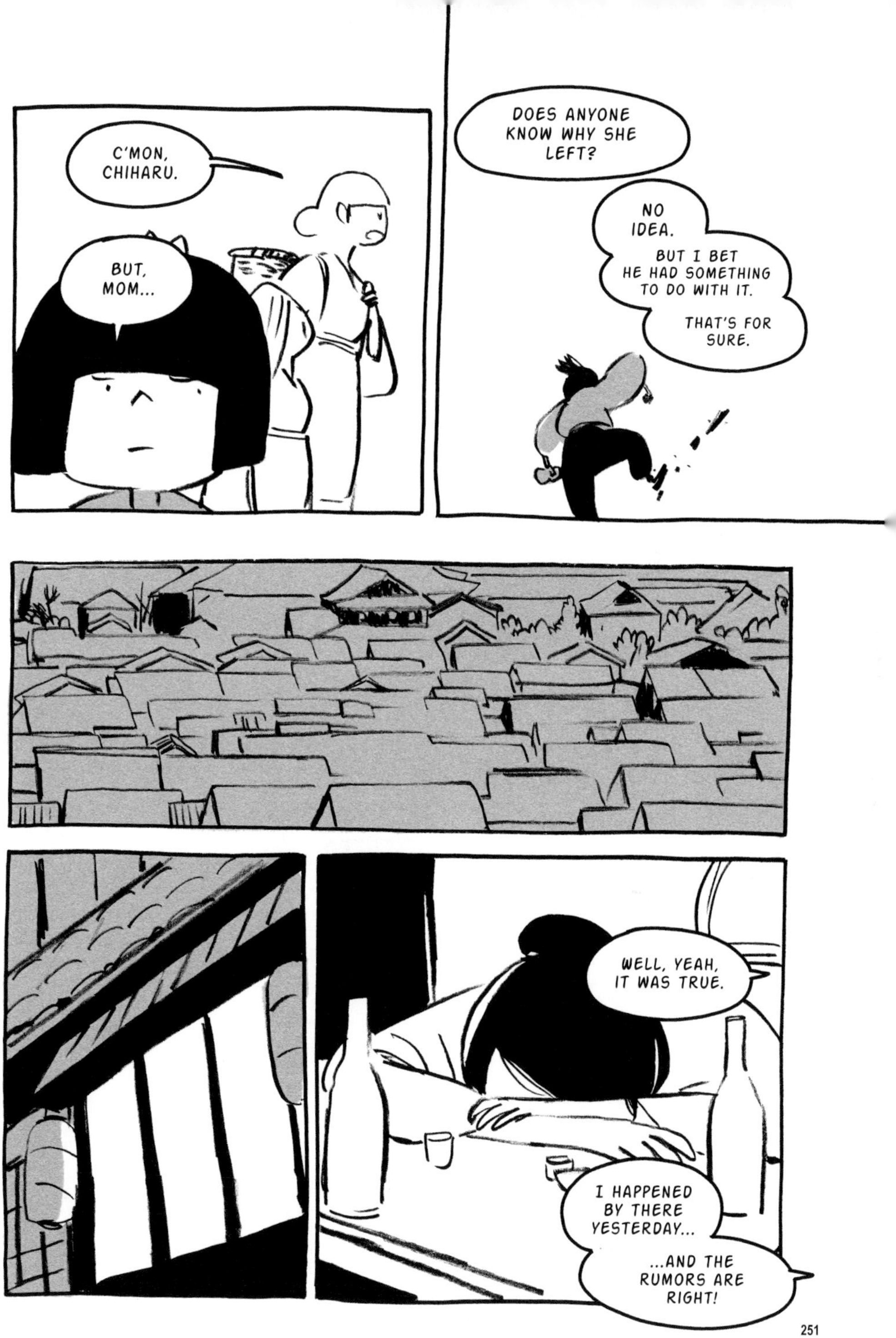
C'MON, CHIHARU.
BUT, MOM...
DOES ANYONE KNOW WHY SHE LEFT?
NO IDEA.
BUT I BET HE HAD SOMETHING TO DO WITH IT.
THAT'S FOR SURE.
WELL, YEAH, IT WAS TRUE.
I HAPPENED BY THERE YESTERDAY...
...AND THE RUMORS ARE RIGHT!

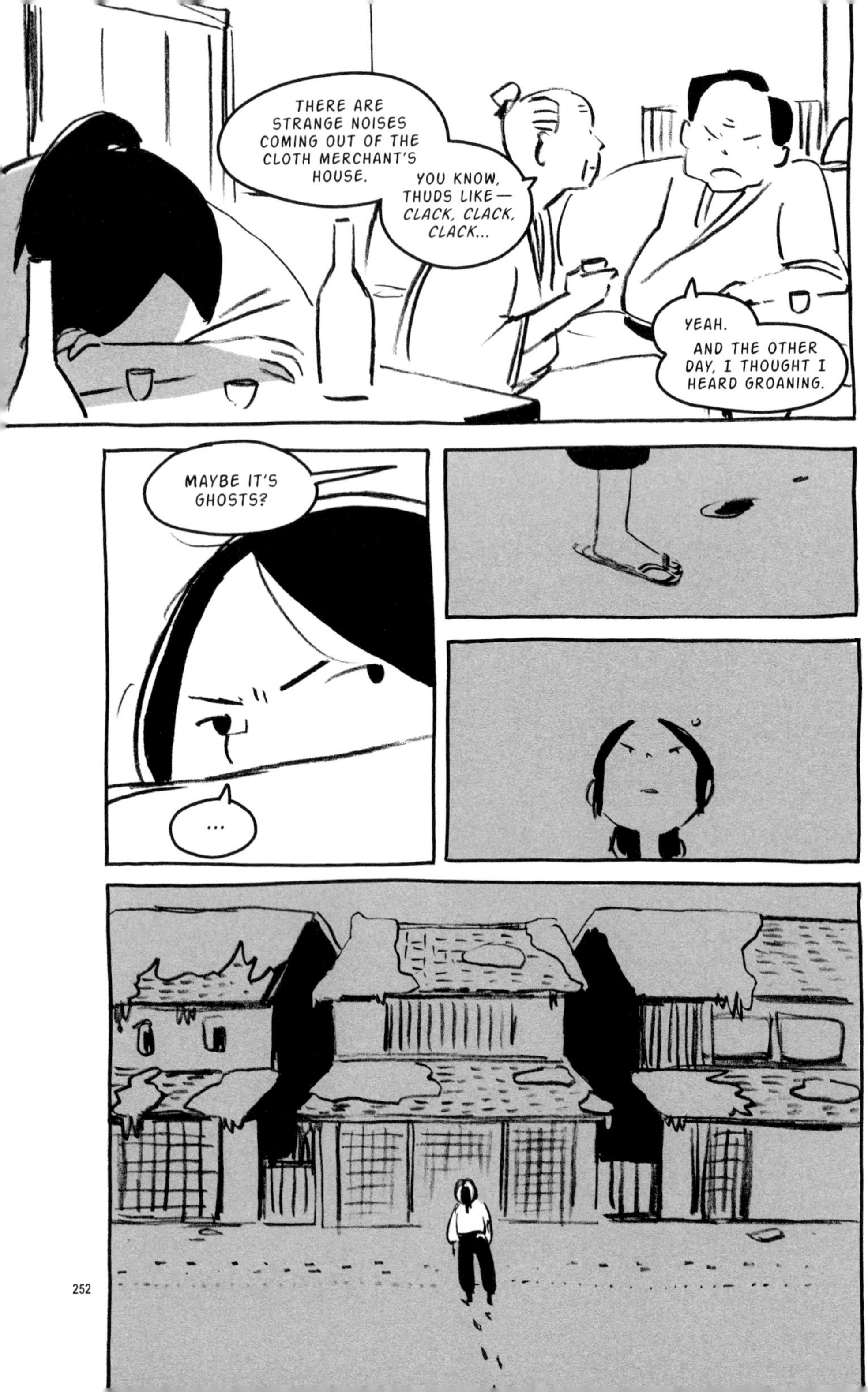
THERE ARE STRANGE NOISES COMING OUT OF THE CLOTH MERCHANT'S HOUSE.
YOU KNOW, THUDS LIKE— CLACK, CLACK, CLACK...
YEAH.
AND THE OTHER DAY, I THOUGHT I HEARD GROANING.
MAYBE IT'S GHOSTS?
...

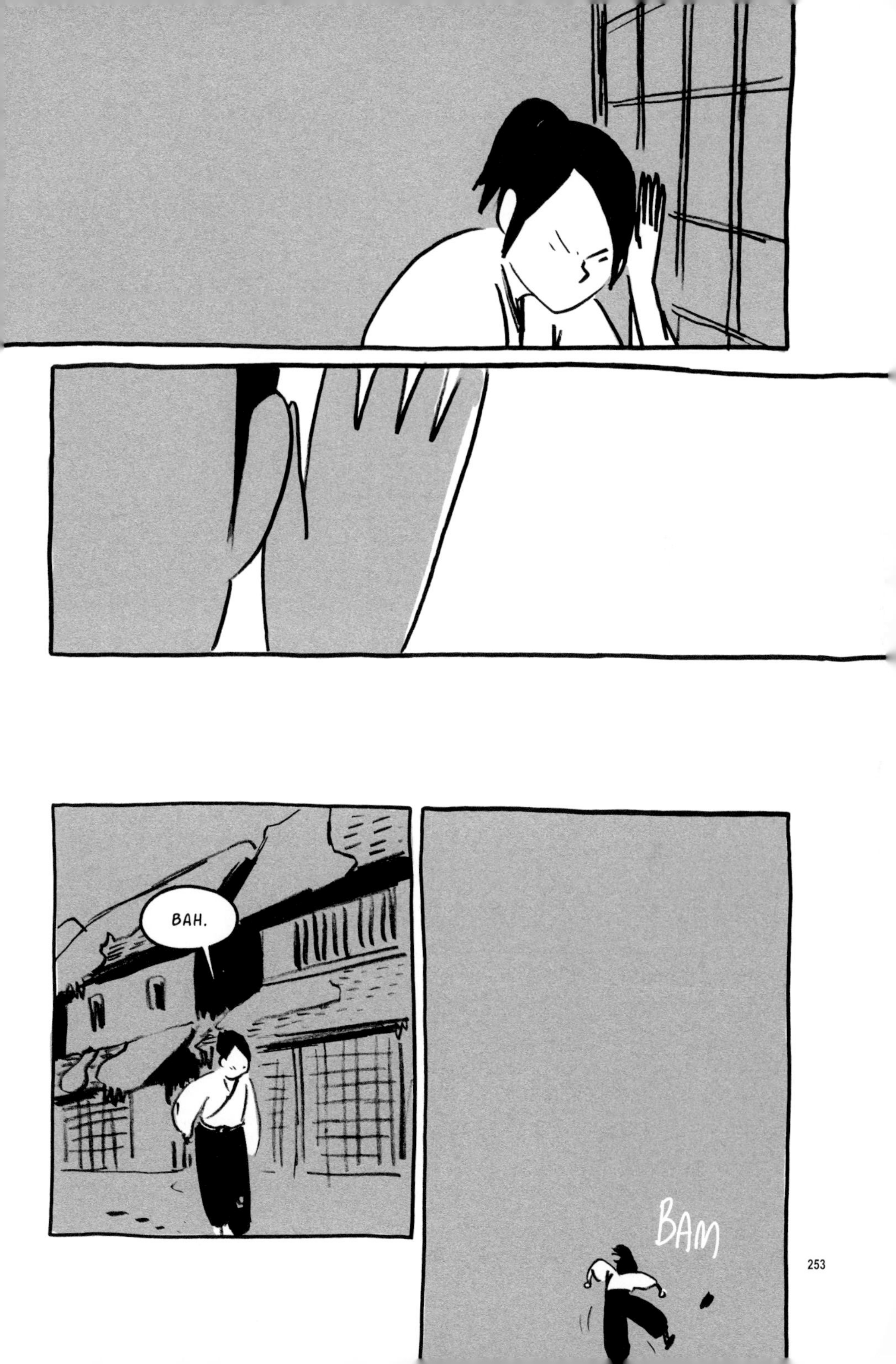
BAH.
BAM

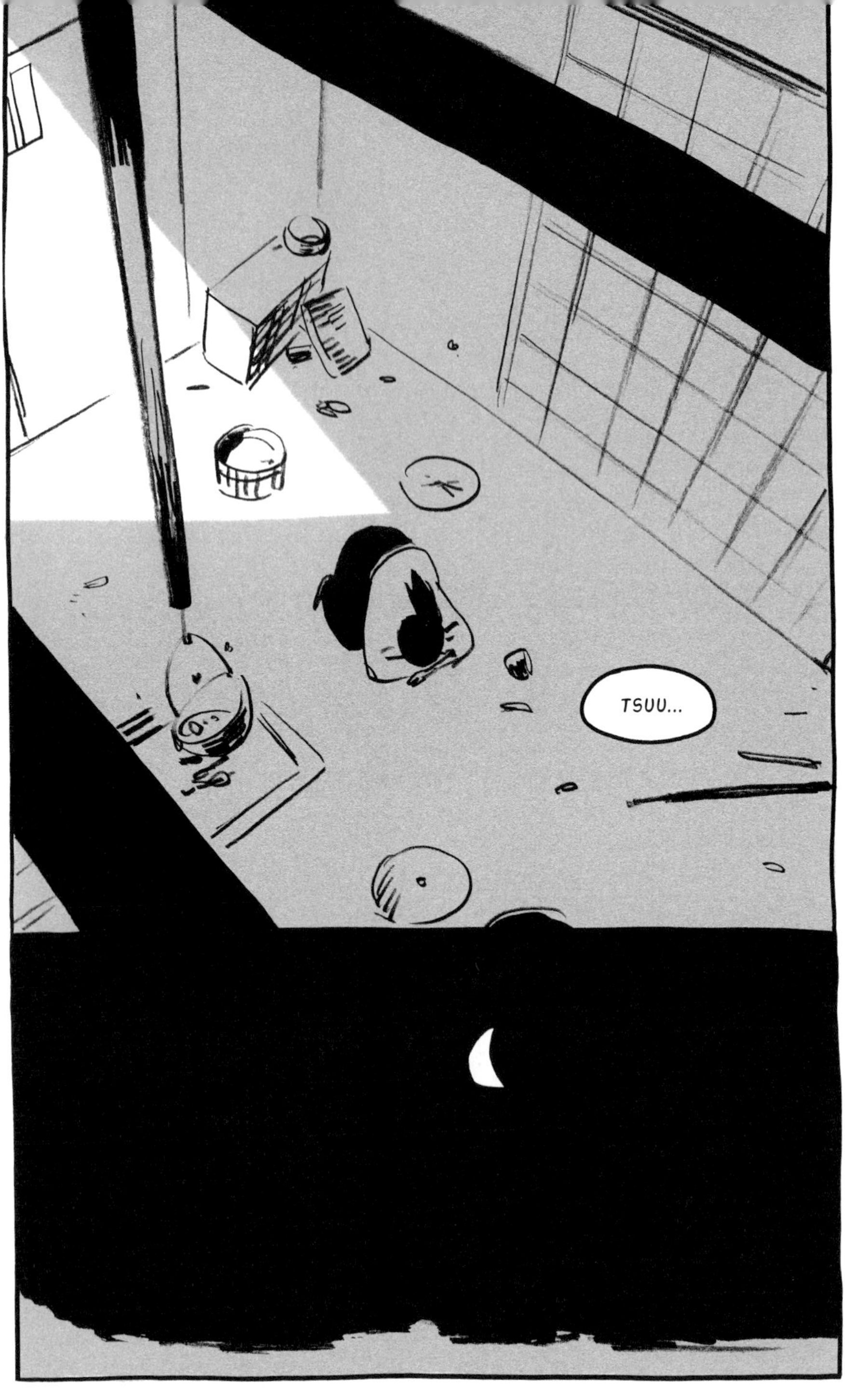
TSUU...

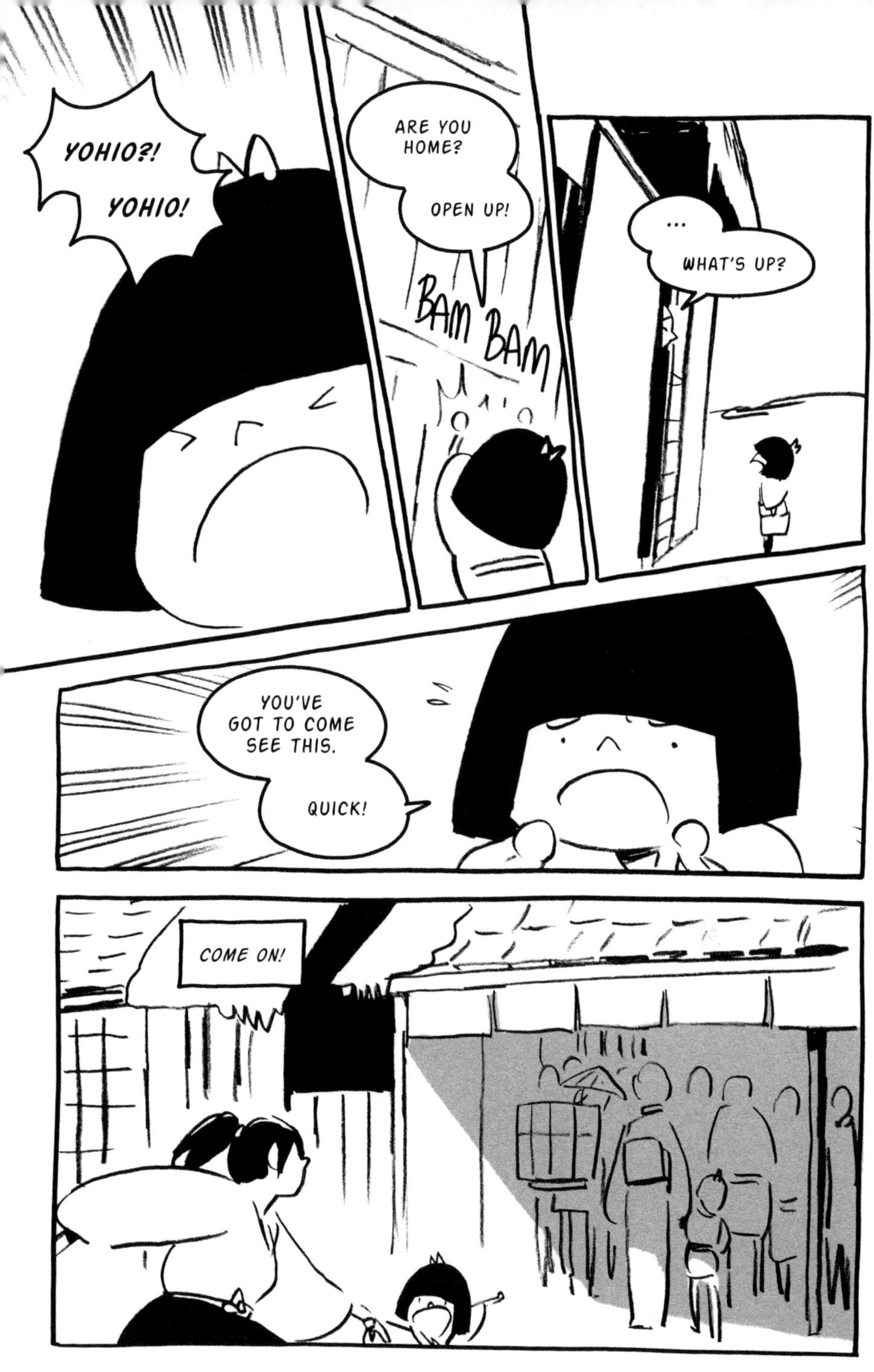
YOHIO?!
YOHIO!
ARE YOU HOME?
OPEN UP!
BAM BAM
...
WHAT'S UP?
YOU'VE GOT TO COME SEE THIS.
QUICK!
COME ON!

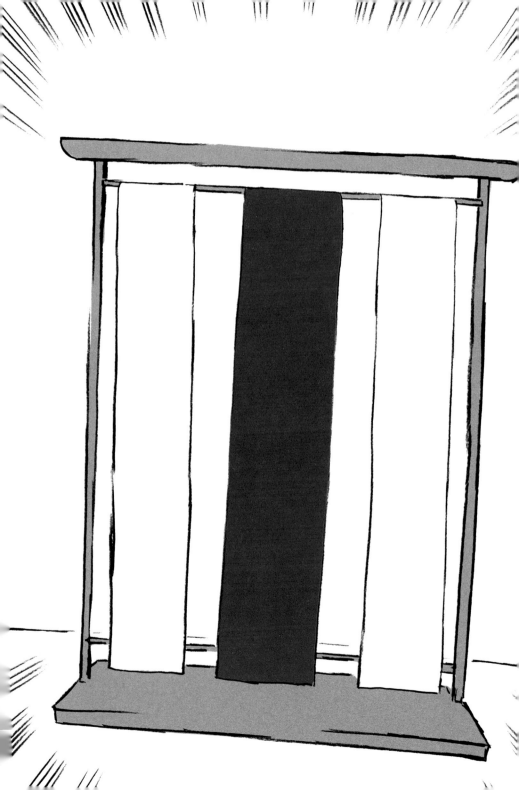

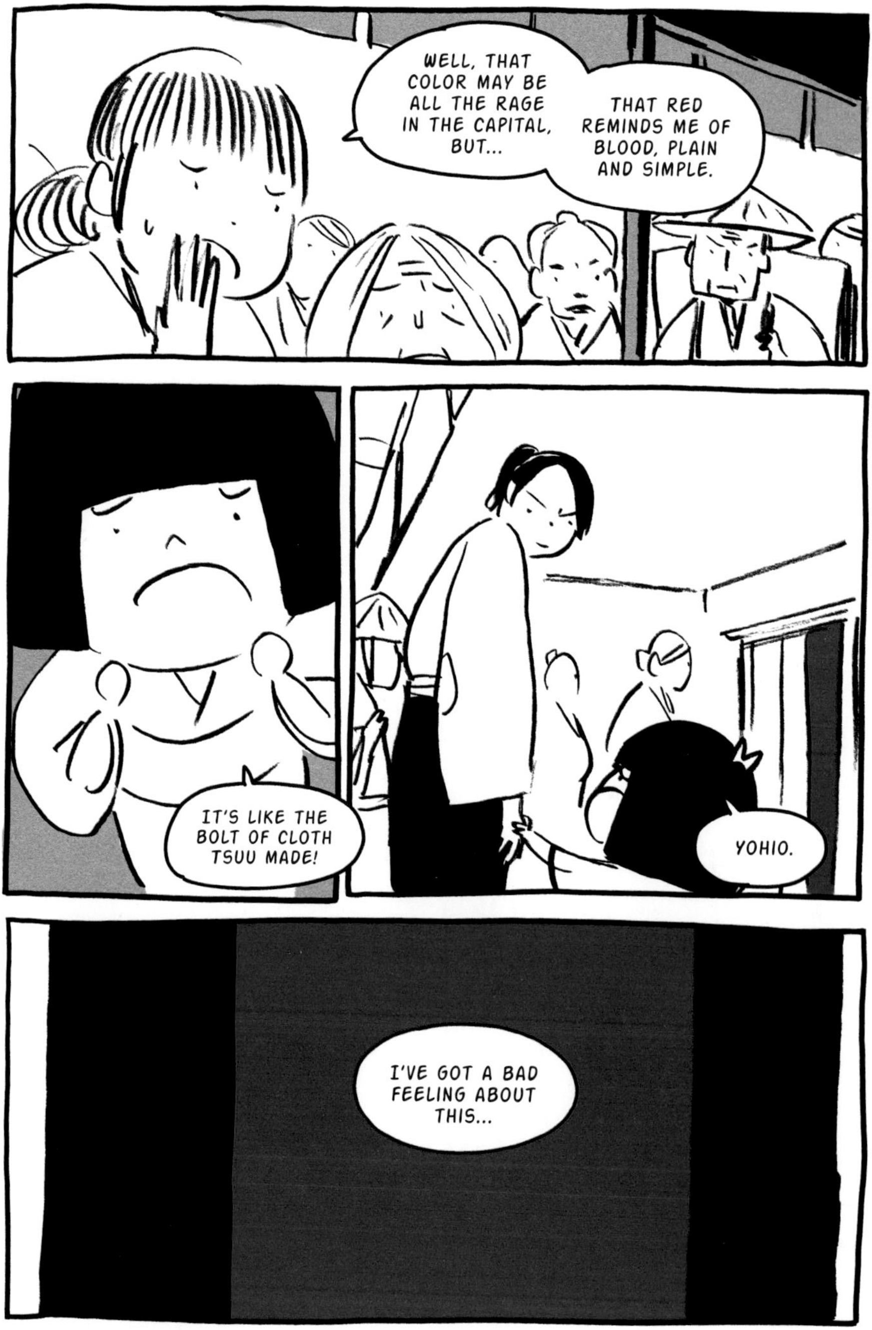
WELL, THAT COLOR MAY BE ALL THE RAGE IN THE CAPITAL, BUT...
THAT RED REMINDS ME OF BLOOD, PLAIN AND SIMPLE.
IT'S LIKE THE BOLT OF CLOTH TSUU MADE!
YOHIO.
I'VE GOT A BAD FEELING ABOUT THIS...

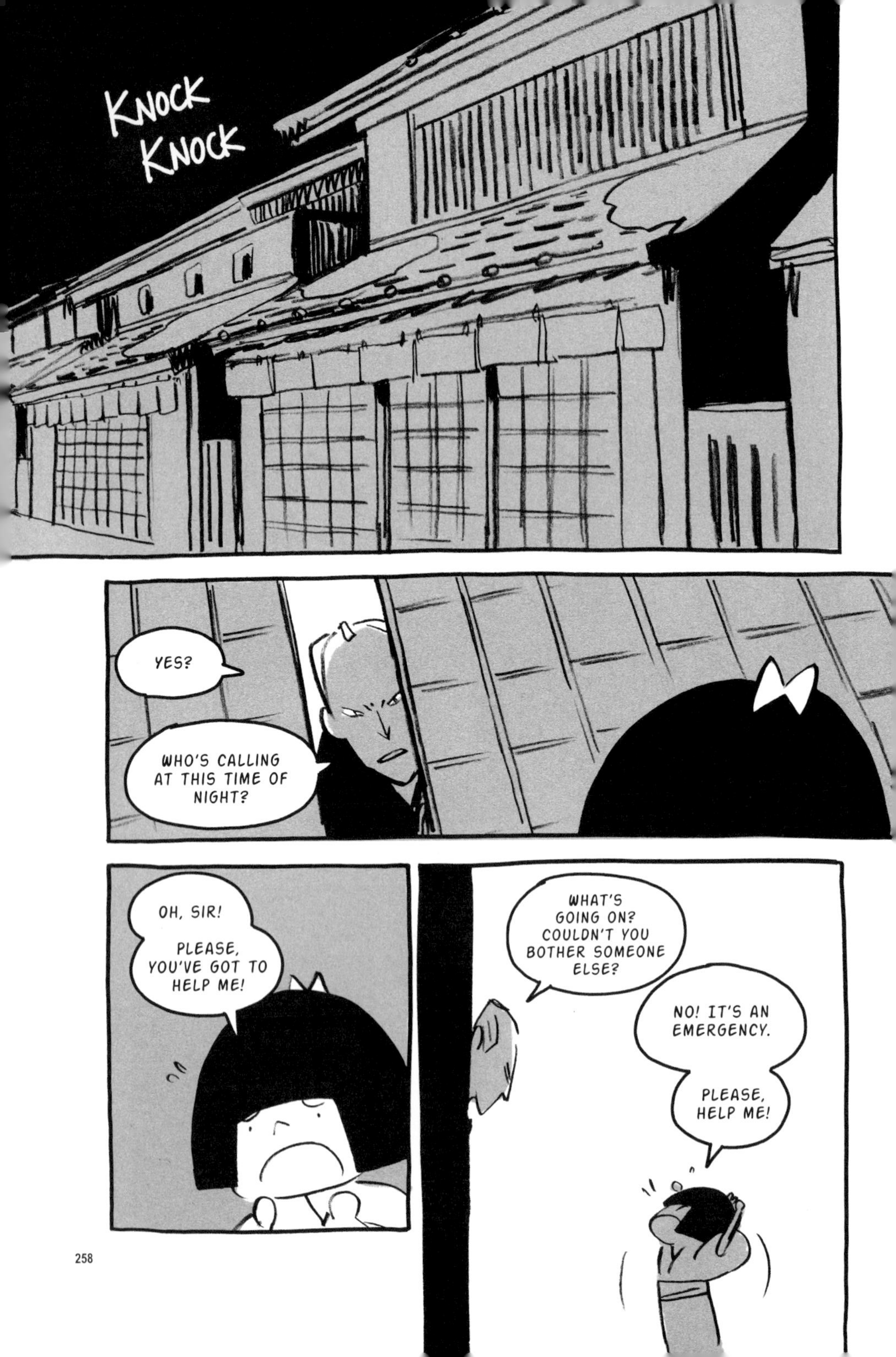
KNOCK KNOCK
YES?
WHO'S CALLING AT THIS TIME OF NIGHT?
OH, SIR! PLEASE, YOU'VE GOT TO HELP ME!
WHAT'S GOING ON? COULDN'T YOU BOTHER SOMEONE ELSE?
NO! IT'S AN EMERGENCY.
PLEASE, HELP ME!

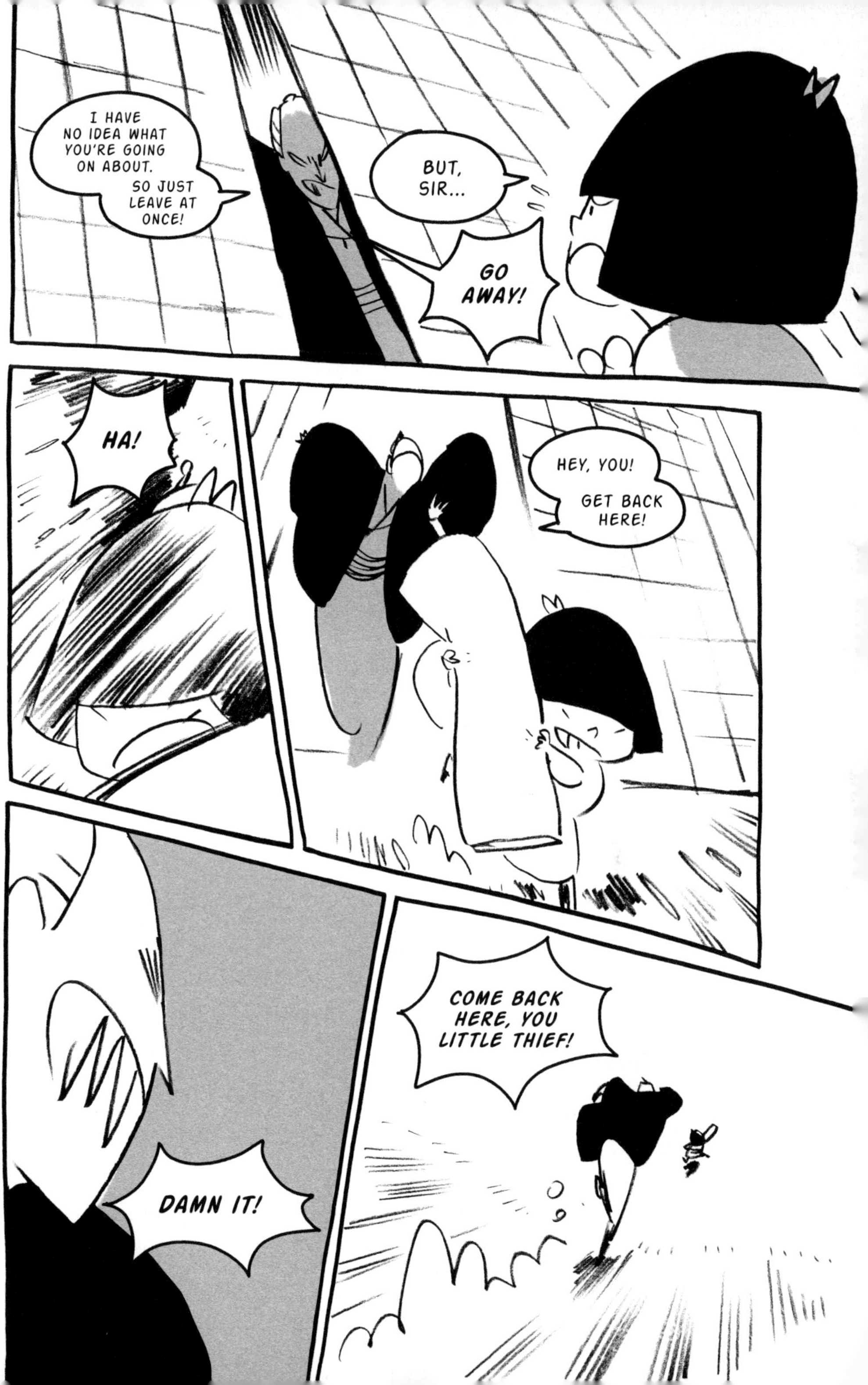
I HAVE NO IDEA WHAT YOU'RE GOING ON ABOUT.
SO JUST LEAVE AT ONCE!
BUT, SIR...
GO AWAY!
HA!
HEY, YOU!
GET BACK HERE!
DAMN IT!
COME BACK HERE, YOU LITTLE THIEF!

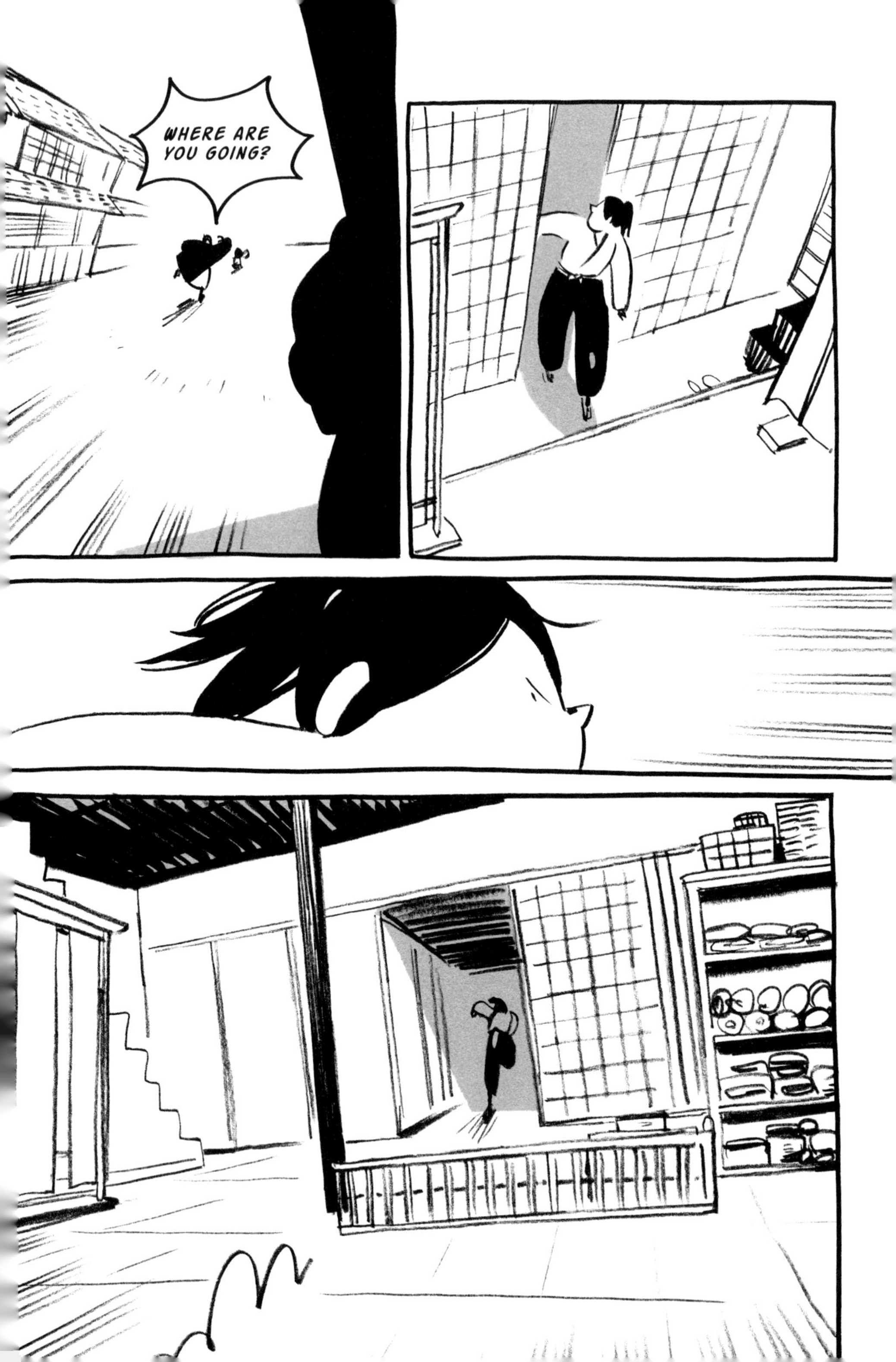
WHERE ARE YOU GOING?

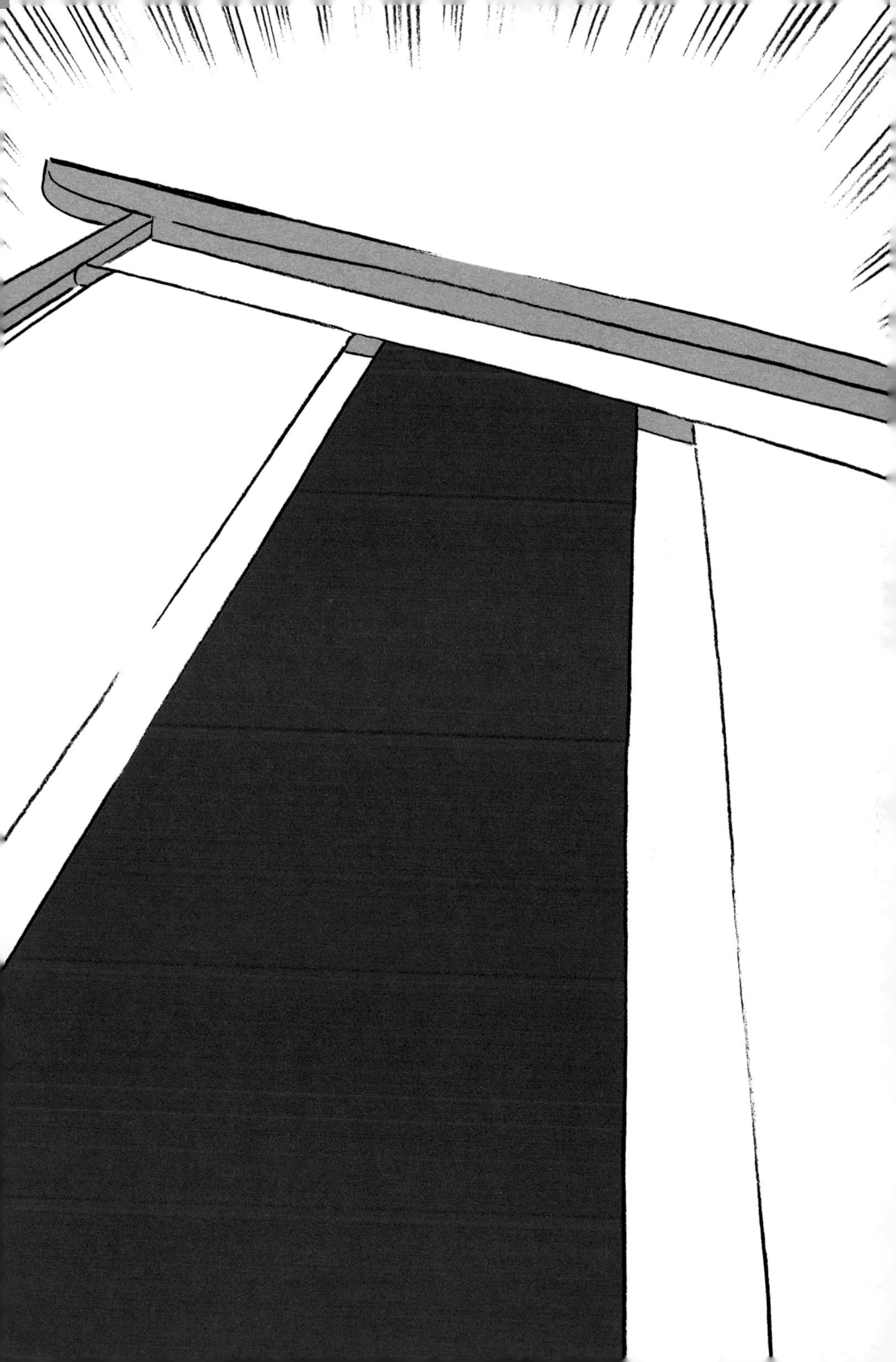

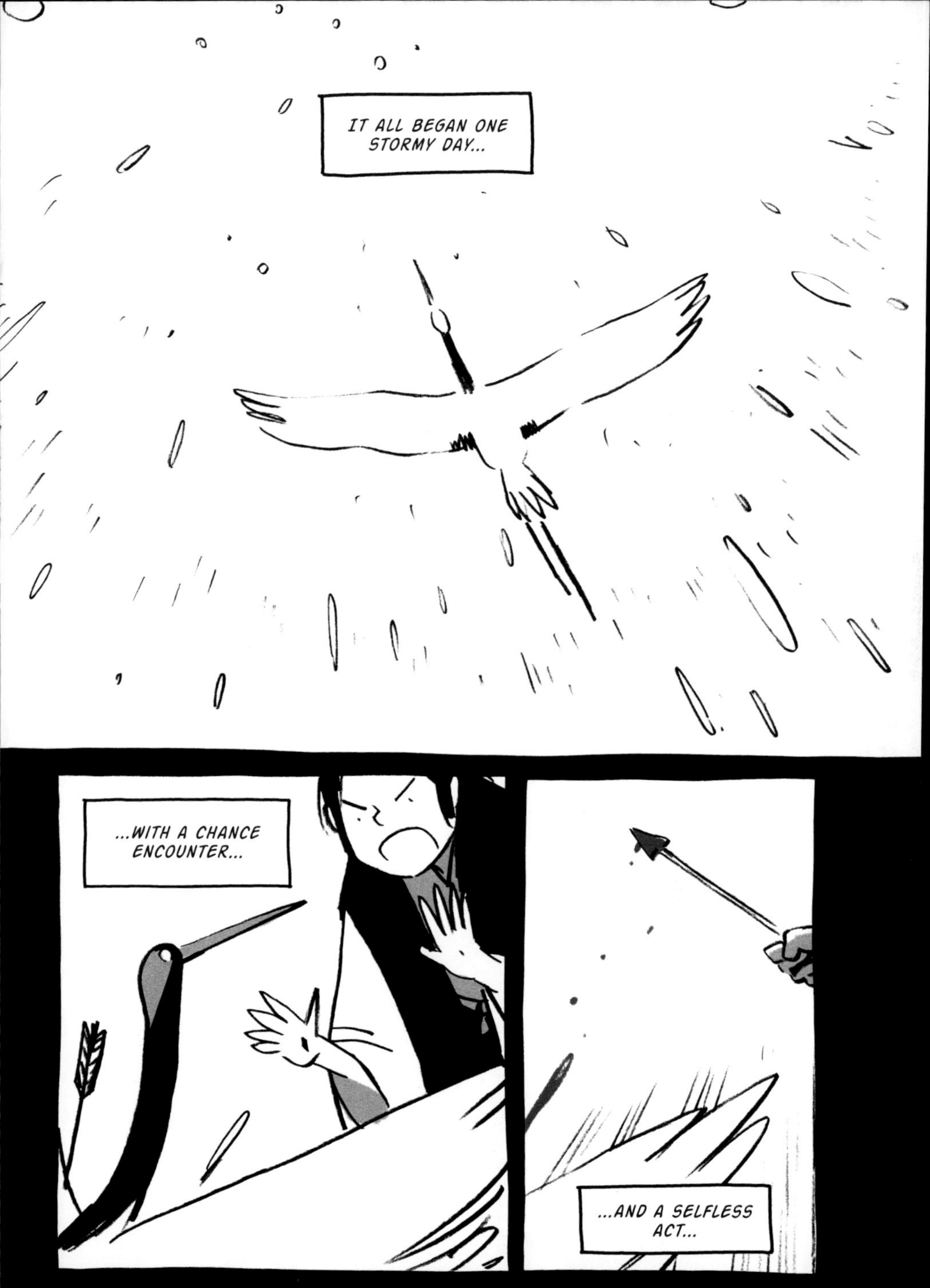
IT ALL BEGAN ONE STORMY DAY...
...WITH A CHANCE ENCOUNTER...
...AND A SELFLESS ACT...

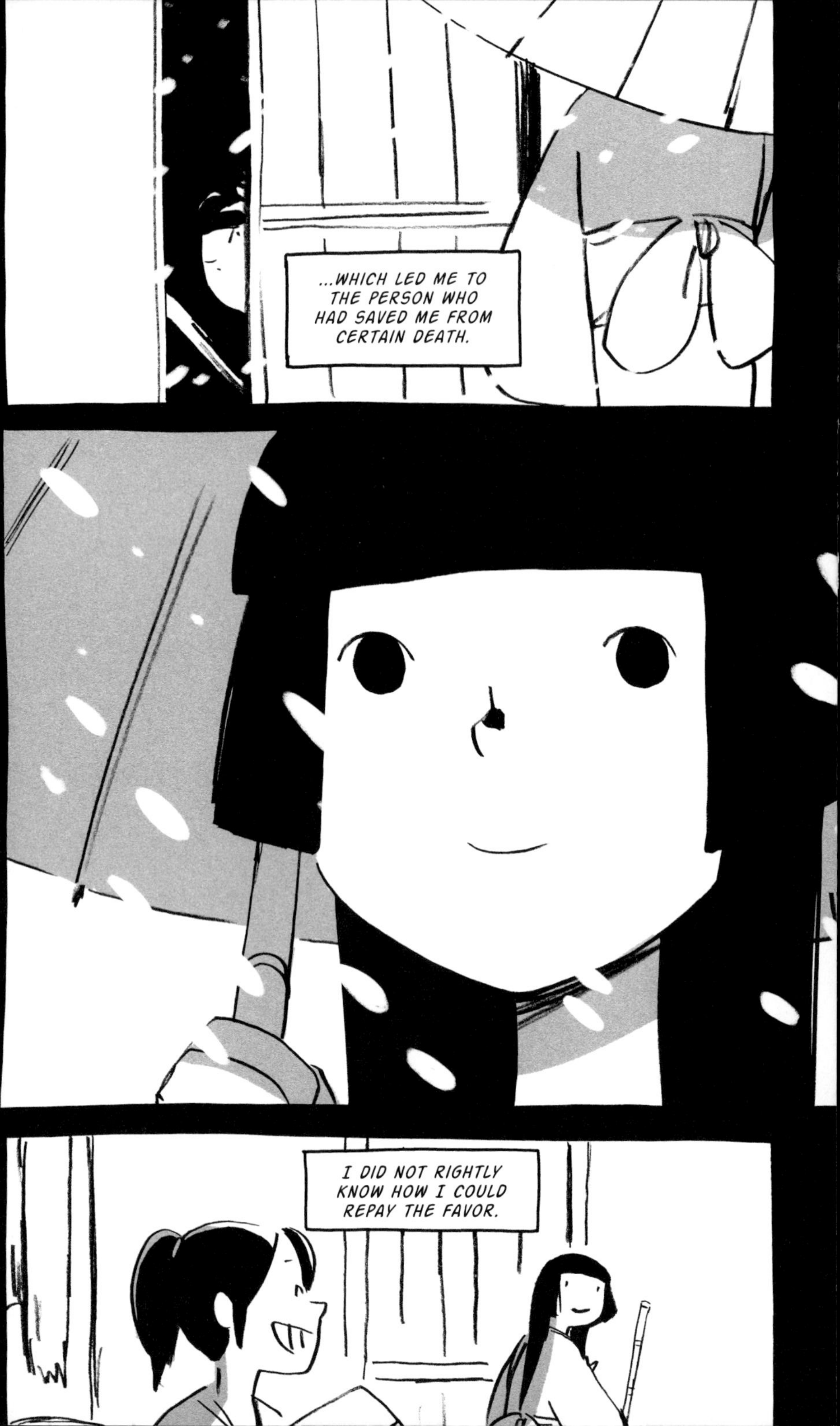
...WHICH LED ME TO THE PERSON WHO HAD SAVED ME FROM CERTAIN DEATH.
I DID NOT RIGHTLY KNOW HOW I COULD REPAY THE FAVOR.

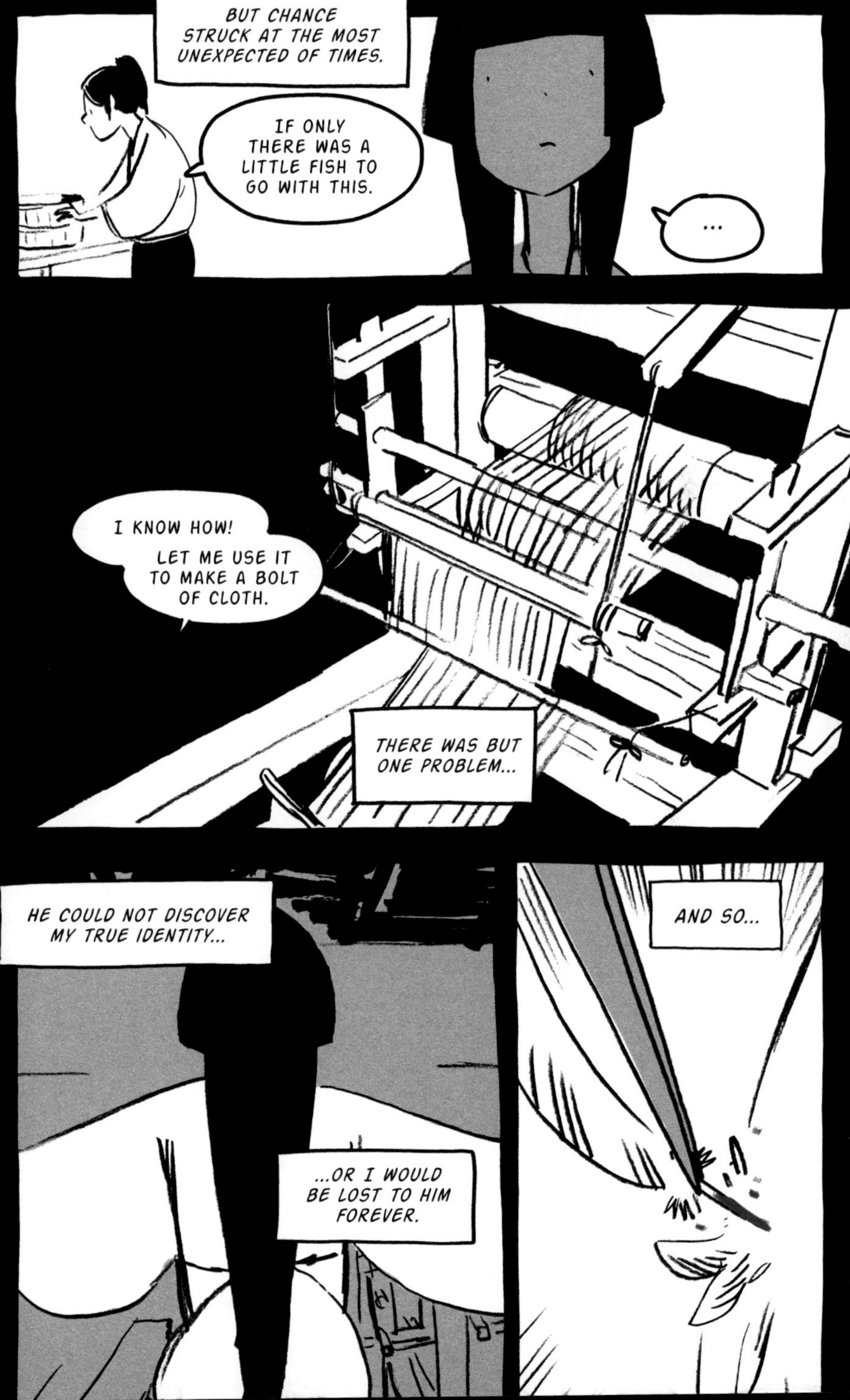
BUT CHANCE STRUCK AT THE MOST UNEXPECTED OF TIMES.
IF ONLY THERE WAS A LITTLE FISH TO GO WITH THIS.
...
I KNOW HOW!
LET ME USE IT TO MAKE A BOLT OF CLOTH.
THERE WAS BUT ONE PROBLEM...
HE COULD NOT DISCOVER MY TRUE IDENTITY...
...OR I WOULD BE LOST TO HIM FOREVER.
AND SO...

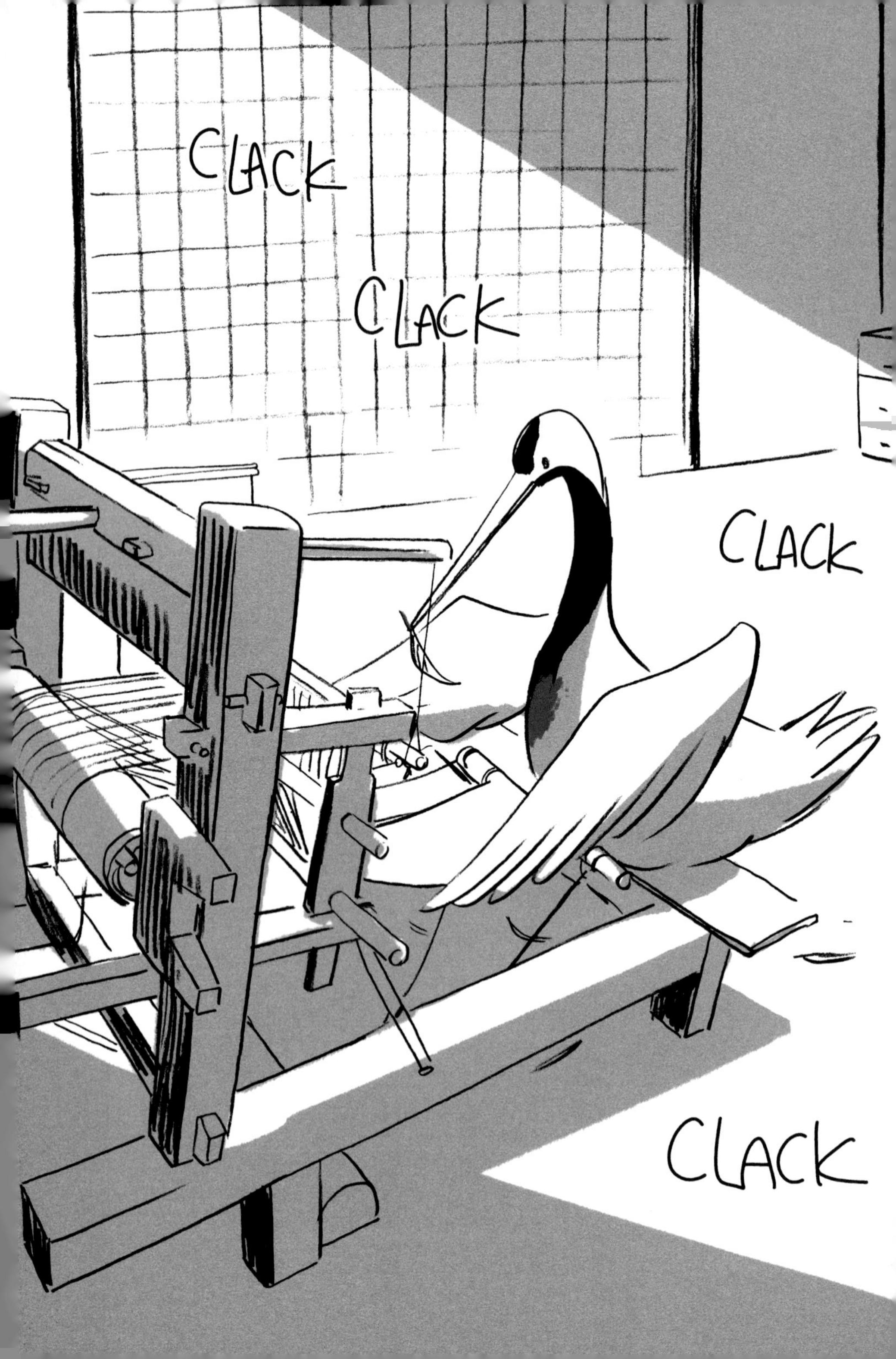
CLACK
CLACK
CLACK
CLACK

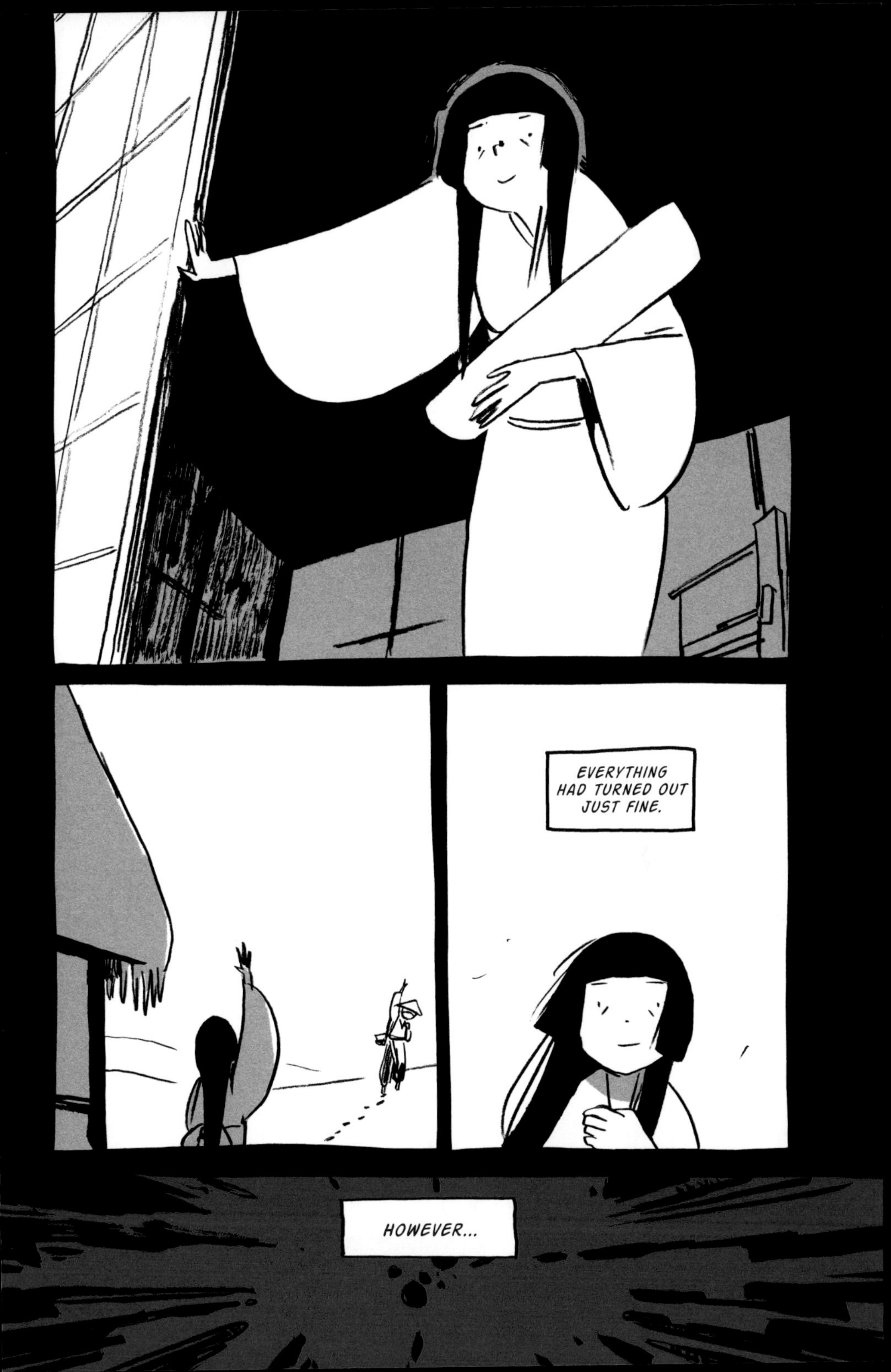
EVERYTHING HAD TURNED OUT JUST FINE.
HOWEVER...

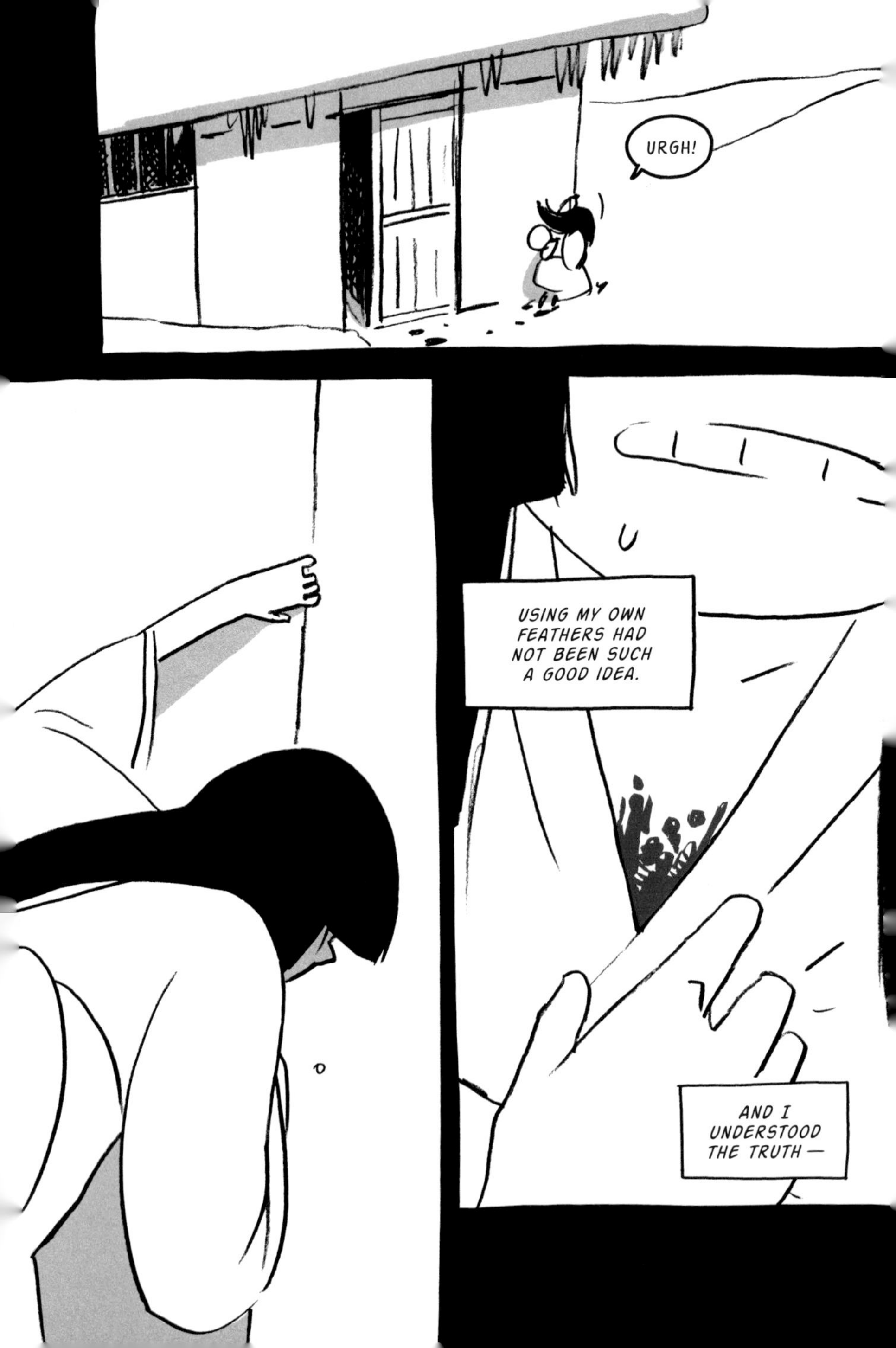
URGH!
USING MY OWN FEATHERS HAD NOT BEEN SUCH A GOOD IDEA.
AND I UNDERSTOOD THE TRUTH —

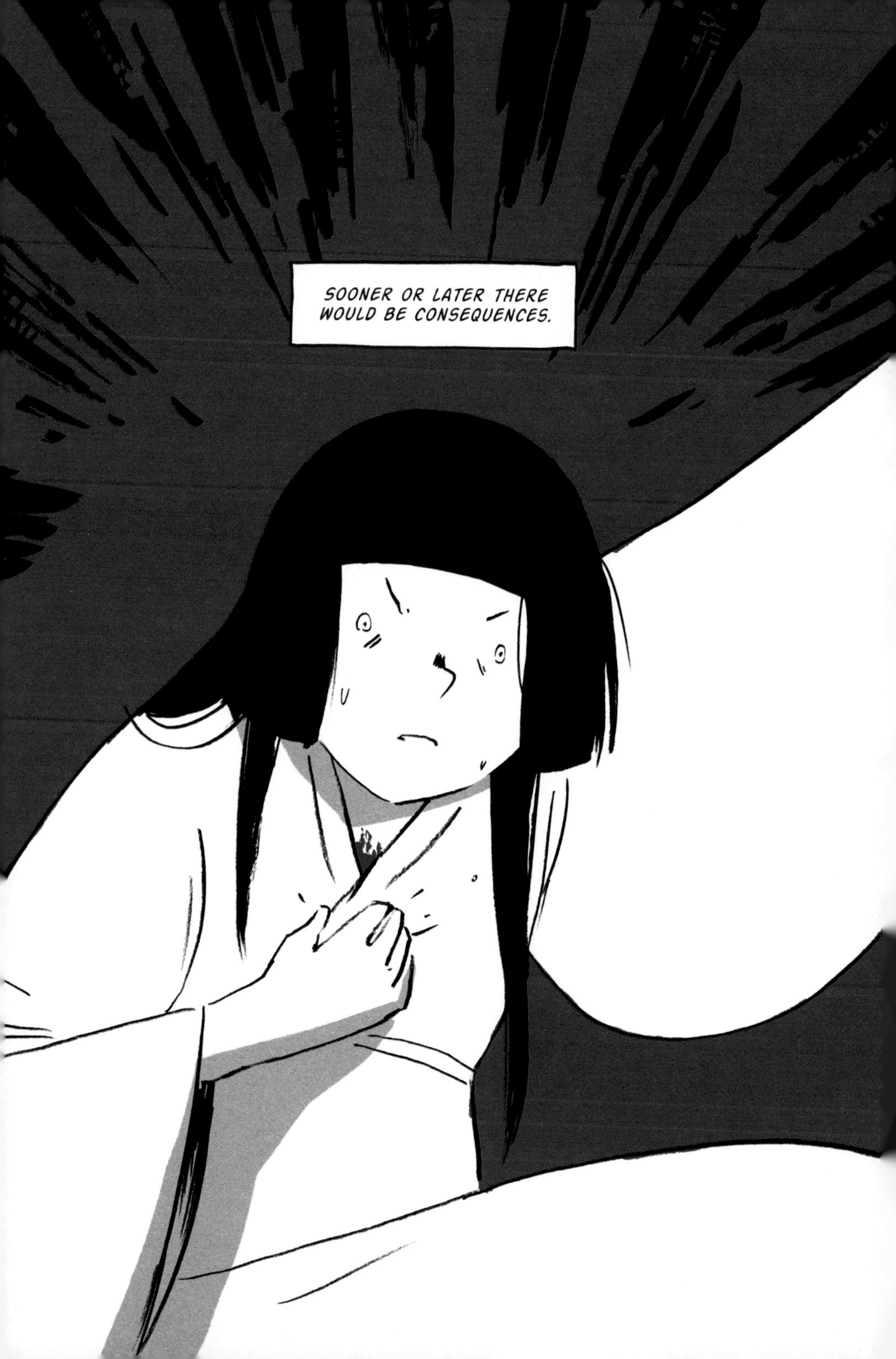
SOONER OR LATER THERE WOULD BE CONSEQUENCES.

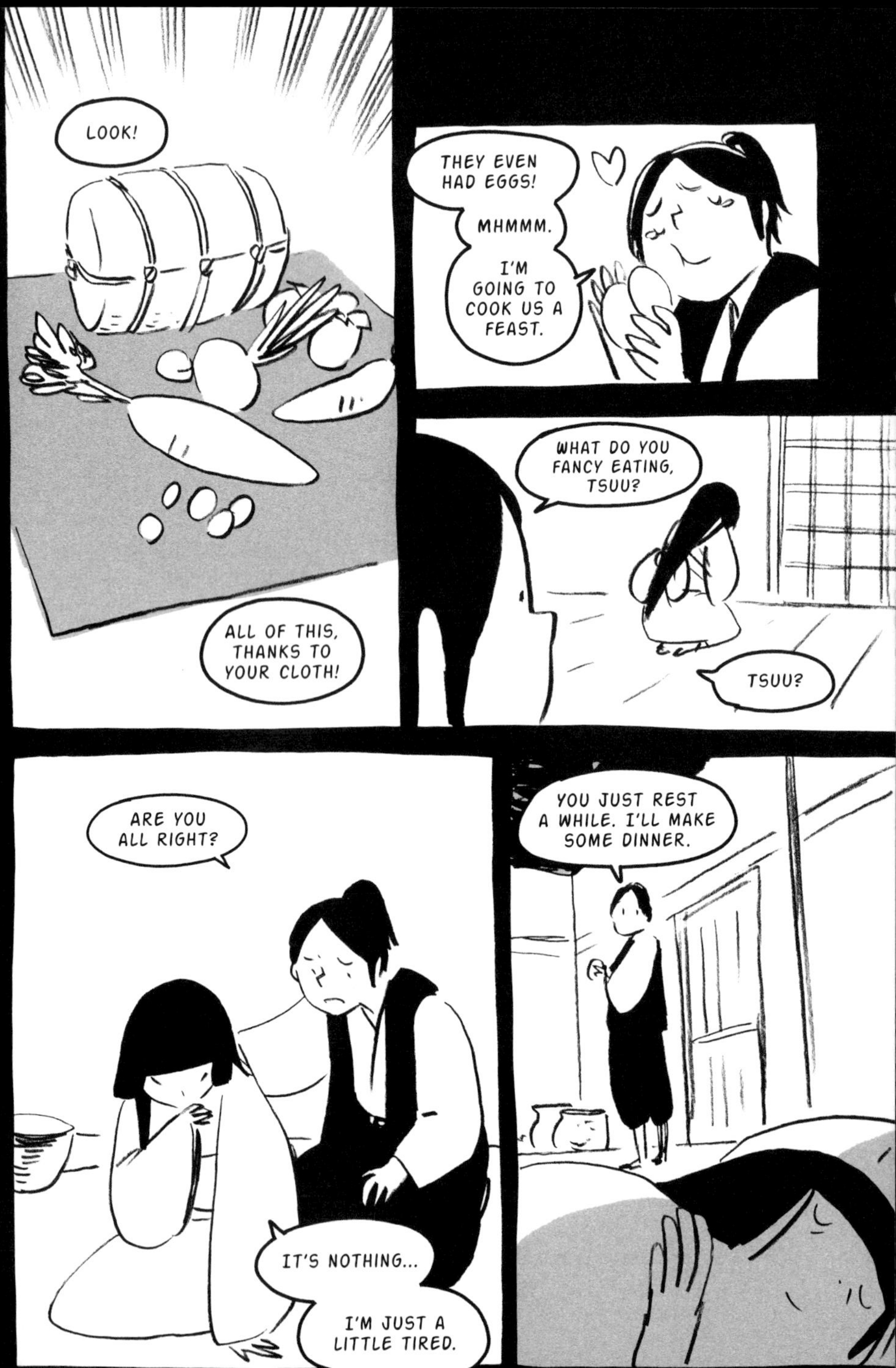
LOOK!
ALL OF THIS, THANKS TO YOUR CLOTH!
THEY EVEN HAD EGGS!
MHMMM.
I'M GOING TO COOK US A FEAST.
WHAT DO YOU FANCY EATING, TSUU?
TSUU?
ARE YOU ALL RIGHT?
IT'S NOTHING...
I'M JUST A LITTLE TIRED.
YOU JUST REST A WHILE. I'LL MAKE SOME DINNER.

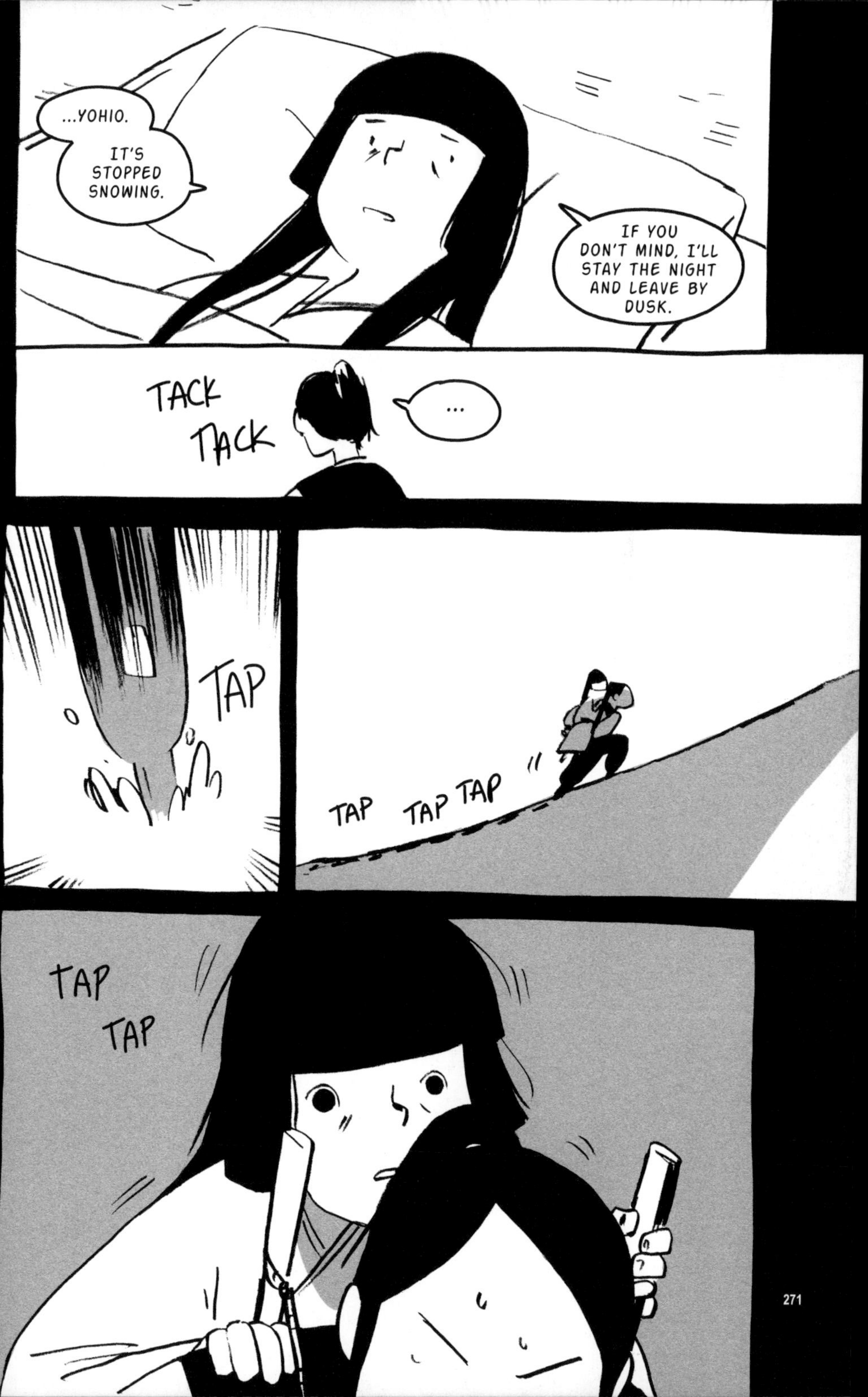
...YOHIO.
IT'S STOPPED SNOWING.
IF YOU DON'T MIND, I'LL STAY THE NIGHT AND LEAVE BY DUSK.
TACK TACK
...
TAP
TAP TAP TAP
TAP TAP

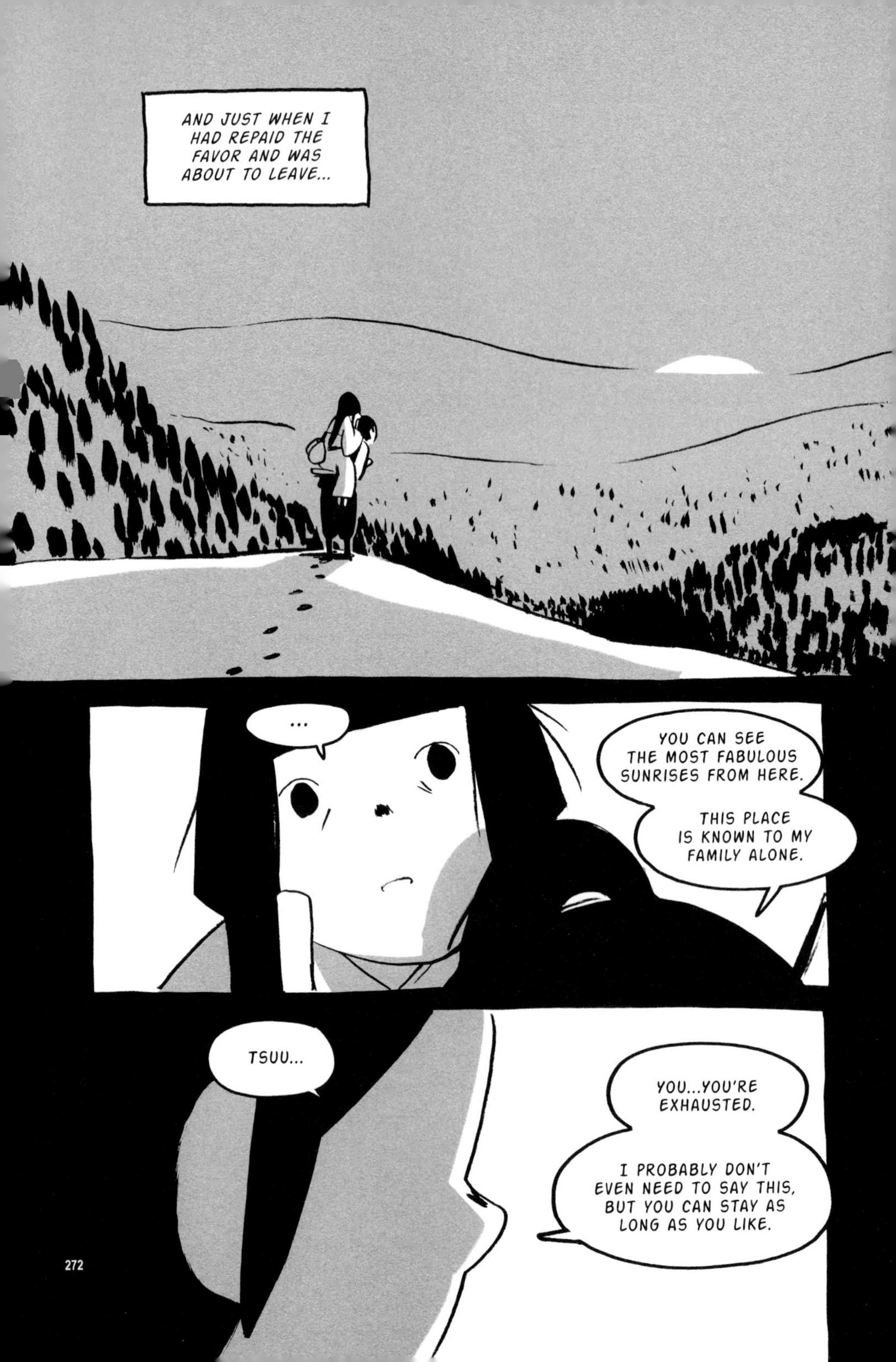

AND JUST WHEN I HAD REPAID THE FAVOR AND WAS ABOUT TO LEAVE...
...
YOU CAN SEE THE MOST FABULOUS SUNRISES FROM HERE.
THIS PLACE IS KNOWN TO MY FAMILY ALONE.
TSUU...
YOU...YOU'RE EXHAUSTED.
I PROBABLY DON'T EVEN NEED TO SAY THIS, BUT YOU CAN STAY AS LONG AS YOU LIKE.

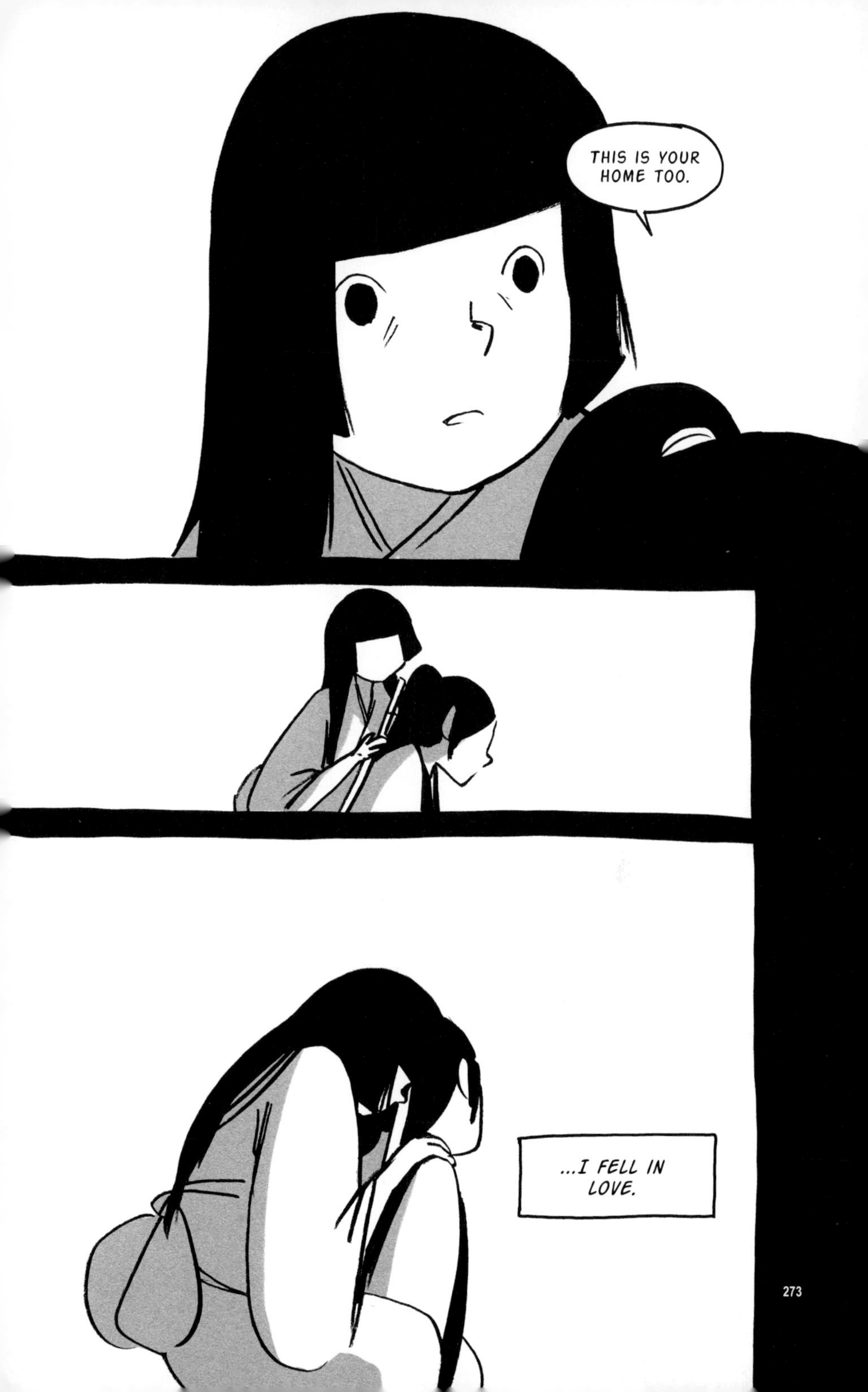
THIS IS YOUR HOME TOO.
...I FELL IN LOVE.

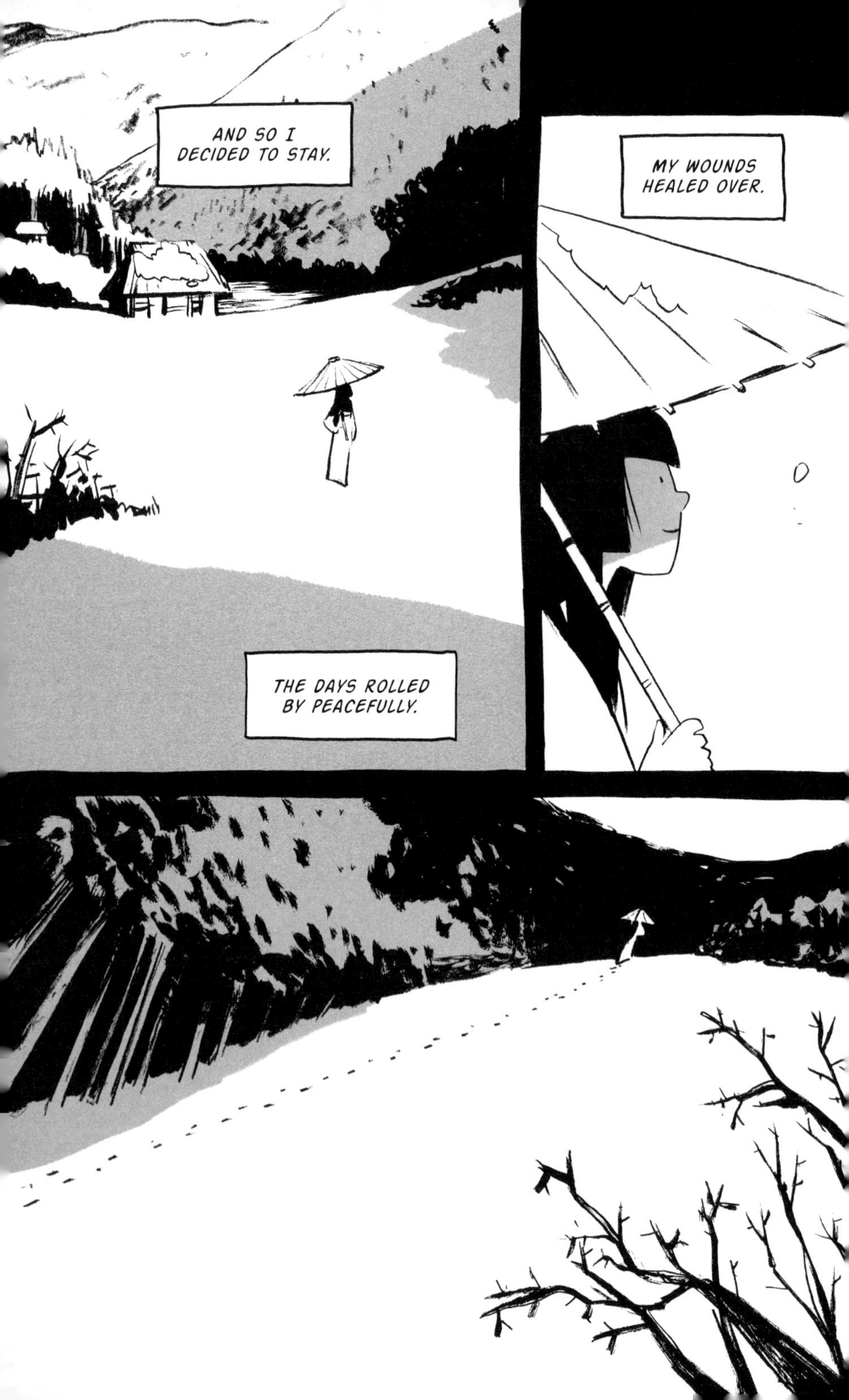
AND SO I DECIDED TO STAY.
MY WOUNDS HEALED OVER.
THE DAYS ROLLED BY PEACEFULLY.

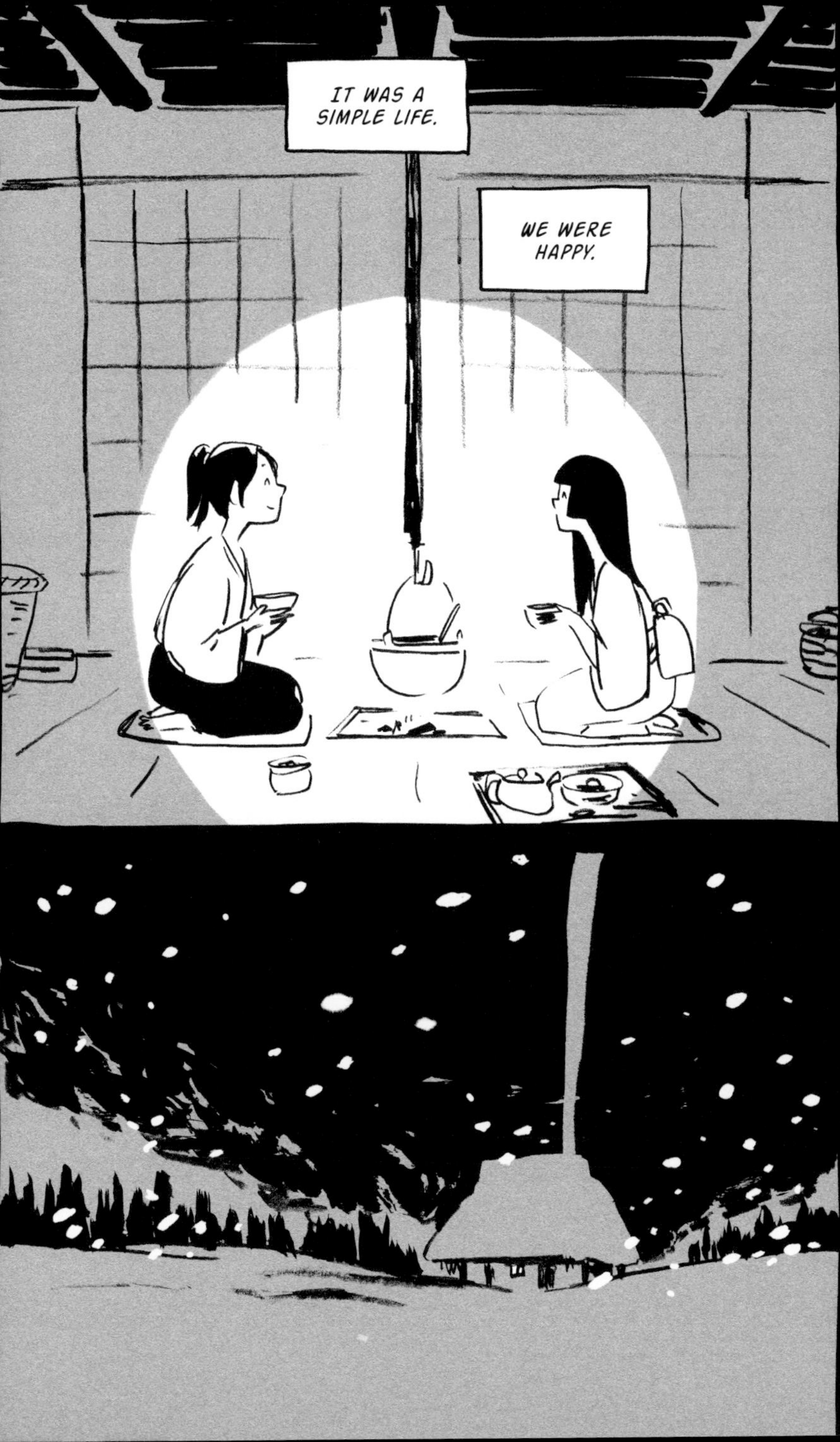
IT WAS A SIMPLE LIFE.
WE WERE HAPPY.

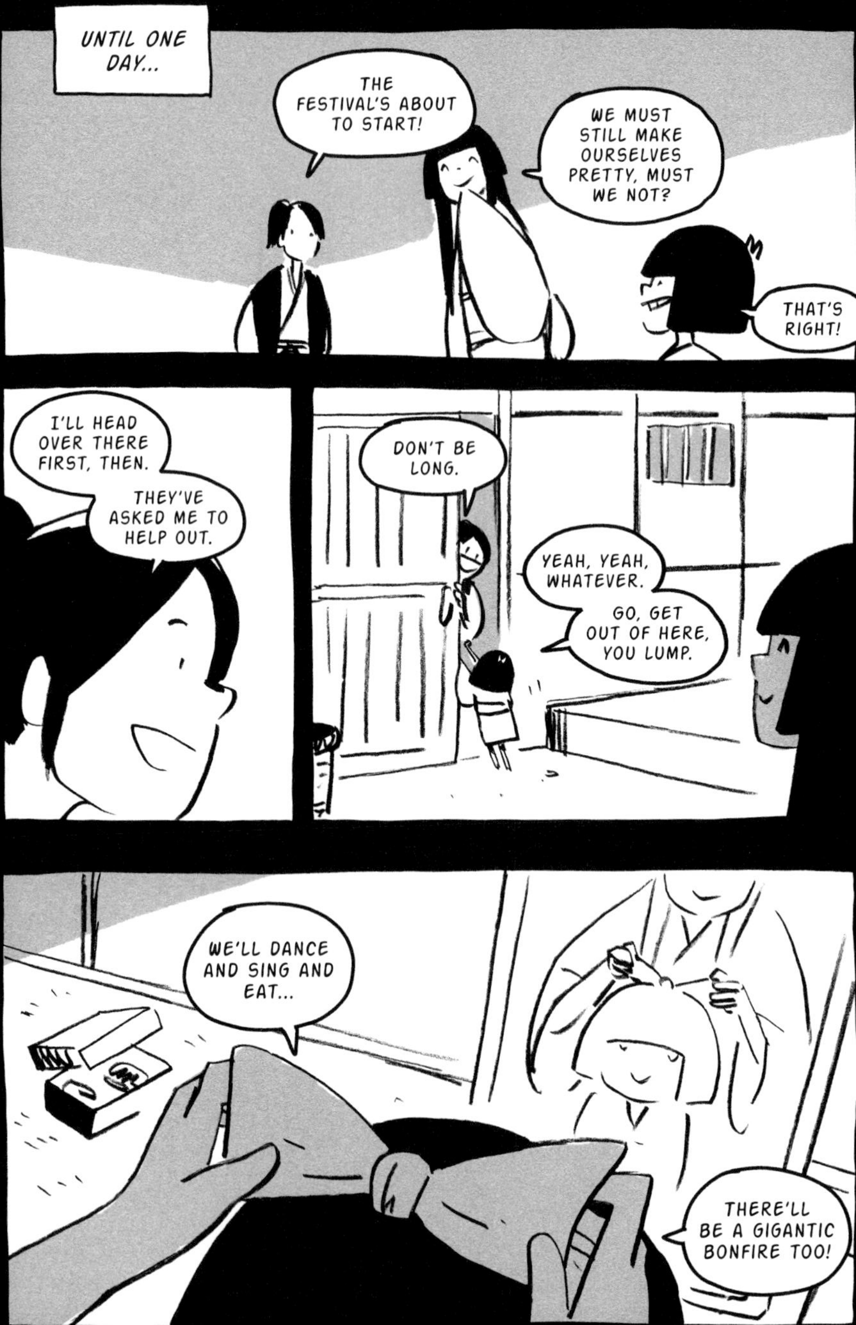
UNTIL ONE DAY...
THE FESTIVAL'S ABOUT TO START!
WE MUST STILL MAKE OURSELVES PRETTY, MUST WE NOT?
THAT'S RIGHT!
I'LL HEAD OVER THERE FIRST, THEN.
THEY'VE ASKED ME TO HELP OUT.
DON'T BE LONG.
YEAH, YEAH, WHATEVER.
GO, GET OUT OF HERE, YOU LUMP.
WE'LL DANCE AND SING AND EAT...
THERE'LL BE A GIGANTIC BONFIRE TOO!

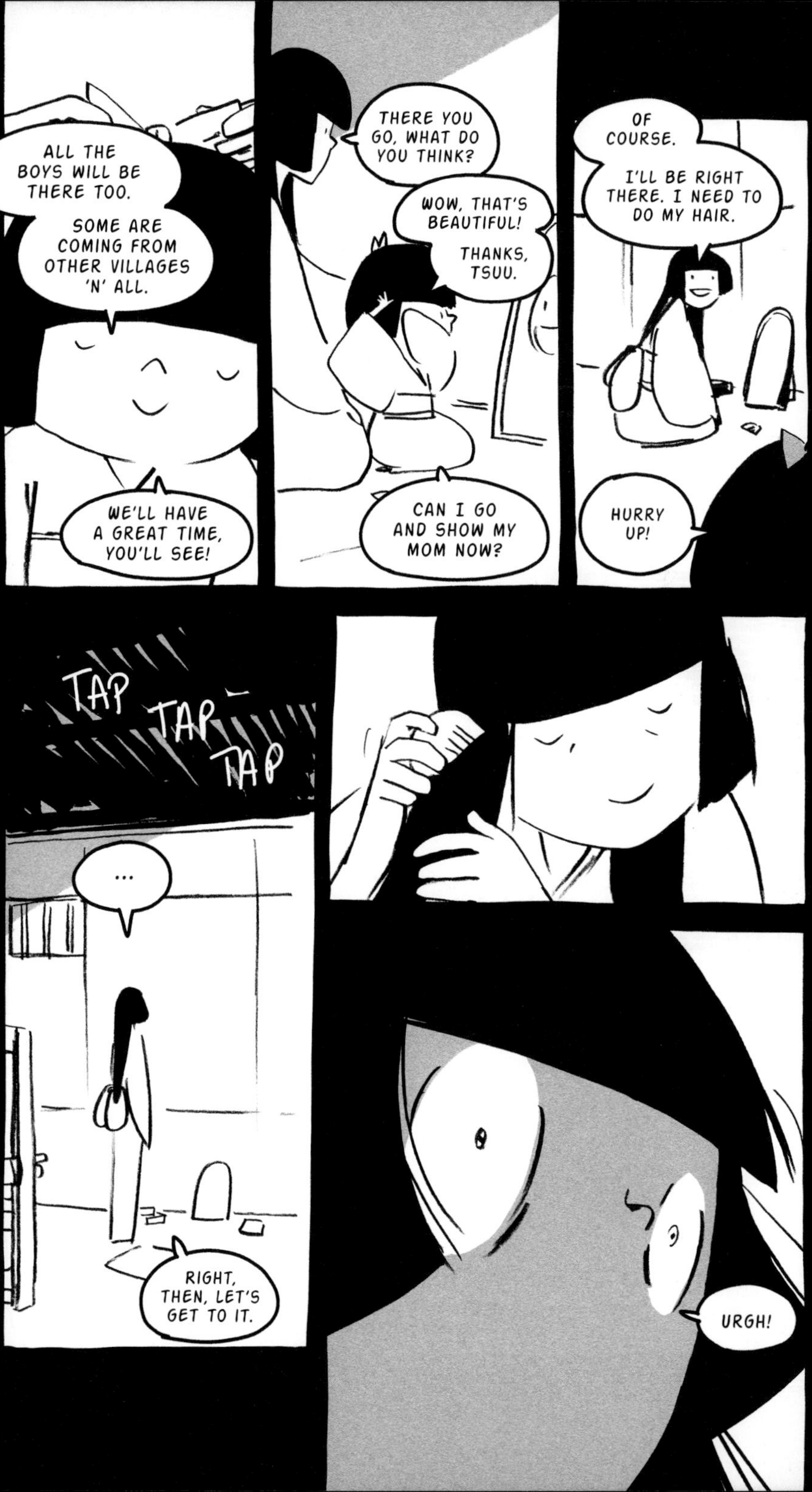
ALL THE BOYS WILL BE THERE TOO.
SOME ARE COMING FROM OTHER VILLAGES 'N' ALL.
WE'LL HAVE A GREAT TIME, YOU'LL SEE!
THERE YOU GO, WHAT DO YOU THINK?
WOW, THAT'S BEAUTIFUL!
THANKS, TSUU.
CAN I GO AND SHOW MY MOM NOW?
OF COURSE.
I'LL BE RIGHT THERE. I NEED TO DO MY HAIR.
HURRY UP!
TAP TAP TAP
...
RIGHT, THEN, LET'S GET TO IT.
URGH!

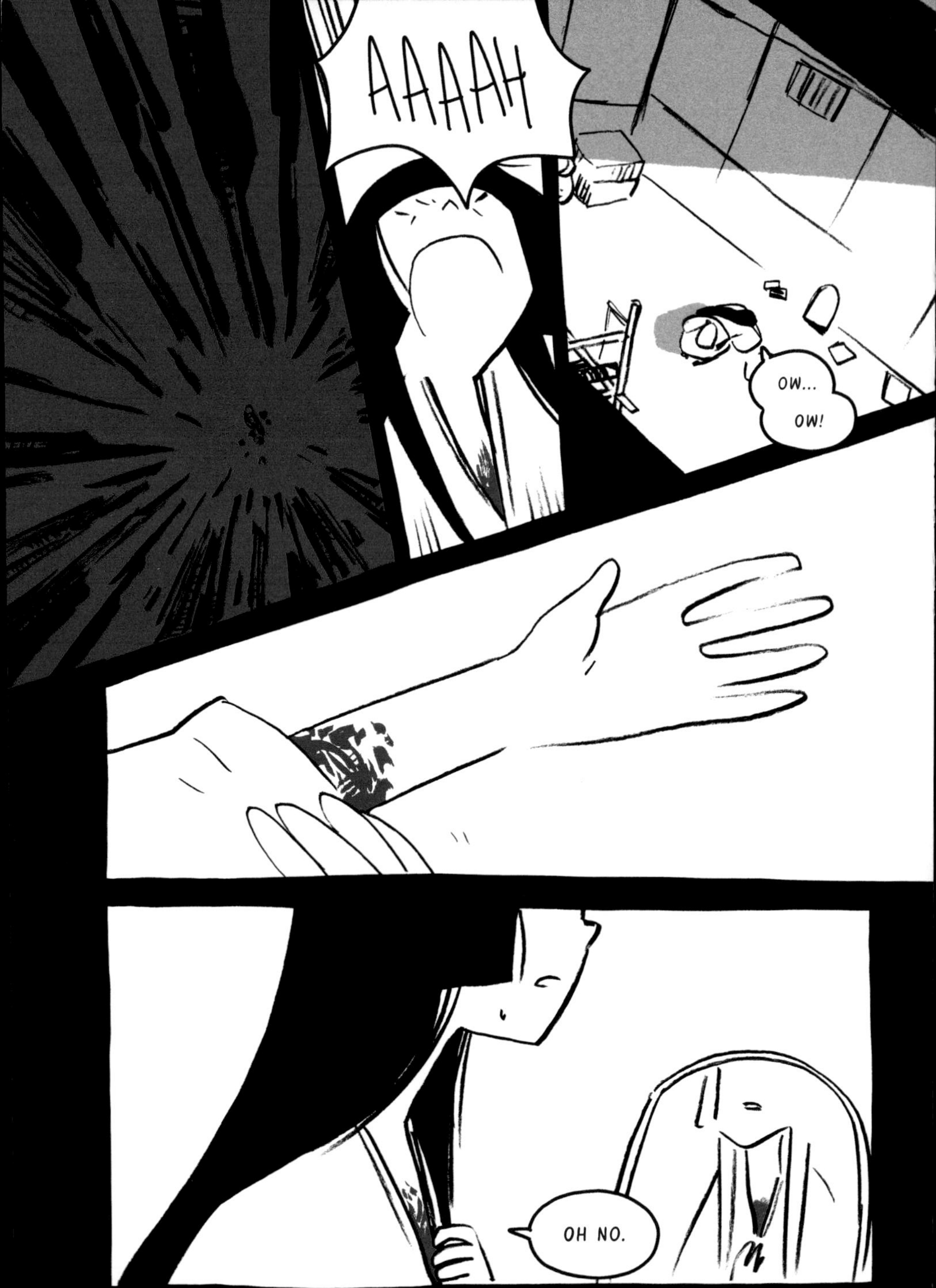
AAAAH
OW... OW!
OH NO.

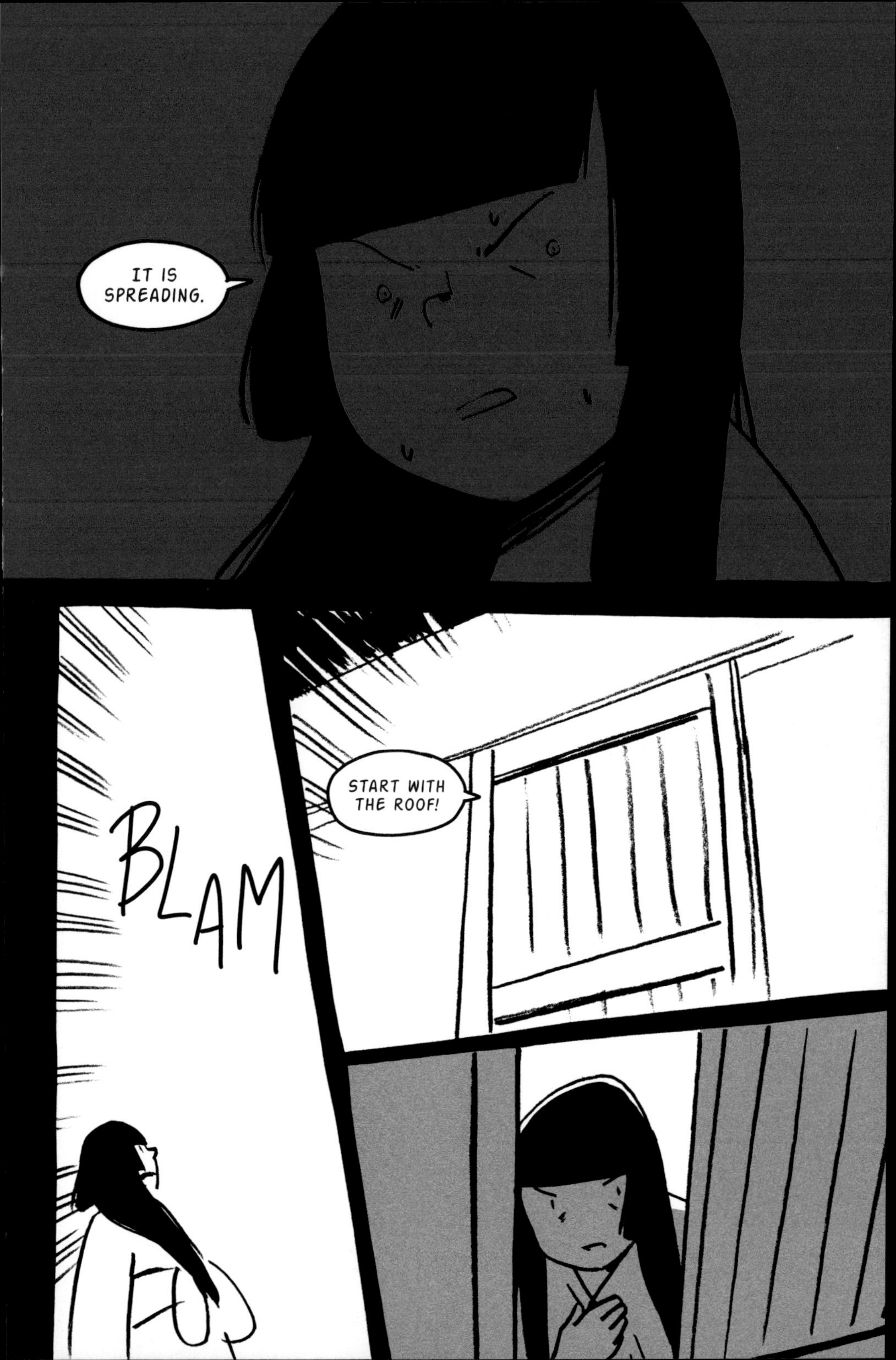
IT IS SPREADING.
START WITH THE ROOF!
BLAM
FU

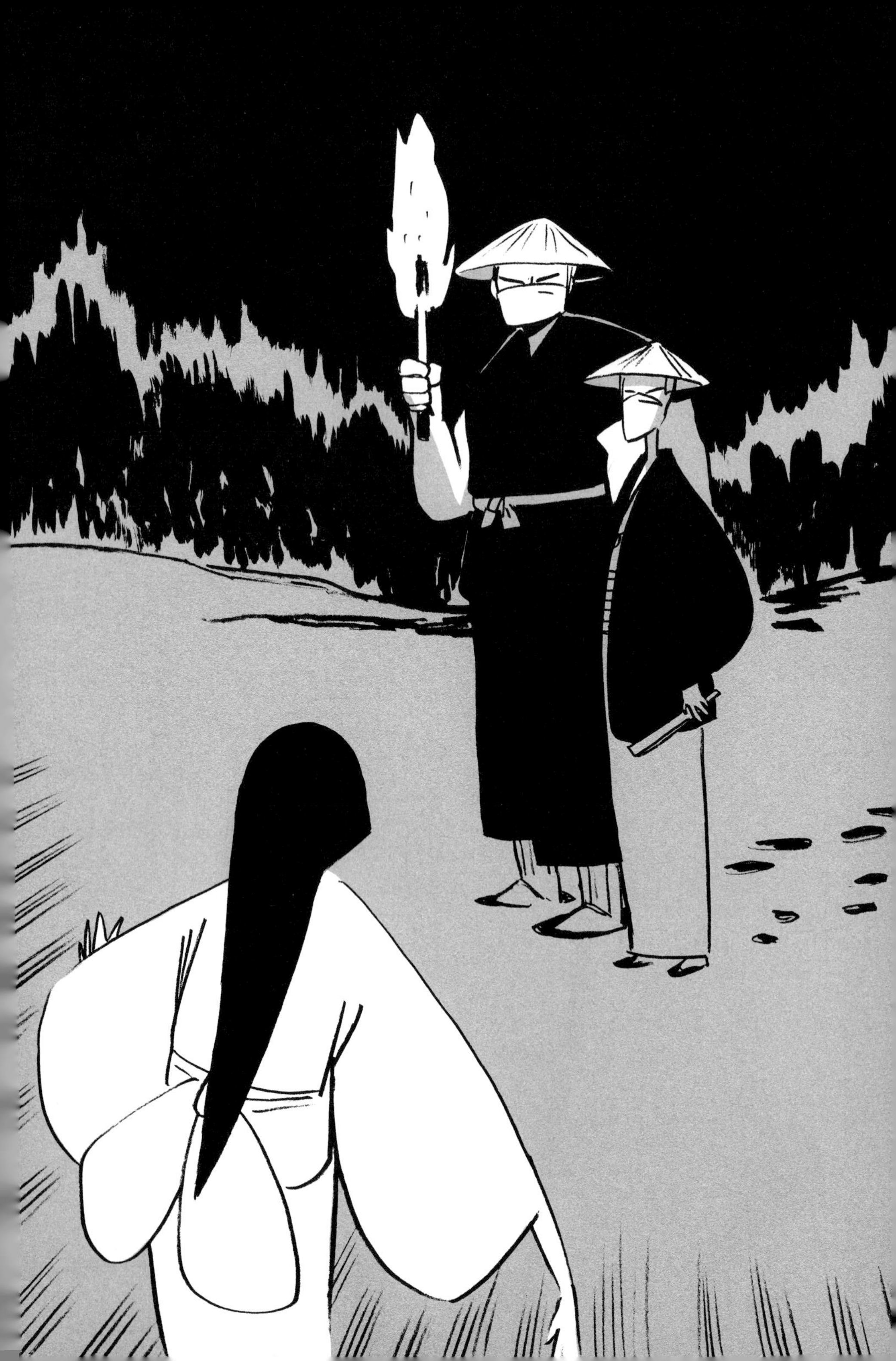

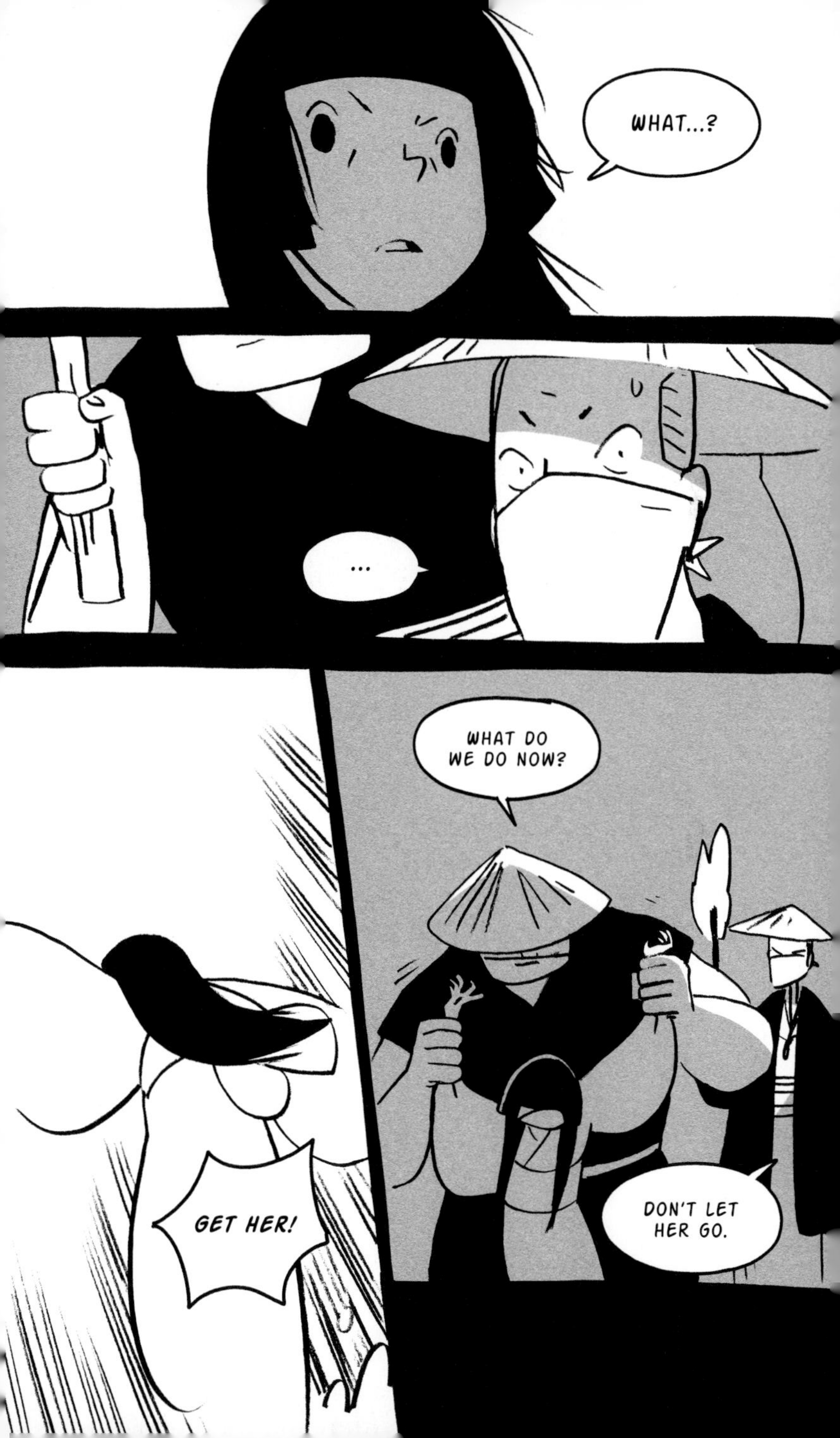
WHAT...?
...
WHAT DO WE DO NOW?
GET HER!
DON'T LET HER GO.

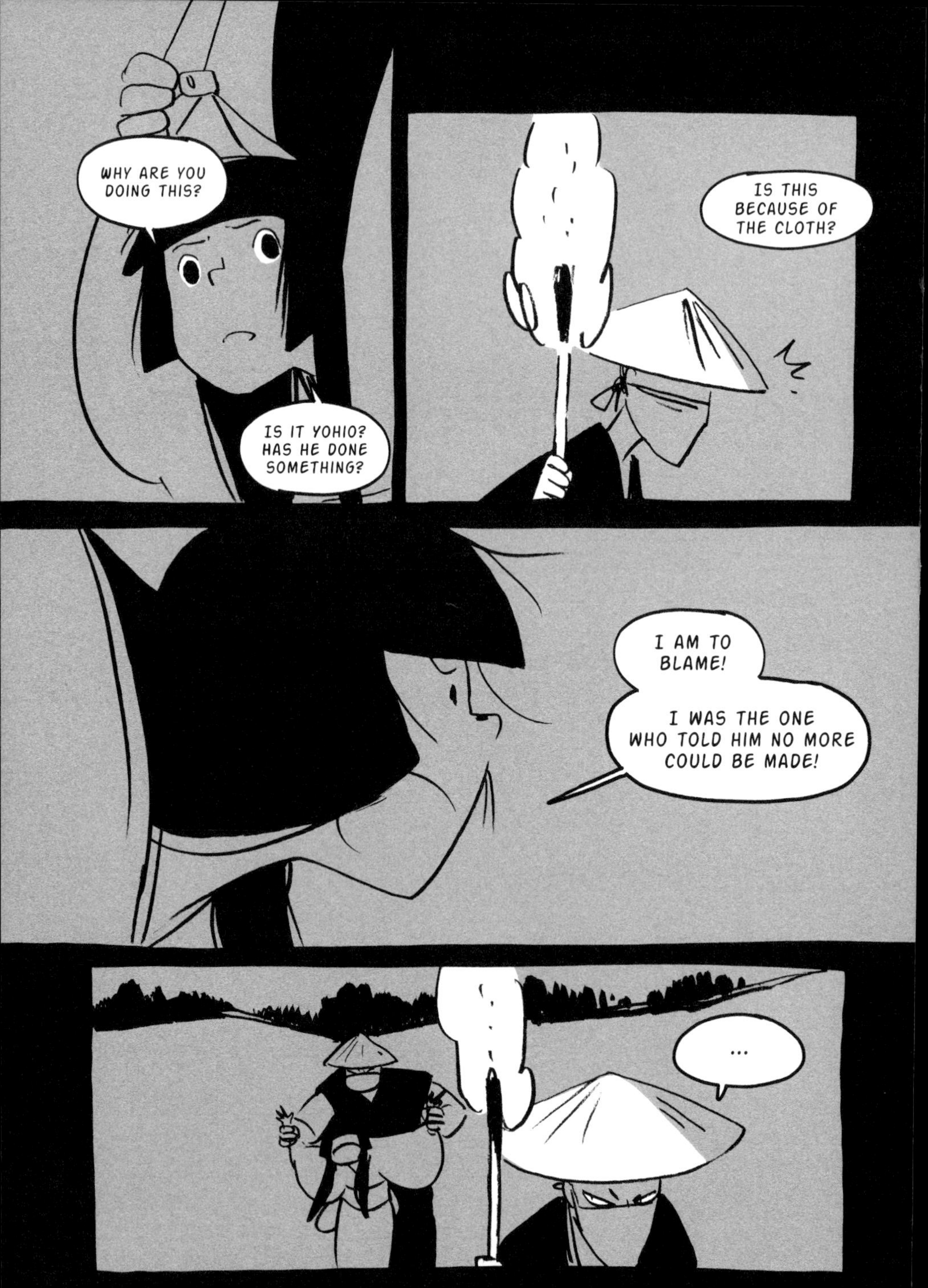
WHY ARE YOU DOING THIS?
IS IT YOHIO? HAS HE DONE SOMETHING?
IS THIS BECAUSE OF THE CLOTH?
I AM TO BLAME!
I WAS THE ONE WHO TOLD HIM NO MORE COULD BE MADE!
...

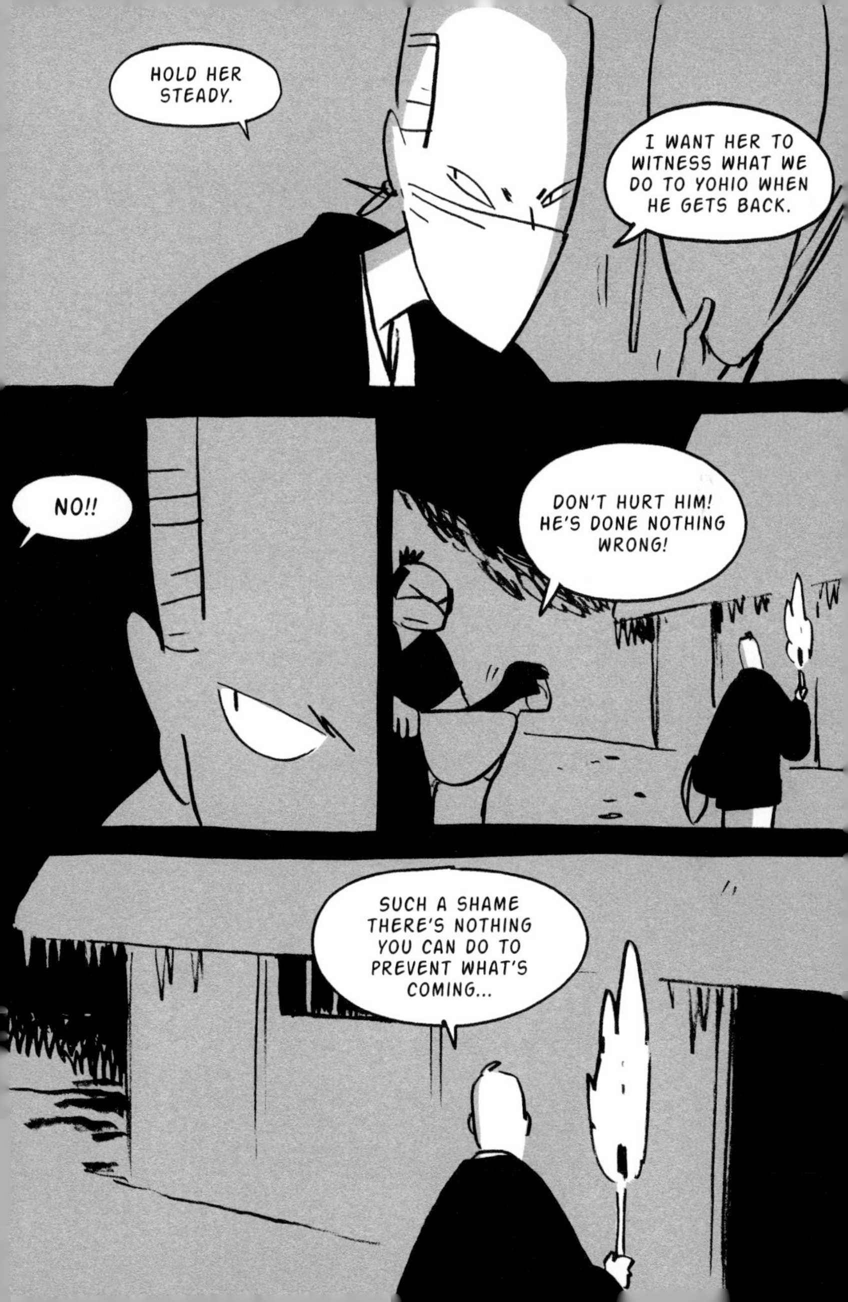
HOLD HER STEADY.
I WANT HER TO WITNESS WHAT WE DO TO YOHIO WHEN HE GETS BACK.
NO!!
DON'T HURT HIM! HE'S DONE NOTHING WRONG!
SUCH A SHAME THERE'S NOTHING YOU CAN DO TO PREVENT WHAT'S COMING...

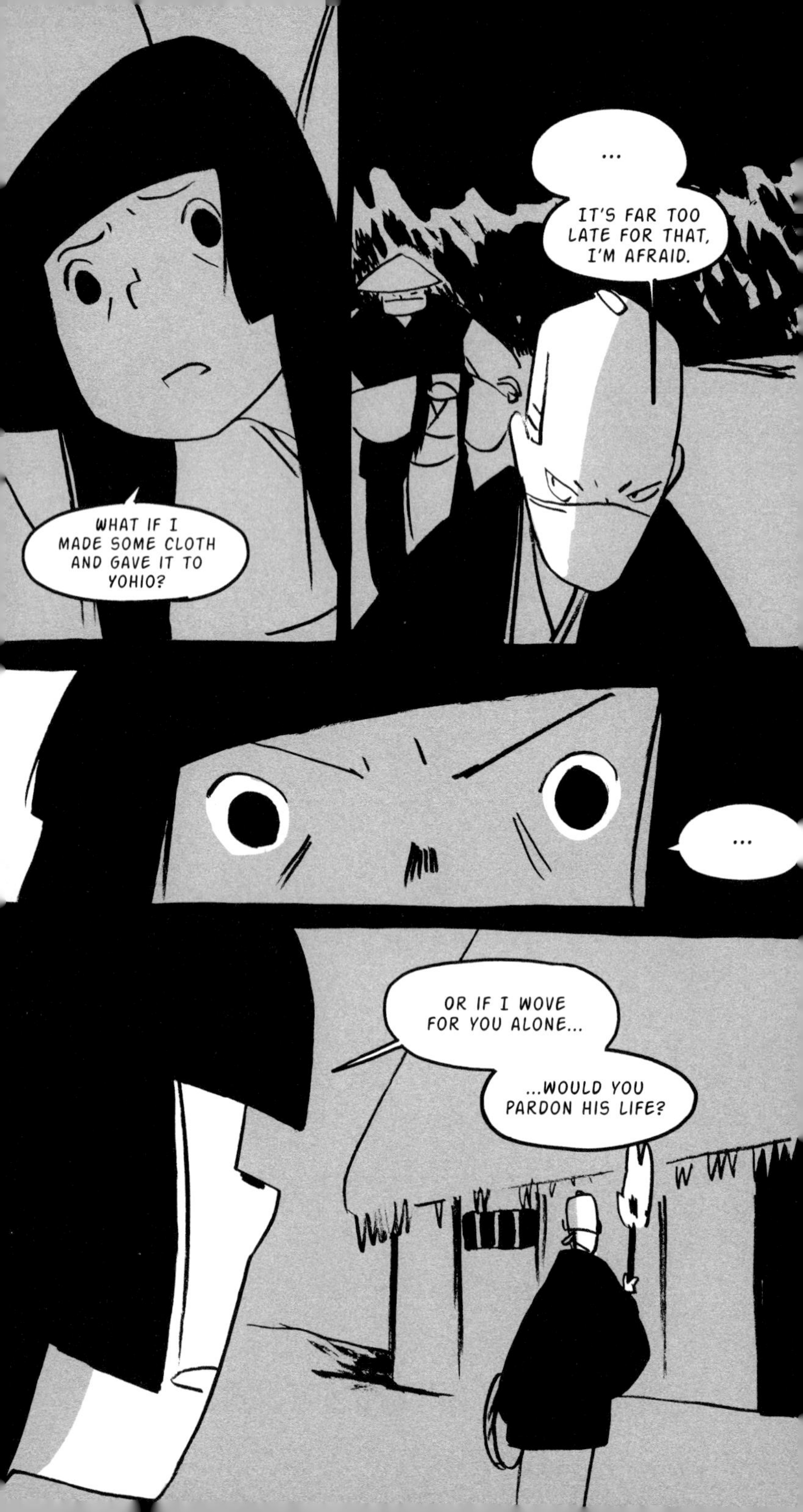
...
IT'S FAR TOO LATE FOR THAT, I'M AFRAID.
WHAT IF I MADE SOME CLOTH AND GAVE IT TO YOHIO?
...
OR IF I WOVE FOR YOU ALONE...
...WOULD YOU PARDON HIS LIFE?

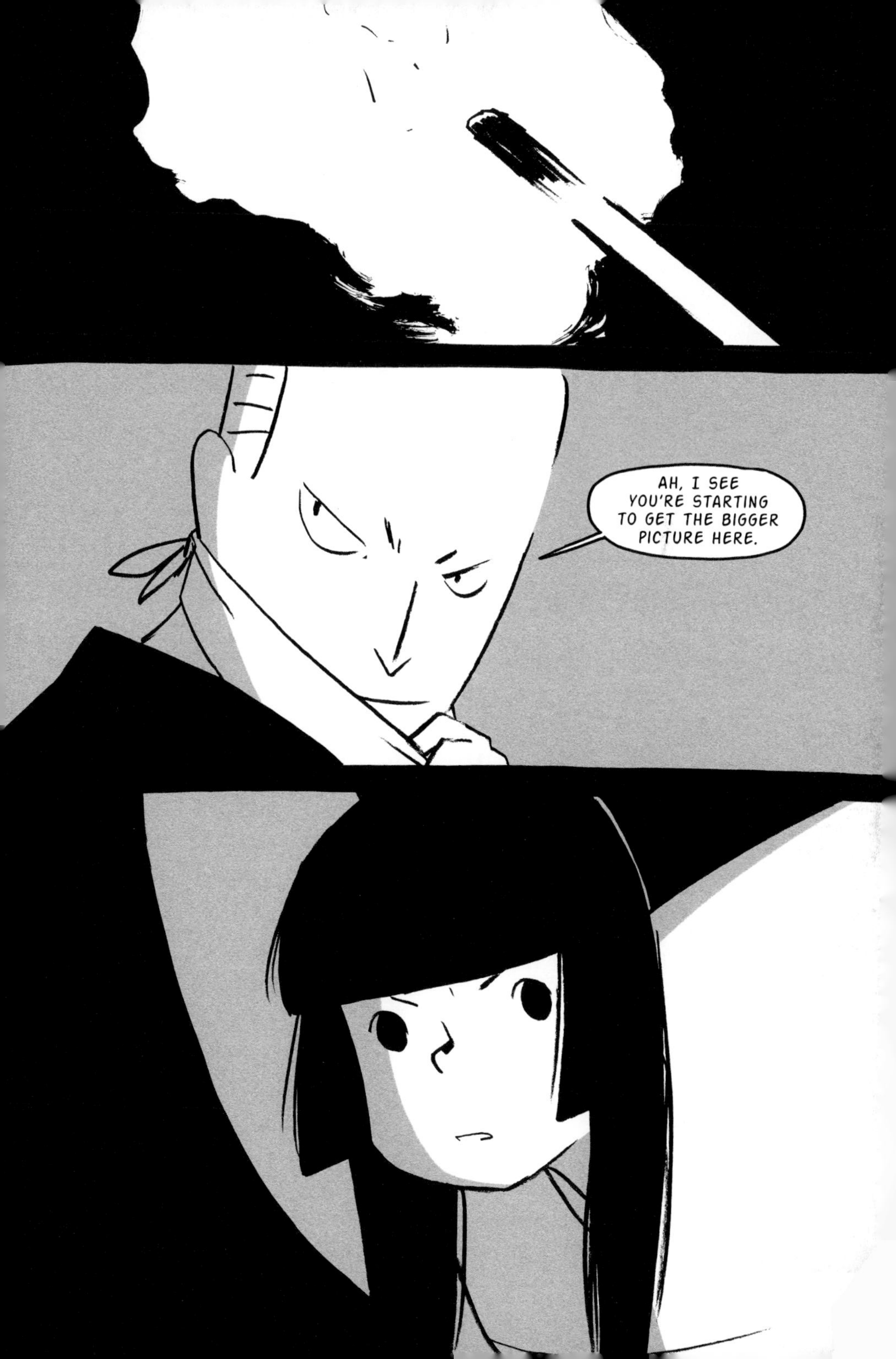
AH, I SEE YOU'RE STARTING TO GET THE BIGGER PICTURE HERE.

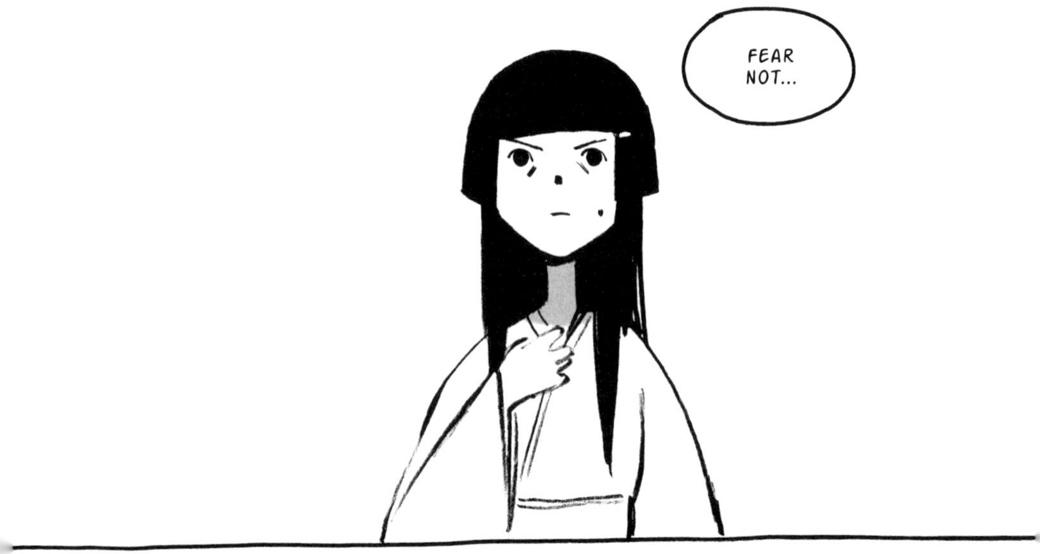
FEAR NOT...

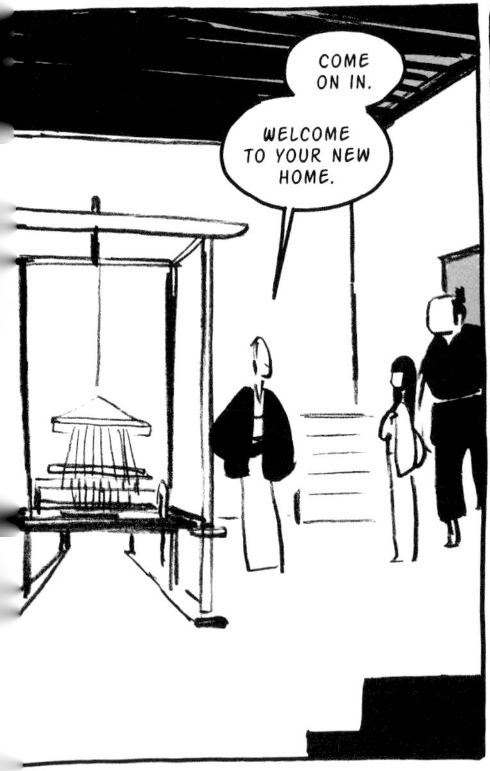
COME ON IN.
WELCOME TO YOUR NEW HOME.

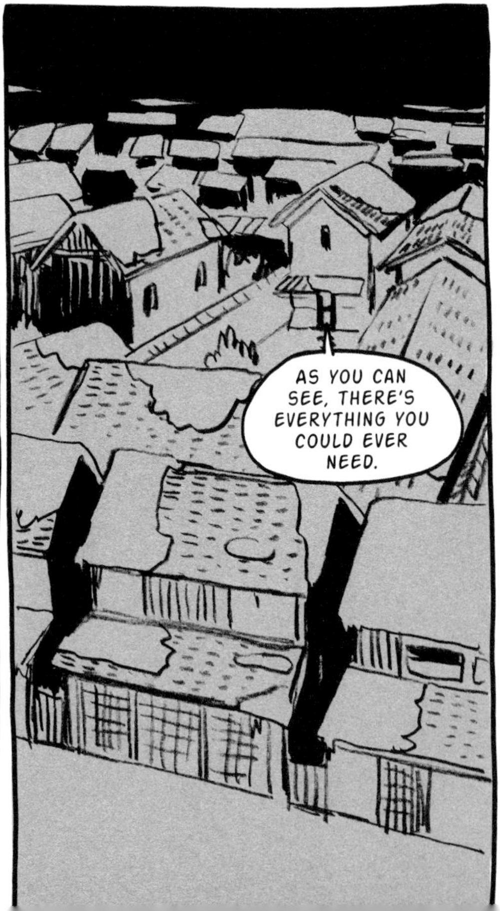
AS YOU CAN SEE, THERE'S EVERYTHING YOU COULD EVER NEED.

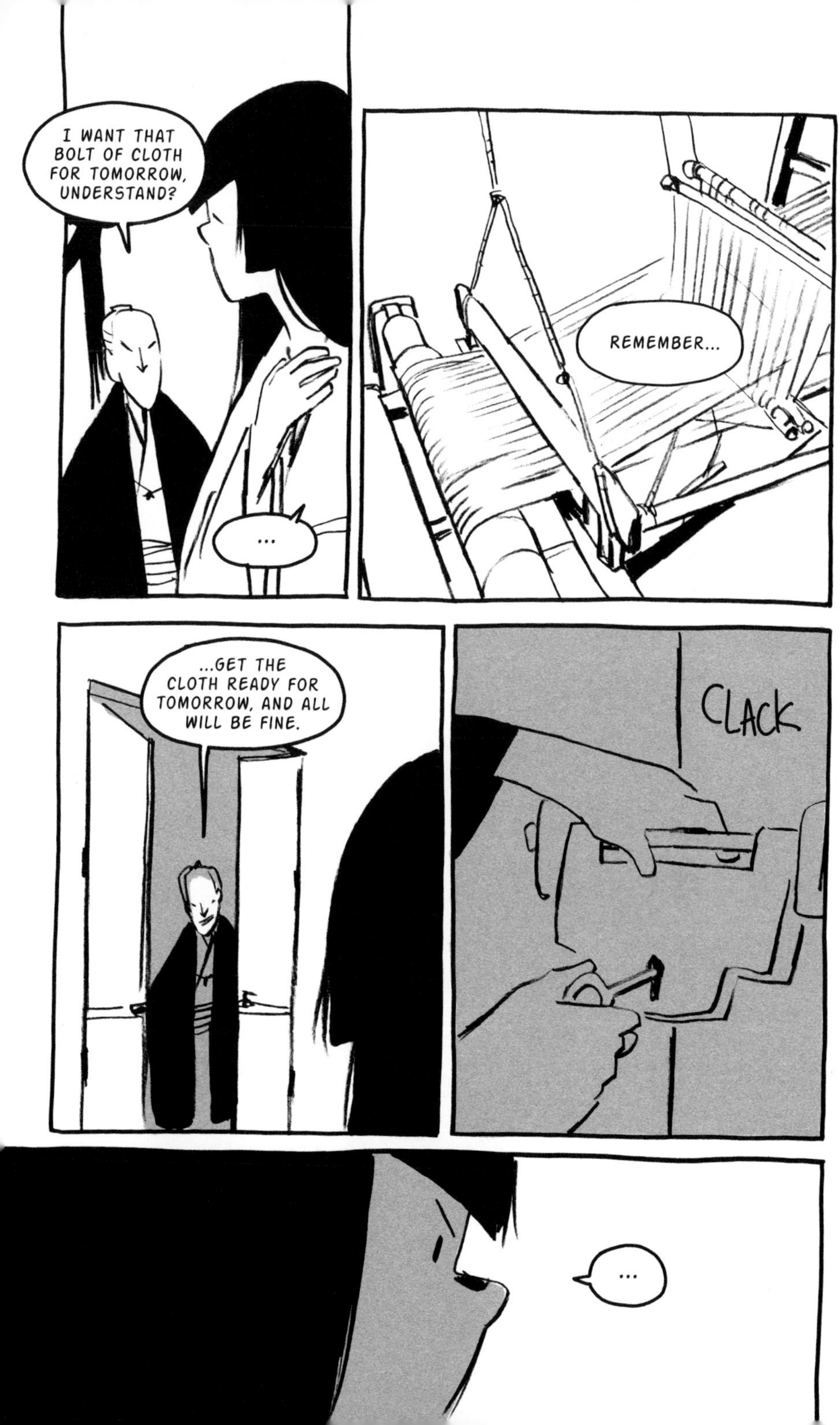
I WANT THAT BOLT OF CLOTH FOR TOMORROW, UNDERSTAND?
...
REMEMBER...
...GET THE CLOTH READY FOR TOMORROW, AND ALL WILL BE FINE.
CLACK
...

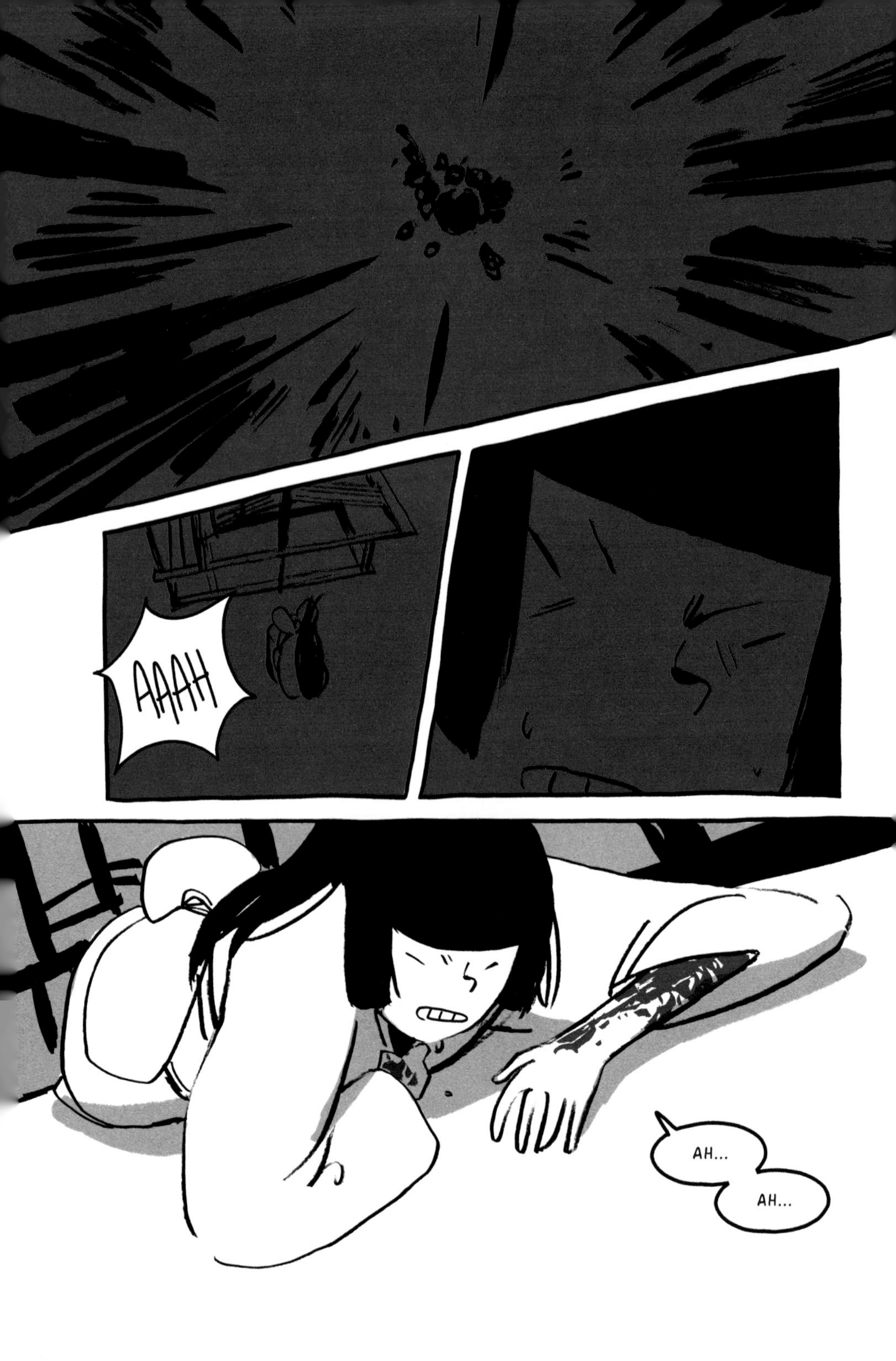
AAAH
AH...
AH...

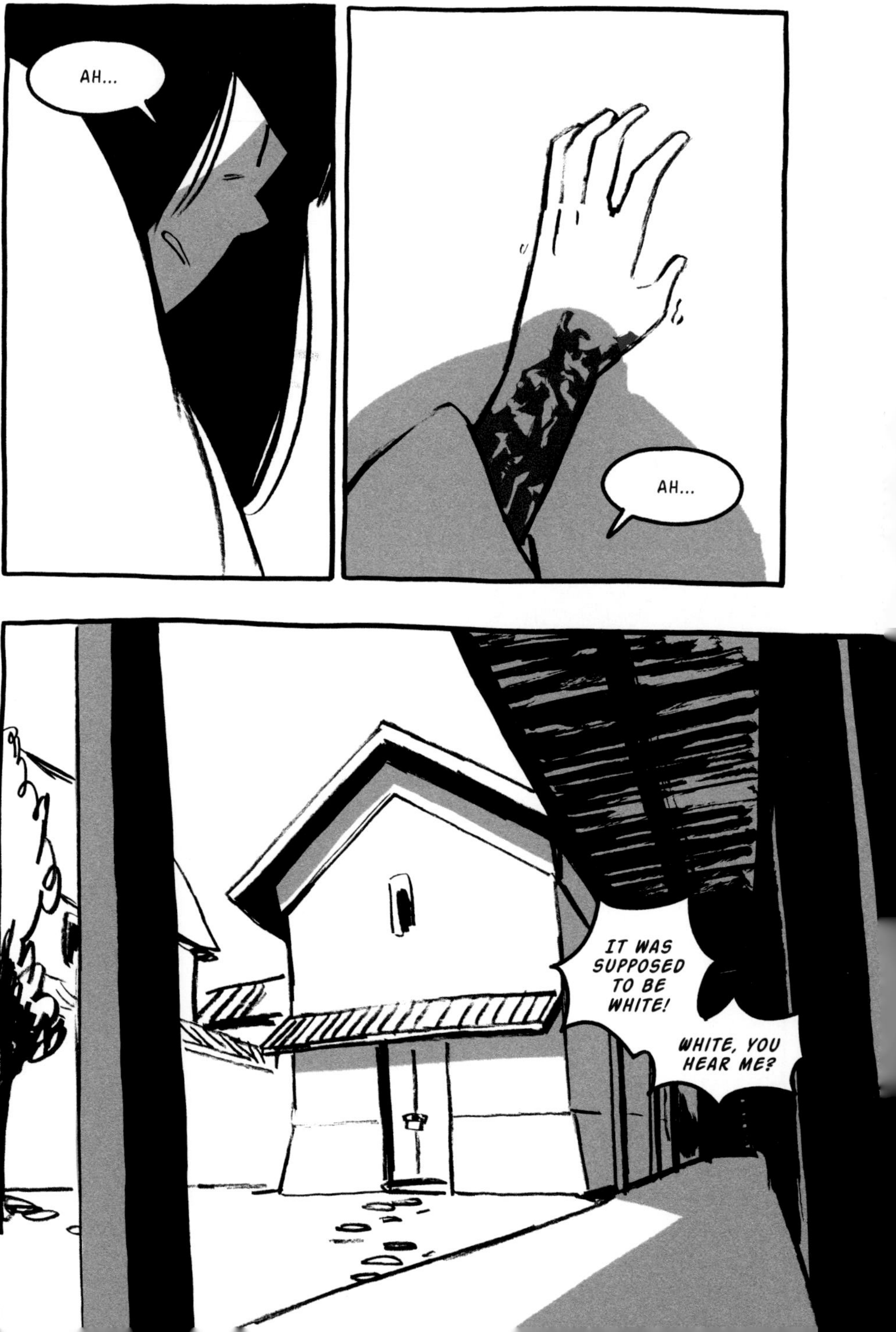
AH...
AH...
IT WAS SUPPOSED TO BE WHITE!
WHITE, YOU HEAR ME?

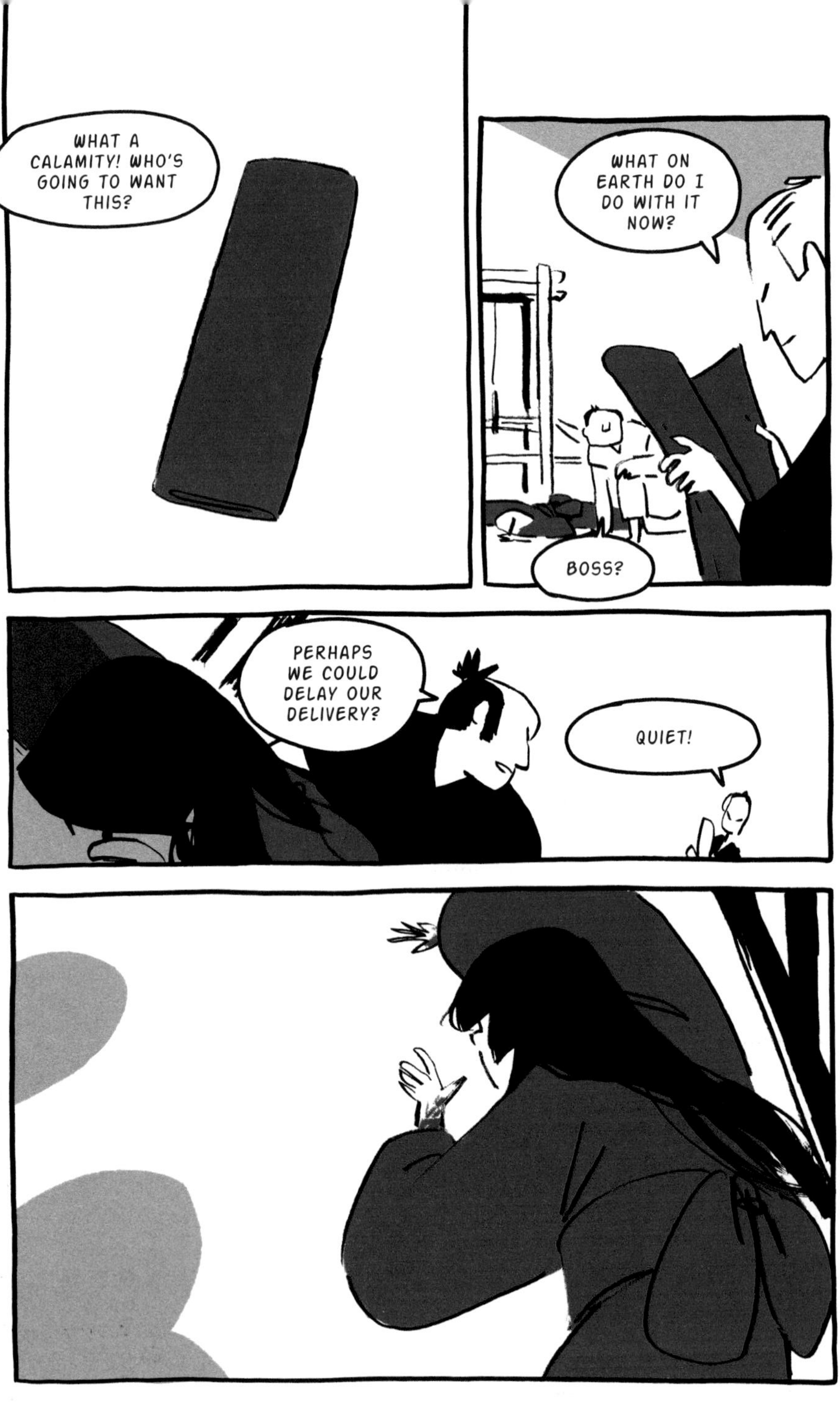
WHAT A CALAMITY! WHO'S GOING TO WANT THIS?
WHAT ON EARTH DO I DO WITH IT NOW?
BOSS?
PERHAPS WE COULD DELAY OUR DELIVERY?
QUIET!

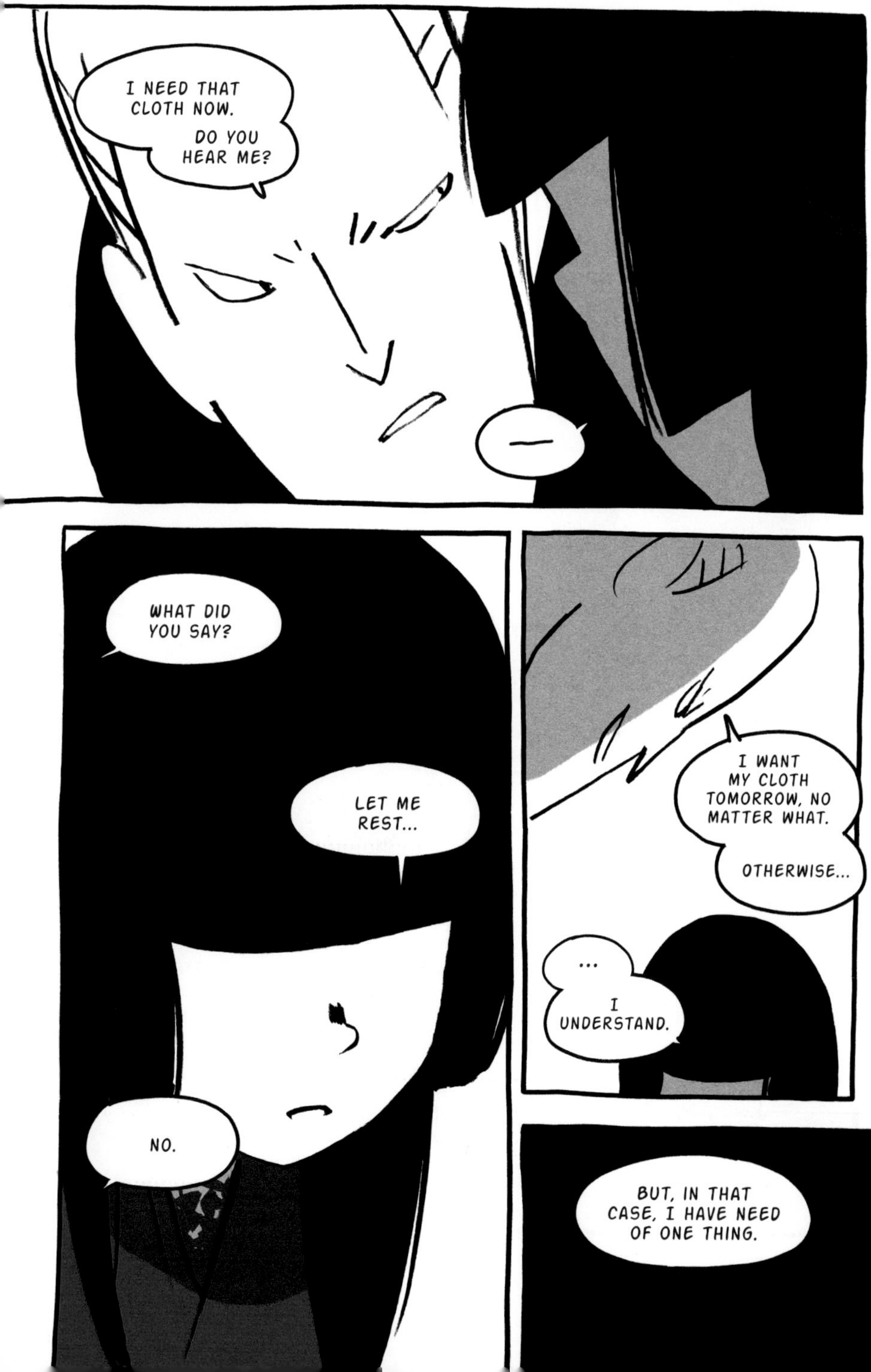
I NEED THAT CLOTH NOW.
DO YOU HEAR ME?
—
WHAT DID YOU SAY?
LET ME REST...
NO.
I WANT MY CLOTH TOMORROW, NO MATTER WHAT.
OTHERWISE...
...
I UNDERSTAND.
BUT, IN THAT CASE, I HAVE NEED OF ONE THING.

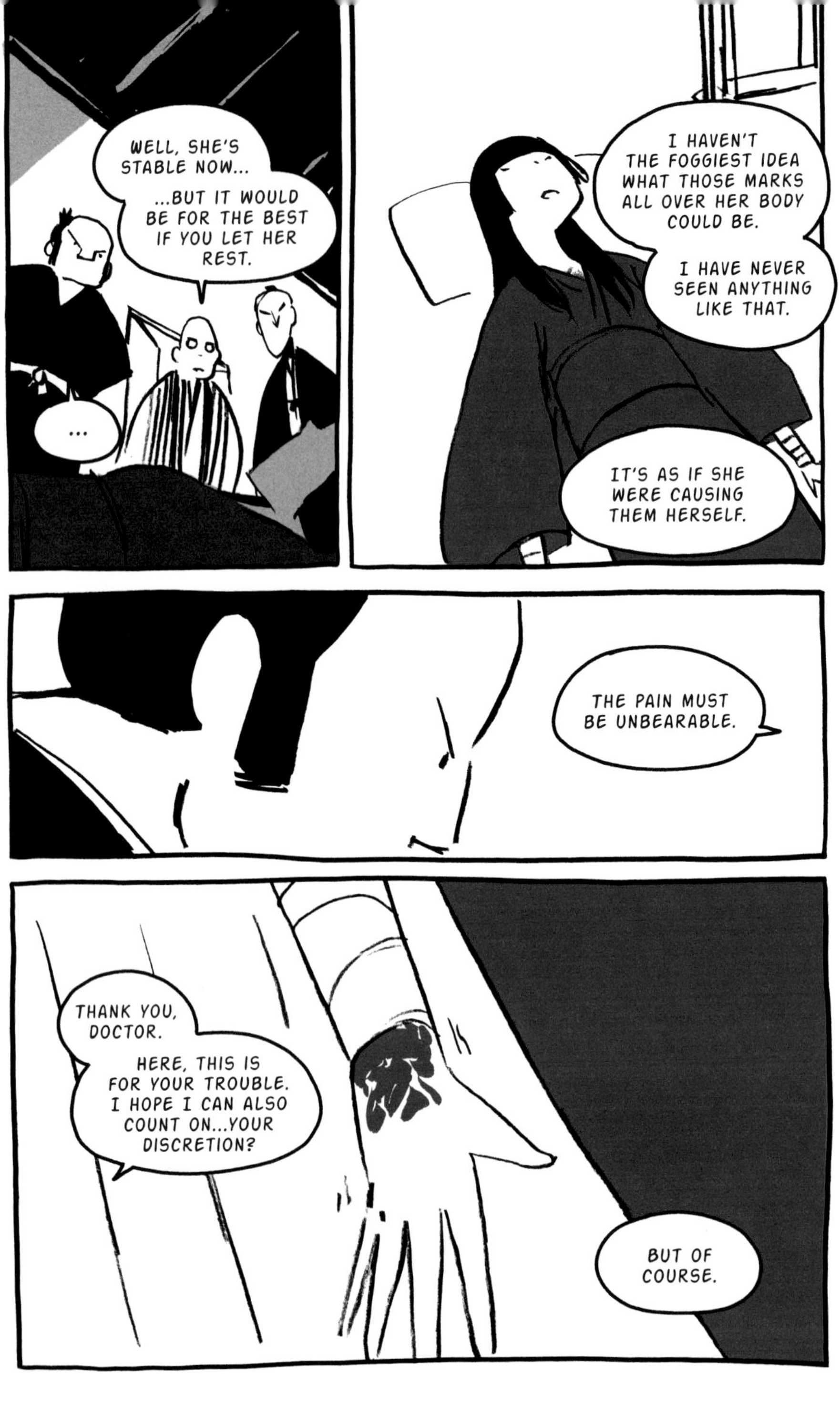
WELL, SHE'S STABLE NOW...
...BUT IT WOULD BE FOR THE BEST IF YOU LET HER REST.
...
I HAVEN'T THE FOGGIEST IDEA WHAT THOSE MARKS ALL OVER HER BODY COULD BE.
I HAVE NEVER SEEN ANYTHING LIKE THAT.
IT'S AS IF SHE WERE CAUSING THEM HERSELF.
THE PAIN MUST BE UNBEARABLE.
THANK YOU, DOCTOR.
HERE, THIS IS FOR YOUR TROUBLE. I HOPE I CAN ALSO COUNT ON...YOUR DISCRETION?
BUT OF COURSE.

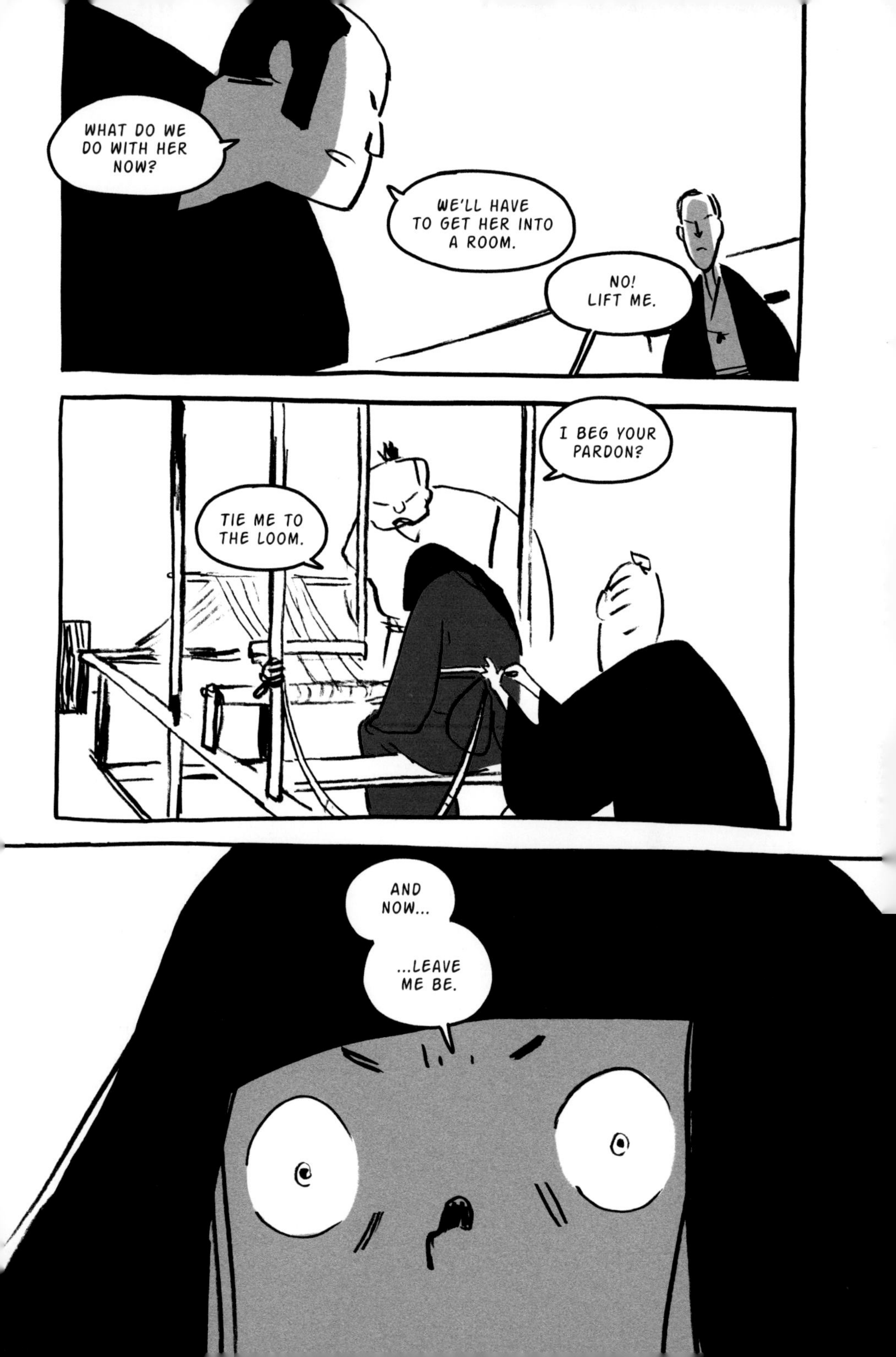
WHAT DO WE DO WITH HER NOW?
WE'LL HAVE TO GET HER INTO A ROOM.
NO! LIFT ME.
I BEG YOUR PARDON?
TIE ME TO THE LOOM.
AND NOW...
...LEAVE ME BE.

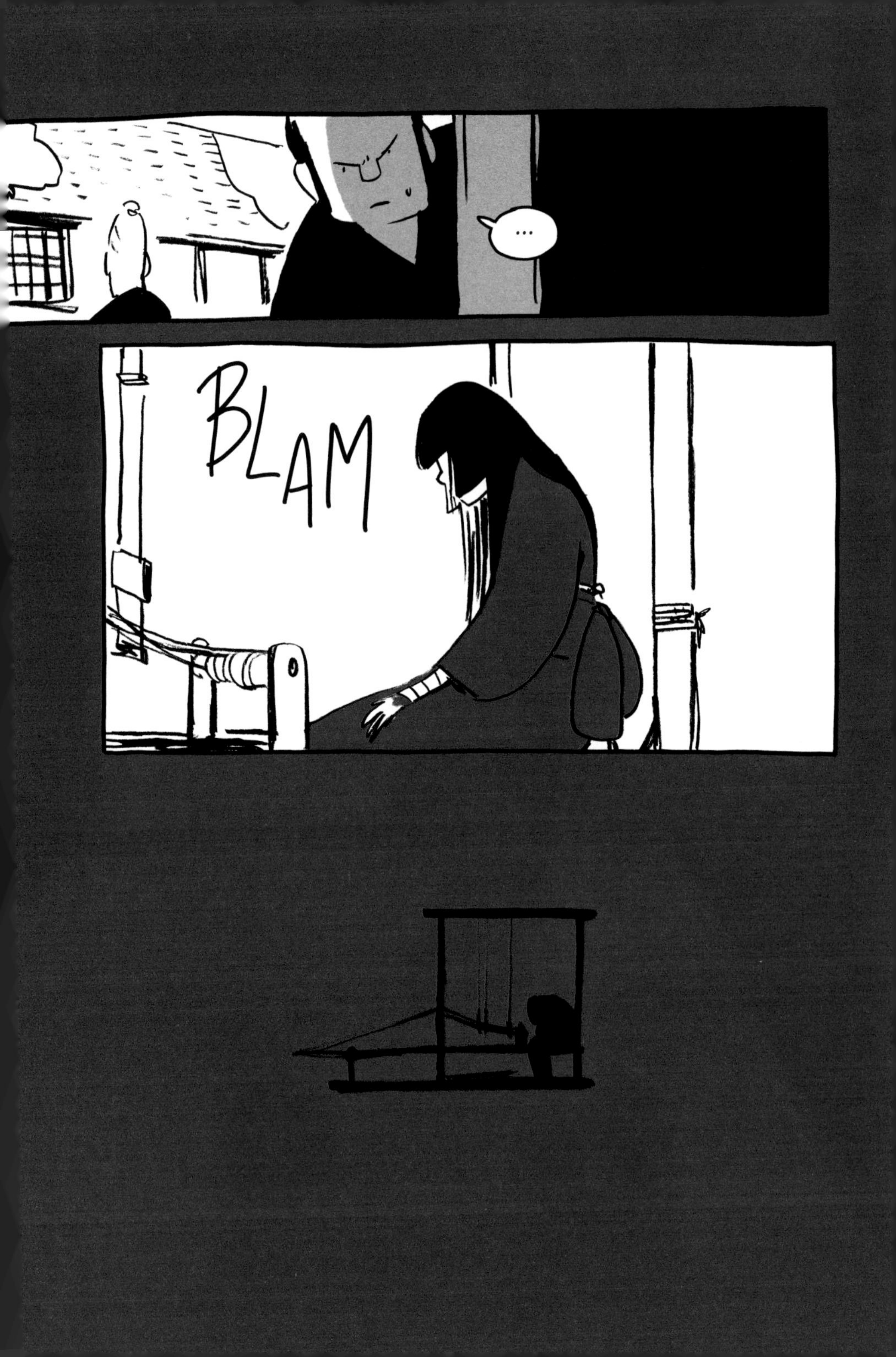
...
BLAM

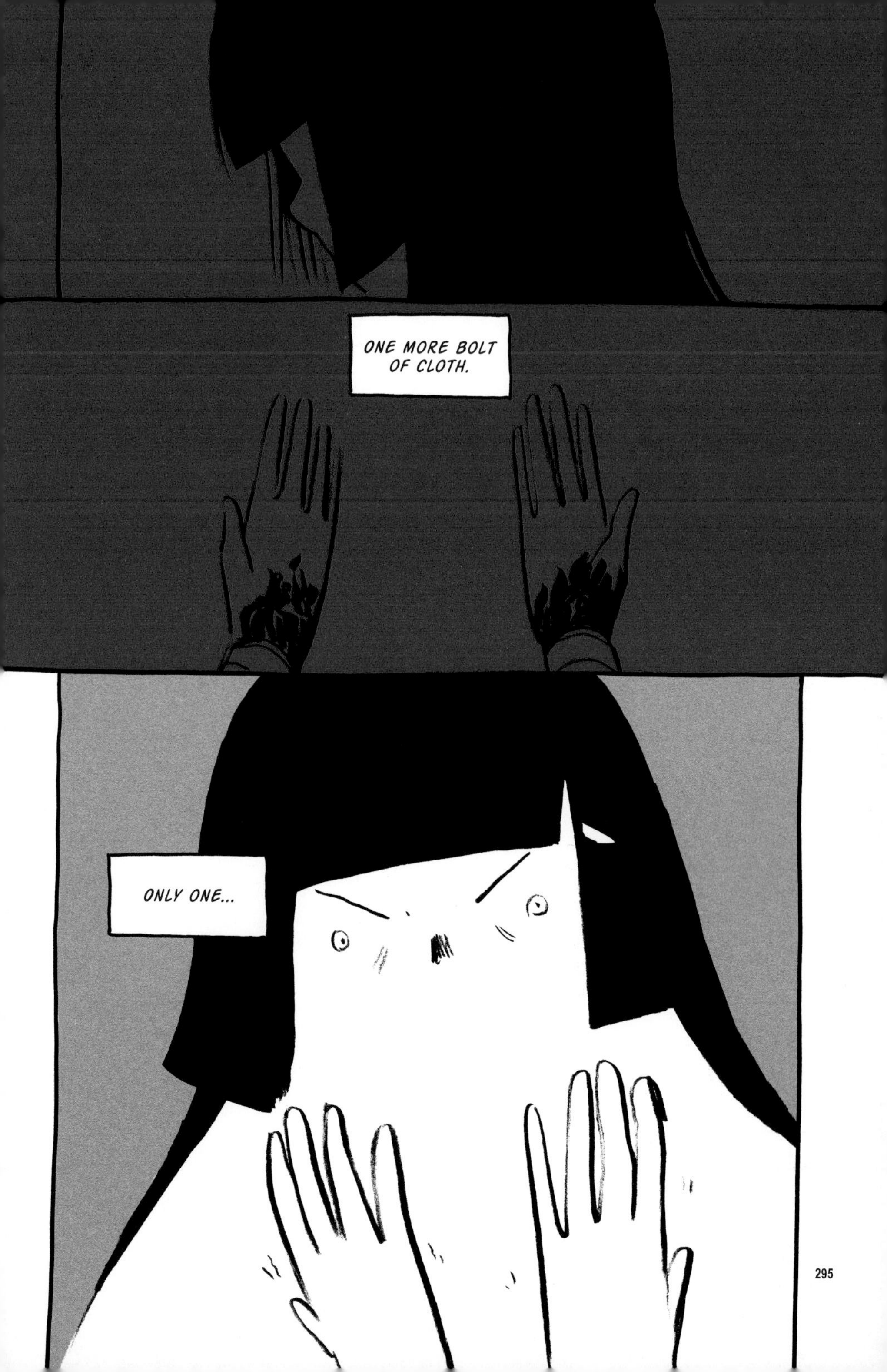
ONE MORE BOLT OF CLOTH.
ONLY ONE...

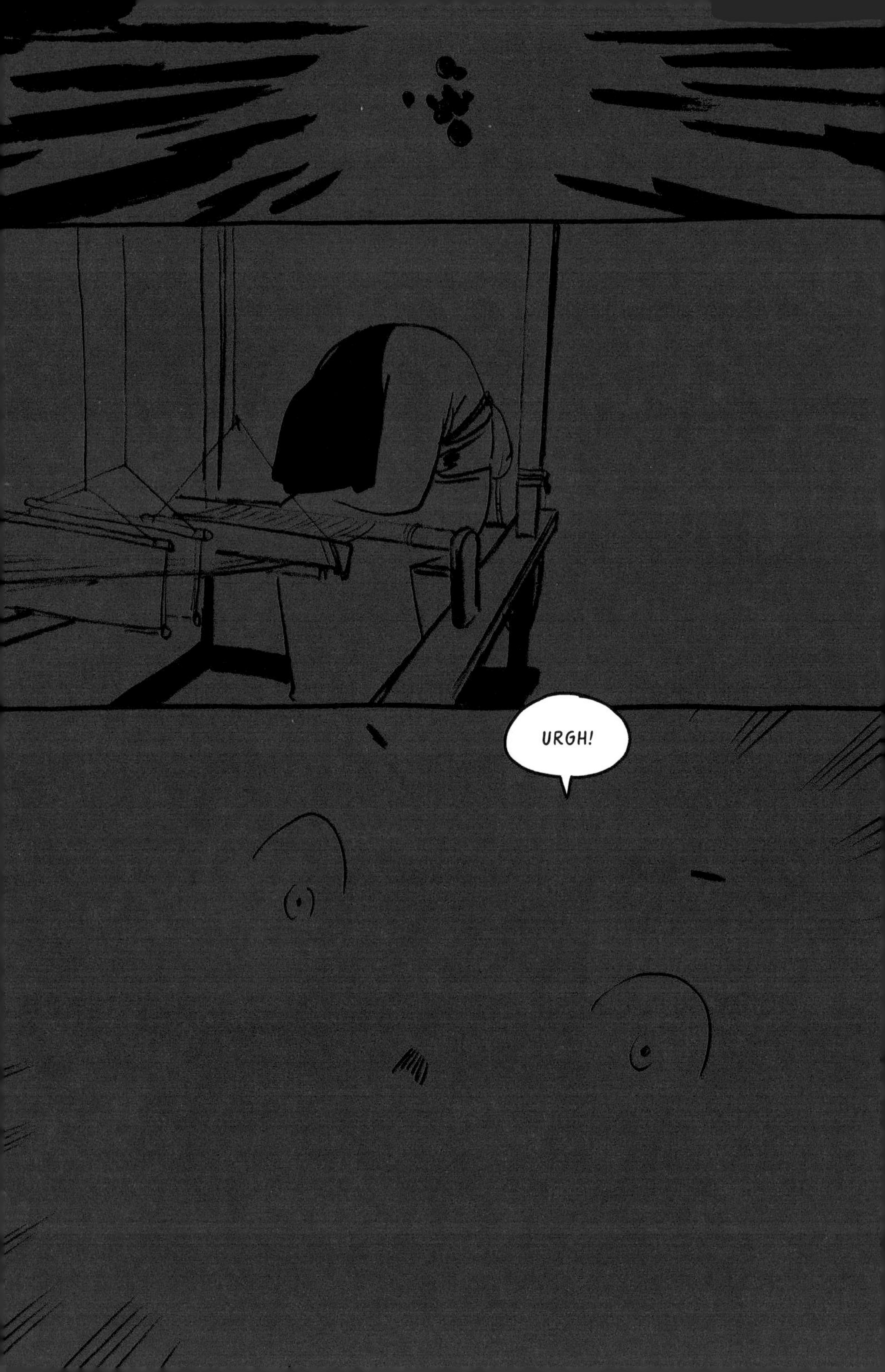
URGH!

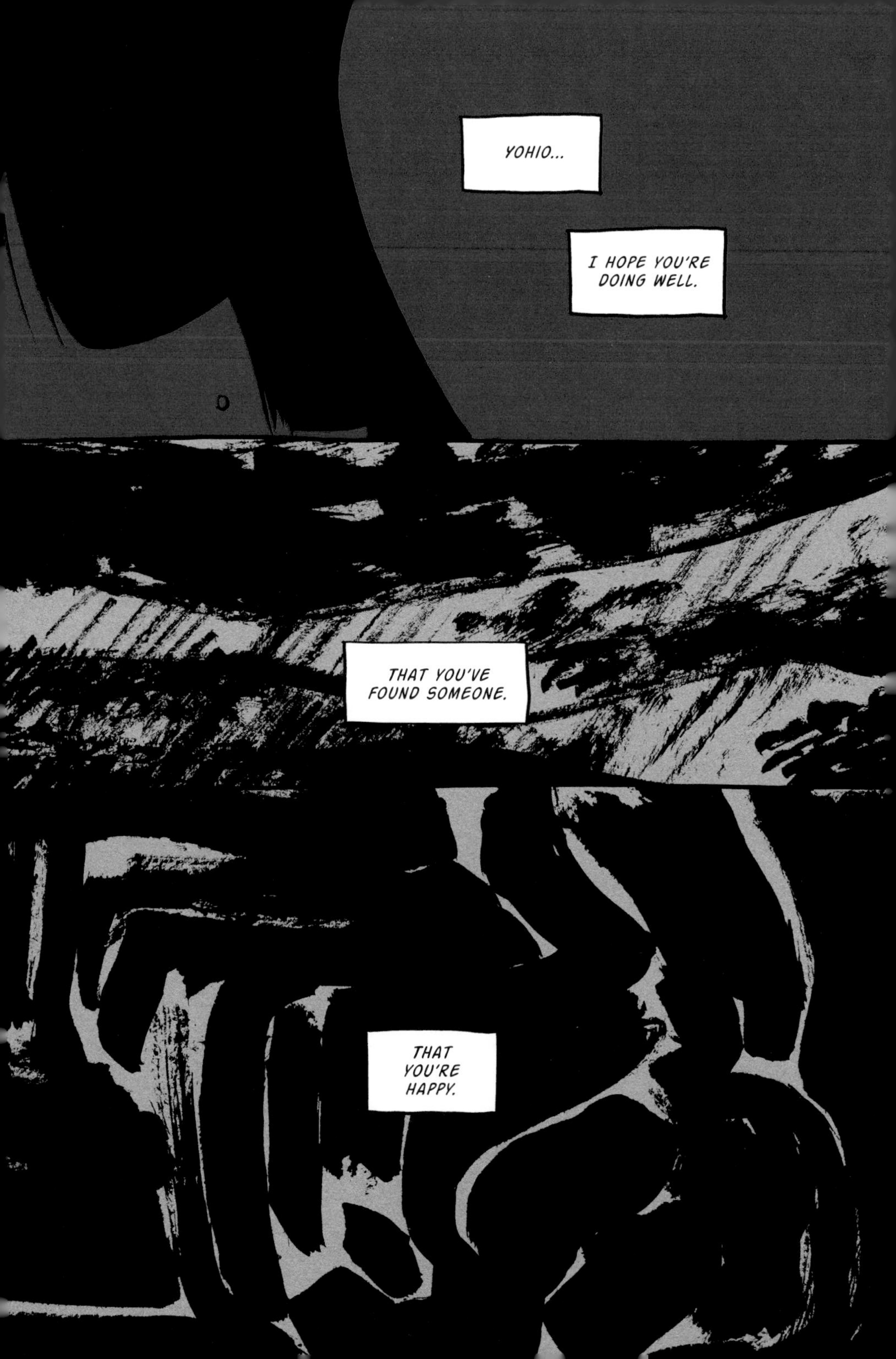
YOHIO...
I HOPE YOU'RE DOING WELL.
THAT YOU'VE FOUND SOMEONE.
THAT YOU'RE HAPPY.

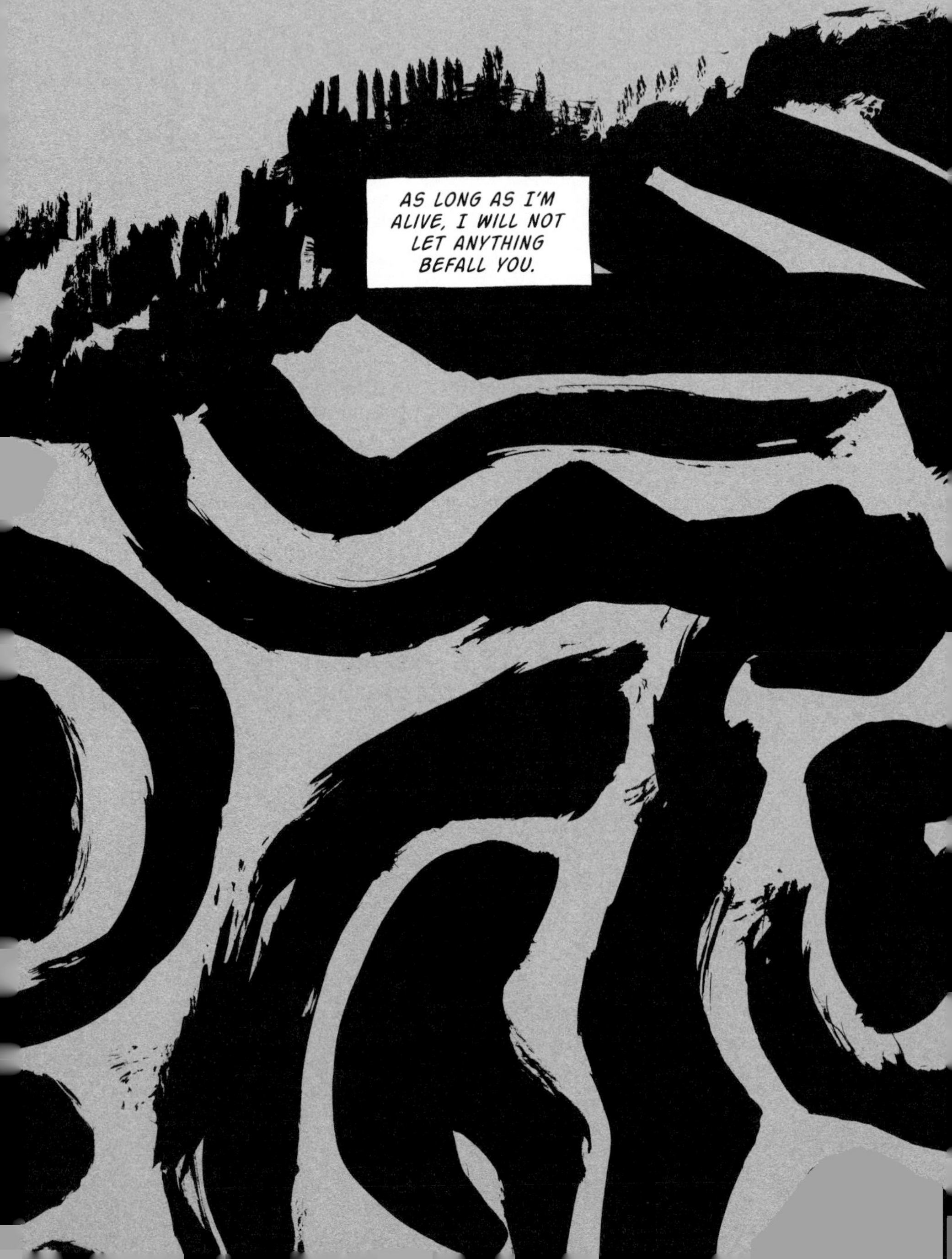
AS LONG AS I'M ALIVE, I WILL NOT LET ANYTHING BEFALL YOU.

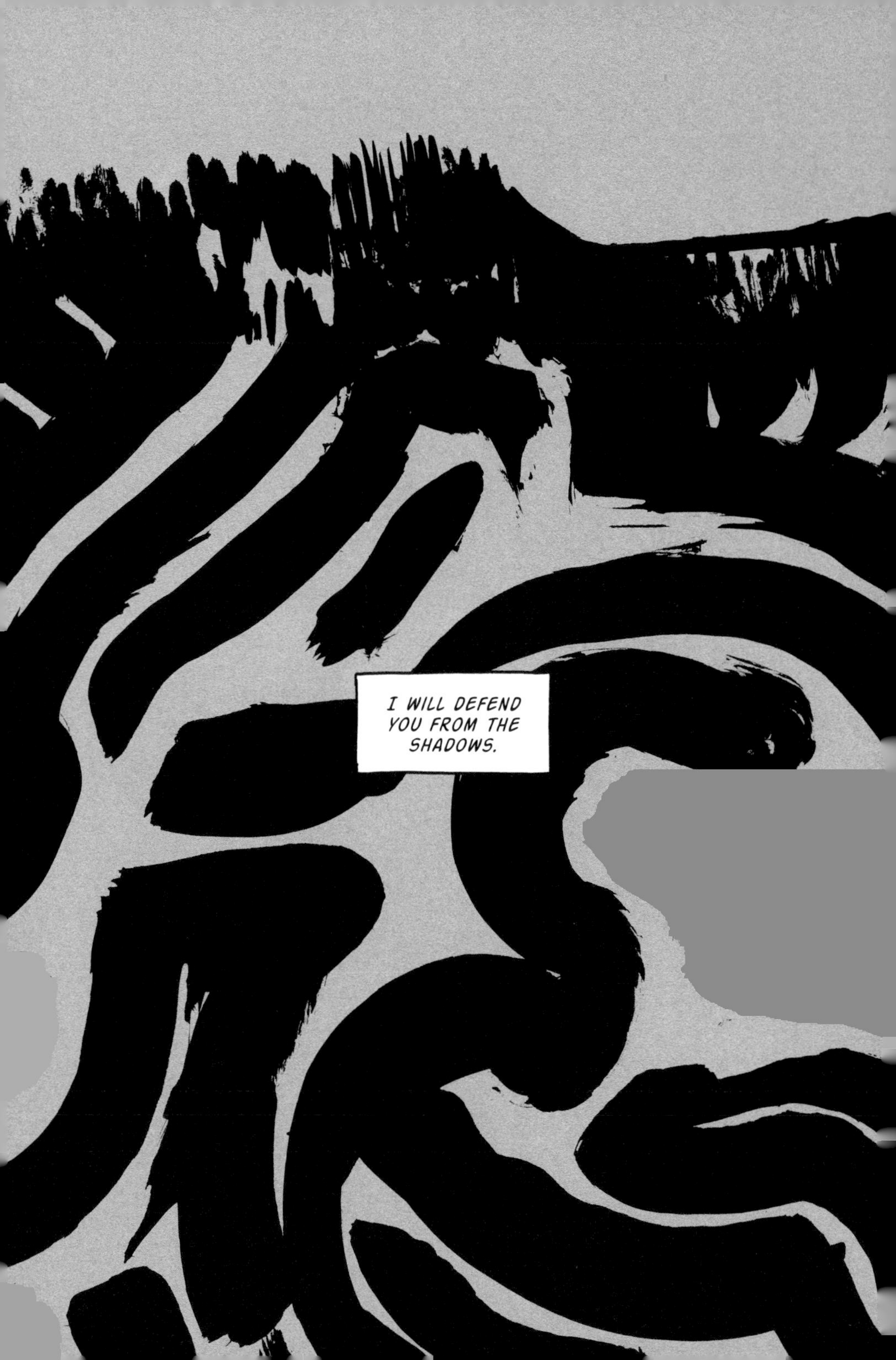
I WILL DEFEND YOU FROM THE SHADOWS.

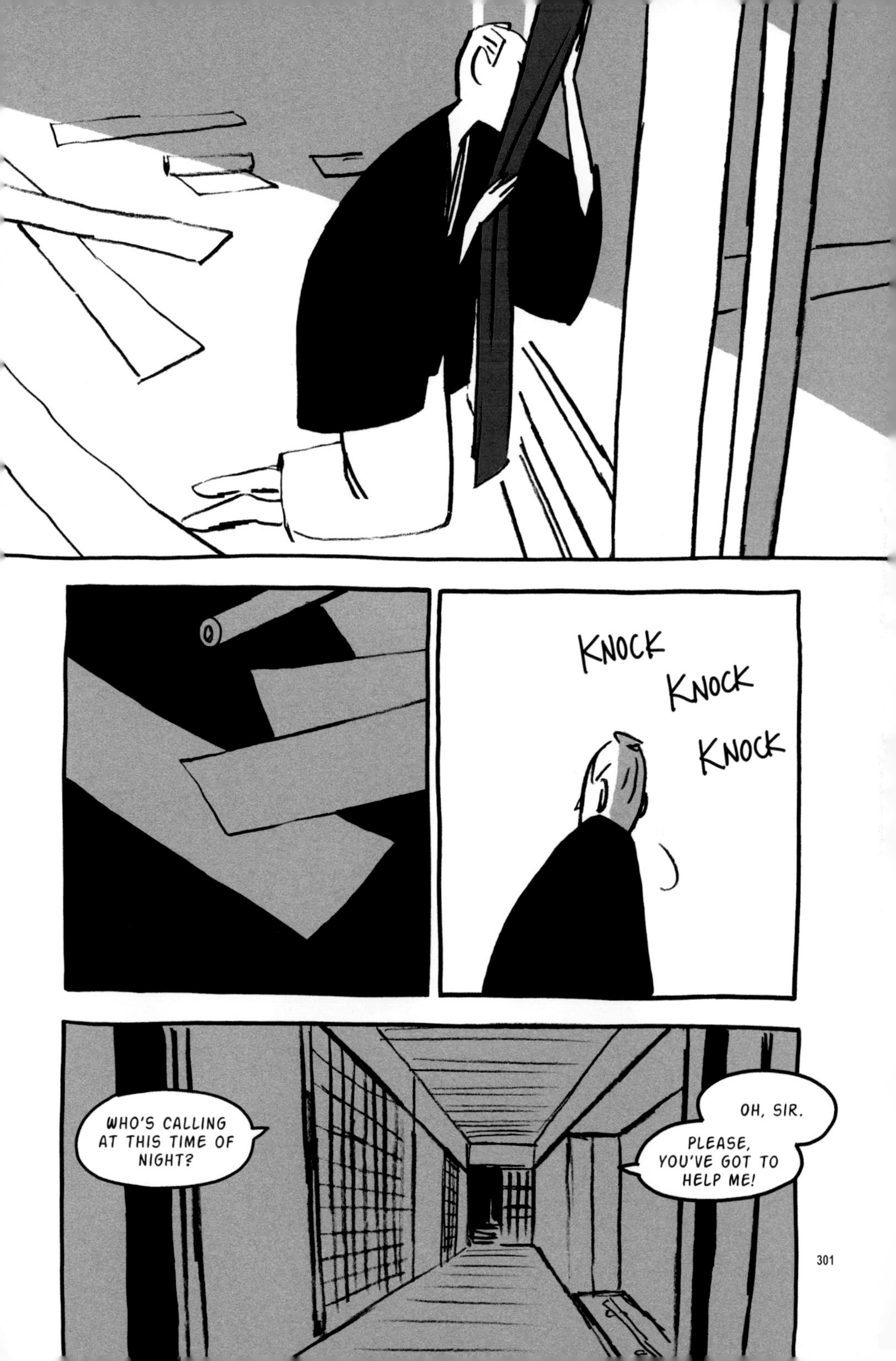
KNOCK
KNOCK
KNOCK
WHO'S CALLING AT THIS TIME OF NIGHT?
OH, SIR.
PLEASE, YOU'VE GOT TO HELP ME!

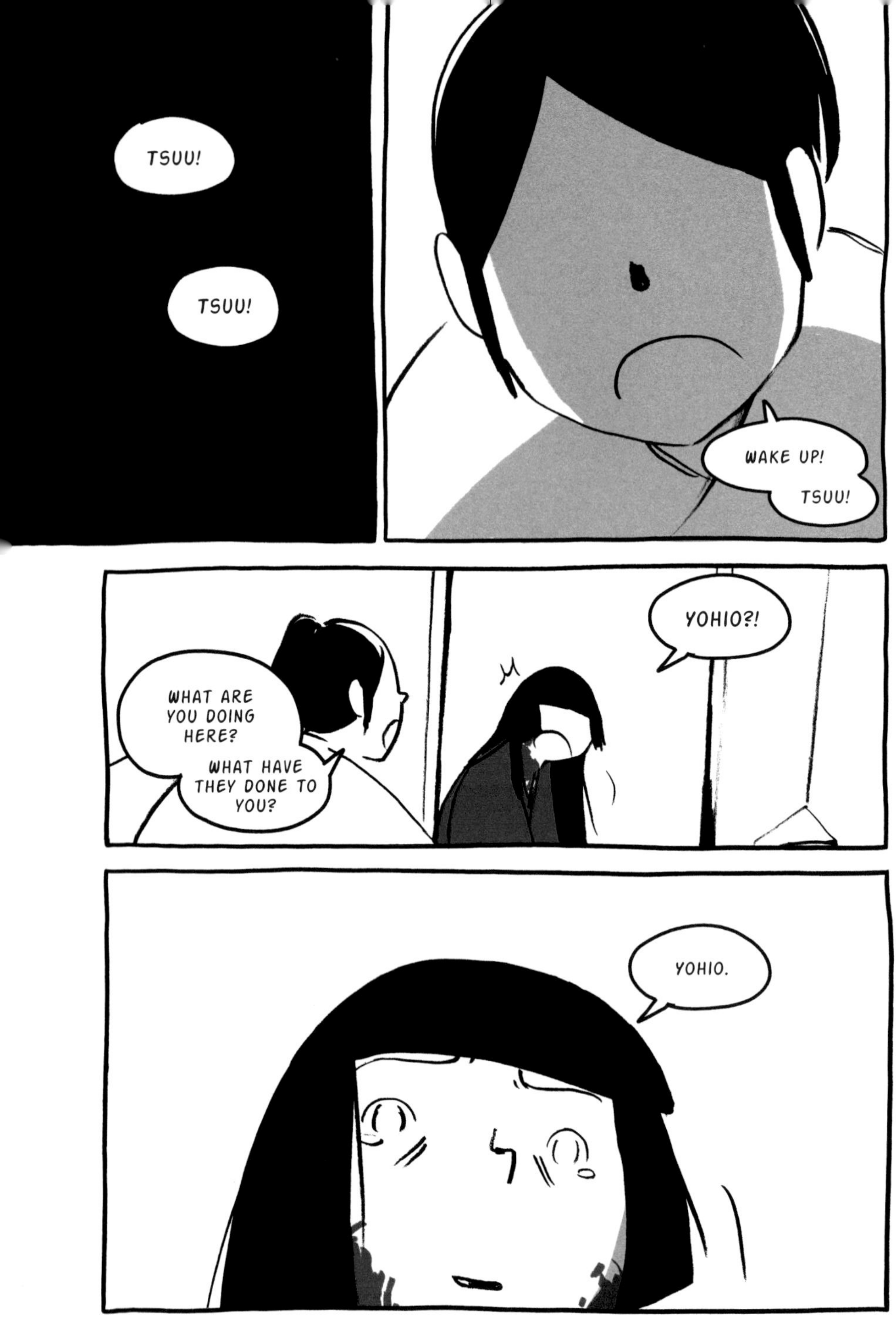
TSUU!
TSUU!
WAKE UP!
TSUU!
YOHIO?!
WHAT ARE YOU DOING HERE?
WHAT HAVE THEY DONE TO YOU?
YOHIO.

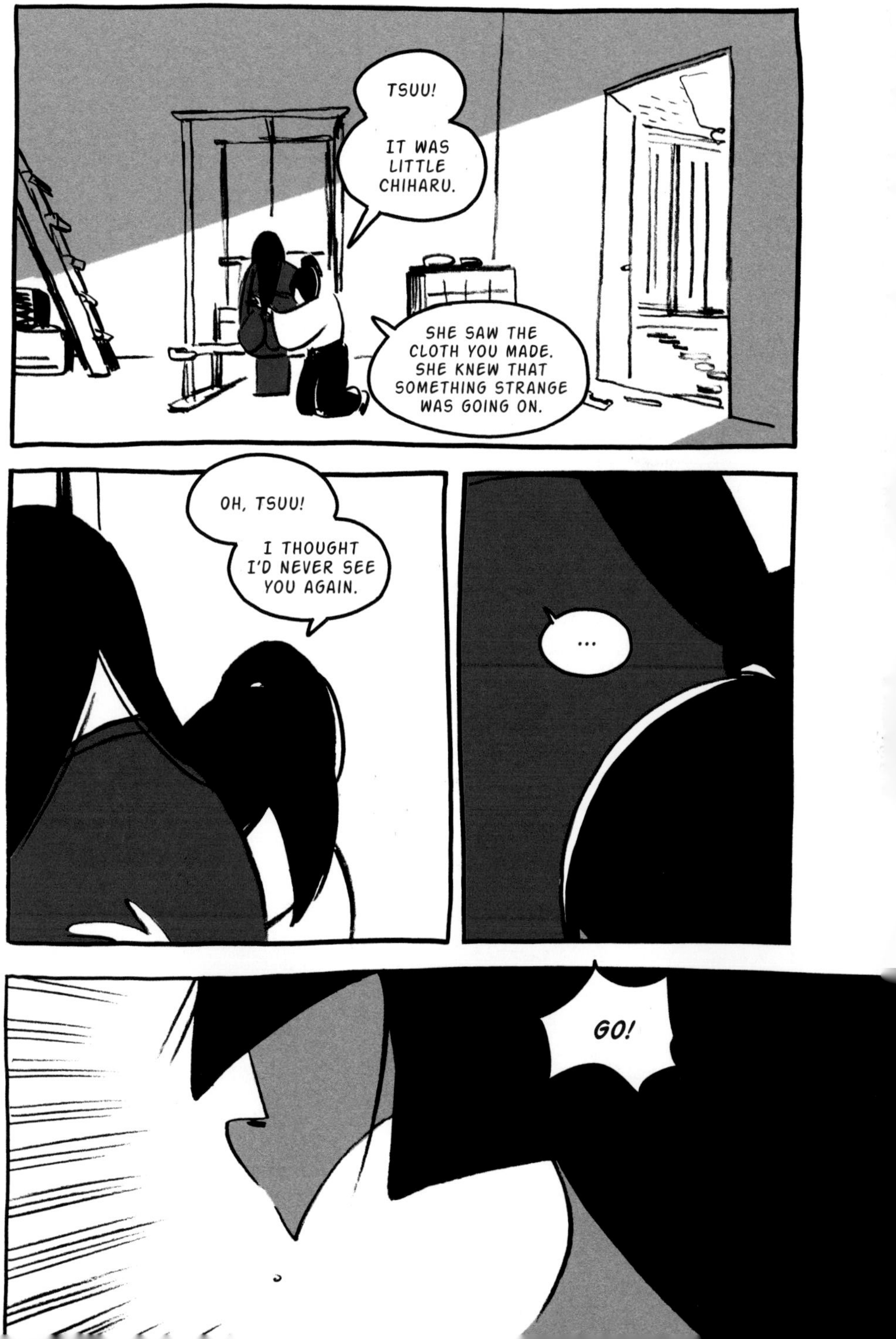
TSUU!
IT WAS LITTLE CHIHARU.
SHE SAW THE CLOTH YOU MADE. SHE KNEW THAT SOMETHING STRANGE WAS GOING ON.
OH, TSUU!
I THOUGHT I'D NEVER SEE YOU AGAIN.
...
GO!

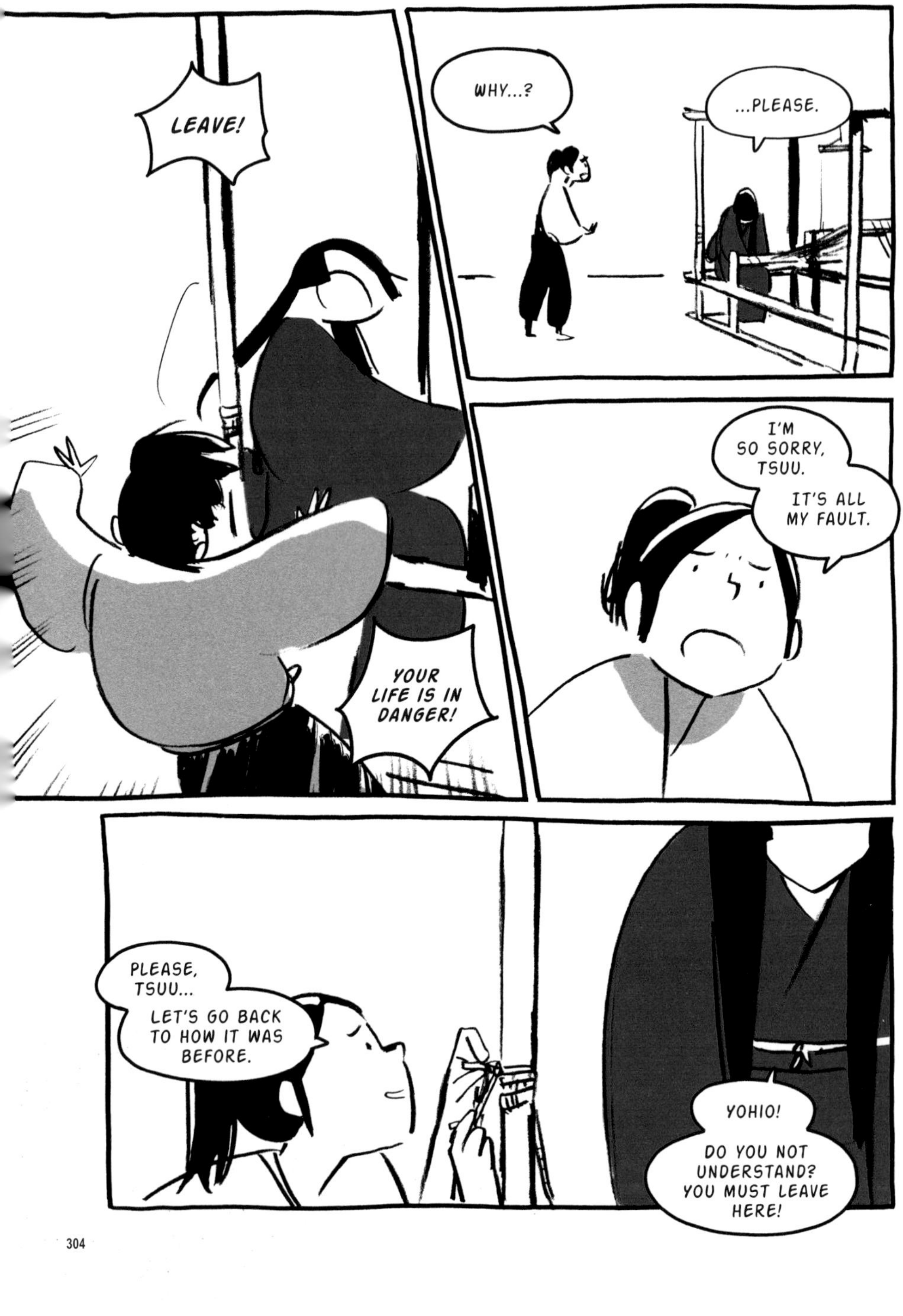

LEAVE!
YOUR LIFE IS IN DANGER!
WHY...?
...PLEASE.
I'M SO SORRY, TSUU.
IT'S ALL MY FAULT.
PLEASE, TSUU...
LET'S GO BACK TO HOW IT WAS BEFORE.
YOHIO!
DO YOU NOT UNDERSTAND? YOU MUST LEAVE HERE!

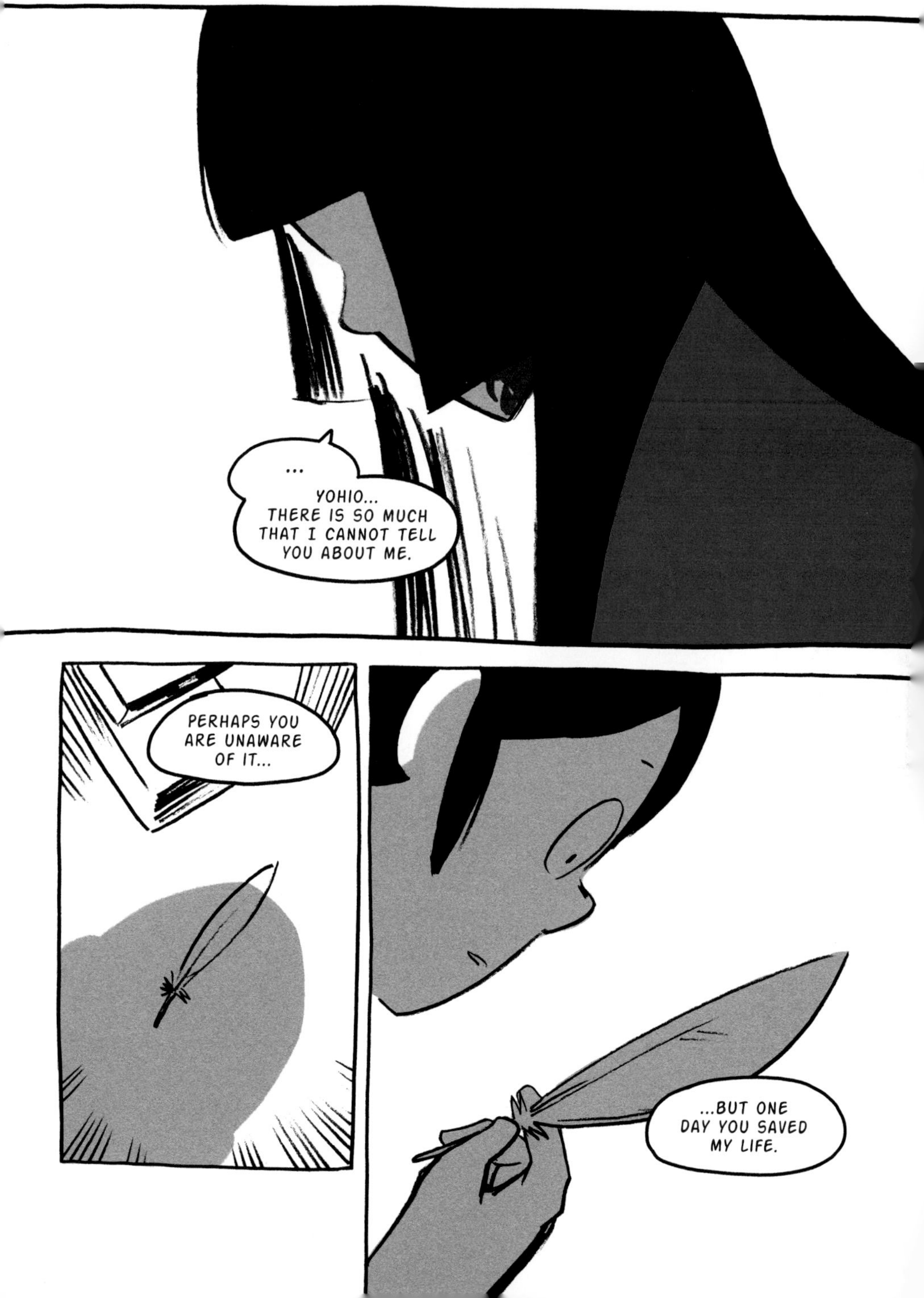
...
YOHIO...
THERE IS SO MUCH
THAT I CANNOT TELL
YOU ABOUT ME.
PERHAPS YOU
ARE UNAWARE
OF IT...
...BUT ONE
DAY YOU SAVED
MY LIFE.

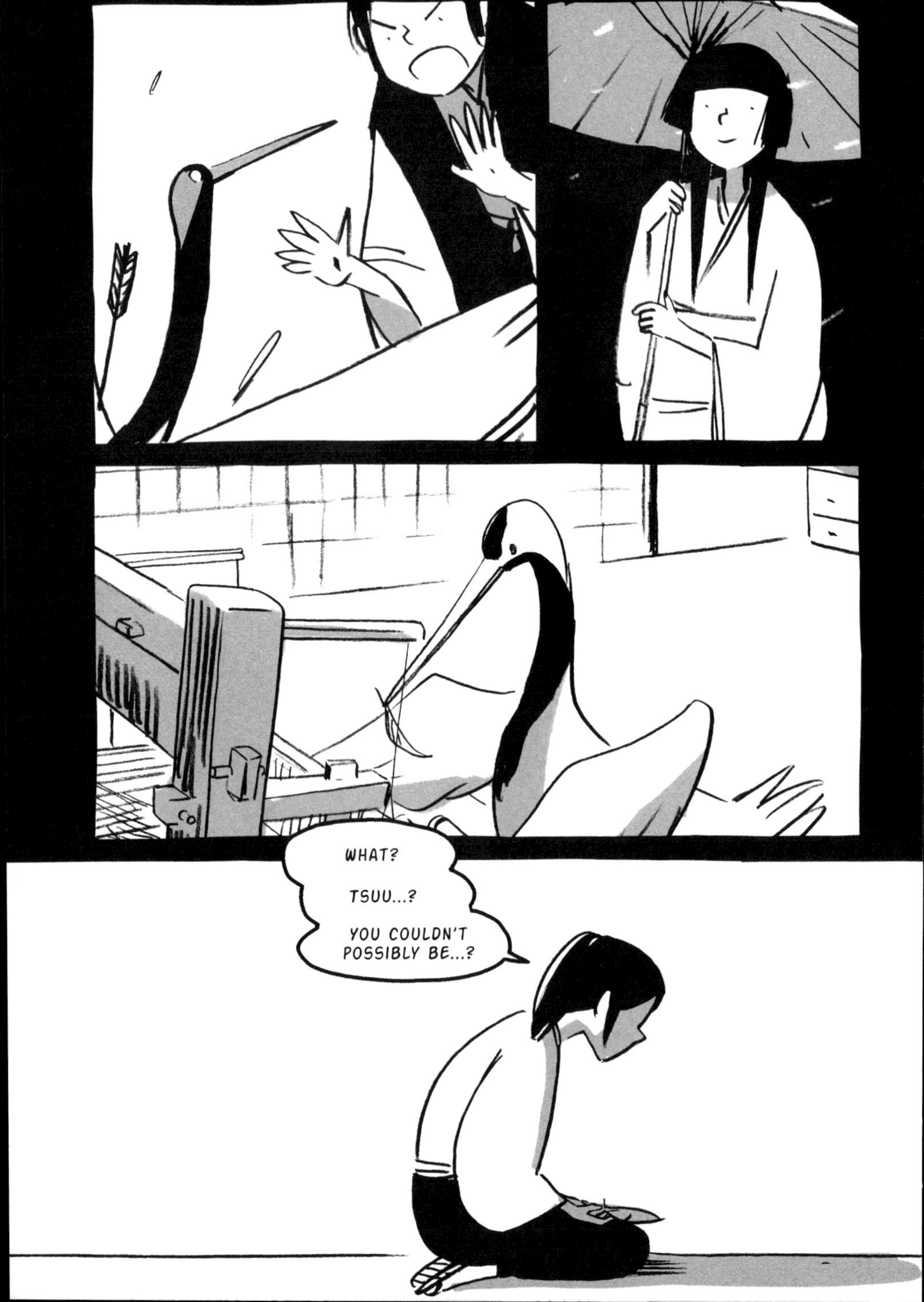
WHAT?
TSUU...?
YOU COULDN'T POSSIBLY BE...?

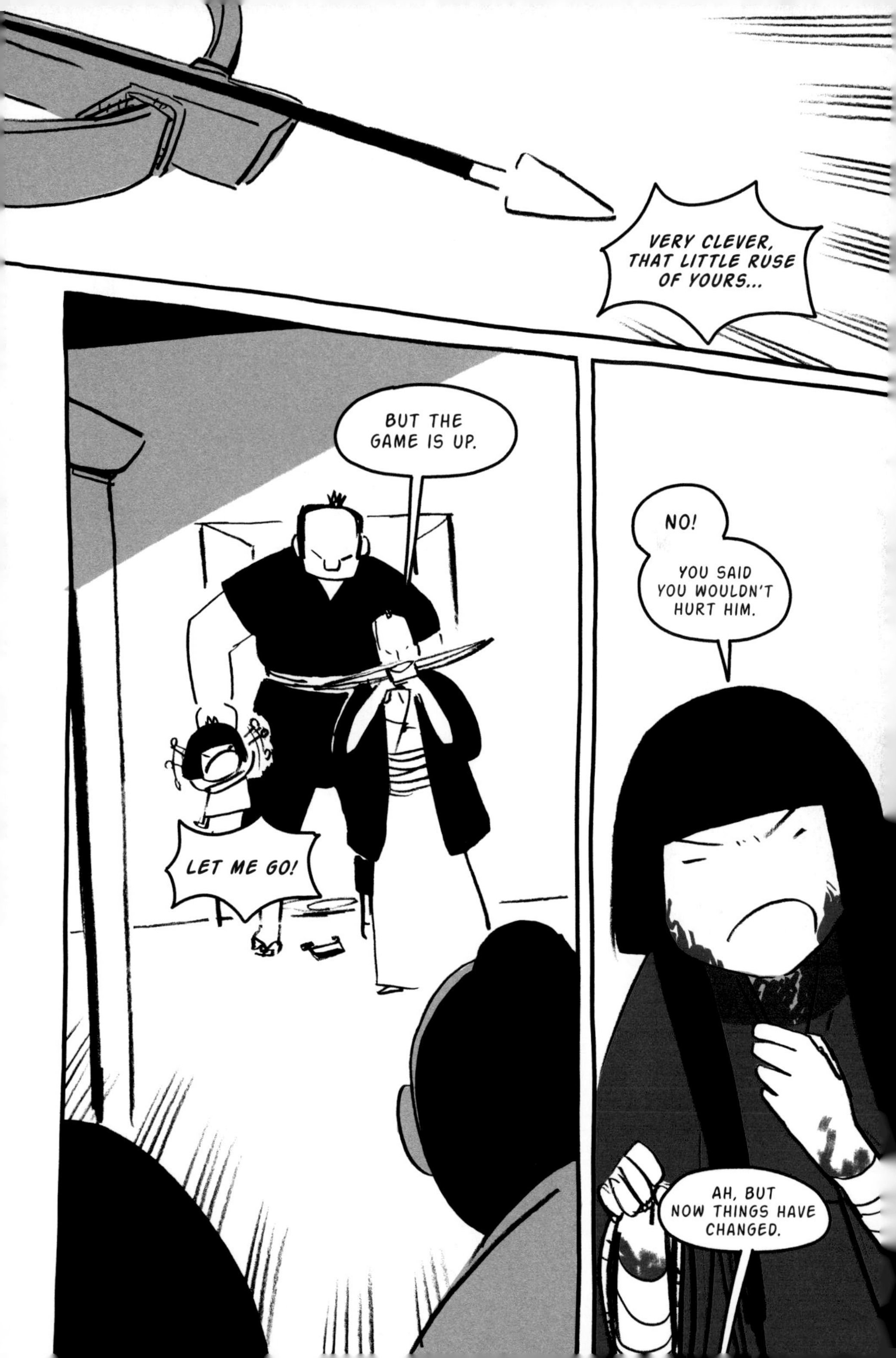
VERY CLEVER, THAT LITTLE RUSE OF YOURS...
BUT THE GAME IS UP.
LET ME GO!
NO!
YOU SAID YOU WOULDN'T HURT HIM.
AH, BUT NOW THINGS HAVE CHANGED.

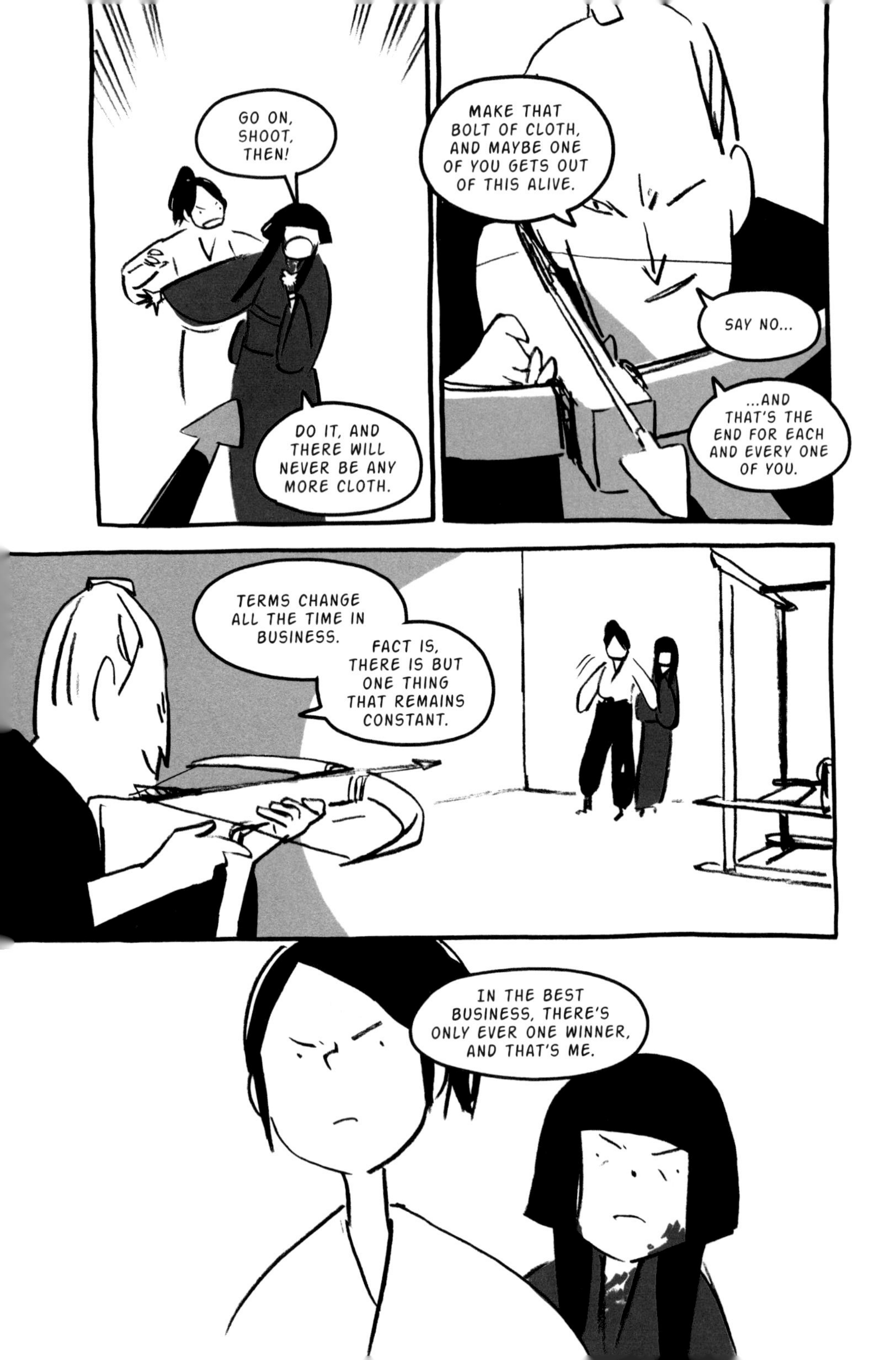
GO ON, SHOOT, THEN!
DO IT, AND THERE WILL NEVER BE ANY MORE CLOTH.
MAKE THAT BOLT OF CLOTH, AND MAYBE ONE OF YOU GETS OUT OF THIS ALIVE.
SAY NO...
...AND THAT'S THE END FOR EACH AND EVERY ONE OF YOU.
TERMS CHANGE ALL THE TIME IN BUSINESS.
FACT IS, THERE IS BUT ONE THING THAT REMAINS CONSTANT.
IN THE BEST BUSINESS, THERE'S ONLY EVER ONE WINNER, AND THAT'S ME.

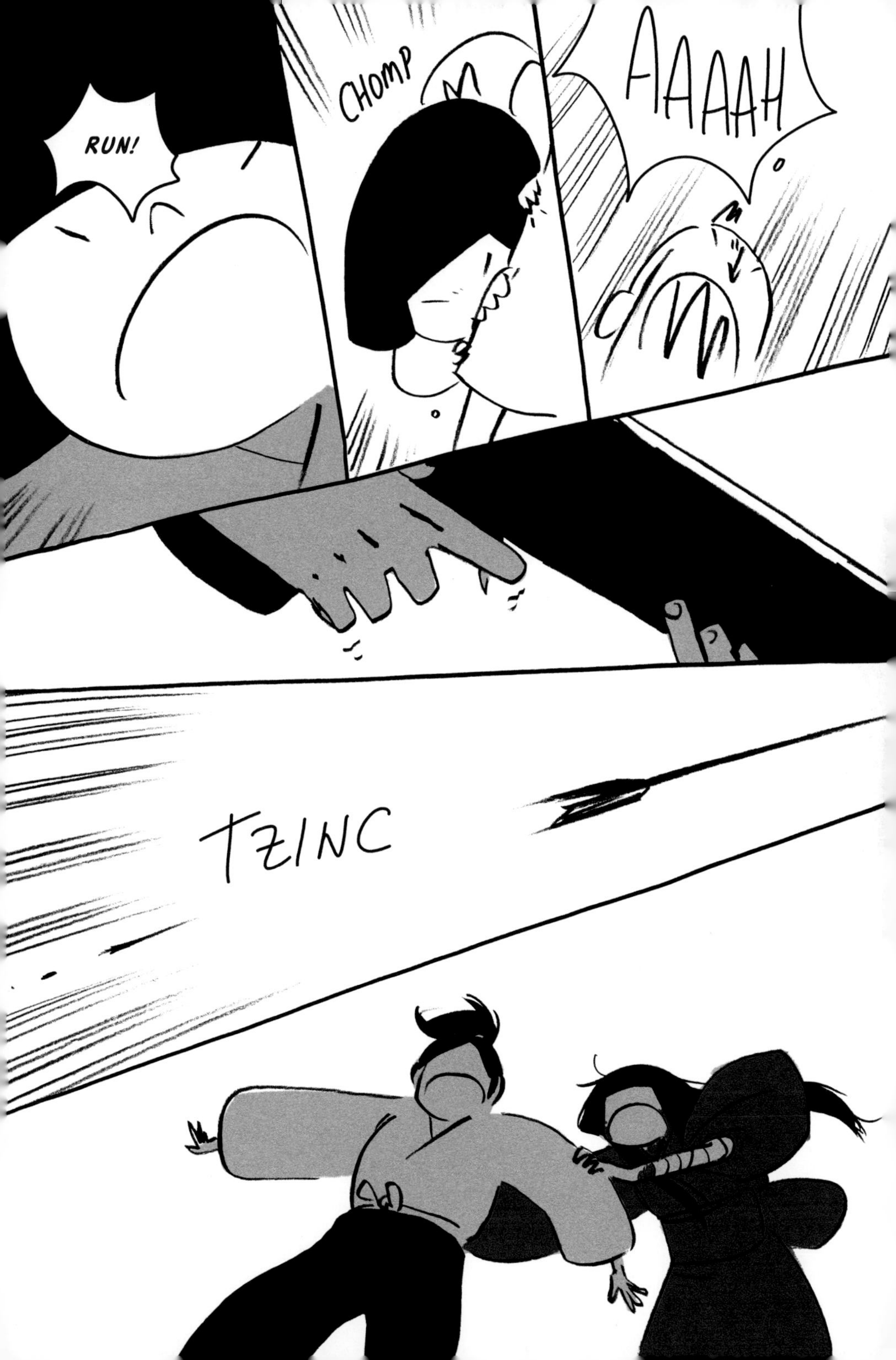
RUN!
CHOMP
AAAAH
TZINC

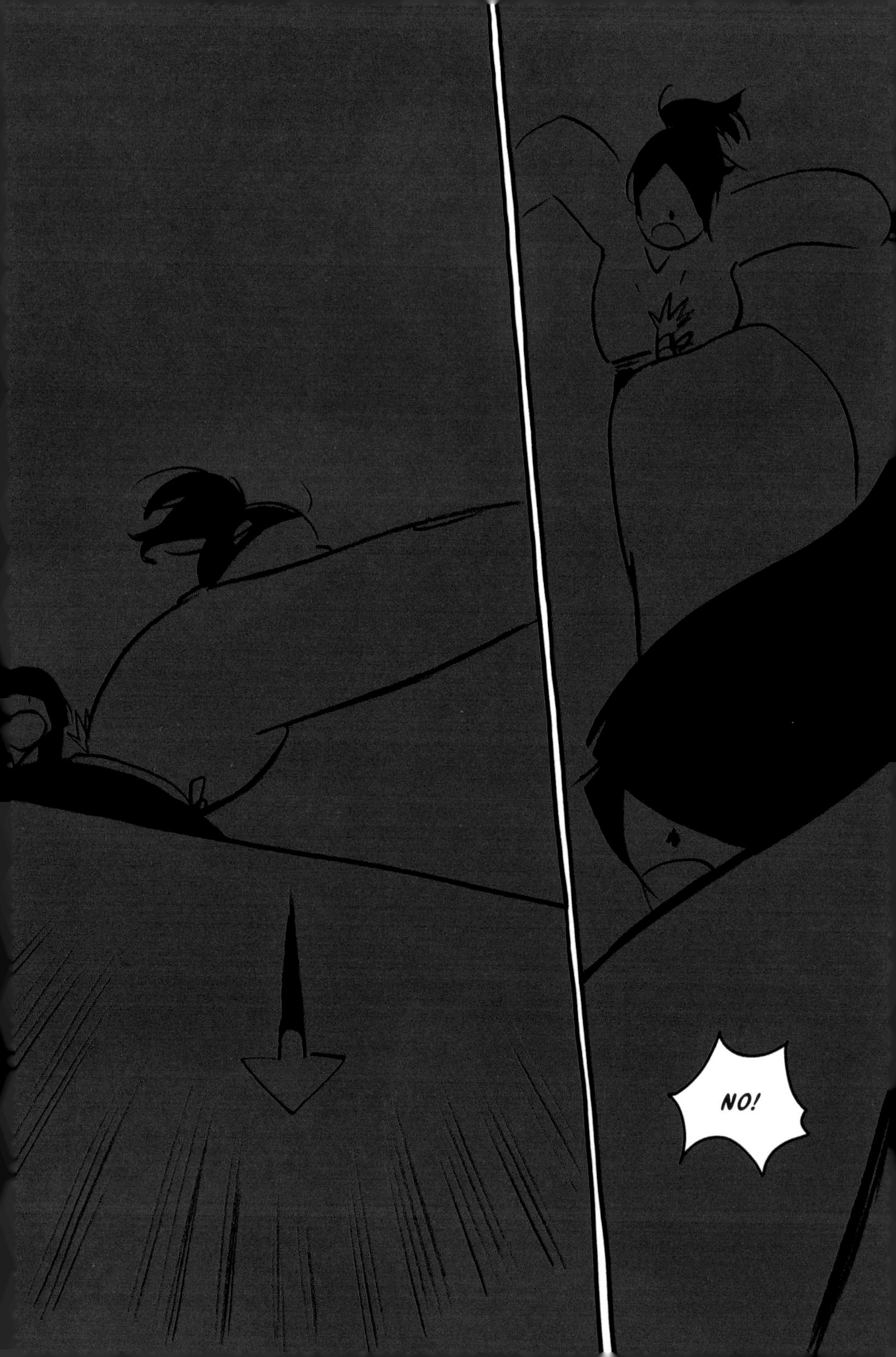
NO!

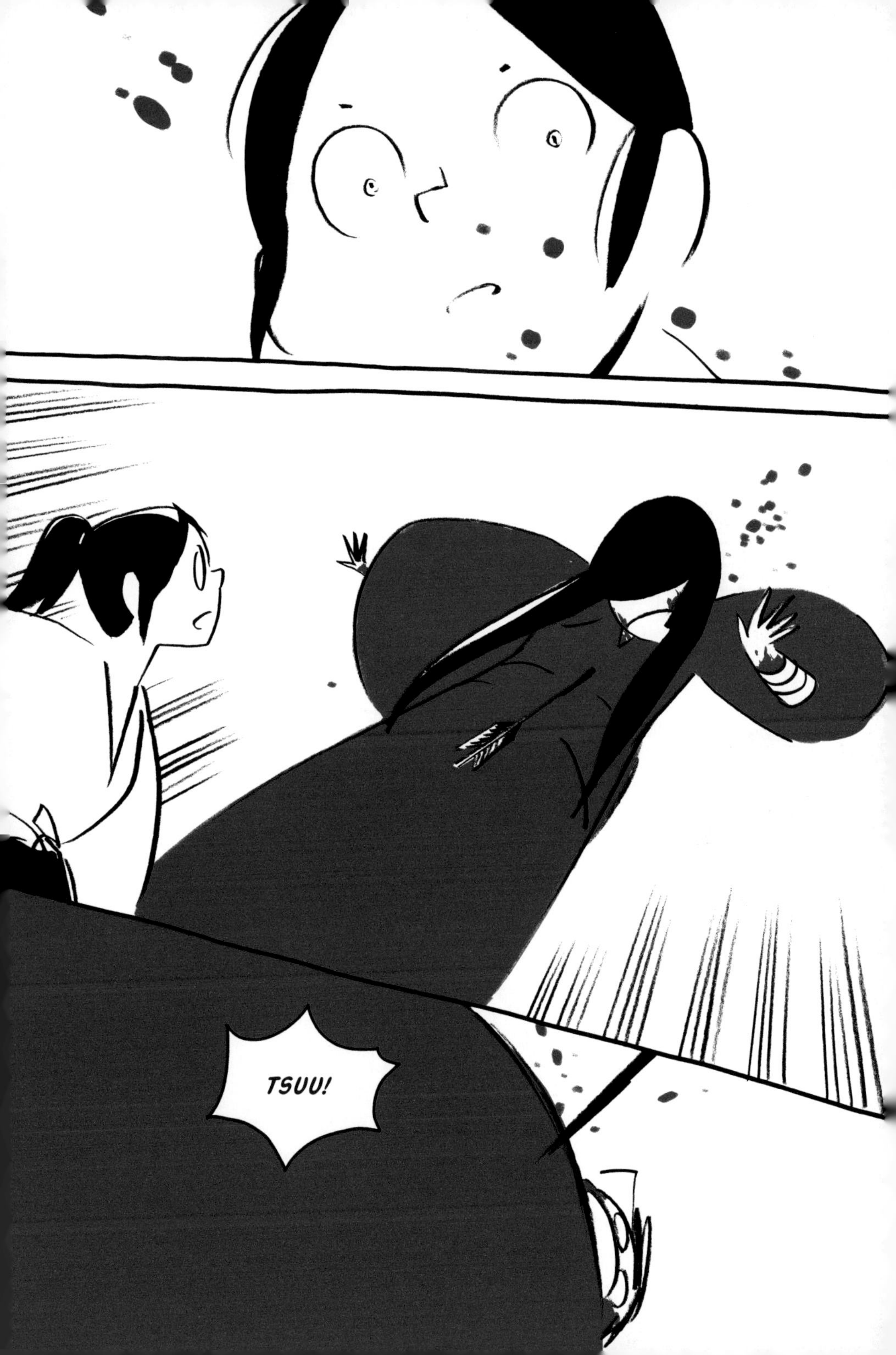
TSUU!

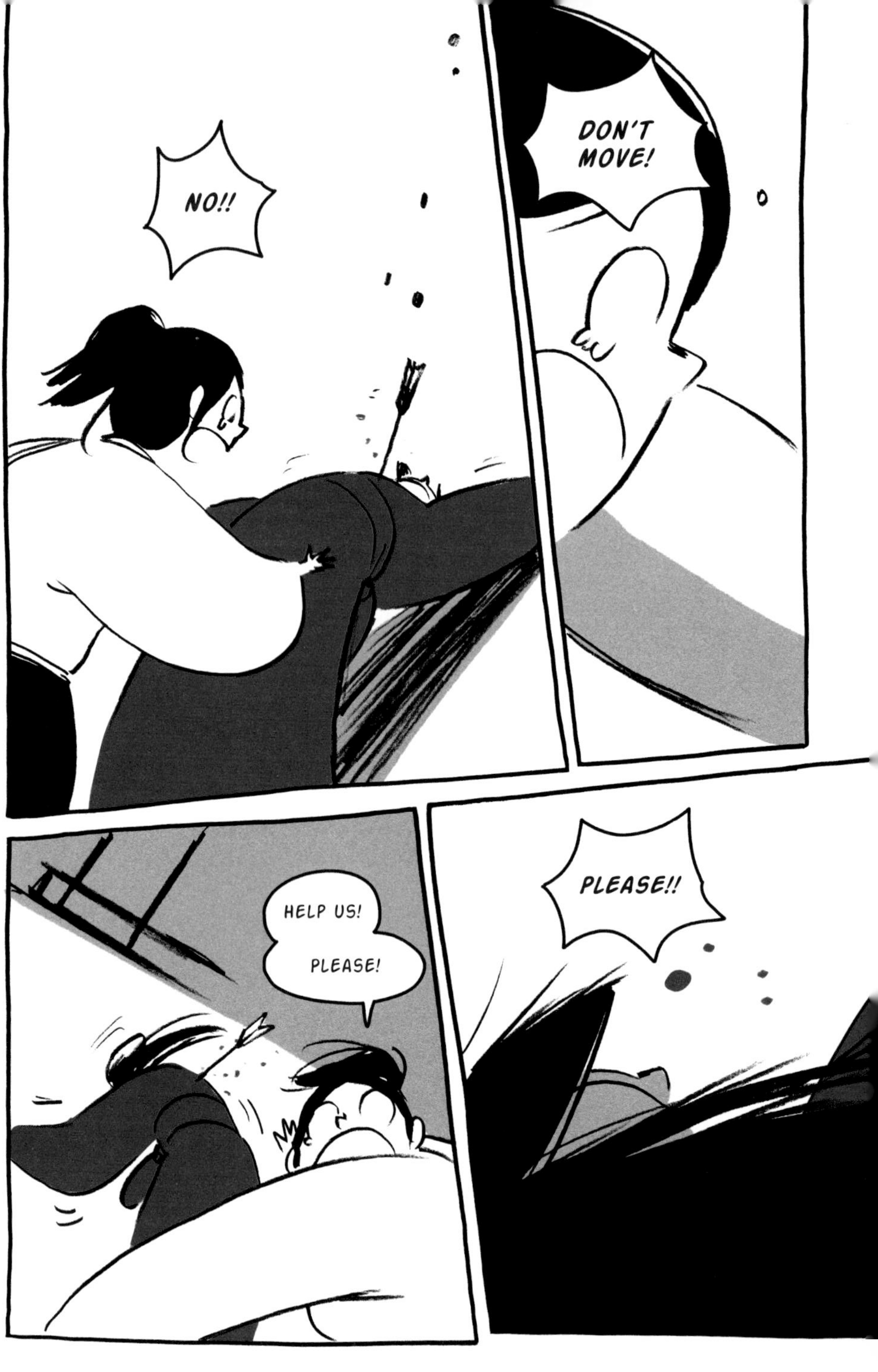
NO!!
DON'T MOVE!
HELP US!
PLEASE!
PLEASE!!

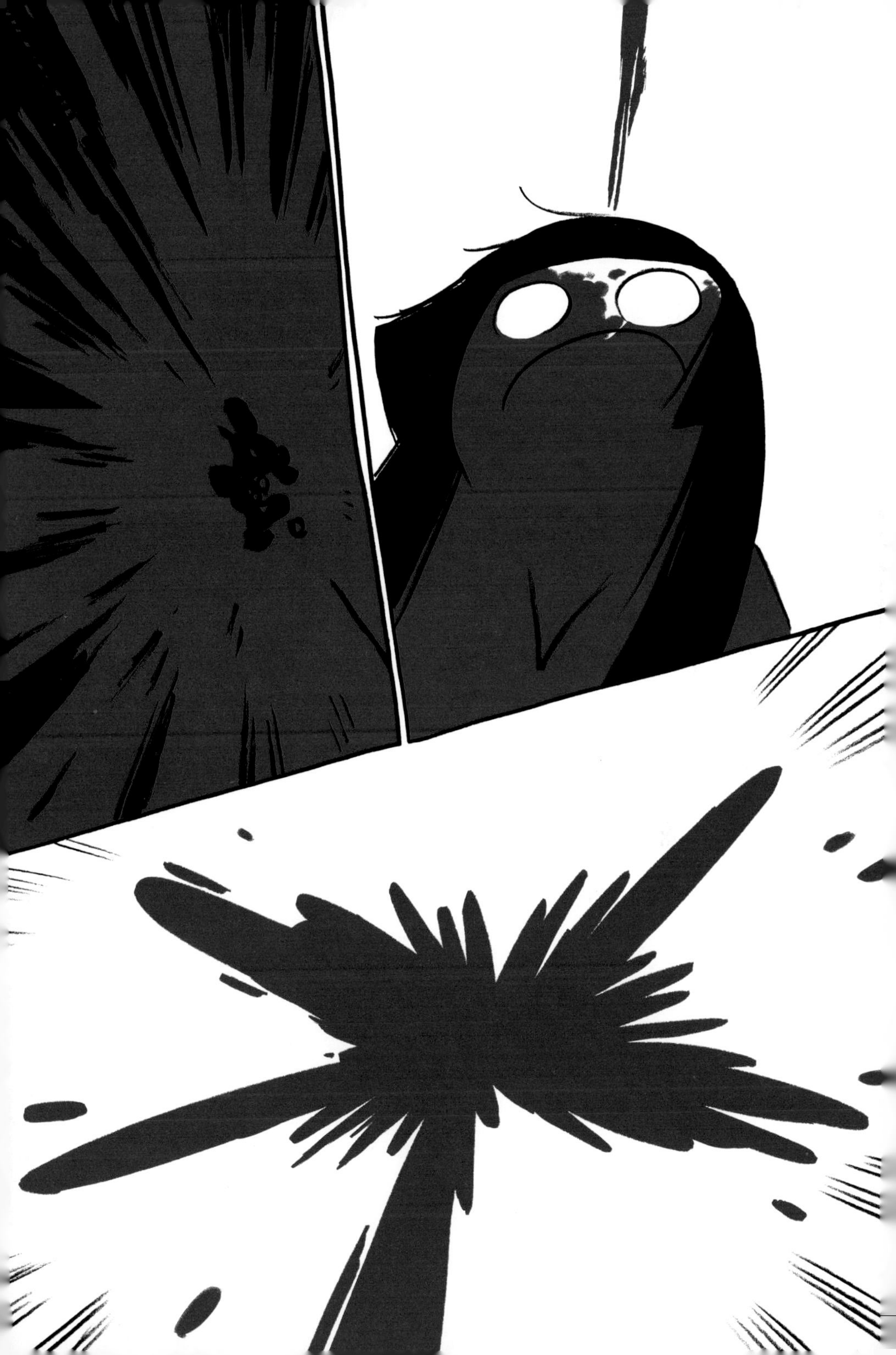

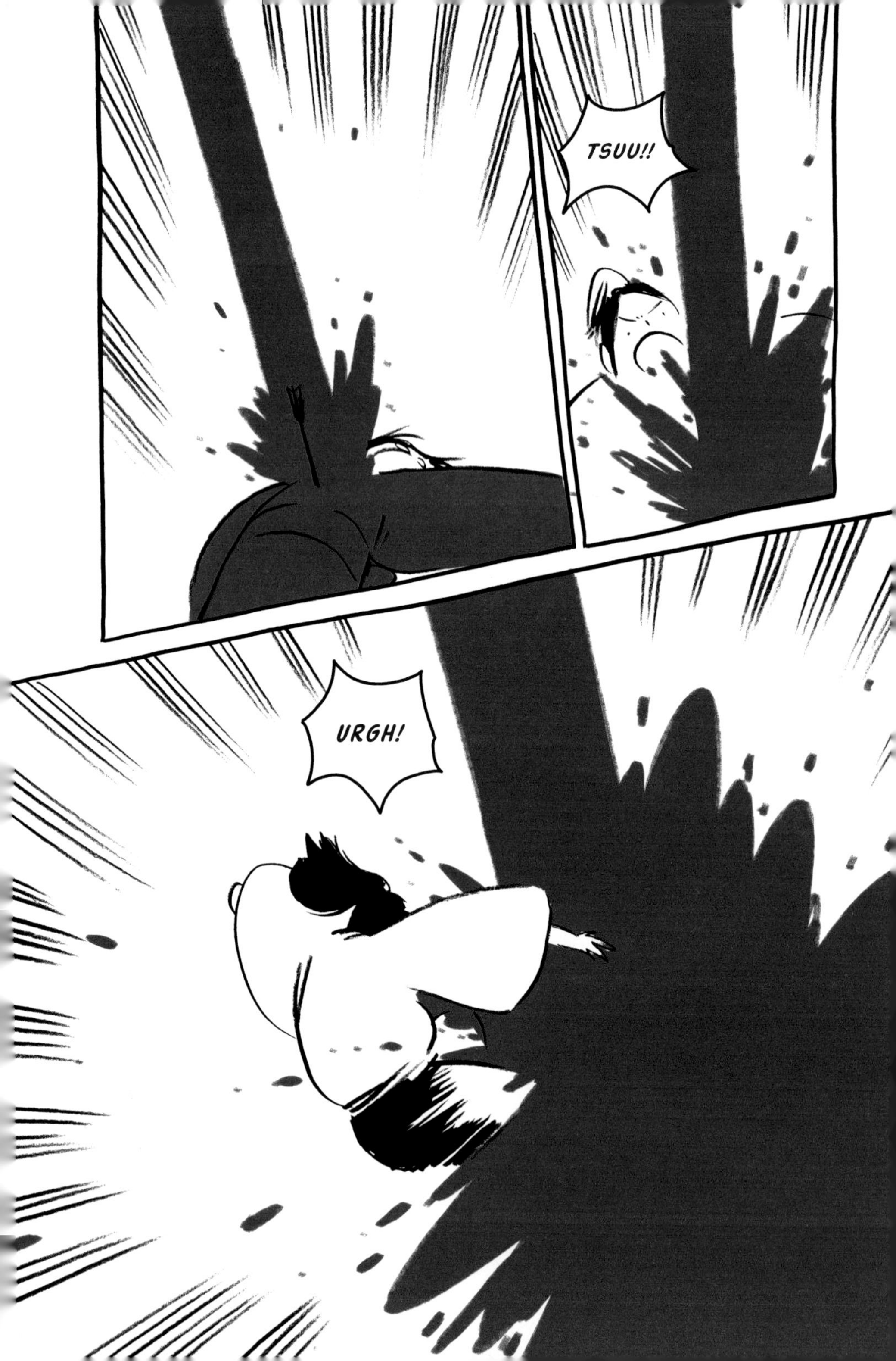
TSUU!!
URGH!

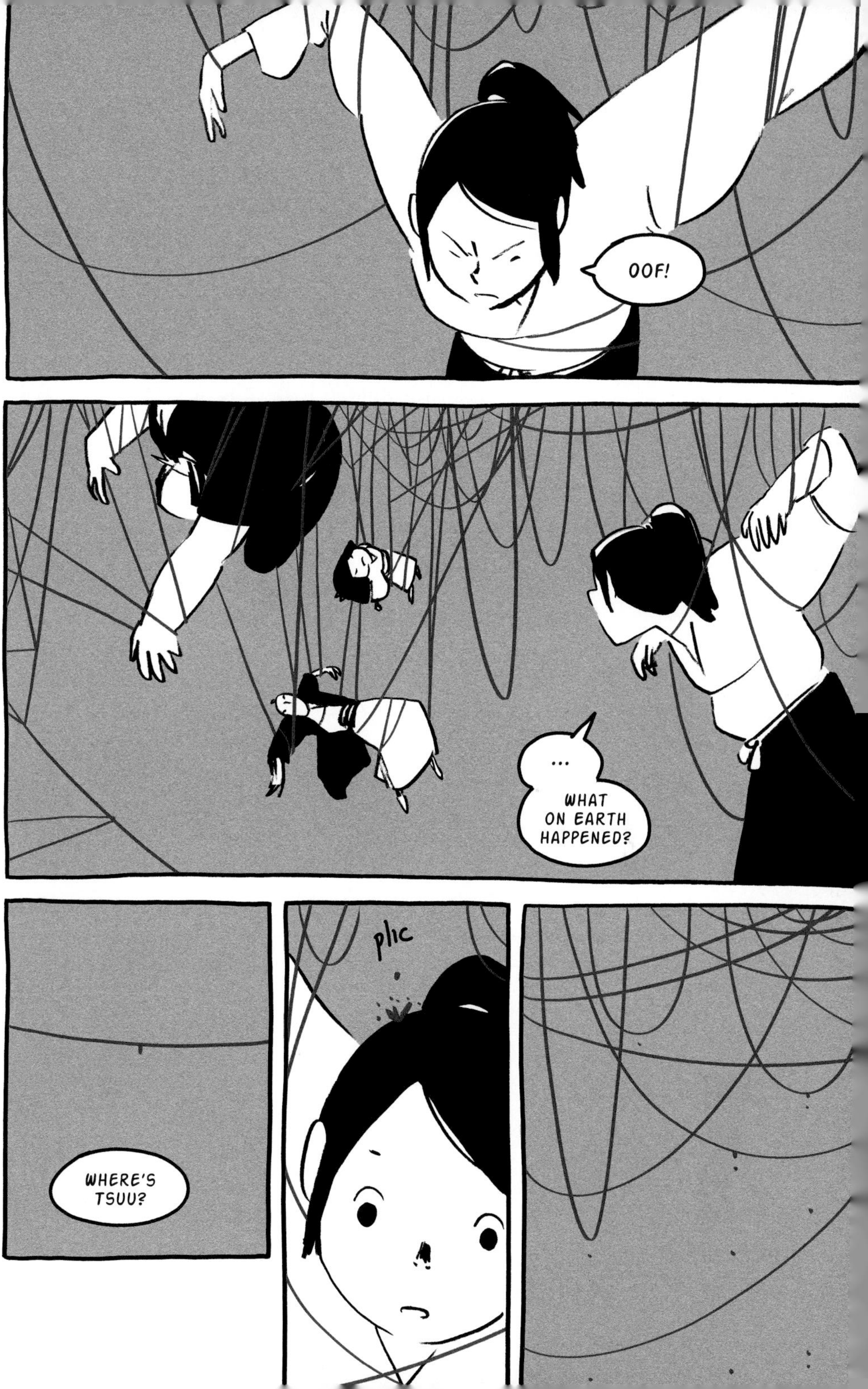
OOF!
...
WHAT ON EARTH HAPPENED?
WHERE'S TSUU?
plic

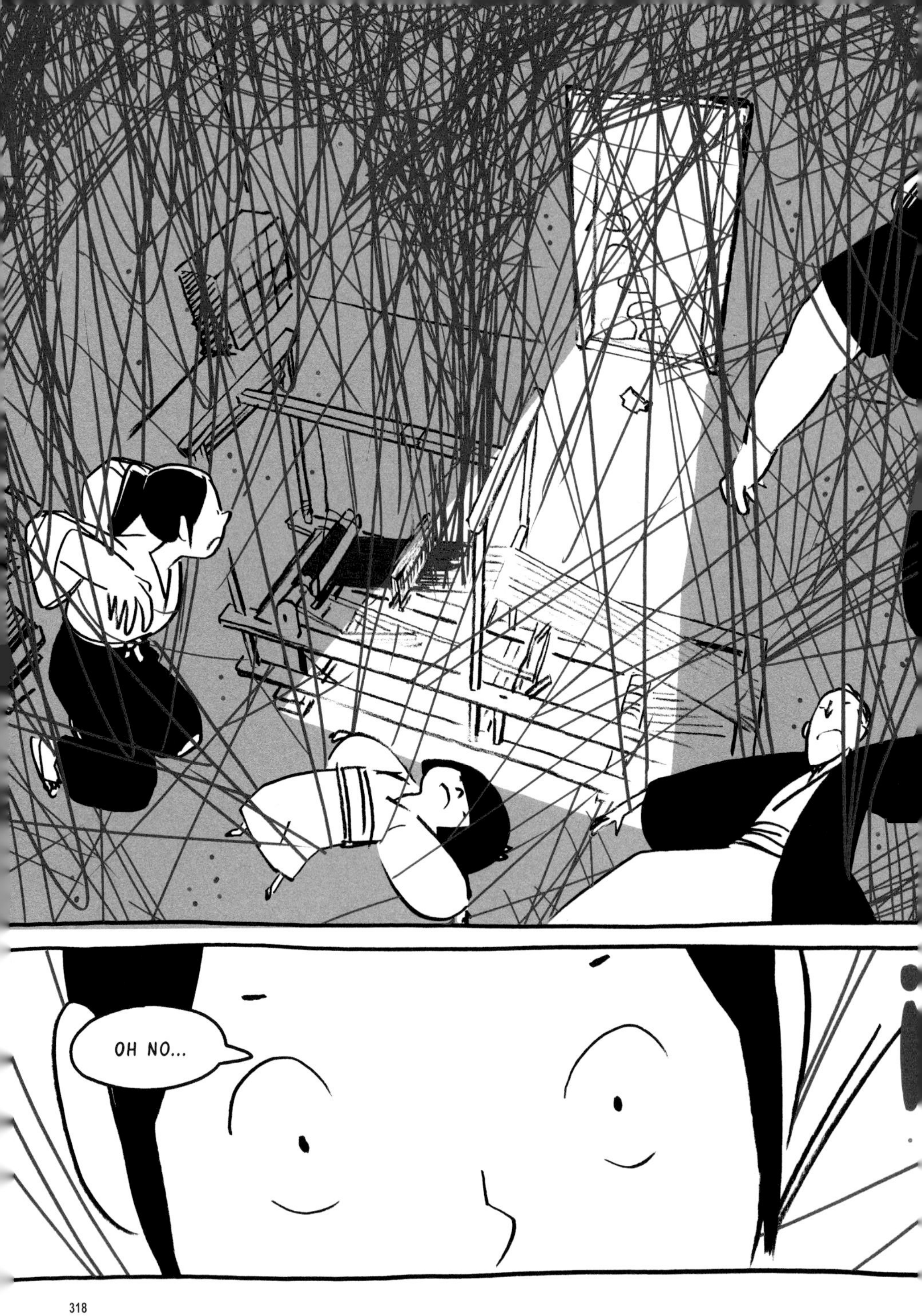
OH NO...

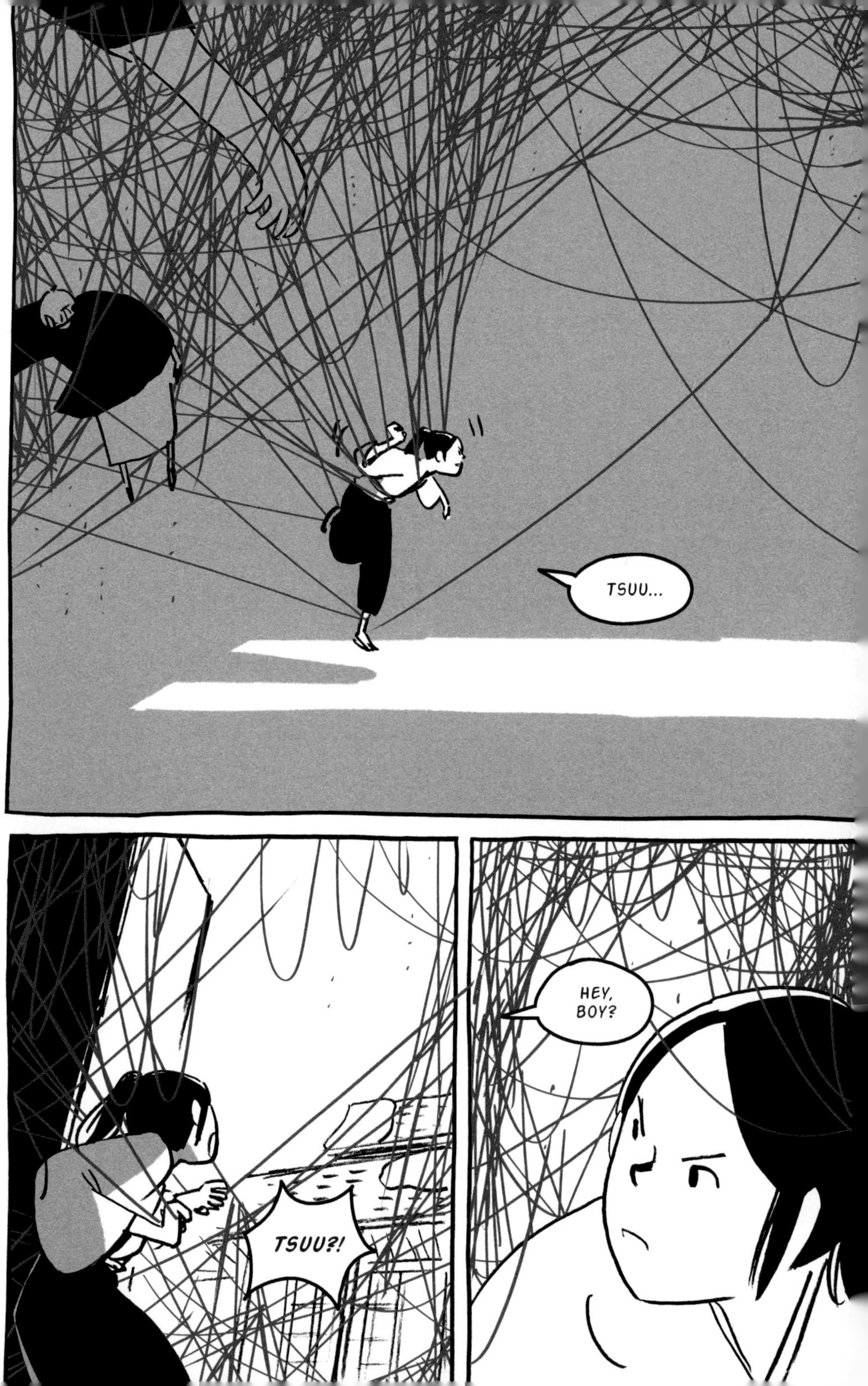
TSUU...
TSUU?!
HEY, BOY?

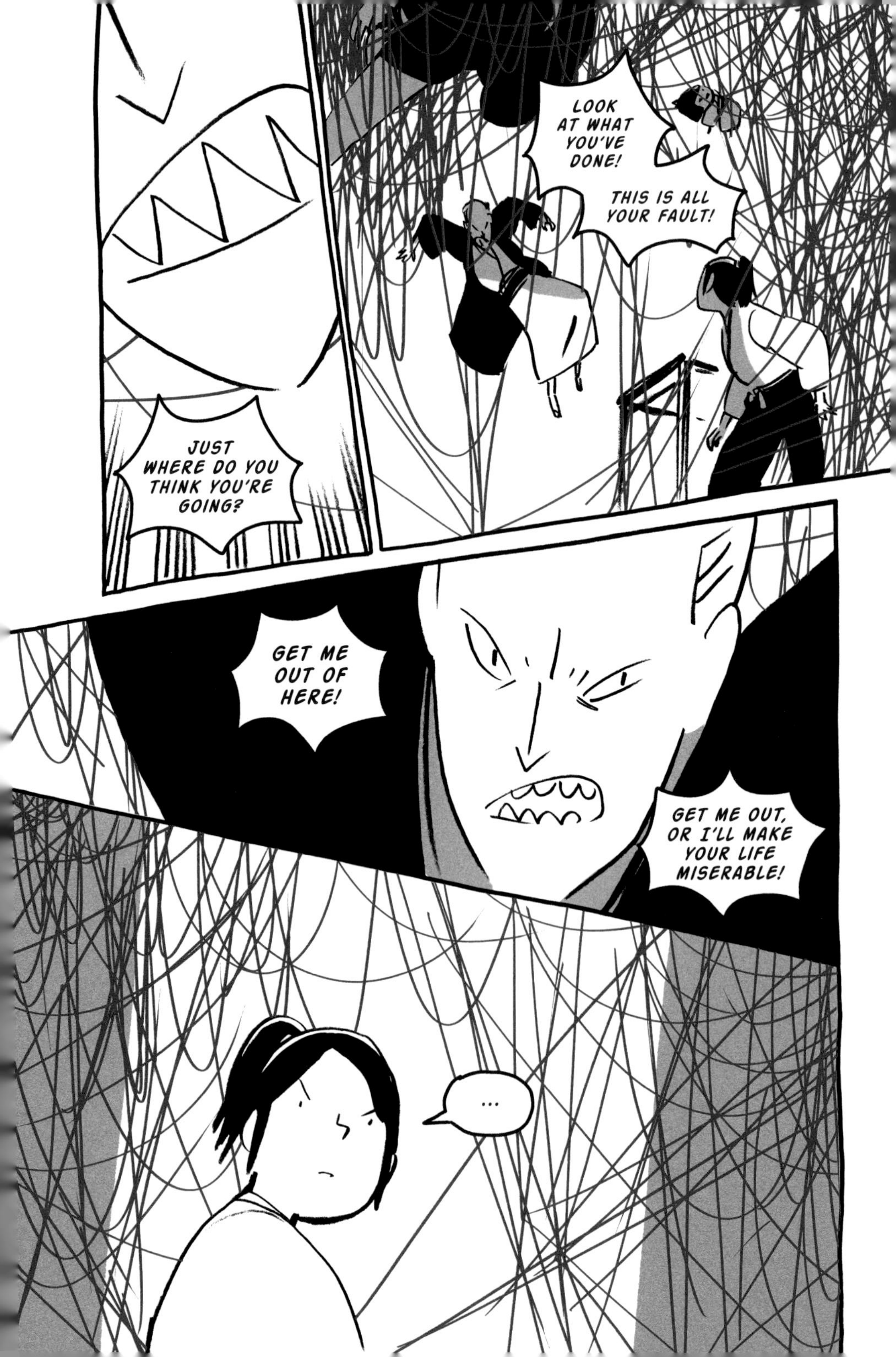
JUST WHERE DO YOU THINK YOU'RE GOING?
LOOK AT WHAT YOU'VE DONE!
THIS IS ALL YOUR FAULT!
GET ME OUT OF HERE!
GET ME OUT, OR I'LL MAKE YOUR LIFE MISERABLE!
...

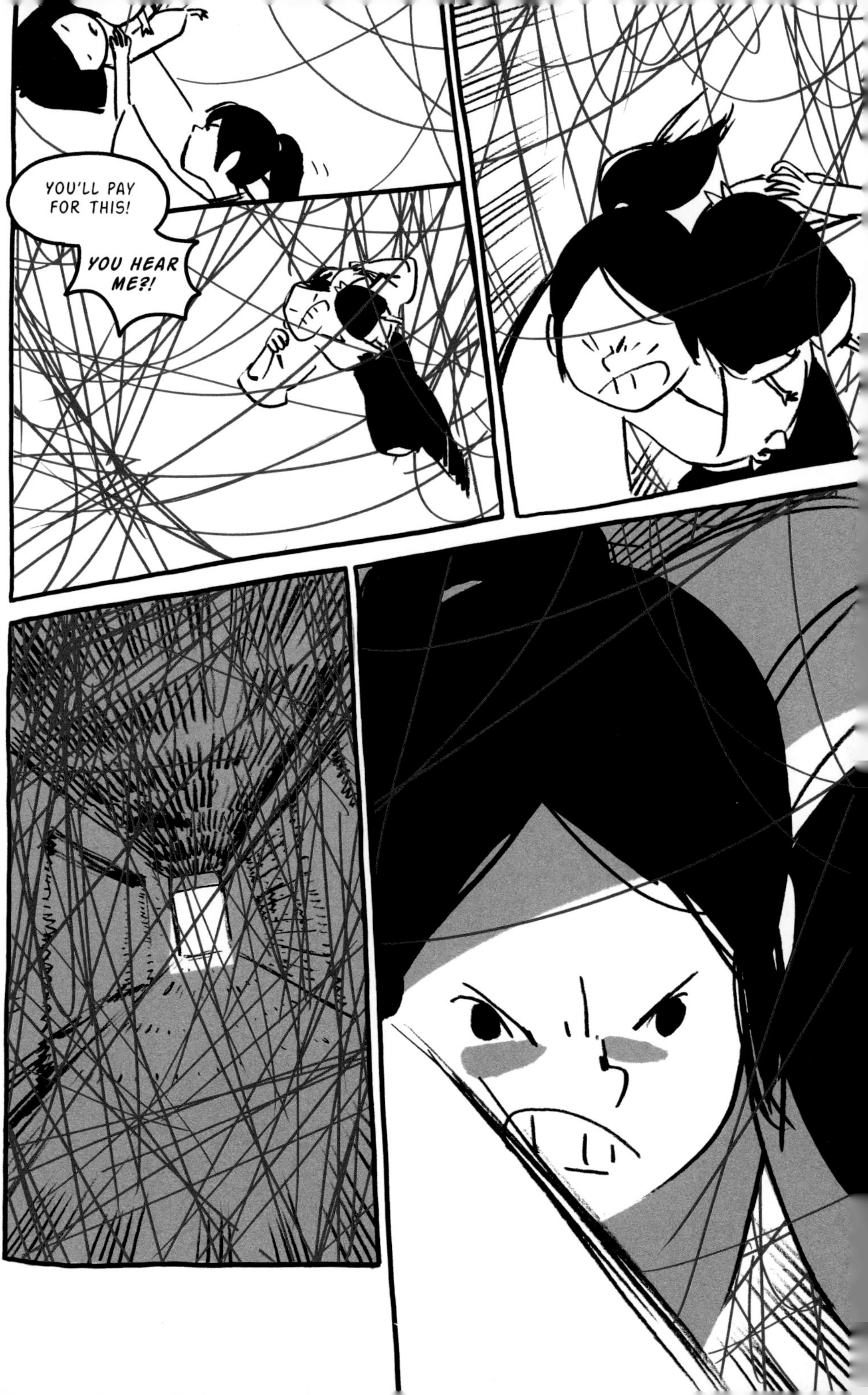
YOU'LL PAY FOR THIS!
YOU HEAR ME?!

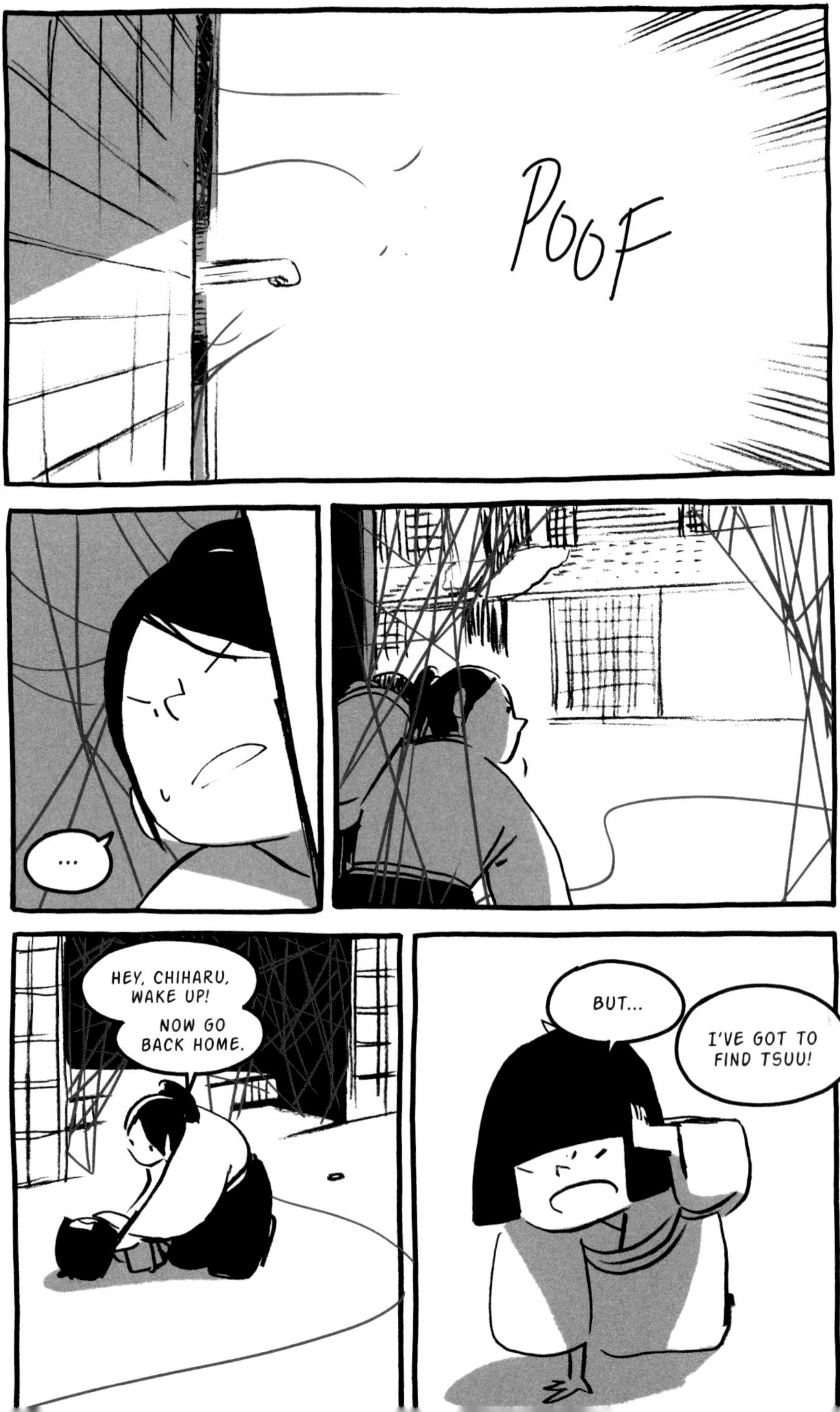
POOF
...
HEY, CHIHARU, WAKE UP!
NOW GO BACK HOME.
BUT...
I'VE GOT TO FIND TSUU!

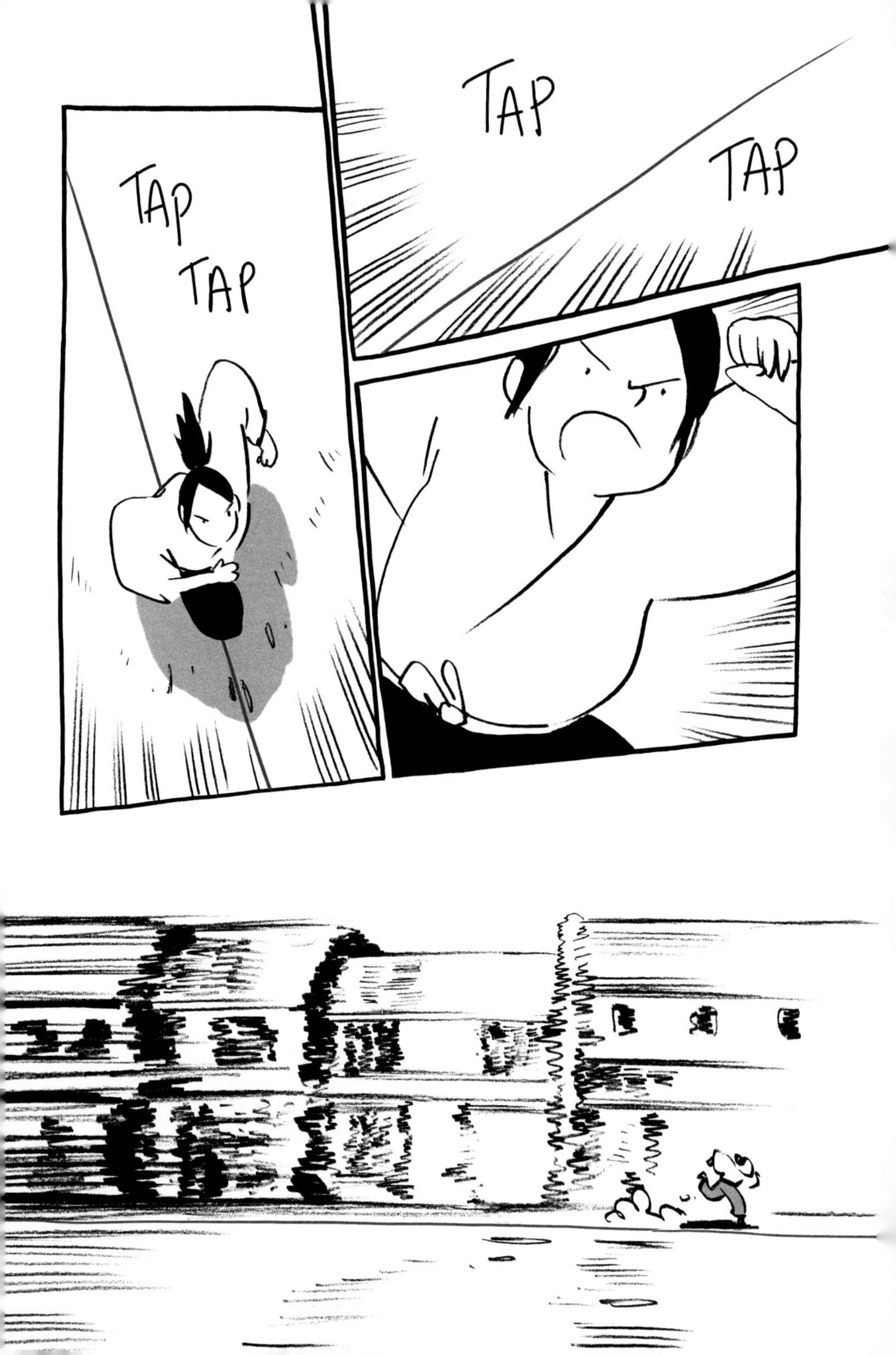

TAP
TAP
TAP
TAP

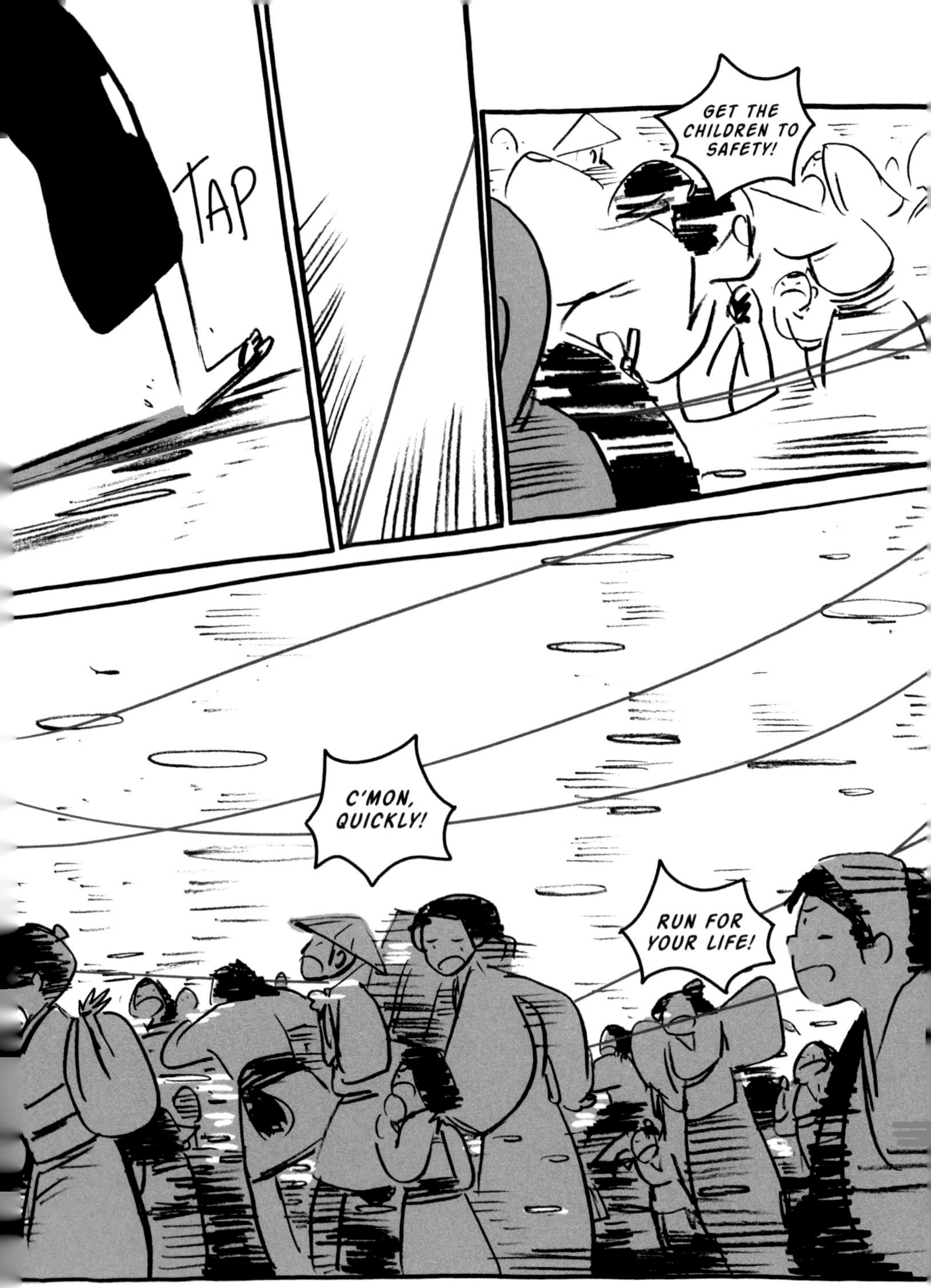
TAP
GET THE CHILDREN TO SAFETY!
C'MON, QUICKLY!
RUN FOR YOUR LIFE!

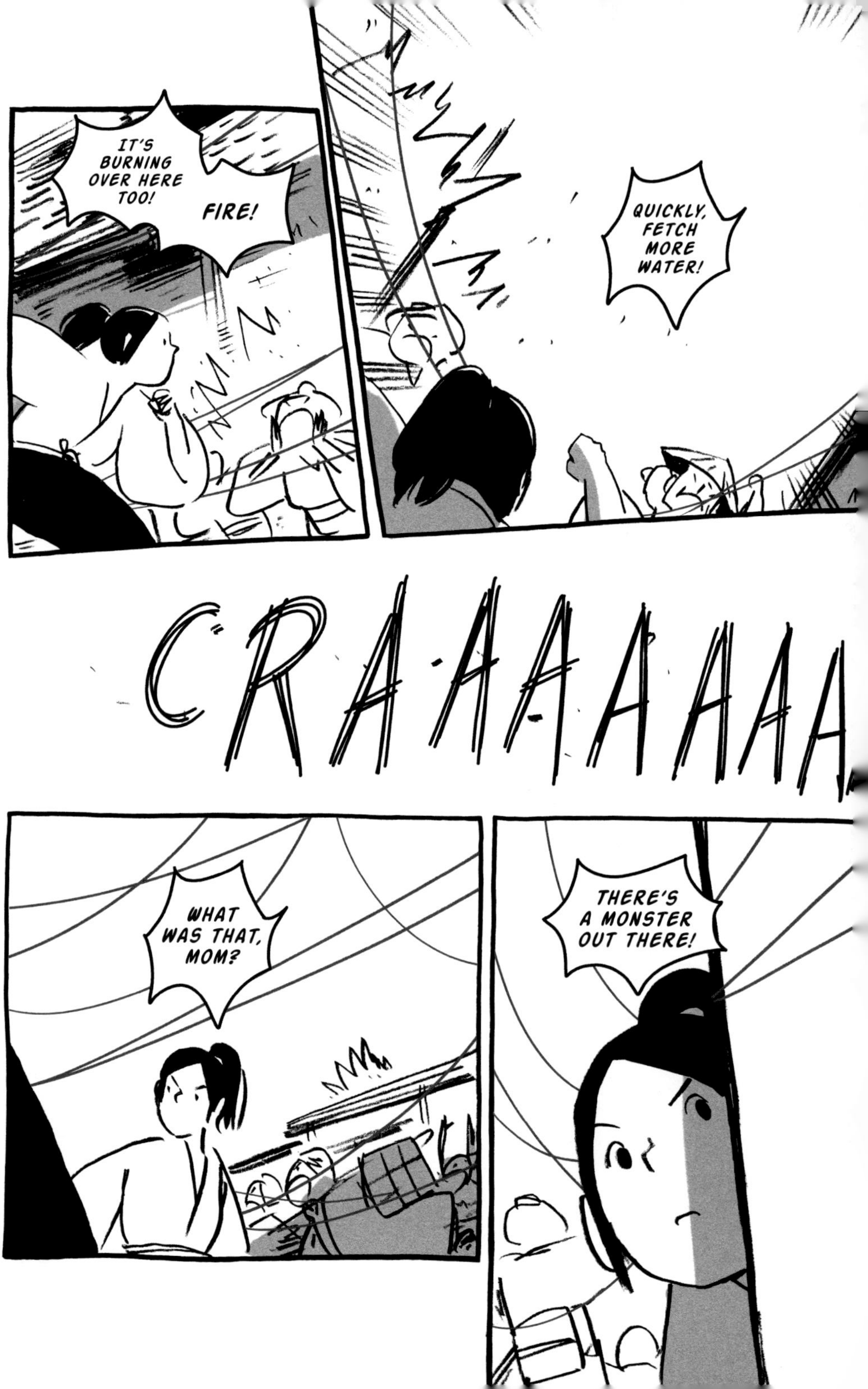
IT'S BURNING OVER HERE TOO!
FIRE!
QUICKLY, FETCH MORE WATER!
CRAAAAAAA
WHAT WAS THAT, MOM?
THERE'S A MONSTER OUT THERE!

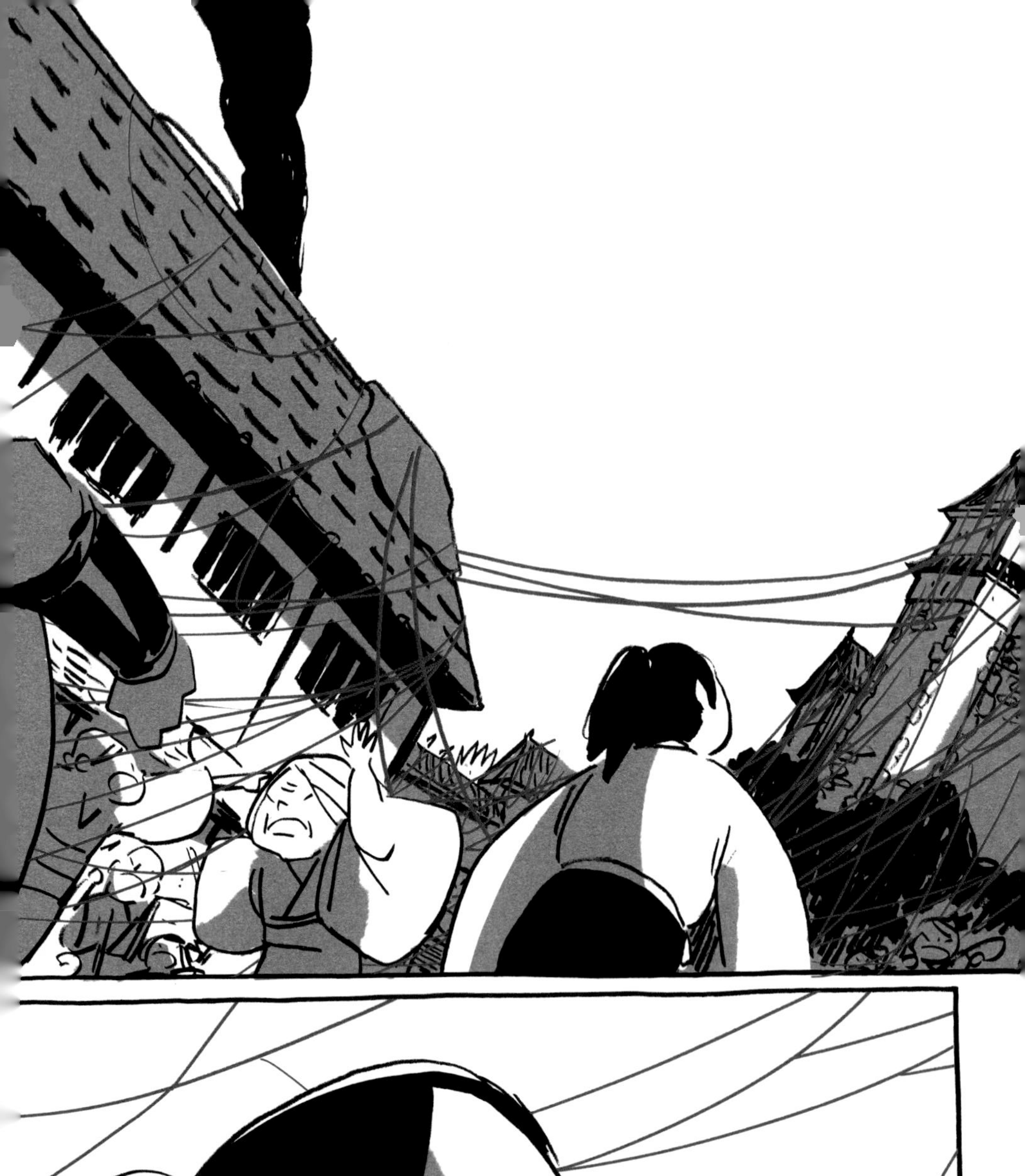

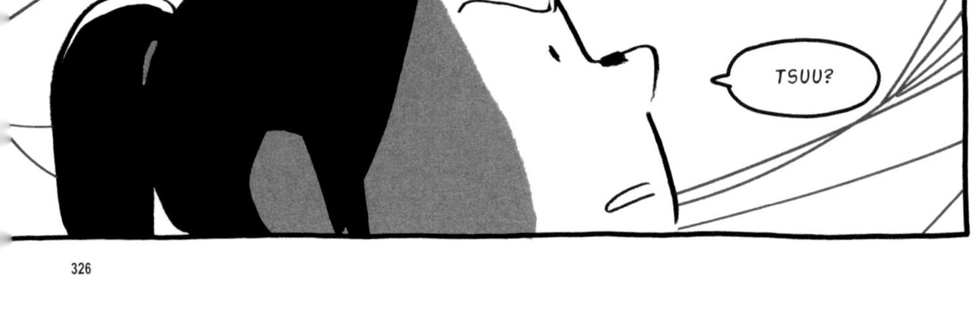
TSUU?

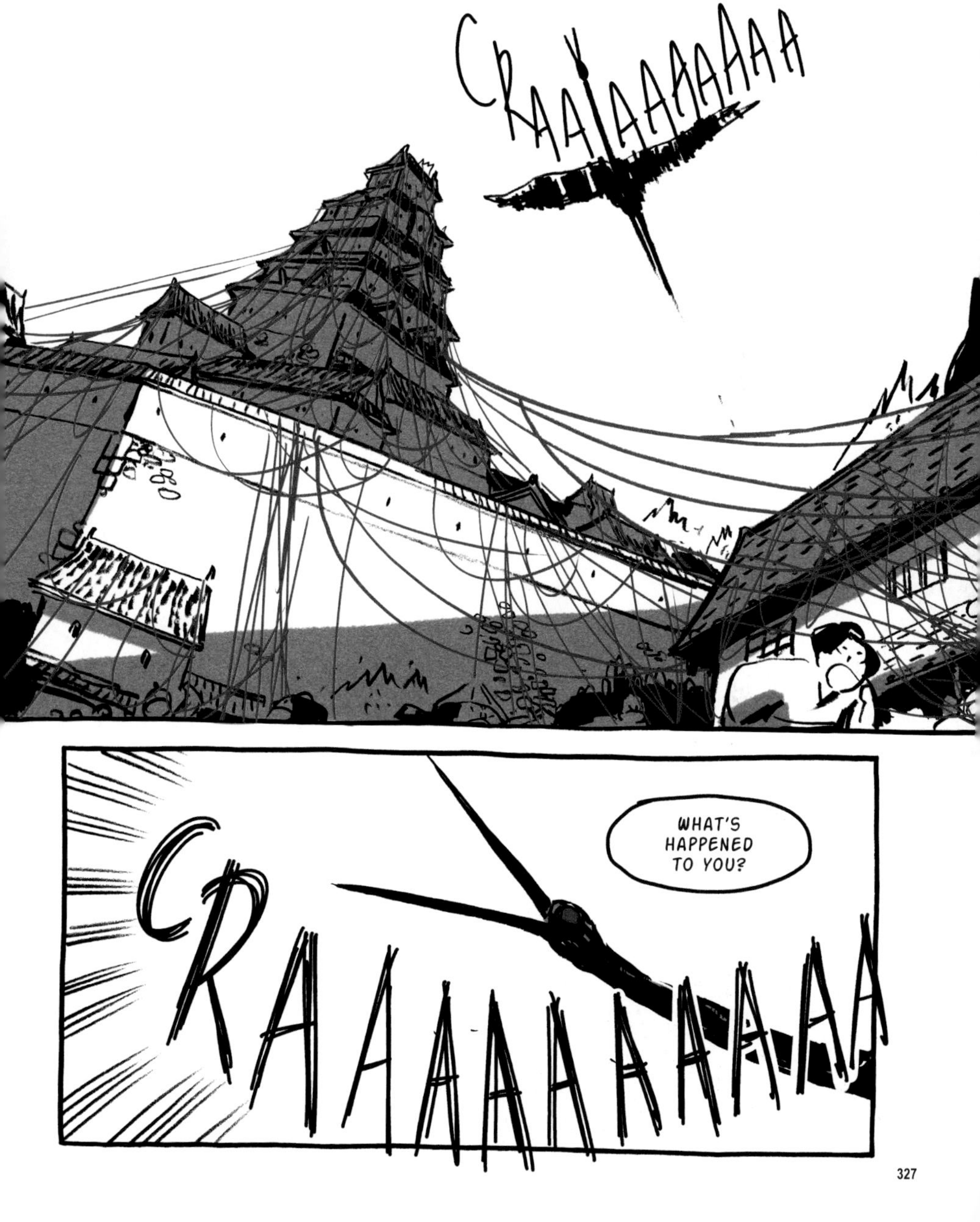
CRAAAAAAAAAA
WHAT'S HAPPENED TO YOU?
CRAAAAAAAAAA

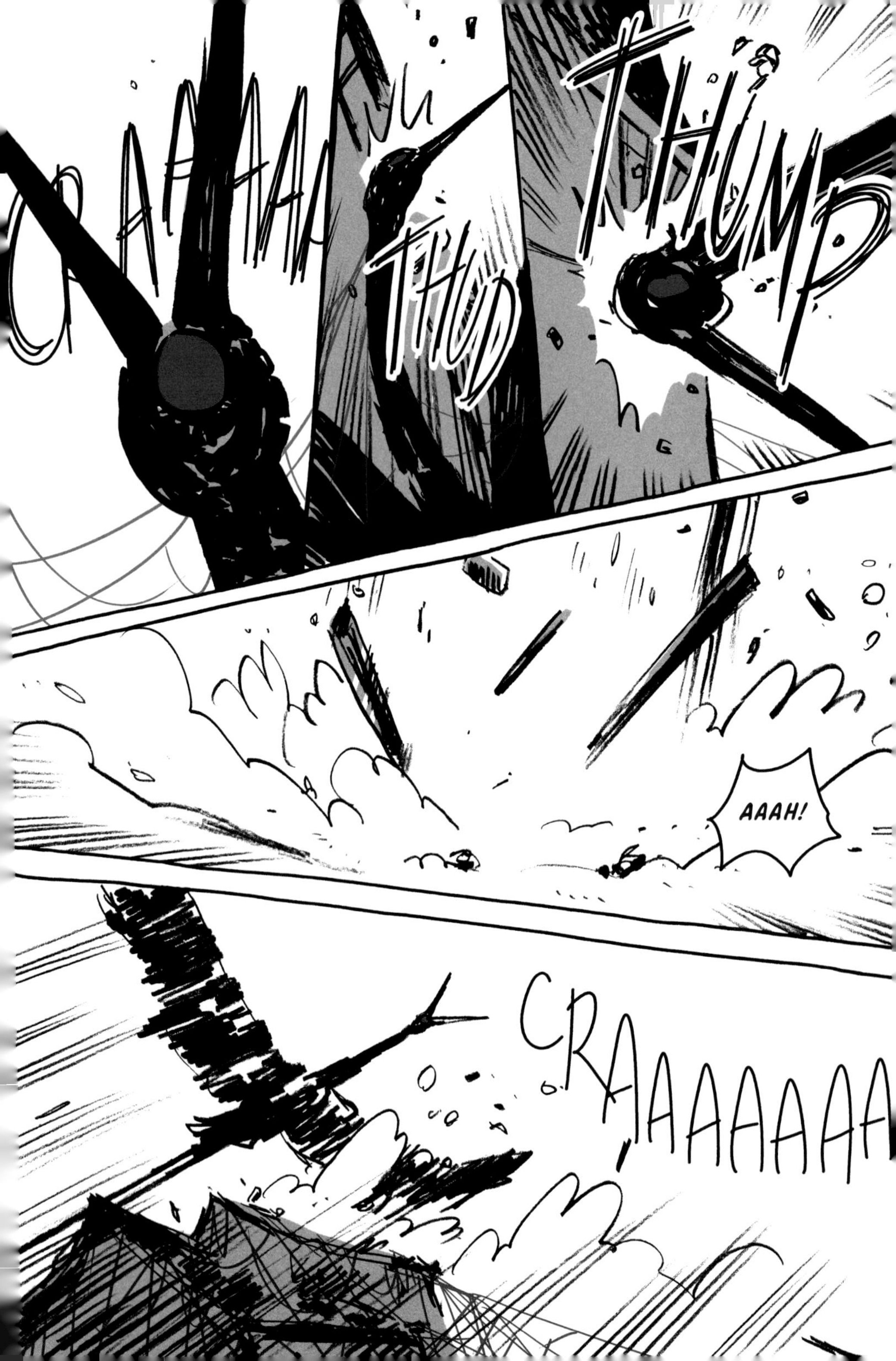
CRAAAAAAA
THUD
THUMP
AAAH!
CRAAAAAAA

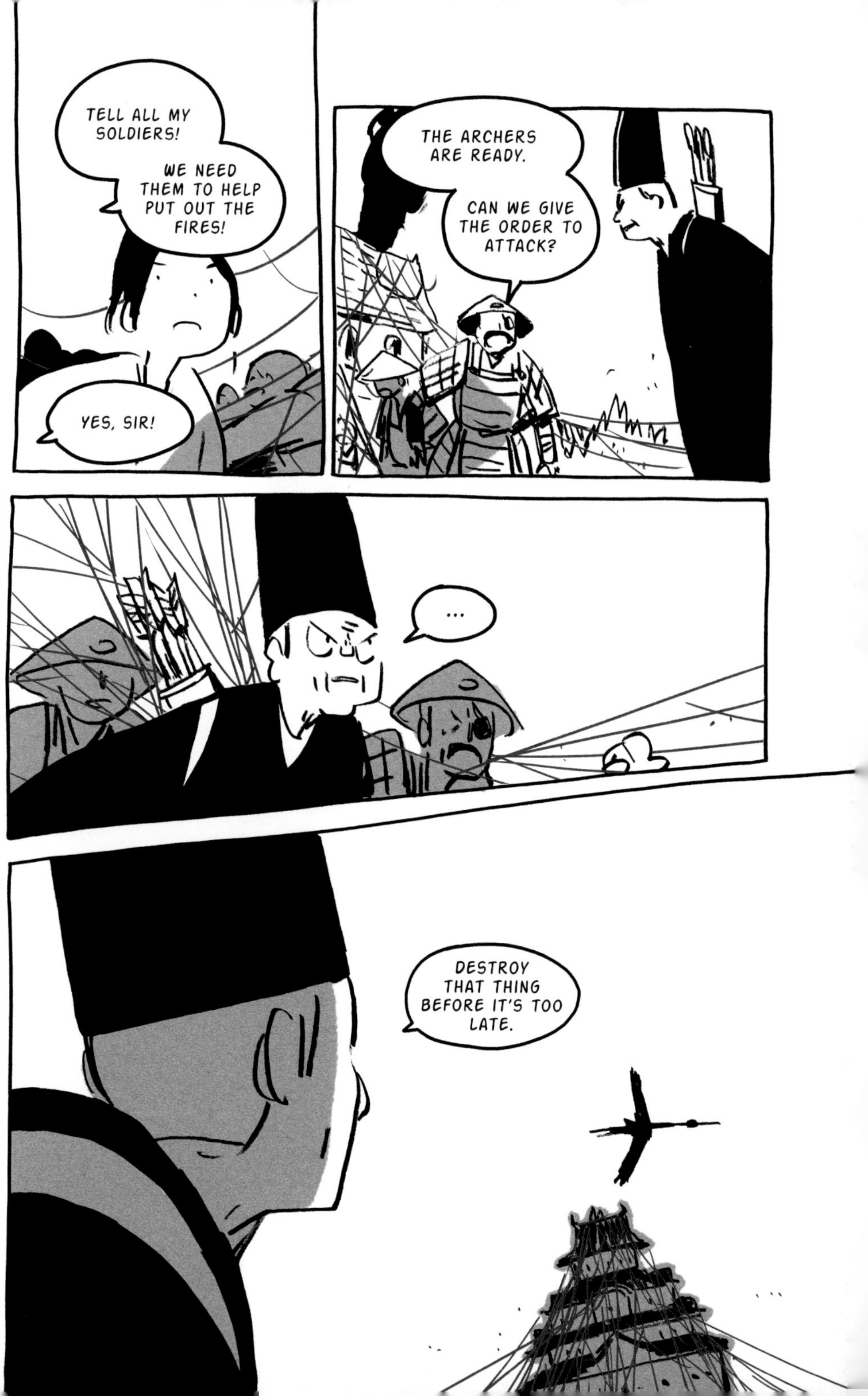
TELL ALL MY SOLDIERS!
WE NEED THEM TO HELP PUT OUT THE FIRES!
YES, SIR!
THE ARCHERS ARE READY.
CAN WE GIVE THE ORDER TO ATTACK?
...
DESTROY THAT THING BEFORE IT'S TOO LATE.

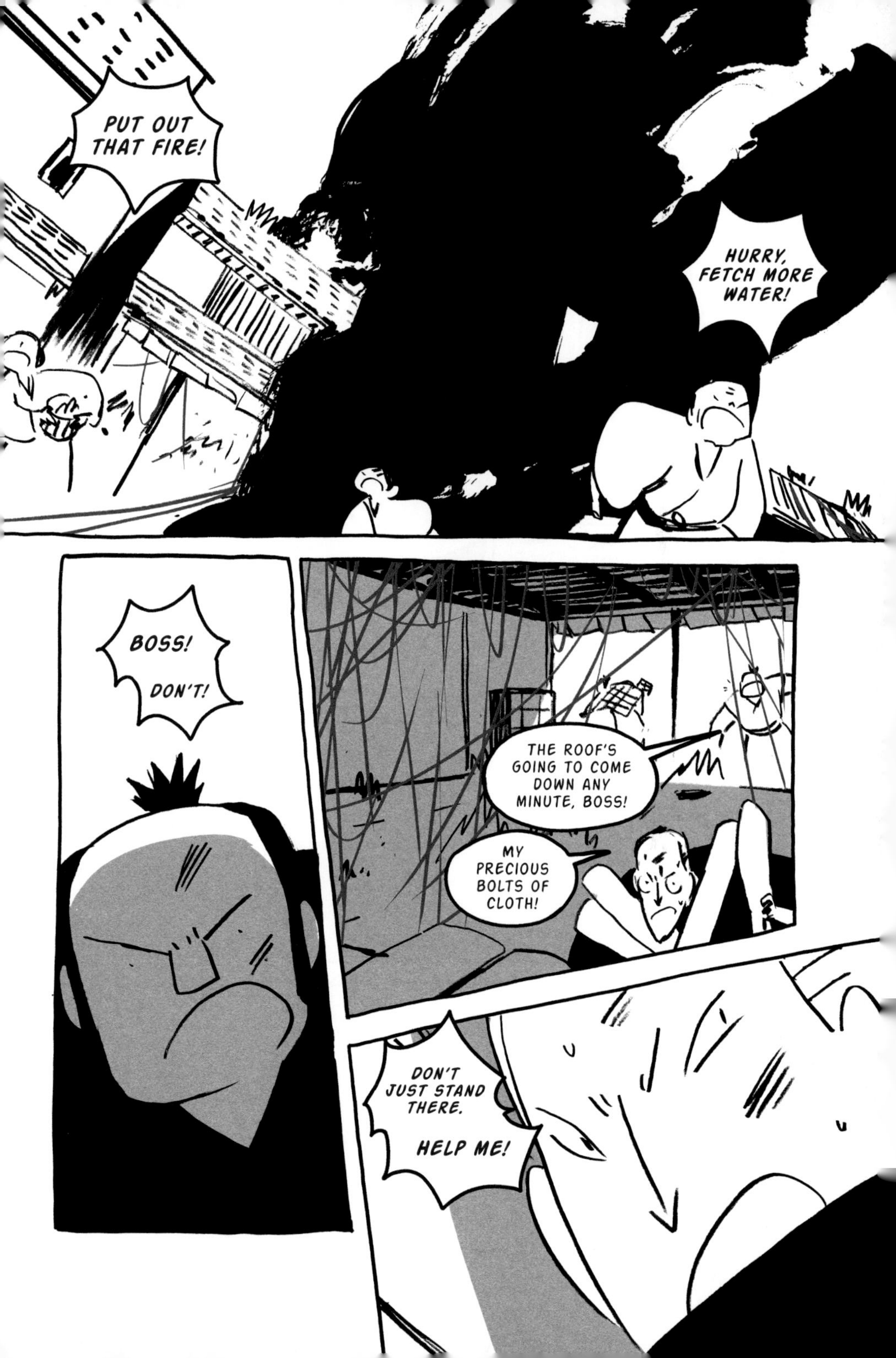
PUT OUT THAT FIRE!
HURRY, FETCH MORE WATER!
BOSS! DON'T!
THE ROOF'S GOING TO COME DOWN ANY MINUTE, BOSS!
MY PRECIOUS BOLTS OF CLOTH!
DON'T JUST STAND THERE.
HELP ME!

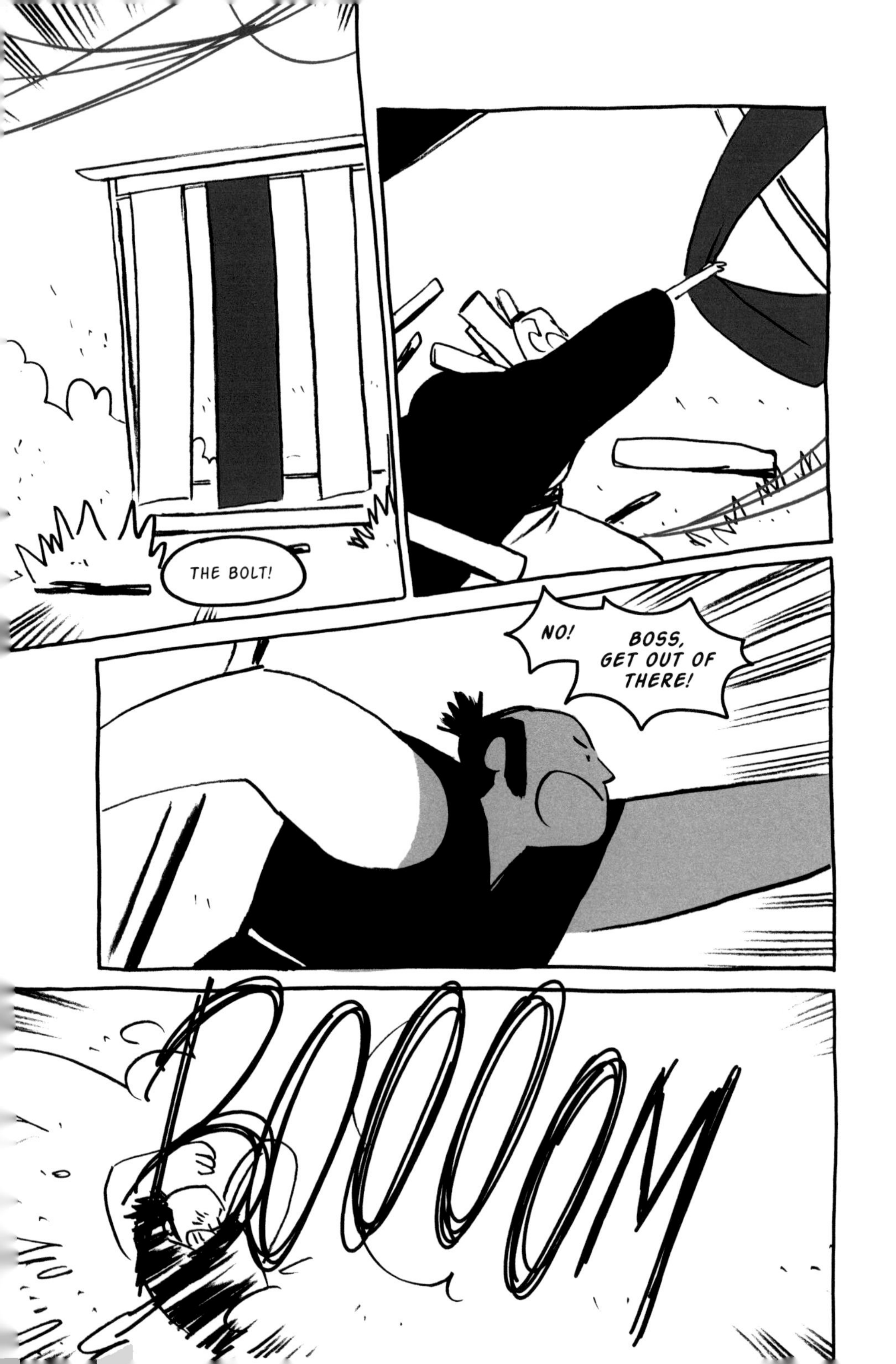
THE BOLT!
NO!
BOSS, GET OUT OF THERE!

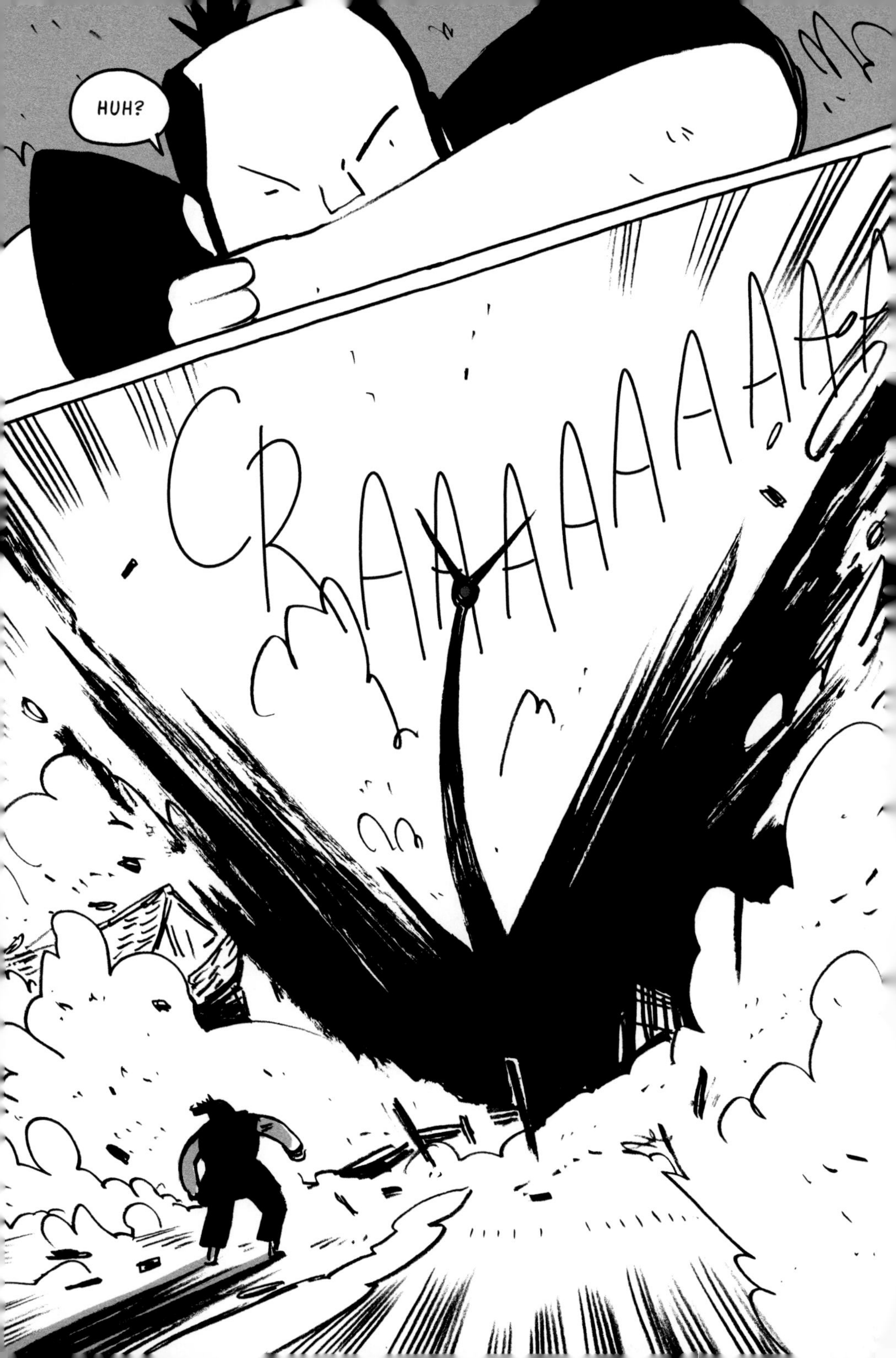
HUH?

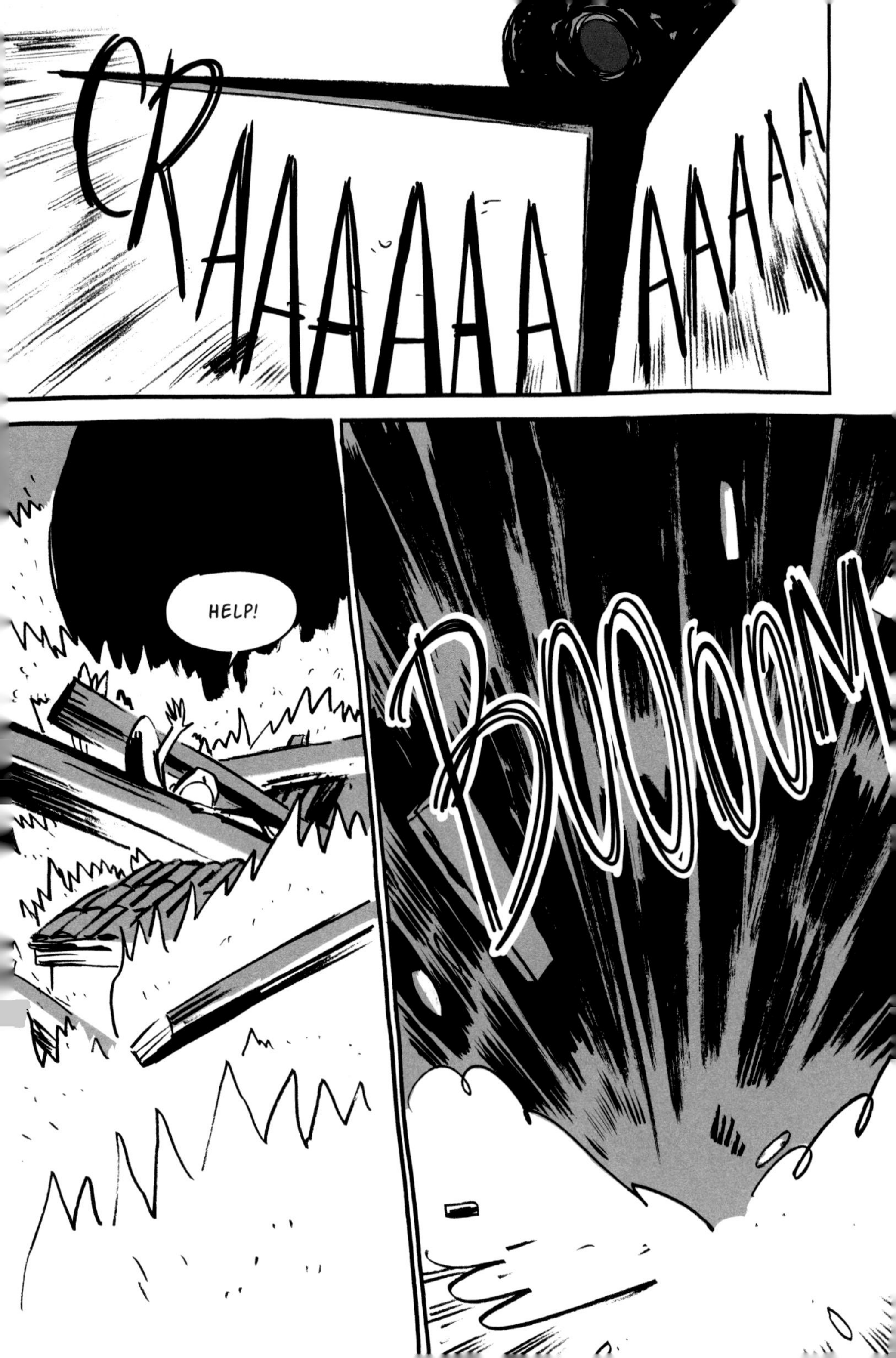
CRAAAAAAAAAA
HELP!
BOOOOOM

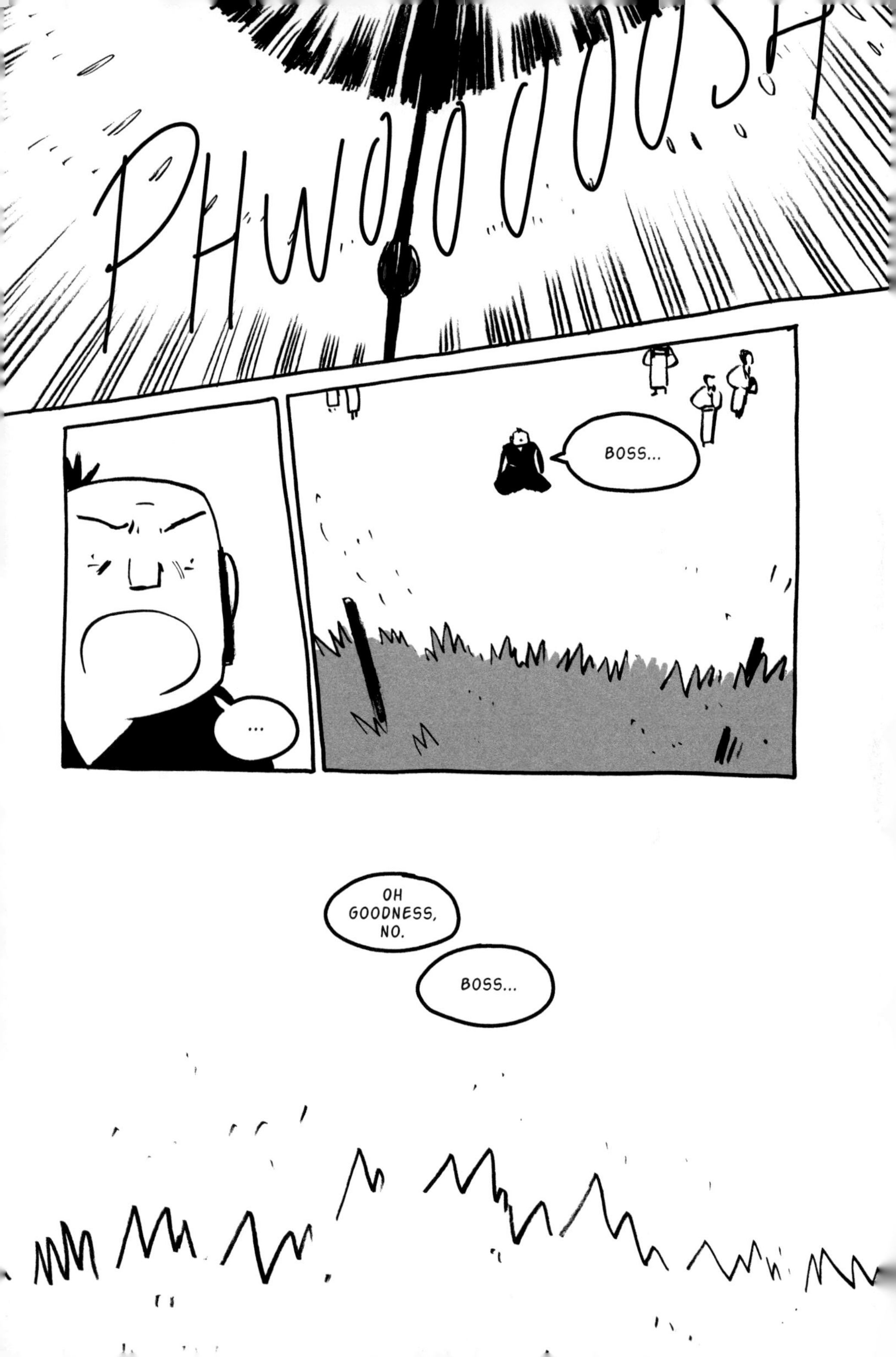
PHWOOOOOSH
BOSS...
...
OH GOODNESS, NO.
BOSS...

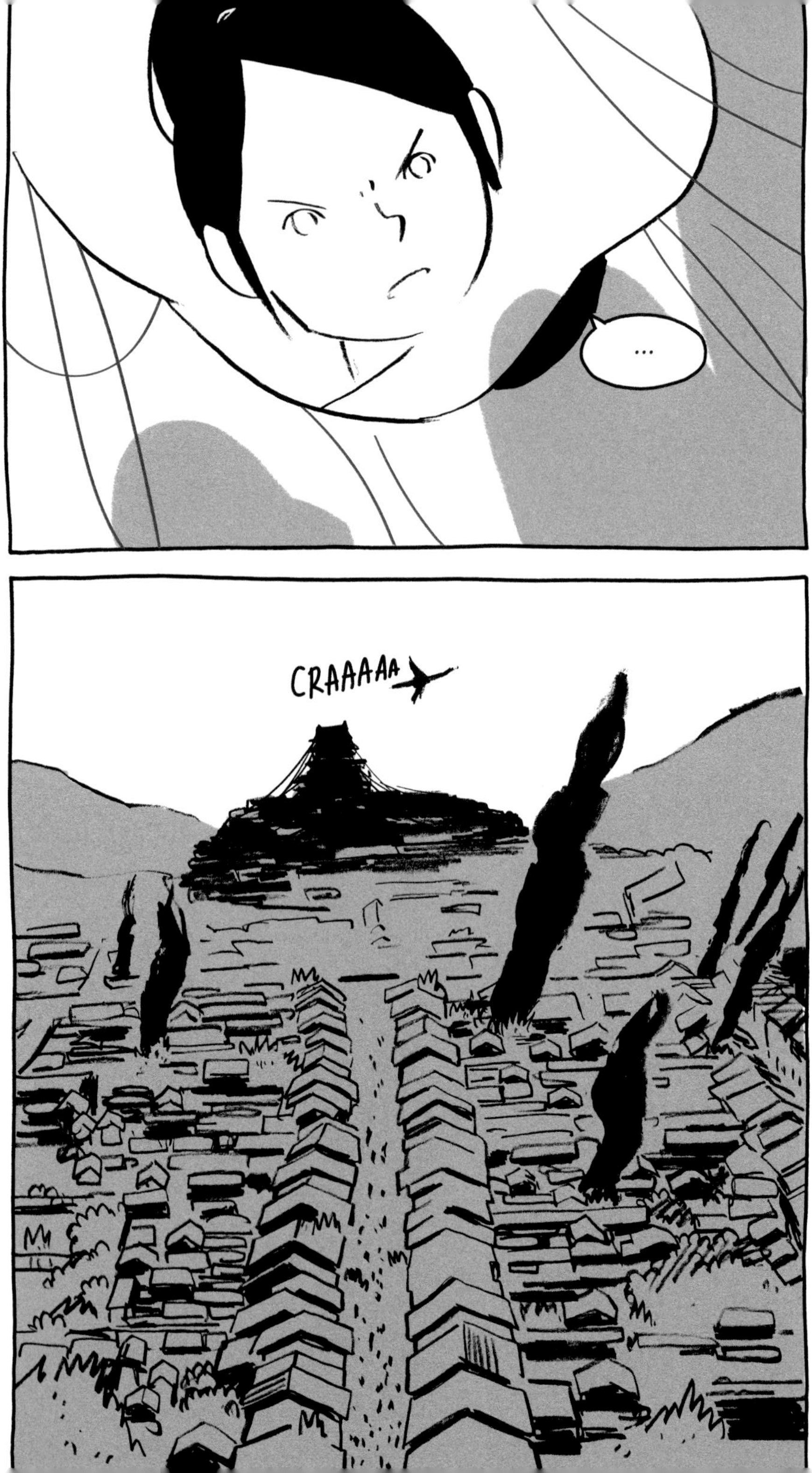
...
CRAAAAA

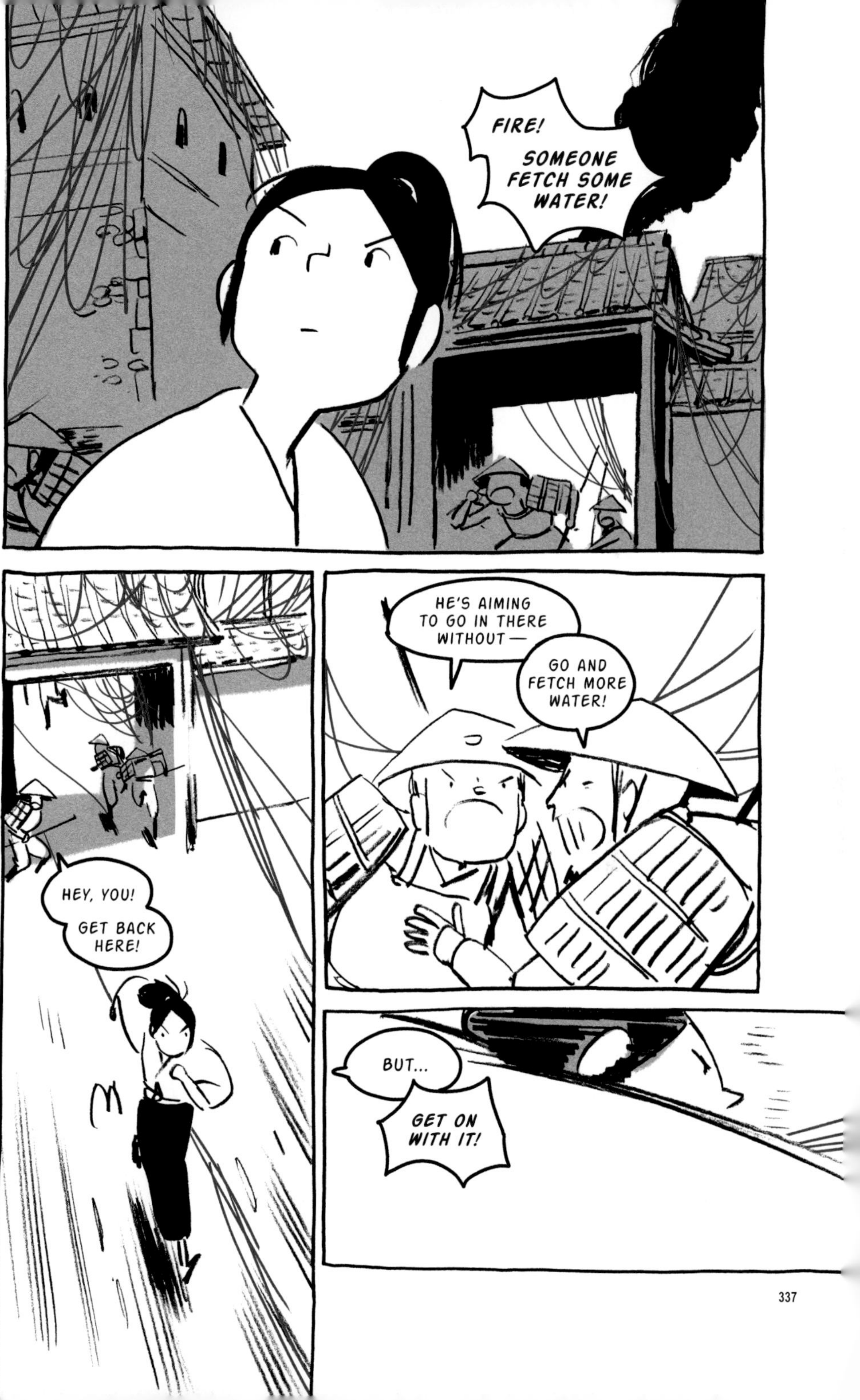
FIRE!
SOMEONE FETCH SOME WATER!
HEY, YOU!
GET BACK HERE!
HE'S AIMING TO GO IN THERE WITHOUT—
GO AND FETCH MORE WATER!
BUT...
GET ON WITH IT!

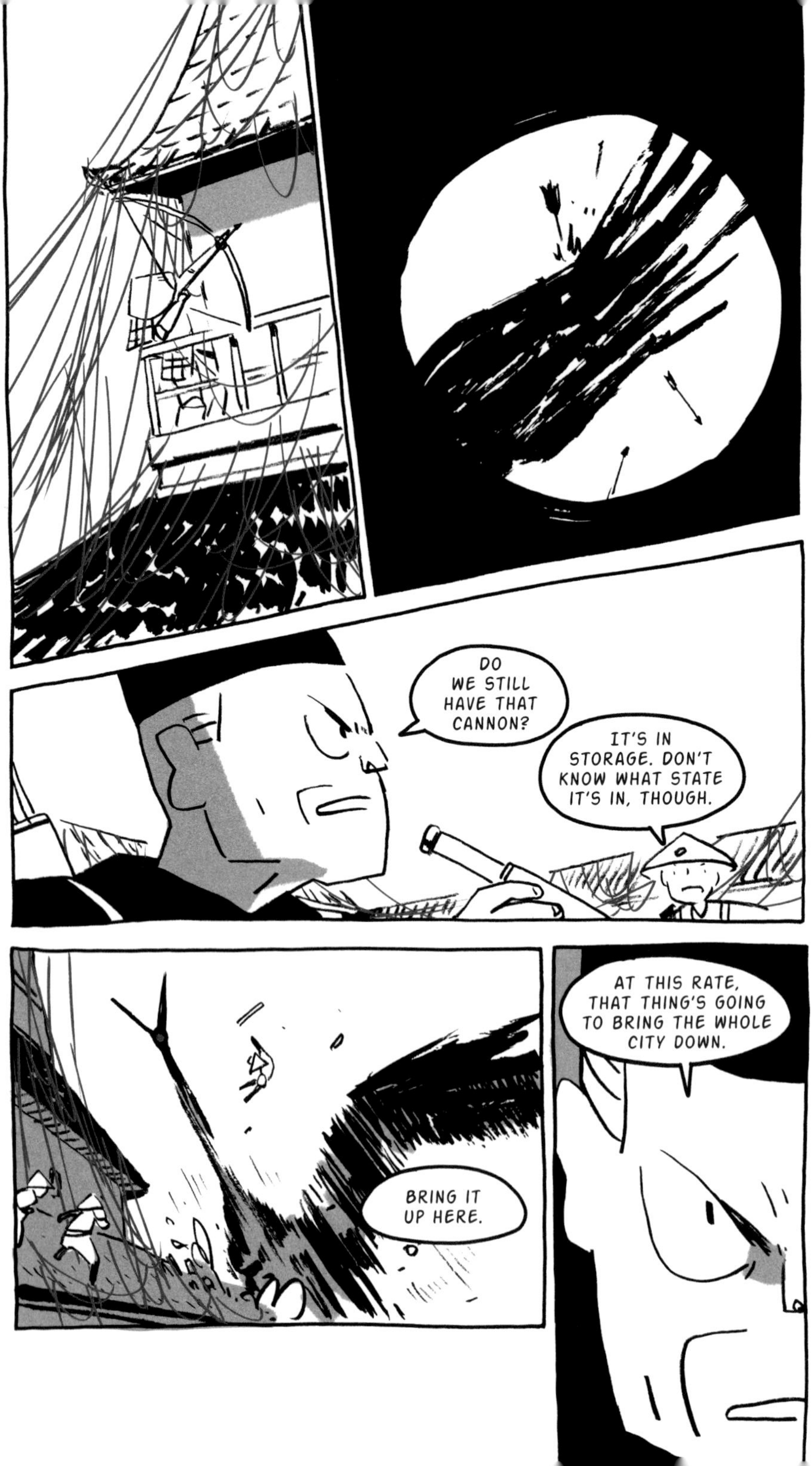
DO WE STILL HAVE THAT CANNON?
IT'S IN STORAGE. DON'T KNOW WHAT STATE IT'S IN, THOUGH.
AT THIS RATE, THAT THING'S GOING TO BRING THE WHOLE CITY DOWN.
BRING IT UP HERE.

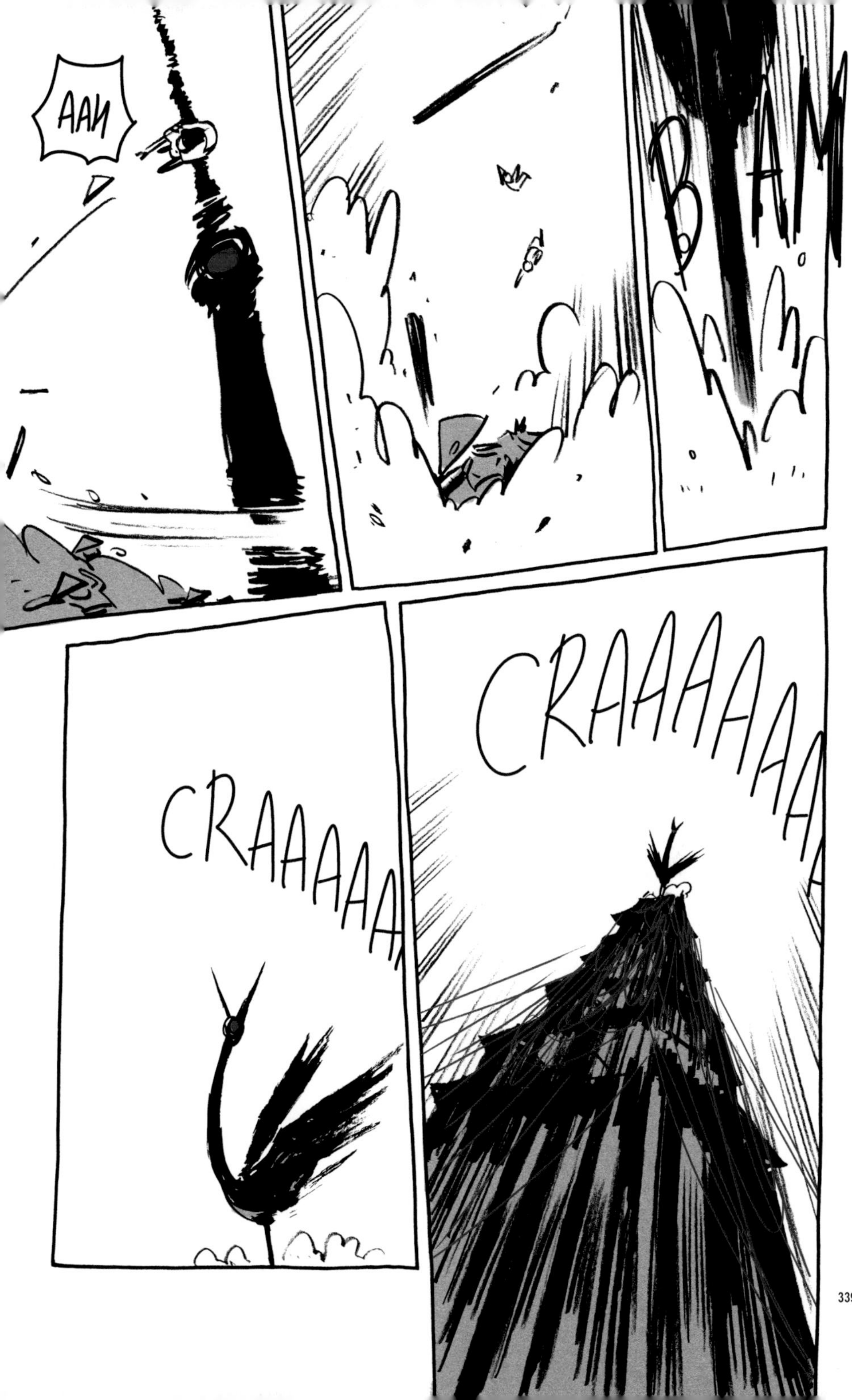
AAH
BAM
CRAAAAAA
CRAAAAAAAA

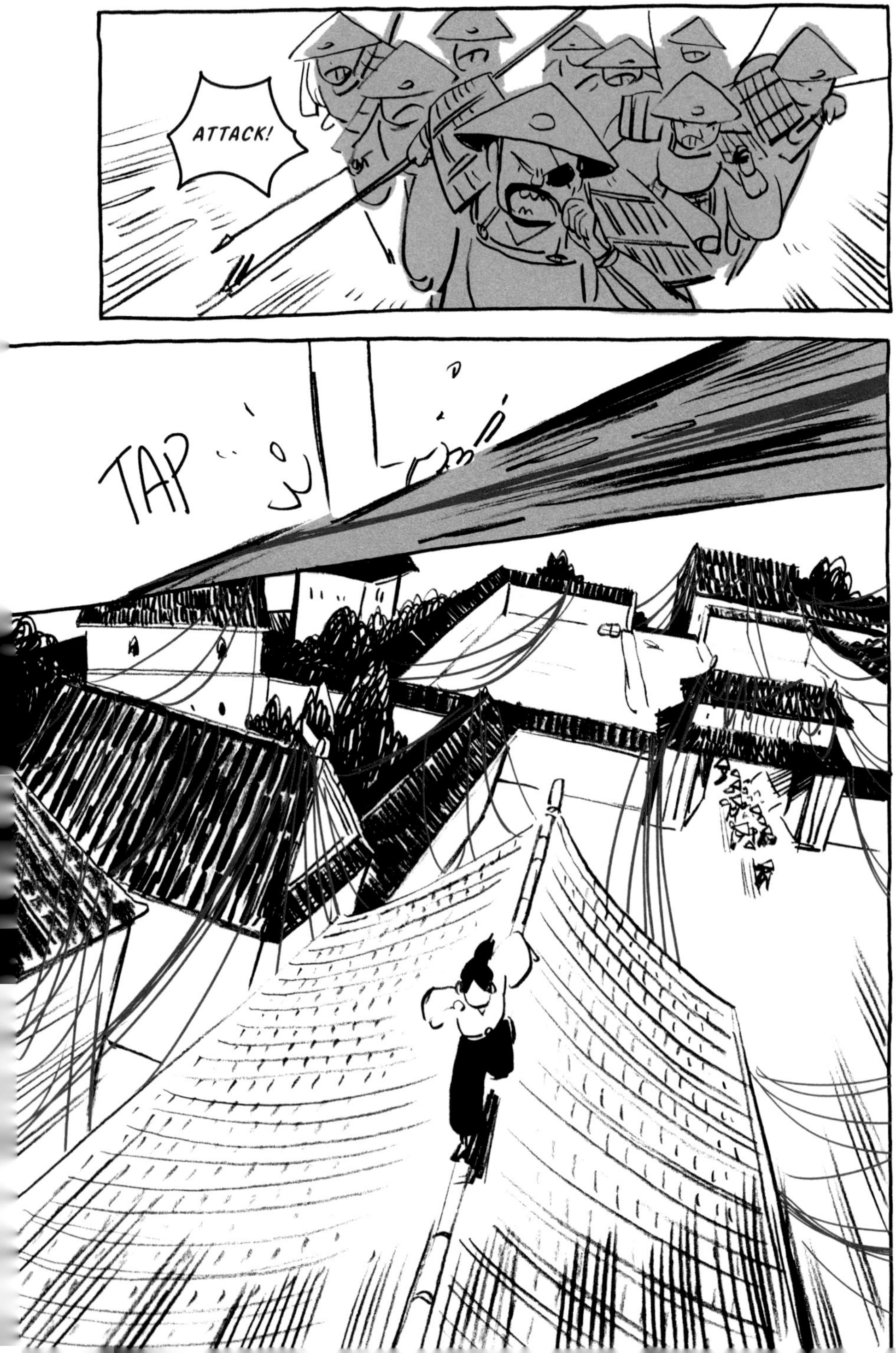
ATTACK!
TAP

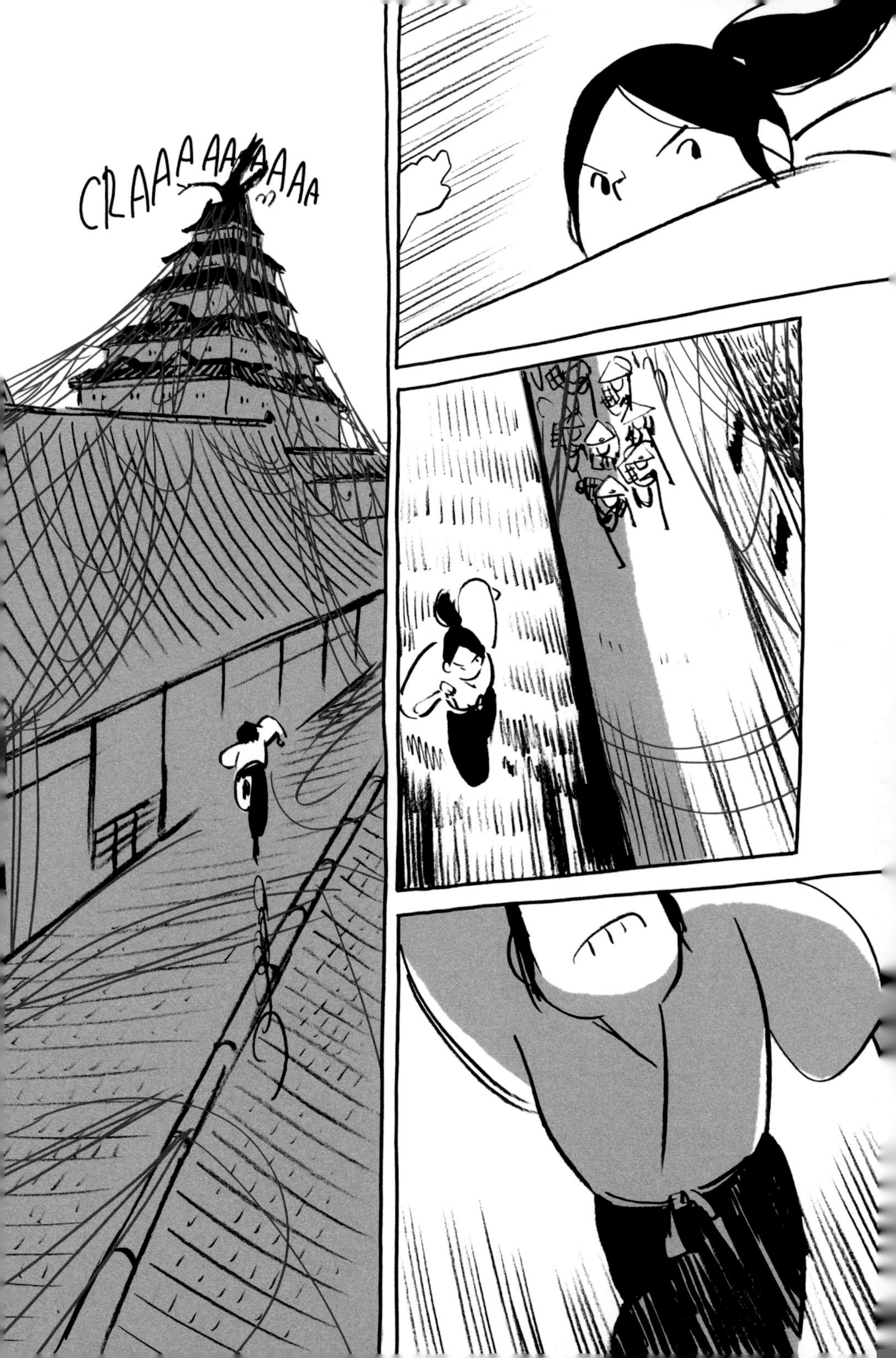
CRAAAAAAAAAA

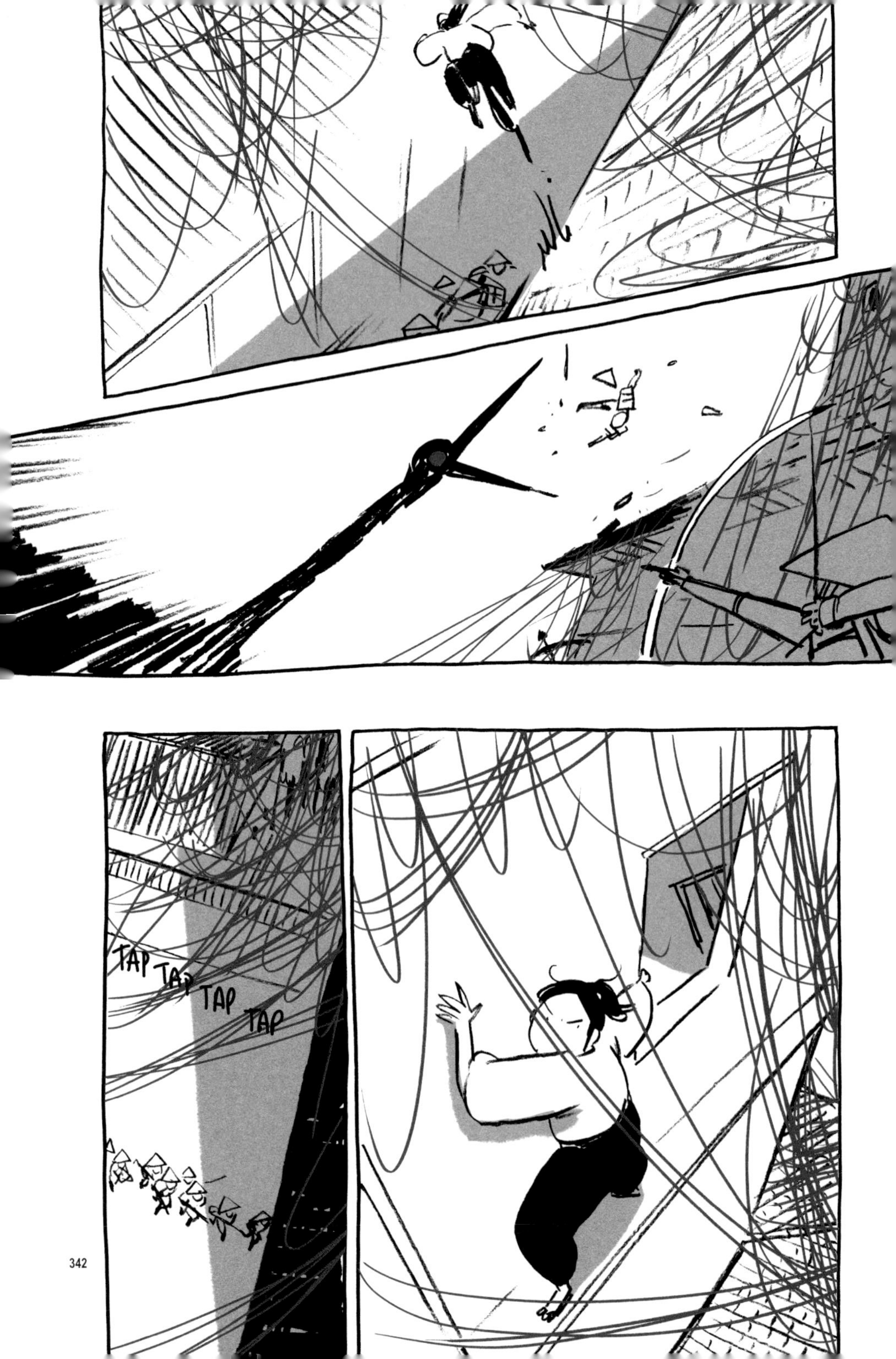
TAP TAP TAP TAP

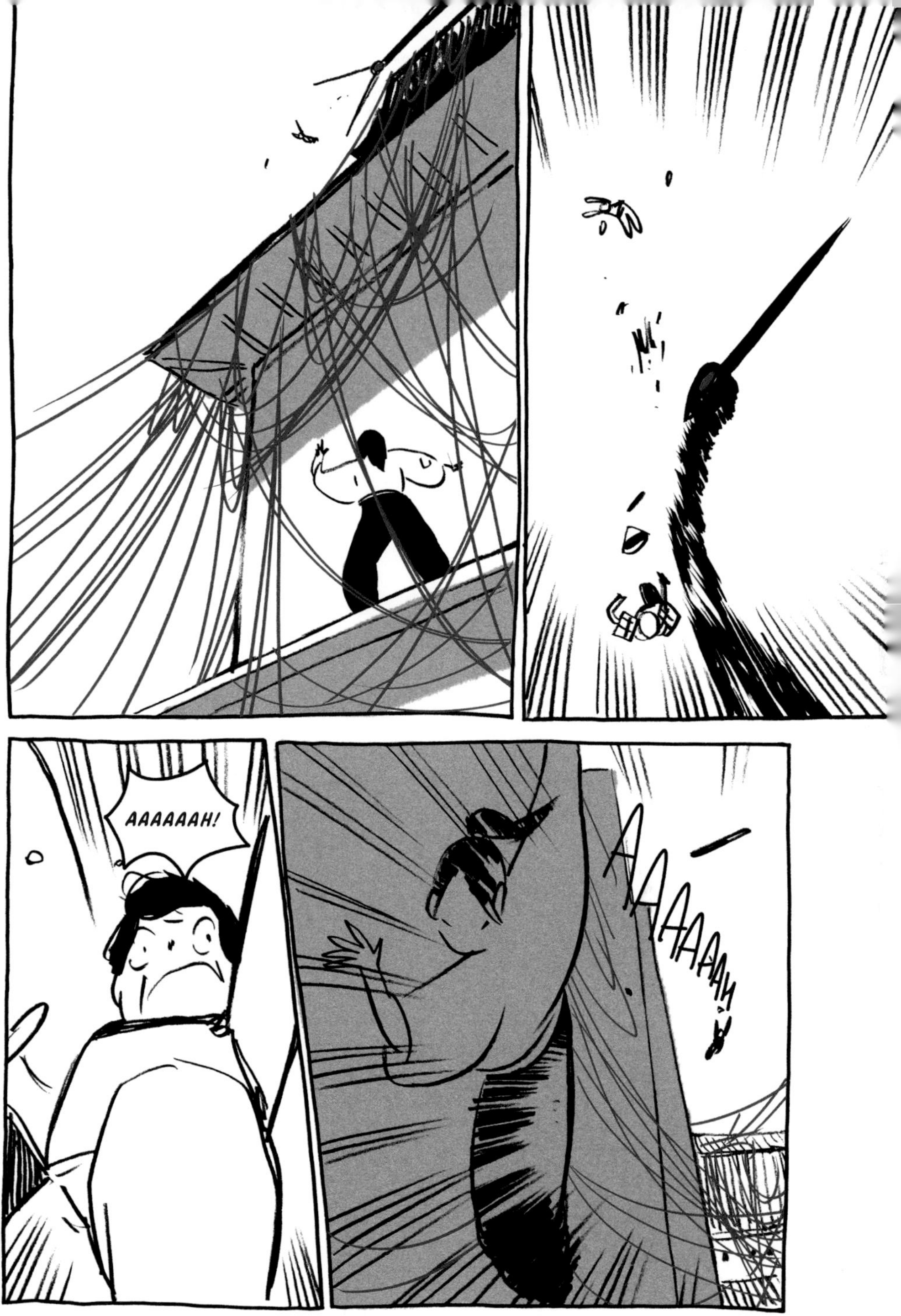
AAAAAAH!
AAAAAAAH

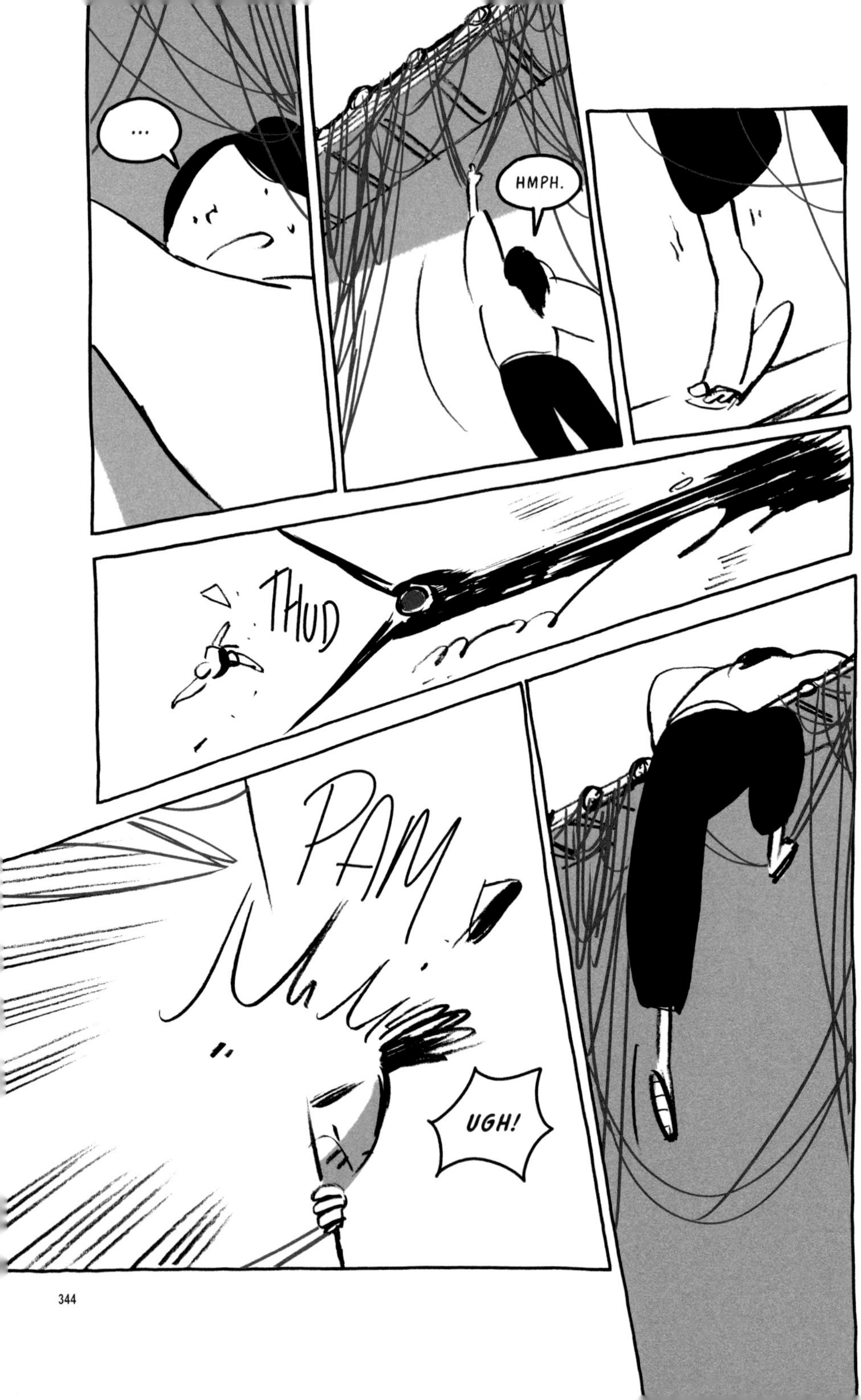
...
HMPH.
THUD
PAM
UGH!

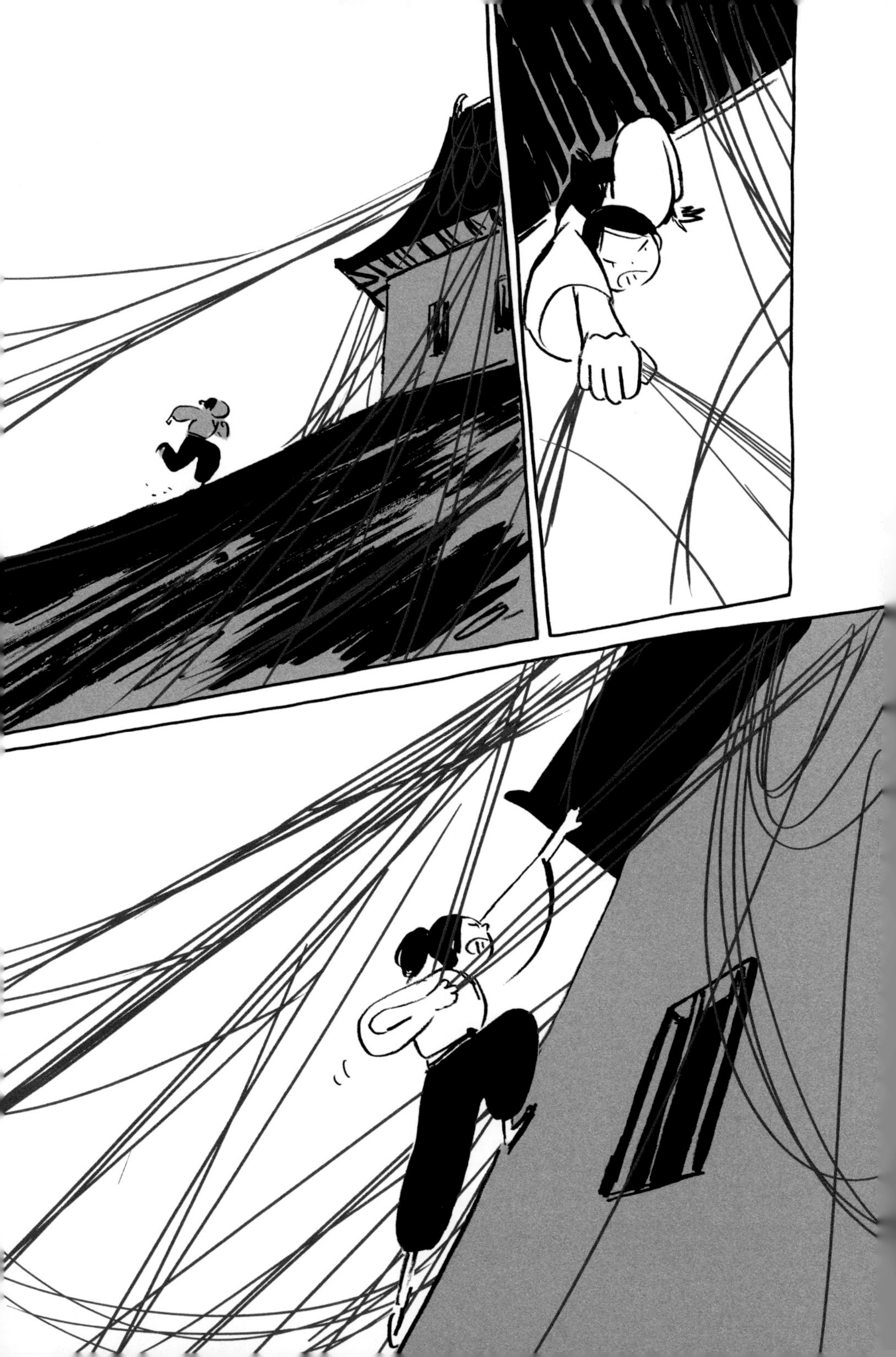

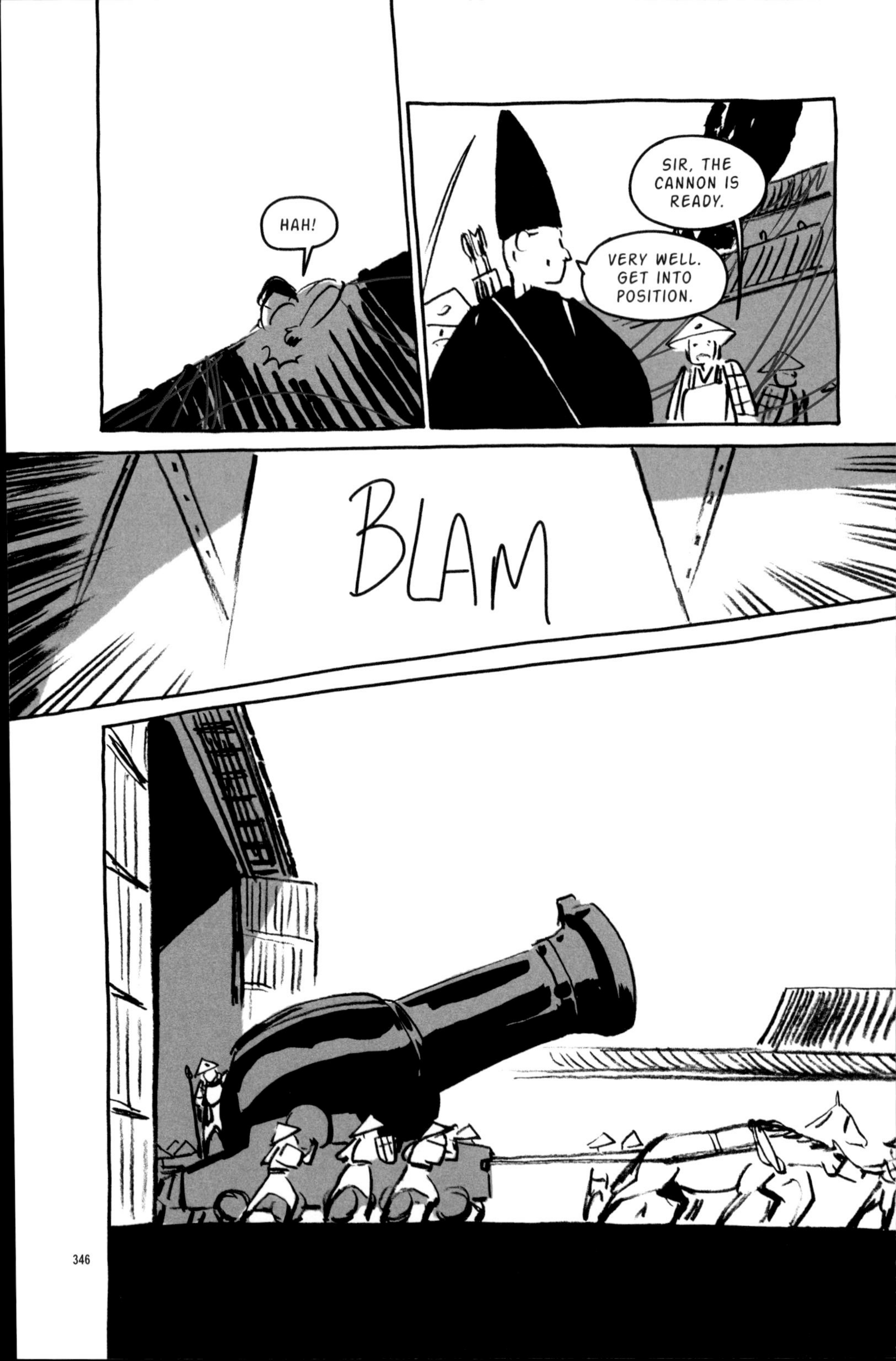
HAH!
SIR, THE CANNON IS READY.
VERY WELL. GET INTO POSITION.
BLAM

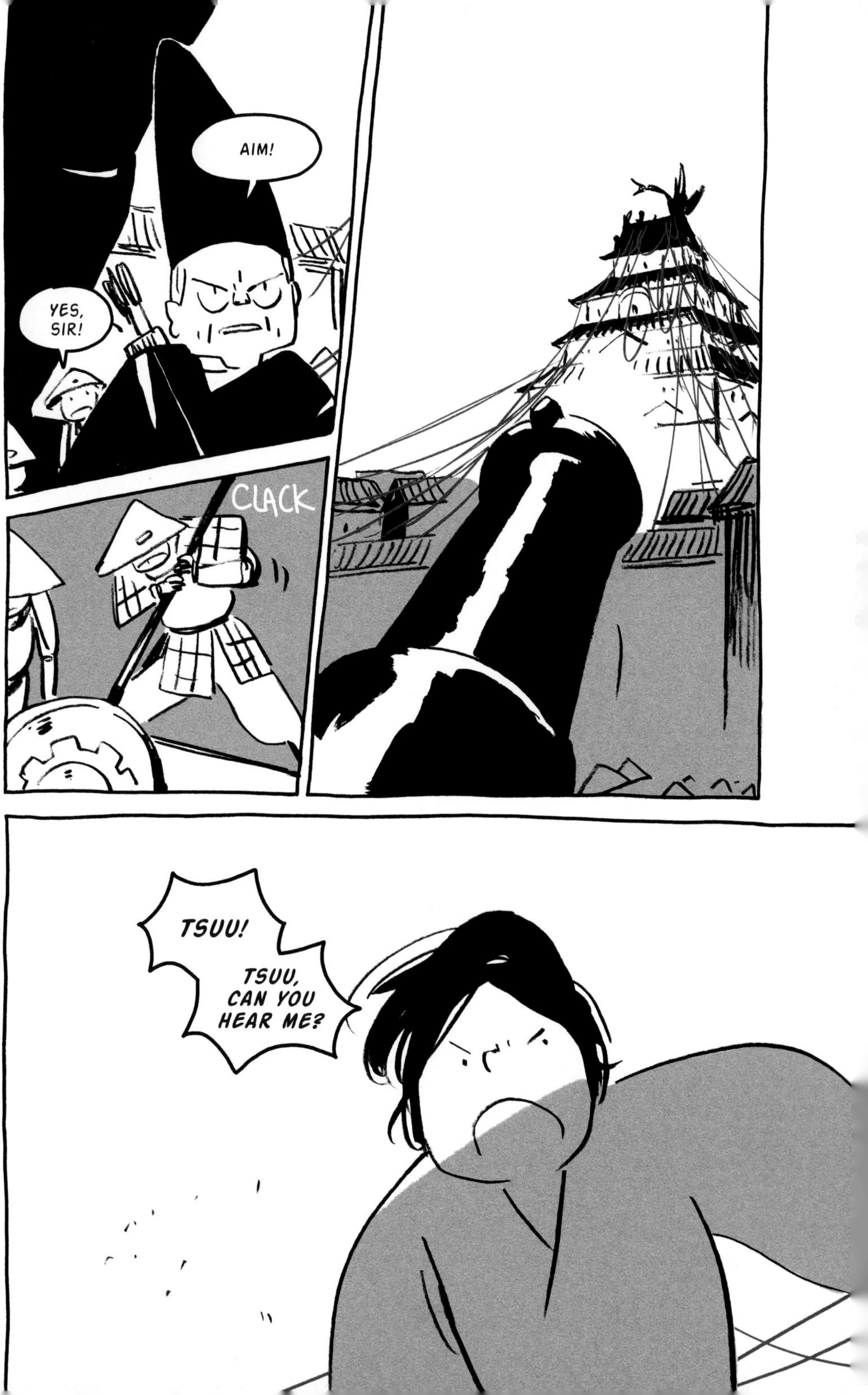
AIM!
YES, SIR!
CLACK
TSUU!
TSUU, CAN YOU HEAR ME?

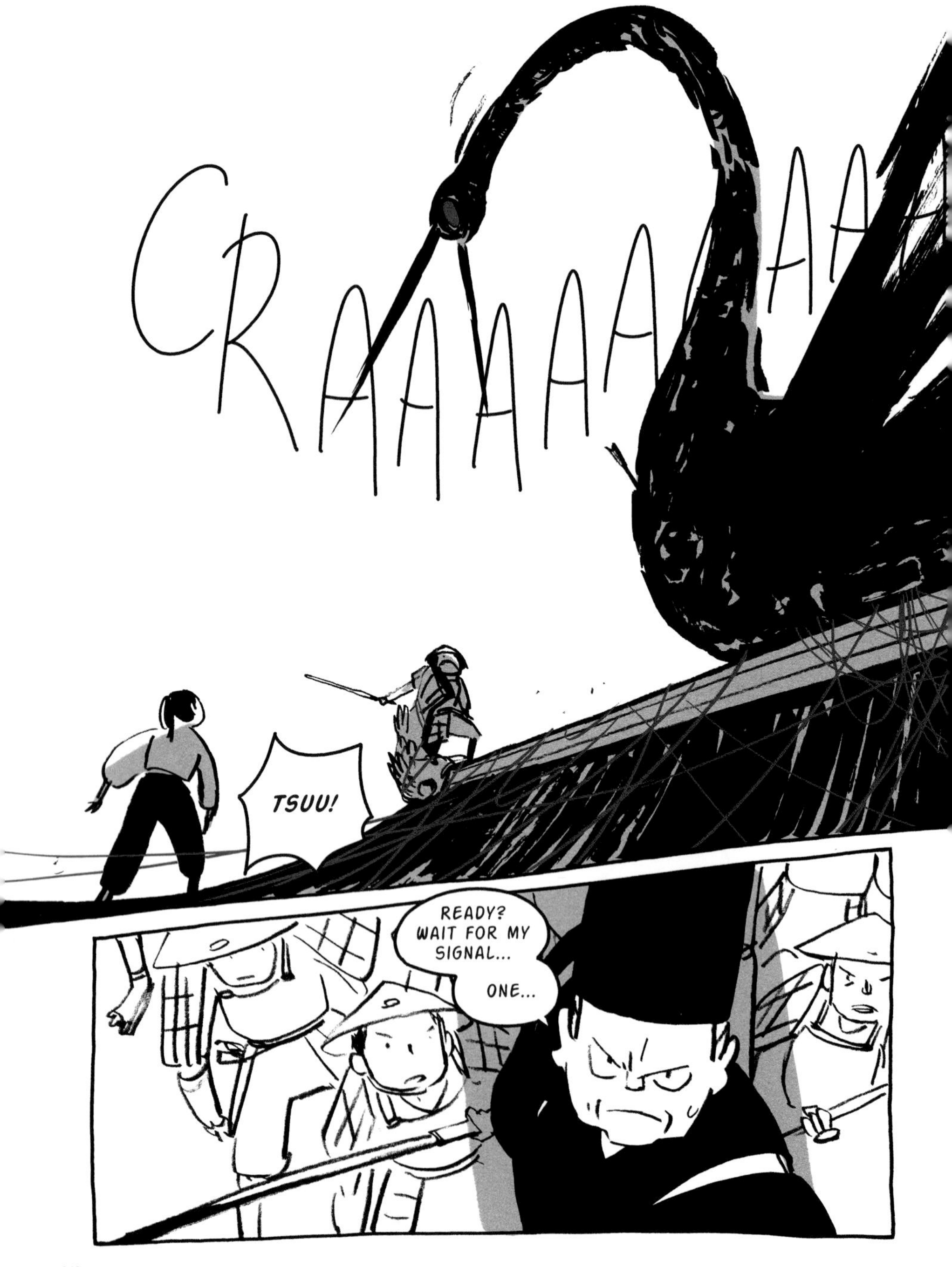
CRAAAAAAAAA
TSUU!
READY? WAIT FOR MY SIGNAL...
ONE...

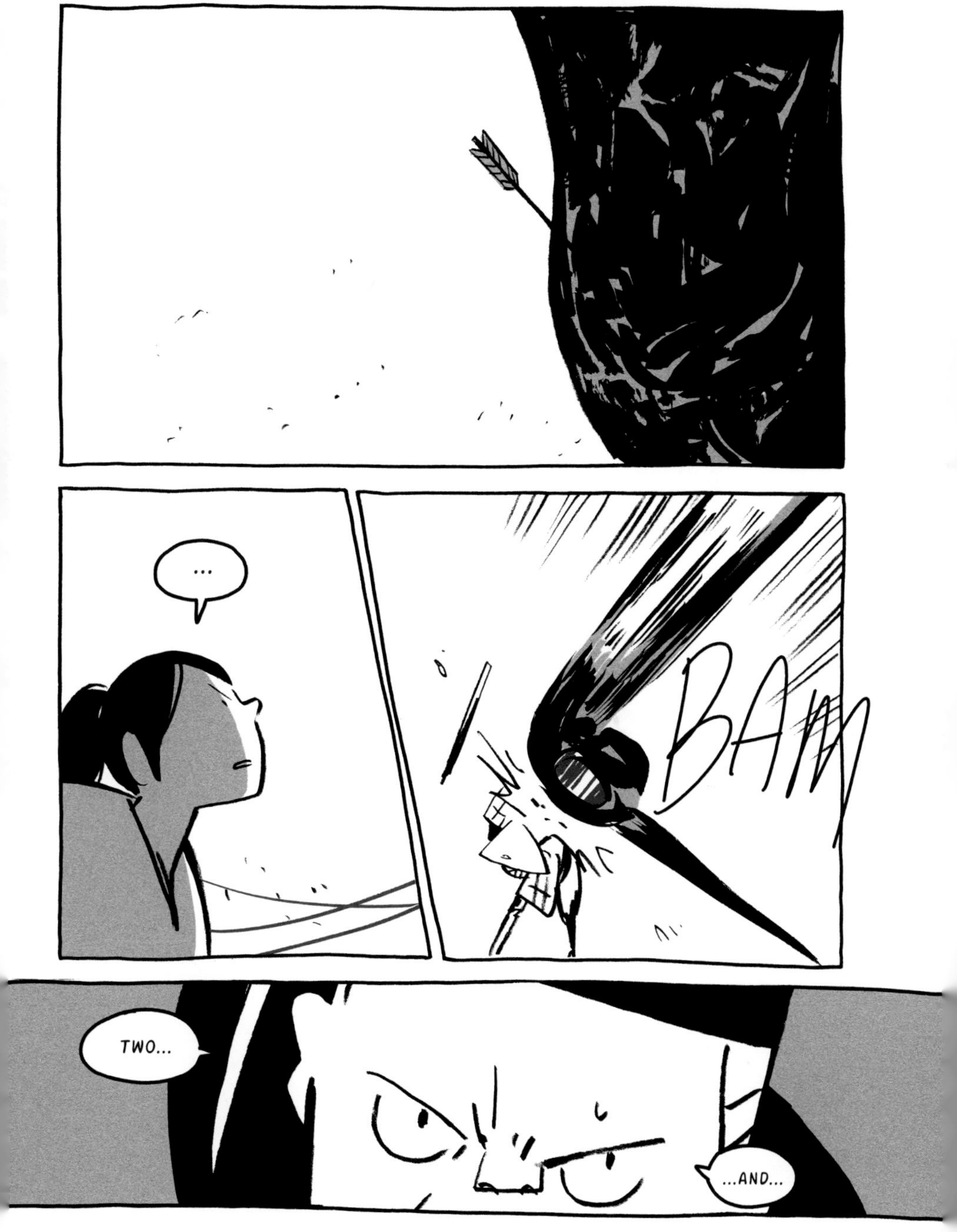
...
BAM
TWO...
...AND...

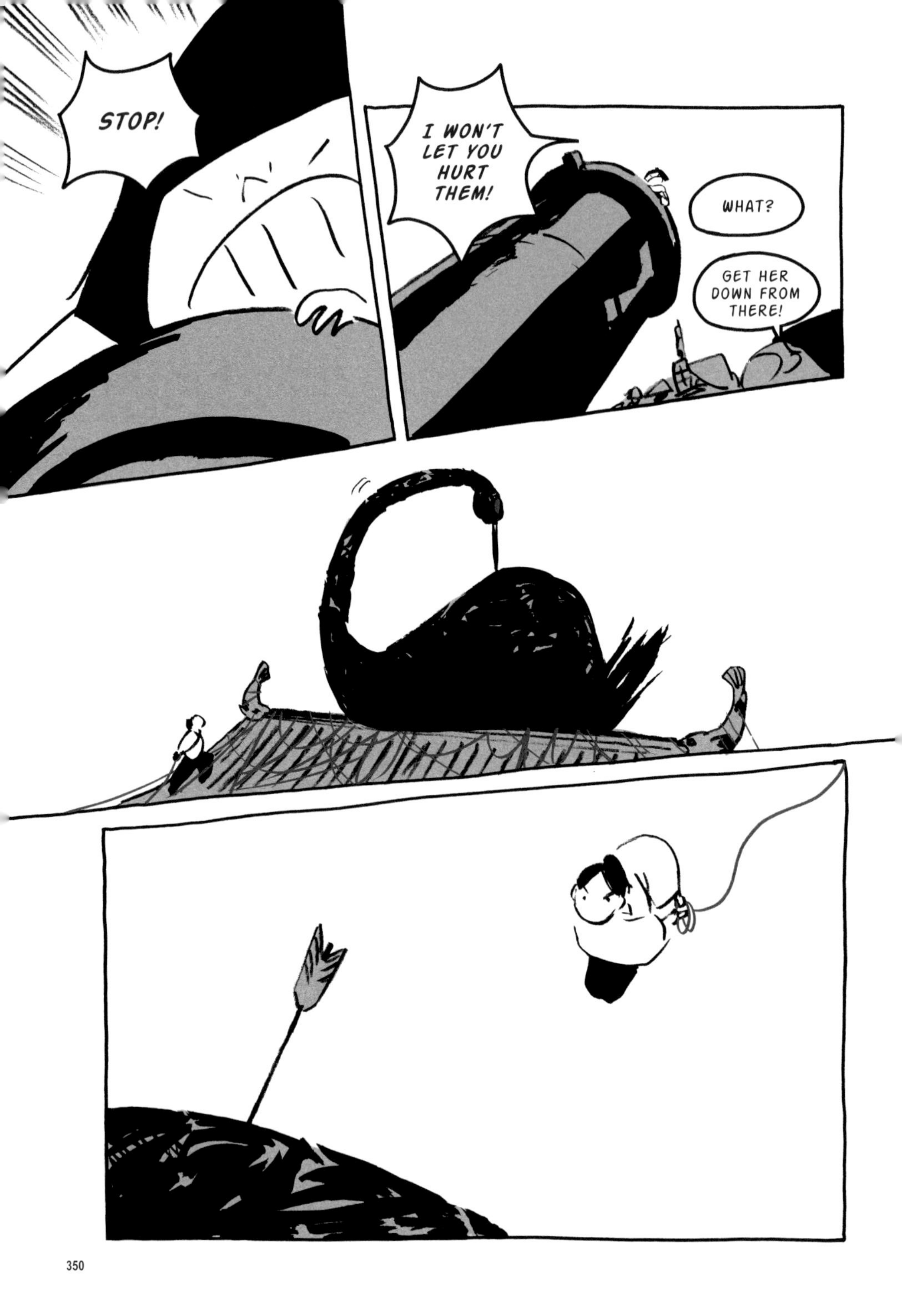
STOP!
I WON'T LET YOU HURT THEM!
WHAT?
GET HER DOWN FROM THERE!

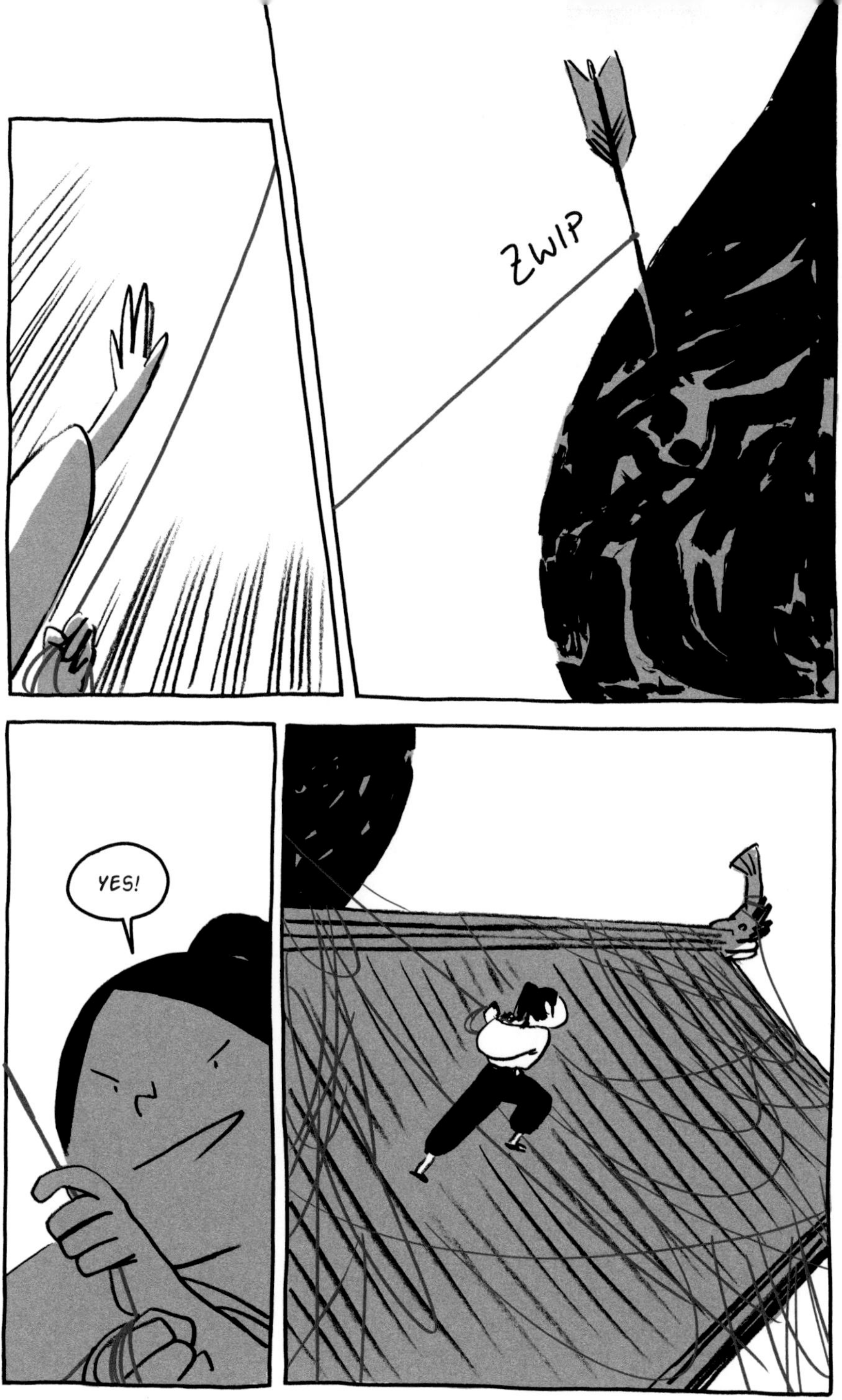
ZWIP
YES!

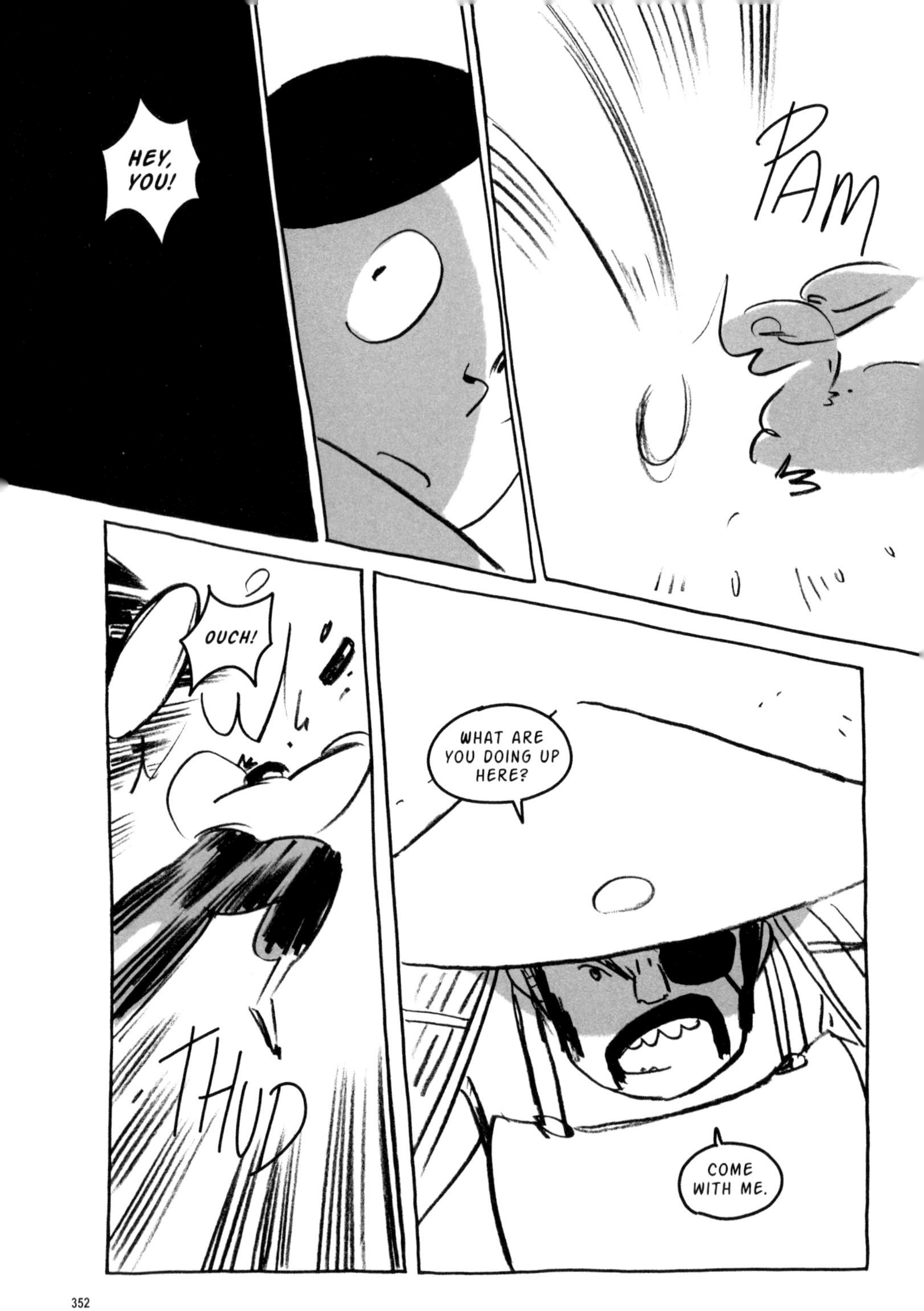
HEY, YOU!
PAM
OUCH!
THUD
WHAT ARE YOU DOING UP HERE?
COME WITH ME.

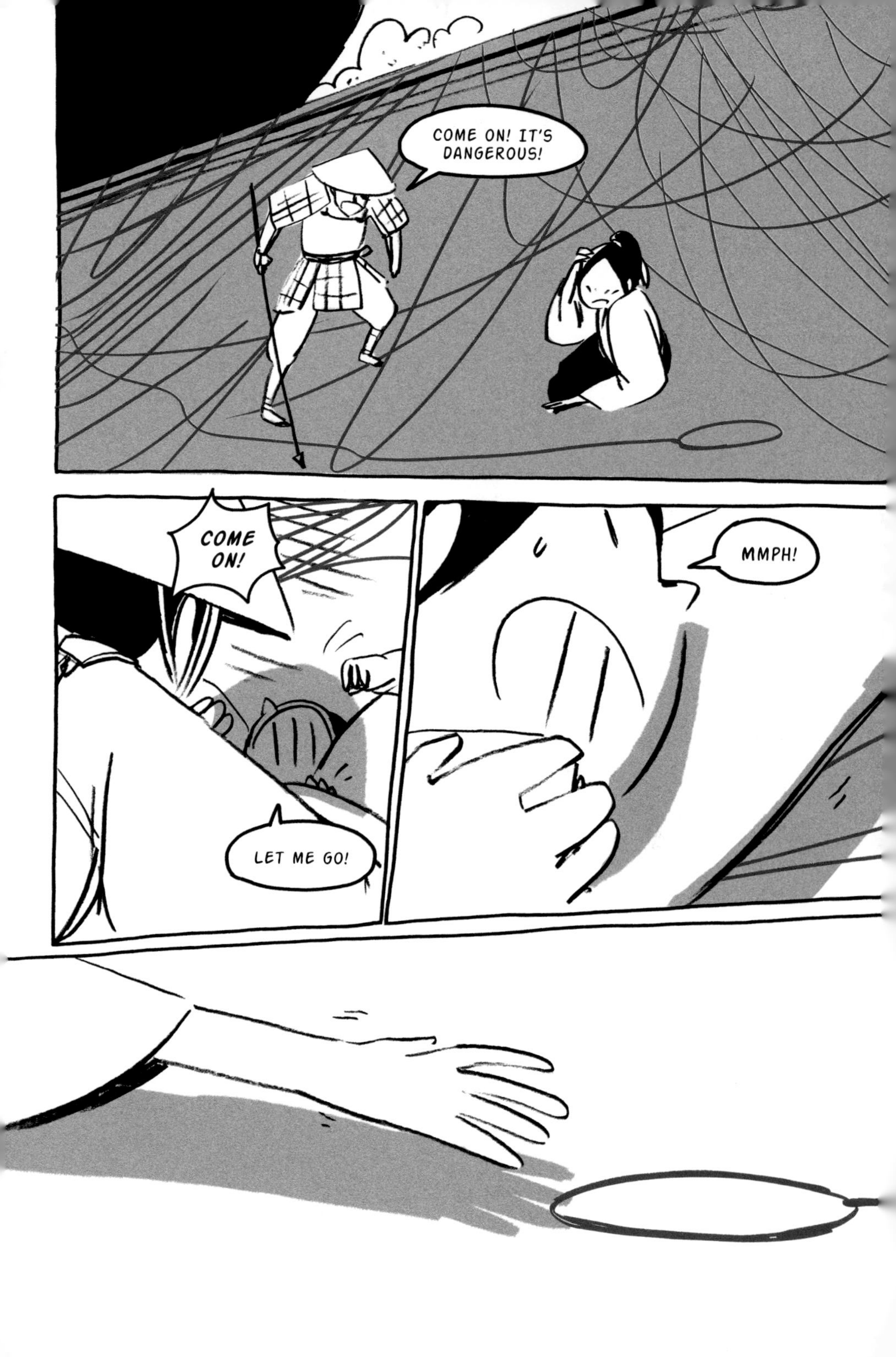
COME ON! IT'S DANGEROUS!
COME ON!
LET ME GO!
MMPH!

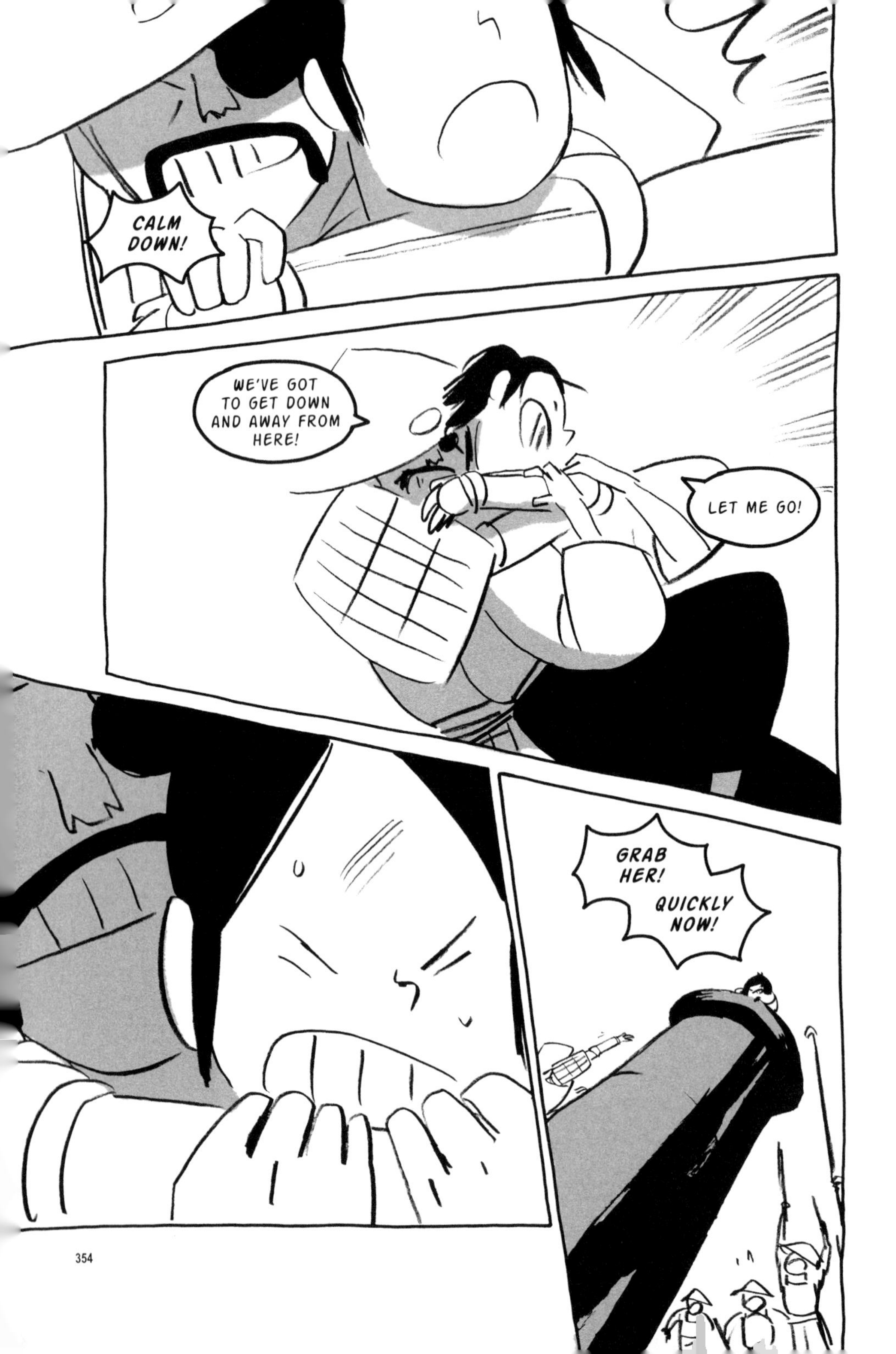
CALM DOWN!
WE'VE GOT TO GET DOWN AND AWAY FROM HERE!
LET ME GO!
GRAB HER! QUICKLY NOW!

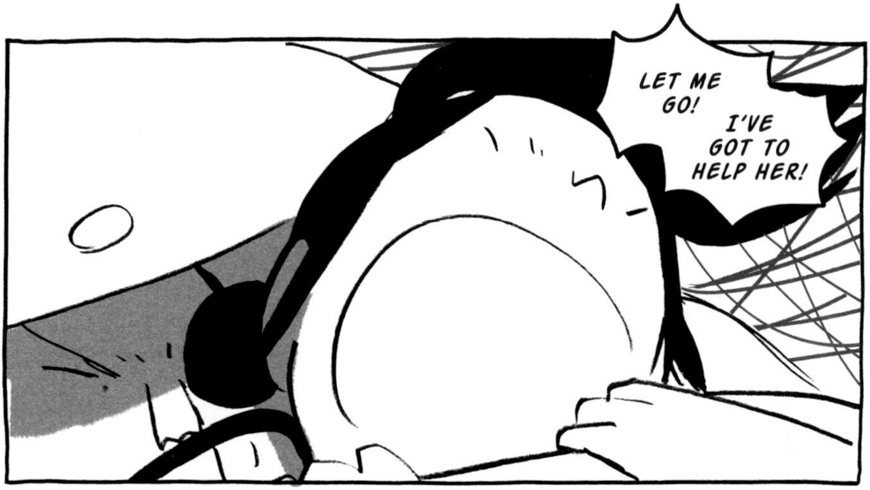
LET ME GO! I'VE GOT TO HELP HER!

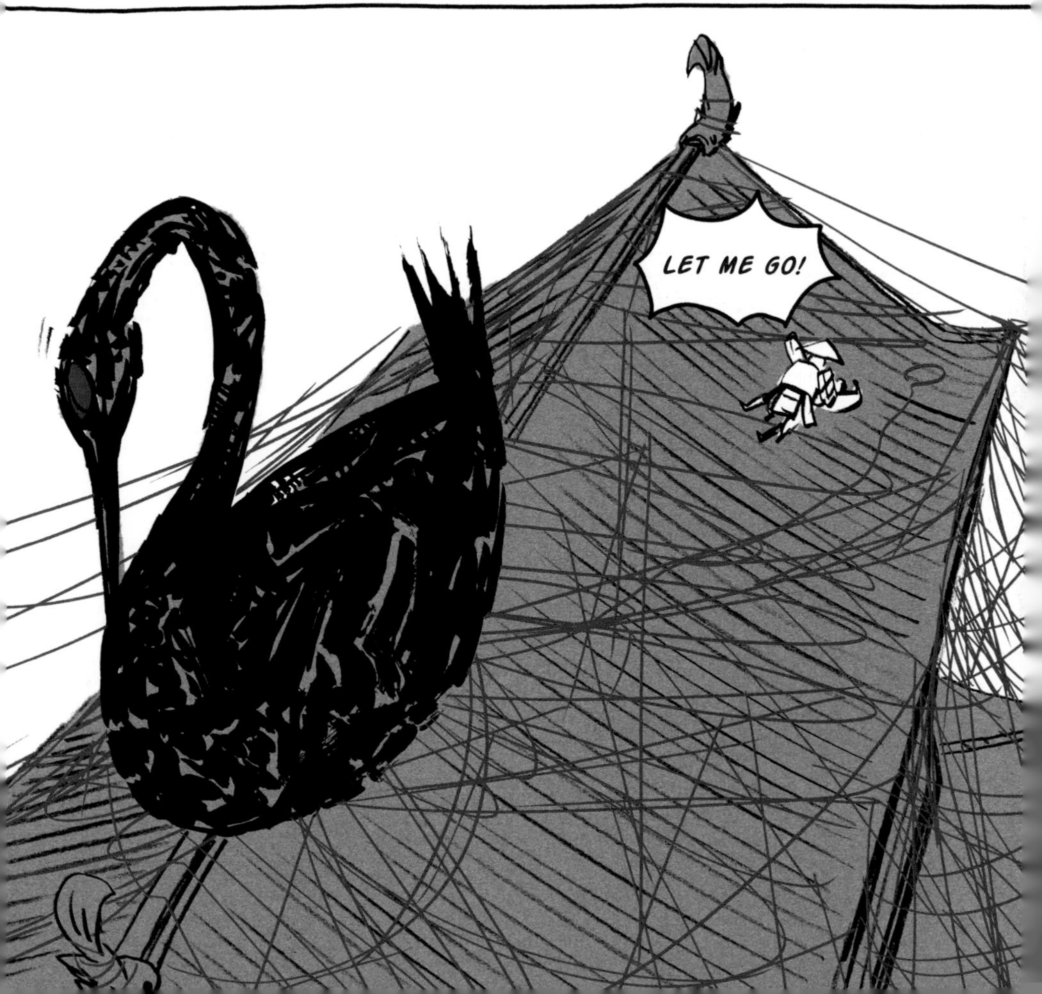
LET ME GO!

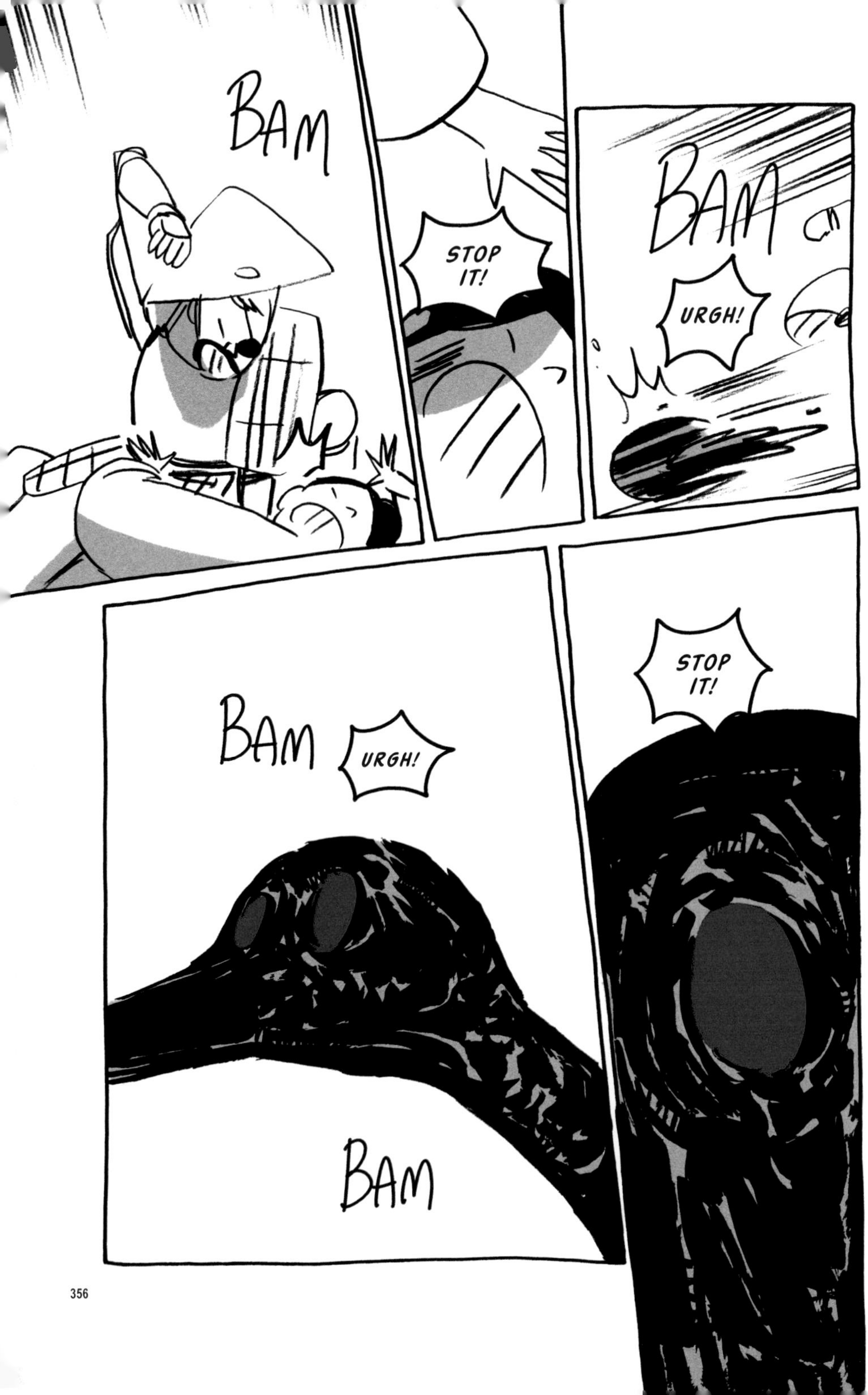
BAM
STOP IT!
BAM
URGH!
BAM
URGH!
BAM
STOP IT!

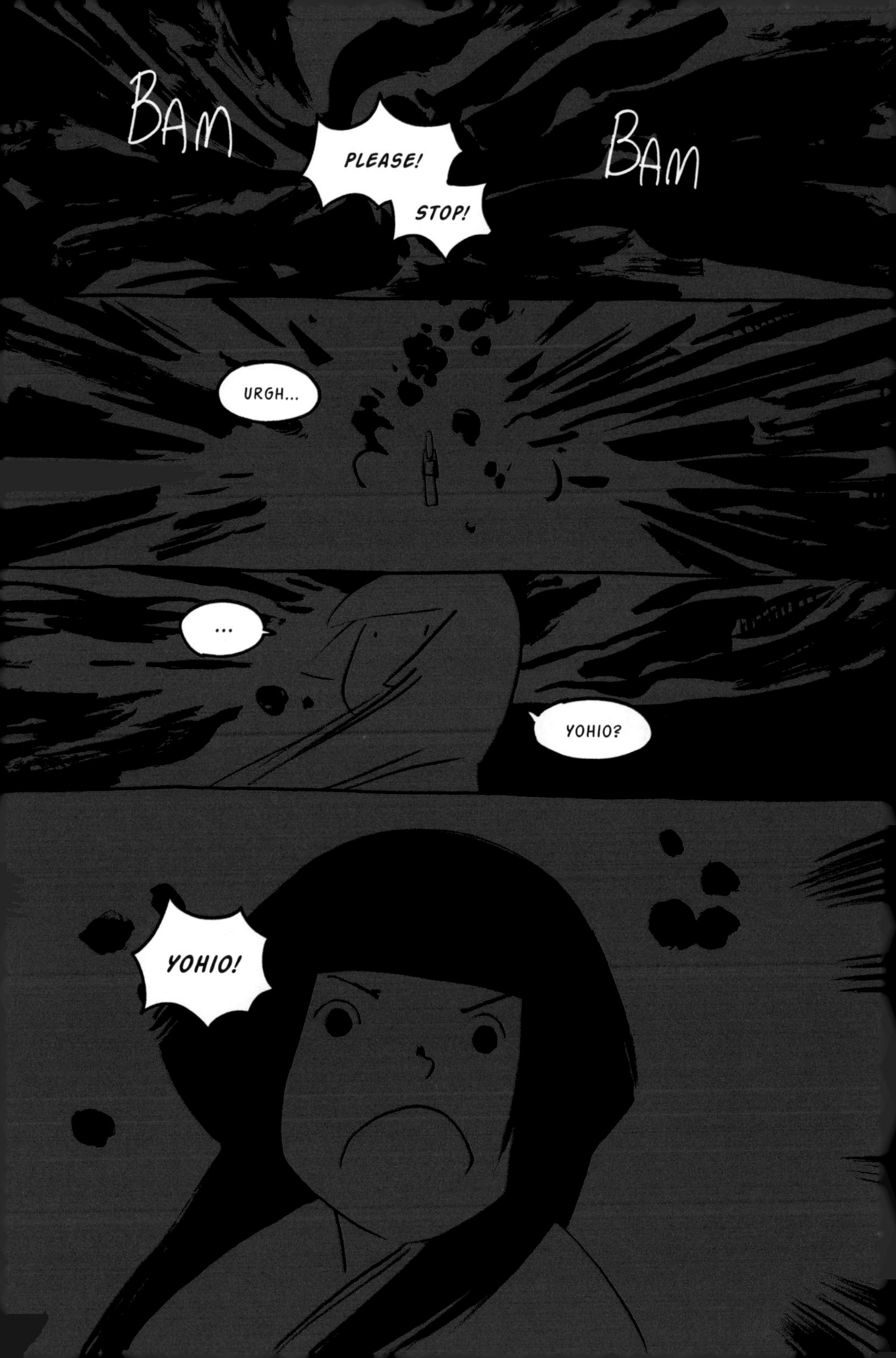
BAM
PLEASE!
STOP!
BAM
URGH...
...
YOHIO?
YOHIO!

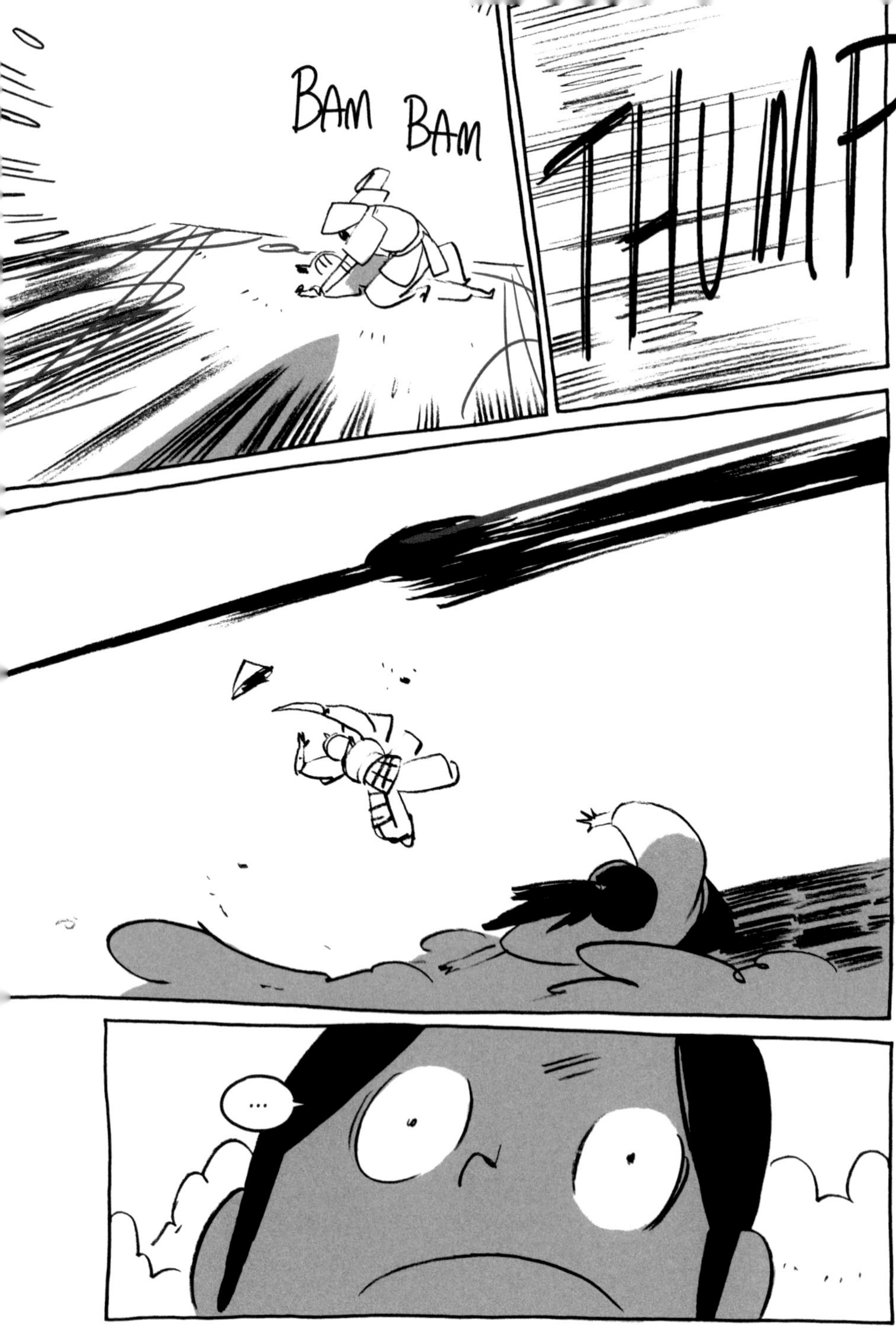
BAM BAM
THUMP
...

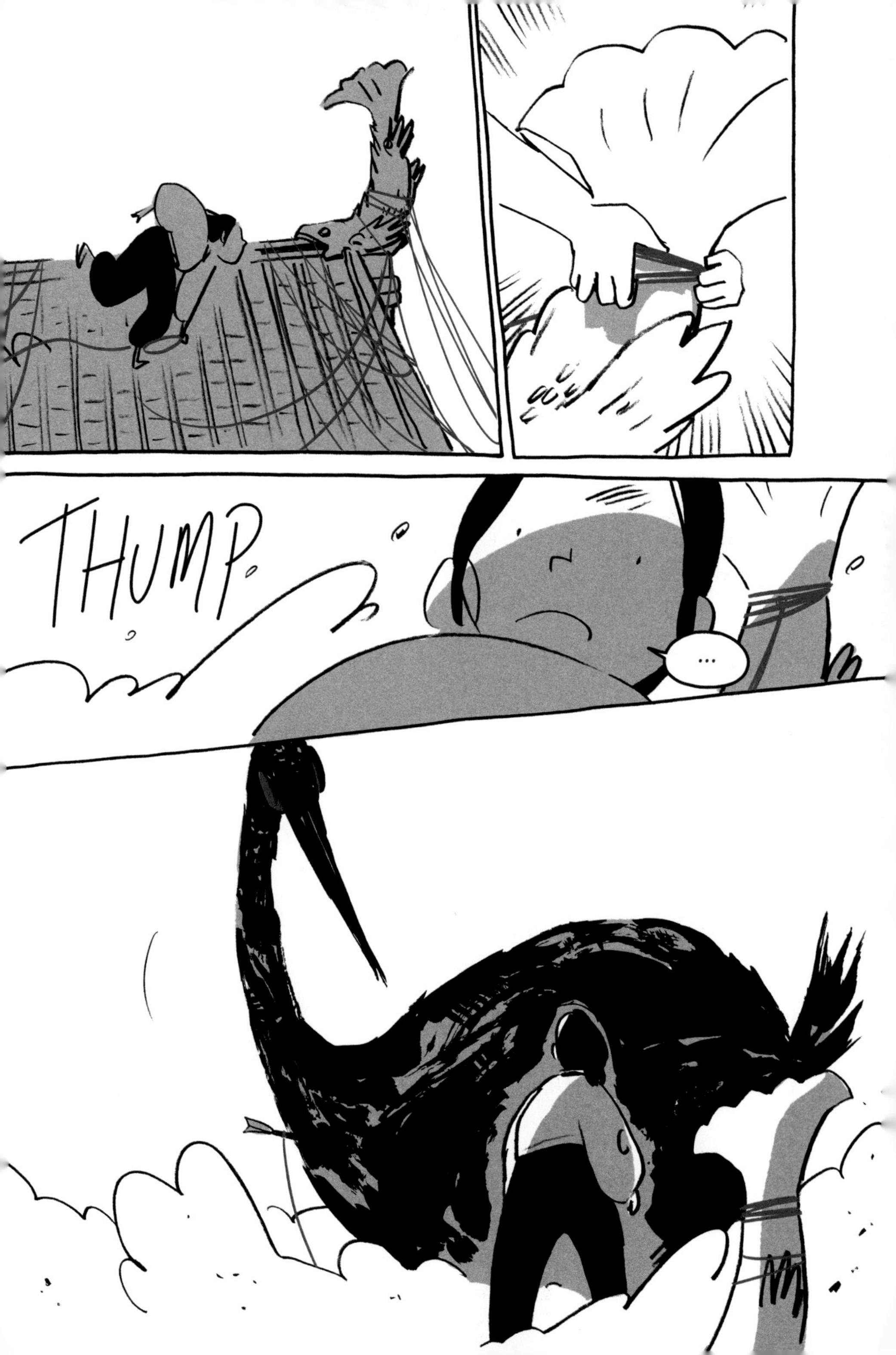
THUMP
...

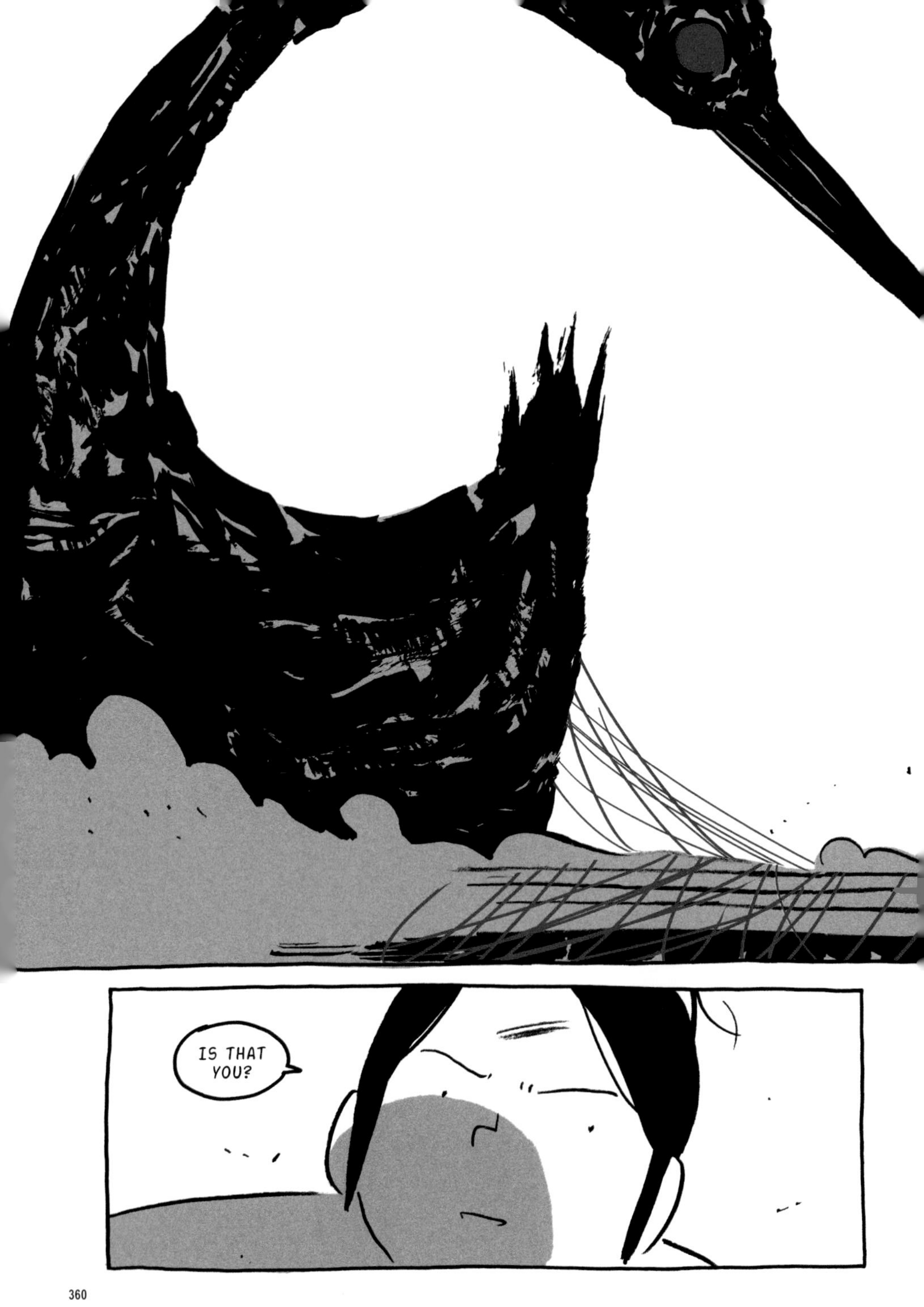
IS THAT YOU?

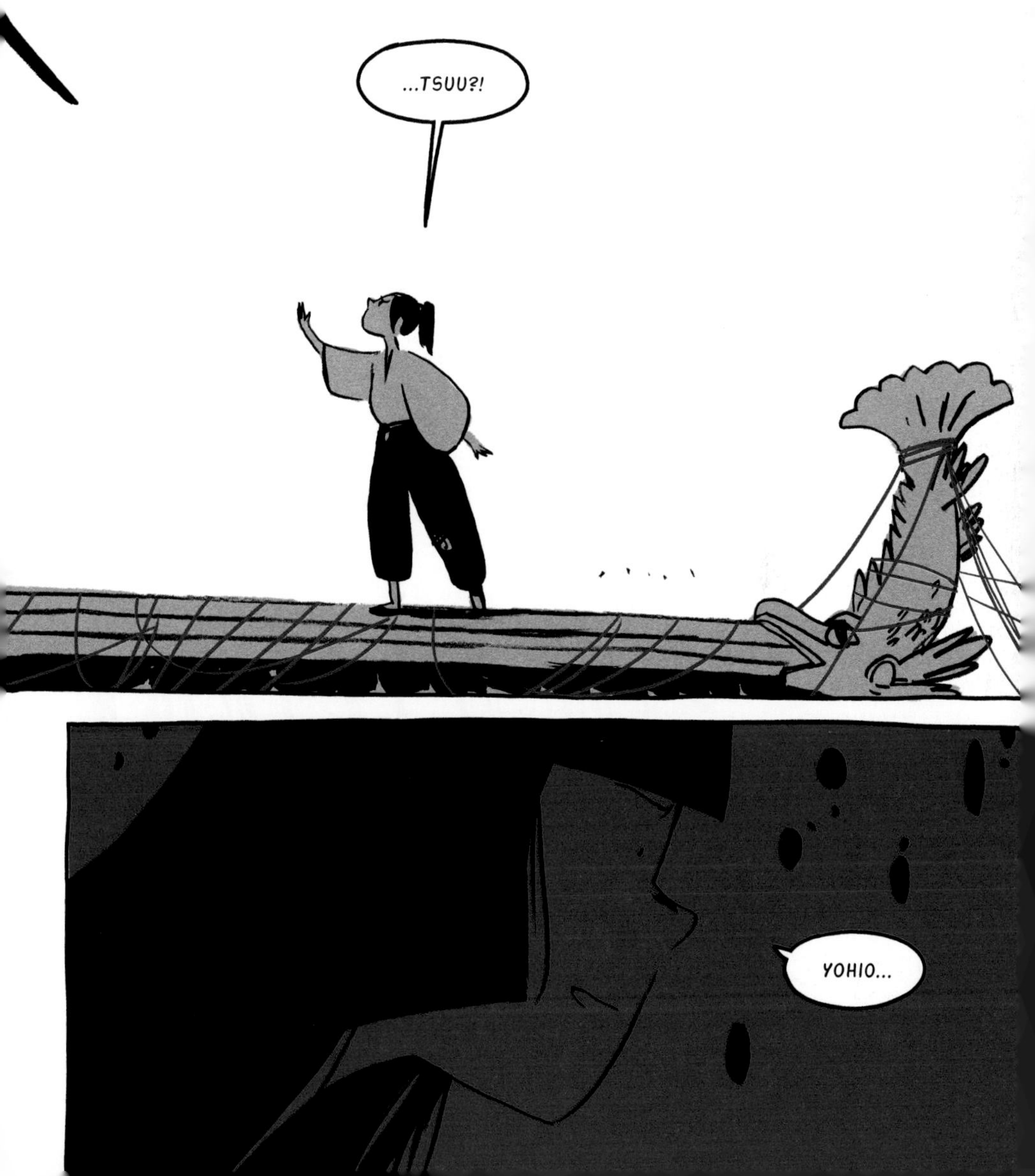
...TSUU?!
YOHIO...

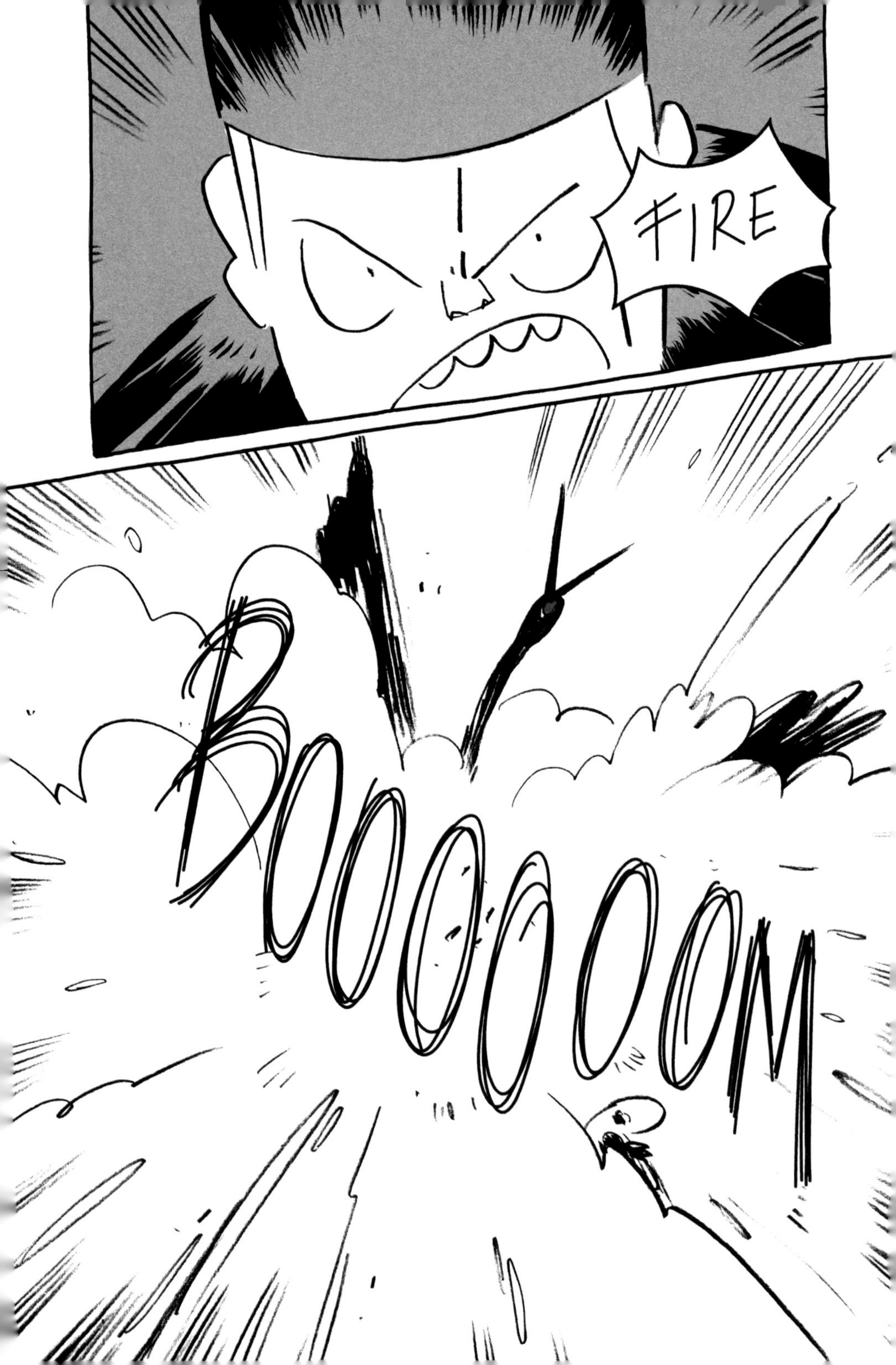
FIRE
BOOOOOOM

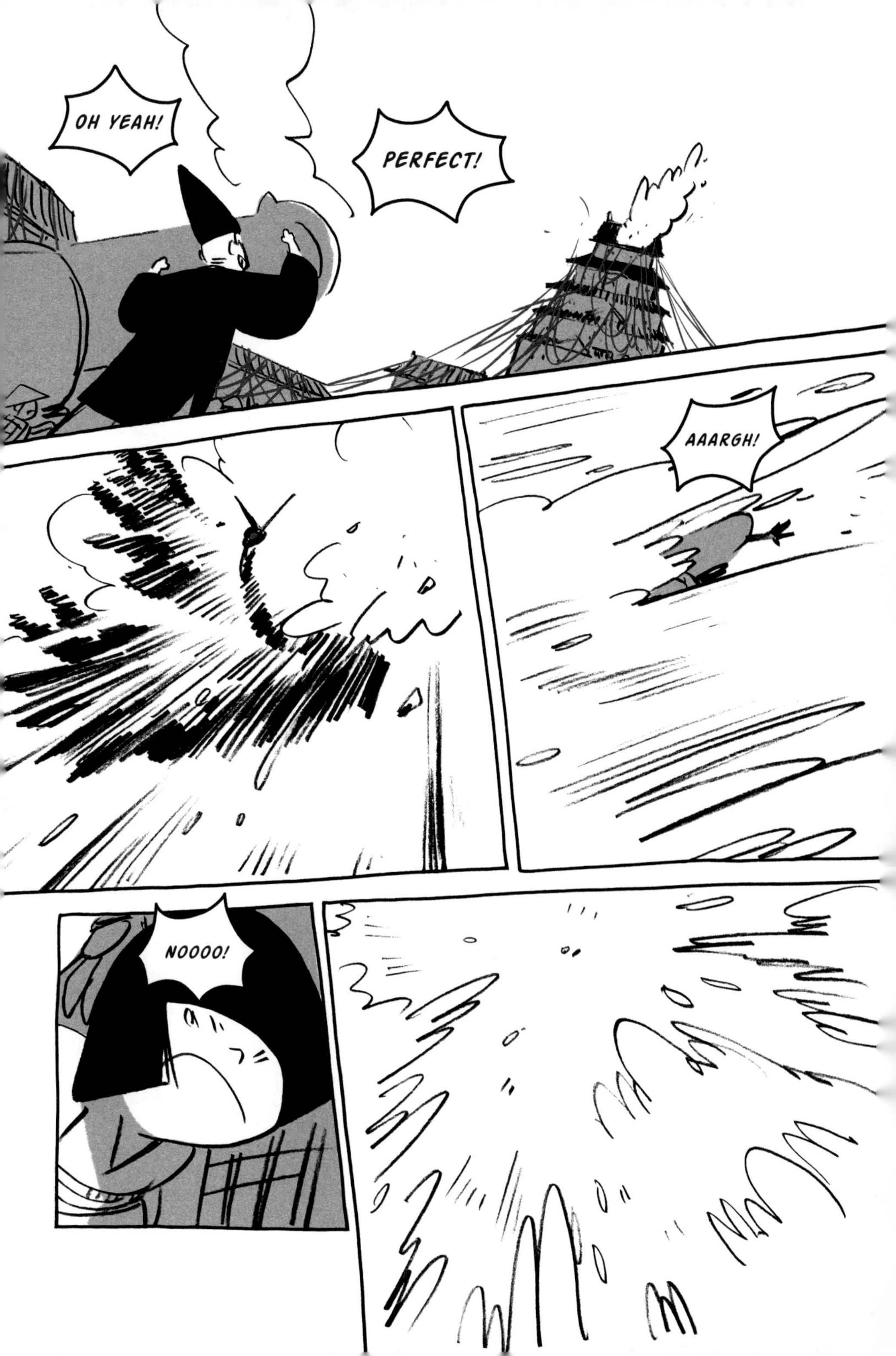
OH YEAH!
PERFECT!
AAARGH!
NOOOO!

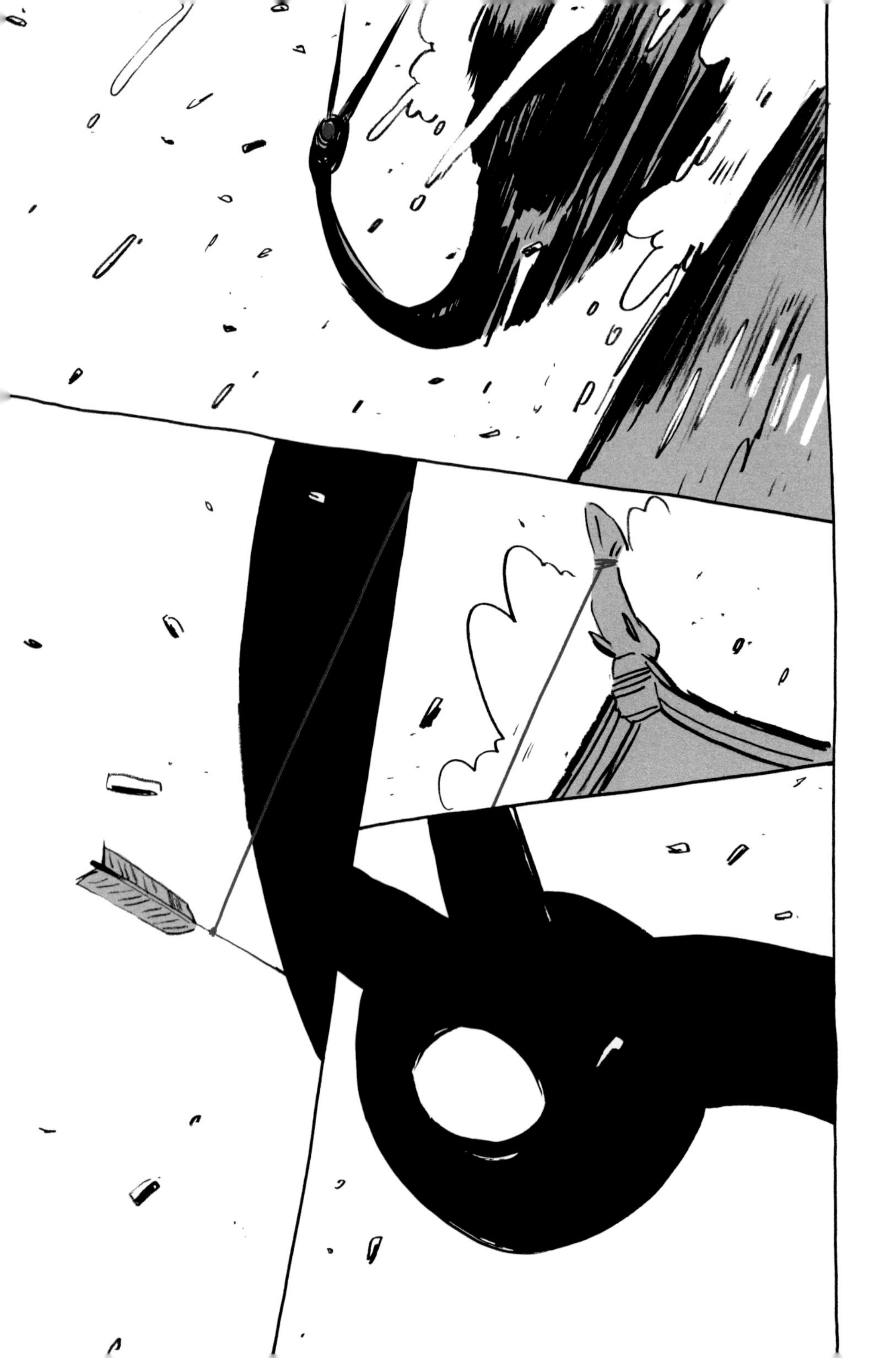

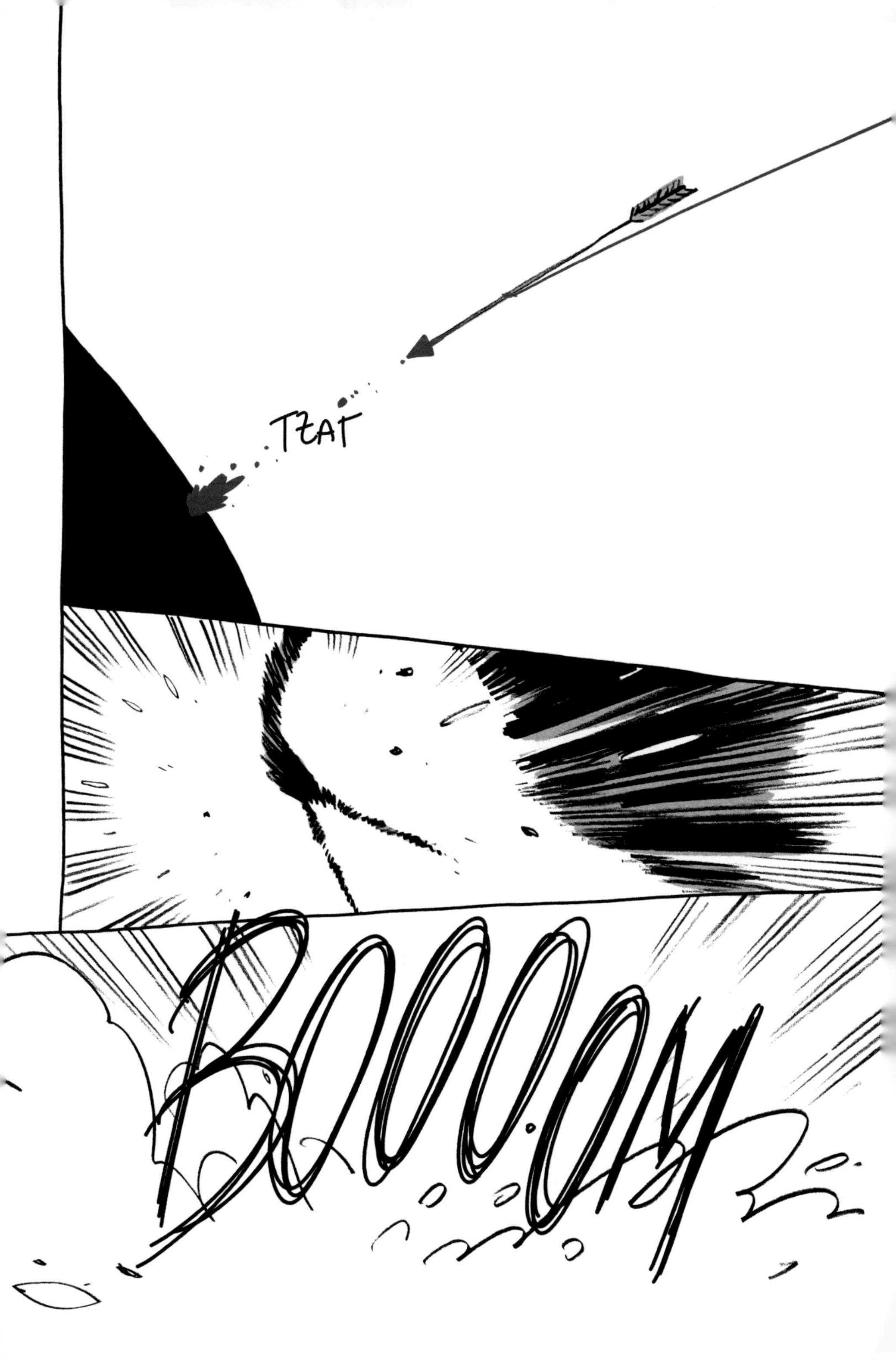
TZAT
BOOOOM

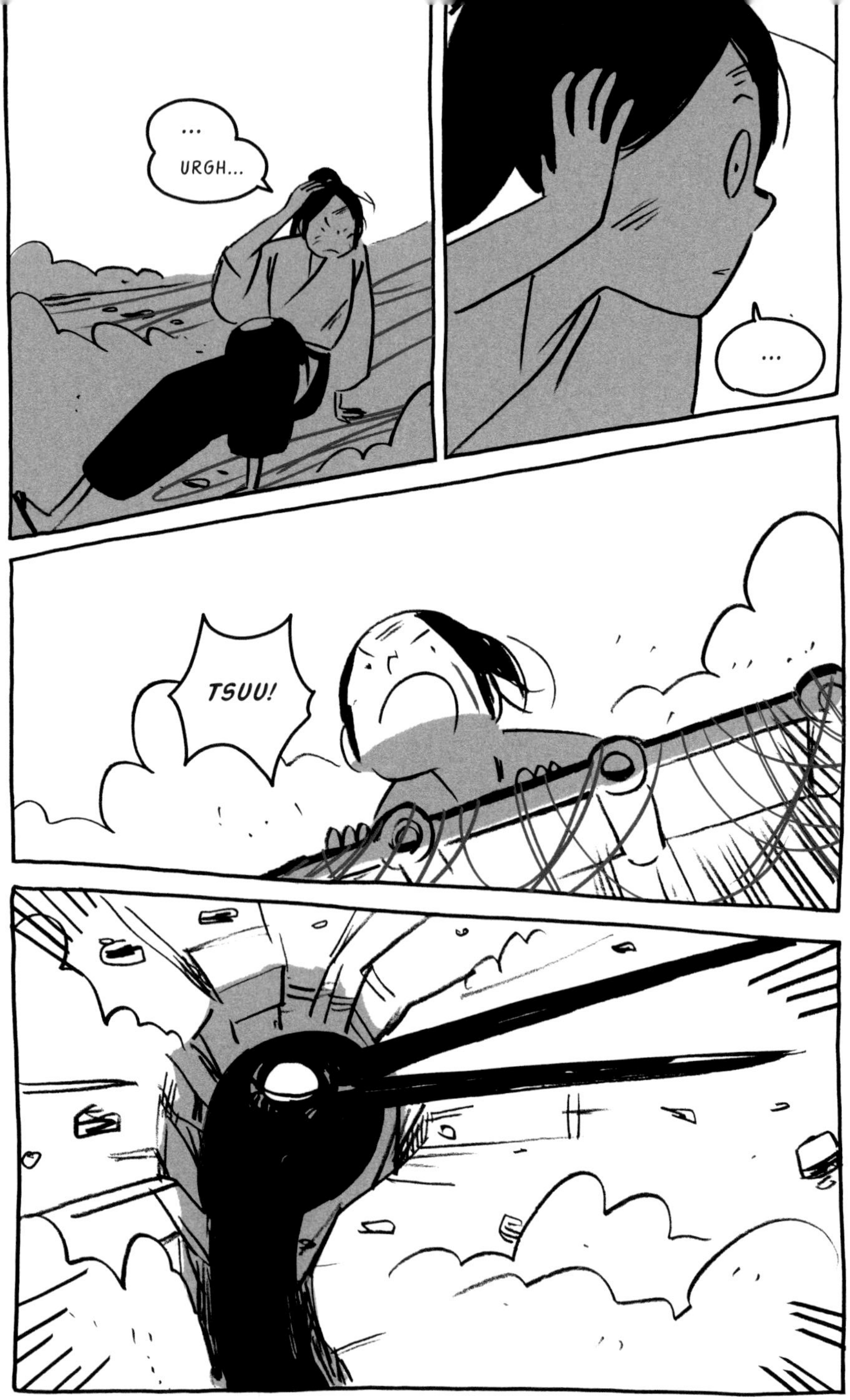
...
URGH...
...
TSUU!

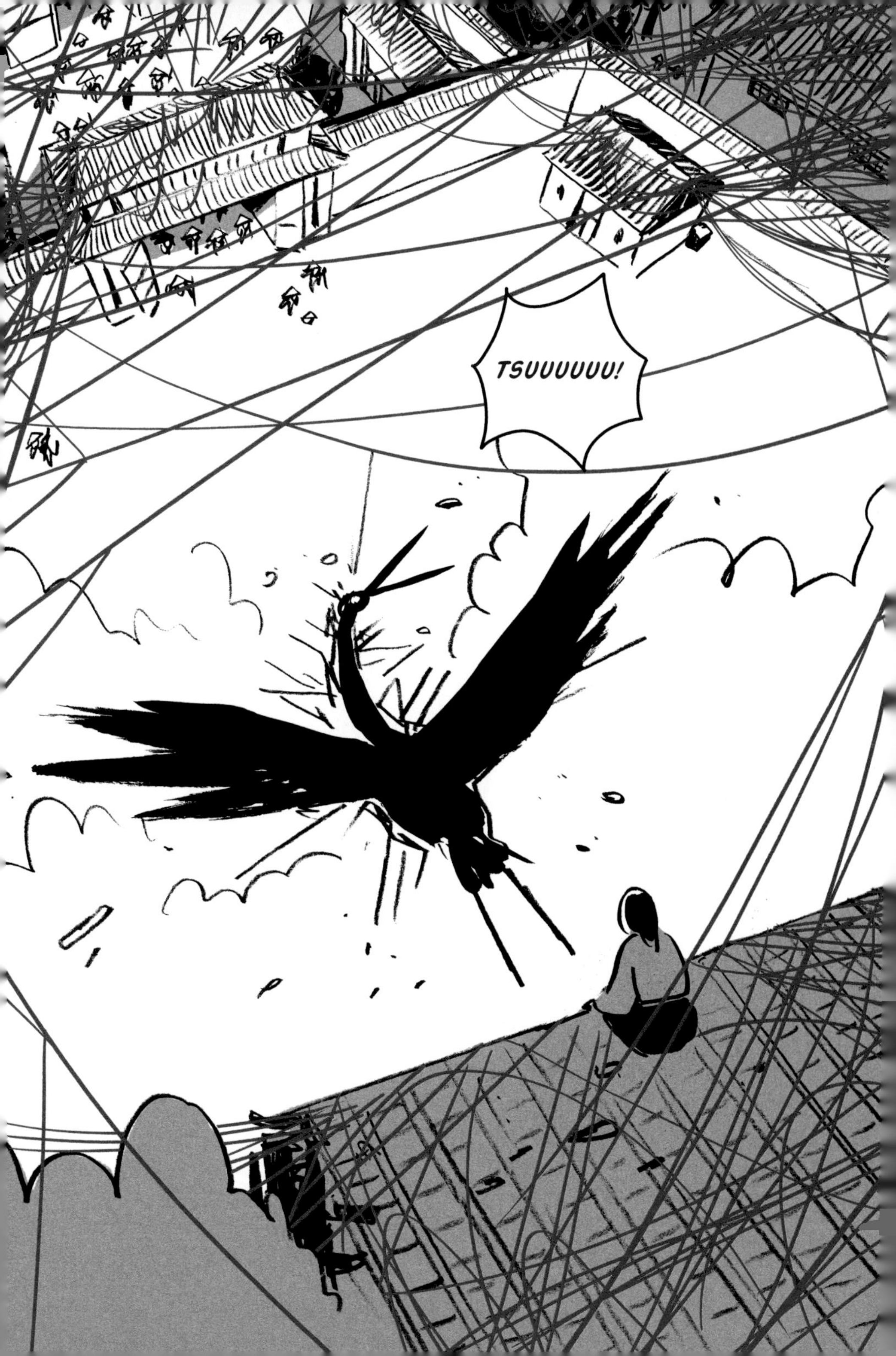
TSUUUUUU!

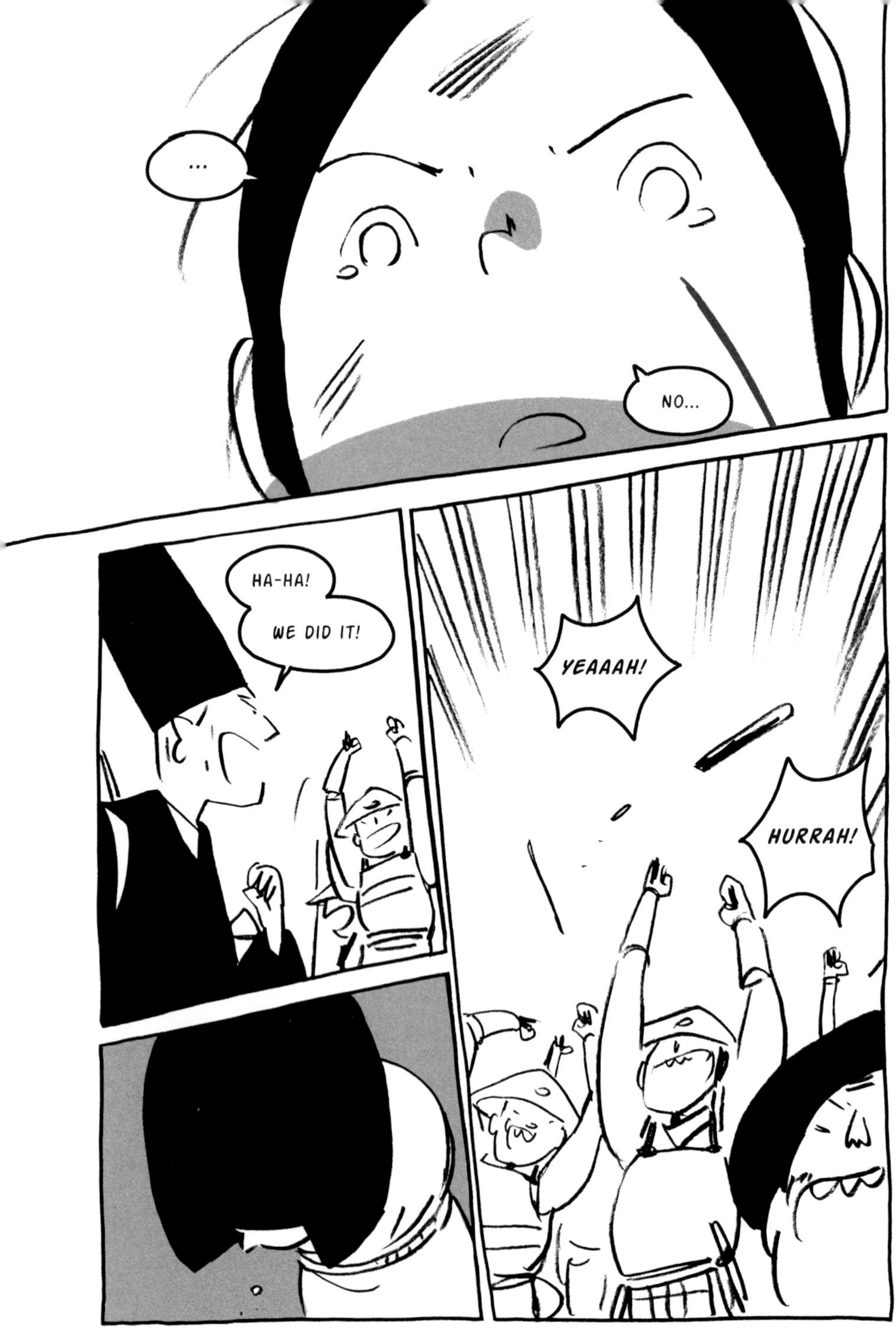
...
NO...
HA-HA!
WE DID IT!
YEAAAH!
HURRAH!

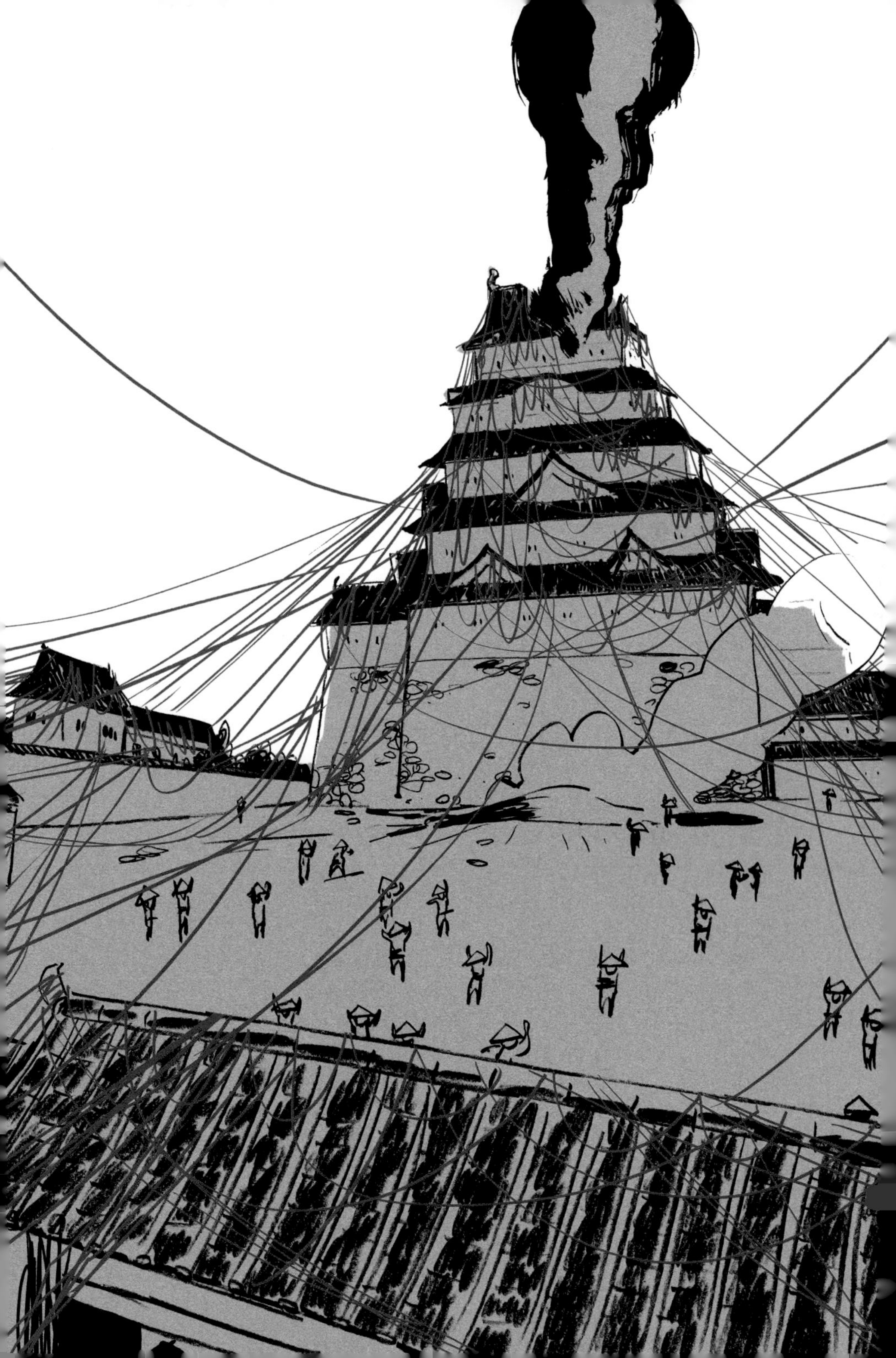

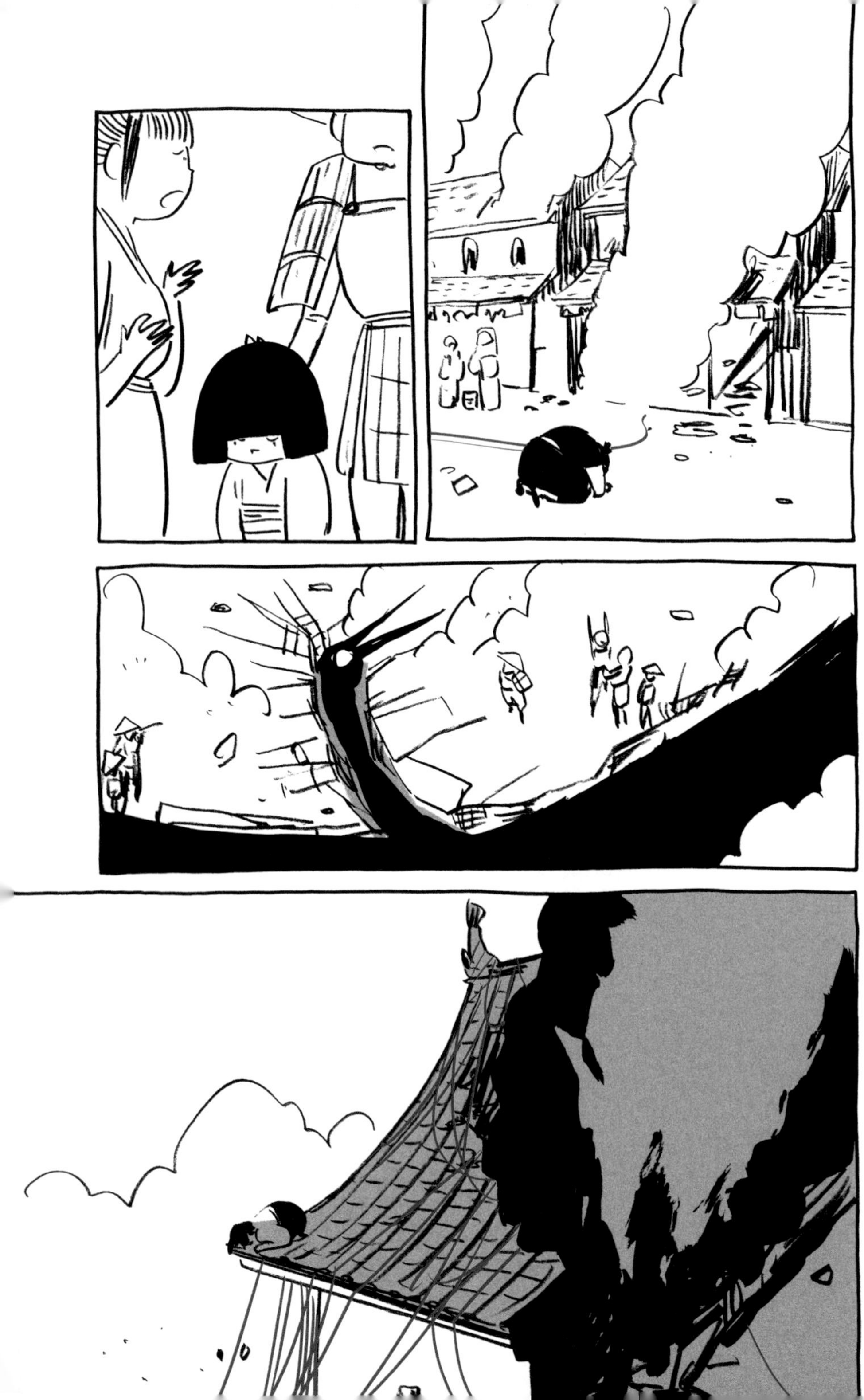

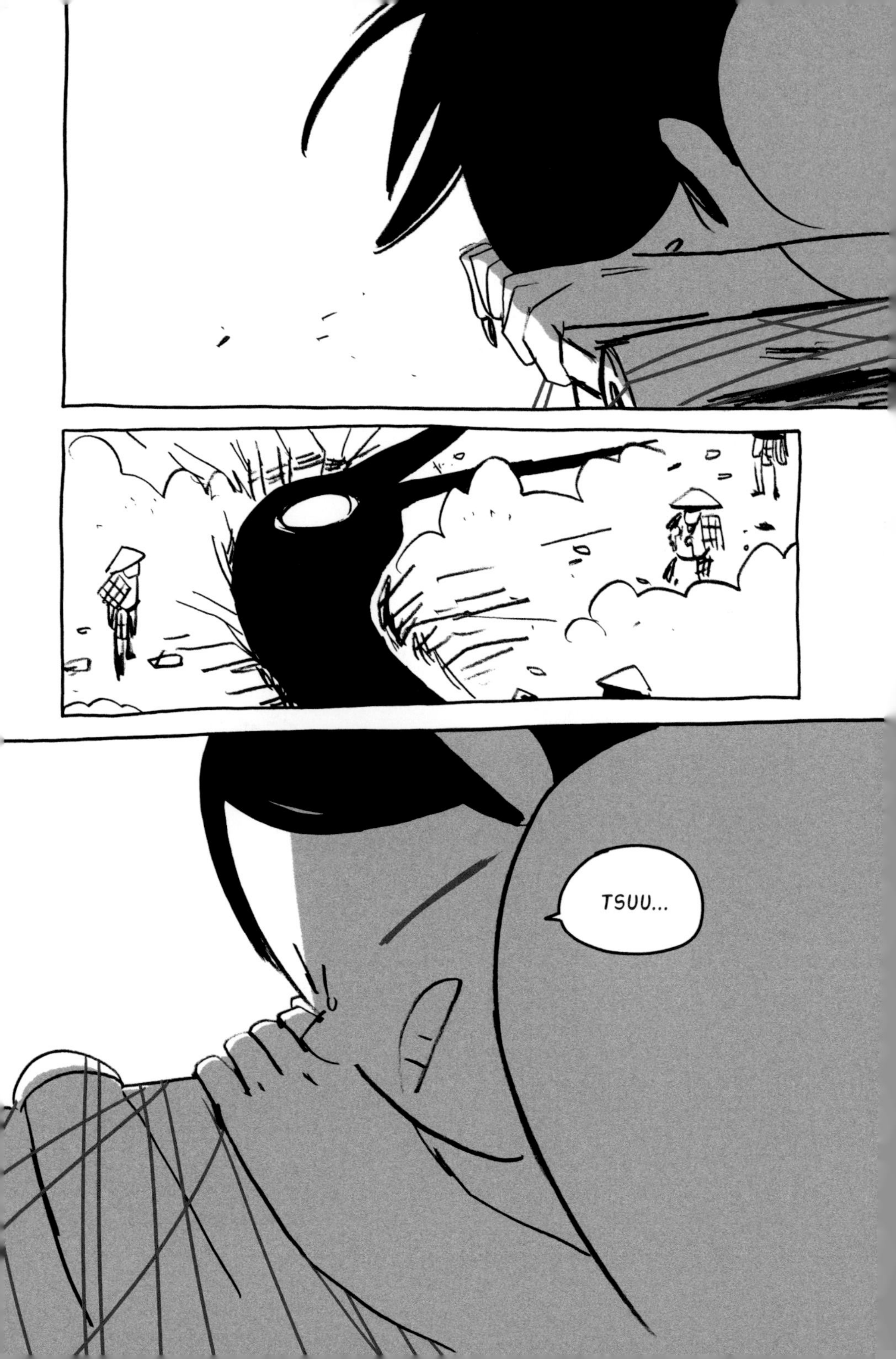
TSUU...

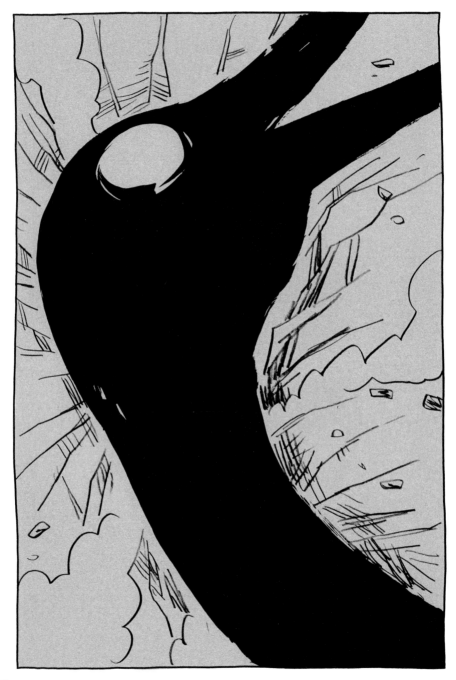

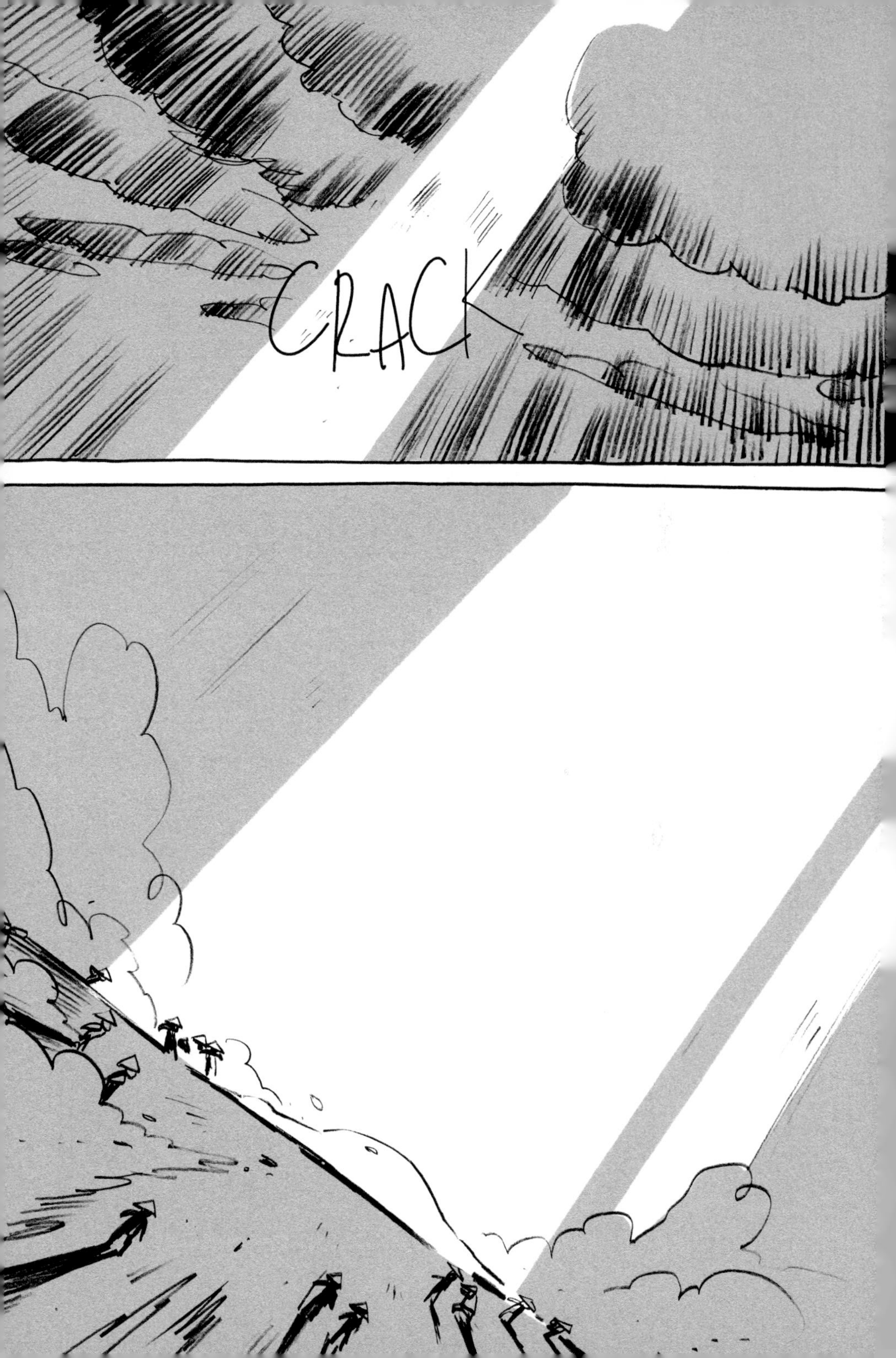
CRACK

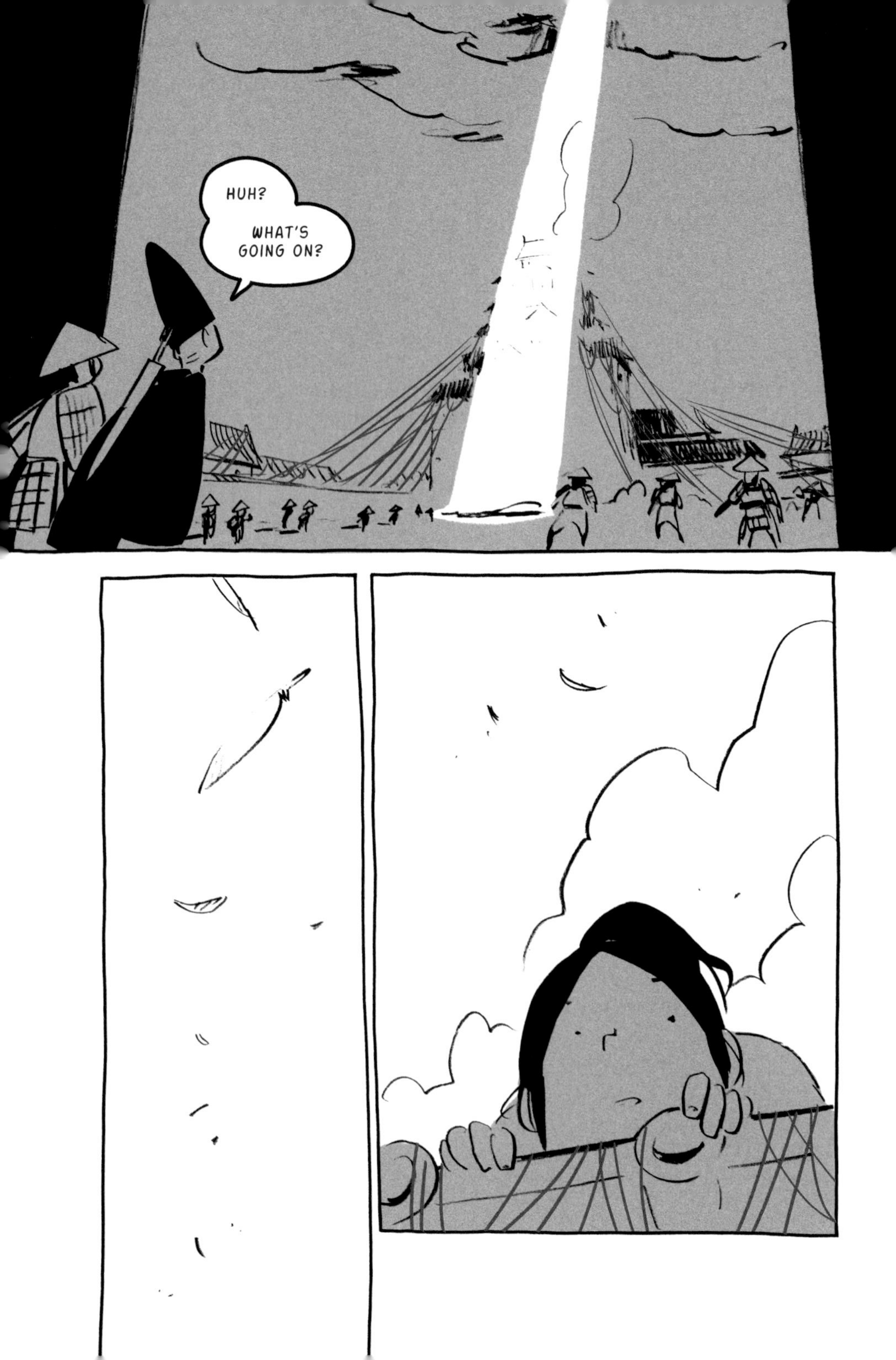
HUH?
WHAT'S GOING ON?

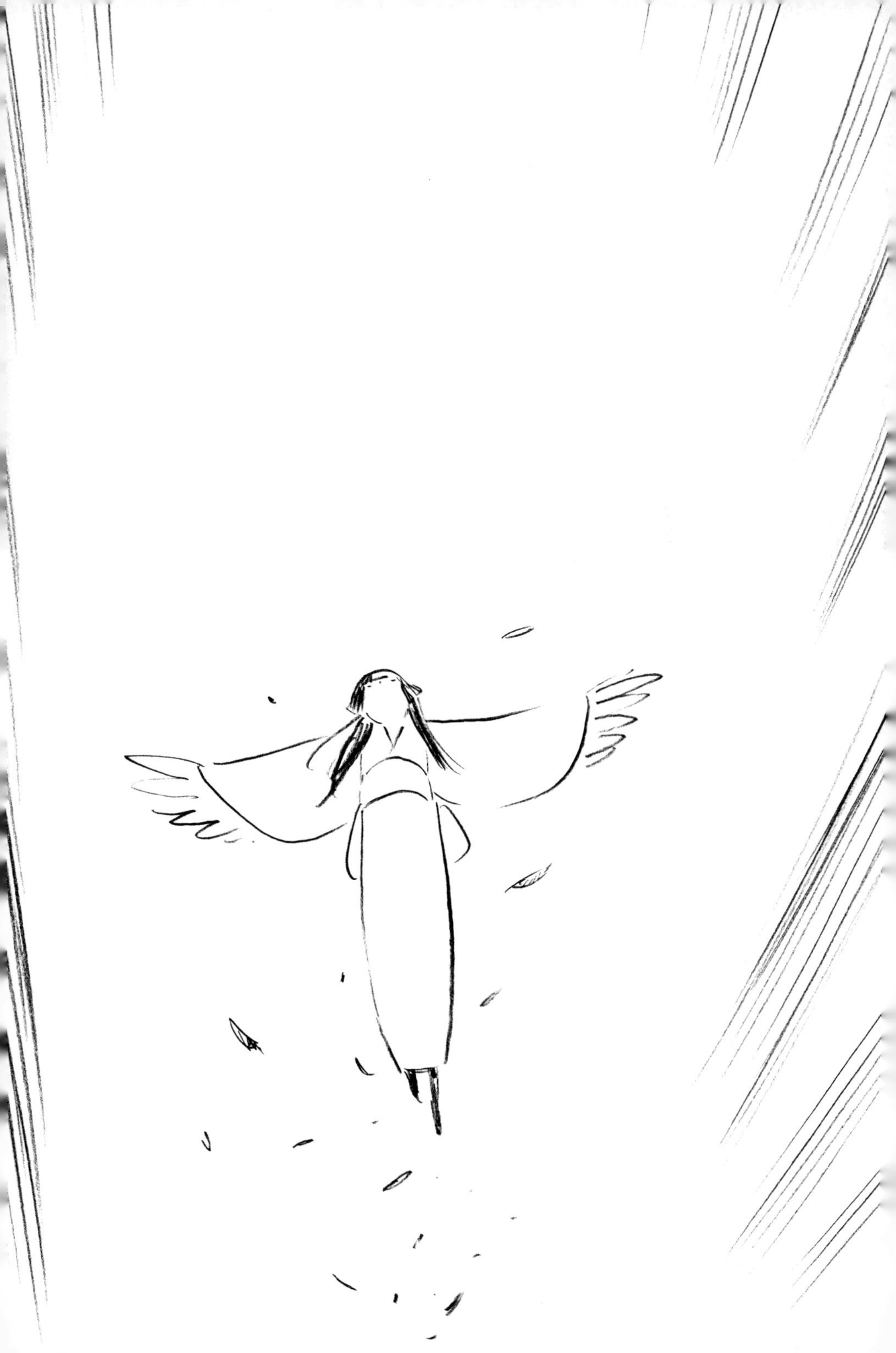

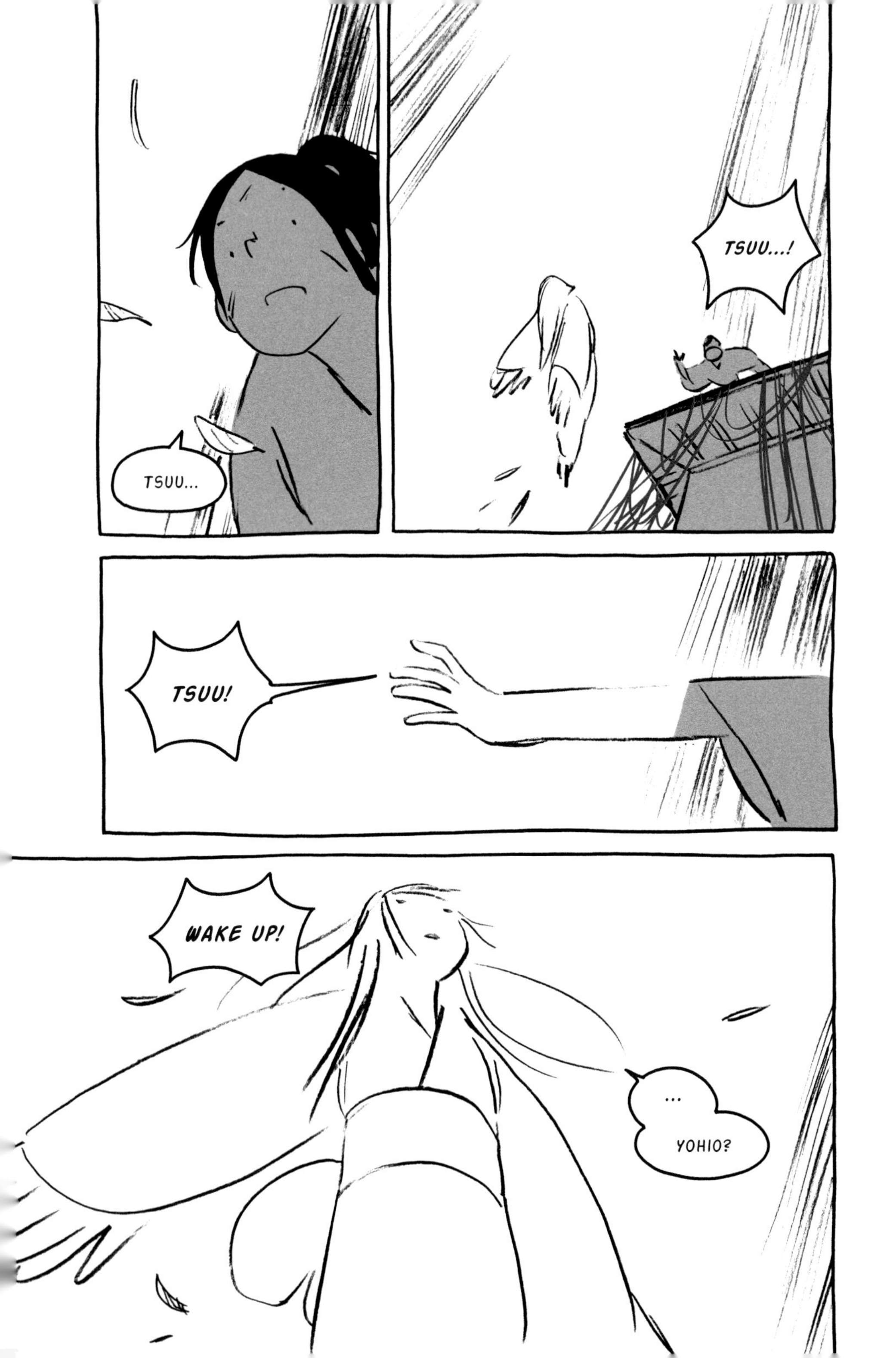
TSUU...
TSUU...!
TSUU!
WAKE UP!
...
YOHIO?

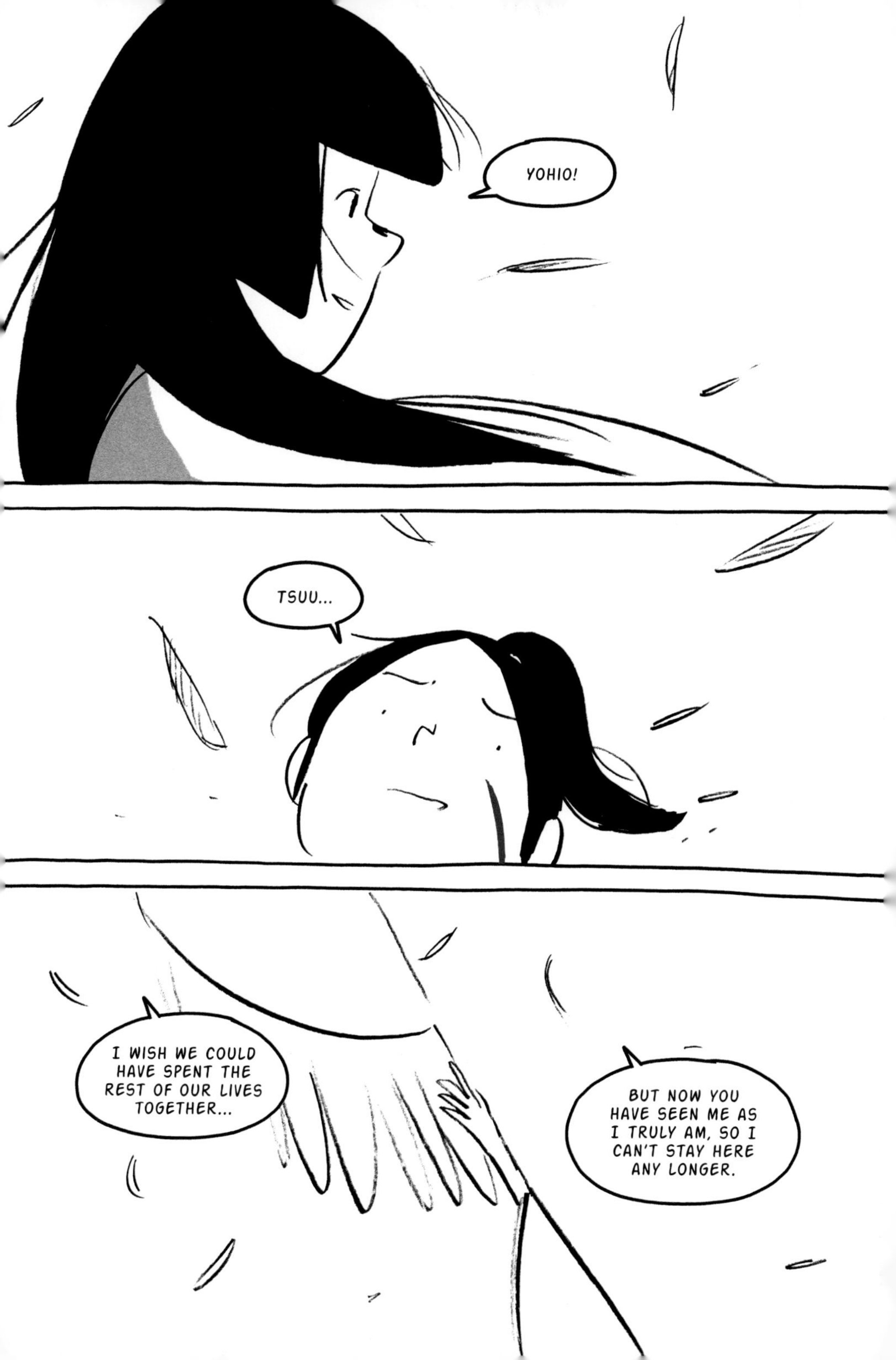
YOHIO!
TSUU...
I WISH WE COULD HAVE SPENT THE REST OF OUR LIVES TOGETHER...
BUT NOW YOU HAVE SEEN ME AS I TRULY AM, SO I CAN'T STAY HERE ANY LONGER.

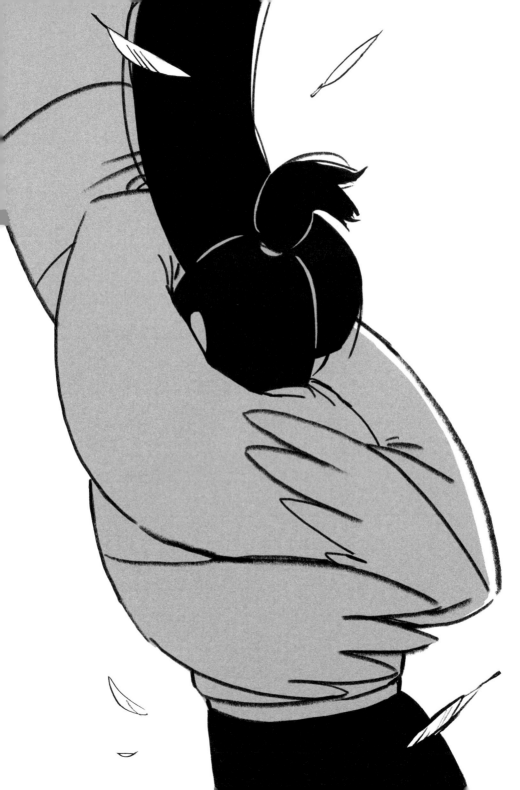

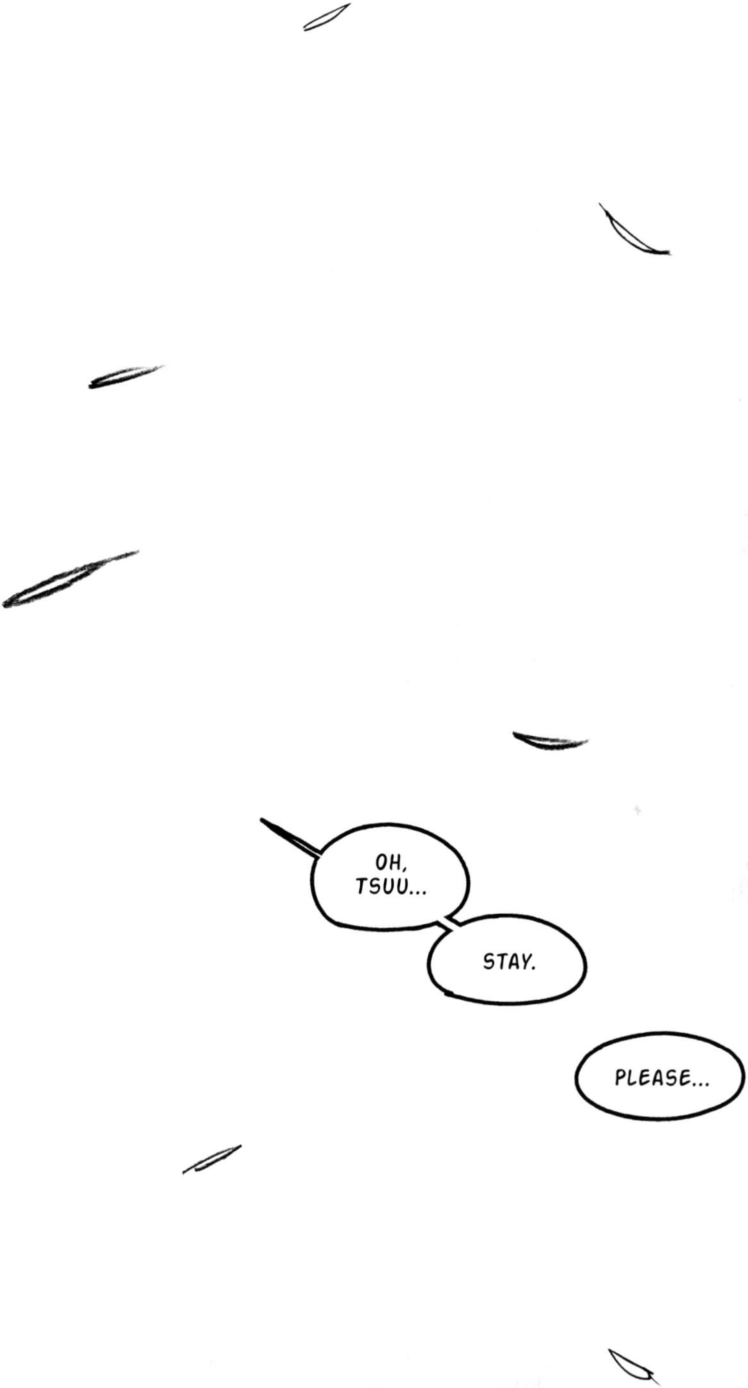
OH, TSUU...
STAY.
PLEASE...

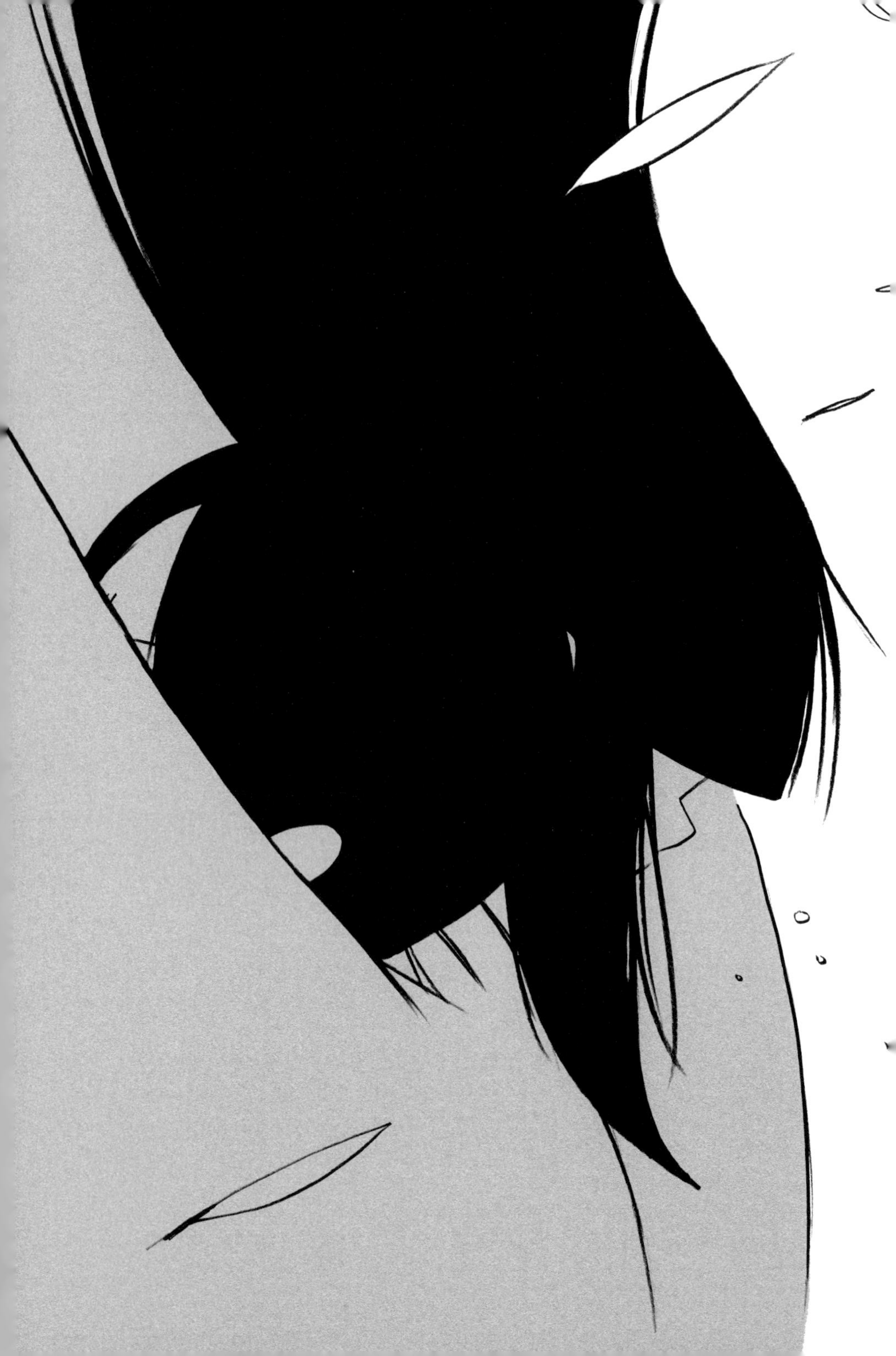

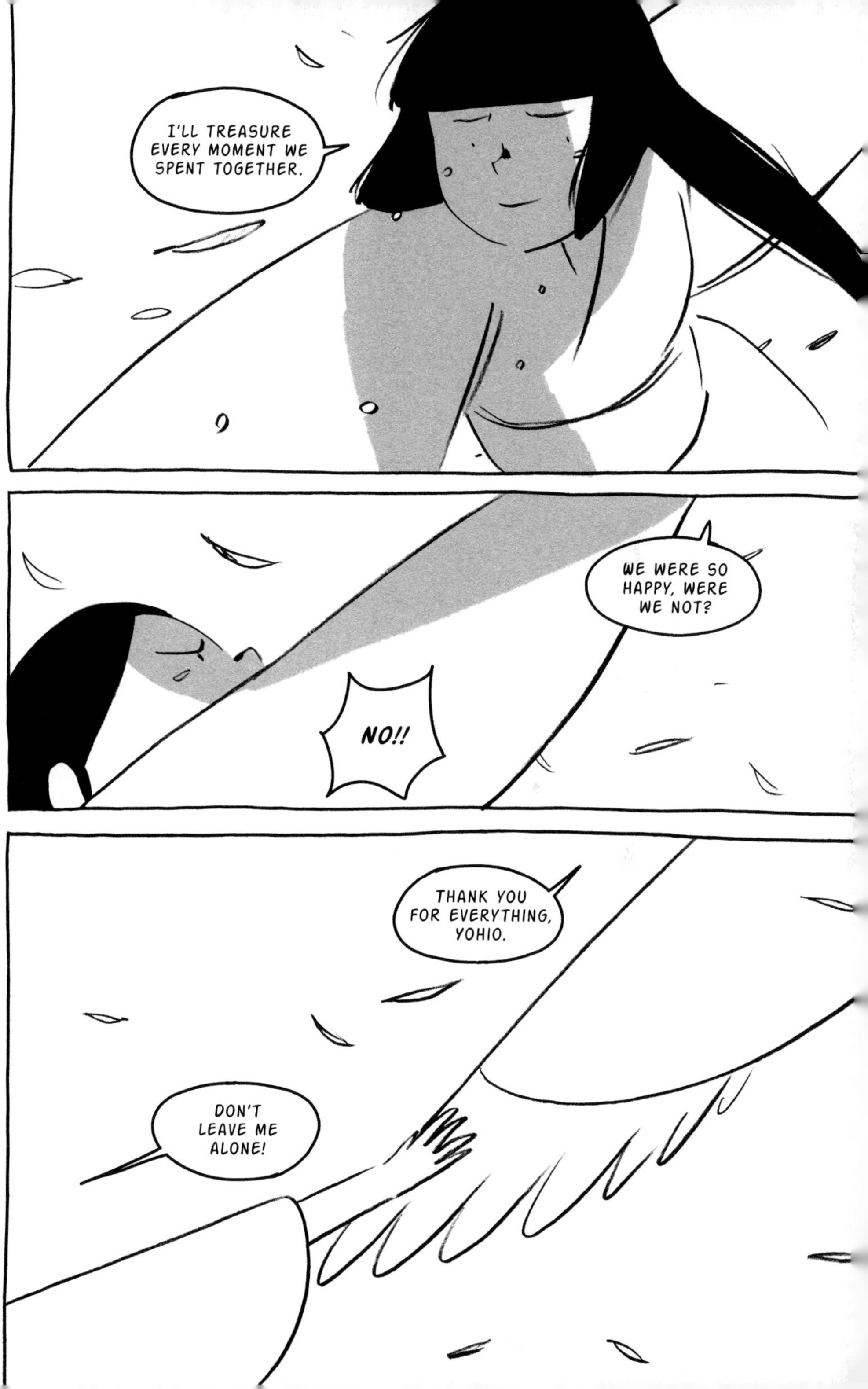
I'LL TREASURE EVERY MOMENT WE SPENT TOGETHER.
WE WERE SO HAPPY, WERE WE NOT?
NO!!
THANK YOU FOR EVERYTHING, YOHIO.
DON'T LEAVE ME ALONE!

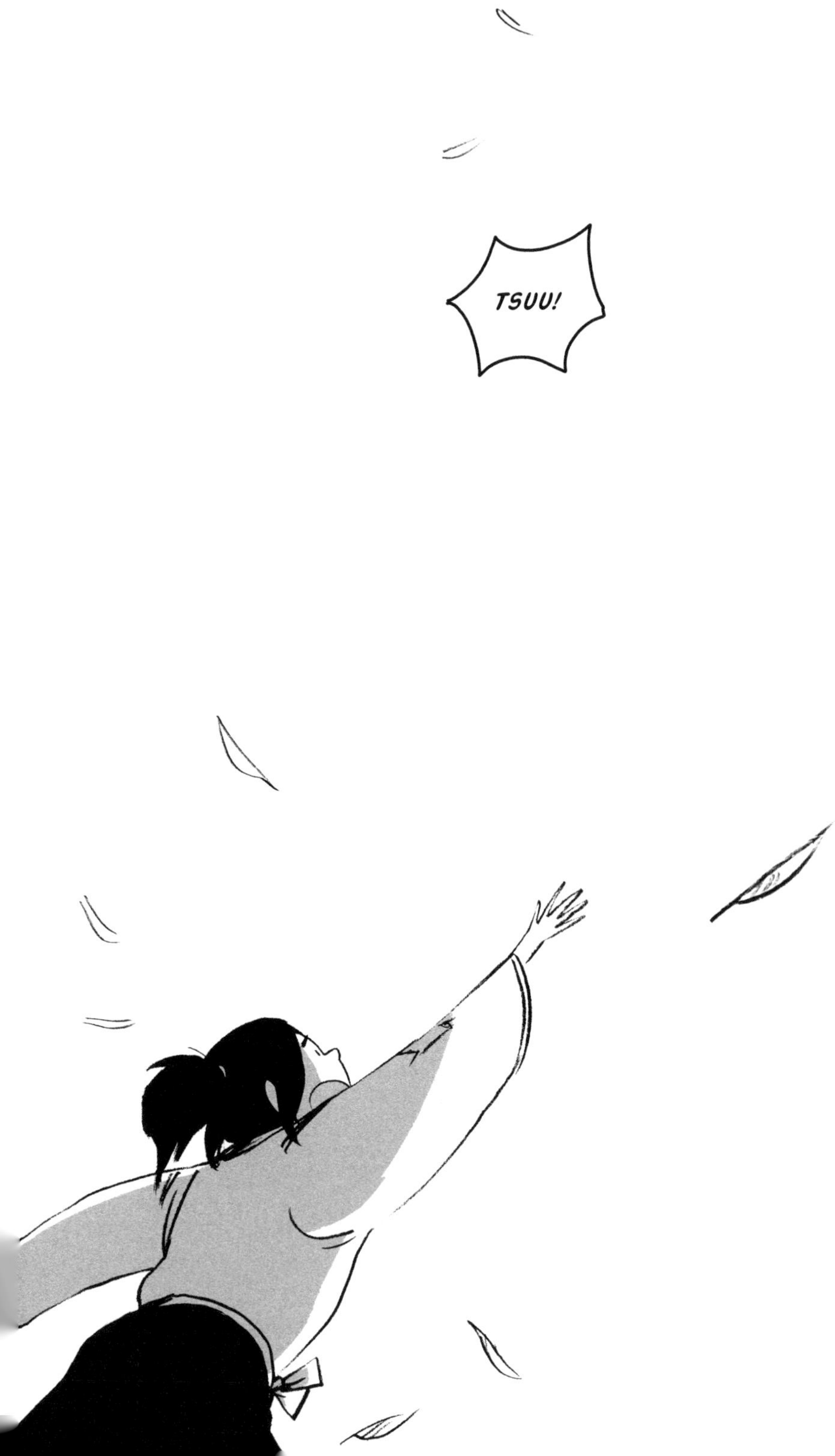
TSUU!

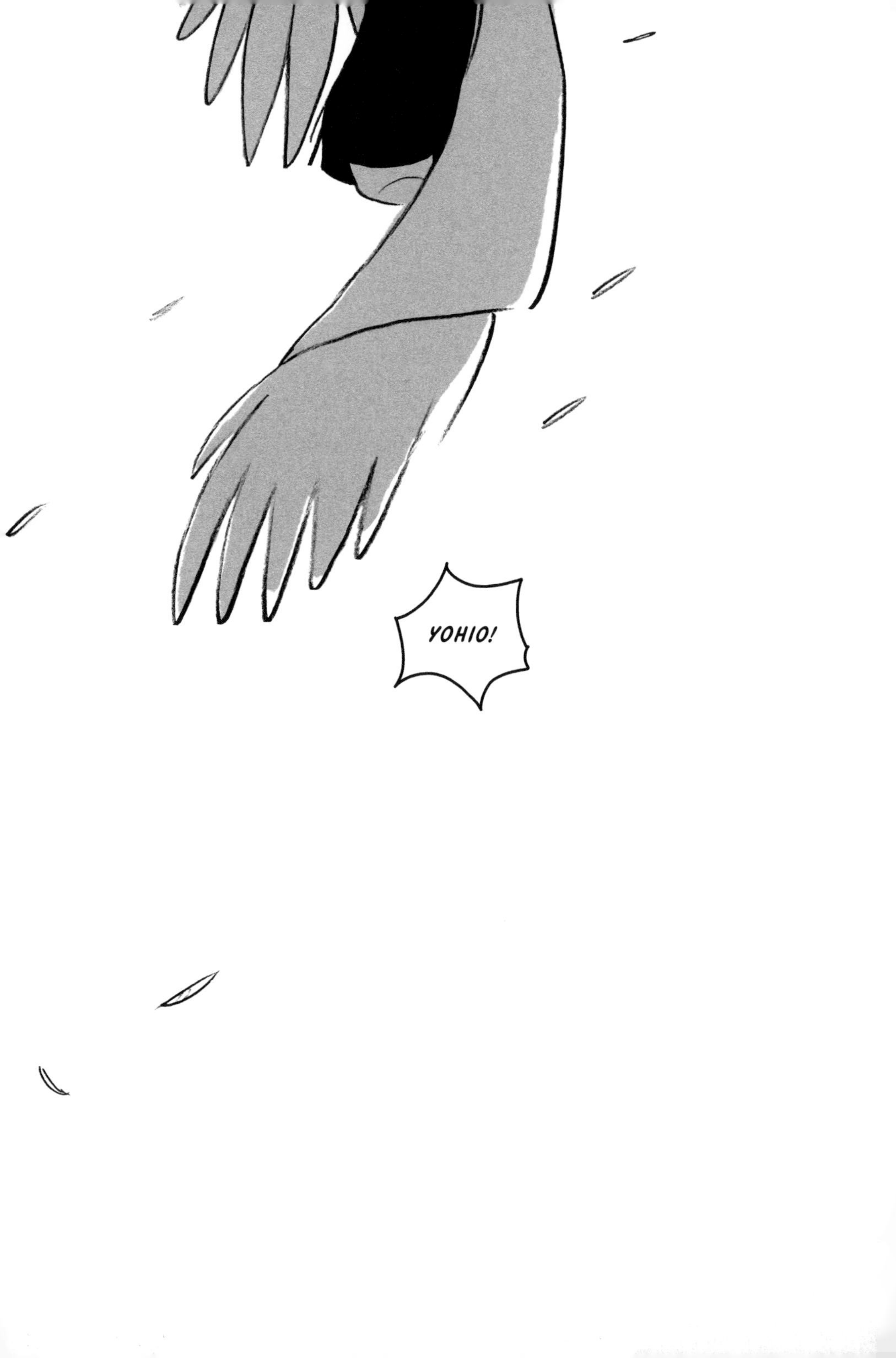
YOHIO!

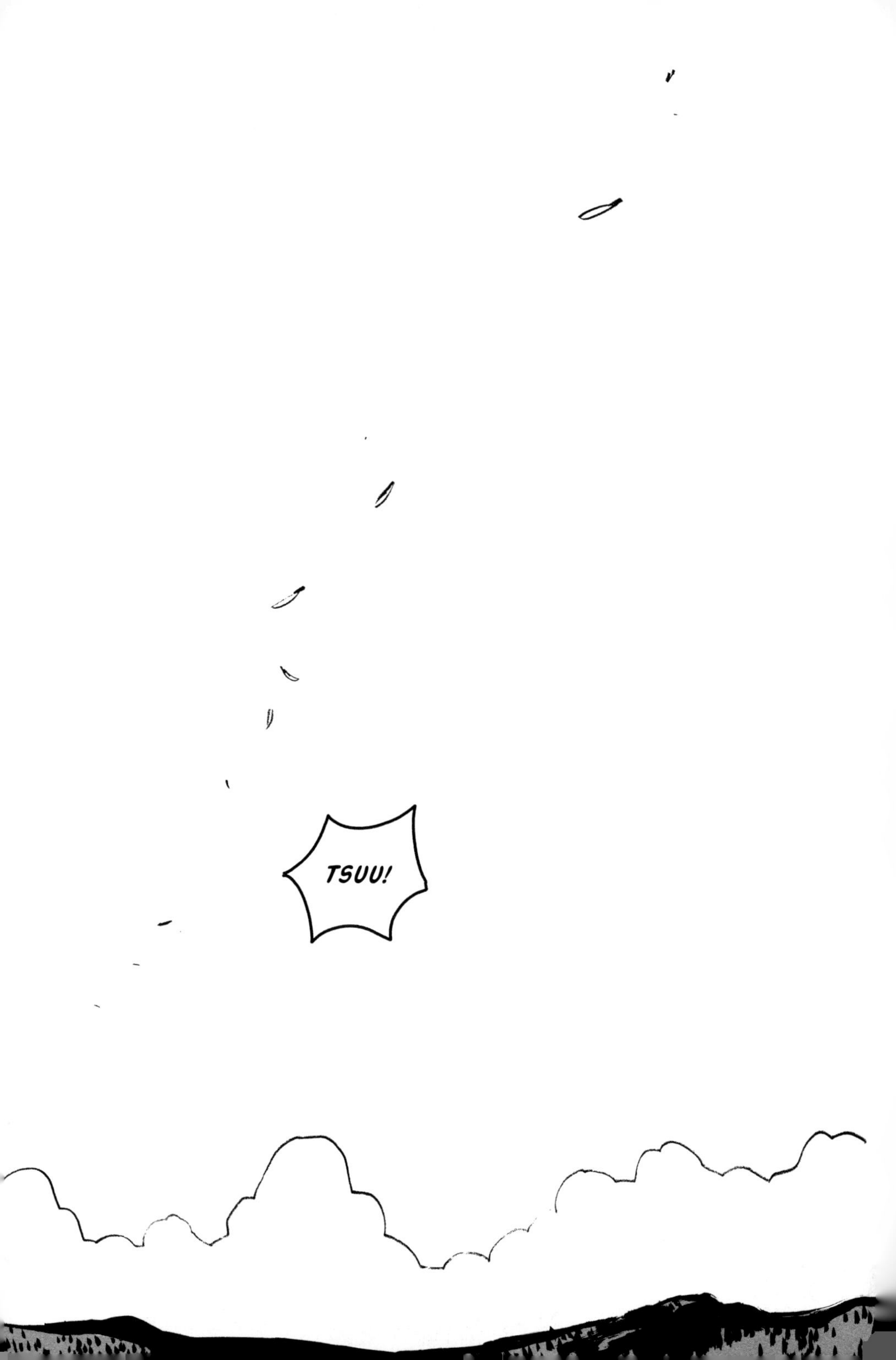
TSUU!

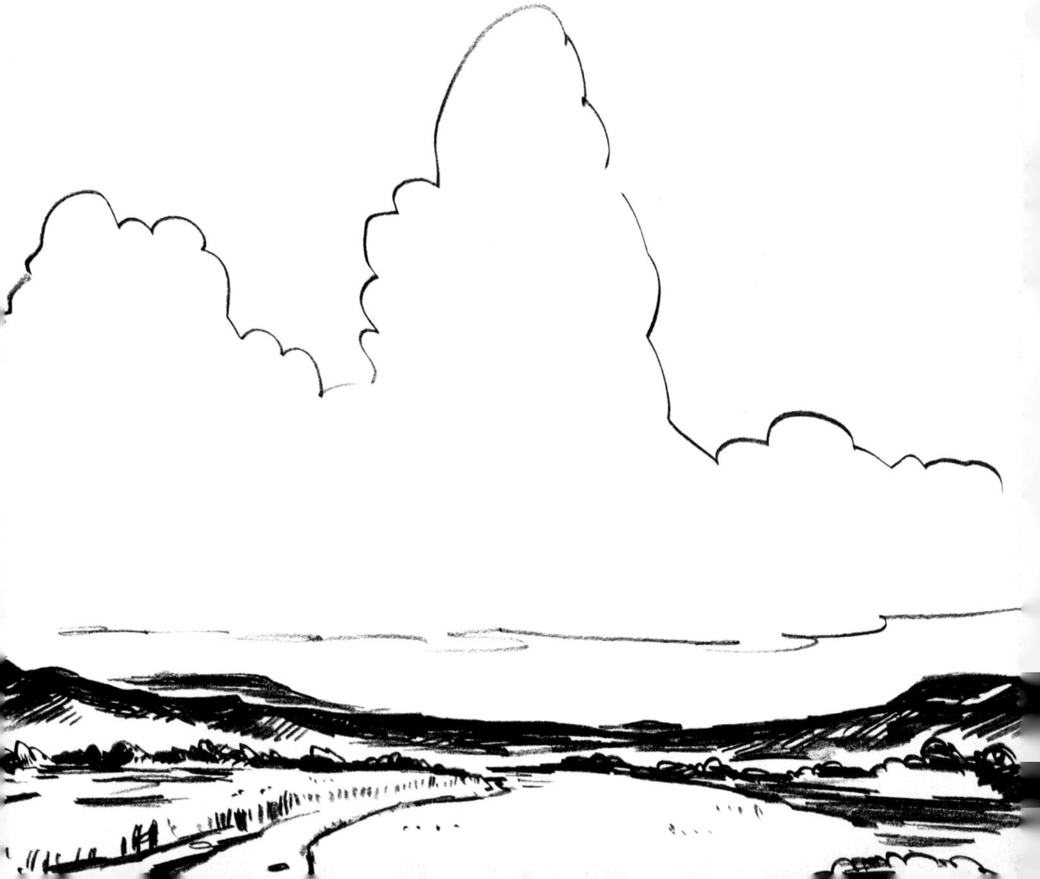

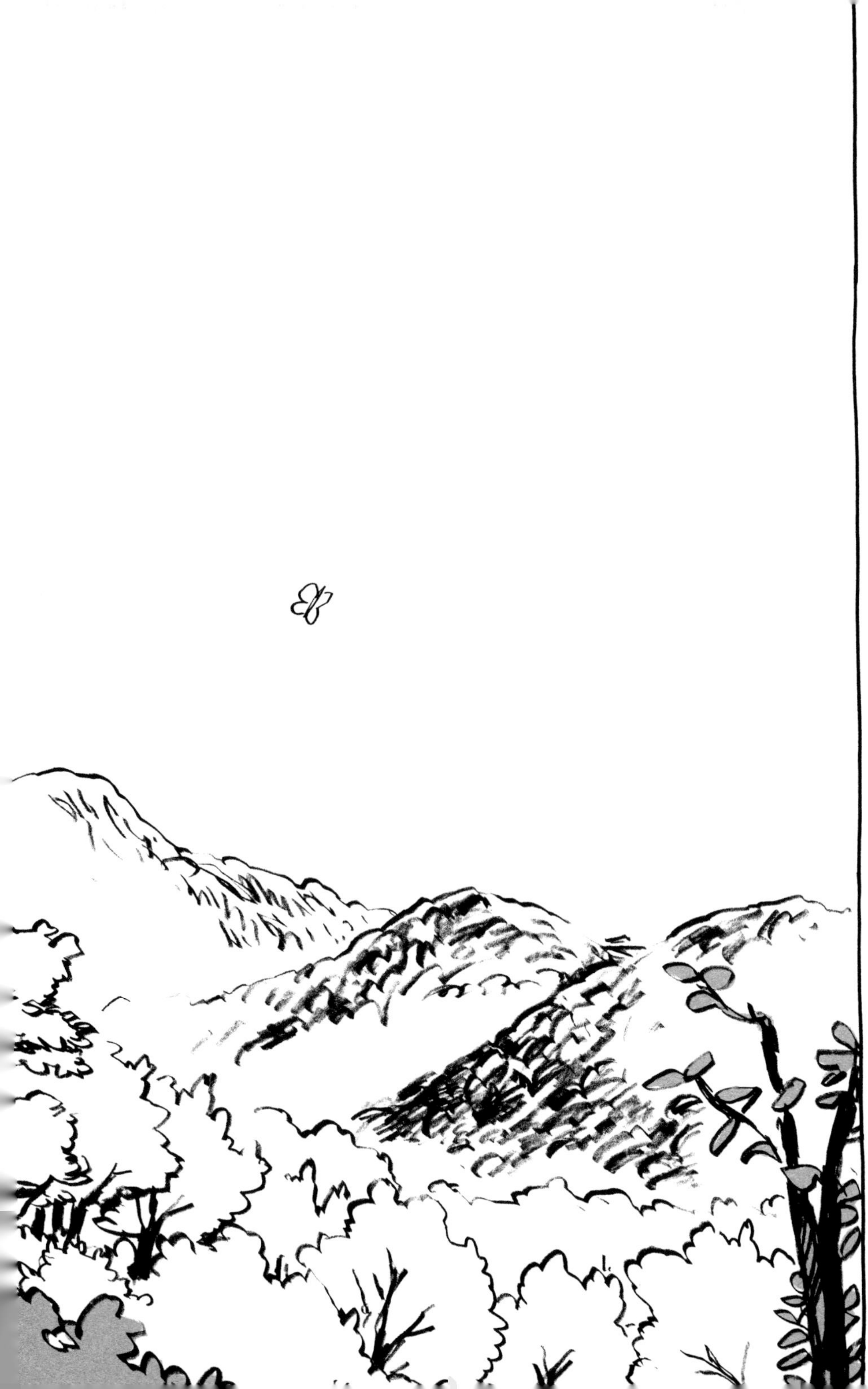

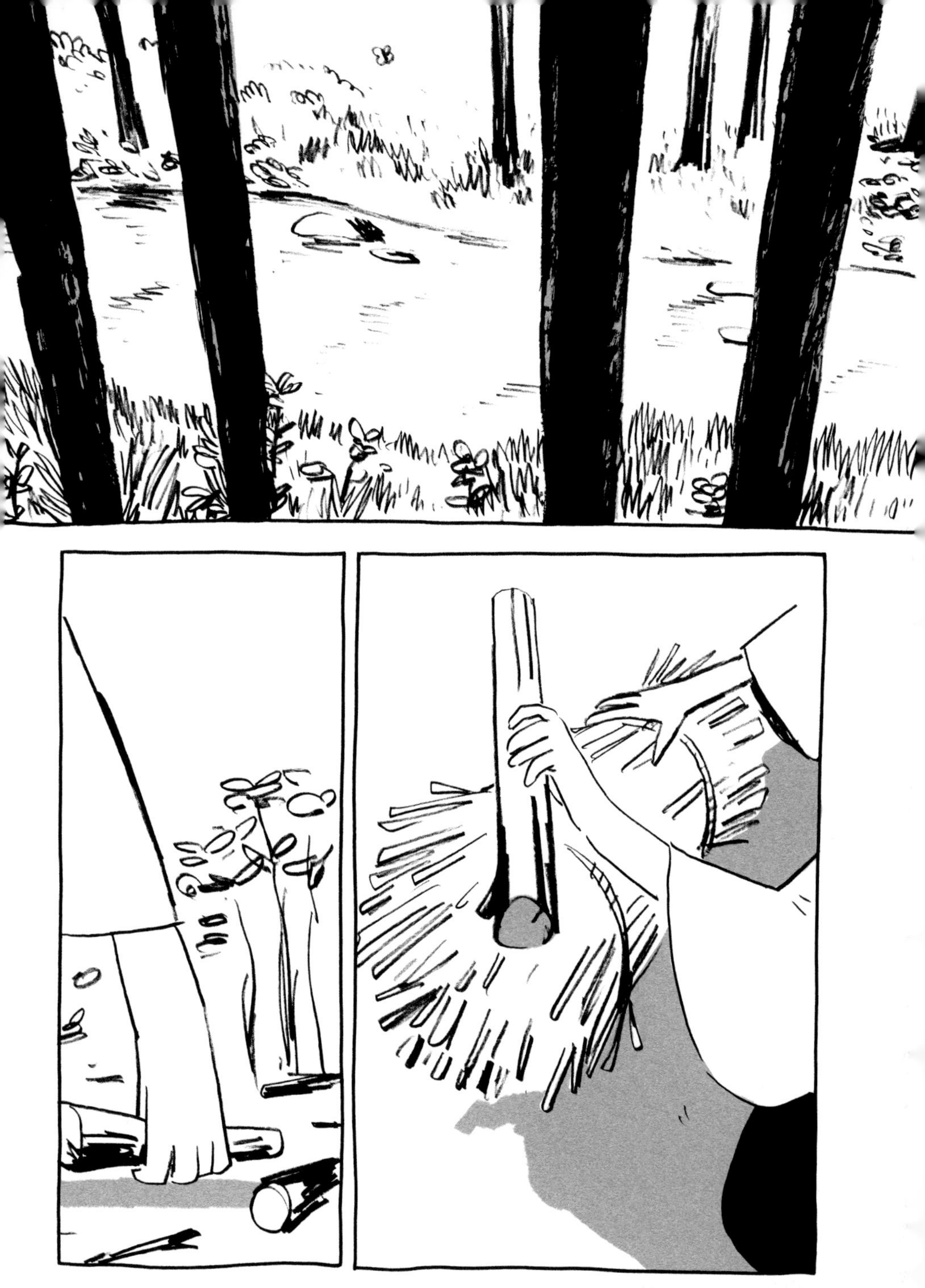

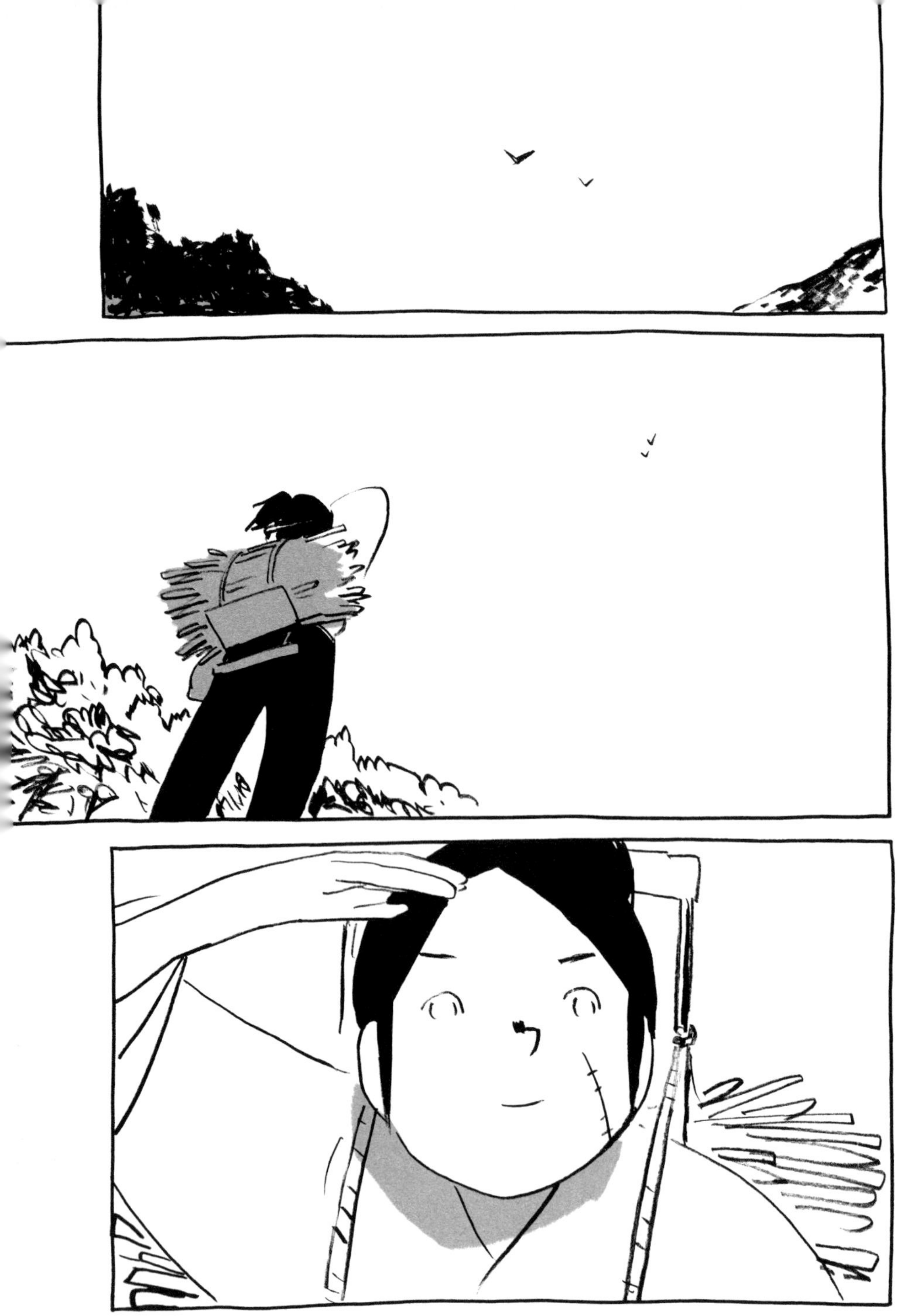

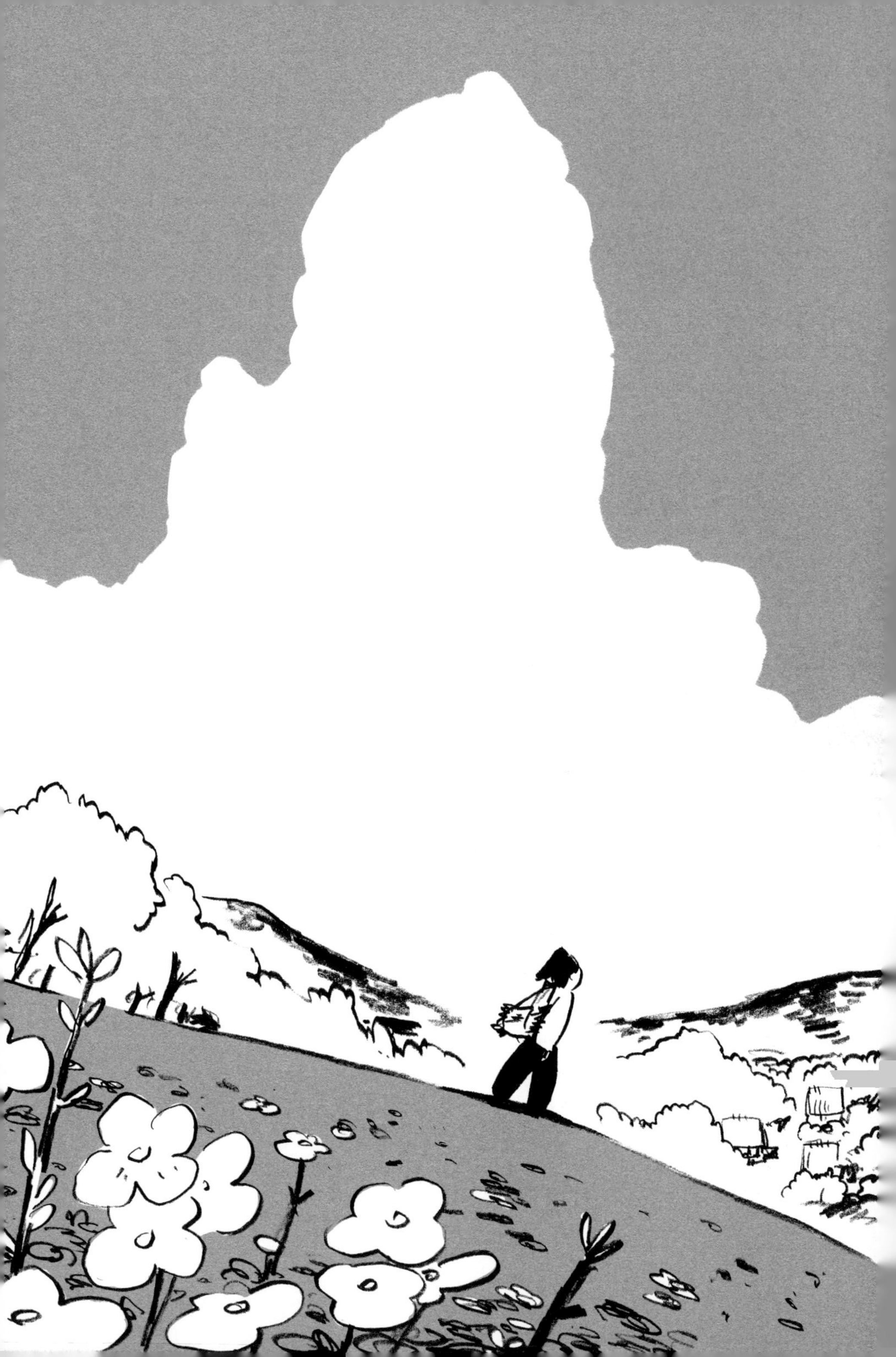

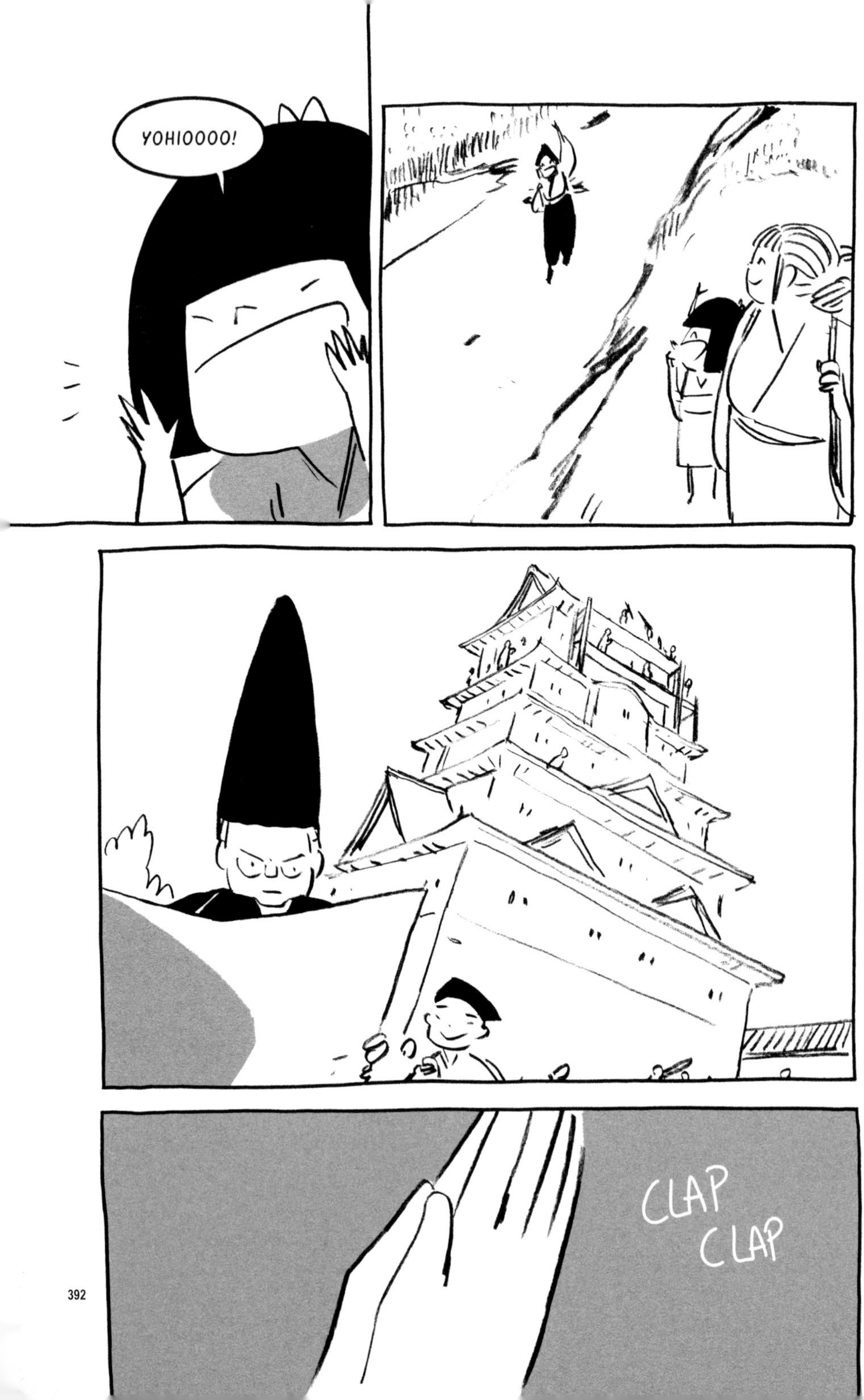
YOHIOOOO!
CLAP
CLAP

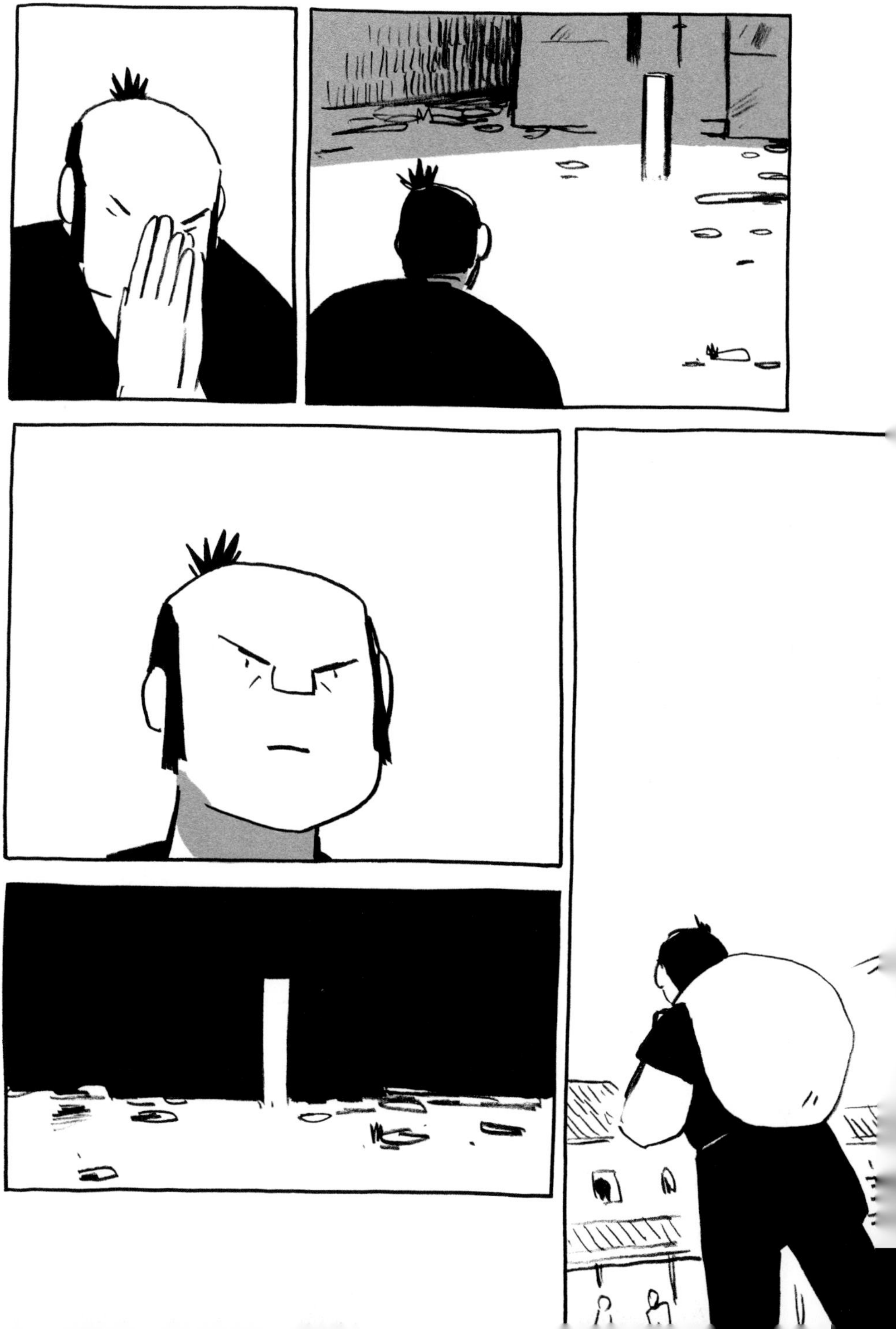

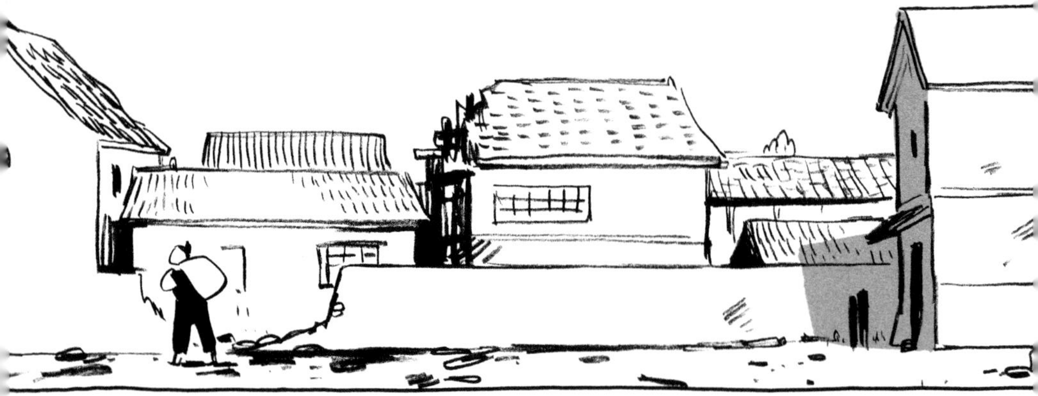

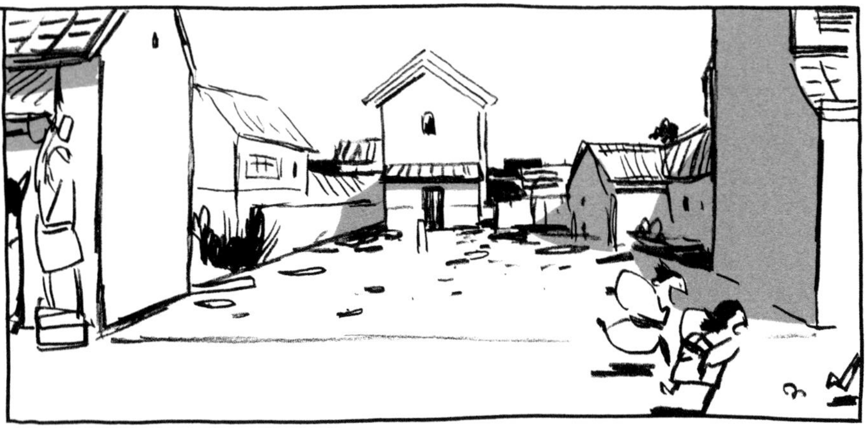

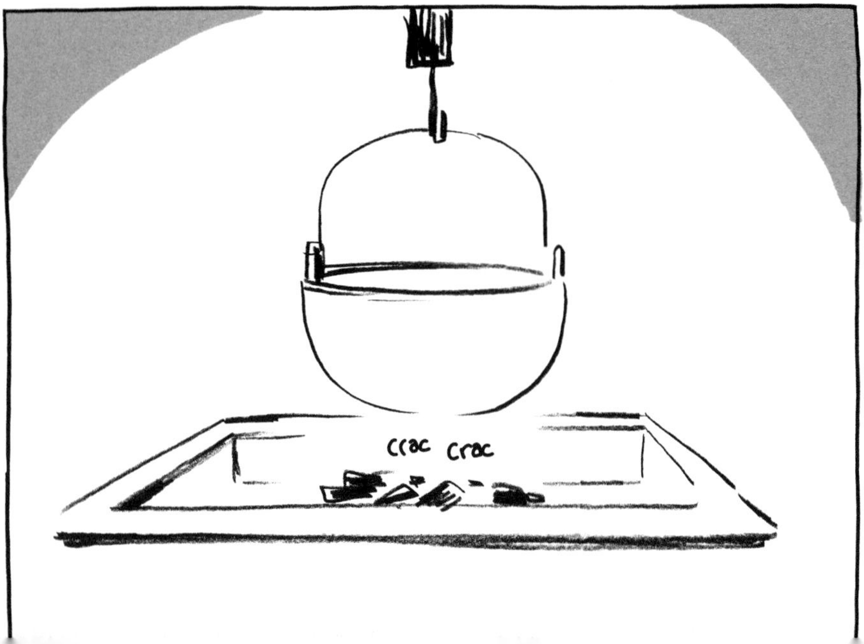
crac crac

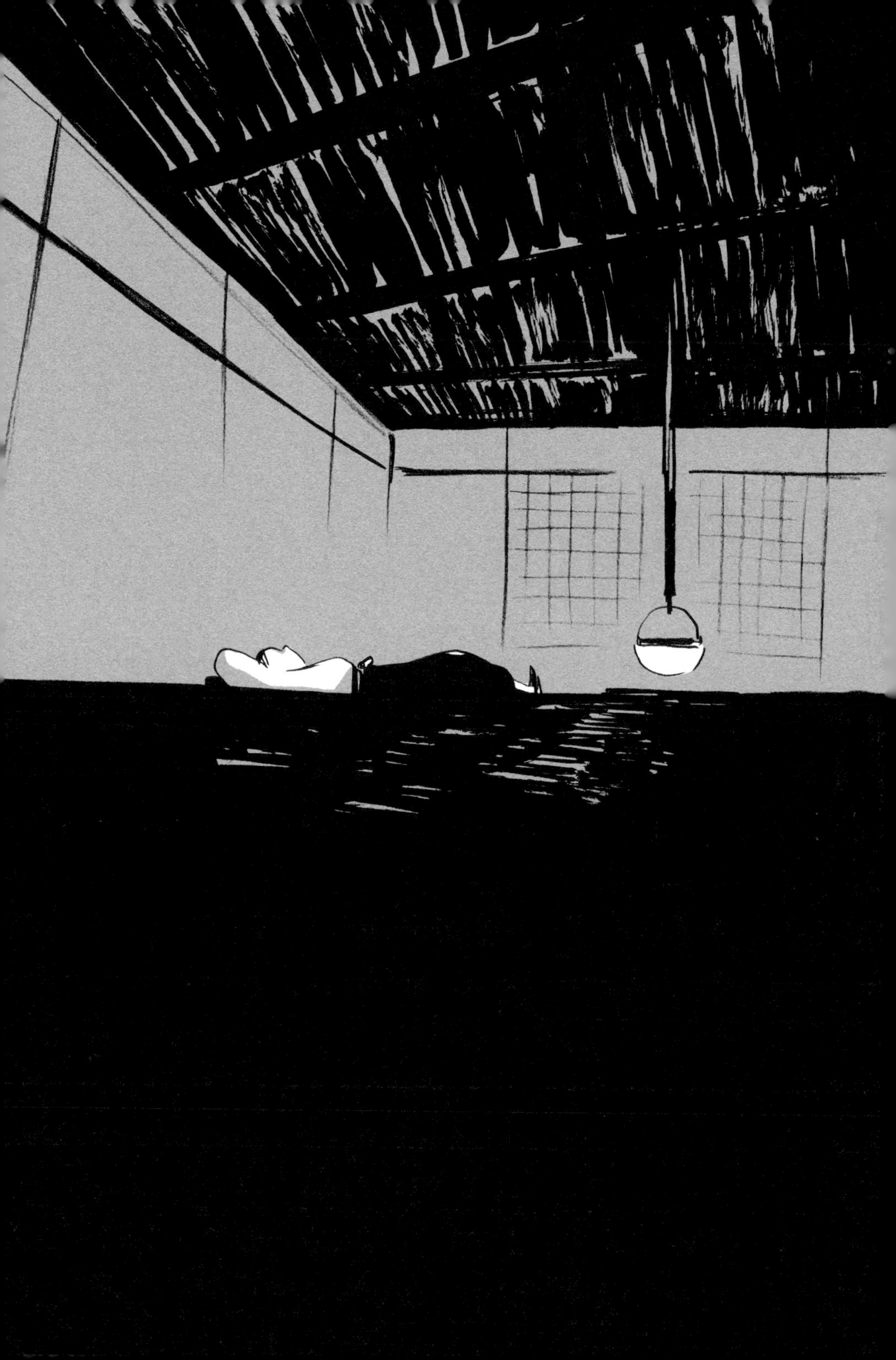

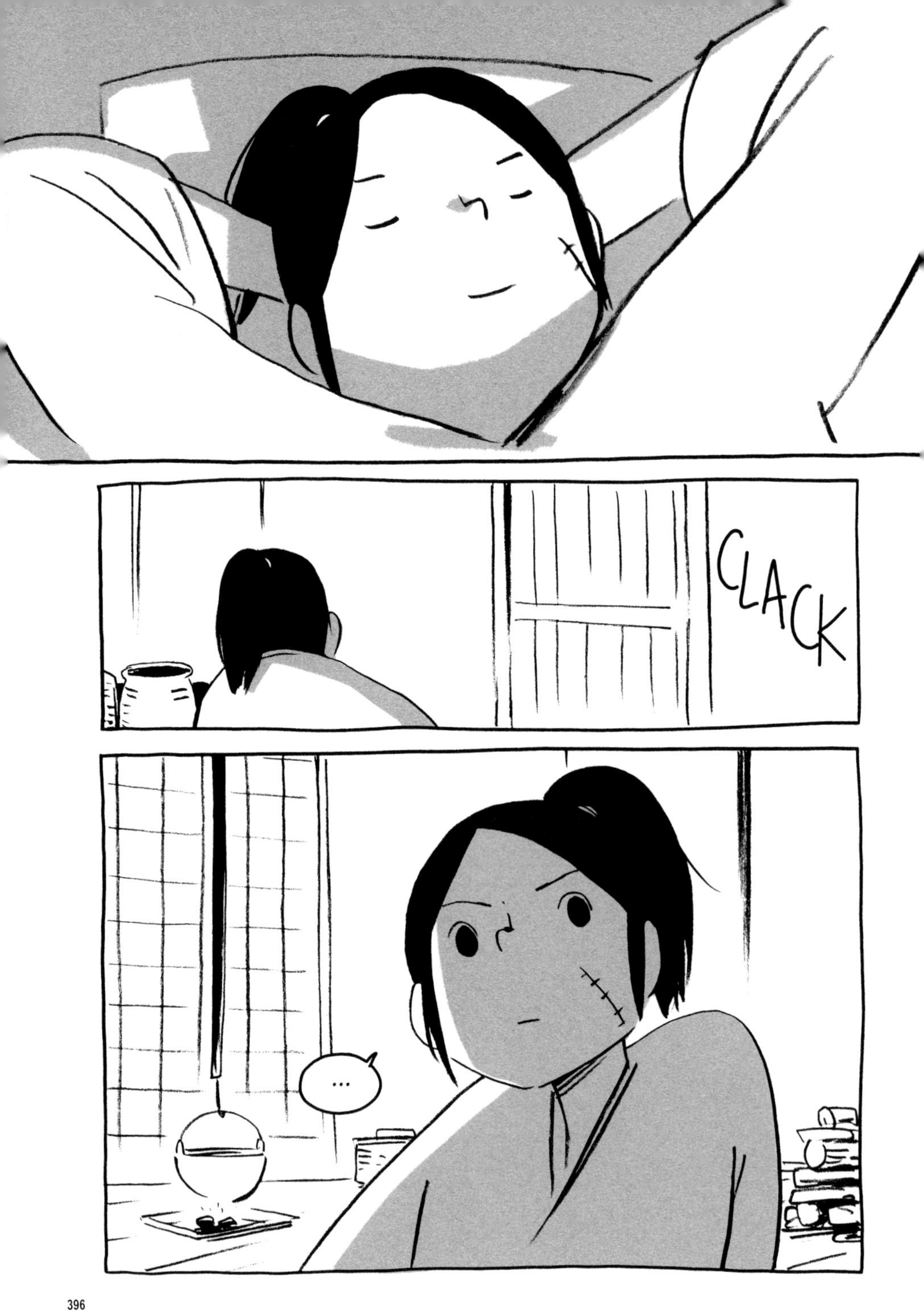
CLACK
...

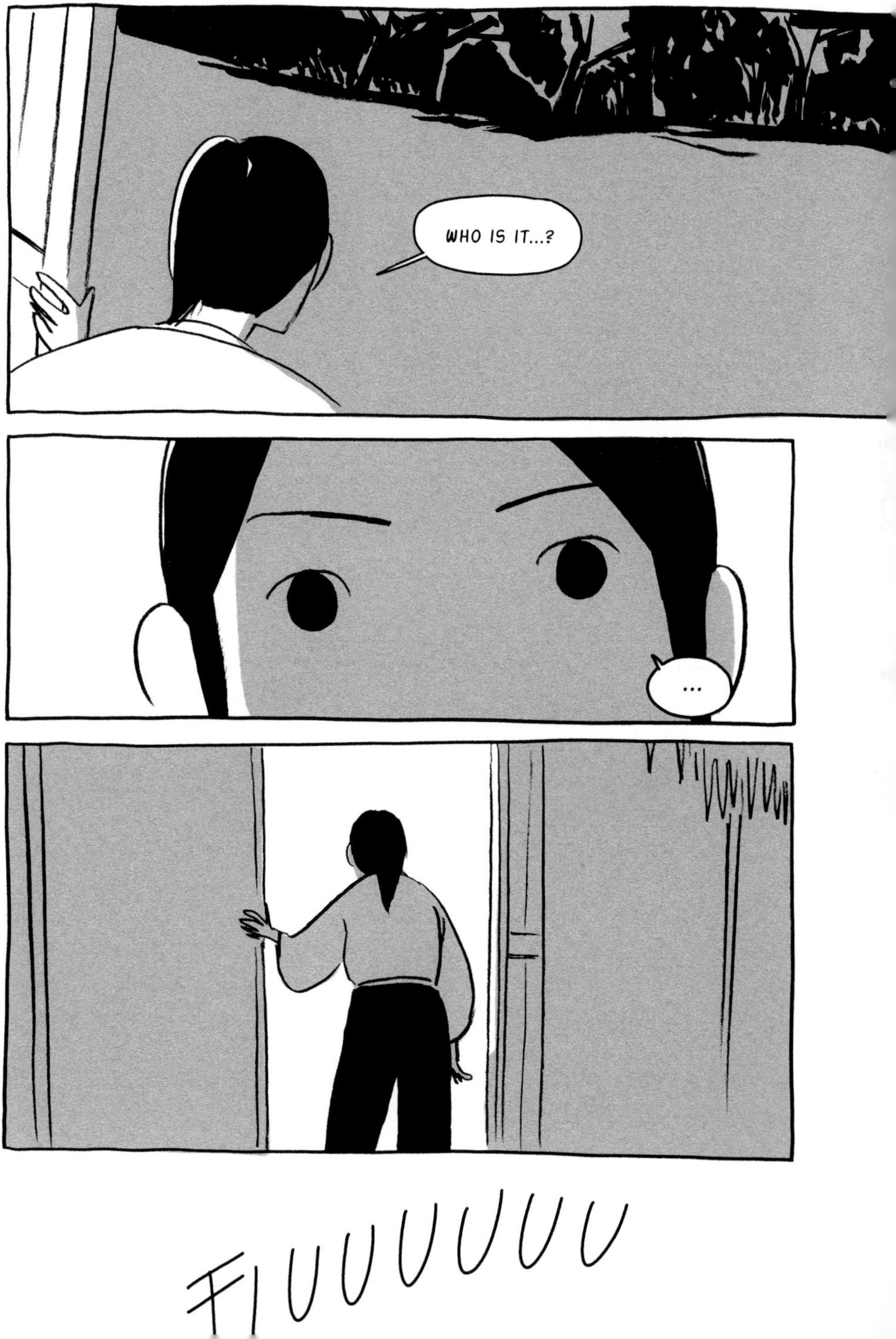
WHO IS IT...?
...
FIUUUUUU

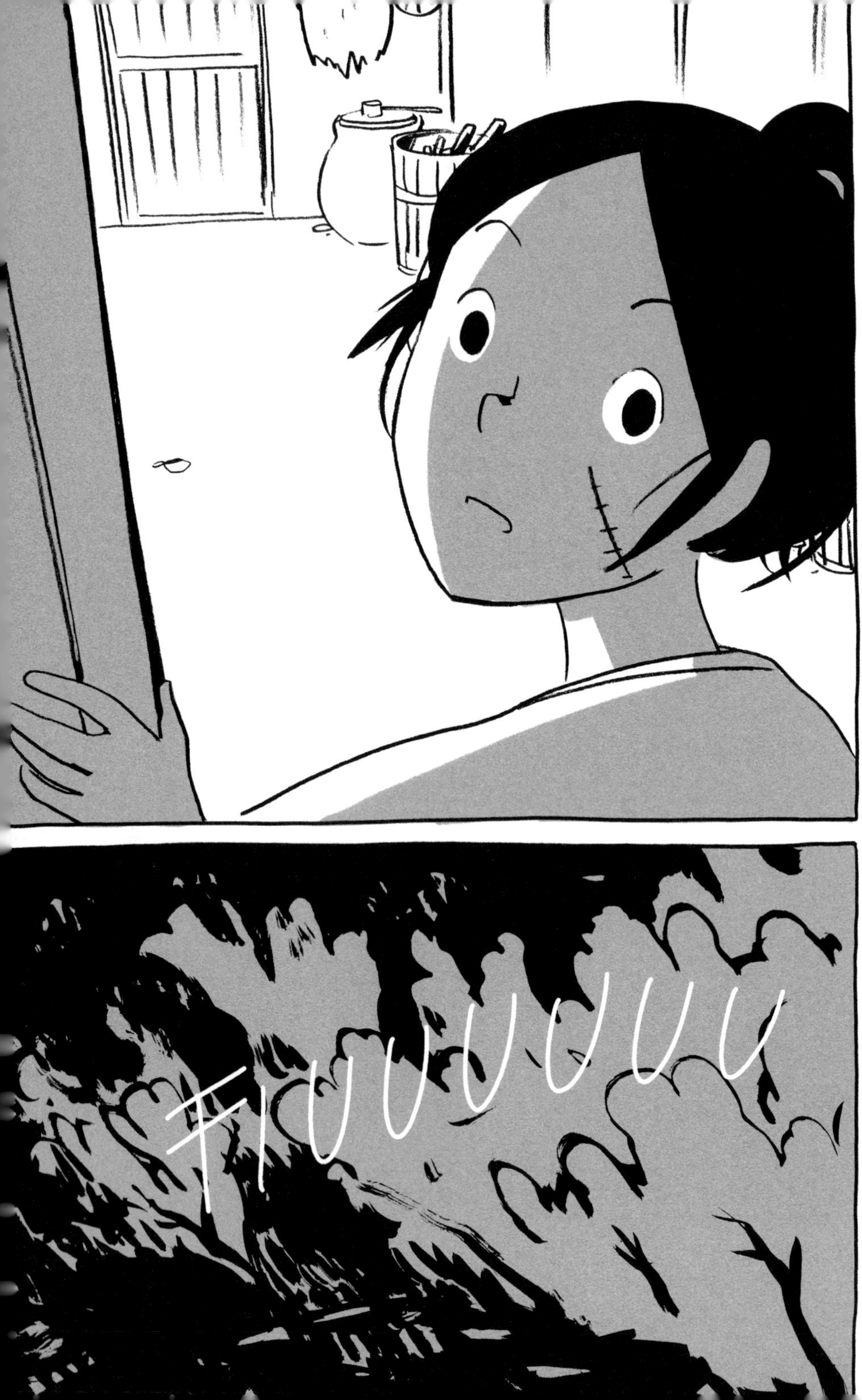
FIUUUUUUU

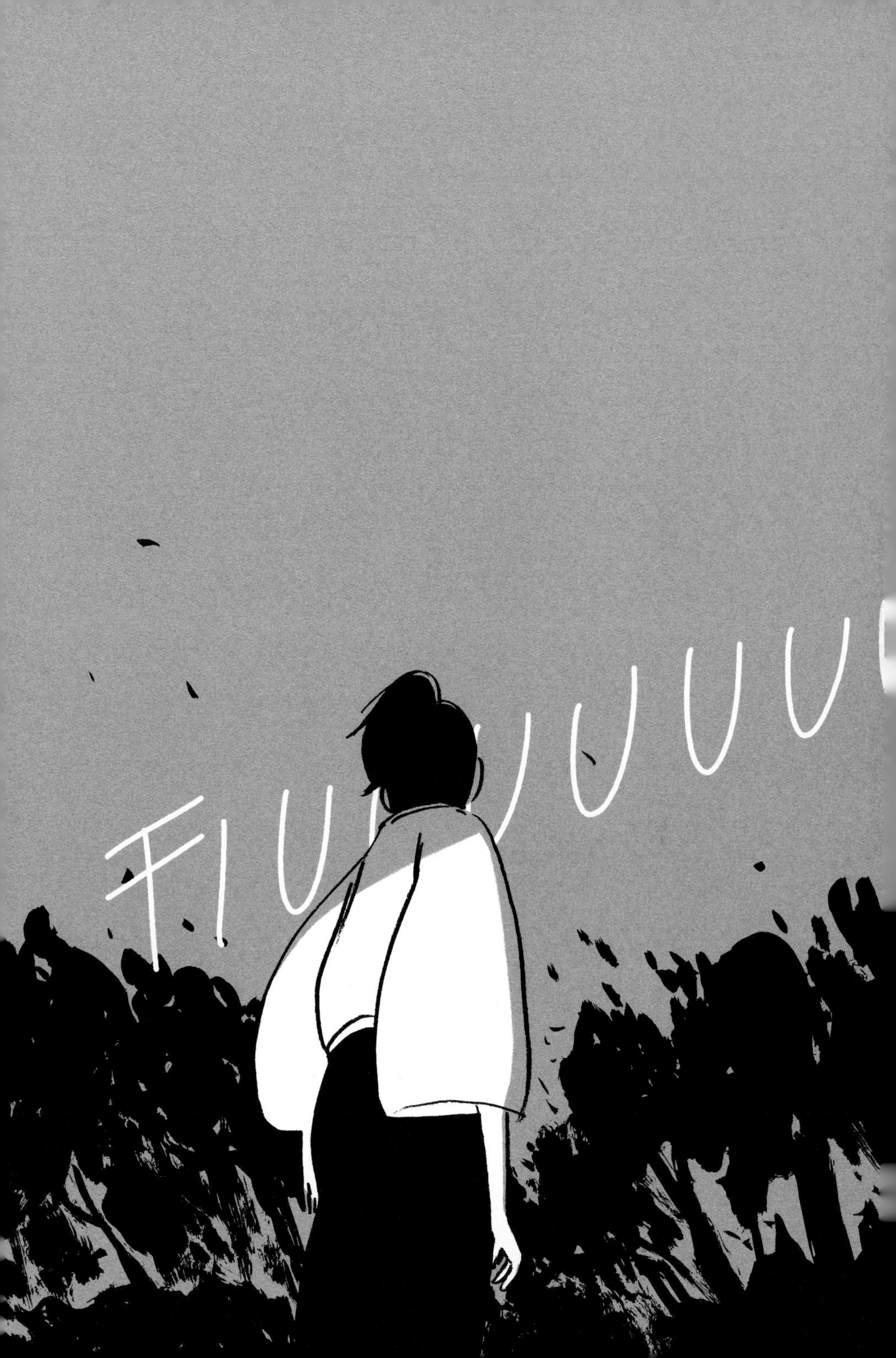
FIUUUUUUU

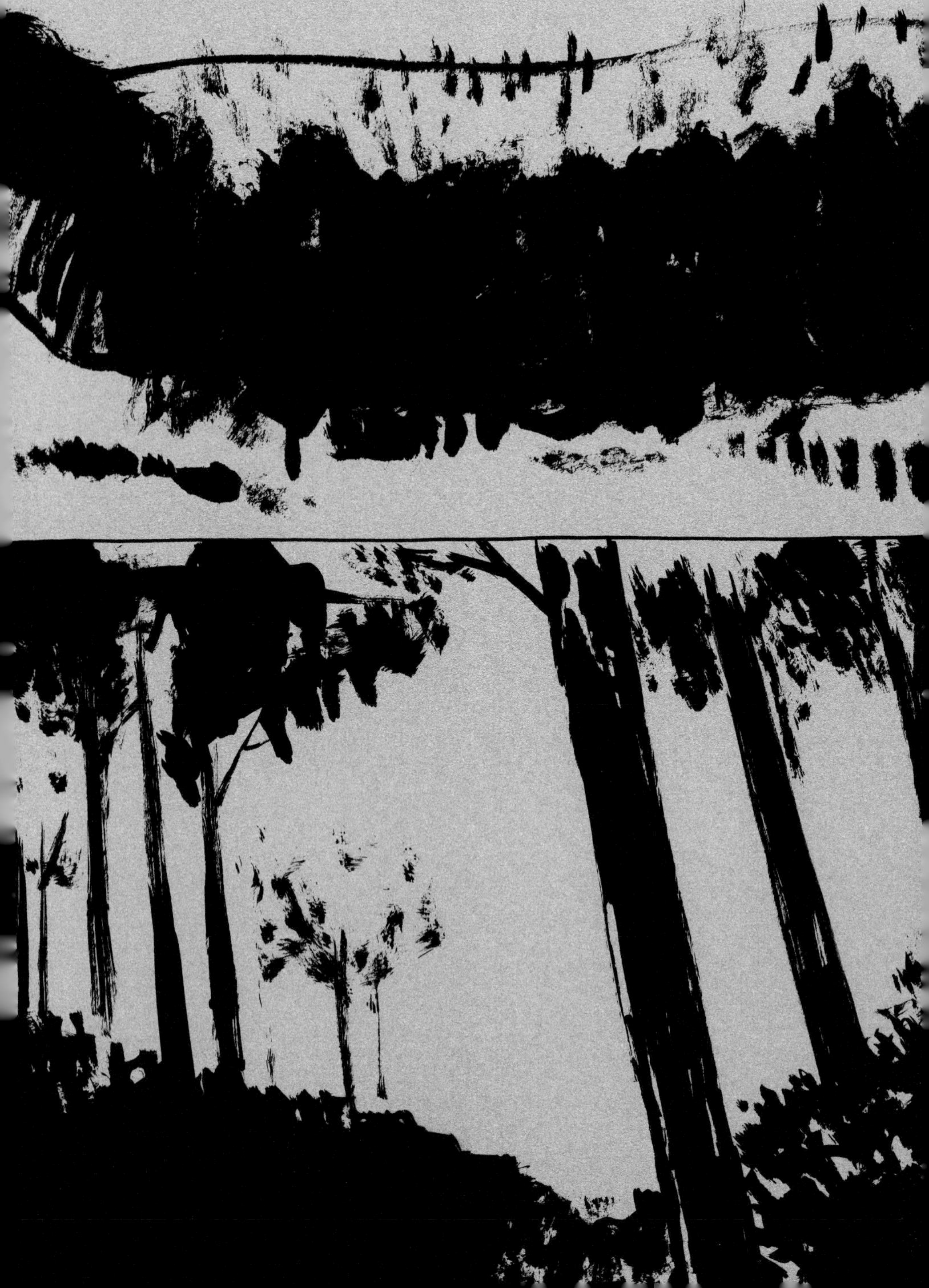

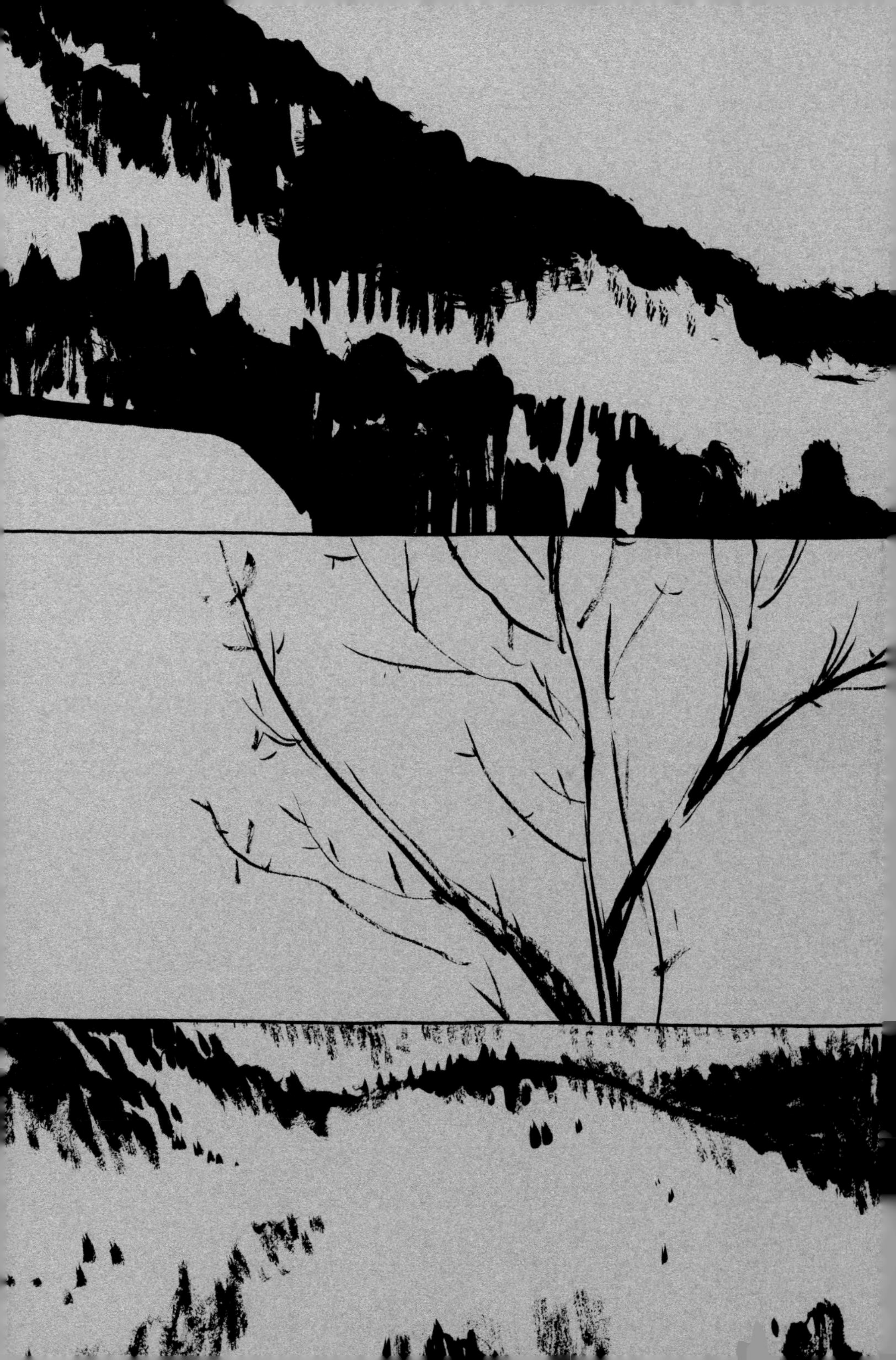

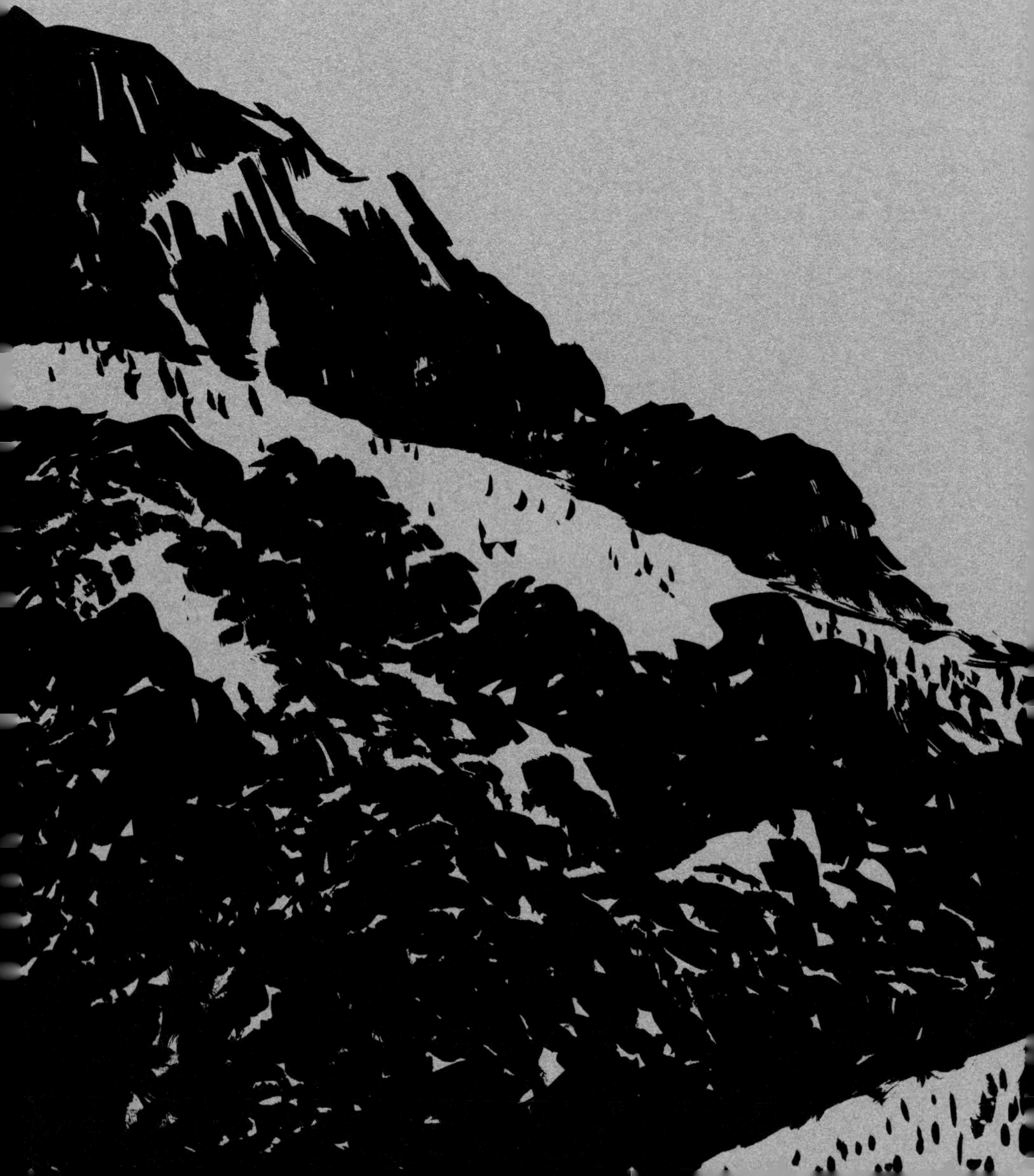

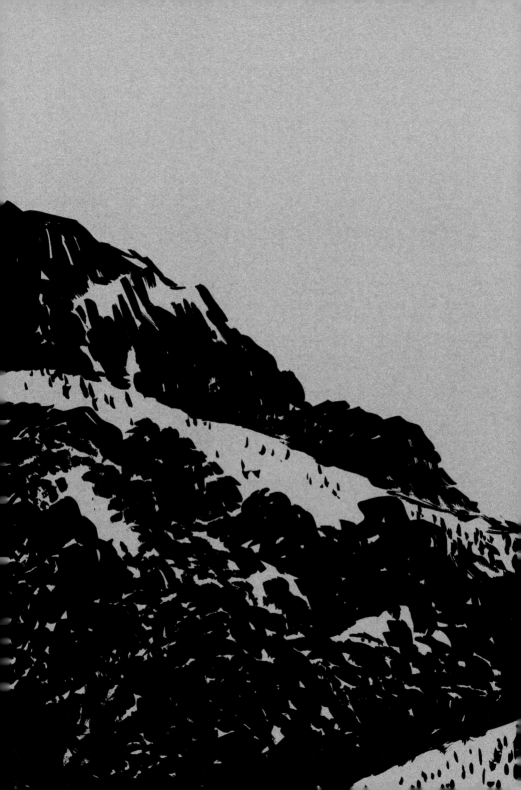

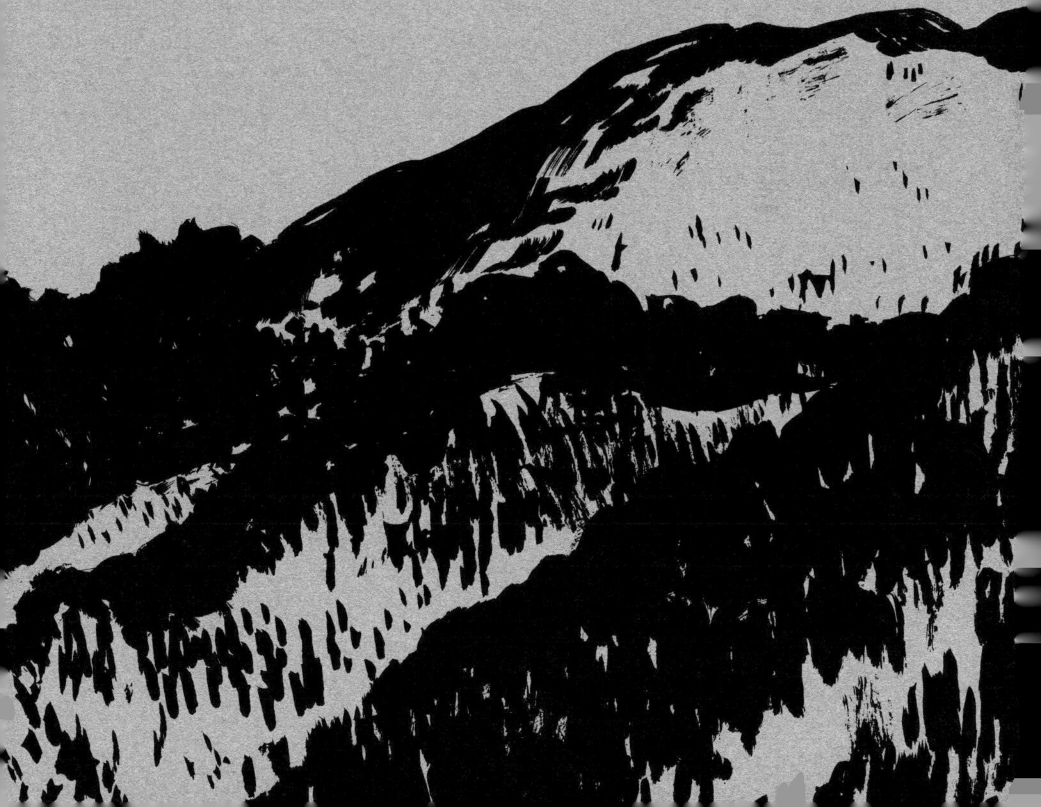

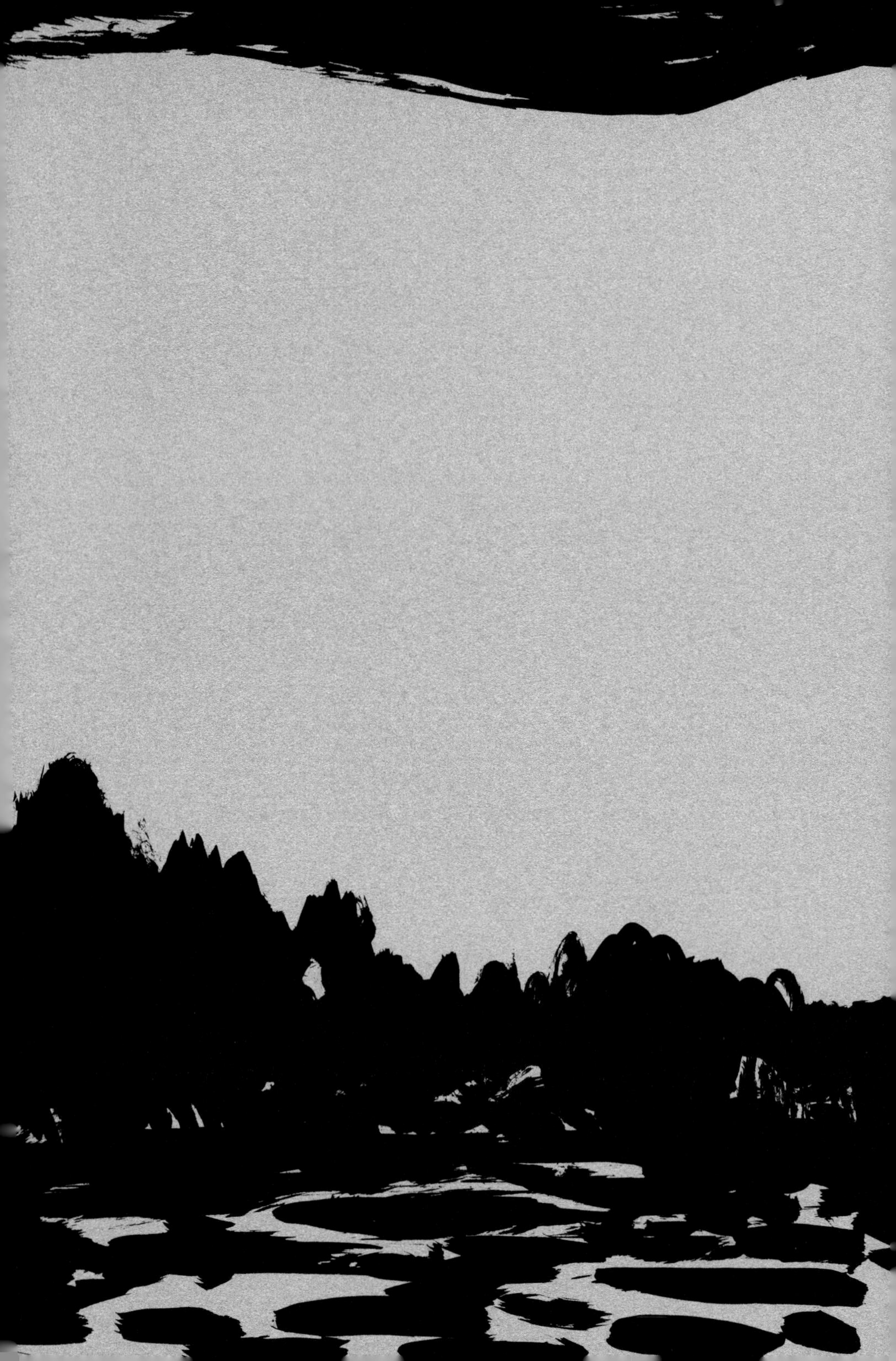

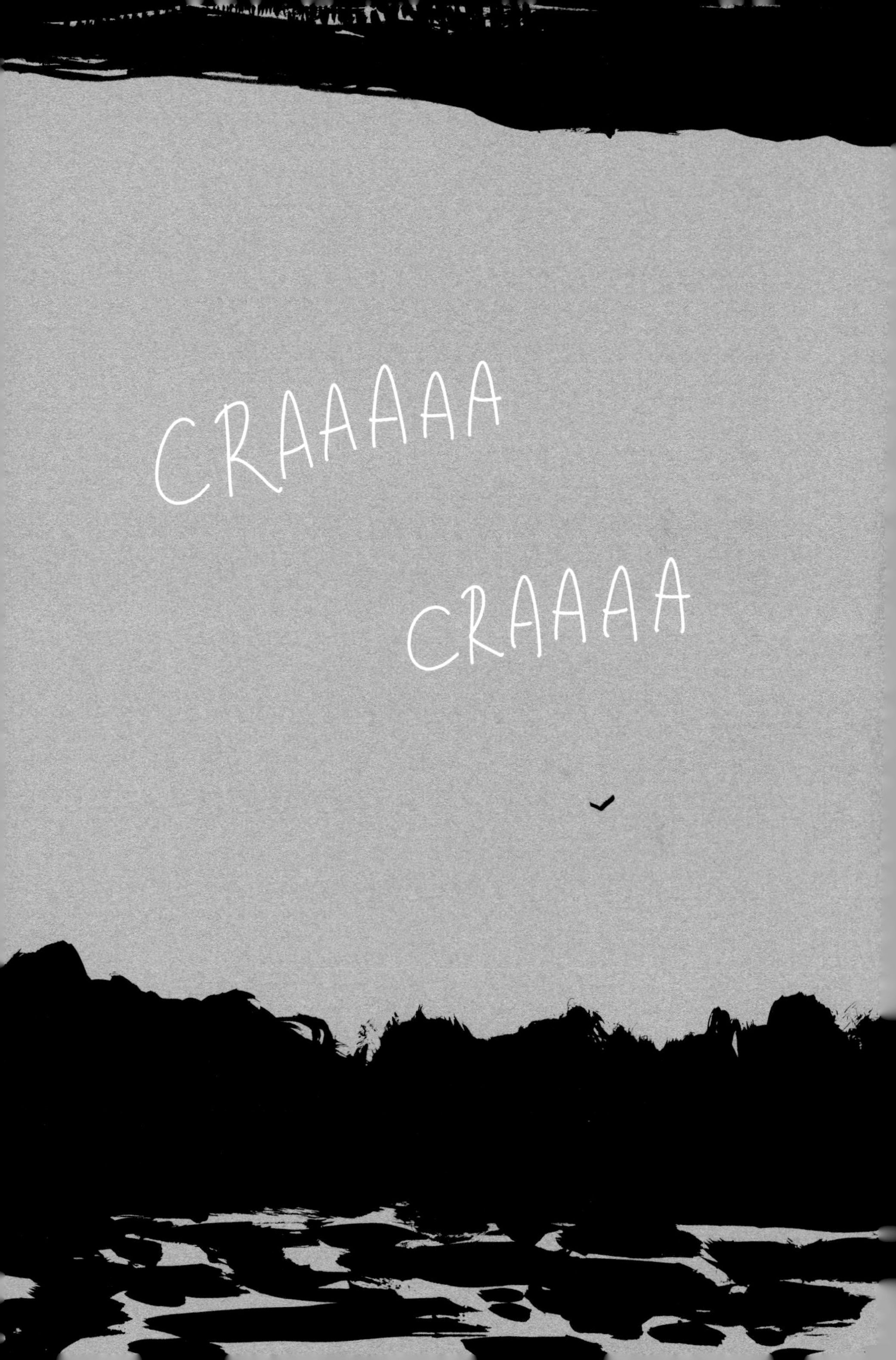
CRAAAAAA
CRAAAAA

CLOSING WORDS

Japan has a repertoire of very well-known folk tales by the name of *mukashi banashi*, some of which date back a thousand or more years. They range from epic tales to comical sketches and have been loved and cherished by many generations. They are also some of the stories my parents used to read me when I was a kid.

I took as a premise the legends of "Urashima Taro," "Ikkyu-san," and "The Crane Wife," reimagining and giving them new endings. Each one of these legends has a version that's the most well known by the general public, though there are many variants depending on the region or age.

These are some of the sources I used as references:

"Never Open It"
Urashima Tarō by Miyoko Matsutani and Chihiro Iwasaki, Kaiseisha (1967)
Urashima Tarō by Shirou Tokita and Fuku Akino, Fukuinkan Shoten (1974)
Urashima Tarō by Haruo Yamashita and Kinji Ishikura, Kaiseisha (1990)

"Empty"
Ikkyū-san (chapter 1) by Toei Animation (1975)
Busu by Rintaro Uchida and Yoshifumi Hasegawa, Poplar Sha (2007)
Busu by Izumi Motoshita and Yuki Sasameya, Kodansha (2007)

"The Promise"
Yūzuru / Hikoichi Banashi by Junji Kinoshita, Shinchosha (1954)
Tsuru Nyōbō by Sumiko Yagawa and Suekichi Akaba, Fukuinkan Shoten (1979)
Tsuru by Kon Ichikawa, Toho (1988)
Tsuru no Ongaeshi by Miyuki Iso and Ken Kuroi, Shogakukan (2010)

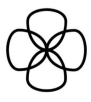

ACKNOWLEDGEMENTS

This book has been possible thanks to the help of many people.

"Never Open It" was the first story I worked on. I started it at an illustration workshop at the Itabashi Art Museum in Tokyo under the tutelage of Steven Guarnaccia.

I worked on the first draft of "Empty" at The Animation Workshop in Viborg, Denmark, where I was able to use a table and work among their students.

I developed "The Promise" during a workshop at the Atlantic Center for the Arts in Florida. I am very grateful to Matt Madden and all the participants (Amanda Andrei, Dave Drayton, Nadia Moujalli, Kevin Ottemfox, Jason Robinson, Linda Rodriguez, and Christina Tran) for all their ideas and comments. I worked on the rest of the tale while staying in an apartment in Paris that the Fagniez family gracefully let me use. A big nod also to Chiharu Shiota, whose work provided inspiration for some of this story.

A bunch of people put in time and effort to read the various versions of each story and were kind enough to provide comments that took the stories to the next level. In alphabetical order: Javier Bolado, Cécile Brun, Arnaud Bureau, Guillermo Capacés, Est Em, Pierre Fagniez, Daniel Gutiérrez Alias, Chihiro Inoue, Eri Kageyama, David López, Miho, Takeshi Miyazawa, Ota, Miguel Porto, Emma Ríos, Alfonso Salazar, Daniel Seijas, Josh Tierney, Yumetaro Toyoda, Cristina Triana, Christine Wang, Yun Watanabe, Sho Yamada, and Miki Yamamoto.

These folks assisted in the production of this book in a variety of ways: Lucía Álvarez Rovira, Ran Atsumori, Stephen Blanford, Daniel Gutiérrez Alías, Eri Kageyama, Chihiro Inoue, Antonio Núñez Sánchez, Sekine Shinichi, and Cristina Triana.

And a big thank you to Judy Hansen for all her hard work in finding the right publisher.

This collection was drawn with Tombow Mono 100 6B pencils, inked in Winsor & Newton Indian Black and Deleter 135g paper, and touched up using Clip Studio Paint and Photoshop in the Hayashi-san Studio in Tokyo.

KEN NIIMURA is a Spanish-Japanese cartoonist and illustrator.

He is the author of *Henshin* (2014), *Umami* (2018, winner of the Eisner Award for Best Digital Comic), and *Never Open It* (2021). He is also the co-creator of *I Kill Giants*, written by Joe Kelly (2009, winner of the International Manga Award), which was adapted into a film starring Zoe Saldana.

Ken Niimura's work has been translated into twelve languages. He lives in Tokyo.

NEVER OPEN IT

THE TABOO TRILOGY

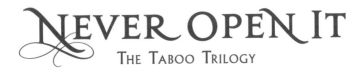